MANAGEMENT SCIENCE

CONCEPTS, INSIGHTS, AND APPLICATIONS

MANAGEMENT SCIENCE

CONCEPTS, INSIGHTS, AND APPLICATIONS

JOELEE OBERSTONE

McLAREN COLLEGE OF BUSINESS
UNIVERSITY OF SAN FRANCISCO

WEST PUBLISHING COMPANY

ST. PAUL   NEW YORK   LOS ANGELES   SAN FRANCISCO

Cover: Private Collection, New York. Courtesy M. Knoedler & Co., Inc., NY.
Composition: Alphatype and Graphic Typesetting Services
Illustrations: Teshin Associates and Barbara Barnett

COPYRIGHT © 1990   By WEST PUBLISHING COMPANY
50 W. Kellogg Boulevard
P.O. Box 64526
St. Paul, MN 55164–1003

LIBRARY OF CONGRESS CATALOGING-IN-PUBLICATION DATA

Oberstone, Joelee.
  Management science / Joelee Oberstone.
      p.   cm.
  Includes bibliographical references.
   ISBN 0–314–47360–2
   1. Industrial project management.   I. Title.
T56.8.O24 1990   89–70747
658.4′03—dc20   CIP

The author and the publisher of *Management Science: Concepts, Insights, and Applications* wish to acknowledge the protection under copyright, registered trademark, or established use of the names of the following products cited in the text:

Actsim
ALPAL
AMPS
Arborist
Big ALPAL Versions 1.0, 2.0
Computer Models for Management Science (CMMS) Versions 1, 2
Confidence Factor
Confidence Factor Version 2
Crystal Ball
DATA
Decision Analysis Techniques
Decision Analyst
DecisionMap
Decision 1-2-Tree
Decision Support Modeling Version 1
DSM
Excel
Excel 1.5
Expert Choice
Extend
FLP
Harvard Project Manager
Lightyear
LINDO/PC
Lotus 1-2-3
LP/80
LP83
LP88

MacProject
Management Science and the Microcomputer
Management Science Models and the Microcomputer Version 2
Microcomputer Models for Management Decision-Making (MMMDM)
Microcomputer Models for Management Decision-Making (MMMDM) Version 1.2
Microcomputer Software for Management Science and Operations Management Versions 6, 8, 9
Microcomputer Software for Management Science and Operations Research
MicroGANTT
Micro Manager Version 1.2
MicroManager
Micro-PASSIM
Microsoft Project
Microsolve Version 1
Microsolve Student Version, rev. ed.
Microsolve/Goal Programming Via Multiplex-1
MicroTSP
Milestone
Minuteman Software
MIP83

MP7-MIPROG
Mr. Quarter Master
NETSOLVE
PC Model
Primavera Project Manager
Programs for Quantitative Analysis in Management
Quantitative Systems for Business (QSB)
Quantitative Systems for Business (QSB) Versions 2.0, 3.0
Quatro
Riskcalc
Siman
SIMPLE 1
Simscript II.5
Simulations
Slam II
SmartForecasts
SOLON
StatView 512+
StatView + Microcomputer Program
STORM Versions 1,2
Supertree
TSA88

(Continued following Index)

DEDICATION

- To my children,
  Max (''King of All Wild Things'')
  and Sami ("What's Dat?")
  who make each day a joy to wake up to and
  who keep me constantly aware of what is
  really important in life.
- For my wife, confidant, nurse, laughing partner,
  nutritionist, alter ego, periodontist,
  and best friend, Bekka.
- To my stepfather, Bernard, an insightful,
  considerate, gentle man of wit and humor
  whom I love and respect.
- To my dear friend and master teacher,
  Michel Thomas.
- To the memory of my loving parents,
  Florence and Marvin,
  who are with me in my heart, forever.

CONTENTS IN BRIEF

CONTENTS

CHAPTER 7
Special Linear Resource Allocation Models
Transportation Method, Assignment Method, Integer Programming, and De Novo Programming   215

CHAPTER 8
Linear Distribution Networks
Shortest Route, Minimal Spanning Tree, Maximal Flow, and Transshipment Models   257

CHAPTER 9
Goal Programming
Multiple Objective Resource Allocation Methods   295

PREFACE

INTENDED AUDIENCE

This textbook is primarily intended for use in a first course in management science or quantitative business methods. Although it is planned primarily for students of business and management, it is also suitable for quantitative courses in urban planning, public administration, economics, and health care planning. The self-initiating working manager who may not have time for a normal course in management science and prefers to learn on his or her own will also find this book useful.

Management Science: Concepts, Insights, and Applications can be effective in supporting either a one or two semester course at the graduate or upper division undergraduate level, depending on the number of techniques studied and the depth to which each is explored.

Another business executive totally overwhelmed by his left brain.

PHILOSOPHY

This is not a book about number-crunching. It does not pretend to present a panacea for *solving* difficult problems. My intention has been, instead, to provide the university student and on-the-job manager with practical, useful, analytical tools that can serve as potentially powerful *supplements* to common sense. Thus, this textbook can be used as a source for alternative approaches to decision making based solely on managerial prerogatives or gut-level feelings as well as decision making that involves applying technocratic solutions to human problem settings. (The former approach rarely provides satisfactory relief because the problems are typically fuzzy and ill-defined, while the latter approach forces rigid, inflexible problem characterizations that defy the human condition.) It does not attempt to replace subjective values or human judgment; rather, it aims to *enhance* their effectiveness through the employment of useful methodologies that, *over the long run*, will provide more impressive results than "shooting from the hip."

In addition, this textbook focuses on the conceptual understanding, formulation, microcomputer solution, and interpretation of contemporary managerial problems. The book consistently takes the position that management science solutions to complex problems are really *educated estimates*: The parameter values used to define each problem are, in actuality, uncertain. As a result, the importance of examining each problem solution to determine how sensitive (or resilient) it is to such estimates is consistently emphasized.

PURPOSE

With few exceptions, management science books reinforce the forbidding image that the field of quantitative methods has earned over the last four or so decades. How fre-

quently does one encounter students actually looking forward to taking a course in statistics or management science? My guess is very rarely. But few will argue the value of those managerial techniques. So why does this paradox exist? It is my feeling that it is not the analytical tools that are at fault, but the stiff, intimidating, and distant manner in which these materials are traditionally presented. The intent of this book is to provide a highly readable, understandable text for students and managers interested in being able to *apply* contemporary, sophisticated analytical techniques.

By premeditated design, the style of this book is more like that of a good magazine than that of a traditional textbook. This style does not involve any sacrifice to the conceptual development and presentation of methodologies. The kinds of problems presented in exploring the various techniques incorporate believable and interesting subject matter. In fact, the majority of problems presented in this textbook are either adaptations of or taken directly from actual occurrences that are either familiar or of more than average interest. For example, there are hundreds of problems to wrestle with—some actual, some hypothetical—such as analyze Coca-Cola's decision to change (or not change) its original cola formula; determine the most profitably production schedule for Apple Computer's multiple product microcomputer line; examine a playwright's decision on whether to produce one of his plays for Broadway, or off Broadway, or not produce it at all; select the lowest rental car fleet cost maintenance program for Avis; and determine a plant location in France for Pepsi Cola that will result in the lowest overall operation and distribution costs. It is my view that if students have problems that are interesting and believable to use as a learning focus, the chances of their grasping the basic concepts and applications are enhanced.

READER PREREQUISITES

This text requires a minimum level of mathematical expertise. An introductory course in algebra is sufficient. The text all but omits model derivations and theory as unnecessary and energy-draining accompaniments to conceptual learning and application skills. Instead, the thrust of the material is toward *problem formulation and solution interpretation skills*. The reason for not incorporating the traditional approach of rigorous model development and manual solution is simple: Virtually no management science problems can be solved this way. The simplified problems that are usually used as examples in most texts deny the complexities of factual problems readers will really encounter.

To help develop model formulation skills, each chapter incorporates an abundance of *examples*, in which situations are explained in painstaking detail from problem formulation through computer solution and interpretation. I believe that the examples in this book represent an advance over the typically trite problem situations usually presented, being based, instead, on "real life" situations that can be counted on to command interest. It is hoped that this version of the example approach will involve readers more readily in the material, thus facilitating learning.

Manual solutions to well-formulated problems are of secondary importance in this book; the emphasis is refocused on *microcomputer solutions*. A summary listing of available microcomputer software is provided at the end of each chapter. Additionally, the final chapter in the book illustrates, in considerable detail, the *use* of these software packages in solving some of the examples presented in the text.

TEXT ORGANIZATION

The text opens with three chapters on decision analysis. No matter what type of problem is tackled, the outcome will necessitate a decision. Decision analysis provides the manager with invaluable strategies for approaching problems and working through implications. It provides a methodology for organizing the many considerations typically comprising even the most simple problem setting. The third chapter adds an additional refinement to the decision making process, as it explains how to examine and choose between strategies that are composed of multiple criteria. Chapter 3 also includes a unique extension of multiattribute utility methods: stochastic MAUM.

The next six chapters (Chapters 4–9) focus on the allocation of scarce resources: linear, integer, specialized (transportation and assignment), network, and goal programming methods. These important techniques are among the most pervasive types of analytical models used in management settings. Included in this six-chapter cluster is a resource allocation method that challenges some basic tenets of traditional resource allocation: de novo programming.

The use of Markov analysis is presented in Chapter 10 to illustrate its significant value in addressing optimum maintenance policy considerations (and also to emphasize its serious limitations in solving the traditional "brand switching" problem). Forecasting methods are examined in Chapter 11 to see how predictions of short, medium, and long-range changes in the business marketplace are made. Queueing analysis—the analytical study of waiting lines—is examined in Chapter 12, followed by inventory management (Chapter 13) and project management (Chapter 14). Monte Carlo simulation (Chapter 15) is presented as a viable alternative to the types of management science tools that are seen as having severe application limitations: queueing models, project management (PERT/CPM) systems, and inventory management systems.

Since the use of computers—especially microcomputers—plays such a crucial role in modern organizations, Chapter 16 is dedicated to reviewing the use of some of the different management science microcomputer software available. It is anticipated that a rapid increase in kinds of software available will provide a considerably broader array of products than is available at the time of this writing. Even so, the general illustration of how to use the different types of management science software will continue to be of value to the reader. In addition, many of the existing software packages will continue to be successful, even if they are not standards in the marketplace. The Epilogue closes the book with an overview of the future directions of management science: expert systems and decision support systems.

As I have noted, every chapter in the book includes numerous examples. The early exampless are comparatively simple, but by the close of the exercise segment, the examples closely approximate real-world dilemmas.

The text is roughly organized into four material clusters: (1) decision methods: Chapters 1–3; (2) linear resource allocation methods: Chapters 4–9; (3) The stochastic/deterministic variety pack: Chapters 10–15; and (4) overview subjects (Chapter 16 and Epilogue). The order in which these clusters can be presented in a course is flexible: cluster 1, 2, or 3 can be selected to introduce a course. There are, however, a few constraints regarding the order of the materials taught *within* each cluster. Although the decision regarding how many of these chapters are to be taught is at the discretion of the instructor, an order of coverage within the decision analysis cluster (Chapters 1–3), the linear resource allocation cluster (Chapters 4–9), and the stochastic/deterministic variety pack is strongly recommended. I advise including at the least Chapters 1 and 2 and 4–6; further, within the third cluster, the chapter on Monte Carlo simulation (Chapter

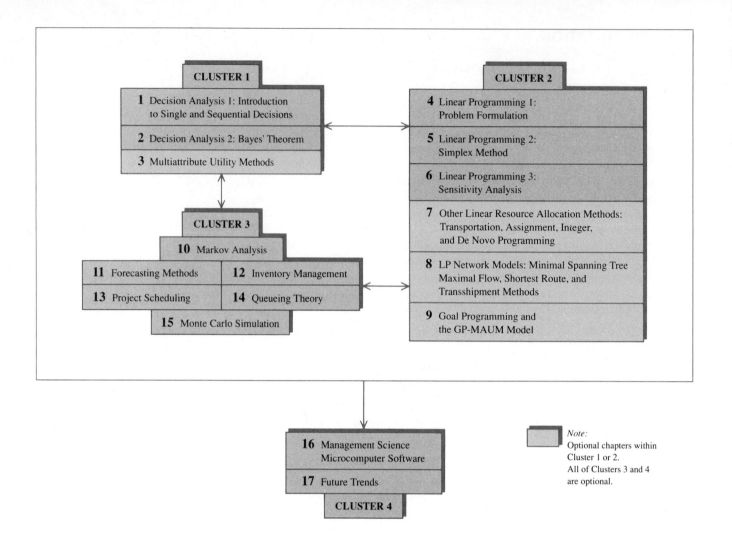

CLUSTER 1

1 Decision Analysis 1: Introduction to Single and Sequential Decisions

2 Decision Analysis 2: Bayes' Theorem

3 Multiattribute Utility Methods

CLUSTER 3

10 Markov Analysis

11 Forecasting Methods

12 Inventory Management

13 Project Scheduling

14 Queueing Theory

15 Monte Carlo Simulation

CLUSTER 2

4 Linear Programming 1: Problem Formulation

5 Linear Programming 2: Simplex Method

6 Linear Programming 3: Sensitivity Analysis

7 Other Linear Resource Allocation Methods: Transportation, Assignment, Integer, and De Novo Programming

8 LP Network Models: Minimal Spanning Tree Maximal Flow, Shortest Route, and Transshipment Methods

9 Goal Programming and the GP-MAUM Model

16 Management Science Microcomputer Software

17 Future Trends

CLUSTER 4

Note:
Optional chapters within Cluster 1 or 2.
All of Clusters 3 and 4 are optional.

FIGURE 1

Text Organization.

15) is intended to be presented *after* any combination of the chapters on queueing (Chapter 12), inventory management (Chapter 13), and project management (Chapter 14) that the instructor wishes to incorporate. Finally, cluster 4 should be saved to close out the course materials. An illustration of this flexible text organization is shown in Figure 1.

Most of the techniques of management science evolved from the efforts of a small group of scientists who worked on the deployment of allied forces and weaponry during World War II. Although some of these methods have origins considerably older than the 1940s, most of their refinements and application techniques are very contemporary. A brief history of the various tools and their origins is usually given in the introduction to each chapter.

CARTOONS

You will notice a liberal sprinkling of cartoons throughout the text. Although the cartoons were chosen primarily because they are funny (and represent the works of my very favorite cartoonists), there are other important reasons for including them. First,

the material is very demanding, so a distraction now and then is greatly appreciated. The cartoons were selected also because often they embody a particular concept being discussed and, thereby, may help the reader to retain the material. Lastly, the cartoons serve as a gentle reminder to me not to take the subject matter of any book—including this one—too seriously. Management science is important, but it isn't AIDS or cancer research.

The final version of this book has received the valued insight of many individuals that helped me to reshape my early manuscript efforts. The reviewers of the various manuscript drafts include:

Deep inside, Brian wondered if the other guys really listened to his ideas or regarded him only as comic relief.

Burt Madden
University of Arkansas
at Little Rock

Myron Cox
Wright State University

Kenneth Foresythe
St. Cloud University

Dinesh S. Dave
Marshall University

Carl H. Naeher
State University College
at Buffalo

Carol B. Diminnie
St. Boneventure University

Cathleen M. Zucco
Le Moyne College

Khalid R. Mehtadbin
College of St. Rose

John F. Hofmann
Humboldt State University

Richard K. Hay
Pittsburgh State University

Michael G. Sklar
University of Georgia,
Athens

Carol Lee Stamm
Western Michigan University,
Kalamazoo

Robert L. Armacost
Marquette University

David W. Ashley
University of Missouri,
Kansas City

Milan Zeleny
Fordham University

Neil B. Marks
Miami University

A. J. Roayaéi
California State University,
Los Angeles

Peter B. Barr
University of South Carolina,
Conway

William E. Stein
Texas A & M University

David Aviel
California State University,
Hayward

M. Albohali
Indiana University of Pennsylvania

Jonathan M. Furdek
Purdue University

Sohail S. Chaudhry
University of Wisconsin,
La Crosse

Hope M. Baker
University of North Carolina,
Greensboro

Additionally, a special handful of reviewers provided helpful suggestions and information that exceeded anything that I could have anticipated. This special group of reviewers consists of:

Paul A. Rubin, Michigan State University

Peter M. Ellis, Utah State University, Logan

Shirley A. Hopkins, University of Denver

Thomas L. Case, Georgia Southern College, Statesboro

Finally, my gratitude and appreciation to the wonderful production team at West Publishing—the people who literally put this book together. They have my undying respect for always providing me with the necessary resources and support—both physical and emotional—to develop a textbook that I am proud of (and allowing me—even encouraging me—to use my beloved cartoons). This group includes: Janet Bollow, Jan Lamar, Melody Rotman, Ann Swift, and particularly Clyde Perlee, Editor and Chief (a prince).

Joelee Oberstone

MANAGEMENT SCIENCE

CONCEPTS, INSIGHTS, AND APPLICATIONS

CHAPTER 1

DECISION ANALYSIS: PART 1

AN INTRODUCTION TO SINGLE-STAGE AND
MULTIPLE-STAGE (SEQUENTIAL) DECISIONS

1.1 INTRODUCTION

Decision analysis is a technique that we can use to organize the many considerations involved in the choice among two or more options so that we can make an intelligent selection—one that is compelling and defensible. Decision analysis neither functions as a number-crunching tool nor attempts to ignore the fact that human decisions often are highly subjective and sometimes can be emotionally charged. Instead, decision analysis attempts to incorporate these visceral realities within an objective framework, so that the process can be understood, and the chances for informed dialogue preserved.

To grasp the materials covered in this chapter—as well as in the next one—you will find it helpful to have a basic (*very* basic) understanding of probability. Most readers will have already taken a course in statistics, which covers the concepts of probability. However, for those people who either (1) have never been exposed to, or (2) are experiencing the dreaded "memory fade" phenomenon with, these materials, a brief review of probability is presented in Appendix A.

1.2 THE PURPOSE OF RATIONAL DECISION ANALYSIS

The use of rational decision analysis does not in itself guarantee a "good decision." In fact, in any single instance, a manager using intuition could conceivably make a decision that results in an ultimate outcome more desirable than the outcome of one made by a manager using the most sophisticated of rational decision processes. The outcome of an *individual* case, however, is not what concerns us. Rational decision analysis, *over the long term*, will give "batting averages" that are considerably more impressive than are those of the more visceral approaches.

1.3 APPLICATIONS OF DECISION ANALYSIS

Examples of the application of decision analysis are numerous. Consider the following:

■ Decision analysis can help health professionals to determine whether a person should receive the swine influenza vaccination (Zalkind and Shachtman, 1980).

- Risk analysis using decision trees can help regulatory bodies to assess the safety of nuclear facilities (Judd and Weissenberger, 1982).
- Decision trees can help managers to do on-line product planning (Ulvila, et al., 1975).
- A decision analysis model can help doctors to diagnose and treat undifferentiated liver disease in conjunction with jaundice (De Rivera, 1980).
- Decision analysis can help lawyers to determine when a company should go to court in a legal dispute (Bodily, 1979).
- Decision analysis can help hotel managers to set a reservation policy (Williams, 1977).
- Decision analysis can help marketing staff to develop an airlines discount-coupon program (Digman, 1980).
- Decision analysis can help us to glean a lesson from the Iran hostages rescue operation (Saaty, et al., 1982).
- A decision model can help us to assess the implications of the *Bakke* decision in implementing affirmative-action programs (Solomon and Messmer, 1980).

1.4 WHEN DOES USE OF DECISION ANALYSIS MAKE SENSE?

Many decisions involve only minor considerations and influence only small amounts of resource allocation. For these types of decision settings, it is not worth your time to attempt to formalize the decision process. In addition, people tend to deal quite well with simple, unencumbered issues. Other decisions, however, do involve considerable complexity, and correspondingly large resource allocations ride on the ultimate outcome. If you do not attempt to organize the intricacies of such problems by using a formal approach, the quality of your ultimate choice will tend to be poor. People have a limited capacity to assimilate the often-large number of key factors describing a given problem. Rational decision methods provide such an organizational structure.

1.5 THE ELEMENTS OF DECISION MAKING

All decision problems contain five basic elements: (1) decision maker, (2) alternative acts or strategies, (3) future events, (4) event probabilities, and (5) outcome payoffs. We shall discuss each of these important decision components in detail.

1. *Decision maker*. Any individual or group of people who have the authority of selection are viewed as the decision maker, D.

2. *Acts*. The set of acts, alternatives, options, or strategies used to solve or remedy the problem in question are given by A, where

$$A = (a_1, a_2, \ldots, a_i, \ldots, a_m)$$

and there is a total of "m" acts from which to select (a_i is the ith act). The act is *within the control* of the decision maker, since D is free to select any single act desired.

3. *Events*. After the decision maker, D, selects the preferred act, certain future conditions will ultimately determine the "goodness" of this selection. These conditions are referred to as "future states of nature," but are simply events that matter at the

time the selected specific act is being implemented. If there are n possible states or events, the total set of these events is given by S, where

$$S = (s_1, s_2, \ldots, s_j, \ldots, s_n)$$

and there is a total of n future events that can occur (s_j is the jth event). The different types of events that might affect the selected act could include economical, political, social, moral, military, legal, physical, technological, or environmental factors. In decision analysis, these events are mutually exclusive and, theoretically, collectively exhaustive. In reality, the events may be highly interrelated, may overlap significantly, and certainly are not exhaustive. More practically, a set of events usually consists of the event most likely to occur (often the existing or prevailing state), the event that will most positively affect the act, the event that will most negatively affect the act, and, if desired, several events intermediate between these extremes. An important property of these events is that *they are beyond the control of the decision maker*. The best that D can do with respect to the future events is to attempt to anticipate them (as described earlier).

4. *Probabilities of occurrence for future events.* Since "nature" is associated with events that occur in the future, the specific event that does prevail cannot, in real-world problem settings, be known for sure. There is, therefore, a likelihood or probability linked with every future event, P. That is, for each s_j there is a probability that that event will occur, denoted p_j. The probability of any individual event occurring, p_j, is between 0 and 1. The sum of the probabilities of all the events that comprise the set of interest is given by

$$\sum_{j=1}^{n} p_j = p_1 + p_2 + \cdots + p_j + \cdots + p_n = 1.0$$

The set of probabilities, P, is given by

$$P = [p_1, p_2, \ldots, p_j, \ldots, p_n]$$

Typically, probabilities used in business settings are generated from expert opinion or forecasts (subjective) or are supported by empirical evidence (objective).

5. *Outcomes.* Each combination of a selected act and the prevailing event at the time of implementation results in a specific outcome or payoff, o_{ij}. The outcome can be calculated in terms of costs, benefits, or other measures of worth.

Next, we shall examine the caliber (quality) of the information available for making a decision.

1.6 LEVEL OF KNOWLEDGE

A decision maker's ultimate selection is heavily colored by the caliber or quality of the evaluative information available. The quality of the decision-making information is also referred to as the *level of knowledge* of the problem.

In particular, the quality of the estimated probabilities is crucial. The attractiveness of each alternative hinges on which future event might prevail at the time the selected alternative is implemented. Traditionally, decisions may be examined under three dif-

ferent levels of knowledge. These levels are, in decreasing order of available information, (1) certainty, (2) risk, and (3) uncertainty.

1. *Decisions under certainty.* Each alternative results in the same specifically known outcome. Only *one* future event is possible, and it will occur with certainty. It therefore has an associated probability of 1.00.

2. *Decisions under risk.* Each alternative may result in more than one outcome because more than one future event is possible. Each event has a known (or presumably known) probability of occurrence associated with it. These probabilities can be either derived objectively or assessed subjectively. Subjective probabilities are far more common in business than are objective probabilities.

3. *Decisions under uncertainty.* Each alternative may result in more than one outcome because more than one future event (or state) is possible. However, the probabilities associated with each event are unknown, and there is no possible way to obtain them.

Many books on decision methods have a separate discussion for each of these three different information settings. In this book, we shall focus solely on decisions under risk. There are several reasons for this narrow concentration. First, we will rarely, if ever, encounter a future event that will occur "for sure" in a complex, real-life decision setting. Unfortunately, life is just not that convenient. Further, if we assume that we are going to the trouble of using decision methods because the allocation of resources warrants that effort, then it should also be important enough to *refine* decisions under uncertainty: We *must* make the best possible educated estimates of an event's likelihood of occurrence. We can make those estimates by digging into the problem more deeply, by interviewing experts to get a consensus of opinion, or by consulting a psychic. *Nevertheless, we must make them.* Even though these probabilities that we ultimately develop are among the weakest (and are often *the* most criticized) links in decision methods, there are ways to account for and overcome this apparent vulnerability. We shall discuss and illustrate these buttressing methods later in this chapter.

In the next two sections, we shall examine the two basic methods of rational decision analysis: single-stage decisions under risk using decision matrices and multiple-stage or sequential decisions using decision trees.

1.7 DECISION MATRICES FOR SINGLE-STAGE DECISIONS

To solve a single-stage decision problem, we commonly use a *decision matrix*—an organizing tool that helps us to illustrate, in tabular form, the set of competing alternatives under consideration, the possible future conditions or events that might occur, and the effects of these events on the ultimate worth of each alternative. Let's look at an example of how decision matrices can be used to appraise a complex decision setting effectively.

EXAMPLE 1.1 NBC TELEVISION NETWORK PROGRAMMING EMPHASIS

It is not likely that the highly subjective, confidential information used by each television network to determine the "new season's lineup" would be made public. Nevertheless, let us imagine that the National Broadcasting Company (NBC) television network is assessing the emphasis they wish to have for the next season of programming. The

programming emphasis chosen is crucial, since it will create a priority for the specific types of shows that the network will choose to produce and to distribute to their affiliates. The success of these selections will be, in turn, largely at the mercy of the taste of the viewing audience—a truly forbidding circumstance when you consider the kinds of shows that have been wildly popular over the past decade (e.g., "A Team," "Duke's of Hazzard," "Starsky and Hutch," "Hello Larry," "Hogan's Heroes," and "The Dating Game"). Further, NBC knows that it cannot assume that a format that has been successful in the past will continue to be popular: Tastes change from one season to another; what is hot in one season may be "old hat" in the next. If NBC judges these anticipated viewer desires correctly, and selects programs carefully to fit them, the crucial Nielsen ratings should prove to be quite favorable and the network will earn a significant chunk of the hundreds of millions of advertising dollars spent during the season (the per-minute advertising rates that the network can set for each show are greatly influenced by the show's "Nielsen"). If the programs are not successful, many network jobs—both in front of and behind the cameras, as well as in the mahogany-paneled upstairs offices—will be eliminated or restaffed. Let's pose the following decision setting envisioned by the NBC programmers:

A TV network programmer prepares for another day at the office.

1. NBC is considering the three different emphases: (1) educational, cultural (e.g., great literature, classic theater, arts and music, science); (2) escapist entertainment (e.g., talk shows, game shows, situation comedies, movies without a message); and (3) realistic adventure/action, sports, contemporary humor (e.g., police, doctor, and law dramas; message comedy shows; news specials).

2. The preference of the viewing audience for next season will fall into one of three possible categories: (1) high-end, top-quality dramas; hard news; and documentaries; (2) light entertainment, such as "glitsy" talk shows hosted by celebrities discussing noncontroversial subjects, soap operas, and "happy-talk news"; and (3) middle-of-the-road mix of sports, news, dramas, and comedy specials.

The resultant potential payoffs that might occur for each combination of programming emphasis and viewer preference are shown in Table 1-1. The values located within each cell represent the network's estimated profits ($+$) or losses ($-$) in millions of dollars that would result from a specific combination of programming emphasis (alternative) and viewer preference (event). The table only provides an illustration of the potential

TABLE 1-1

Payoff Matrix of Likely Net Profits for NBC Television Programming-Emphasis Selection for New Season, As Influenced By Viewer Preference ($1 Million).

Network Programming Emphasis, a_i*	Viewing Audience Preference, s_j**		
	s_1	s_2	s_3
a_1	−500	1100	500
a_2	1250	−800	350
a_3	500	−250	700

*a_1 = high-end, top-quality dramas, news, and documentaries; s_2 = light entertainment, such as "glitsy" talk shows hosted by celebrities discussing noncontroversial subjects, and soap operas; s_3 = middle-of-the-road mix of sports, news, dramas, and comedy specials.

**s_1 = escapist entertainment (e.g., talk shows, game shows, situation comedies, movies without a message); a_2 = educational, cultural (e.g., great literature, classic theatre, arts and music, science); a_3 = realistic adventure/action, sports, contemporary humor (e.g., police, doctor, and law dramas; message comedy shows; news specials).

outcomes that might occur; it does not dictate the ultimate selection. The actual selection traditionally is dependent on the likelihood of each viewer preference actually occurring and the network programmers' *style of selection*.

Styles of Selection

There are three basic selection strategies we can use to assess competing alternatives under risk environments:

- The most probable future
- The principle of expected values
- The principle of paranoia (minimum regret)

To use any of these selection techniques to evaluate NBC's various programming emphases, we must first find a way to generate probability estimates of the viewer preference (future events). Suppose that a panel of knowledgeable people agrees on the following estimates of the three different event probabilities: $p_1 = .30$, $p_2 = .30$, $p_3 = .40$. Now, let us examine a number of ways in which decisions can be made, based on the philosophy or style of the decision maker.

TABLE 1-2

NBC Television Network Payoff Matrix for the Most Probable Future ($1 Million).

Emphasis, a_i	Middle-of-the-Road Preference, s_3
a_1	500
a_2	350
→ a_3	700

The Most Probable Future This approach assumes that the event with the highest probability of occurrence will, in fact, occur. In our example, this event is s_3: There is a 40 percent chance that the viewer preference will be for a mixed offering of programs. The "best" selection would be, in this case, a_3: the largest value is listed under this type of viewer preference—$700 million—in Table 1-2, the NBC *payoff matrix*.

The Principle of Expected Values Every programming emphasis, a_i, has associated with it an expected value (average payoff), EV_i. The principle of expected values uses a probability-weighted average equal to the sum of the products of each possible combination of payoff and probability (in general, expected values either maximize profits or minimize costs):

$$EV_i = \sum_{j=1}^{n} p_{ij} v_{ij}$$

or

$$EV_i = p_{i1} v_{i1} + p_{i2} v_{i2} + \cdots + p_{in} v_{in}$$

where

p_{ij} = probability of occurrence for the jth event of the ith alternative

v_{ij} = payoff (or value) associated with the jth event of the ith alternative

For the NBC decision matrix, the EVs for the three programming strategies are

$$EV_1 = (.30)(-500) + (.30)(1100) + (.40)(500) = 380$$
$$EV_2 = (.30)(1250) + (.30)(-800) + (.40)(350) = 225$$
$$EV_3 = (.30)(500) + (.30)(-250) + (.40)(700) = 355$$

We see immediately that the optimum strategy to employ based on the principle of expected values is a_1, which has the maximum EV of $380 million.

The Principle of Paranoia (Minimum Regret)   If the decision environment is one in which the decision maker D must worry about punitive retribution (e.g., loss of a job) based on the difference in outcomes between the strategy *actually* selected and the *optimum* strategy selection—the one you would have made if you had had the ability to predict accurately the future audience preference—then there is a selection style the decision maker will love! This principle is given by the relationship

$$r_{ij} = o_j^* - o_{ij}$$

where

r_{ij} = regret associated with the actual selection of programming emphasis, a_i, when audience preference, s_j, occurs

o_j^* = best outcome that can occur under audience preference, s_j

o_{ij} = actual outcome associated with selected programming emphasis, a_i, when audience preference, s_j, occurs

Notice that the paranoia approach is identical to the expected-value method except that it uses a table of "hindsight" values rather than of direct payoffs.

Here's how to use this approach:

Step 1. For each audience preference, s_j, *determine the best outcome value* that could occur (this value represents the alternative you would select if you knew that this audience preference would definitely occur).

Step 2. Using this payoff value, o_j^*, as a baseline value, *calculate the difference* between this payoff and the other programming strategies for the *single audience preference under examination*. This calculation will give you the regret value for each programming strategy, a_i, under that specific audience preference, s_j.

Step 3. *Repeat steps 1 and 2* until you have exhausted all possible viewing audience preferences. This process results in a new matrix that represents the regret you would experience if you made a nonoptimum decision (the cell with zero values indicates the optimum selections under specific audience preferences). This regret matrix is shown in Table 1-3.

Step 4. Now calculate the *expected regret* you would experience for each programming emphasis by including the likelihood of each audience preference occurring. These expected regret values are given by the relationship

$$ER_i = \sum_{j=1}^{n} p_j r_{ij} \qquad \text{for each } i\, [i = 1, 2, \ldots, m]$$

TABLE 1-3

Regret Matrix for NBC Television Programming.

Network Programming Emphasis, a_i	Viewing Audience Preference, s_j		
	s_1	s_2	s_3
a_1	1750	0	200
a_2	0	1900	350
a_3	750	1350	0

Using our previous estimates of the chances associated with the three audience preferences (states of nature), we find the following results:

$$ER_1 = (.30)(1750) + (.30)(0) + (.40)(200) = 605$$
$$ER_2 = (.30)(0) + (.30)(1900) + (.40)(350) = 710$$
$$ER_3 = (.30)(750) + (.30)(1350) + (.40)(0) = 630$$

The optimum selection under the paranoia setting is, accordingly, a_1, since that choice minimizes your expected regret, at \$605 million.

So, which of the three methods we have examined is the best? The answer is that there is no "best" method. Each decision setting is unique. Every manager must assess each problem based on the characteristics of the specific situation, not on a preconceived style. In fact, the decision setting often is not at all suited for any of these three techniques. In particular, these methods do not address such issues as how to compare competing alternatives when the problem consists of *sequential decision* considerations. We'll turn to this important area now.

1.8 DECISION TREES FOR MULTIPLE-STAGE (SEQUENTIAL) DECISIONS

For those problems that require a sequence of decisions, the most useful method to employ is the *decision tree*. The decision tree is a tool we use to clarify the choices, risks, and outcomes inherent in the problem. It provides a chronological display of each factor we believe to be pertinent to the problem and gives us an opportunity to examine the various alternatives with considerable clarity. A decision tree illustrating a problem in which the strategy to market or not to market a new product (and whether or not to use surveys to judge the mood of the potential consumer population) is shown in Figure 1-1. We'll make a more detailed inspection of the use of decision trees by working through an example.

EXAMPLE 1.2 UNITED AIRLINES DISCOUNT-COUPON PROMOTIONAL PROGRAM

By the early 1980s, it was common practice for many airline companies to attract new customers by offering various types of promotional programs. One of the most common promotions was to issue heavily discounted coupons to customers during a regular, nondiscounted flight, which the customers could use to purchase tickets for a future flight (Digman, 1980). Suppose, as an illustration, that United Airlines is considering a promotional campaign designed to enhance their domestic market position. It is on the verge of developing a coupon that will allow a person to purchase a round-trip ticket to Hawaii for only \$100. The company will give one coupon to any customer who purchases a round-trip, regular-fare ticket on any United flight of at least 400 miles (one-way's distance). United managers believe that an attractive promotional program such as this one will help them to improve the company's position in the highly competitive, high-volume market of the western United States. Specifically, United's managers reason that they will certainly keep their present passengers as well as attract away from their competitors a large number of new passengers who will "come over" just to take advantage of the Hawaii ticket offer. They also believe that a significant percentage of these new customers will continue to fly United, and to spend revenues on nondis-

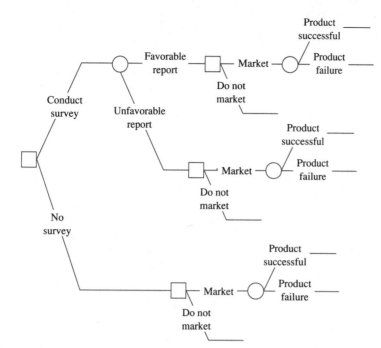

counted, regular flights, for long enough to offset any losses anticipated by the discounted Hawaiian flights.

The managers know from industry experience that, in the aggregate, similar discount-ticket strategies are successful only 31 percent of the time. Since the marketing and advertising costs associated with this campaign are estimated at $18.5 million, they want to organize the various considerations comprising this decision so they can scrutinize the program for financial payoffs over a 12-month period—the anticipated life of the program. They estimate that, if this program is successful, it will generate $43.5 million in revenues during the year. If it is unsuccessful, only $10 million will be generated. United is faced with an immediate decision between two possible strategies concerning the promotional program: (1) do nothing—forgo the program, or (2) market the new program at a cost of $18.5 million.

DECISION-TREE DESIGN

If you were serving as an advisor to United Airlines on this important promotional program, how would you use the information you have to guide you in making an intelligent recommendation? Regardless of the method or the decision you suggest to United, what will you be able to say about the *considerations* comprising your assessment? Will you be able to *show* United why you selected a specific option? Can you *defend* the approach you offer? If these questions embarrass or worry you, then you are probably not using an adequate decision-making process, in which case you will certainly never be able to make your selection clear either to yourself or other people. The rest of this chapter focuses on the development of such a process.

Let's start by developing an illustration of the information that we have.

1. Determine the *initial* alternatives. In this example, we know that United Airlines either will do nothing or will market the program. Alternatives—often referred to as acts, strategies, decisions, options, and so on—always emanate from an *act* (or *decision*) *node*, symbolized by a *square*. So we begin drawing the tree by forming a square with two possible paths, as shown in Figure 1-2.

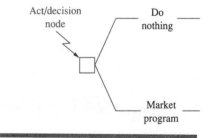

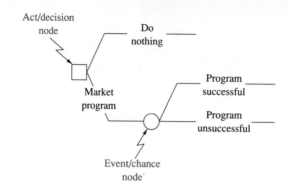

2. Estimate the consequences of selecting each alternative. We can view these consequences as potential events or future conditions that will contribute to the ultimate value (in dollars or in some other measure of worth) of our selection. These consequences, more often referred to as *events*, are illustrated by (what else?) *event (or chance) nodes*. These event nodes are symbolized by *circles*. For our problem, the only act that has associated with it future events is United deciding to market the program. If we select the "do nothing" act, there are no further options. So, we can extend the tree by identifying, chronologically, the possible events that come with the decision to market the program. Of course, this event must be the ultimate success or failure of the program.[1] The complete tree is shown in Figure 1-3. This tree is a chronological snapshot, sequentially flowing from left to right, illustrating all the options available from the information contained in the brief problem scenario. Even though it does not yet contain the quantitative data necessary to support a cogent decision, it nevertheless provides significant insight regarding the complex sequence of considerations; insight that would be difficult to glean from a typical discussion or written description of the problem. However, we need more information. What analytical operations can we use to evaluate competing alternatives?

EXPECTED VALUES

One of the most common standards to use in comparing competing, sequential decision alternatives is the *criterion of expected value*, *EV* (also called the expected monetary value, *EMV*). The *EV* method identifies the alternative that has the highest "average payoff." This average payoff is simply the sum of the products of the probability of an event occurring, times the payoff associated with that event. It is given by the relationship

$$EV_i = \sum_{j=1}^{n} p_{ij} v_{ij}$$

or

$$EV_i = p_{i1} v_{i1} + p_{i2} v_{i2} + \cdots + p_{in} v_{in}$$

---

[1] In actuality, there could be far more than the two diametric outcomes of success and failure; it would be more realistic to include an array of probabilities—a probability distribution of possible dollar outcomes. However, this added complexity would tend to distract your attention from the primary intent of this exercise, which is to explain the process of structuring and analyzing decision trees. We shall add complexity to our models soon enough.

where

p_{ij} = probability of occurrence for the jth event of the ith alternative

v_{ij} = payoff (or value) associated with the jth event of the ith alternative

Although a decision tree flows chronologically from left to right, the expected-value method uses a *folding-back* process that moves from right to left. You will always initiate the folding-back procedure from the *terminal nodes* of each branch in the tree (i.e., the nodes at the far right or end of each tree branch). For this United Airlines example, there is a .31 probability that the program will be successful, P(successful), and will generate $25 million if United decides to market it (i.e., $43.5 million in revenues less $18.5 million in marketing costs). However, there is also a likelihood that the program will not be successful. Since the sum of the probabilities of any event (chance) node must be equal to 1.00, the probability that the promotion will be unsuccessful, P(unsuccessful), is

$$P(\text{unsuccessful}) = 1 - P(\text{success})$$
$$= 1 - .31$$
$$= .69$$

Therefore, there is a .69 (or 69 percent) chance that the program will "bomb" and will cost the airline $8.5 million (i.e., $10.0 million in revenues less the $18.5 million in marketing costs). The full decision-tree design, incorporating all of the probabilities and payoffs, is given in Figure 1-4. How can we use this information to evaluate the goodness (intelligence) of committing to the promotional ticket program without knowing for sure what the ultimate outcome will be? We simply calculate what we would expect *on the average*: We pretend that we have a very large (nearly infinite) number of opportunities to take the same gamble, and we calculate what we would make (or lose) over the long haul. The expected value of marketing the promotional program provides this information. Starting at the terminal nodes of the "market" branch reveals the following expected value:

$$EV_{\text{market}} = P(\text{successful}) \cdot \text{successful payoff} + P(\text{unsuccessful}) \cdot \text{unsuccessful payoff}$$
$$= (.31)(25,000,000) + (.69)(-8,500,000)$$
$$= 7,750,000 - 5,865,000$$
$$= \$1,885,000$$

This calculation means that, *if* United Airlines decides to market this program, it can expect an average payoff of about $1.89 million. The alternative strategy—that of doing nothing (not marketing the program)—is, simply:

$$EV_{\text{do nothing}} = (1.00)(0) = \$0$$

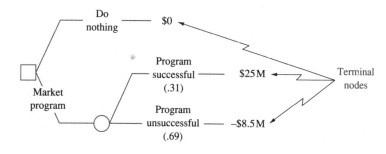

FIGURE 1-4

Complete Decision Tree for United Airlines.

The probability of 1.0 in this case represents the *certainty*, if you choose, of not marketing the program; it does not represent the *probability* of an event because it is a *decision*. The expected-value calculations are illustrated in Figure 1-5. For the specific parameters of the United Airlines problem, the most desirable option is to market the program, since a rational decision maker will always maximize positive expected values or minimize negative expected values. Notice that there is a *double hashmark* on the "Do nothing" act in Figure 1-5. This notation means that the act is not competitive—there is at least one other alternative that is more attractive. Whenever you fold back, you must always use this hashmark notation to signify the elimination of all act branches that are nonoptimal. These hashmarks will identify the precise actions to employ, from the beginning to the end of the optimal strategy. View them as road signs that direct you precisely to where you wish to go.

Although the program appears attractive to the United Airlines managers responsible for assessing its potential, they understand that, in reality, the program will either make $25 million or lose $8.5 million: They have only one opportunity to undertake this project. Because of the large potential loss, and the greater than two-thirds chance that the project will fail, they are understandably concerned about proceeding. In fact, the managers are leaning toward dropping the promotion. Just as they are deciding to forgo the series, however, new information for them to consider is received. In particular, they are told that a professional market-research consulting group is available to conduct a survey on United's promotional program. The company would report to the managers whether it believes this *particular* program has a favorable or unfavorable market prognosis. Past experience with this consulting group has shown that, when they write favorable reports, the programs are ultimately successful 85 percent of the time. When they write unfavorable reports, the programs are successful only 8 percent of the time. This consultant group has a record of writing favorable reports for similar projects about 30 percent of the time. The marketing study will cost United $500,000; the fee includes a survey, an assessment, and a written report. Now, how can these new data be incorporated so that United can select the most promising strategy?

Let's start by sketching the new tree (Figure 1-6). Of course, the tree is not entirely new; it simply has an additional option—the two original strategies remain unchanged. Notice how much more complex the problem has become. If we hire the consultants, they will issue a report reflecting the survey findings—either favorable (forecasting the program will be successful) or unfavorable (suggesting an ultimately unsuccessful program). When it receives the report—favorable or unfavorable—United must decide to market or to drop the program. If the program is dropped, a dead-end is reached and there are no further situations to consider. If the program is marketed, it will either succeed or fail.

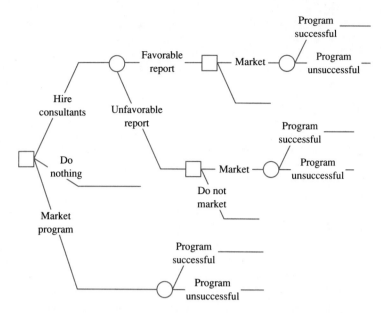

Before we go back to the tree and examine it in greater detail, let's develop a simple notation method for labeling the acts and events. This will make the tree easier for us to "read" and understand. We'll eliminate the cumbersome, long-hand writing scribbled all over the tree, which is tiresome to decipher. We'll select the following symbols arbitrarily for the various acts and events associated with this tree:

N: Do nothing

M: Market program

M': Do not market (drop) program

H: Hire consultants

F: Consultants write favorable report

F': Consultants write unfavorable report

S: Program is successful

S': Program is unsuccessful

This notation uses a prime (" ' ") to denote the *negative* or undesirable side of an outcome when an event or act has two situations that are opposite in meaning. Now we can relabel our tree with a less cumbersome branch and node format, as shown in Figure 1-7.

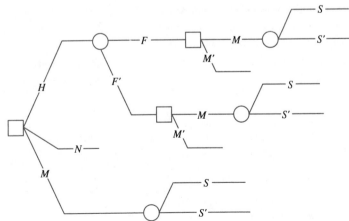

FIGURE 1-7

Shorthand Branch and Node Notation for United Airlines Decision Tree.

Although we can understand an uncluttered tree more easily than we can one with a great deal of verbiage, we still need to label each event in the tree in appropriate *probabilistic notation*. We know that the probability of a promotional program in the airlines industry being successful (with no additional information) is .31. This is given by the expression

$$P(S) = .31$$

This term is called a *marginal probability* because it represents the chance of a single, independent event occurring (it is also called a *prior probability* because no events occur prior to it). The same logic holds for the likelihood that the program will be unsuccessful, $P(S')$. Even for the "hire consultant" act, H, the early events are also marginal probability events [i.e., $P(F)$ and $P(F')$]. However, the *outcome* or *terminal events* (the last event along any specific path in the tree) of this act are *not* marginal. The probabilities of the program becoming successful or not successful are preceded by the earlier *predictive events* and are called *conditional probabilities*. These earlier or predictive events are literally predicting the ultimate outcome of the program. Accordingly, the product of this prediction—the reports—are presumably providing the manager with *imperfect information* regarding the chances of success for this *specific* program, and not just the aggregate chances of *any* program in general. [2]

Now let's examine how to interpret conditional probabilities so that, as an example, the given and later events are placed in the proper order.

PROBABILITY NOTATION AND INTERPRETATION

The United Airlines program has conditional probabilities given by $P(S/F)$, $P(S'/F)$, $P(S/F')$, and $P(S'/F')$. For example, $P(S/F')$ represents the probability of the program ultimately becoming successful *after* an unfavorable report is written by the consulting group [i.e., $P(S/F')$ is also read "the probability of becoming successful, *given* an unfavorable report was written]. The new tree, with appropriate probabilistic labeling, is shown in Figure 1-8.

The next step is to incorporate all our event probabilities and anticipated outcomes for each act. We have been given the following probabilities data for marketing the program outright:

$$P(S) = .31$$

Those for hiring the market research consultants are

$$P(S/F) = .85$$
$$P(S/F') = .08$$

It is crucially important to understand *how to interpret conditional probabilities* from the case study text. There is a simple method that relies on only English grammar and sentence structure. Here's how it works:

1. Any sentence that contains a probability described by *two* events is a conditional probability. The structure of this kind of sentence will always be compound; that is,

---

[2] An analogous situation would be predicting the chance of success in a particular game for a baseball player who is a "switch hitter"—a player who bats left-handed against right-handed pitchers and right-handed against left-handed pitchers—with an *overall* batting average of .300. However, his batting average is .318 left-handed and .265 right-handed (i.e., he bats left-handed more often than right-handed because there are more right-handed pitchers than left-handed pitchers). If you were asked, "What are the chances of this player getting a hit in his next official at bat in tonight's game?" you would answer ".300." However, if, after assessing the pitching rotation of the opposing team, you discovered that a left-handed pitcher would be starting the game, you would answer .265—a 35 point difference from your earlier, less informed response!

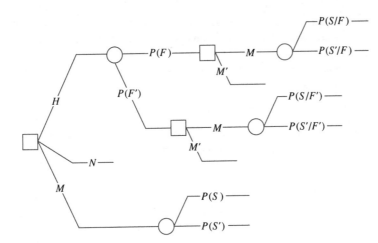

it will comprise a *dependent* and an *independent phrase*. The two types of phrases are easy to identify: An independent phrase (clause) is a *complete* thought and can stand as a complete sentence (even though it is part of a larger sentence), whereas a dependent phrase is simply an *incomplete* thought.

2. Divide the sentence into its dependent and independent components. As an example, here is the following sentence paraphrase concerning the consultant group performance in the United Airlines example: "For those reports that were *favorable*, the programs were ultimately *successful* 85 percent of the time." We can divide this sentence into its two parts (keep in mind that the sentence discussed *two events*—a sure sign that we are dealing with a conditional probability). These two parts are, without worrying about which one is the dependent or independent phrase,

"For those reports that were favorable"

and

"the programs were ultimately successful 85 percent of the time."

Clearly, "for those reports that were favorable" is *not* a complete thought, whereas "the programs were ultimately successful 85 percent of the time" definitely is! Now here is the rule:

| The independent phrase becomes the first term written in the conditional probability statement while the dependent phrase is the given event—the term written after the slash ("given" sign). |

This rule can be represented in a general expression for a conditional probability in terms of these two types of sentence phrases:

Complete thought   Incomplete thought

$$P(\text{independent phrase}/\text{dependent phrase})$$

So, for our example, the dependent phrase is talking about the favorable report, F, whereas the independent phrase deals with the ultimately successful program, S. We can now write the conditional probability as

$P(S/F) = .85$

That's all there is to it. But just to play it safe, let's examine the other conditional probability. The relevant sentence says, paraphrasing, "When the consultants wrote

unfavorable reports, the programs were successful only 8 percent of the time." The two phrases are, then, "When the consultants wrote unfavorable reports" *and* "the programs were successful only 8 percent of the time."

Do you see that the first phrase is an incomplete thought, whereas the second one is not? So, we write this conditional probability as

$$P(S/F') = .08$$

It is also important to understand that whether the dependent or independent phrase is presented first or last in the sentence structure is irrelevant. The results will be the same.

Now we have enough information to complete the calculations for the third act in the tree. The final version of the United Airlines decision tree is shown in Figure 1-9. The folding-back process reveals that, if the report is favorable, United should market the new program, since the *EV* for this branch is $19.475 million, compared to a $500,000 loss if United doesn't market the program. If the report is unfavorable, it is best to drop the program (do not market), since the *EV* for this branch is only a $500,000 loss, compared to an *EV* of −$6.32 million if it is marketed. The sum of the products of the .30 likelihood of a favorable report times the *EV* of $19.475 million, plus the .70 chance of an unfavorable report times the −$500,000 *EV*, results in an *EV* of $5.49 million for the act of hiring the consultant group. And, of course, this is the most attractive act among the three considered.

Let's summarize the steps we took in designing and evaluating the decision tree:

Step 1. List the initial competing strategies that you are considering. Typically, the manager is weighing a problem that can be generally characterized as "do something," "don't do something," or "seek imperfect (expert/diagnostic/forecast) information." Examples include (1) marketing or not marketing one or more products; (2) expanding or not expanding a business; (3) investing or not investing in one or more business opportunities; (4) developing or not developing one or more products; (5) drilling for or not drilling for oil, and (6) hiring or not hiring a consultant.

Step 2. Determine the consequences that could result from the selection of each strategy under consideration. This step will require that you anticipate future con-

---

FIGURE 1-9

Final Version of United Airlines Decision Tree.

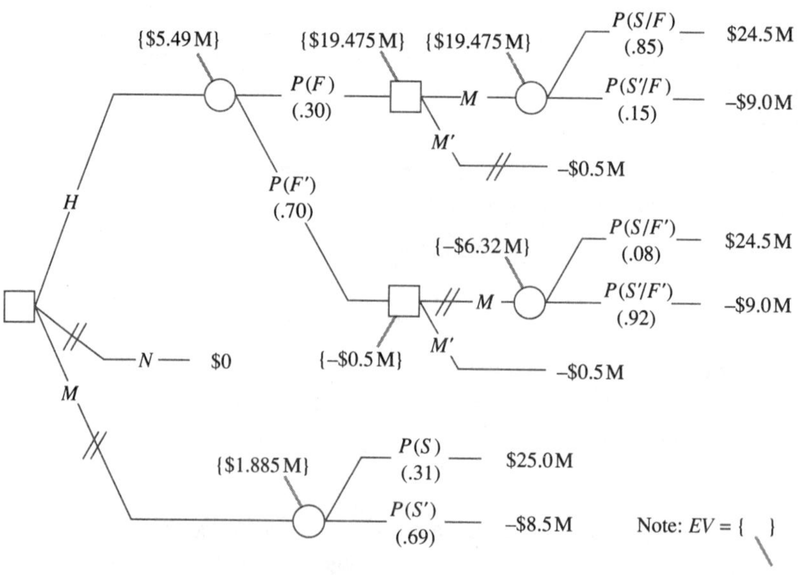

ditions—events beyond your control that could conceivably affect the goodness of your selection. Examples include (1) the product is successful or not successful; (2) business increases, stays the same, or decreases; (3) you strike oil (gusher, moderate, trickle) or you don't strike oil; (4) the consultant's report is favorable or unfavorable; and (5) the diagnostic test is positive or negative.

Step 3. After describing each event in step 2, determine if the relevant branch terminates or if there is a second act or event that follows. Repeat steps 1 and 2 as needed. This iteration should complete the layout of the tree.

Step 4. Label the tree using appropriate probability notation. Be sure that an event that is preceded by a forecast event is represented as a conditional probability, not as a marginal probability. Conditional probabilities must be present in any strategy that uses forecasts (imperfect information). If there is only one stage of events along a specific branch, you must represent it as a marginal probability. Marginal probabilities occur when a particular strategy does not use forecasts. Make sure that the sum of the probabilities at each event node sums to one.

Step 5. Include the payoffs associated with each terminal event node. Be sure that all termination events have payoffs assigned to them.

Step 6. Calculate the expected value for each branch of each strategy. Begin by folding back from the payoff values at each terminal node. As you fold back to an decision node, be sure to eliminate all nonoptimal branches (only the maximum *EV* "survives" at each act node). The optimal strategy is the one with the largest positive expected value for profit-maximization problems, or the one with the smallest negative expected value for cost-minimization problems.

Even though hiring the consultant group appears to be the best way to proceed, some members of United's management team are uncomfortable with the idea of paying $500,000 for the consultant's services. "Too much money!" they argue, "It's not worth it." This brings us to a very important consideration: When you are considering consulting costs or internal costs associated with digging out "better data," how do you determine what is a *reasonable* amount to spend? The concept of the *value of imperfect information* is our next subject.

EXPECTED VALUE OF IMPERFECT INFORMATION (*EVII*)

If a forecast is not 100 percent reliable, it is viewed as imperfect information.[3] The question is really: How imperfect is the forecast? It is crucial to have a reasonable understanding of the reliability of the predictions you are considering using in any prominent decision. This is true regardless of whether you are paying significant consulting fees for the prediction service or if that service is "free" (e.g., inhouse studies are often myopically viewed as free). Nevertheless, a manager can make a terrible decision with an expensive forecast just as well as she can with an inexpensive forecast.

With respect to decision trees using expected values, what reliability would you like your forecaster to have? That's easy, right? One-hundred percent! OK, no argument. Now tell me what forecast reliability would be the worst? Zero percent? Wrong! These

---

[3] The term "imperfect information" can be semantically misleading. A forecaster who is 95 percent accurate is providing imperfect information; he is also providing a very reliable forecast.

two extreme forecasters would provide information that would either be always correct or always wrong. The former forecaster is 100 percent reliable; the latter is 0 percent reliable. However, in forecasts that concentrate on only binomial (two-event) outcomes, a prediction that is always wrong is just as good as a prediction that is always correct (and you can probably purchase the services of the forecaster with 0 percent reliability considerably cheaper than you can those of his infallible counterpart)! The worst forecaster—the one that provides the manager with the least amount of help—would provide you with the same probabilities as those you would gain from flipping a fair coin. So, the 50 percent favorable, 50 percent unfavorable forecaster is the least helpful.

Consider the consultant group that United Airlines is considering hiring. The consultant group is not infallible: Promotional programs are successful 85 percent of the time it forecasts successful outcomes. In other words, their predictions are wrong 15 percent of the time when it forecasts favorable (successful) outcomes. Also, programs are successful in 8 percent of those instances in which it predicts unsuccessful outcomes. It is clear that this consulting group not only is fallible, but also has different reliabilities in predicting successful versus unsuccessful outcomes (i.e., there is a 15 percent error rate for favorable forecasts, and an 8 percent error rate for unfavorable forecasts). However imperfect, the consultant's forecast can be of significant value when *compared to making the decision to market or not to market the new program without this information.* Therefore, *the expected value of imperfect information is the difference between the expected value of the alternative incorporating an expert forecast source* (e.g., marketing consultant) *and the expected value provided by the next best available alternative.* That is,

$$EVII = \left(\begin{array}{c} \text{expected value of} \\ \text{using ''expert'' forecast} \end{array} \right) - \left(\begin{array}{c} \text{expected value of next-best alternative,} \\ \text{e.g., general market data, ''in-house''} \\ \text{forecast capabilities} \end{array} \right)$$

For the United Airlines example, the first term on the right-hand side of the equation is the EV found when the consultant group is employed:

$$\left(\begin{array}{c} \text{expected value of} \\ \text{using ''expert'' forecast} \end{array} \right) = EV_{\text{consultant}} = \$5,492,500$$

The "next-best alternative" is the EV resulting from the rather general market information that suggests that similar promotional programs are successful only 31 percent of the time:

$$\left(\begin{array}{c} \text{expected value of} \\ \text{next-best alternative} \end{array} \right) = EV_{\text{market (no consultant)}} = \$1,885,000$$

Therefore, the expected value of the imperfect information is the difference (monetary advantage gained) between the expected value of using the consulting group and the expected value found from the next-best alternative: immediately marketing the program,

$$
\begin{aligned}
EVII &= 5,492,500 - 1,885,000 \\
&= \$3,607,500
\end{aligned}
$$

This analysis suggests that using the expertise of the consulting group provides United Airlines with an additional expected value of $3.61 million over what it could hope to achieve "going it alone"—using only the general market data for similar promotional programs. Keep in mind that this value already *includes* the $500,000 fee that would be paid to the consulting group. However imperfect the information provided by the consulting group's forecast, it provides a considerable advantage beyond the data on the

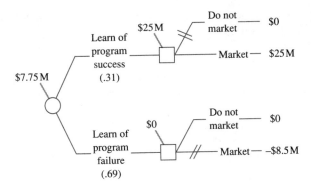

general market success-failure rate. Do not, however, interpret the $3.61 million as a justifiable fee that could be paid to gain this improved position: What is gained is merely the improvement in expected values provided by the use of consulting group; what the group should be paid is a separate issue.

Now that we've examined the value of using imperfect information, let's explore the ultimate question: What is the value of possessing perfect forecast data?

EXPECTED VALUE OF PERFECT INFORMATION (*EVPI*)

The value of a manager to a company is typically appraised in light of how well she handles risky decision settings. If there were a way for a manager to know what the ultimate outcome would be ahead of time—that is, prior to committing to a strategy, decisions would always be successful—her job would be a veritable piece of cake. Wouldn't it be a relief for United Airlines managers to know whether their promotional marketing plan would be successful or not *before* they decided to commit the investment monies needed for marketing, advertising, hiring a consultant and so on?

Infallible information—information with 100-percent reliability—is called *perfect information*. Risk is virtually eliminated. Perfect information does not, however, provide the manager with the ability to manipulate the ultimate outcome. On the contrary, perfect information simply places the manager in the position of learning—prior to selecting a strategy—whether that strategy will be successful. The chances of occurrence of such strategies are unaffected. An illustration of a perfect-information decision tree for United Airlines management is shown in Figure 1-10. Realistically, managers are rarely, if ever, privy to such an ideal set of data.[4] So why spend time discussing perfect information?

The answer is that perfect information provides the manager with the upper-bound value of how much improvement is possible above and beyond an imperfect decision setting. Since perfect information cannot manipulate the chances of occurrence for the different outcomes, it must incorporate these probabilities into an expected value of perfect information, *EVPI*. This value provides the manager with the very best outcome that is possible and serves as a point of comparison with the expected values of the actual alternatives used in the problem. Therefore, the expected value of perfect information is the difference between the expected value of knowing what the outcome will be

---

[4] The majority of perfect-information examples in business seem to fly in the face of ethical behavior and fair play. If you consider, for example, such situations as insider trading in the stockmarket and inside tips on competitive contract awards, you will have a pretty good idea of why perfect information is such a squeamish issue. Anyone privy to such information has a huge and almost certainly unfair advantage over any "competition."

ahead of time and the expected value of the next-best strategy, which does not have this infallible information:

$$EVPI = \begin{pmatrix} \text{expected value of alternative} \\ \text{employing infallable information} \end{pmatrix} - \begin{pmatrix} \text{expected value of} \\ \text{next-best alternative} \end{pmatrix}$$

For the United Airlines example, the *EV* of the next best alternative would be that of the consulting group: $5.49 million. Therefore, the ultimate amount of improvement above present capabilities would be

$$EVPI = 7,750,000 - 5,492,500$$
$$= \$2,257,500$$

| 1.9 | PRACTICAL PROBABILITY CONSIDERATIONS FOR DECISION-TREE ASSESSMENTS

One of the most important pieces of information for an organization to take into consideration is the *general* success experienced in the marketplace for similar products: the *prior probability* of market success, $P(S)$, and failure, $P(S')$ for two-event outcomes. [5] If greater insight is desired, the company can conduct its own inhouse study or hire an experienced consulting firm to make a forecast based on expert opinion or market-survey data. Regardless of who conducts the forecast, its purpose is to provide specialized information regarding this *particular* product—not regarding the general line of similar products. If the study is conducted skillfully—if the history of the forecaster's previous performance on particular products has been demonstrated to be reliable—the information gathered will provide more accuracy than was previously available.

What is meant by *forecast accuracy*? Simply this: If a forecast predicts a favorable outcome, $P(F)$, the actual outcome should be successful, $P(S/F)$ proportion of the time. If the forecast is unfavorable, $P(F')$, the outcome should be unsuccessful, $P(S'/F')$ proportion of the time. It is important to note that, in the latter probability, $P(S'/F')$, the organization does not *desire* to experience failure (be unsuccessful) after an unfavorable report—clearly there are instances in which a company will choose to proceed even after a negative evaluation in the hopes that it might get lucky. Nevertheless, if the organization discovered that after unfavorable forecasts it actually *was* successful a significant portion of times, wouldn't it be reasonable to assume that it would experience a loss of confidence in the credibility of the forecast? So the issue is the *believability* or *degree of reliability* of forecast information. Accordingly, the probability of the product being successful after a favorable forecast, $P(S/F)$, must at least be higher (more accurate) than merely the prior probability of success experienced in the general marketplace, $P(S)$:

$$P(S/F) > P(S)$$

---

[5] As mentioned in an earlier footnote in this chapter, it is more likely that a sophisticated study would use a probability distribution of three to five events, rather than these simplified success-failure combinations. Our intent is to clarify specific points.

Alternately, the chances of being unsuccessful after an unfavorable forecast should be, at the minimum, more accurate (have a higher probability) than the prior (marginal) probability of being unsuccessful in the general marketplace, $P(S')$:

$$P(S'/F') > P(S')$$

If these conditions are not true, the survey is not justifiable. The reason for purchasing (or not purchasing) imperfect information is now established. Next, it is important to understand the interrelationships between the forecaster's prediction and the forecaster's reliability.

There is a specific consistency that must be maintained in *each branch* of the great majority of decision trees: The marginal probability of success and failure—$P(S)$ and $P(S')$—must be the same. *In other words, for each option of a given decision tree, the sum of the joint probabilities along every path leading to success (or failure) must be equal to the prior probability of success (or failure).* The reason for this is that *the forecast is assumed to not influence marketplace behavior* (i.e., there exists an independence between prediction and the prior probabilities). People who ultimately purchase the product do so based on the merits of the product and on the advertising and marketing skills of the manufacturer: their behavior is not due to the forecast—which almost certainly was conducted long before the consumers' ultimate decisions. This fact does not suggest, however, that different forecast sources must have similar reliabilities; clearly, they do not. Some are more accurate than are others. Compare, for example, the prior (marginal) probabilities of success, $P(S)$, and failure, $P(S')$, with the accuracy of the forecast probability for success and failure, $P(S/F)$ and $P(S'/F')$, in the United Airlines example:

$$P(S) = .31$$
$$P(S') = .69$$

and

$$P(S/F) = .85$$
$$P(S'/F') = .92$$

United Airlines knows that if it receives a favorable report from the consultant, its chances for success increase from .31 (69 percent chance of being wrong) to .85 (15 percent chance of being wrong). If the prediction is unfavorable, the probability for an unsuccessful program increases from .69 (31 percent chance of being wrong) to .92 (8 percent chance of being wrong). These are the consultant's historic forecast performance accuracies. Even though, based on this consultant's performance, the accuracy of the forecast increases, the probability of success in each branch remains the same: .31. So, for the branch in which no consultant is used, if United decides to promote the program, the probability for success, $P(S)$, is .31. Even if the improved forecast accuracies of the consultant are used, the probability of success is still .31. That is, the chance for success when imperfect information is purchased is equal to the sum of the joint probabilities of each path leading to success:

favorable prediction followed
by successful outcome

/

$$P(S) = P(F)P(S/F) + P(F')P(S/F')$$

/

unfavorable prediction followed
by successful outcome

Suppose that we don't know that $P(S)$ is .31. Using the consultant alternative alone, we can sum these joint probabilities and solve the equation for $P(S)$. The results are

$$P(S) = (.30)(.85) + (.70)(.08)$$
$$= .255 + .056$$
$$= .311 \approx .31$$

The consistency of the prior probability of success—the realization that it cannot change by virtue of forecast information—is an important concept to grasp; it will play a major role in most of the decision-tree problems that managers encounter in business and in many of the more advanced examples presented in the next chapter.

1.10 SENSITIVITY ANALYSIS

The effectiveness of decision analysis hinges on the accuracy of the human judgments that estimate such critical tree elements as the probabilities and payoffs. It is, therefore, essential to determine just how sensitive these estimates are. More specifically, *it is essential to find out by how much these estimates can vary before the strategy originally selected is no longer preferred.*

The process of decision-tree sensitivity analysis is not difficult. A probability or payoff value that is suspect or questionable is varied, while all other parameters are held constant. This allows the manager to determine the range over which the parameter in question can vary without changing the alternative selection. If there is more than one parameter that is to be scrutinized, this process is repeated. It is even possible to conduct the sensitivity analysis for two or more variables at a time; however, this approach may be self-defeating because it is not possible to detect the proportional contribution to the aggregate change of the individual parameters being examined. An example of sensitivity analysis using the United Airlines example will help to clarify these ideas.

EXAMPLE 1.3 SENSITIVITY ANALYSIS APPLIED TO UNITED AIRLINES PROGRAM

Suppose that, in the initial United Airlines scenario (Example 1.2), the likelihood of success, $P(S)$, for the discount-ticket program is somewhat fuzzy (i.e., the interpretation of what is successful and what is not is, to some degree, a matter of judgment). What if $P(S)$ were some value different from the 31 percent originally estimated? Would it make a difference with respect to which strategy would ultimately be selected? Would United hire the consultants or not? At what different value of $P(S)$ would United become indifferent between the two strategies (i.e., what is the exact value of $P(S)$ that would result in identical *EV*s for the two strategies)? The solution to this important question requires that different values of $P(S)$ be tested. In addition, all other decision-tree probabilities that are affected by any change in $P(S)$ must be adjusted. Remember, the internal consistency of the tree requires that the joint probabilities in the hire consultant branch, H, that lead to successful outcomes must sum to the marginal probability of success. That is,

$$P(S) = P(F) P(S/F) + P(F') P(S/F')$$

If the initial conditional probabilities of $P(S/F)$ and $P(S/F')$ are still acceptable, then changes in $P(S)$ will also require adjustments in $P(F)$ and $P(F')$. Since

$$P(F') = 1 - P(F)$$

then

$$P(S) = P(F)P(S/F) + [1 - P(F)]P(S/F')$$

It is now possible to solve for $P(F)$ and $P(F')$ for a given value of $P(S)$ using trial-and-error methods. We also can solve the equation for $P(F)$ explicitly:

$$P(F) = \frac{P(S) - P(S/F')}{P(S/F) - P(S/F')}$$

After we obtain the solution, the only remaining step is to calculate the EVs of the competing strategies. In this way, we will be able to see the effect of the probability changes on expected value. A plot of EV versus $P(S)$ will illustrate this relationship clearly. The point of intersection of any two EV lines will give the exact value of $P(S)$ at which these two strategies are equal. Let's walk through this process. We already know that

$$P(S) = .31$$
$$P(F) = .30$$
$$P(F') = .70$$
$$EV(M) = \$1,885,000$$
$$EV(H) = \$5,490,000$$

So, let's try $P(S) = .50$. Now,

$$P(F) = \frac{.50 - .08}{.85 - .08} = \frac{.42}{.77} = .54$$

$$P(F') = 1 - .54 = .46$$

and

$$EV(M) = \$8,250,000$$
$$EV(H) = \$10,290,000$$

With a higher likelihood of market success, the improved information strategy has less effect.

Next, let $P(S) = .75$. Now,

$$P(F) = \frac{.75 - .08}{.85 - .08} = \frac{.67}{.77} = .87$$

$$P(F') = 1 - .87 = .13$$

and

$$EV(M) = \$16,625,000$$
$$EV(H) = \$16,870,000$$

The expected values of the two strategies are now almost equal. Rather than calculate a fourth set of data, let's plot those we already have (Figure 1-11). This figure illustrates that the value of $P(S)$ at which the two strategies become equal (the value at which we

FIGURE 1-11

Sensitivity Analysis of Changes in the Probability of Program Success, $P(S)$, for United Airlines.

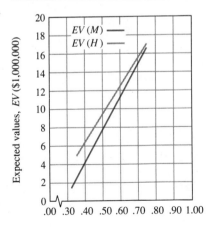

Probability of program success, $P(S)$

become indifferent) is approximately .78. So, our original estimate of .31 could increase by about 250 percent before the original selection became invalid! This finding should be comforting news to the analyst. Of course, the selection of parameters on which to perform sensitivity analysis is not necessarily a clearcut choice in many cases (e.g., it would also have been possible to do a sensitivity analysis on another probability or on a particular cash flow; however, the process would have been the same as the one just illustrated). As usual, it is the *sensitivity of the manager* that ultimately makes these delicate selections.

1.11 A FEW PRACTICAL RULES OF THUMB

Every decision tree has alternatives that fall into one or more of the following three model types:

1. "Do nothing" model: Forgo whatever it is you are considering doing (e.g., don't market the product, don't produce the play, don't drill for oil).

2. "Take the plunge" model: Do whatever you are considering doing without seeking improved information. You will have no need to revise probabilities (e.g., market the product, produce the play, drill for oil).

3. "Seek imperfect information" model: Prior to deciding to "do nothing" or "take the plunge," obtain better information so that you can make a more informed decision (e.g., hire the market-research firm to conduct survey, use the diagnostic test).

Absolutely every act in every decision tree falls into one of these three different "types." So now you have a helpful design guideline to use during the embryonic stages of your tree.

1.12 MICROCOMPUTER SOFTWARE FOR DECISION ANALYSIS

The availability of microcomputer software changes dramatically each year. The following list represents the decision-analysis software available for decision trees and decision matrices at the time of this book's printing. More information regarding the system compatibility and operating requirements is provided in Chapter 16.

- *Arborist*. (Texas Instruments.) Chicago: Scientific Press.
- *Computer Models for Management Science*. Englewood Cliffs, NJ: Prentice-Hall.
- *The Confidence Factor*. Irvine, CA: Simple Software.
- *DATA*. Boston: Tree Age.
- *Decision Analysis Technique*. Alburg, VT: Lionheart Press.
- *Decision 1-2-Tree*. Cambridge, MA: FAST Decision Systems, Inc.
- *Micro Manager*. Madison, WI: William C. Brown.
- *Riskcalc*. Belmont, MA: Riskcalc Associates.
- *Supertree*. Menlo Park, CA: SDG Decision Systems.

1.13 | MICROCOMPUTER-SOFTWARE SOLUTIONS FOR DECISION-MATRIX AND DECISION-TREE PROBLEMS

The microcomputer-software packages presented in Section 1.12 are only a sampling of the variety of products available for solving decision-analysis problems. Let's look at an illustration of how two such products can be used to evaluate the kinds of problems discussed in this chapter.

Microcomputer Solutions for a Decision Matrix

The main menu of the *Computer Models for Management Science* software package (Erikson and Hall) is shown in Table 1-4. The program's options menu from the decision-analysis module (DECS) is illustrated in Table 1-5.

Now let's solve the NBC television network problem (Example 1.1), shown in Table 1-1, using this software.

Since we are going to be entering data for the first time, we select option 1—keyboard entry. The data-entry process consists of inputting the values for each payoff

---

TABLE 1-4

Main Menu of *Computer Models for Management Science* (Erikson & Hall) Software Package.

```
            COMPUTER MODELS FOR MANAGEMENT SCIENCE
                    ***** MAIN MENU *****

-------------------------------------------------------------------
     1  =  LINP...LINEAR PROGRAMMING        8  =  DTRE...DECISION TREE MODELS
     2  =  INTP...INTEGER PROGRAMMING       9  =  MRKV...MARKOV MODELS
     3  =  TRAN...TRANSPORTATION MODEL     10  =  INVN...INVENTORY MODELS
     4  =  ASGT...ASSIGNMENT MODEL         11  =  QUES...QUEUEING MODELS
     5  =  PERT...PROJECT SCHEDULING       12  =  DATA...DISKETTE MANAGEMENT
     6  =  NETW...NETWORK MODELS           13  =  QUIT...(EXIT TO DOS)
     7  =  DECS...DECISION MODELS
-------------------------------------------------------------------
```

TABLE 1-5

Program Options Menu for the Decision-Analysis Module of the *Computer Models for Management Science* (Erikson & Hall) Software Package.

```
                    DECISION MODELS
              ***** PROGRAMS OPTIONS MENU *****
        ---------------------------------------------
            1 = ENTER PROBLEM FROM KEYBOARD
            2 = ENTER PROBLEM FROM DATA DISK
            3 = ENTER EXAMPLE PROBLEM
            4 = VIEW CURRENT PROBLEM
            5 = EDIT CURRENT PROBLEM
            6 = VIEW DATA DISK DIRECTORY
            7 = RUN PROBLEM
            8 = RETURN TO MAIN MENU
            9 = QUIT (EXIT TO DOS)
        ---------------------------------------------
```

TABLE 1-6

Data Entry of NBC Television Study Using the *Computer Models for Management Science* Software Package.

```
ENTER NUMBER OF STATES (1 TO 15): 4
ENTER NUMBER OF ALTERNATIVES (1 TO 15): 4
DECISION UNDER RISK (R) OR UNCERTAINTY (U): R
IS THE PROBLEM TYPE MAXIMIZATION  (1) OR MINIMIZATION (-1): 1


                          PAYOFF TABLE*
              PAYOFF FROM EACH ALTERNATIVE
                        STATE               1
           2        3        4
           1     175.00     5.00 -110.00   190.00
           2     -50.00   -80.00   50.00  -100.00
           3     -25.00   160.00    0.00   -20.00
           4      80.00    25.00  150.00    70.00

                      STATE #1=  .5
                      STATE #2 = .2
                      STATE #3 = .2
                      STATE #4 = .1
```

*The payoff table row-column arrangement of the original payoff matrix in Table 1-1 is opposite to that of this computer package.

matrix cell (row, column) and for each of the three states of nature. The entire data entry for the NBC case is shown in Table 1-6. The results (computer output) are shown in Table 1-7.

Microcomputer Solutions for Decision Trees

There are a number of microcomputer software products that offer decision-tree programs. We'll use a typical representative of this group, *Micro Manager* (Lee and Shim), to illustrate the solution of the United Airlines study (Example 1.2, Figure 1-9).

The prompted input style of this software package requires that each decision (act), chance (event), and terminal node (outcome) be numbered for every branch in the tree. The United Airlines decision tree is shown in Figure 1-12 using the branch and node numbering system necessary to run this particular package. The data entry is shown in Table 1-8. The computer solution to the United Airlines decision tree is given in Table 1-9.

TABLE 1-7

Solution of NBC Television Study Using the *Computer Models for Management Science* Software Package.

```
           --DECISION MAKING UNDER RISK RESULTS--
    -----------------------------------------------------
            EXPECTED VALUE OF EACH ALTERNATIVE
            80.50          21.00      -30.00
    78.00
               OPTIMAL ALTERNATIVE : A1
    EXPECTED PAYOFF WITH PERFECT INFORMATION: 152.00
    -----------------------------------------------------
                   --END OF ANALYSIS--
```

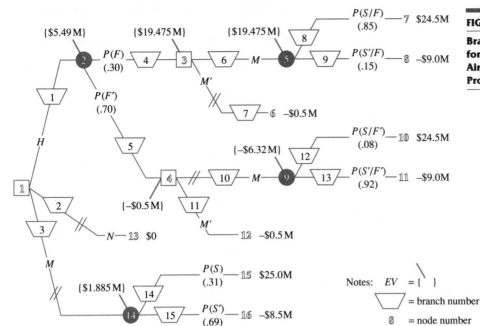

FIGURE 1-12

Branch and Node Numbering System Used for Microcomputer Solution of United Airlines Discount-Coupon Promotional Program.

Notes: $EV = \{\quad\}$

$\underline{\quad\diagdown}$ = branch number

⑧ = node number

TABLE 1-8

Data Entry for United Airlines Study Using the _Micro Manager_ (Lee & Shim) Software Package.

```
          1. NUMBER OF BRANCHES
          2.  FOR EACH BRANCH
                 STARTING NODE NUMBER
                 ENDING NODE NUMBER
                 PROBABILITY (0 AT DECISION NODE)
                 CONDITIONAL PAYOFF (0 IF NOT APPLICABLE)

PROGRAM:  DECISION TREE

                 ***** INPUT DATA ENTERED *****

     TOTAL NUMBER OF BRANCHES:   15
          BRANCH      NODES      PROBABILITY CONDITIONAL PAYOFF

            #1        1--->2        .00          0.00
            #2        1--->13       .00          0.00
            #3        1--->14       .00          0.00
            #4        2--->3        .30          0.00
            #5        2--->4        .70          0.00
            #6        3--->5        .00          0.00
            #7        3--->6        .00         -0.50
            #8        5--->7        .85         24.50
            #9        5--->8        .15         -9.00
            #10       4--->9        .00          0.00
            #11       4--->12       .00         -0.50
            #12       9--->10       .08         24.50
            #13       9--->11       .92         -9.00
            #14       14--->15      .31         25.00
            #15       14--->16      .69         -8.50
```

TABLE 1-9

Solution of United Airlines Study Using the *Micro Manager* (Lee & Shim) Software Package.

```
                    *****  PROGRAM OUTPUT  *****


EVALUATED DECISION TREE
      ----------------------------------------------------------------------
              BRANCH    NODES     PROBABILITY    CONDITIONAL PAYOFF
      ----------------------------------------------------------------------
               #1      1--->2      DECISION          5.49 *
               #2      1--->13     DECISION          0.00
               #3      1--->14     DECISION          1.89
               #4      2--->3      .30               5.84
               #5      2--->4      .70              -.35
               #6      3--->5      DECISION         19.48 *
               #7      3--->6      DECISION         -.50
               #8      4--->9      DECISION        -6.32
               #9      4--->12     DECISION         -.50 *
               #10     5--->7      .85              20.83
               #11     5--->8      .15              -1.35
               #12     9--->10     .08               1.96
               #13     9--->11     .92              -8.28
               #14     14--->15    .31               7.75
               #15     14--->16    .69              -5.86
      ----------------------------------------------------------------------
            *  INDICATES PREFERRED DECISION BRANCHES AND PAYOFFS

EXPECTED PAYOFF OF THE SOLUTION =      5.49
```

1.14 EXERCISES

1-1 A private investor is interested in investing $250,000 in one of three different opportunities during the next year: (a_1) property, (a_2) stock market, and (a_3) gold. At the end of the 12 month period, she will "cash in" her holdings and reexamine what to do for the next year. The three possible states of nature that might occur during the present 12-month period are: (s_1) dollar falls substantially, interest rates rise dramatically, stock market drops precipitously, and gold price soars; (s_2) foreign deficit improves slightly, stock market increases slightly, property holds, gold price decreases slightly; (s_3) foreign deficit decreases dramatically, property values rise sharply, gold price decreases moderately, and stock market improves moderately. The investor estimates that the chances of occurrence for each of the future states of nature are .30, .50, and .20 for s_2, s_2, and s_3, respectively. The payoff, in $1000 of net profit, for each combination of investment alternative and future state of nature is illustrated in Table 1-1.1 for the $250,000 investment. Design the decision matrix and determine which investment you would advise the investor to make, basing your decision on

1. The most likely future.
2. Playing the averages.
3. The principle of paranoia (minimum regret).

TABLE 1-1.1

Net Profit Payoff Matrix for Investor ($1000).

Investment Type Selected, a_i	Future Financial States, s_j		
	s_1	s_2	s_3
a_1	0	35	100
a_2	−50	30	50
a_3	100	−25	−60

1-2 A wildcat oil company, J. J. Cord, is trying to determine whether it should invest the necessary monies to drill (a_1) or not drill (a_2) on land it has leased on the northeastern Louisiana border. The company tells you that one of three possible outcomes will occur if it drills: hit a gusher (s_1), average strike (s_2), or hit a dry hole (s_3). Their surveyors estimate, based on a visual inspection of the land and previous empirical data from other drilling attempts in the immediate area, that the chances for these three possible outcomes are $p_1 = .15$, $p_2 = .70$, and $p_3 = .15$. The decision matrix illustrating probable net profit resulting from each combination of drilling decision and future state of nature is shown in Table 1-2.1. For

TABLE 1-2.1

Net Profit Payoff Matrix for J. J. Cord Wildcat Oil Company ($1000).

Option Selected, a_i	Future Drilling Outcome, s_j		
	s_1	s_2	s_3
a_1	900	100	−300
a_2	0	0	0

each of the three styles of decision making under risk illustrated in Section 1.7, determine whether you would drill or not.

1-3 Illustrate and solve Exercise 1-1 as a decision tree.

1-4 Illustrate and solve Exercise 1-2 as a decision tree.

1-5 Over the past 3 years, weather forecasts for Honolulu during the month of March have predicted the likelihood of rain to be .73. When the prediction was for rain, rain actually occurred 84 percent of the time during this time period. However, rain fell on 34 percent of the occasions for which the forecast was for no rain.

GUINDON 3 17 © R. Guindon.

"As you can see by the map, North and South Dakota will be moving into the nineteen-fifties while parts of Florida can expect more of the nineteen-thirties."

ASSIGNMENT

Assume that the weather forecast included only the climate events of rain or no rain. What percent of the time did it actually rain in Honolulu during March over this 3-year period?

1-6 A San Francisco metals broker has just acquired an option to buy 400,000 tons of tungsten ore from the Thailand government for $10 per ton, which is well below the current world market price for this ore. Since other brokers have not yet received the same option, the broker thinks he must make a decision immediately if he is not to lose this opportunity. He is quite certain that he can get about $15 per ton for the ore if he is able to import it, but there is a catch. The United States government may refuse to grant an import license. If this happens, the contract will be annulled and a penalty of $1.50 per ton will be imposed on the broker.

The broker knows that, if he acts now, prior to the decision of the United States government ruling on the acceptability of the transaction, he is virtually guaranteed the rights to the tungsten ore. Based on previous rulings, the chance that the government will approve the license is about 50 percent. However, if the broker waits for government approval before committing to the ore purchase (the ruling is a license approval), he will no longer have the inside track; there will be many other metals brokers with whom he must now contend. In fact, the chances of his being able to purchase the ore in this more highly contested setting will be only one in three.

ASSIGNMENT

1. Using only your intuition—ignoring the techniques discussed in this chapter—how would you advise the broker? Are you able to incorporate *all* of the information provided in the problem using an intuitive approach?

2. Using decision-tree analysis, draw the various options available to the broker. Which strategy provides the highest expected value? Is this expected value what the broker can expect to make (or lose) on this particular venture? Explain your answer.

1-7 The Ford Motor Company manufactured the Pinto automobile from 1970 to 1977. During this period, the Pinto developed a serious problem: Because the rear bumper was believed by many to be inadequately separated from the adjacent gas tank, the gas tank would rupture as a result of moderate rear-end impact or rollover, and would burst into flame. Certain experts concluded that the problem of gas-tank rupture could be resolved if a small, inexpensive metal baffle was placed between the interior of the rear bumper and the gas tank. In this way, much of the shock of a rear-end collision or rollover would be absorbed by the new part.

A national magazine reproduced an alleged Ford internal memorandum that included dollar estimates of the worth of human life lost on the highway as well as Ford's own inhouse estimates regarding the number of accidents that were anticipated to result in death, serious injury, or simple property loss if no changes were made in the gas-tank design (Dowie, 1977). The article suggested that the final decision boiled down to one of two possible alternatives for Ford:

1. Recall the Pinto as well as other Ford models of compacts and light trucks that also had the same potential safety defect. The recall would include 11 million compact cars and 1.5 million light trucks manufactured by Ford in previous years. The replacement part would cost Ford an estimated $11 per car or light truck.

2. Ignore the design-defect recall and defend themselves against any litigation that might be brought against them on a case-by-case basis. The article also reported that Ford estimated that an equal number of burn deaths and serious burn injuries were likely to occur—180 of each. Further, Ford also projected 2100 burn-destroyed vehicles. The projected costs associated with each death, serious burn, and destroyed vehicle were $200,000, $67,000, and $700, respectively.

Assume that the data presented here are accurate. Use decision-tree analysis, and the given estimates of deaths, injuries, and property damage, to illustrate Ford's choices and determine what the company is likely to conclude based solely on the assumption that the expected monetary values are appropriate. Assume that Ford anticipates a worst-case scenario of having to replace the part on all 12.5 million vehicles if it chooses option 1.

1-8 In 1986, a Texas jury awarded the Pennzoil Corporation $10.3 billion after deciding that Texaco, Inc. had illegally interfered with Pennzoil's takeover of Getty Oil Company. The U.S. Supreme Court had agreed to hear an appeal in June 1988. On November 19, 1987, Texaco refused the following offer from Pennzoil Corporation: Texaco was to make a binding out-of-court settlement with Pennzoil, and was to make initial payment to Pennzoil for 5 billion dollars, and was to forgo any further court appeals of the $10.3-billion ruling already made in favor of Pennzoil. Texaco refused this out-of-court settlement offer. Assume that Texaco's options were either (1) to wait for the U.S. Supreme Court to rule on the case, or (2) to accept Pennzoil's $5 billion settlement. Assume further that if Texaco waits for the U.S. Supreme Court to act, the ruling will be either a reversal or an upholding of the earlier judgment.

1. What is your estimate of Texaco's likelihood of obtaining a Supreme Court ruling overturning the standing lower court ruling if it refuses the out-of-court settlement offer from Pennzoil? Assume that a favorable judgment would release Texaco of all financial responsibility to Pennzoil.

2. Assume instead that there is considerable uncertainty regarding both the chances of a favorable Supreme Court ruling and Texaco's financial costs associated with this favorable ruling; that is, it is possible that the Supreme Court will only lessen Texaco's fine to some value lower than the $10.3 billion, rather than necessarily eliminate the financial penalty altogether. Illustrate a sensitivity analysis for both the probability of a favorable finding and the payoff costs associated with this ruling.

1-9 Assume that it is now late 1987. Suppose that the Olympic Games Committee (OGC) has just hired you to help them with a number of very serious problems. First, the South Korean government is in political turmoil, facing continuing charges of corruption and nondemocratic practices. Second, the Soviet bloc countries are less than pleased with the selection of Seoul as the 1988 Summer Olympic Games site because, if they attend, they could be viewed as legitimizing the Western-aligned South Korean government.

The OGC believes that there is a significant chance that the Soviet bloc countries will boycott the Olympics if the Games are held in Seoul (no such boycott is likely to occur if the Games are moved to one of several alternatives sites—with the possible exception of a boycott by the South Koreans). If the site is not changed, the result could be a significant decrease in attendance and thus loss of revenues. However, moving the

Games with so little time left could result in poor attendance (and revenues) because attendees will be faced with readjusting travel plans, accommodations, and so on. Because of the volatile sentiments of the Soviet bloc countries, the OGC is considering moving the Games to a less controversial site. They wish to examine the facts as closely as possible, but time is running out. The OGC must make a decision within a few days. Here are the specific considerations the OGC thinks are important:

1. Three points are relevant if the Games are kept in Seoul. First, the chance of a Soviet bloc boycott is estimated to be 40 percent. Second, the likelihood for success in Seoul is .70 if the Soviet bloc does not boycott the Games; if the bloc does boycott, the probability of success decreases to .30. Third, the gross profits associated with successful and unsuccessful outcomes with no boycott are estimated to be $1 billion and −$300 million, respectively. Conversely, the gross profits associated with successful and unsuccessful outcomes when there is a boycott are $750 million and −$600 million, respectively.

2. If the Games are moved to another site at this late date, the OGC estimates that the chance for a financially successful Olympiad would be about 40 percent and that the gross profits associated with this outcome would be approximately $500 million. A financially unsuccessful Olympiad at the new site would bring in an estimated loss of $300 million. There is no chance of a Soviet bloc boycott if the site is moved.

1. Using decision-tree analysis and expected values, determine what strategy the OGC should employ.

2. What change in the likelihood in a Soviet bloc boycott would cause the OGC to become indifferent to the site selection?

1-10 The Oklahoma Crude Oil Company (OCOC) was established shortly after the OPEC boycott precipitated the oil crisis in the United States during the mid-1970s. OCOC leases land solely to explore for oil reserves, not to run the long-term oil-field operations. The typical mode of operation is to lease the land short-term, run seismic tests, and drill. If oil is discovered, OCOC will obtain a long-term lease on the land, then will sell the development rights to an oil refining company.

During OCOC's first year of operation, one project after another led to dry wells. Now, the net liquid assets of the company have shrunk to $275,000, and the president, George C. Scott, is very concerned. "George, we're close to going broke," says Vice President, Jack Palance. "We need to study the alternatives, try to define the possible outcomes in terms of their associated probabilities and payoffs, and then make our decision thoughtfully. We don't have enough money to survive another bad decision." George agrees, "You're right. If we fail this time, we're back hustling life insurance!"

The situation to which Scott and Palance are referring is on an option that OCOC purchased 4 weeks ago for $25,000. The option gives the company the right to make tests and to drill for oil over a 7-week period. Until the option expires, OCOC can

sign a long-term lease agreement on the property for a fixed fee of $250,000. The current short-term option expires in 3 weeks, and until now OCOC has not conducted tests or initiated drilling operations. This land represents the only business opportunity that OCOC is presently considering.

Palance plays with the brass oil rig paperweight on his desk while he thinks over the situation. Finally, he says, "George, I think we have three choices. Either we let the current option run out, or we order seismic tests, or we take a chance and drill without any initial testing. Our geologist thinks that there is a twenty-percent chance that any tests conducted in this region covered by the option will result in positive test results."

Scott thinks for a moment, then asks, "If our seismic tests are positive and we drill, what is your best guess for the probability that we will find oil?"

"If I were forced to give you a number now, I would guess 80 percent," says Palance.

"What if we get a negative seismic result? Should we consider drilling under those conditions?" asks Scott.

"I don't know," answers Palance. "Our chances of finding oil given a negative test result drop to five percent. It doesn't sound too promising under those conditions."

"Hold on, Jack," exclaims Scott. "This decision is too important for us to attempt to assess it in our heads. We need more than dialogue to examine our situation. Let's take a look at the likely payoffs and costs."

"According to the best information available," Palance replies, "a seismic test will cost us seventy-five thousand dollars, and drilling a well will run another two-hundred thousand dollars. Both can be completed in about ten days. If we are lucky and strike oil, we can sell the rights to this land for about one and a half million bucks."

Scott ponders the situation. Finally, he looks over to Palance and says, "I must tell you that I feel overwhelmed. What do you think we should do?"

Palance replies, "The chances of striking oil don't seem very good if we just go ahead and drill. Because of this, I favor taking a test first. In my opinion, this is the safest approach. The seismic test at least provides us with valuable insight. I think that it will pay for itself! In fact, after speaking to our geologist, I believe that the chance that a seismic test will be positive is actually closer to 30 or 40 percent, rather than 20 percent. Our geologist was probably too restrained in his estimate. We ought to consider getting rid of him if we survive the next couple of weeks!"

ASSIGNMENT

1. Structure this problem as a decision tree and determine, on the basis of expected values, what decision you would recommend to OCOC.

2. How did you, as the decision analyst, deal with the difference in judgment between the geologist and Jack Palance? What is the shortcoming, if any, of the expected-dollar-payoff criterion when it is used to reach a decision in this case?

1-11 A successful entrepreneur must decide about an investment opportunity she has open to her. She believes that the invest-

ment could be a flop, be good, or be terrific, with respective probabilities of .38, .48, and .14. If the investment flops, the revenues for the investment will be about $100,000; if it is good, the revenues will be $500,000; and if it's terrific, $1,250,000 in revenue will be generated. The initial investment requires that she spend $350,000. At an additional cost of $50,000, she can hire an investment consultant to analyze the situation and to provide a report that will suggest whether the investment will be wise or not wise. The consultant's reports are denoted by the following notation: W = wise investment, W' = unwise investment. The notation for the actual investment outcomes are: O_1 = flop, O_2 = good, and O_3 = terrific. Past experience with the consultant has shown the following results:

1. When the reports suggested a wise investment, the results were good 53 percent of the time and flopped 13 percent of the time.
2. The outcomes were terrific 8 percent and good 47 percent of the time when the consultant predicted that the investment was unwise.

ASSIGNMENT

1. Sketch the decision tree and determine what strategy the tycoon should incorporate in this risky investment opportunity using expected values.
2. Is the $50,000 consultant fee a fair price? From a theoretical standpoint, exactly how much could the consultant justifiably expect to be paid?

1-12 The metals broker in Exercise 1-6 is interested in reassessing his earlier estimates. In particular, he would like to know by exactly how much the following parameters could change before the change causes him to select a different strategy:

1. The probability of the government approving the import contract
2. The actual per-ton price that he could obtain for the tungsten
3. The actual per-ton price that he would have to pay for the tungsten
4. The probability of winning the contract if he decides to wait and to see what the government decision will be.

1-13 A small, regional soft-drink manufacturer is considering expanding its bottling plant. Company sales had grown gradually over the company's 20 year existence, until 3 years ago. At that time, the company received great publicity in a national weekly news magazine that identified numerous public figures as avid drinkers of the company's famed Diet Chocolate Mousse soda (e.g., Wayne Newton, Sammy Davis, Junior, Barry Manilow). Since that article hit the newsstands, sales have doubled during each of those 3 years! The existing facility is running at almost the production capacity; if demand continues at anything near the present rapid growth rate, the company will not be able to handle it. The company's market analysts suggest, however, that the demand may level out during the near future, or even may decrease depending on the impact of the rapidly growing sparkling water, seltzer, and fruit

TABLE 1-13.1

Annual Company Revenues ($10 Million) As a Function of Demand and Plant Size for Soft-Drink Manufacturer.

Present Demand	Unchanged	Expanded
Decreased	8	−5
Unchanged	13	5
Increased	15	28

juice industry. The estimated company revenues for these different levels of sales for both the existing plant and proposed expanded plant are shown in Table 1-13.1. The company estimates that the probabilities of the demand decreasing, remaining constant, or increasing are .15, .60, and .25 respectively. Amortized expansion costs are estimated at $7 million per year over the next 5 years. The company president would like to know whether to expand the plant.

ASSIGNMENT

Design a decision tree and determine what the optimal strategy is for the company based on a 5-year planning horizon (assume that the values in Table 1-13.1 represent the average revenues generated over that 5-year time period).

1-14 A meat packing company is concerned that the sodium nitrite preservative it uses in its bacon products is carcinogenic (cancer-causing). Although there has been no formal investigation to date, the Food and Drug Administration (FDA) is about to begin tests. The findings of these tests will be either favorable (i.e., approve the nitrites) or unfavorable (i.e., ban the nitrites). The FDA's history of testing similar meat nitrites indicates that there is a 75 percent chance that the FDA will rule favorably (i.e., will find the existing nitrites safe for human consumption). Fortunately, the company has a substitute for these nitrites and is considering immediately replacing the potentially carcinogenic preservative with this new ingredient. This move would avoid a quick—and expensive—changeover if the FDA bans the nitrites later. The conversion, if done now, will cost the company approximately $5 million. Of course, the company can choose to do nothing and hope that the FDA will issue a favorable test finding. If this happens, the company will sustain no costs. If, however, the FDA issues an unfavorable report, the company would have to recall all nitrite products from the markets and, in addition, close down production until the new preservative can be introduced. The associated costs for such an outcome are estimated at $15 million, which includes lost sales, consumer ill-will, and the overtime and downtime expenses of the conversion to the new preservative.

ASSIGNMENT

1. Using decision-tree analysis and the principle of expected values, what would you suggest that the company do?
2. By how much can the estimate that there is a 75 percent chance of the FDA ruling favorably *be in error* before your optimum strategy is affected? Include illustrations in your answer.
3. By how much can the $15 million conversion-cost estimate vary before your optimum strategy changes? Include illustrations in your answer.

1-15 Calculate the value of perfect information for the San Francisco metals broker of Exercise 1-6.

1-16 What is the value of perfect information for the Oklahoma Crude Oil Company, versus the imperfect information as given in Exercise 1-10?

1-17 What is the value of perfect information for the imperfect information given in Exercise 1-11?

1-18 What is the value of perfect information for the soft-drink manufacturer, versus the imperfect information given in Exercise 1-13?

1-19 What is the value of perfect information for the meat packing company in Exercise 1-14?

REFERENCES

1. Bodily, Samuel E. "When Should You Go to Court?" *Harvard Business Review* 59 (No. 3: May–June 1981): 103–113.
2. Clarke, John R. "The Application of Decision Analysis to Clinical Medicine." *Interfaces* 17 (No. 2: March–April 1987): 27–34.
3. De Rivera, Daniel Peña Sanchez. "A Decision Analysis Model for a Serious Medical Problem." *Management Science* 26 (No. 7: July 1980): 707–718.
4. Digman, Lester A. "A Decision Analysis of the Airline Coupon Strategy." *Interfaces* 10 (No. 2: April 1980): 97–101.
5. Dowie, Mark. "Pinto Madness." *Mother Jones* 11 (No. 8: September–October 1977): 18–32.
6. Judd, Bruce R., and Stein Weissenberger. "A Systematic Approach to Nuclear Safeguards Decision-Making." *Management Science* 28 (No. 3: March 1982): 289–302.
7. Saaty, Thomas L., Luis G. Vargas, and Amos Barzilay. "High-Level Decisions: A Lesson from the Iran Hostage Rescue Operation." *Decision Sciences* 13 (No. 2: April 1982): 185–206.
8. Solomon, Robert J., and Donald J. Messmer. "Implications of the Bakke Decision in Implementing Affirmative Action Programs: A Decision Model." *Decision Sciences* 11 (No. 2: April 1980): 312–324.
9. Ulvila, Jacob W. "Postal Automatic (ZIP + 4) Technology: A

Decision Analysis." *Interfaces* 17 (No. 2: March–April 1987): 27–34.

10. Ulvila, Jacob W., Rex V. Brown, and Karale S. Packard. "A Case in On-Line Decision Analysis for Product Planning." Paper presented at the ORSA/TIMS National Convention, Chicago, Arpil 30, 1975.

11. Williams, Fred E. "Decision Theory and the Innkeeper: An Approach for Setting Hotel Reservation Policy." *Interfaces* 7 (No. 4: August 1977), pp. 18–30.

CHAPTER 2

DECISION ANALYSIS: PART 2

PROBABILITY REVISION AND BAYES' THEOREM

| 2.1 | REVISING PRIOR PROBABILITIES USING BAYES' THEOREM

The common expression "on second thought" is typically used when an earlier assessment or view is *revised*. Usually, this revision is based on improved insight gained from additional information that was either not used or not available during the earlier assessment. Another familiar illustration of this process is seen when the odds (or point differential) on an upcoming sporting event dramatically change because a key athlete for one team has been injured. The revision reflects the use of this latest important news, because the athlete's injury provides the decision maker with *imperfect information*.

The revision of prior probabilities is a crucial tool in business. That is why imperfect information sources such as diagnostic tests or consultant inputs are used. However, sometimes these data are presented in a form that is not immediately usable. For example, it is quite possible that the probability information regarding the United Airlines consultant group's predictive performance on earlier marketing-program assessments (Example 1.2) could have been presented in a very different way. The information could have been given like this:

The experience with this consulting group has taught us that, for those programs that became successful, favorable reports had been written 82 percent of the time. Favorable reports were also written 7 percent of the time when the program ultimately failed.

Do you notice something different about the way in which these two probability statements are presented? If you carefully dissect each statement, you will find that the given events—the ones that must come *before* the present events—are the success or failure of the program. That is,

$$P(F/S) = .82$$

and

$$P(F/S') = .07$$

How can you know this information *prior* to receiving the favorable report? In fact, what sense does it make to know what the ultimate destiny of the program is *before* receiving the report? Well, it doesn't make sense unless you know that *nonchronological* probabilities such as these simply represent *historical* information. They are probabilities, collected over some period of time, representing the diagnostic accuracy or "track record" of the predictive source, such as a consultant, or survey findings, or a

You know how it goes, civilization kept encroaching and I kept retreating farther and farther until finally I said to myself, "you'd better rethink your life while there's still time . . ."

diagnostic medical test. The reason they are in *reverse order* is that they were compiled *after* the ultimate outcomes of success and failure were known. The reverse order just represents another way in which conditional probabilities can be presented. Of course, since these probabilities are not in real time (they are nonchronological), they cannot be used directly in a decision tree that requires a chronological flow of acts and events. In fact, it is not possible to solve the decision tree for the consultant group using these probabilities. What needs to be accomplished now is to devise some technique for unraveling these nonchronological data. They must be turned around or reversed, so that they can be incorporated into the decision tree.

The process used to accomplish this critical step borrows from one of the most important concepts in decision analysis: Bayes' theorem. This powerful tool was developed by Thomas Bayes in the eighteenth century as a method to facilitate the revision and improvement of earlier probabilities established prior to the availability of new information. This procedure of updating old information with the latest available information is a common practice in business—or should be, if the business is to survive. The general form of Bayes' theorem is

$$P[A_i/B] = \frac{P[A_i]P[B/A_i]}{\sum\limits_{j=1}^{n} P[A_j]P[B/A_j]}$$

where

$P[A_i/B]$ = probability that the ith event will actually occur given that event B has already occurred. An example, in terms of the TV series (Example 1.1), might be the chance that the show will be successful given that the consultant wrote an unfavorable report [i.e., $P(F/S')$]. This term is also referred to as a *posterior probability*.

$P[A_i]$ = probability that the ith event will actually occur without the results of the prediction event, B. For the TV series example, this could be the prior probability of success without the help of the consultant [i.e., $P(S)$].

$P[B/A_i]$ = probability that prediction B will occur given that the ith event has already occurred. Another example would be the probability that the consultant will assess a series as a favorable investment given that the series was, in fact, already successful [i.e., $P(F/S)$]. This information is taken from historical records, such as data taken from other similar series over past seasons.

$\sum\limits_{j=1}^{n} P[A_j]P[B/A_j]$ = the sum of the probabilities of all the ways in which the prediction, B, can occur and there are n different terminal events. This denominator term in Bayes' equation is also the *marginal probability of prediction* B. For example, it represents all the ways in which favorable forecasts, $P(F)$, can be made for the TV series example—in the cases of both successful outcomes and unsuccessful outcomes.

$$\sum\limits_{j=1}^{2} P(S_j)P(F/S_j) = P(S)P(F/S) + P(S')P(F/S') = P(F)$$

A visual representation of Bayes' theorem is shown in Figure 2-1. The use of this important theorem is far less imposing than this brief presentation indicates. An illustration of the application of Bayes' theorem to the United Airlines problem (Example 1.2) will help to clarify the process considerably.

FIGURE 2-1

Pictorial Representation of Bayes' Theorem.

Given the ultimate outcome, such as the chance of being successful (or not), what proportion of times were the predictions accurate (or not)? These are the conditional probabilities in non-chronological time.

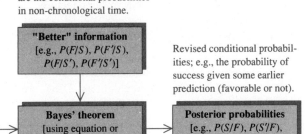

"Better" information [e.g., $P(F/S)$, $P(F'/S)$, $P(F/S')$, $P(F'/S')$]

Early estimates of the states of nature, such as the chances of being successful or not.

Revised conditional probabilities; e.g., the probability of success given some earlier prediction (favorable or not).

Prior probabilities [e.g., $P(S)$, $P(S')$]

Bayes' theorem [using equation or reverse tree]

Posterior probabilities [e.g., $P(S/F)$, $P(S'/F)$, $P(S/F')$, $P(S'/F')$]

The given information for the consultant group has already been stated as

$$P(S) = .31$$
$$P(F/S) = .82$$
$$P(F/S') = .07$$

We already know that the two conditional probabilities are not readily usable since it is impossible, in real time, to have the success or failure of the series preceding a favorable or unfavorable report. We need only to examine Figure 1-8 briefly to see that what we eventually desire to know is $P(S/F)$, $P(S'/F)$, $P(S/F')$, and $P(S'/F')$. What we have been given is the reverse of this information. So, what we are going to do is to incorporate a device called a *reverse tree*. A reverse tree will make it possible to take historical conditional probabilities that are not in true chronological order and to transform (revise) these data into real-time probabilities through the use of Bayes' theorem. First, let's draw the reverse tree for the United Airlines problem (Figure 2-2).

FIGURE 2-2

Reverse Tree for United Airlines.

1. The reverse tree always begins with the marginal, prior probabilities, and

2. progresses to the nonchronological conditional probabilities that must be revised.

3. The joint probabilities are formed by multiplication of the prior and nonchronological conditional probabilities. These joint probabilities are the key elements in Bayesian revision; they have all the information you will require to solve for any real-time conditional probability needed for the decision tree.

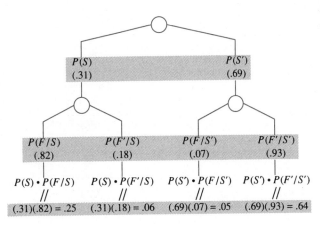

When we incorporate a reverse tree, there are several useful points for us to remember:

1. Only events and their associated probabilities are shown on reverse trees. Any intermediate acts that might appear in the decision tree are omitted.

2. The tree typically has a top-down architecture, starting with the marginal probabilities of the terminal (last) events [i.e., $P(S)$ and $P(S')$]. The primary reason for this vertical layout is that it provides an immediate distinction from the decision tree.

3. The prediction events follow the terminal events and are expressed as non-chronological conditional probabilities. These are the probabilities that you are going to revise [e.g., $P(F/S)$, $P(F'/S)$, $P(F/S')$, $P(F'/S')$].

4. The sum of the probabilities at each event fork must total 1.00. That's how the values for $P(S')$, $P(F'/S)$, and $P(F'/S')$ were found, even though they were not provided in the problem statement.

5. All possible combinations of *joint probabilities* along each of the four paths in the tree are calculated. These joint-probability values are used extensively in the Bayes' theorem equation:

$$P(S)P(F/S) = (.31)(.82) = .25$$
$$P(S)P(F'/S) = (.31)(.18) = .06$$
$$P(S')P(F/S') = (.69)(.07) = .05$$
$$P(S')P(F'/S') = (.69)(.93) = .64$$

6. Finally, we can employ Bayes' theorem to reverse the nonchronological conditional probabilities into real-time values that, in turn, we can plug into the decision tree. These reversed values—which will be slightly different from the probabilities provided in the original version due to rounding error associated with two-decimal-place accuracy—are

$$
\begin{aligned}
P(S/F) &= \frac{P(S)P(F/S)}{P(S)P(F/S) + P(S')P(F/S')} \\
&= \frac{.25}{.25 + .05} \\
&= \frac{.25}{.30} \\
&= .83
\end{aligned}
$$

$$
\begin{aligned}
P(S/F') &= \frac{P(S)P(F'/S)}{P(S)P(F'/S) + P(S')P(F'/S')} \\
&= \frac{.06}{.06 + .64} \\
&= \frac{.06}{.70} \\
&= .09
\end{aligned}
$$

$$P(S'/F) = \frac{P(S')P(F/S')}{P(S')P(F/S') + P(S)P(F/S)}$$

$$= \frac{.05}{.05 + .25}$$

$$= \frac{.05}{.30}$$

$$= .17$$

$$P(S'/F') = \frac{P(S')P(F'/S')}{P(S')P(F'/S') + P(S)P(F'/S)}$$

$$= \frac{.64}{.64 + .06}$$

$$= \frac{.64}{.70}$$

$$= .91$$

Now we have sufficient information to fill in all the probabilities and payoffs necessary to evaluate the competing alternatives of the program. Since the only difference between these probabilities and those given earlier is merely the form of presentation (the first set is given in chronological time, whereas the last set is not) and a small rounding error, the solution of the tree can still be represented by the results in Figure 1-9.

2.2 MORE EXAMPLES OF DECISION-TREE DESIGN AND EVALUATION

It is challenging to design a decision tree accurately based solely on the contents of a paragraph or two of text. There are no equations to guide you. You must use common sense and be almost preoccupied with the specific details of the problem statement or scenario. That is not to suggest that you must become so bogged down in the details of the problem that you lose a sense of overview or read information into it that isn't there. The only way you will become proficient in designing and evaluating decision trees is through the experience you gain in wrestling with numerous examples. So that's just what we are going to do now.

EXAMPLE 2.1 THE PRO TENNIS MANAGER STUDY

One day, a well-known sports manager hears about a new, young tennis pro trying the professional circuit for the first season. The manager knows that, historically, young, unestablished tennis pros have a very low likelihood of being successful in the sport—something like 15 percent of them ever "make it." The manager surmises that, if he offers the athlete a contract and it is accepted, he will probably have to spend about $100,000 per year to pay for his player's development and living costs for each of the next 5 years. If the athlete becomes successful, the manager estimates that the player will return total revenues of about $1,200,000 over this same 5-year period. If he is un-

What Jimmy Connors might look like if he were a parking lot attendant.

successful, he will probably return a total of about $150,000 over the next 5 years. The manager is almost certain that, if he decides to offer the athlete a contract immediately, the contract will be accepted. However, if he waits, there is about one chance in three of his not being able to convince the athlete to sign with him (i.e., it is possible that if this young tennis player does well in a major tournament just 2 weeks from now, other managers will take notice and will attempt to sign him also). In the past, the manager has been reasonably accurate in predicting talent. His judgment regarding an ultimately successful tennis pro has been correct 75 percent of the time (i.e., his view toward the player was favorable when, in fact, that player was ultimately successful). He also assessed players unfavorably about 85 percent of the time when they were ultimately unsuccessful. Design the decision tree and then determine what you would do, on the basis of expected values, if you were the manager.

SOLUTION

The initial step you must take is to identify the immediate alternatives that are available. These options appear to be

1. Do nothing.
2. Take the plunge; sign him to a contract immediately.
3. Take your time; assess the player's potential carefully even though you may lose him (seek imperfect information).

The notation used is:

N: Do nothing; forgo opportunity.

C: Offer athlete contract.

C': Do not offer athlete contract.

W: Wait and assess athlete first.

F: Favorable assessment.

F': Unfavorable assessment.

A: Athlete accepts contract offer.

A': Athlete does not accept contract offer.

S: Athlete successful.

S': Athlete not successful.

The tree for these options is shown in Figure 2-3. There are several important points regarding the tree design. First, there are two ways in which the player is not signed when the manager waits to assess his talent, W:

1. The manager may decide against a contract offer, C'.
2. The player may decide not to accept the contract, A'.

This highlights a significant point about the general philosophy of decision trees: Each tree represents the viewpoint of a specific individual or group. In this particular setting, we are representing the *manager's* decision tree. That is why C' represents an act; the manager has the control to do whatever he thinks is best regarding the decision of whether to attempt to sign the player. However, the actual signing, A, or not signing, A', is out of the manager's control. That's why, from the manager's perspective, it is viewed as an event fork. Another important point is that the ultimate success or failure of the athlete in the W act is a conditional event, but only because of the manager's assessment of his potential (favorable or unfavorable); it is not considered conditional because of the preceding event regarding the athlete's decision to sign or not. In fact, there

FIGURE 2-3

Basic Structure of Decision Tree for Pro Tennis Manager.

N

C — P(S) —

P(S') —

W

P(S/F)

P(S'/F) —

P(A)

P(A') —

C

P(F) — C' —

P(F')

C' —

C

P(A') —

P(A)

P(S /F') —

P(S'/F')

can be no success or failure regarding the athlete in the *W* branch of the tree *unless* he signs! Thus, the problem is *contingent on — not conditional to* — his signing. Now let's evaluate the tree using the expected-value (*EV*) method. The given probabilities are

$$P(S) = .15$$
$$P(A) = .67$$
$$P(F/S) = .75$$
$$P(F'/S') = .85$$

Do you see that the given conditions of the two conditional-probability terms are the ultimate success or failure of the investment? Did you correctly determine this fact on your own? Since the conditional probabilities are nonchronological—it is impossible for you to know the ultimate outcome of the player's fortune prior to your having made an assessment of his talent—you will need a reverse tree (Figure 2-4). As always, we start at the top with the marginal probability of successful and not-successful outcomes. The joint probabilities of each of the four branch paths in the tree are

$$P(S)\,P(F/S) = (.15)(.75) = .11$$
$$P(S)\,P(F'/S) = (.15)(.25) = .04$$
$$P(S')\,P(F/S') = (.85)(.15) = .13$$
$$P(S')\,P(F'/S') = (.85)(.85) = .72$$

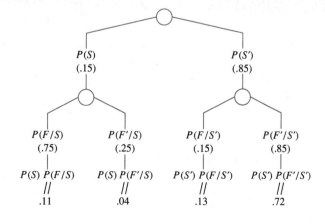

FIGURE 2-4

Reverse Tree for Pro Tennis Manager.

Next, we use Bayes' theorem to find our posterior probabilities:

$$P(S/F) = \frac{.11}{.11 + .13} = .46$$

$$P(S/F') = \frac{.04}{.04 + .72} = .05$$

From these two calculations, we can find every other probability that we need to solve the tree. That is, solving for $P(S'/F)$ gives us

$$P(S/F) + P(S'/F) = 1$$
$$P(S'/F) = 1 - P(S/F)$$
$$= 1 - .46$$
$$= .54$$

Similarly, for $P(S'/F')$,

$$P(S'/F') = 1 - P(S/F')$$
$$= 1 - .05$$
$$= .95$$

Also, the denominators of the Bayes' calculations provide the marginal probabilities of the predictions, $P(F)$ and $P(F')$. These values are

$$P(F) = .24$$
$$P(F') = .76$$

The completed decision tree is shown in Figure 2-5. This illustration reveals that the best act, from the viewpoint of the manager, is to wait, W. Then, if the assessment is favorable, you should attempt to sign the athlete. If the assessment is unfavorable, don't make a contract offer. Do you follow the mathematics of folding back along each branch? The expected value for the alternative of an outright contract offer, C, is found from

$$EV_c = (.15)(700,000) + (.85)(-350,000)$$
$$= -\$192,500$$

Folding back on the W alternative gives us the following results:

1. If, after a favorable assessment, a contract is offered and the player signs, the expected value is

$$EV = (.46)(700,000) + (.54)(-350,000)$$
$$= \$133,000$$

However, this EV does not take into consideration the one-third chance that the player will decide not to sign with the manager. The expected value of offering the contract after a favorable assessment—taking into account the likelihood of both an acceptance and a rejection—is

$$EV = (.67)(133,000) + (.33)(0)$$
$$= \$89,110$$

Since the EV of offering the player the contract (C) is greater than that of not offering him the contract (i.e., $\$89,110 > \$0$), eliminate C' from further consideration. Therefore, if the review is favorable, you will offer him the contract.

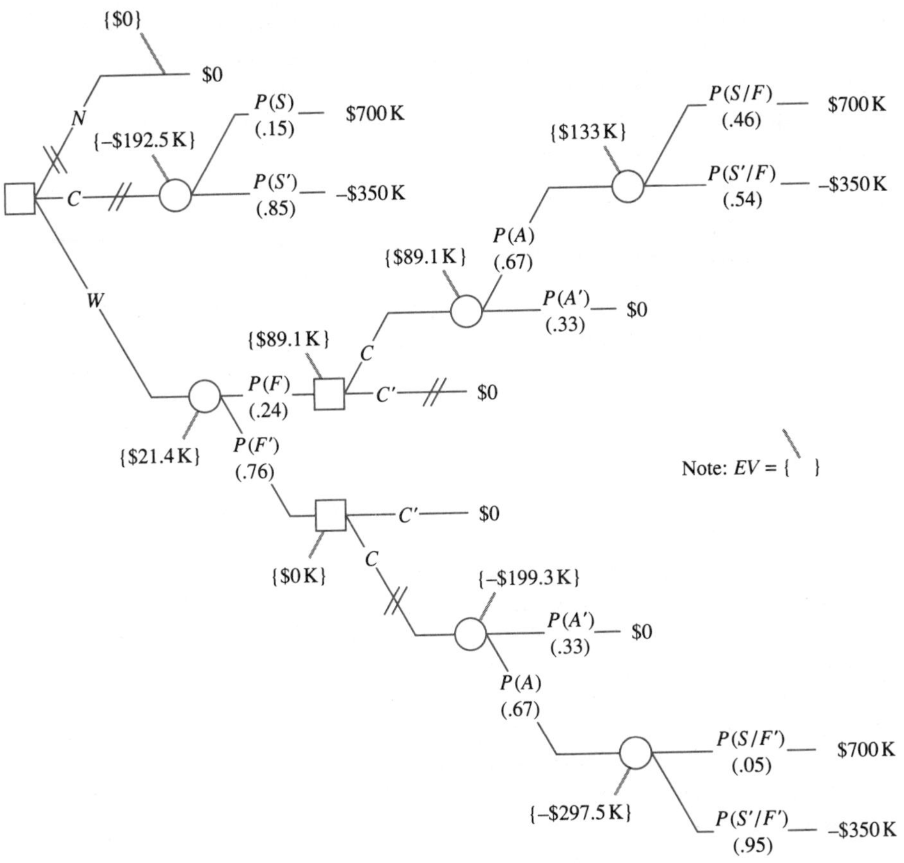

FIGURE 2-5

Completed Decision Tree for Pro Tennis Manager.

Note: $EV = \{\quad\}$

2. For the unfavorable-assessment branch of the W strategy (F'), the expected value is

$$EV = (.05)(700,000) + (.95)(-350,000)$$
$$= -\$297,500$$

if the player signs. There is also, as in the favorable-assessment branch, a one-third chance that he won't sign. So, if you offer him the contract after an unfavorable assessment, the expected value is

$$EV = (.67)(-297,500) + (.33)(0)$$
$$= -\$199,325$$

Since this is less desirable than is not offering the contract, C', eliminate C from this branch; i.e., if your findings are unfavorable, do not offer a contract. The best EV you can hope for in this branch is that of no contract offer ($\$0$). The resultant EV for the W alternative can now be calculated as

$$EV_w = (.24)(84,110) + (.76)(0)$$
$$= \$20,261$$

Since the EV of this act exceeds that of all others, select W.

Before leaving this example, it would seem for us advantageous to illustrate once again the internal consistency of the probabilities. You were told that the chance of the young tennis pro being ultimately successful, $P(S)$, was .15. Remember that $P(S)$ can also be found from the alternative in the problem that attempts to obtain imperfect infor-

mation—i.e., prediction or survey. So, from the W act, it is also possible to determine the probability of success as the sum of the joint probabilities along all paths that lead to success. [Of course, the probability of an unsuccessful outcome, $P(S')$, can be found in the identical manner.] The sum of these two joint probabilities will yield the marginal probability of success. So,

$$
\begin{aligned}
P(S) &= P(F)P(S/F) + P(F')P(S/F') \\
&= (.24)(.46) + (.76)(.05) \\
&= .110 + .038 \\
&= .148 \approx .15
\end{aligned}
$$

Always remember that the probabilities of almost every decision tree are interrelated to a logical internal consistency (the exceptions to this relationship will be illustrated in the next case study). Now let's try the next case.

EXAMPLE 2.2 THE REALTY COMPANY LITIGATION STUDY

"The jury has found you not guilty, but I'm going to give you 2 years just to be on the safe side."

A large realty company has been sued in two related legal actions for unfair competition and has retained a law firm to represent it in the litigation. For each of the lawsuits, the company may settle out of court. The trial dates for the two suits are far enough apart that there is no chance of the cases overlapping. Preparation costs (including discovery costs and attorney's fees) for either of the trials are anticipated to be approximately equal, at $35,000 each. However, if the company wishes to go to trial with both cases, the preparatory information of the first trial could be used in the second trial, decreasing the litigation costs of the latter trial to $21,000. Of course, the company could avoid both of these costs by settling out of court.

If the realty company decides to go to trial in the first case, the outcome will be that it either wins (W) or loses (L). If the company prevails in the first case, it will incur no liability for damages. If it loses, however, it will have to pay $700,000 in damages. The out-of-court settlement costs would be $350,000. The law firm, on examination of the case evidence, estimates that the likelihood of prevailing in the first legal action is approximately .60.

The second case can be settled out of court for a cost of $210,000. If it is not, there will be a trial, which will result in one of three possible outcomes:

1. The suit is dismissed for failure to state a cause of action; the company incurs no monetary liability (dismissal).

2. The company is adjudicated negligent in its business dealings and is required to pay $175,000 in direct damages (negligent).

3. The company is found liable for intentional unfair competitive practices and must pay $175,000 in direct damages plus punitive damages of $140,000, for a total of $315,000 (intentional).

The likelihoods of these different outcomes in Case 2 depend largely on the result of Case 1, because the findings of the first case are anticipated to set an important legal precedent. The law firm's estimation of the chances of the three outcomes of Case 2 under the various potential results of Case 1 is shown in Table 2-1. Solve the decision tree and select the optimum strategy for minimizing the company's expected losses.

SOLUTION

The tree design for this problem is reasonably demanding, so let's examine its development carefully. There are two cases to be managed; however, they must be done in

TABLE 2-1

Assessed Likelihoods of Possible Outcomes of Case 2, As Influenced by Outcome of Case 1

	Outcome of Case 2		
Outcome of Case 1	*Dismissal*	*Negligent*	*Intentional*
Settle out of court	.30	.30	.40
Win (W)	.70	.20	.10
Lose (L)	.10	.50	.40

series. Case 1, therefore, must be concluded *prior* to the start of Case 2. So, a tree design that presents both cases being tried in parallel would constitute a major error in logic. What we have to do first, then, is to decide how to handle the first case. You know that there are two options: (1) go to trial, or (2) settle out of court. The notation for the first stage of the decision tree is given by

T_1: Try Case 1.

S_1: Settle Case 1 out of court.

and is shown in Figure 2-6. If we choose to try Case 1, T_1, then the next outcome that will occur will be the result of the trial: We either win or lose the case. Winning or losing is, of course, an *event*, since it is out of our control. We add this new notation:

W_1: Win Case 1.

L_1: Lose Case 1.

Figure 2-7 illustrates the second stage of the tree design.

We have identified all considerations of Case 1, so we are ready to turn to Case 2. The considerations for this case are the same as those at the beginning of Case 1. The initial question is still whether the case should be tried or should be settled out of court. That question exists regardless of the outcome of the first trial. Always leave yourself every possible option—don't preclude anything. Use the folding-back process to eliminate the weaker options. The notation for the third stage of the decision tree (Figure 2-8) is

S_2: Settle Case 2 out of court.

T_2: Try Case 2.

D: Verdict for Case 2 is "dismissal."

N: Verdict for Case 2 is "negligent."

I: Verdict for Case 2 is "intentional."

Now let's complete the S_1 branch. We face the dilemma of either going to trial or settling out of court with Case 2. The concluding portion of the S_1 branch is very similar to the T_1 branch, although it is not identical because the probabilities are not conditional.

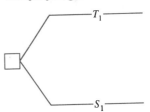

FIGURE 2-6

First-Stage Decision Tree for Realty Company Litigation.

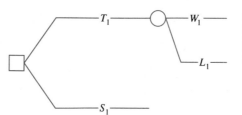

FIGURE 2-7

Second-Stage Decision Tree for Realty Company Litigation.

FIGURE 2-8

Third-Stage Decision Tree for Realty
Company Litigation.

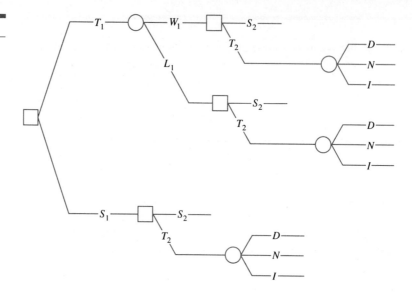

The fourth and final stage of the decision-tree design is shown in Figure 2-9. Notice that the end events in the T_1 branch are all *conditional probabilities*: The outcome of the second trial is dependent on that of Case 1 because "the first case is anticipated to set an important legal precedent." So, the result of a Case 1 trial will serve as a legal barometer for Case 2. Conversely, if Case 1 is settled out of court, we have no information by which to gauge the outcome of the second trial. That is why these probabilities are all *marginal*. It is now possible to plug in given probability and cost information and fold back on the tree (Figure 2-10). Note that all probabilities given are chronological; therefore, no reverse tree for Bayes' theorem is needed. The decision, based on expected-value analysis, would be to go to trial with Case 1 and, if you win, to try Case 2; if you lose Case 1, settle Case 2 out of court.

FIGURE 2-9

Fourth-Stage Decision Tree for Realty
Company Litigation.

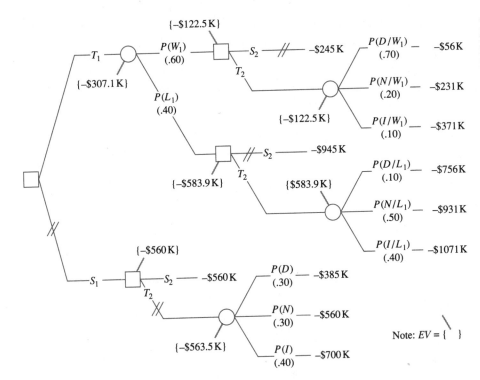

Note: $EV = \{\quad\}$

Several interesting elements evolve out of this case study. The first regards the preparation costs of the two trials:

1. Case 1 trial costs are $35,000, but this fee also covers some of the preparatory work that would be required if you also were to take Case 2 to trial. Accordingly, because the two cases share $14,000 in preparation costs, the second case would have a trial cost of $21,000 if you went to trial with Case 1. If Case 1 were settled out of court, the court costs for Case 2 would be the full $35,000.

2. The second unique characteristic of this problem is that there is no internal consistency among the probabilities, since the outcome of Case 1 *influences* (sets a precedent for) Case 2. *So, the only time that a decision will* not *have internal consistency is when earlier events can affect the likelihood of occurrence of later events; (i.e., dependent event settings). This type of sequential problem is rare.*

EXAMPLE 2.3 THE HEALTH WAYS NUTRITION COMPANY STUDY

The Health Ways Nutrition Company (HWNC) would like to market a new banana-flavored diet drink that will either be successful, S, or be a failure, S'. HWNC is facing a dilemma, however, with regard to the most sensible way to go about this business venture. It must make one of three possible choices:

1. a_1: Immediately market or do not market the product without any prior assessment.

2. a_2: Hire Informed Sources, Inc., to do a market survey first.

3. a_3: Hire Rumor Has It, Inc., to conduct a market survey first.

"How much longer did he tell you to stay on this banana diet?"

The product, HWNC estimates, will gross $4,500,000 or $500,000, depending on whether it is a success or failure, respectively, *if it is marketed now*. However, if HWNC waits for a survey, they are more than likely to have to share the early market with competitors. They anticipate that their expected gross revenue would then decline to an estimated $2,700,000 or $200,000 for successful and failure outcomes, respectively. The marketing costs associated with the product are $1,600,000, regardless of when it is marketed.

If Informed Sources conducts the survey, the likelihood of product success is .90 and .30 for favorable and unfavorable reports, respectively. Historically, Informed Sources has written favorable reports 42 percent of the time. Its fee for the survey is $60,000.

Rumor Has It has written favorable reports 18 percent of the time when the product was a failure and 82 percent of the time when it was a success. Its fee for the survey is $50,000.

What decision would you make if you were asked to assess the options for HWNC?

SOLUTION

The toughest part of this problem will be to interpret accurately the types of probabilities given. In addition, you will have to incorporate the methods discussed earlier in this chapter regarding internal-consistency relationships among the various probabilities. The design of the decision tree is given in Figure 2-11. This decision tree is essentially identical to the TV series decision tree. Let's examine the probability information that is given, and determine what information is missing. The statements concerning the conditional probabilities and the interpretation of each follow.

FOR INFORMED SOURCES:

■ "The likelihood of product success is .90 for favorable results."

Independent phrase = "the likelihood of product success is .90"
Dependent phrase = "for favorable results"

■ "The likelihood of product success is .30 for unfavorable results."

Independent phrase = "the likelihood of product success is .30"
Dependent phrase = "for unfavorable results"

FOR RUMOR HAS IT:

■ "RHI has written favorable reports 18 percent of the time when the product was a failure."

Independent phrase = "RHI has written favorable reports 18 percent of the time"
Dependent phrase = "when the product was a failure"

■ "RHI has written favorable reports 82 percent of the time when the product was a success."

Independent phrase = "RHI has written favorable reports 82 percent of the time"
Dependent phrase = "when the product was a success"

The interpretations for these conditional statements, as well as the remaining marginal-probability statement, are

$$P(S/F_2) = .90$$
$$P(S/F_2') = .30$$
$$P(F_2) = .42$$
$$P(F_3/S') = .18$$
$$P(F_3/S) = .82$$

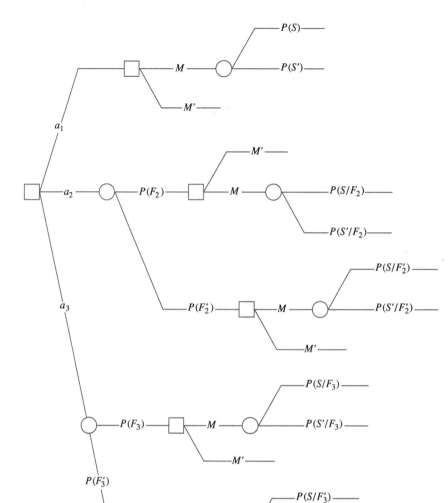

FIGURE 2-11

Basic Decision Tree Design for Health Ways Nutrition.

Can you see the new wrinkle added in the probability notation? To be able to distinguish immediately which alternative each probability addresses, we subscript the predictive events—F and F'—with the same number as that alternative. So, the first three probabilities in the set of the five given are associated with Informed Sources (a_2), and the last two refer to Rumor Has It (a_3). A closer examination of this information reveals that Informed Sources will not require a reverse tree, because its conditional probabilities are chronological (the given events are the predictions). However, Rumor Has It has given events that are the ultimate success or failure of the product. These probabilities will require a reverse-tree diagram and Bayes' theorem. There is also no information regarding the marginal probabilities of success or failure for a_1. Obviously, it is necessary to find these values based on the internal consistency of the probabilities.

To determine the value of $P(S)$ or $P(S')$, we must use the a_2 information. Specifically, from a_2 we know that

$$P(S) = P(F_2)P(S/F_2) + P(F_2')P(S/F_2')$$

These are all the paths for a_2 that lead to ultimately successful outcomes. Plugging in the given values, we find

$$P(S) = (.42)(.90) + (.58)(.30)$$
$$= .55$$

The chance of not being successful, $P(S')$, is

$$P(S') = 1 - P(S)$$
$$= .45$$

Next, $P(S)$ and $P(S')$ must be used in a_3's reverse tree, which is given in Figure 2-12. The joint probabilities for the tree are

$$P(S)P(F_3/S) = (.55)(.82) = .45$$
$$P(S)P(F_3'/S) = (.55)(.18) = .10$$
$$P(S')P(F_3/S') = (.45)(.18) = .08$$
$$P(S')P(F_3'/S') = (.45)(.82) = .37$$

When we substitute these probabilities into Bayes' theorem, we can find the chronological values needed for the basic decision tree. So, for a_3,

$$P(S/F_3) = .85$$
$$P(S'/F_3) = .15$$
$$P(S/F_3') = .21$$
$$P(S'/F_3') = .79$$

We find the marginal probabilities for favorable and unfavorable reports from the denominators of the Bayes' equations (identical to earlier examples):

$$P(F_3) = .53$$
$$P(F_3') = .47$$

We can now fill in all the probabilities and payoff values needed to solve the decision tree, as displayed in Figure 2-13. The decision for this problem is to forgo any survey and to market immediately. The early market edge combined with the volatility of the market—neither a_2 nor a_3 provides information that predicts market reaction with sufficient reliability—make a_1 the most desirable strategy.

FIGURE 2-12

Reverse Tree for a_3 Branch of Health Ways Nutrition.

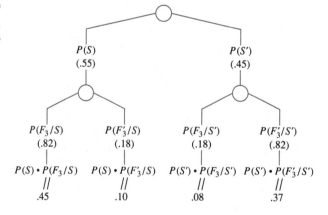

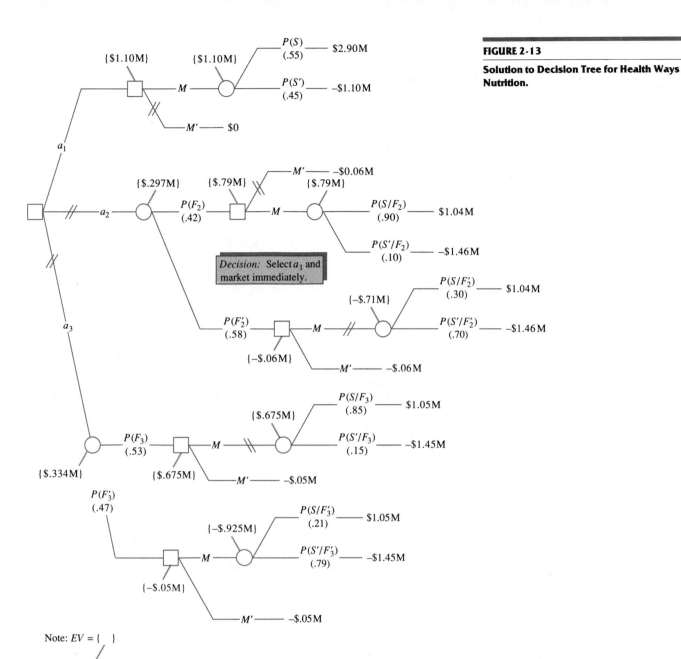

FIGURE 2-13

Solution to Decision Tree for Health Ways Nutrition.

Decision: Select a_1 and market immediately.

Note: $EV = \{\ \}$

EXAMPLE 2.4   THE PUBLIC TELEVISION PROGRAM STUDY

A public television station is considering the development of a new collection of programs similar to the prestigious PBS award winning series, "The Ascent of Man," which was hosted by the late Jacob Bronowski. The station is quite concerned, of course, about whether this series will be able to generate sufficient funds (public memberships, new private-sector grants, etc.) to warrant its production, since its federal subsidies have been reduced acutely. The station is considering using several strategies to determine what ultimately to do about the potential series:

a_1: Decide immediately whether to produce the series.

a_2: Produce and test market a single pilot in several representative market cities, to gauge audience response to the show before making the decision whether to produce the complete series.

a_3: Pay a professional marketing group to assess the likely outcome of the proposed series.

The station has considerable data it has collected regarding these three approaches:

1. The program would either be successful or not successful. Successful programs generate an average of $18 million in revenues, whereas unsuccessful ones provide only $4 million. Similar programs have been successful 34 percent of the time.

2. Total production costs associated with the complete series will be $10 million. A pilot costs $1 million to produce but will be used as one show in the series; if the complete series is marketed using this strategy, this pilot cost is included in the $10 million. Traditionally, pilot programs, although expensive, yield the most accurate predictions. That is, 86 percent of successful series had favorable survey findings on their pilots. However, 14 percent of failed series also received favorable surveys based on their pilots. (Typically, the predictions based on the pilot are either "favorable" or "unfavorable.")

3. The professional market-survey approach will cost $.5 million. In the past, 62 percent of the series that were given favorable reports by this company were successful. This group has written unfavorable surveys in 51 percent of the cases that they have served as consultants.

Let's suppose that you have been hired by the station as a consultant to help them to decide what to do. What would you suggest?

SOLUTION

The decision tree consists of two alternatives that seek imperfect information and one that makes the immediate decision either to produce the series or not to produce it. The given information concerning probabilities and cash is as follows:

$$P(S) = .34 \qquad M = \$10,000,000$$
$$P(F_2/S) = .86 \qquad M' = \$0$$
$$P(F_2/S') = .14 \qquad S = \$18,000,000$$
$$P(S/F_3) = .62 \qquad S' = \$4,000,000$$
$$P(F_3) = .51$$
$$a_1 = \$0$$
$$a_2 = \$1,000,000$$
$$a_3 = \$500,000$$

There are two tasks that we need to do first. The probability data for the pilot show, a_1, require Bayes' theorem. Also, no conditional probabilities are provided in the unfavorable-report branch of the professional marketing group, a_3. We can solve for either one of these probabilities first. Let's arbitrarily decide to design the reverse tree for a_2. Since the probability of success is known, this is a simple task (Figure 2-14). We find the conditional probabilities by calculating one from each of the favorable- and unfavorable-report findings branches.

$$P(S/F_2) = \frac{P(S)\,P(F_2/S)}{P(S)\,P(F_2'/S) + P(S')\,P(F_2/S')} = \frac{.29}{.38} = .76$$

$$P(S/F_2') = \frac{P(S)\,P(F_2'/S)}{P(S)\,P(F_2'/S) + P(S')\,P(F_2'/S')} = \frac{.05}{.62} = .08$$

Next, we solve for one of the conditional probabilities in the unfavorable branch of a_3. If $P(S/F_3')$ is arbitrarily selected, then we know that

$$P(S) = P(F_3)\,P(S/F_3) + P(F_3')\,P(S/F_3')$$

The only unknown quantity in this equation is $P(S/F_3')$, so let's solve the equation for that term:

$$P(S/F_3') = \frac{P(S) - P(F_3)\,P(S/F_3)}{P(F_3')}$$

Substituting in the given probability information for the three probabilities on the right-hand side of the equation gives

$$P(S/F_3') = \frac{.34 - (.49)(.62)}{.51}$$

$$= \frac{.34 - .30}{.51}$$

$$= \frac{.04}{.51}$$

$$= .08$$

Now there is sufficient information for us to complete the tree and to calculate the expected values for each competing action. The results of these calculations are shown in Figure 2-15. These findings suggest that the station should test market a single pilot first, then should produce the new series only if the audience response is favorable.

EXAMPLE 2.5   THE BROADWAY PLAY EXERCISE

A playwright is developing a three-act comedy that deals with some of his favorite topics—fear of death, the likelihood of eternal nothingness, the ineptitude of male sexual performance, and Manhattan. He wants to produce the play on Broadway. He is

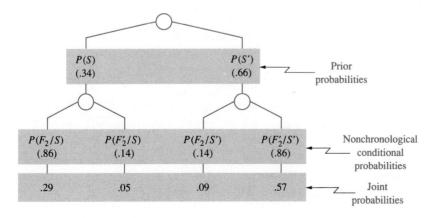

FIGURE 2-14

a_2 Branch of the Reverse Tree for TV Station.

FIGURE 2-15

Solution to TV Station Decision Tree.

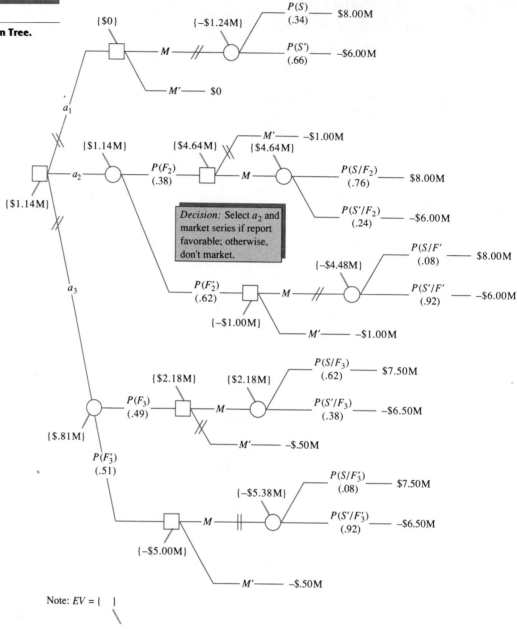

Note: $EV = \{\ \ \}$

naturally concerned with the long-run success or failure of his play, since the play will be expensive to produce, and he doesn't want to risk putting up his money if there is only a low probability of a return on this investment.

His immediate options are as follows:

1. Decide whether to produce the play, without assessing its chances for success.

2. Hire critic Albert Branch (the most influential play reviewer) to read and assess the script, then decide whether to produce the play. Mr. Branch's fee is $25,000.

3. Hire critic Charles Saylor (not as influential as Branch but, nevertheless, a well-known reviewer of Broadway plays) to read and assess the script, then decide whether to produce the play. Mr. Saylor's fee is $15,000.

4. Open the play off-Broadway (way off-Broadway, like Philadelphia, maybe) to get feedback in lieu of Mr. Branch's or Mr. Saylor's script reviews. This way, the playwright will be able to *see* the impact of the play on the audience and can make any changes he believes are necessary. He will be in a better position to assess, for himself, his chances of success.

The playwright estimates that the play, if it goes into production for Broadway immediately, will return revenues of \$950,000 or \$180,000 if it is a success or failure, respectively. If he decides to hire either Branch or Saylor to review the script, the production will be delayed for about 6 weeks while he makes changes in response to their suggestions. This will lose the "early market edge" for the playwright, because he knows that another comedy will also be coming out shortly, resulting in both plays sharing a near-common audience market. Accordingly, our playwright's comedy would then return revenues estimated at about \$690,000 or \$120,000 for successful or unsuccessful outcomes, respectively. The costs for a Broadway production of the play, if the play is produced immediately, are estimated at \$250,000. If he waits for either Charles Saylor or Albert Branch to review the script, the additional time will increase this cost to \$335,000—exclusive of either critic's consulting fees.

The playwright's business manager has done some research regarding how successful the two critics have been in their previous consulting jobs. He has developed the following information:

- If Branch reviews the script, the chances that the play will be unsuccessful are 17 percent and 83 percent for favorable and unfavorable reviews, respectively (based on Mr. Branch's history of past predictions). Charles Saylor, on the other hand, has written favorable reviews 91 percent and 29 percent of the time when the play was a success and failure, respectively. As mentioned, Mr. Branch and Mr. Saylor's fees for reviewing the script are \$25,000 and \$15,000, respectively. In the past, Mr. Branch has written unfavorable reports 70 percent of the time.
- If the playwright's comedy opens off-Broadway initially, this additional production will increase the cumulative production costs through the Broadway opening to \$410,000. He thinks that this is still a viable alternative because, when he used this method in the past, 80 percent of those plays he predicted would be successful were, 90 percent of the plays he predicted would be failures were.

    Our playwright comes to you for advice.

SOLUTION

To solve this case, you will need to use everything you have learned. There is no superfluous information in this problem; however, there is just enough to get by on. First, design the basic decision tree (Figure 2-16). We shall use the following notation:

a_1: Immediately decide whether to produce.

a_2: Hire Albert Branch to review play.

a_3: Hire Charles Saylor to review play.

a_4: Introduce play off-Broadway first.

B: Produce play on Broadway.

F: Favorable review.

S: Successful outcome (long run).

FIGURE 2-16

Basic Decision Tree for Broadway Play.

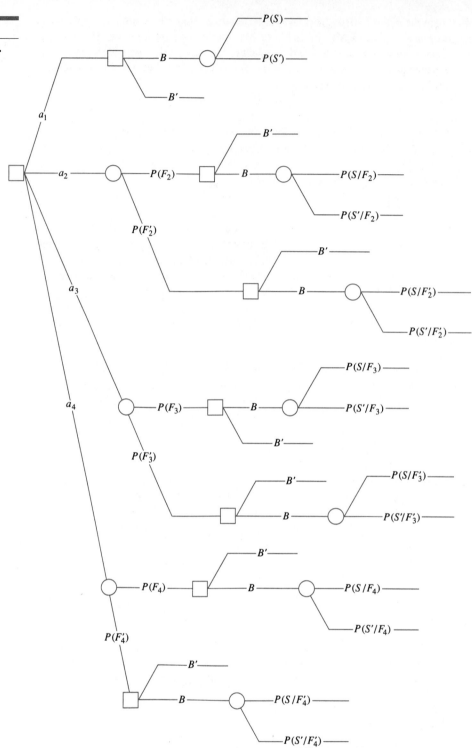

The given probability data for Albert Branch (a_2) are:

$$P(S'/F_2) = .17$$
$$P(S'/F_2') = .83$$
$$P(F_2') = .70$$

Every probability for Branch uses given information that is in chronological order. No reverse tree is needed, and the probabilities can be plugged directly into the decision tree. This is fortunate, because the problem does not explicitly provide you with the marginal probability of success, $P(S)$; we must calculate $P(S)$ from Branch's data. Also, later you will see why we can't use Saylor's data to generate this marginal probability. The marginal probability for success, then, using a_2 data, is

$$P(S) = P(F_2)P(S/F_2) + P(F_2')P(S/F_2')$$
$$= (.30)(.83) + (.70)(.17)$$
$$= .37$$

Next, let's look at the given information regarding Saylor's performance, a_3:

$$P(F_3/S) = .91$$
$$P(F_3/S') = .29$$

Since the Saylor conditional probabilities are nonchronological, we'll use a reverse tree to revise them (Figure 2-17). Now we can use the tree to provide the real-time conditional probabilities for the Saylor alternative. The Bayes' revision for $P(S/F_3)$ is

$$P(S/F_3) = \frac{P(S)P(F_3/S)}{P(S)P(F_3/S) + P(S')P(F_3/S')}$$
$$= \frac{(.37)(.91)}{(.37)(.91) + (.63)(.29)}$$
$$= \frac{.34}{.34 + .18} = .65$$

Similarly, that for $P(S/F_3')$ is

$$P(S/F_3') = \frac{P(S)P(F_3'/S)}{P(S)P(F_3'/S) + P(S')P(F_3'/S')}$$
$$= \frac{(.37)(.09)}{(.37)(.09) + (.63)(.71)}$$
$$= \frac{.03}{.03 + .45}$$
$$= \frac{.03}{.48} = .06$$

The denominators of these probabilities also provide the marginal probabilities of favorable and unfavorable reviews by Saylor:

$$P(F_3) = .52$$
$$P(F_3') = .48$$

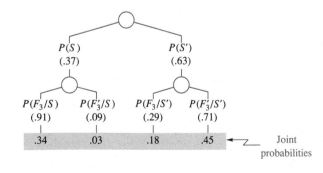

FIGURE 2-17

Reverse Tree for Saylor Branch (a_3) of Broadway Play.

FIGURE 2-18

"Produce Off-Broadway First" (a_4) Branch of Broadway Play.

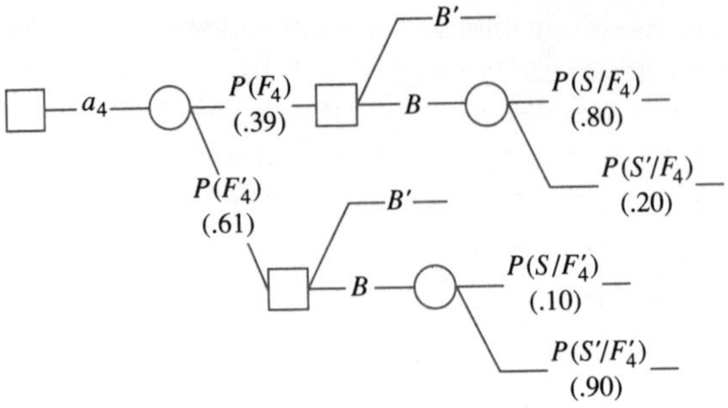

At this point, we have calculated all the probabilities for the tree except for the marginal probabilities of the playwright giving favorable and unfavorable reviews to his own work (a_4). We know from the problem statement that

$$P(S/F_4) = .80$$
$$P(S'/F_4') = .90$$

Interpreting these values was a little tricky. The phrase "of those plays he predicted would be successful" tells you the given condition was a favorable review; that is, not that the play *was* successful, but that the playwright *predicted* that it would be successful. The playwright is simply making a prediction *in terms of the ultimate outcome*.

Now we can calculate the only missing probabilities: $P(F_4)$ and $P(F_4')$ for the off-Broadway branch of the playwright's tree. Since we know the values for $P(S)$ and $P(S')$, we can calculate the missing values readily from the a_4 action shown in Figure 2-18. We know that

$$P(S) = P(F_4)(.80) + P(F_4')(.10)$$

Since $P(F_4')$ can be expressed in terms of $P(F_4)$, the last equation can be rewritten such that it is composed of only one unknown variable and can therefore be solved explicitly. First,

$$P(F_4') = 1 - P(F_4)$$

Substituting this expression into the $P(S)$ equation along with the value of $P(S) = .37$, it is possible to solve for the probability of a favorable review by the playwright:

$$
\begin{aligned}
P(S) &= (.80)P(F_4) + .10[1 - P(F_4)] \\
&= .80P(F_4) + .10 - .10P(F_4) \\
&= .70P(F_4) + .10
\end{aligned}
$$

Solving for $P(F_4)$ gives us

$$
\begin{aligned}
P(F_4) &= \frac{P(S) - .10}{.70} \\
&= \frac{.37 - .10}{.70} \\
&= \frac{.27}{.70} = .39
\end{aligned}
$$

And, of course,

$$P(F_4') = 1 - P(F_4) = .61$$

The solved decision tree is shown in Figure 2-19. It suggests that the playwright should forgo any reviews and should produce the Broadway play immediately [$EV(a_1) =$ $214,900].

FIGURE 2-19

Solution to Decision Tree for Broadway Play.

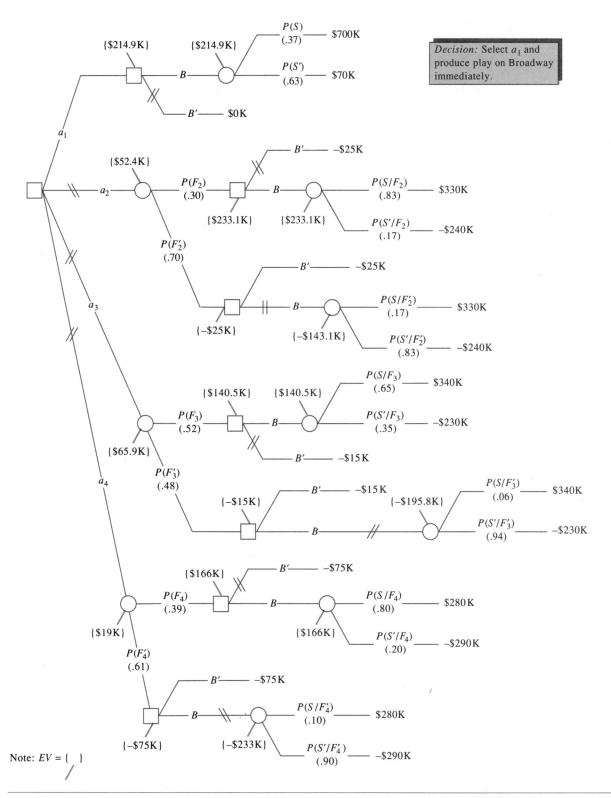

Decision: Select a_1 and produce play on Broadway immediately.

Note: $EV = \{\ \}$

$\mid 2.3 \mid$ DECISION TREE ANALYSIS USING EXPECTED UTILITY

Up to now, we have employed only one method to assess the relative merit of competing actions in decision trees—that of expected values. The reason we focused exclusively on this approach is that it allowed us to become familar with the complex process of designing and evaluating decision trees, without clouding the technique with nonessential considerations. However, at this point, it is important that you become aware of another way to evaluate decision trees. This method does not require additional mathematical skills and is, in fact, nearly identical to the expected-value approach. The interrelationship of probabilities remains the same, as does the folding-back process. The only difference is that we will not fold back on dollars with this new method. Instead, we will establish a barometer of measurement that will be more representative of how humans function in risk settings. This evaluative concept is called the method of *expected utilities*.

Utility may be viewed as the worth or value an individual, group, or organization assigns to a particular outcome under uncertain conditions, or under risk. An example will help us to understand this new approach.

EXAMPLE 2.6   PETRO ENTERPRISES WILDCAT OIL-DRILLING STUDY

In 1967, John S. Hammond III published an important paper in the November–December issue of the *Harvard Business Review* that analyzed a decision-making technique that seemed to come closer to the way people behave when faced with choices involving risk. The paper is entitled, "Better Decisions with Preference Theory" (Hammond, 1967).

Although Hammond contended that he did not originate or develop the methodology, he presented the concepts in such a concise, articulate, and understandable way that the popularity of the technique grew immediately. In fact, there are at least 10 management science books that have, except for minor variations, plagiarized this paper in the form of case studies or problems. What higher form of flattery is there?

Briefly, Hammond discussed the situation of a small wildcat oil-drilling organization called Petro Enterprises. This company, with assets of only $130,000, has to face three immediate choices:

1. Let expire a nontransferable, short-term option it has on a specific piece of land.

2. Exercise its right, prior to the option expiration, to drill immediately. The result will be "oil" or "no oil."

3. Pay to have a seismic test conducted and, based on the results—which will either be favorable or unfavorable—decide at that time whether to drill.

The rest of the information pertinent to the problem is

- The seismic test costs $30,000.
- The drilling costs $100,000.
- If oil is found, Petro is guaranteed a $400,000 sale to a large oil firm for its drilling rights. If no oil is found, Petro will have to absorb all costs through this point in time; no revenues are anticipated.
- The geologist for Petro believes that, based on this property's geological characteristics, there is a .55 chance that, if a well is drilled, oil will be discovered.

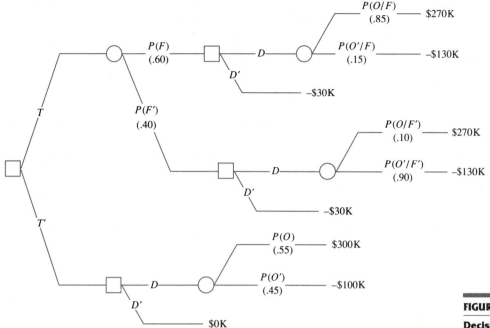

FIGURE 2-20

Decision Tree for Petro Enterprises.

■ Data concerning the accuracy of the seismic test indicate that, if the seismic test is favorable, the chance that oil will be found is .85; if it is unfavorable, the chance for oil drops to .10.

■ Previous use of this seismic test has shown that it gives favorable results 60 percent of the time.

SOLUTION

The decision tree for this problem should be relatively easy for you to design—especially after all the experience you've had by now. Further, all of the probabilities are in real time; none require use of Bayes' theorem. The Petro decision tree is shown in Figure 2-20, and the folded-back results are given in Figure 2-21.

In folding back this tree, we are shown the primary point Hammond was making: If you follow expected-value methods to the hilt, you must select the outright drilling for oil without the seismic test. After all, the seismic-test action has an expected value that is $6000 less than that of the outright-drilling approach. But Hammond then asks the reader to consider the logic of making this selection: *Regardless of the risk involved,* you must always opt for the strategy that maximizes your expected payoff! Hammond has raised a valuable point of human behavior in decision making: *We are not insensitive to risk.* Just think, for a slightly higher *EV* ($120,000 versus $114,000), the decision maker runs a 45 percent risk of coming up with a dry well after accumulating $100,000 in drilling costs. For an additional $30,000 investment, it is possible to cut this risk to one-third of the original value for a positive seismic test (of course, a negative test would strongly suggest that the project should be discontinued, since the revised chance of striking oil would only be 10 percent). It appears that the expected-value method, although analytically sound, does not replicate human attitudes toward risk.

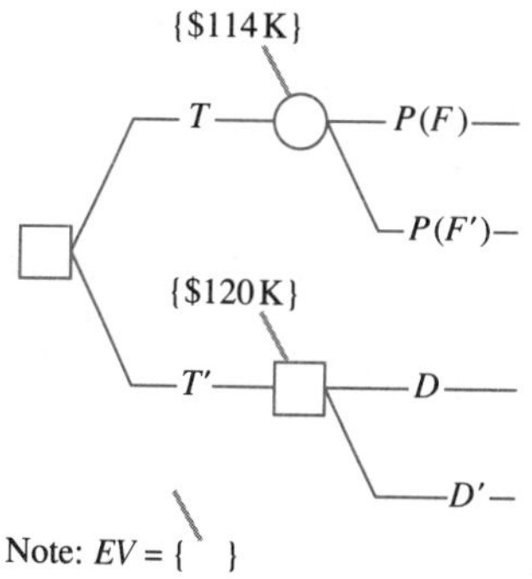

To further illustrate why the expected-value method does not represent, in most situations, how rational people behave, we will suppose you are faced with the following situation. You have a single opportunity to make one of two investments. One provides

FIGURE 2-21

Expected-Value Solution to Petro Enterprises Decision Tree.

{$114K}

T — P(F)—

— P(F')—

{$120K}

T' — D —

— D'—

Note: *EV* = { }

an almost "can't lose" situation, and returns a modest amount of money. The other carries a much greater risk, but has a much higher potential payoff. That is:

Investment 1: You have a .90 chance of making $1000, and a .10 chance of making nothing.

Investment 2: You have a .01 chance of making $100,000, and a .99 chance of making nothing.

Which one would you prefer? The expected value of investment 1 is $900, whereas that of investment 2 is $1000. Most people, after examining the odds, would choose investment 1, even though it has a lower *EV*. If, however, you preferred investment 2, consider this next set of investments.

Investment 3: You have a .90 chance of making $10,000, and a .10 chance of making nothing.

Investment 4: You have a .001 chance at $10 million, and a .999 chance of making nothing.

The *EV*s are $9000 and $10,000 for investments 3 and 4, respectively. Do you still prefer the investment with the higher *EV*? If so, it is quite easy to continue to increase the risk–payoff combinations to such ridiculous heights that, sooner or later, any rational person will forgo any investments that are associated with minuscule probabilities of attainment *no matter how large the dollar payoff may be*! She or he will instead prefer an investment that yields a lower *EV* but has a more assured likelihood of success. Why is this the case? Because people make decisions, in almost all situations, which reflect their *preference* for the "investment," or the investment's *worth* to them, rather than the expected value. This more realistic concept is called the *method of expected utilities*.

The only additional information that the expected-utility (*EU*) approach requires compared to the expected-value method is a utility or preference curve illustrating the relative worth of different levels of attainment of the measurement criterion (usually in dollars). For Hammond's example, a utility curve representing Petro's chief executive officer's (CEO's) preference for attaining various dollar payoffs was generated. A replica of this curve is shown in Figure 2-22.

The process used to generate this utility curve is intricate, consisting of a series of questions given the CEO regarding the amount of money that he would require to forgo

FIGURE 2-22

Utility Curve for Petro's CEO.

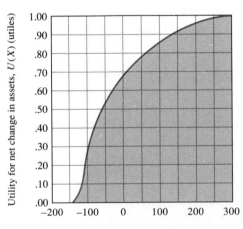

Net change in liquid assets, X (in $ thousands)

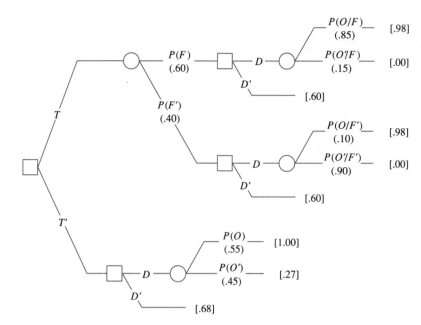

various risk-payoff gambles. This approach, called the *reference-lottery method*, need not be used in developing utility curves. Rather, it is just as acceptable to draw or sketch the utility curve. Typically, the best feasible outcome (the highest payoff attainable) receives a utility value of 1.00 utile, whereas the worst outcome (the lowest payoff attainable) is assigned a value of .00 utile. The next step is to determine an outcome to which you would be indifferent—about which you'd be neither pleased nor displeased—and to assign to it a value of .50 utile. You now have three points on the utility curve. If the curve you sketch has inflection points, it is strongly advisable to explain them in a brief scenario—preferably within the figure of the utility curve. Also, the point spread used for the utility of your goal, $U(X)$, is arbitrary: A scale of .00 to 1.00 is quite common, but it could be from 1 to 100, from -10 to $+10$, or whatever.

Now let's use the preference curve for Petro Enterprise's CEO to evaluate the available options using expected utility. We need to convert the payoff values—in this case, dollars—into their corresponding utility values. This conversion is simple; we take four steps:

Step 1. Determine the point on the x axis that corresponds to the dollar payoff value of interest.

Step 2. Find the point where this x coordinate intercepts the utility curve (move up from the x axis to the curve).

Step 3. At this point of intersection, move horizontally across to your left until you intersect the vertical utility axis. Record this utility value $U(X)$.

Step 4. Use this new utility value to replace the original dollar value you used in Step 1.

If, for example, we use Figures 2-20 and 2-22, we can convert the original tree with dollar payoffs to one in terms of utile payoffs, as shown in Figure 2-23. Folding back on these utility values *exactly* as we have before in calculating *EV*s gives us the result in terms of expected utility, as shown in Figure 2-24. Therefore, the expected-utility

{.74}
T — P(F)—
— P(F')—

{.68}
T' — D—
— D'—

Note: $EU = \{\ \ \}$

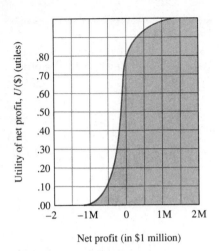

FIGURE 2-25

Management's View of the Utility of Various Monetary Outcomes for Health Ways Nutrition Company.

method indicates that the CEO, given his attitude toward money and associated risks, would be best served if the seismic test were conducted first—quite a different result from that we got using the original *EV* method. Let's do another example using expected utility to make sure the process is clear.

EXAMPLE 2.7   HEALTH WAYS NUTRITION STUDY REVISITED

Suppose that Health Ways Nutrition, discussed earlier in Example 2.3, has decided to reassess its earlier decision by using the *EU* method. A new utility curve representing top management's attitude toward money and risk is shown in Figure 2-25. Does this new method cause a shift in strategy?

SOLUTION

The results of converting the dollar-payoff values shown in the previous HWN decision tree of Figure 2-13 to their corresponding utile values is illustrated in Figure 2-26. You can see that the *EU* results suggest that the company should hire Rumor Has It, Inc. (Actually, the decision among the three actions is very close, indicating a need for a "second cut," more detailed analysis.) Notice the contrast with the expected-value method, in which marketing without a survey was the clear choice for a_1; the 45 percent chance of having an unsuccessful outcome was overshadowed by the $2.9 million payoff if the product became successful. The other alternatives did not have the same level of reward given the product's success, but the chance of unsuccessful outcomes were only 10 and 15 percent for alternatives a_2 and a_3, respectively. However, only the expected-utility method was sensitive enough to register this attractive risk reduction in the strategy evaluation.

2.4   MICROCOMPUTER SOFTWARE SOLUTIONS TO BAYESIAN DECISION TREES

Almost all of the decision-analysis software listed in Section 1.12 contains a module that performs Bayesian or reverse-tree–type calculations. One of these software modules is contained in *Quantitative Systems for Business* (*QSB*; Chang and Sullivan). Within the Decision and Probability Theory module option of their main menu, they offer Bayesian analysis. Let's illustrate how this module works by using it to solve for the revised probabilities of the PBS Example 2.4 shown in Figure 2-14.

Most software packages require that you provide the "states of nature" or prior/outcome probabilities, as well as the "alternative" values or forecast/prediction probabilities. The states of nature, S_1 and S_2, represent the prior/outcome event probabilities of being successful $P(S)$ and of being unsuccessful $P(S')$, respectively. The different alternatives, A_1 and A_2, are associated with the forecasts or predictions, $P(F)$ and $P(F')$, respectively. The cell values in the probability matrix represent the nonchronological conditional probabilities associated with the different forecast- and outcome-event combinations; e.g., the cell values of S_1 and A_1 correspond to $P(F/S)$; the S_2 and A_1 cell is $P(F/S')$.

The data entry information used from the PBS example is

$$P(S) = .34$$
$$P(F/S) = .86$$
$$P(F/S') = .14$$

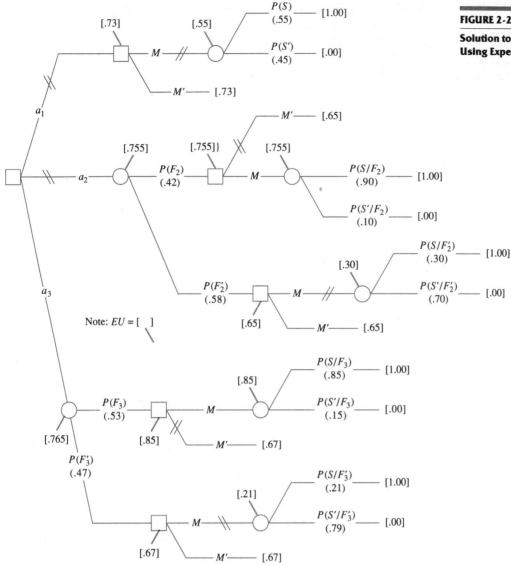

FIGURE 2-26

Solution to Health Ways Nutrition Using Expected Utilities.

Note: $EU = [\quad]$

The resulting joint probabilities and posterior (revised) probabilities for this example are shown in Table 2-2.[1] So, the *QSB* software uses the two nonchronological probabilities (1) to form a Bayesian probability matrix, (2) to calculate the joint probabilities of the reverse tree, (3) to generate the marginal probabilities for each "alternative"—the probabilities associated with the forecast or prediction and, finally, (4) to determine the revised conditional probabilities Just to make sure we know how to use this important program, let's do one more example. First, the revised probabilities for the Broadway play (Example 2.5) will be calculated and then the entire decision tree will be solved.

[1]The slight differences between the values found in Table 2-2 and those calculated earlier during the initial solution of the PBS decision tree can be attributed to the 4 decimal places of accuracy that the computer program employs versus the 2 decimal places of accuracy typically used throughout the decision analysis chapters.

The two nonchronological conditional probabilities and the marginal prior probability in the Charles Saylor branch, a_3, are used to determine the revised conditional probabilities needed to solve the decision tree. These values are

$$P(S) = .37$$
$$P(F_3/S) = .91$$
$$P(F_3/S') = .29$$

The posterior probabilities are now generated from the Bayesian analysis module in the *QSB* package (Table 2-3). The microcomputer solution to this example is now easy to obtain. Let's arbitrarily use the *Micro Manager* software package for the solution phase of this problem. The data entry for the Broadway play is shown in Table 2-4, and the solution to the tree is presented in Table 2-5.

2.5 SUMMARY AND CONCLUSIONS

Use of decision analysis—especially the more sophisticated techniques, such as decision-tree methods and utility analysis—is resisted by a large number of organizations because of what is considered the "highly subjective nature" of the approach. The arguments people make against using decision analysis suggest that they view the estimations needed for the probabilities and payoffs as simply esoteric guesswork. Also, they think that the procedures used to develop utility curves for individuals and organi-

---

TABLE 2-2

Public Television Station Example Solution, Using the Bayesian Analysis Module of the *Quantitative Systems for Business* (QSB) Microcomputer Software Package (Chang & Sullivan)

STATES OF NATURE	ALTERNATIVE A1	A2
S1	.86	.14
S2	.14	.86

STATES OF NATURE	JOINT PROBABILITES OF ALTERNATIVE A1	A2
S1	.2924	.0924
S2	.0476	.5676

ALTERNATIVE	MARGINAL PROBABILITY
A1	.3400
A2	.6600

STATES OF NATURE	POSTERIOR (REVISED) PROBABILITES OF ALTERNATIVE A1	A2
S1	.7599	.0773
S2	.2401	.9227

TABLE 2-3

Broadway Play Example, Using the Bayesian Analysis Module of the *Quantitative Systems for Business* (QSB) Microcomputer Software Package (Chang & Sullivan) to Determine the Posterior Probabilities of the Saylor Branch

STATES OF NATURE	ALTERNATIVE A1	A2
S1	.91	.09
S2	.29	.71

STATES OF NATURE	JOINT PROBABILITES OF ALTERNATIVE A1	A2
S1	.3367	.0333
S2	.1827	.4473

ALTERNATIVE	MARGINAL PROBABILITY
A1	.5194
A2	.4806

STATES OF NATURE	POSTERIOR (REVISED) PROBABILITIES OF ALTERNATIVE A1	A2
S1	.6482	.0693
S2	.3518	.9307

TABLE 2-4

Data Entry for the Broadway Play Example, Using the Decision-Tree Module of *Micro Manager* (Lee & Shim)

PROGRAM: DECISION TREE

***** INPUT DATA ENTERED *****

BRANCH	NODES	PROBABILITY	CONDTIONAL PAYOFF	BRANCH	NODES	PROBABILITY	CONDTIONAL PAYOFF
#1	1--->2	.00	0.00	#20	18--->20	.48	0.00
#2	1--->7	.00	0.00	#21	19--->21	.00	0.00
#3	1--->18	.00	0.00	#22	19--->24	.00	-15.00
#4	1--->29	.00	0.00	#23	20--->25	.00	-15.00
#5	2--->3	.00	0.00	#24	20--->26	.00	0.00
#6	2--->4	.00	0.00	#25	21--->22	.65	340.00
#7	3--->5	.37	700.00	#26	21--->23	.35	-230.00
#8	3--->6	.63	-70.00	#27	26--->27	.06	340.00
#9	7--->8	.30	0.00	#28	26--->28	.94	-230.00
#10	7--->9	.70	0.00	#29	29--->30	.39	0.00
#11	8--->10	.00	-25.00	#30	29--->35	.61	0.00
#12	8--->11	.00	0.00	#31	30--->31	.00	-75.00
#13	9--->14	.00	-25.00	#32	30--->32	.00	0.00
#14	9--->15	.00	0.00	#33	32--->33	.80	280.00
#15	11--->12	.83	330.00	#34	32--->34	.20	-290.00
#16	11--->13	.17	-240.00	#35	35--->36	.00	-75.00
#17	15--->16	.17	330.00	#36	35--->37	.00	0.00
#18	15--->17	.83	-240.00	#37	37--->38	.10	280.00
#19	18--->19	.52	0.00	#38	37--->39	.90	-290.00

TABLE 2-5

Solution to Broadway Play Example, Using the
Decision-Tree Module of *Micro Manager* (Lee & Shim)

```
                    *****  PROGRAM OUTPUT  *****

                         EVALUATED DECISION TREE

-----------------------------------------------------------------------------
BRANCH  NODES  PROBABILITY  CONDITIONAL  BRANCH  NODES  PROBABILITY  CONDITIONAL
                             PAYOFF                                   PAYOFF
-----------------------------------------------------------------------------
 #1    1--->2   DECISION      214.90 *    #20   18--->20   .48         -7.20
 #2    1--->7   DECISION       52.43      #21   19--->21  DECISION    140.50 *
 #3    1--->18  DECISION       65.86      #22   19--->24  DECISION    -15.00
 #4    1--->29  DECISION       18.99      #23   20--->25  DECISION    -15.00 *
 #5    2--->3   DECISION      214.90 *    #24   20--->26  DECISION   -195.80
 #6    2--->4   DECISION        0.00      #25   21--->22   .65        221.00
 #7    3--->5    .37          259.00      #26   21--->23   .35        -80.50
 #8    3--->6    .63          -44.10      #27   26--->27   .06         20.40
 #9    7--->8    .30           69.93      #28   26--->28   .94       -216.20
#10    7--->9    .70          -17.50      #29   29--->30   .39         64.74
#11    8--->10  DECISION      -25.00      #30   29--->35   .61        -45.75
#12    8--->11  DECISION      233.10 *    #31   30--->31  DECISION    -75.00
#13    9--->14  DECISION      -25.00 *    #32   30--->32  DECISION    166.00 *
#14    9--->15  DECISION     -143.10      #33   32--->33   .80        224.00
#15   11--->12   .83          273.90      #34   32--->34   .20        -58.00
#16   11--->13   .17          -40.80      #35   35--->36  DECISION    -75.00 *
#17   15--->16   .17           56.10      #36   35--->37  DECISION   -233.00
#18   15--->17   .83         -199.20      #37   37--->38   .10         28.00
#19   18--->19   .52           73.06      #38   37--->39   .90       -261.00
-----------------------------------------------------------------------------

          EXPECTED PAYOFF OF THE SOLUTION =   214.90
```

zations are too abstract to allow accurate representation. (Even if they could be represented, these values would change over time, so—people ask—why bother?)

Criticisms such as these fail to recognize several important points. First, human decisions *are* subjective. There is simply no way to escape that fact. The purpose of decision analysis is to provide an objective framework within which these subjective decisions can be guided intelligently. Second, regardless of whether a person has tried to articulate the problem analytically, *a decision is going to be made!* At least, with the identification of the parameters that were used to guide the decision, it is possible to have a frame of reference for understanding the selection process (even at a much later date), and to use it as a vehicle for meaningful dialogue. Without it, only guesswork and conjecture prevail.

2.6 EXERCISES

2-1 Empirical data gathered from records associated with the Insight Consulting Group (ICG) of Baltimore, Maryland, show the following previous history on marketing forecasts dealing with assessing the likely success or failure of a beauty-industry product:

1. Favorable reports were written for 78 percent of the products that were ultimately successful.
2. Favorable reports were written for 22 percent of those products that were ultimately unsuccessful.

ASSIGNMENT

1. Given that the probability of success for a beauty-industry product is 28 percent, draw the reverse tree for ICG.
2. Determine the proportion of ICG's reports that are favorable and unfavorable reports.
3. If ICG writes a favorable report, what are the chances that the product will be successful?
4. If ICG writes an unfavorable report, what are the chances that the product will be successful?
5. What is ICG's reliability when it writes favorable reports?
6. What is ICG's reliability when it writes unfavorable reports?

2-2 Use the algebraic form of Bayes' theorem to solve Exercise 2-1.

2-3 The results of a lie-detector test are not admissible evidence in court. Typically, these tests label as untruthful 96 percent of the statements that are actually lies. Unfortunately, these same tests label as untruthful 11 percent of statements that are true. Suppose that a person in a civil case insists on taking a lie-detector test, even though the findings are not admissible evidence. Based on hours of interviews by opposition lawyers, the test results indicate that she lies 20 percent of the time. Answer the following questions after laying out the reverse tree:

1. The lie-detector test has just indicated that the person lied. What is the likelihood that the lie detector is incorrect (i.e., that this is a *false-negative* result)?
2. The lie-detector test has just indicated that the person told the truth. What is the likelihood that the lie detector is incorrect (i.e., that this is a *false-positive* result)?

2-4 Solve Exercise 2-3 using the algebraic form of Bayes' theorem.

2-5 Suppose that the ABC television network wants to market a classical dramatic series using an actor better known for his action series. Because of this major shift in emphasis, from what this actor is known for, ABC is concerned about whether the viewing audience will accept this actor in this very different type of role. ABC predicts that the series will be either successful or unsuccessful. If it is a success, it is expected to generate revenues of $23,500,000 for the season; if it fails, it will bring in only $7,500,000.

The network is faced with an immediate decision. It must choose one of three possible actions:

1. Pay for a professional market survey at a cost of $1,250,000.

"Well, we've tried every device and you still won't talk—every device, that is, except this little baby we simply call 'Mr. Thingy.'"

Chuck Norris, concerned about being typecast, does Hamlet.

2. Do an in-house market survey at a cost of $400,000.

3. Market immediately.

The marketing cost is estimated at $11,250,000. If the series is market surveyed, the results will be classified as either favorable or unfavorable, and ABC will have to decide whether to market or to drop the series. If a professional firm conducts the survey, the probability of product success is 0.80 for a favorable survey report; if unfavorable, the estimated success is only 0.05. The network's past in-house experience has indicated that its surveys are favorable only 60 percent of the time when the series, in fact, becomes successful. However, the survey results are also favorable 30 percent of the time when the ultimate outcome of the series is failure. From past experience, the probability of a new series becoming a success is estimated to be .10.

ASSIGNMENT

1. Using the principal of expected values, draw the decision tree and determine which action is most desirable.

2. Calculate by how much the estimated probability of the series being successful can be in error without causing the existing optimum solution to change.

3. Calculate by how much the marketing cost can change without causing the existing optimum strategy to change.

2-6 The small, regional soft-drink manufacturer introduced in Exercise 1-13 is considering hiring a consulting firm to study the idea of plant expansion. The consultants will provide the company CEO with a strategy report in 30 days for a fee of $500,000. The report will either suggest that expansion is a good idea because the market growth looks strong (i.e., favorable findings), or that expansion is not the correct approach for the time being because the market may level off or decline (i.e., unfavorable findings). A little research on the part of the CEO and her staff reveals that these consultants write favorable reports on similar market studies about 73 percent of the time when the outcome has been one of strong market growth; 17 percent of the time, they predict market growth when, in fact, the market volume decreases.

ASSIGNMENT

Using expected values, determine whether hiring the consulting group provides the CEO with a strategy stronger than the one you determined in Exercise 1-13.

2-7 A vice president of operations thinks that the company should be more sophisticated to its approach in dealing with the preservative issue presented in Exercise 1-14. Specifically, the VP wants the company to conduct its own in-house testing program immediately, to determine whether the preservative is a potential health hazard. He believes that deciding what to do about the preservative without conducting any of its own tests leaves the company in a highly unreliable situation.

This proposed in-house test uses a process identical to the one employed by the FDA. The test yields positive findings 95 percent of the time when the substance is truly a cancer-causing agent; it also provides negative findings 90 percent of

the time when the substance is, in fact, noncarcinogenic. If the company chooses to initiate this in-house testing program, the test results will almost certainly provide the same findings that the FDA will ultimately discover and rule on. In this way, the company can determine—prior to the actual FDA ruling—whether they are likely to be faced with a preservative ban. The testing program would cost the company $1,700,000.

ASSIGNMENT

Illustrate the in-house testing program using decision-tree analysis. Based on expected values, does the new in-house testing strategy look more attractive than do the options in Exercise 1-14?

2-8 A private pharmaceutical laboratory, Fantasia, Inc., is considering developing a new orally administered drug that it believes will virtually eliminate symptoms of glaucoma. There are no foreseeable competitors. The FDA requires sufficient developmental safeguards before it will approve this drug and allow marketing by Fantasia. The FDA will give a 19-year, exclusive-production-rights contract to Fantasia if and when it successfully fulfills the developmental criteria. After that, the market will be open to everyone. Fantasia is wrestling with the problem of selecting the most attractive testing and manufacturing procedures for demonstrating the safety and efficacy of this medication. It can use several different development techniques. The more traditional approach, a_1, is totally acceptable to the FDA as long as all the criteria are met. There is an alternative approach, a_2, however, which Fantasia is tempted to use because it results in much higher profits (due to dramatically lower development costs) if the FDA does not disallow its use. And so here is the dilemma Fantasia must resolve:

1. It must contend with the normal worries concerning the production, marketing, and sales of its new product. Success is not guaranteed simply because it can develop and market this drug. Fantasia also knows that the drug could be a resounding failure.

2. If Fantasia selects the traditional FDA-approved development method (a_1), the total development and production costs to the company, exclusive of market survey, will be $8,300,000. No FDA challenge would occur in this instance.

3. If the alternative method is used (a_2), the total post-development and production costs to the company drop to $4,500,000. The problem Fantasia foresees is that there is a 10 percent chance that the FDA will disallow the method's use. In this case, since the decision to produce and market the drug is made prior to the FDA ruling, all program-development and production costs (including the survey expense) will be lost and the drug will not be marketable. At this point, Fantasia would have to start all over again with the traditional development program, which it will not have enough funds to do.

4. Fantasia knows that it must assess the development of this new product just as it does any other product; i.e., it will have to conduct a consumer survey among the medical profession to determine whether doctors would be likely to prescribe the drug (favorable or unfavorable response). Although it can also decide not to develop the medication (a_3), *it cannot proceed* with either a_1 or a_2 *without a survey.* Also, physicians will want to see the initial research findings generated from the specific development program used (either a_1 or a_2), and the degree of receptiveness of the physicians may vary slightly with the development method was employed. These survey costs are, on the average, $1,000,000, exclusive of the other marketing expenses.

5. Products developed with the traditional method (a_1) have historically demonstrated ultimate success 81 and 13 percent of the time when favorable and unfavorable physician-survey responses resulted, respectively.

6. Physicians have anticipated successful outcomes in 88 and 10 percent of those instances in which products developed with the alternative method (a_2) actually succeeded and failed, respectively.

7. If the product succeeds, Fantasia anticipates $17,500,000 in revenues over the 19-year period. If it is not successful, the revenues are approximated at $5,800,000. In the past, 68 percent of similar types of medication products have succeeded.

ASSIGNMENT

You have been hired as consultant to the Fantasia CEO, to help her understand the problem so that she can make the most enlightened decision possible with the information available.

1. Design the decision tree for this case illustrating all probability and payoff values.

2. Using the principle of expected values, what strategy would you suggest that Fantasia select?

2-9 Although the details surrounding Apple Computer's decision to develop and market the Macintosh microcomputer are not available, it is interesting to speculate about some of the landmark decisions leading up to this remarkable product. The data that follow are purely conjectural.

First, the company had to consider whether it was sensible to add a new model to their already extensive line of Apple home computers. If this was judged to be a good idea, then one of the next decisions may have been to determine whether the market for the graphical-interface orientation of its new Macintosh computer would attract and compete for the same market as that of the IBM-PC, or whether it would attract a different group of buyers. This point would be particularly important to Apple because, if the market was predicted to be a different segment, then it would feel freer (and probably would prefer) to develop its own unique, advanced disk operating system (DOS). However, this advanced system would be incompatible with the key-stroke oriented IBM Microsoft DOS and, if the market was assessed to be a common one, the incompatibility of operating systems would result in an estimated loss of 67 percent of potential buyers who would be unwilling to purchase the incompatible and software-lean Macintosh system. Conversely, if the market comprised a separate population of buyers, the unique Macintosh operating system would clearly enhance and solidify the Macintosh's position.

Apple estimated that the cost of developing and marketing their advanced operating system would be $80 million, whereas using standard PC-DOS (IBM-compatible) would cost closer to $20 million. Further, Apple realized that it could select either design and simply introduce it into the marketplace on completion without conducting a market survey of consumers and retailers, *or* it could conduct this survey before beginning development. If Apple moved quickly, it could capture whatever potential early market existed. However, conducting and analyzing the survey would require 4 to 6 months of additional time and would, in the case of the advanced operating system, decrease this advantageous early position in the marketplace. In all strategies, however, Apple wished to have the option of not marketing their product if they so chose. No marketing costs would be incurred in this situation unless the strategy included using the survey (later marketing strategy).

The forecast Macintosh sales revenues for the early marketing (without the marketing survey) and later marketing (with the marketing survey) are shown in Table 2-9.1 for the ad-

TABLE 2-9.1

Macintosh Sales Revenues As Influenced by System Design and Early versus Later Marketing Strategies

Macintosh System Selected	Sales Revenues Generated ($ Millions)			
	Early Marketing		Later Marketing	
	Successful	Unsuccessful	Successful	Unsuccessful
Standard	100	50	100	50
Advanced	800	50	500	30

vanced and standard operating systems, for both successful and unsuccessful outcomes.

The cost of a sophisticated market survey was estimated at $3,000,000 and would be the same regardless of which system-design approach was selected. Apple's past experience with surveys on advanced or evolutionary products had resulted in predictions that suggested unsuccessful outcomes for 75 percent of the products that ultimately failed. These same surveys have also predicted unsuccessful results for 20 percent of the product that, in fact, were successful. Marketing surveys performed for products that use the standard operating system have resulted in successful outcomes on 15 percent of those occasions in which the survey reports suggested an unfavorable result. Unfavorable reports for the standard design have been written about 60 percent of the time.

One of the most important marketing properties that Apple had to acknowledge was that the probabilities of successfully marketing an advanced or innovative, versus that for an established or standardized, product are *very different*. Expensive, breakthrough products in the home-computer field have traditionally met with initial market skepticism, whereas the standard product usually has not (the consumer feels a natural reluctance to invest hard-earned money in a product that may be viewed initially as a "gimmick"). Because of the greater risk involved in successfully introducing an innovative product, Apple estimated that its chances of successfully marketing an advanced microcomputer product is about 20 percent, whereas the more standard designs will succeed about 35 percent of the time.

Suppose that Steven Jobs, then president of Apple Computers, had hired you to tell him how to proceed with Macintosh. Using the method of expected values, what would you have told him? Should Apple have marketed the Macintosh? If so, should they have used the standard or advanced system design? Should they have conducted the survey, thereby losing the early market edge?

2-10 Suppose that, at the time you worked for Apple in Exercise 2-9, you also collected information regarding Mr. Jobs' attitude toward risk in terms of his personal utility for various financial outcomes that the Macintosh might have demonstrated (Figure 2-10.1). Although you didn't use that information, you decide now to re-solve the original problem using the method of *expected utilities*. What effect, if any, does this new approach have on your findings, when contrasted with the results you developed in Exercise 2-9? Show all your work.

2-11 Referring back to Exercise 2-9, discuss briefly (in no more than a few sentences) what you would have done if

1. The information regarding the probabilities of success for the standard and advanced systems was not available and there was no other source you could use?

2. Mr. Jobs told you that Apple Computers was not in a high-liquid-asset position, had maturing loans it had to pay soon, and therefore could not afford to employ any strategy that might lose more than $1,500,000?

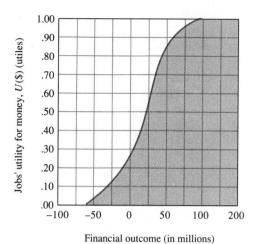

FIGURE 2-10.1

Steven Jobs' Utility Curve for Financial Outcome of the Macintosh Operating-System Study.

Review the findings you developed for Parts 1 and 2, and assume that Apple *did not* do any extensive surveys that would have delayed the introduction of the Macintosh. Do you think that

3. Apple Computers used expected-value or expected-utility analysis in their actual decision (assuming that it used one or the other)? Explain your answer briefly.

2-12 [1] At about 2:30 A.M., a 28-year-old woman is brought into the emergency room at the University of California at San Francisco (UCSF) Hospital. She tells the emergency-room receptionist that she has been experiencing sharp chest pains on her right side since about midnight. The examining physician sees that the pain is especially acute when the woman tries to take a deep breath. Over the last 48 hours, the woman has had chills and muscular aches, as well as coughing (flecks of blood have been discovered in her sputum). To complicate the diagnosis, the physician learns that the woman has just returned to the United States on a 16-hour flight from Rome; the woman was essentially immobile during the entire flight because she felt ill.

The woman's medical history suggests that she has been very healthy all her life. She has never been married and has had no children. The only medication she has been taking over the last 30 months is birth-control (estrogen) pills. Because of these data, the physician believes that the woman probably has a viral infection contracted in Europe. However, there is also

[1] This problem was adapted from P. H. Hill, H. A. Bedon, R. A. Chechile, W. J. Crochetiere, B. L. Kellerman, D. Ounjian, S. G. Pauker, S. P. Pauker, and J. Z. Rubin, *Making Decisions: A Multidisciplinary Introduction* (Reading, MA: Addison-Wesley, 1979).

concern that the combination of the birth-control pills and lengthy plane ride may have resulted in a pulmonary embolism—a blood clot probably originating in a vein in the leg that is passed to main artery in the lung. The physician makes the following immediate assessment of the woman's situation:

1. If the patient has, in fact, experienced an embolism, give her the appropriate medication and treatment.
2. If the patient has, in fact, a virus, don't give her any special medication. Send her home to rest, drink fluids, and take aspirin.

For this specific medical history, the physician assesses the likelihood of the pulmonary embolism to be about 50 percent. If the embolism has, in fact, occurred, the appropriate treatment is to give the patient an anticoagulant agent such as Coumadin. (This type of medication "thins" the blood so that the existing embolism is dissolved and the chances of further clotting are minimized.) Without the medication, there is a 50 percent chance of reembolization (i.e., that the patient will experience two embolisms); the chance of reembolization is only 15 percent with the medication. In addition, there is a slight (5 percent) risk that the use of an anticoagulant could cause hemorrhaging *regardless* of whether the patient has experienced an embolism or not.

The physician has discussed this problem with the woman and has developed an evaluation for the potential outcomes, as shown in Table 2-12.1.

ASSIGNMENT

1. Illustrate the decision tree for this problem.
2. Using the quality-of-life index (QLI) developed with the woman, determine the optimum treatment strategy for the physician to employ.

2-13 [2] Exercise 2-12 assumed that there were treatment options other than to prescribe (or not to prescribe) the anticoagulant. However, there is an additional alternative that aids diagnosis—the pulmonary angiogram. In this procedure, a long, plastic tube (catheter) is inserted into a vein in the patient's groin. This tube is then passed through the heart and into the pulmonary artery. At this point, a radiopaque dye is injected into the artery, and X-ray images are obtained. This procedure determines whether a pulmonary embolism is present, as a clot can be visualized clearly. Once again, however, as with almost all medical procedures, there is a 1 percent chance of incurring complications, such as hemorrhage, infection, vessel rupture, or cardiac arrhythmia. The patient assessments of these new outcomes using the pulmonary angiogram for diagnosis are shown in QLI units in Table 2-13.1.

ASSIGNMENT

1. Draw the new decision tree showing the pulmonary angiogram diagnostic test.
2. Determine the optimum strategy for the physician to employ using the QLI values established by the patient.

[2] This problem was adapted from Hill et al., *Making Decisions: A Multidisciplinary Introduction* (Reading, MA: Addison-Wesley, 1979).

TABLE 2-12.1

Quality-of-Life Outcome Ratings

Outcome	Quality-of-Life Index, QLI
No problems	100
Hemorrhage	20
Another embolism	20
Hemorrhage + second embolism	

2-14 By the end of 1984, the Coca-Cola Bottling Company was on the verge of making a monumental change in their historically successful cola-drink product: It was assessing the possibility of retiring its 99-year-old formula for Coca-Cola. The primary reason that Coca-Cola considered this possible change was the result of recent market tests. These tests, although not conducted using random participant-selection procedures, had shown that about 55 to 60 percent of the 50,000 people who had taken comparative taste tests (between the original Coke formula and the new version of Coke) preferred the newer formula. This newer formula was less carbonated and was sweeter than the original was, and was deemed to be more attractive to the huge "young-adults" portion of the multibillion-dollar soft-drink market. Although there was no market survey regarding possible shifts by its current consumers to other cola manufacturers, Coca-Cola was so taken with the results of the comparative taste tests that, in February 1985, it decided to dump the old formula and aggressively to market the *New Coke*. This is where our story begins.

On July 10, 1985, all three television networks suggested in their nightly news reports that the uproar from the thousands of old customers who preferred the original cola (referred to by Coca-Cola as the *Classic* version), along with the lagging sales of the reformulated *New Coke* formula, had caused the Coca-Cola top management to reconsider their earlier strategy. Although the underlying strategy of this event continues to be a subject of conversation in marketing and advertising circles, it

TABLE 2-13.1

Quality-of-Life Outcome Ratings

Outcome	Quality-of-Life Index, QLI
1. Do not do pulmonary angiography	
1.1 Give anticoagulant	70
1.2 Do not give anticoagulant	40
2. Do pulmonary angiography	
2.1 Angiogram complication	
2.1.1 Emboli present; give anticoagulant	10
2.1.2 No emboli present; do not give anticoagulant	20
2.2 No angiography complication	
2.2.1 (same as 2.1.1)	50
2.2.2 (same as 2.1.2)	100

has never been clearly established whether Coca-Cola actually intended to eliminate "Old Coke" completely and to replace it with "New Coke," or whether the company merely feigned the removal of the original Coke as a part of a clever advertising ploy to set the stage for the reintroduction of that product. Let's pretend, for the sake of argument (and to create an interesting exercise), that the news regarding Coca-Cola's concern over the sluggishness of sales of its new product was, in fact, correct and that the following hypothetical scenario is true.

Coca-Cola is now studying three possible new strategies:

a_1: Hang in with *New Coke*. *Classic Coke* is dead—long live *New Coke*.

a_2: Drop *New Coke*. Face it, we made a disastrous mistake. We're going back to the original formula. H. L. Menken said, "No one ever lost money underestimating the taste of the American public."

a_3: Why not have it both ways? We'll keep *New Coke and* bring back the original *Classic Coke*.

Traditionally, the chance of any new cola drink being successful is estimated to be about 15 percent. However, Coca-Cola is not just *any* cola company. Market analysts thought that, with Coca-Cola's name behind the product, *this* new cola, even after its shaky start, stood a slightly better chance of being successful, ultimately. In fact, the market analysts thought that the chances for market success for strategies a_1 and a_2 were .18 and .25, respectively (based on similar old and new cola-marketing programs conducted in the past).

It was estimated that the different strategies would incur significantly different marketing costs and also would generate different revenue levels for successful and unsuccessful outcomes. More particularly, the likely revenues and marketing costs associated with the three strategies were estimated as shown in Table 2-14.1.

Coca-Cola considered hiring Pollster Associates to conduct extensive marketwide surveys to assess the chances of its product strategies—something it had neglected to do prior to switching formulae. However, some of the "old-line" management still were not convinced that expensive market surveys need to be conducted. After all, they had made plenty of good decisions in the past without employing esoteric MBA techniques. The younger, more enlightened managers were uncomfortable with the older manager's attitude. As a result, the company had to assess whether it should hire Pollster Associates to conduct the market surveys, or whether it should market one of the three strategies without a survey.

Data were collected regarding previous, similar market-survey experience of Pollster Associates. The following information was determined:

1. For new products, like *New Coke*, of those occasions in which the firm forecasts successful outcomes, 30 percent result in failure; 20 percent of Pollster Associates surveys resulted in favorable forecasts for these new, single-product surveys.

2. For remarketing established product lines, like *Classic Coke*, Pollster Associates has forecast unsuccessful outcomes in 30 percent of those instances in which the product was, on the contrary, successful; for those programs that ultimately failed, Pollster Associates predicted success 10 percent of the time.

3. Multiple- or mixed-product marketing situations—such as marketing *Classic* and *New Coke* together—are a bit trickier to assess. It is more difficult to determine the combined effect of two products than to assess the individual effects of two separately marketed products. For this reason, Pollster Associates has more difficulty assessing this mode of marketing (the other leading market-survey firms also experience this difficulty). In the past, mixed products have proven unsuccessful 40 percent of the time that the survey report suggested a favorable situation; mixed products were also successful 18 percent of the time that the survey suggested an unfavorable setting. Multiple-product surveys making unfavorable forecasts were written 67 percent of the time.

Coca-Cola estimated that the survey costs associated with the three strategies would be $8,000,000 and $6,000,000 for market assessments of strategies a_1 and a_2, respectively, and $19,000,000 for the market survey of strategy a_3 (Table 2-14.2).

ASSIGNMENT

Using decision-tree methods, answer the following questions (illustrate all your work). Translate these following statements ("cut and pasted" from the preceding problem text) into appropriate probability notation by filling in the blanks between the parentheses (be sure to use the suggested subscript notation):

1. "Traditionally, the chance of any new cola drink being successful is estimated to be about 15 percent." Ans: $P(\ )$ = .15

2. "the chances for market success for strategies a_1 and a_2, were .18 and .25, respectively." Ans: $P(\ ) = .18$ Ans: $P(\ ) = .25$

TABLE 2-14.1

Revenues and Costs for Coca-Cola Product-Marketing Strategies

| Strategy a_i | Revenue Generation | | Marketing Costs |
	Successful	Unsuccessful	
a_1	190,000,000	50,000,000	75,000,000
a_2	230,000,000	40,000,000	50,000,000
a_3	275,000,000	80,000,000	100,000,000

TABLE 2-14.2

Survey Costs Associated with Coca-Cola's Product-Marketing Strategies

Strategy a_i	Survey Costs
a_1	$ 8,000,000
a_2	$ 6,000,000
a_3	$19,000,000

3. "For new products, like *New Coke*, of those occasions in which the firm forecasts successful outcomes, 30 percent result in failures;" Ans: $P(\ ) = .30$

4. "20 percent of Pollster Associates' surveys resulted in favorable forecasts for these new, single-product surveys." Ans: $P(\ ) = .20$

5. "For remarketing established product lines like *Classic Coke*, Pollster Associates has forecast unsuccessful outcomes in 30 percent of those instances in which the product was, on the contrary, successful;" Ans: $P(\ ) = .30$

6. "for those programs that ultimately failed, Pollster Associates predicted success 10 percent of the time." Ans: $P(\ ) = .10$

7. "In the past, mixed products have proven unsuccessful 40 percent of the time that the survey report suggested a favorable situation;" Ans: $P(\ ) = .40$

8. "mixed products were also successful 18 percent of the time that the survey suggested an unfavorable setting." Ans: $P(\ ) = .18$

9. "Multiple-product surveys making unfavorable forecasts were written 67 percent of the time." Ans: $P(\ ) = .67$

For the following four parts, use appropriate decision-tree methods:

10. Design the *portion* of the decision tree that illustrates only the a_1 strategy. Perform the calculations needed to fill in all the probabilities and payoffs in this segment of the tree.

11. Design the *portion* of the decision tree that illustrates only the a_2 strategy. Perform the calculations needed to fill in all the probabilities and payoffs in this segment of the tree.

12. Design the *portion* of the decision tree that illustrates only the a_3 strategy. Perform the calculations needed to fill in all the probabilities and payoffs in this segment of the tree.

13. Select the optimal strategy using the criterion of expected values.

2-15 The CEO of the Fantasia pharmaceutical company (see Exercise 2-8) thinks that a few of the key parameter estimates used in the original problem may be in error. Specifically, she would like to uncover the following information:

1. How much the probability of product success can change before the two development programs (a_1 and a_2) are considered equally attractive.

2. At what probability value of agency disapproval (for a_2) the two programs would become equally attractive.

Determine the values that she seeks.

CHAPTER 3

MULTIATTRIBUTE UTILITY METHODS

A FRAMEWORK FOR ASSESSING COMPETING MULTIDIMENSIONAL ALTERNATIVES

3.1 INTRODUCTION

The two preceding chapters on decision analysis have shown that decision methods can help you to examine complex situations in a well-documented and rational manner. However, these methods are limited to situations in which we are examining the selection of the best alternative *based on a single criterion*—usually either the expected value or expected utility of a given dollar amount. It would be convenient if all decisions concerning the selection of the "best" alternative could be made this simply. Some situations, however, dictate the consideration of *multiple* criteria or attributes. In addition, these attributes often have incommensurate units of measure. So, how can we compare dollars with years or, possibly, with a measure even more diverse, such as an esthetic judgment? The answer lies in the manager's ability to execute two crucial tasks successfully:

1. Devise a common scale of merit against which all attributes may be measured.

2. Collect the appropriate attribute performance data that indicate the *degree* to which each attribute contributes to the overall satisfaction of an alternative. This task is particularly important, since the performance of most attributes is not a binary measurement (e.g., alternative performance is usually not measured as simply as "acceptable" or "not acceptable").

When these two tasks are successfully completed, the set of attribute performance values can be combined to provide an overall measure of worth for each alternative. The technique that accomplishes these critical tasks is called the *multiattribute utility method (MAUM).*[1]

Some employees of *Consumer Reports*, trying to decide the best place to have lunch.

3.2 APPLICATIONS OF MAUM

MAUM has been applied to many significant problems: assessing investment decisions, purchasing a home or car, allocating money to competing projects, evaluating job applicants, comparing different sites for company relocation, selecting advertising

[1]The multiattribute utility method (MAUM) is also referred to as MAUT (multiattribute utility technique) and MAUA (multiattribute utility analysis).

media, choosing a new job, determining which college to attend, and so on. Some excellent application examples from the literature are these:

- Selecting a portfolio of solar energy projects (Kamal, 1981).
- Evaluating an alternative to court adjudication of disputes (Newman and Drew, 1979).
- Evaluating school desegregation plans in Los Angeles (Edwards, 1979).
- Making product-line decisions (Jackson and Shapiro, 1979).
- Evaluating alternative energy systems (Keeney and von Winterfeldt, 1985).
- Generating compromise options for offshore oil drilling (bon Winterfeldt, 1985).
- Evaluating professional football players for the annual NFL draft selection (Oberstone and Newman, 1986).

3.3 THE MAUM PROCESS

If you stop to think about it, there is only a handful of considerations that a manager uses in making a decision regarding competing alternatives characterized by multiple attributes: (1) identify the key attributes to consider in making the decision; (2) select the candidate alternatives you wish to evaluate; (3) determine how important each attribute is; (4) determine how well each alternative performs in each attribute category; (5) select the best alternative. These tasks are precisely those that MAUM performs.

MAUM is a powerful evaluation tool for making subjective comparisons of multiple alternatives characterized by multidimensional attributes. MAUM manages this crucial operation by transforming these noncommensurate factors into a common measure of worth (this transformation procedure is not uncommon; nonmonetary outcomes are often converted into their monetary equivalents)—typically utiles. It is then possible for a manager to compare competing, multidimensional alternatives with a single measure of merit.

The primary parts of MAUM require that (1) each attribute be given a weighting factor to reflect its relative importance to the total scheme of things, and (2) the value of each attribute be established over its possible range of performance—called the attribute *utility function*.

There are many different types of utility functions (linear, nonlinear, logarithmic, etc.).[2] The most resilient or robust model is some form of the *additive utility function* (AUF). The AUF assumes that each attribute is independent of the others in the set. This independence allows each attribute to be separated into its own weighted utility function—individual utility functions are treated as separate commodities. Each attribute's utility function can then be assessed independently of the others before being combined into an aggregate model. The AUF model is given by

$$U[y_1, y_2, \ldots, y_j, \ldots, y_n] = w_1 U[y_1] + w_2 U[y_2] + \cdots + w_n U[y_n]$$

The total worth of an alternative—referred to later in this chapter as the *composite utility*—is therefore equivalent to the weighted sum of the individual AUFs:

$$U[y_1, y_2, \ldots, y_j, \ldots, y_n] = CU[a_i] = \sum_{j=1}^{n} w_j U[y_j]_i$$

[2]Melvin Lifson, *Decision and Risk Analysis* (Boston: Cahners Books, 1972), pp. 95–98.

where

$CU[a_i]$ = composite (additive) utility of the ith alternative.

w_j = weight of importance of the jth attribute.

$U[y_j]_i$ = individual utility of the ith alternative—j^{th} attribute combination.

It can be overly simplistic to assume an additive form of utility function for MAUM problems. Ideally, it is wise to establish first whether the attributes are independent. Unfortunately, validating the property of independence for the utility functions is an extremely arduous operation when there is even a modest sum of attributes in the MAUM model (the complexity grows exponentially with the number of attributes).[3] Because of this, the assumption that the AUF model is appropriate can be accepted (usually in circles where community standards are lower) as an expedient—albeit somewhat risky—first-cut approach to a MAUM problem; if necessary, the form of the utility function can be refined later.[4] For our purposes in this text, *utility functions will be assumed to be additive*. It seems timely, at this point, to include an illustration of this simple yet elegant technique.

EXAMPLE 3.1   FRED KUGELMAN SELECTS THE "BEST" JOB

Fred Kugelman is in the market for a new job. He has interviewed for a number of positions in different companies. Several of these organizations have been quite impressed with his professional and educational qualifications and have made a formal job offer to him. Kugelman would like to assess the relative attractiveness of these competing job offers.

Now, let's switch places with him. If *you* were trying to choose among several job offers, how would you proceed? Would you be concerned only with salary? How about the location of the new job, or the prestige of the organization? Can you see that it is natural to consider multiple attributes when attempting to compare significant options? Here's how MAUM tackles this kind of problem:

Step 1. *Determine the goals of the problem*. This can be a simple statement of need or preference; for example, "Pick the best job offer."

Step 2. *Establish the attribute set* that most aptly reflects the important considerations, in terms of measurable criteria, that can be used to assess how satisfying any ultimate alternative selection is. A maximum of eight to ten attributes will satisfy most situations (sometimes three or four are sufficient). These attributes must be defined operationally to avoid ambiguity. Further, the attributes must be separate from each other (mutually exclusive) or very close to it (e.g., Kugelman would be ill-advised to have two attributes such as "salary" and "benefits"—bonuses, company car privileges, stock options—unless he carefully separated out the overlapping components of each attribute). If you don't check them carefully, nonexclusive attributes can lead to a disproportionate representation of overlapping components in the final MAUM model.

From *The Wall Street Journal* — Permission, cartoon Features Syndicate.

"Tell me about yourself, Kugelman—your hopes, dreams, career path, and what that damn earring means."

---

[3] We test the independence by developing and assessing a series of unidimensional utility functions—a process similar to one used to test the validity of a regression model (i.e., can Y be best predicted by an independent set of X variables, or is the mean of Y just as good?).

[4] It is even quite common for a manager to assume that the model is not only additive, but also *linear*. Examples of the linear additive model include personnel evaluation; financial-institution loan applications; insurance-company risk models; and graduate, law, dental, and medical school admission applications.

TABLE 3-1	
Rank-Ordered Attribute Set for Kugelman's Selection of the Best Job	
Attribute, y_j*	Attribute Rank
Job potential, y_1	1
Annual salary, y_2	2
Job location, y_3	3
Housing conditions, y_4	4

*y_j = j^{th} attribute

TABLE 3-2	
Weighted Attribute Set for Kugelman's Selection of the Best Job. (Weighting Method 4.1)	
Attribute, y_j	Weight of Importance
Job potential, y_1	50
Annual salary, y_2	40
Job location, y_3	20
Housing conditions, y_4	10

Assume, for this job-selection example, that the following four attributes are selected:

1. Job potential, y_1 (growth, company stability, responsibility, and creative freedom on a five-point Likert Scale[5] of 1 = poor; 2 = fair; 3 = average; 4 = good; 5 = excellent).
2. Annual salary, y_2 (dollars per year).
3. Job location, y_3 (parent city's cultural, educational, recreational, and weather profiles measured on the five-point Likert Scale (described in y_1).
4. Housing conditions, y_4 (distance to work, housing type and expense, and neighborhood conditions, measured on the five-point Likert Scale described in y_1).

Step 3. *List the attributes in order of importance.* The rank set for this example is listed in Table 3-1.

Step 4. *Weight the individual attributes to reflect their relative importance to satisfying the problem.*[6] There are several simple, effective approaches:

Method 4.1 Arbitrarily assign 10 points to the least important attribute in the set. Then examine the next least important attribute and assign to it a number of points reflecting how much more important it is than the least important attribute, in terms of a ratio; for example, if it is considered twice as important, give it 20 points. Continue up the list of attributes, comparing each succeeding attribute with the weight of the attribute just beneath it. Next, continue to step 5.

Method 4.2 Imagine you have 100 poker chips. Distribute these chips among the various attributes so that the relative importance of each is reflected in the total number of chips received. Next, continue to step 5.

For our example, suppose that we use the weighting method 4.1 and that the weight assignments are as shown in Table 3-2.

---

[5]A Likert scale is an ordinal scale of measurement commonly used to assess subjective opinions (e.g., 5 = strongly agree; 4 = agree; 3 = undecided; 2 = disagree; 1 = strongly disagree). The number of points on the scale is arbitrary, although usually it is an odd number so that a balanced scale with a midpoint—"undecided," "no opinion," "average," or some other neutral response—is possible.

[6]There are inherent weighting problems that occur when considerable detail has been provided in identifying the underlying value structure of the problem. In particular, if an attribute has been decomposed into a number of subattribute elements, overweighting of these elements—beyond the weight that would have been assigned to the attribute—may occur. For more information see Schoemaker and Waid (1982), and Weber, Eisenfuhr, and von Winterfeldt (1988).

TABLE 3-3

Normalized Weights for Attribute Set for Kugelman's Selection of the Best Job

Attribute, y_j		Weight of Importance	Normalized Weight
y_1		50	42
y_2		40	33
y_3		20	17
y_4		10	8
	Totals	120	100

Step 5. Normalize the weights of step 4 by summing all attribute weights, then dividing each individual attribute by this sum. Next, multiply each attribute value by 100. This step converts the original attribute weights into numbers that sum to 100. That is,

$$\sum_{j=1}^{n} w_j = 100$$

where w_j represents the normalized weight of importance of the jth attribute. Although this is an arbitrary step, it conveniently converts the weights of the attributes onto a scale of 0 to 100. These normalized weight values are shown in Table 3-3.

Step 6. *Define constraint values for all the attributes.* We can view these values as limits on values, or minimum allowable values, which an attribute must attain. If the attribute does not attain the constraint value, the "violated" alternative is weeded out as not viable. This weeding out is done even if, for that alternative, all other attributes perform quite well. (Because of this requirement, it is important not to determine constraint values that are overly extreme.) For our example, suppose the constraints are those of Table 3-4.

Step 7. *Define the utility curves for each attribute.* There are two ways to perform this step.

Method 7.1 Generate utility curves for each attribute by assigning the maximum score on the utility scale to the most desired plausible attribute performance level, and by assigning the minimum utile value to the least desired plausible attribute performance level. This utility scale is an *arbitrarily defined* interval measurement and may range from 0 to 1, 0 to 100, −1 to +1, −5 to +5, or any spread deemed appropriate. The attribute utility curves for the four attributes of the job-selection example are shown in Figures 3-1 to 3-4. A 1 utility scale of 0 to 1 was selected arbitrarily. Next, go to step 8.

Method 7.2 Assign to each alternative–attribute pair a utility score. As an alternative to developing formal utility curves, simply combine steps 7, 8, and 9 and rate each alternative–attribute combination on a scale from 0 to 10 (i.e., 0 represents the least attractive performance realistically imaginable, whereas 10 means that the alternative–attribute performance is the very best you would realistically anticipate). This is similar to some critic ratings of movies or restaurants, which suggest a particular number of points on a scale of 0 to 5 or 0 to 10, or assign a number of stars on a scale of 0 to three or four

TABLE 3-4

Attribute Constraint Values for Kugelman's Selection of the Best Job

Attribute, y_j	Constraint Value, y_j^*
y_1	≥ fair
y_2	≥ \$35,000/year
y_3	≥ average
y_4	≥ fair

*y_j = constraint value of the jth attribute.

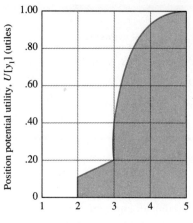

Position potential rating, y_1*

* 1 = poor; 2 = fair; 3 = average;
4 = good; 5 = excellent.

FIGURE 3-1

Kugelman's "Best Job" Utility Curve for Position Potential.

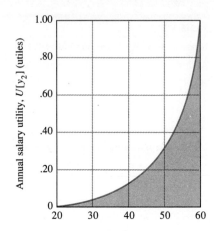

Position rating, y_2 (in $ thousands)

FIGURE 3-2

Kugelman's "Best Job" Utility Curve for Salary.

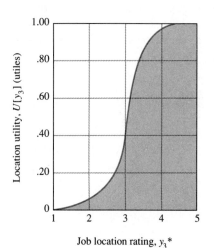

Job location rating, y_3*

* 1 = poor; 2 = fair; 3 = average;
4 = good; 5 = excellent.

FIGURE 3-3

Kugelman's "Best Job" Utility Curve for Location.

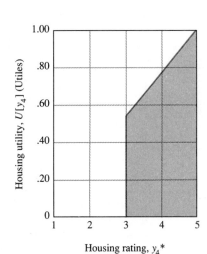

Housing rating, y_4*

* 1 = poor; 2 = fair; 3 = average;
4 = good; 5 = excellent.

FIGURE 3-4

Kugelman's "Best Job" Utility Curve for Housing Conditions.

TABLE 3-5

Attribute Performance Matrix for Kugelman's Selection of the Best Job

| Alternative, a_i | Attribute Performance, y_j | | | | Constraint Violation |
	y_1	y_2	y_3	y_4	
a_1	FAIR	$65,000	POOR	POOR	y_3, y_4
a_2	GOOD	$60,000	GOOD	AVE	NONE
a_3	EXLT	$30,000	EXLT	GOOD	y_2
a_4	FAIR	$58,000	AVE	EXLT	NONE
a_5	EXLT	$70,000	POOR	POOR	y_3, y_4
a_6	GOOD	$46,000	GOOD	GOOD	NONE

stars (e.g., *Michelin Guide* restaurant ratings, *San Francisco Chronicle* movie ratings). Although this latter resolution of utility scoring is quite simple, it lacks the explicit measurement characteristics provided by the formal utility-curve enumeration. Next, go to step 10.

Step 8. *Collect and enumerate the attribute performances for each alternative under consideration.* Display this information in an *attribute performance matrix*, as shown in Table 3-5.

Step 9. *Convert the attribute performance values developed in step 8 to their corresponding utilities for the alternatives not eliminated by constraint violation*, using the utility curves generated in step 7. Present this new information in a *utility matrix*, as shown in Table 3-6.

Step 10. *Calculate the composite utility of each candidate alternative.* Sum the products of attribute weights and utility scores for each remaining alternative. This relationship is given by

$$U[a_i] = \sum_{j=1}^{n} w_j u_{ij}$$

$$= w_1 u_{i1} + w_2 u_{i2} + \cdots + w_n u_{in}$$

where

w_j = normalized weight of the jth attribute

u_{ij} = utility of the jth attribute for the ith alternative

n = total number of attributes

$U[a_i]$ = composite (aggregate) utility of the ith alternative

TABLE 3-6

Utility Matrix for Kugelman's Selection of the Best Job

| Job Offer Alternative a_i | Utility of ith Alternative and jth Attribute, u_{ij} | | | |
	y_1	y_2	y_3	y_4
a_1	CONSTRAINT VIOLATION			
a_2	.90	.90	.97	.50
a_3	CONSTRAINT VIOLATION			
a_4	.10	.70	.45	1.00
a_5	CONSTRAINT VIOLATION			
a_6	.90	.25	.97	.75

The composite utilities for the three remaining job offers can now be calculated easily:

$$U[a_2] = (42)(.90) + (33)(.90) + (17)(.97) + (8)(.50)$$
$$= 87.99 \text{ utiles}$$

$$U[a_4] = (42)(.10) + (33)(.70) + (17)(.45) + (8)(1.00)$$
$$= 42.95 \text{ utiles}$$

$$U[a_6] = (42)(.90) + (33)(.25) + (17)(.97) + (8)(.75)$$
$$= 68.54 \text{ utiles}$$

Step 11. *Choose the alternative with the maximum composite utility, $U[a_i]_{max}$.* Kugelman's search for the best job is over: Kugelman selects a_2.

A pictorial summary of the MAUM process is shown in Figure 3-5. Now let's examine how MAUM can be applied to a different kind of problem setting: program evaluation.

FIGURE 3-5

Multiattribute Utility Method (MAUM) Flowchart.

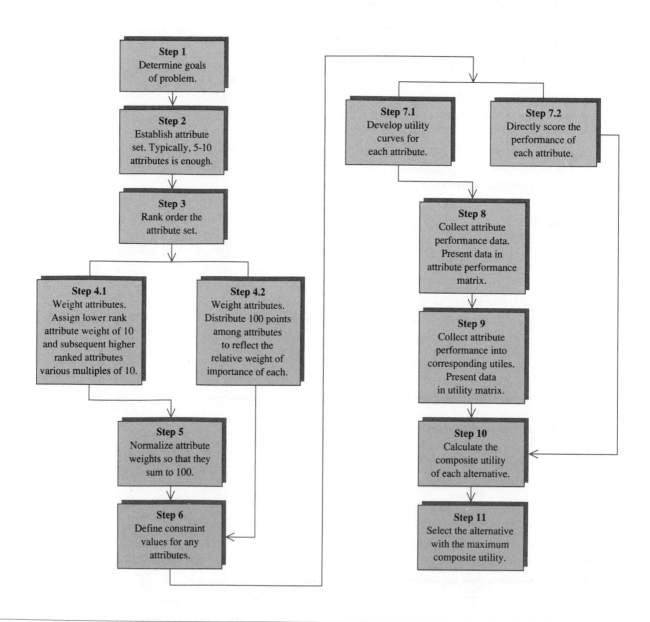

Step 1
Determine goals of problem.

Step 2
Establish attribute set. Typically, 5-10 attributes is enough.

Step 3
Rank order the attribute set.

Step 4.1
Weight attributes. Assign lower rank attribute weight of 10 and subsequent higher ranked attributes various multiples of 10.

Step 4.2
Weight attributes. Distribute 100 points among attributes to reflect the relative weight of importance of each.

Step 5
Normalize attribute weights so that they sum to 100.

Step 6
Define constraint values for any attributes.

Step 7.1
Develop utility curves for each attribute.

Step 7.2
Directly score the performance of each attribute.

Step 8
Collect attribute performance data. Present data in attribute performance matrix.

Step 9
Collect attribute performance into corresponding utiles. Present data in utility matrix.

Step 10
Calculate the composite utility of each alternative.

Step 11
Select the alternative with the maximum composite utility.

3.4 USING MAUM FOR PROGRAM EVALUATION

One of the most useful application areas for MAUM is program evaluation. Even though the MAUM process remains essentially unchanged, it will be helpful to see how this technique is used in this new setting.

EXAMPLE 3.2 NEW ORLEANS LOW-INCOME HOUSING PROJECT

Almost every city in the country has implemented a low-income housing program of some kind since the early 1960s. The provision of safe and decent housing to financially underprivileged individuals and families continues to be one of our most urgent and as yet unsolved urban problems. Let's examine how a typical city might use MAUM to help it select the most promising housing developer out of a large number of hopeful bidders.

Suppose the city of New Orleans, Louisiana, has raised local and federal funding to provide housing for some of its low-income residents. It has just sent out a request for bids on a fixed-price contract to private industry. Those developers who wish to compete for this program will submit proposals to the city outlining what they will provide—for the proposed level of funding—if they are awarded this contract. The city, of course, wishes to award the contract to the bidder who will provide the most outstanding work for this crucial program.

In this particular situation, the alternatives will be the various private-industry builders competing for the public-housing contract award. The 11-step methodology and relevant information for this program follow.

Step 1. The program goals are to provide a given community with a sufficient number of decent, safe, and sanitary federally subsidized housing units to meet current and near-term needs without violation of necessary program constraints (budget, time, personnel, and other limited resources).

Step 2. The city planning department decides that the attributes to be used to evaluate the candidate alternative program bids are

- Total number of standard housing units to be built, y_1
- Median household living area, y_2 (ft^2 housing unit)
- Total program cost, y_3 (millions of dollars)
- Median household rent-to-income ratio, y_4
- Political feasibility index, y_5 (rated on a five-point Likert Scale)
- Housing and neighborhood quality index, y_6 (rated on a five-point Likert Scale)
- Local share of total program cost, y_7 (percent)
- Length of time required to complete program, y_8 (months)

Steps 3, 4, and 5. The attributes are now ranked in order of their relative importance, weighted, and normalized so that the sum of these weights is equal to 100 (Table 3-7).

Step 6. The constraints for the attribute set are given in Table 3-8.

Step 7. The utility curves illustrated in Figures 3-6 through 3-13 represent the eight attributes used in our example. The incorporation of a -5 to $+5$ utility scale is arbitrary. (Note how the attribute constraints are reflected in each curve.)

TABLE 3-7

Ranked and Weighted Attributes for New Orleans Low-Income Housing Project

Attribute, y_j	Attribute Raw Weight	Attribute Normalized Weight, w_j
y_5	80	29
y_6	50	18
y_1	40	14
y_4	40	14
y_8	25	9
y_7	20	7
y_2	15	5
y_3	10	4
Totals	280	100

TABLE 3-8

Attribute Constraint Set for New Orleans Low-Income Housing Project

Attribute, y_i	Constraint Value
y_1	≥ 70 housing units
y_2	≥ 600 ft^2 housing unit
y_3	$\leq \$3,000,000$
y_4	$\leq .45$
y_5	≥ 3.0
y_6	≥ 2.5
y_7	$\leq 50\%$
y_8	≤ 48 months

To make sure that the meaning of each utility curve is clear, let's focus on attribute y_1 (Figure 3-6). How is the shape of this attribute utility curve formed? Imagine that the number of eligible households in the community desiring public housing would fill a 180-unit housing project. A careful study of the community's anticipated growth suggests that that community could not absorb more than 200 housing units; any units in excess of 200 would go unused, resulting in wasted project expenditures. It is also anticipated that any project built with fewer than 70 units would cause great strife in the community arising out of the scarcity of housing opportunities and would be more damaging than would having no project at all (it could suggest "tokenism"). Notice how the utility rapidly decreases when the number of housing units declines toward the minimum number of acceptable units (70 units) and also as superfluous units (more than 200) are added.

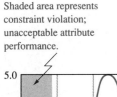

Shaded area represents constraint violation; unacceptable attribute performance.

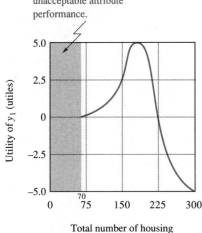

Total number of housing units to be built, y_1

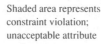

Shaded area represents constraint violation; unacceptable attribute performance.

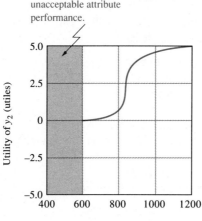

Median household living area, y_2 (ft^2/housing unit)

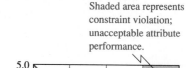

Shaded area represents constraint violation; unacceptable attribute performance.

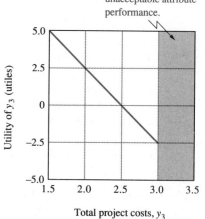

Total project costs, y_3 ($1 million)

FIGURE 3-6

Utility Curve for Number of Housing Units to Be Built for New Orleans Low-Income Housing Project.

FIGURE 3-7

Median Household Living Area (ft^2) for New Orleans Low-Income Housing Project.

FIGURE 3-8

Utility Curve for Total Cost of New Orleans Low-Income Housing Project.

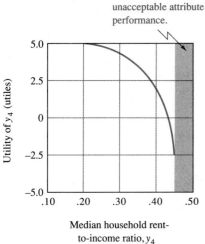

Shaded area represents constraint violation; unacceptable attribute performance.

FIGURE 3-9

Utility Curve for Median Household Rent-to-Income Ratio of New Orleans Low-Income Housing Project.

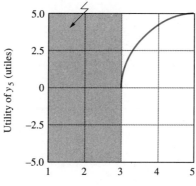

Shaded area represents constraint violation; unacceptable attribute performance.

Political feasibility index, y_5^*

* 1 = poor; 2 = fair; 3 = average; 4 = good; 5 = excellent.

FIGURE 3-10

Utility Curve for Political Feasibility of New Orleans Low-Income Housing Project.

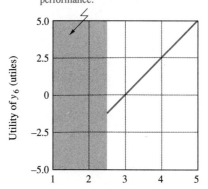

Shaded area represents constraint violation; unacceptable attribute performance.

Housing and neighborhood quality index, y_6^*

* 1 = poor; 2 = fair; 3 = average; 4 = good; 5 = excellent.

FIGURE 3-11

Utility Curve for Housing and Neighborhood Quality Index of New Orleans Low-Income Housing Project.

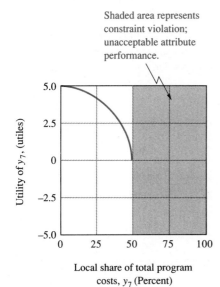

Shaded area represents constraint violation; unacceptable attribute performance.

Local share of total program costs, y_7 (Percent)

FIGURE 3-12

Utility Curve for Percent of Local Share of Total Costs for New Orleans Low-Income Housing Project.

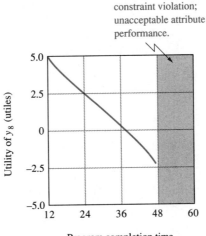

Shaded area represents constraint violation; unacceptable attribute performance.

Program completion time, y_8 (months)

FIGURE 3-13

Utility Curve for Completion Time of New Orleans Low-Income Housing Project.

TABLE 3-9

Attribute Performance Matrix for New Orleans Low-Income Housing Project

Program Plan, a_i	Attribute Performance, y_j							
	y_1	y_2	y_3	y_4	y_5	y_6	y_7	y_8
a_1	100	1000	2.00	.40	4.20	4.00	25	30
a_2	150	700	2.20	.30	3.20	3.00	50	24
a_3	125	900	2.50	.35	4.00	3.50	33	30
Attribute Constraints	$\geqslant 70$	$\geqslant 600$	$\leqslant 3.00$	$\leqslant .45$	$\geqslant 3.00$	$\geqslant 2.50$	$\leqslant 50$	$\leqslant 48$

TABLE 3-10

Utility Matrix for the New Orleans Low-Income Housing Project

Program Plan, a_i	Attribute Utility, $U[y_j]$							
	$U[y_1]$	$U[y_2]$	$U[y_3]$	$U[y_4]$	$U[y_5]$	$U[y_6]$	$U[y_7]$	$U[y_8]$
a_1	.25	4.50	2.50	2.00	4.50	2.50	4.00	1.25
a_2	2.50	0	1.50	4.50	2.50	0	0	2.50
a_3	.50	4.00	0	3.50	4.00	1.25	3.75	1.25
Attribute Weights, w_j	14	5	4	14	29	18	7	9

Step 8. Assume the attribute performance for each of the three program plans is that shown in the attribute performance matrix of Table 3-9. Since all the program plans have attribute performances that exceed the minimum standards of the constraints, each of the programs is a viable candidate.

Step 9. The individual attribute utilities can now be determined for each alternative through the use of the utility–attribute performance relationships illustrated in the utility curves of Figures 3-6 through 3-13. These results are tabulated in the utility matrix of Table 3-10.

Step 10. The composite utility, $U[a_i]$, for each program plan can now be calculated from the general equation. These composite utilities are

$$U[a_i] = \sum_{j=1}^{n} w_j u_{ij}$$
$$= 14u_{i1} + 5u_{i2} + 4u_{i3} + 14u_{i4} + 29u_{i5} + 18u_{i6} + 7u_{i7} + 9u_{i8}$$

So, for the three alternatives,

$$U[a_1] = (14)(.25) + (5)(4.50) + (4)(2.50) + (14)(2.00)$$
$$+ (29)(4.50) + (18)(2.50) + (7)(4.00) + (9)(1.25)$$
$$= 278.75 \text{ utiles}$$

$$U[a_2] = (14)(2.50) + (5)(0) + (4)(1.50) + (14)(4.50)$$
$$+ (29)(2.50) + (18)(0) + (7)(0) + (9)(2.50)$$
$$= 199.00 \text{ utiles}$$

$$U[a_3] = (14)(.50) + (5)(4.00) + (4)(0) + (14)(3.50)$$
$$+ (29)(4.00) + (18)(1.25) + (7)(3.75) + (9)(1.25)$$
$$= 252.00 \text{ utiles}$$

Step 11. The proposal that gives us the maximum composite utility is a_1.

Now let's go through one more illustration of the MAUM process. However, this time we are going to apply MAUM to a process that is concerned with the evaluation and selection of new employees: the annual National Football League draft of college athletes.

EXAMPLE 3.3   EVALUATING PLAYERS FOR THE NATIONAL FOOTBALL LEAGUE (NFL) ANNUAL DRAFT

There are several reasons for using the NFL draft as an example of MAUM. First, professional football is a high-visibility business that attracts an avid audience of tens of millions of television viewers and stadium spectators each season. Second, NFL football is a business that generates hundreds of millions of dollars in annual revenues from network television contracts and gate receipts. Finally, it is easier to learn from an example that is both real and fun to discuss. In our analysis, let's assume the NFL draft currently uses an evaluation procedure that ignores some rational decision considerations, we'll include suggestions on how to refine the existing method by adapting it more closely to the MAUM process.

During the spring of each year, long after the playoffs and Pro Bowl games have been concluded, representatives from each NFL team gather in Manhattan to select college football players in the annual draft. Generally, teams draft in reverse order of their place of finish in the final league standings; that is, the team with the worst season record gets to choose first. So, how does each team determine which player it will select when its turn comes around? Even more important, can MAUM be used to facilitate this process? Let's see.

Step 1. Each team attempts to *draft the best player available*; that is, each wishes to select the individual who can best help the team, on the basis of extensive data, from the thousands of candidate draft choices.

Step 2. Each potential draftee is graded by a set of attributes that reflects the specific position that he is anticipated to play in the NFL. These groups of criteria are sometimes referred to as position-attribute sets. Although there is no standardized set of attributes for each position—the attributes vary only slightly from team to team—there is general agreement. Table 3-11 illustrates the attribute sets for the seven general position categories of potential draftees.

Although many of the attributes are not operationally defined, there is general agreement on what is meant by each criterion. For example, "hands" means the ability of a receiver, running back, or defensive back to catch the football. It could be measured by the percentage of catches out of all passes thrown to him deemed as "catchable." An example of how you might refine the attribute set for the quarterback position is shown in Table 3-12.

Steps 3, 4, 5, and 6. Presently, football teams do not discriminate *explicitly* among attributes, although it is reasonable to assume that there are implicit value systems that color different evaluators' (scouts', director of player personnel's, general manager's, etc.) player assessments. Consequently, the addition of attribute weighting will make the selection process easier to understand. Even the differences of opinion between two or more evaluators can be discussed more meaningfully and resolved more easily when the importance of each attribute is clear. An illustration of what a typical weighting scheme for the quarterback position might look like is shown in Table 3-13.

TABLE 3-11

Attribute Sets for Professional Football Players for the Seven Different Position Categories

PLAYERS GRADED ON FOLLOWING SCALE:

1–2: POOR; UNACCEPTABLE
3–4: SUBSTANDARD; NEEDS SIGNIFICANT IMPROVEMENT TO MAKE ROSTER
5–6: AVERAGE; ROOM FOR IMPROVEMENT; MIGHT POSSIBLY MAKE ROSTER
7–8: VERY GOOD; STARTER QUALITY
   9: OUTSTANDING; PRO BOWL QUALITY

Receivers	Offensive Linemen	Quarterbacks	
Hands	Strength	Arm Strength	
Release	Initial Quickness	Quick Setup	
Quickness	Pass Block	Accuracy Long	
Acceleration	Run Block	Accuracy Short	
Receiving Long	Pulling	Mobility	
Receiving Short	Trap	Running Ability	
Leaping Ability	Downfield	Quickness of Delivery	
Crowd Catching	Explosion	Leadership	
Threat	Position and Sustain		
Running Ability	Punt Snap		
Blocking	Body Control		
Punt Catcher			

Running Backs	Defensive Linemen	Linebackers	Defensive Backs
Elusiveness	Strength	Instincts	M/M Coverage
Initial Quickness	Initial Quickness	Quickness	Quick Feet
Acceleration	Body Control	Reactions	Range
Hands	Pass Rush	Lateral Movement	Closing Quickness
Inside Runner	Disengage	vs Inside Run	Recovery
Outside Runner	Defense Run	vs Outside Run	Ball Reaction
Open Field Runner	Lateral Movement	Strength	Catch-Up Speed
Block Run/Pass	Explosiveness	Pass Drop	Hands
Blocking Effort		Pass Coverage	Punt Catcher
Threat		Hands	
Balance		Blitz/Rush	
Punt Catcher			

Summary:

_____

_____

_____

_____

SCOUT: _____   GAME: _____   DATE: _____   FINAL GRADE: _____

Steps 7, 8, and 9.   Each player is, in fact, given a grade—typically on a scale of 1 to 9 (9 being best)—for his position-attribute set. (Doesn't this seem paradoxical, in light of the fact that the usual player-assessment process does not include the weighting of the individual members of the position-attribute sets?) These grades are then displayed in the player's "report card," as shown in Table 3-14 (a hypothetical example, using Vinnie Testeverde, University of Miami quarterback and Heismann Award winner for 1986, is presented). Even though college football players are apparently not screened based on an articulated set of attribute performance constraints, it is obvious

TABLE 3-12

Operationally Defined Attribute Set for Quarterback Position

Present Attribute Set	Suggested Attribute Set (Definition)
Arm Strength	Mean of longest completed pass for each game during season (yards).
Quick Setup	Mean time from center snap to foot plant of pocket passes (seconds).
Accuracy Long	Percentages of completed passes > 30 yards (%).
Accuracy Short	Percentages of completed passes ≤ 30 yards (%).
Mobility	Percentage of times that quarterback escapes pass rush; defensive player(s) must have broken into pocket (%).
Running Ability	Average per-yard gain on nonsack carries (yards).
Quickness of Delivery	Mean time from foot plant to pass release (seconds).
Leadership	Subjective 1 to 9 score based on scout's impression (subjective Likert-type scale).

TABLE 3-13

Weighted Attribute Set for Quarterback Position

Quarterback Attribute Set	Rank	Weight
Arm Strength: Mean of longest completed pass for each game during season (yards).	5	11
Quick Setup: Mean time from center snap to foot plant of pocket passes (seconds).	4	12
Accuracy Long: Percentages of completed passes > 30 yards (%).	1	20
Accuracy Short: Percentages of completed passes ≤ 30 yards (%).	2	16
Mobility: Percentage of times that quarterback escapes pass rush; defensive player(s) must have broken into pocket (%).	3	15
Running Ability: Average per-yard gain on nonsack carries (yards).	8	6
Quickness of Delivery: Mean time from foot plant to pass release (seconds).	7	9
Leadership: Subjective 1 to 9 score based on scout's impression (subjective Likert-type scale).	6	11

TABLE 3-14

Theoretical Report Card for Vinnie Testeverde (Quarterback)

Quarterback Attribute Set	Score
Arm Strength: Mean of longest completed pass for each game during season (yards).	9
Quick Setup: Mean time from center snap to foot plant of pocket passes (seconds).	7
Accuracy Long: Percentages of completed passes > 30 yards (%).	8
Accuracy Short: Percentages of completed passes ≤ 30 yards (%).	8
Mobility: Percentage of times that quarterback escapes pass rush; defensive player(s) must have broken into pocket (%).	8
Running Ability: Average per-yard gain on nonsack carries (yards).	6
Quickness of Delivery: Mean time from foot plant to pass release (seconds).	8
Leadership: Subjective 1 to 9 score based on scout's impression (subjective Likert-type scale).	9

that, since only a small percentage are ultimately drafted, implicit constraints are used; for example, no team would consider a defensive back who would require more than 4.8 seconds to run 40 yards, or would draft an offensive lineman who did not weigh—or possess the potential to be "built up" to—say, at least 260 pounds.

Although there is no formal development of utility curves for each of the position-attribute sets, it is apparent from the player "report cards" that an assessment of worth, in terms of "grades" or "scores," is being made. Accordingly, these scores can be used to satisfy the individual attribute utility scores.

Step 10. Ultimately, each team boils down the attribute scores for each player into a single figure of merit called the *final grade* or *productivity score*. Once again, this value is often, but not always, a number between 1 and 9. Thus, an overall numerical assessment of "goodness" is made. Unfortunately, there is no defined rationale for how the team reduces the multiple attribute scores for a player into this single grade. This lack of clarity is due in large part to the omission of attribute weighting. If the weighting element were included, the implicit development of the final productivity score could be replaced with the explicit calculation of the composite utility score by use of the following relationship:

$$U_{ik} = \sum_{j=1}^{n_k} w_j u_{ijk} \qquad \begin{array}{l} \text{for each } i\,(i = 1, 2, \ldots, m) \\ \text{and} \quad k\,(k = 1, 2, \ldots, K) \end{array}$$

where

U_{ik} = overall rating of the ith prospective draftee playing the kth position—the composite utility score

n_k = number of attributes for the kth position being assessed

m = total number of players to be assessed

K = total number of positions to be evaluated

w_{jk} = weight of importance of the jth attribute playing the kth position

u_{ijk} = utility score for the ith player on the jth attribute at the kth position

Step 11. The players are grouped by position and are rank-ordered by their composite utility (productivity) score. Individual players' names are then positioned on a wall-sized scoreboard that is divided by each round of the draft. A player's placement on the board represents the team's estimate of the likely round in which the player will be selected. Table 3-15 is an example of such a scoreboard.

The example of the NFL draft has illustrated the versatility of the MAUM process in refining complex, multidimensional decision-making environments.[7]

Until now, we have assumed that MAUM is a deterministic process: The performance of each attribute used to assess the competing alternatives is known with certainty. Unfortunately, this isn't always the case; sometimes, attribute performance cannot be pinned down to a single value. For example, when the likely outcomes of drilling

---

[7]A number of important considerations of this particular problem area have purposely been omitted; they would only complicate the primary purpose of the presentation. An in-depth analysis of applying MAUM to the NFL draft of college football players can be found in Oberstone and Newman (1986).

TABLE 3-15

Partial Reproduction of 1985 Player Productivity Scoreboard Used By NFL Teams as a Guide in the Selection of Players During the Annual Draft

Draft Round	Player Position																	
	Offense							Defense						Special			
	QB	RB	WR	TE	OT	OG	C	DE	DL	OLB	ILB	CB	S	K	P	ST		
1			*RICE, Jerry* *HESTER, Jessie*															
2			*HARRY, Emile*															
3			*SCOTT, Chuck*															
4																		

Draft Round	Wide Receiver Rankings
1	• RICE, Jerry • HESTER, Jessie
2	• HARRY, Emile
3	• SCOTT, Chuck

Offense:
QB = quarterback
RB = running back
WR = wide receiver
TE = tight end
OT = offensive tackle
OG = offensive guard
C = center

Defense:
DE = defensive end
DL = defensive line
OLB = outside linebacker
ILB = inside linebacker
CB = cornerback
S = safety

Special:
K = kicker
P = punter
ST = special teams

Note: The blow-up window indicates that Jerry Rice and Jessie Hester are likely first-round draftees; Emile Harry will probably go in round 2, and so on. Each position for the defense and offense is detailed in a similar fashion. It is typical for many of the NFL teams to conduct numerous "mock" versions of the draft in order to get a better understanding of what players are likely to be available (or not available) during each round of the draft. This exercise helps a team to shape a strategy for the draft.

an oil well are considered, the results do not boil down to merely "strike oil" or "no oil." More likely, there is a *spectrum* of possible outcomes representing a variety of differing levels of success—from zero barrels per day (truly "no oil") to thousands of barrels per day—including many levels in between. If this is the situation, then it is more realistic to represent the performance of such an attribute by an array of discrete performance levels. Stochastic MAUM has the capacity to analyze stochastic, multiattribute problems. We'll discuss that method next.

3.5 | STOCHASTIC MAUM

Although it is convenient to assume that the attribute performance associated with each alternative is known with certainty, it is sometimes inappropriate to do so. The same type of inappropriate simplification is made of statistical data when a point estimate (mean), rather than a confidence-interval estimate, is selected to represent the overall performance of a sample—even though the data exhibit significant variability! For the same reason, the performance of a widely varying attribute can be best portrayed by a finite number of attribute performance levels (and associated probabilities of occurrence) instead of by a single value. *Stochastic MAUM* is a technique that blends the multidimensional features of MAUM with the risk-management capabilities of deci-

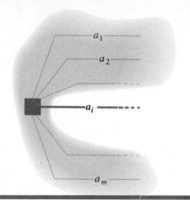

FIGURE 3-14

Specific Alternative Set, a_i, Out of the Total Set of Actions to Be Evaluated for Stochastic MAUM.

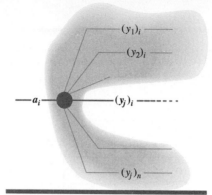

FIGURE 3-15

Specific Attribute, $(y_j)_i$, Out of the Total Attribute Set to Be Evaluated for Stochastic MAUM.

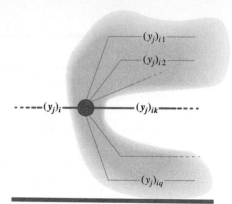

FIGURE 3-16

The kth Level of Performance for Attribute $(y_j)_i$, Associated with Detailed Breakdown of Multilevel Attribute Performance Array.

sion trees to determine from a set of competing alternatives the best alternative on the basis of *maximum expected composite utility*. Let's spend a bit of time here developing the rationale of stochastic MAUM.

First, imagine that you have a number (set) of competing alternatives that you wish to evaluate. Pay particular attention to the ith alternative in the set of m total alternatives shown in Figure 3-14. To compare each of these alternatives without bias, we need to use a common yardstick—a fixed set of attributes. Pretend that there is a total of n attributes in the set. Now, focus on the jth attribute. So now your attention is focused on the jth attribute of the ith alternative, $(y_j)_i$, in Figure 3-15. Notice how the notation is departing from the original MAUM model. Each attribute not only has its own unique identification, j, and is linked to a specific alternative with a second index, i, but also has a *third* index indicating the stochastic properties of the attribute: a subscript referencing the *specific level of performance*, k, out of the total set of possible performance levels, q, that each attribute can potentially deliver! The illustration of the kth level of attribute performance for the ith alternative and j^{th} attribute combination, $(y_j)_{ik}$, is shown in Figure 3-16 (the probability distribution representing the associated probabilities of occurrence for each level of attribute performance for the ith alternative–j^{th} attribute combination, $p(y_j)_{ik}$, is also illustrated).[8] Stochastic MAUM makes it possible to isolate the expected individual attribute contributions to a particular alternative by recognizing that attribute performance is often more accurately represented by a variety of possible outcomes than a single value.

Now let's examine the actual stochastic MAUM process used to evaluate competing alternatives. An illustrative example will be used to help facilitate each step of the process.

EXAMPLE 3.4   GLENN TROTTER REAL-ESTATE INVESTMENT STUDY

Glenn Trotter worked for many years in Manhattan as an extremely successful Wall Street analyst. Unfortunately, the daily pressures of this job became more than Trotter

---

[8]It may be helpful to think of the levels of attribute performance as the future events/states of nature discussed in Section 1.5.

could cope with. He ultimately moved to San Francisco and started a real-estate investment business. Trotter is presently examining three possible investment opportunities:

1. A single-family residence in the Upper Fillmore district, a_1

2. A four-unit rental property in the Marina district in which he would be a 33 percent owner, a_2

3. A three-bedroom townhouse in Opera Plaza near the Civic Center, a_3

Trotter characterizes the most important factors in selecting this type of investment with three attributes. They are, in perceived order of importance,

1. Rate of return on investment, $(y_1)_i$

2. Down payment, $(y_2)_i$

3. Finance rate, $(y_3)_i$

He also decides that he should eliminate any alternative whose performance fails to satisfy a specified minimum (or maximum) expected value. So, Trotter establishes attribute constraints. Specifically, any alternative will be eliminated if one or more of the following three "minimum" performance standards are not met:

1. Provide at least an expected 12 percent rate of return

2. Require no more than an expected $200,000 for his share of the down payment (and all associated finance charges)

3. Require no more than an expected 12 percent interest rate on the loan

Further, Trotter assigns the relative weights of importance for the attributes at: 50, 35, and 15 percent for the rate of return, down payment, and finance rate, respectively.

So, let's begin the stochastic MAUM evaluation process for Trotter's problem.

Step A. Perform steps 1 through 7 as described for the deterministic MAUM process (Section 3.3). The alternatives, attribute weights, constraints, and utility curves are described in Tables 3-16 and 3-17, and in Figures 3-17 through 3-19.

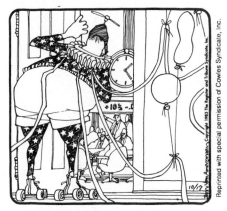

Glenn Trotter, just before he lost his clout as a high-powered Wall Street analyst.

TABLE 3-16

Alternatives for Property Investment

Alternative, a_i	Name
a_1	Single-family home
a_2	4-unit apartment house
a_3	Single-family townhouse

TABLE 3-17

Attributes for Property Investment

Attribute, y_j	Name	Weight of Importance	Constraint Value
y_1	Rate of return	50%	$\geq 12\%$
y_2	Down payment	35%	$\leq \$200,000$
y_3	Finance rate	15%	$\leq 12\%$

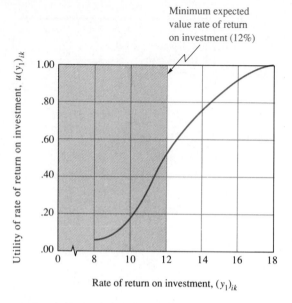

Minimum expected value rate of return on investment (12%)

FIGURE 3-17

Utility for Rate of Return on Investment for Property Investment.

The likely minimum rate of return on the investment is not known with certainty. Therefore, each investment alternative has a probability distribution associated with it that can be best represented by an expected value of rate of return. This expected value will, in turn, be converted to an expected utility to represent the value of this attribute contribution to the overall worth of the alternative with which it is associated.

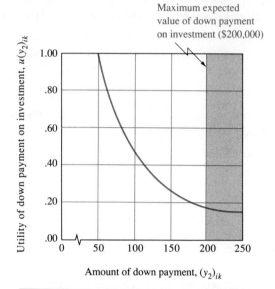

Maximum expected value of down payment on investment ($200,000)

FIGURE 3-18

Utility of Down Payment for Property Investment.

The likely maximum down payment on the investment is not known with certainty. Therefore, each investment alternative has a probability distribution associated with it that can be best represented by an expected value of down payment. This expected value will, in turn, be converted to an expected utility to represent the value of this attribute contribution to the overall worth of the alternative with which it is associated.

FIGURE 3-19

Utility of Finance Rate for Property Investment.

The likely maximum finance rate on the investment is not known with certainty. Therefore, each investment alternative has a probability distribution associated with it that can be best represented by an expected value of finance rate. This expected value will, in turn, be converted to an expected utility to represent the value of this attribute contribution to the overall worth of the alternative with which it is associated.

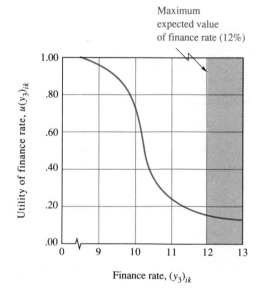

Maximum expected value of finance rate (12%)

Step B. Determine an array of performance values (a probability distribution) for each attribute. (This is the point of departure between the deterministic process described in Section 3.3 and the stochastic MAUM approach.) The number of different possible performance levels will depend on the specific problem setting: three to five "states" should be sufficient.[9] Display this information in a *stochastic attribute performance matrix*.

Mr. Trotter estimates that the likely, feasible range of attribute values for (1) rate of return, $(y_1)_{ik}$, is between 9 and 18 percent; that for (2) down payment, $(y_2)_{ik}$, is between \$50,000 and \$250,000; and that for (3) finance rate, $(y_3)_{ik}$, is between 9 and 13 percent. He subjectively develops discrete probability distributions—using expert opinion to guide these judgments—for each combination of alternative and attribute performance over the range of values just estimated. Trotter decides to use four or five levels of attribute performance for each attribute. This information is shown in Figure 3-20.

Step C. Make sure that the expected value of each attribute, $EV(y_j)_i$, is sufficient to satisfy any performance constraint that may be associated with it. We accomplish this step by calculating the *expected value* of each attribute, which we do by multiplying the values of the performance array, $(y_j)_{ik}$, by their corresponding probabilities, $P(y_j)_{ik}$. This calculation will help us to determine whether any minimum or maximum expected attribute performance standard is violated. Eliminate from further consideration any alternative that has one or more violation of the expected attribute value constraints. So, for a minimum expected attribute value,

$$EV(y_j)_i = \sum_{k=1}^{K} P(y_j)_{ik} \cdot (y_j)_{ik} \geqslant (y_j)_{min}$$
$$\text{for each } i \ (i = 1, 2, \ldots, m) \text{ and } j \ (j = 1, 2, \ldots, n)$$

For a maximum expected attribute value,

$$EV(y_j)_i = \sum_{k=1}^{K} P(y_j)_{ik} \cdot (y_j)_{ik} \leqslant (y_j)_{max}$$
$$\text{for each } i \ (i = 1, 2, \ldots, m) \text{ and } j \ (j = 1, 2, \ldots, n)$$

The expected-value calculation of the rate-of-return attribute for the Upper Fillmore, single-family residence property, $(y_1)_1$, is

$$EV(y_1)_1 = (.20)(9) + (.30)(12) + (.30)(15) + (.20)(18)$$
$$= 13.5\%$$

The expected values for all combinations of alternatives and attributes are calculated, with results as shown in Figures 3-21 through 3-23. Trotter discovers that there are no attribute-constraint violations in his study.

---

[9]One way of developing this attribute performance array might be to examine the following issues:

1. What is the most optimistic yet feasible performance you might expect for this combination of attribute and alternative, and what is the likelihood of this performance actually being delivered?
2. What is the most pessimistic yet feasible performance you might expect for this combination of attribute and alternative, and what is the likelihood of this performance actually being delivered?
3. What is the most likely performance you might expect for this combination of attribute and alternative, and what is the likelihood of this performance actually being delivered?

Finally, if you wish, you could develop intermediate states between the most likely and two most extreme values.

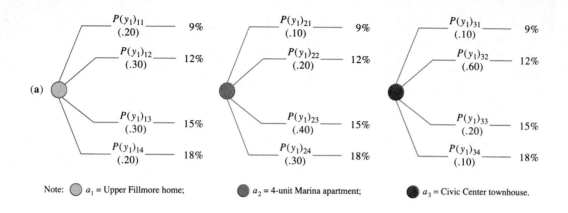

Note: ⬤ a_1 = Upper Fillmore home;　　⬤ a_2 = 4-unit Marina apartment;　　⬤ a_3 = Civic Center townhouse.

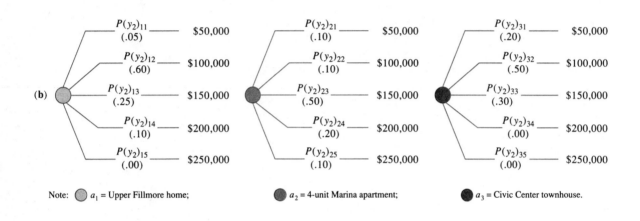

Note: ⬤ a_1 = Upper Fillmore home;　　⬤ a_2 = 4-unit Marina apartment;　　⬤ a_3 = Civic Center townhouse.

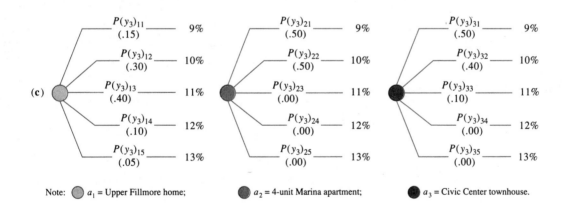

Note: ⬤ a_1 = Upper Fillmore home;　　⬤ a_2 = 4-unit Marina apartment;　　⬤ a_3 = Civic Center townhouse.

FIGURE 3-20

(a) Discrete Probability Distribution of Rate-of-Return Attribute, $(y_1)_{lk}$. (b) Discrete Probability Distribution of Down-Payment Attribute, $(y_2)_{lk}$. (c) Discrete Probability Distribution of Finance-Rate Attribute, $(y_3)_{lk}$.

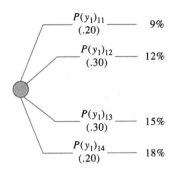

$$EV(y_1)_1 = (.20)(9) + (.30)(12)$$
$$+ (.30)(15) + (.20)(18)$$
$$= 13.5\%$$

FIGURE 3-21

Expected Value of Rate-of-Return Attribute, $(y_1)_i$.

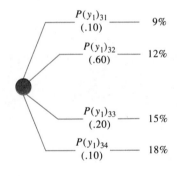

$$EV(y_1)_2 = (.10)(9) + (.20)(12)$$
$$+ (.40)(15) + (.30)(18)$$
$$= 14.7\%$$

$P(y_1)_{31}$
(.10) ——— 9%

$P(y_1)_{32}$
(.60) ——— 12%

$P(y_1)_{33}$
(.20) ——— 15%

$P(y_1)_{34}$
(.10) ——— 18%

$$EV(y_1)_3 = (.10)(9) + (.60)(12)$$
$$+ (.20)(15) + (.10)(18)$$
$$= 12.9\%$$

Note: ⬤ a_1 = Upper Fillmore home;   ⬤ a_2 = 4-unit Marina apartment;   ⬤ a_3 = Civic Center townhouse.

Attribute constraint value: $(y_1)_i \geq 12\%$

FIGURE 3-22

Expected Value of Down-Payment Attribute, $(y_2)_i$.

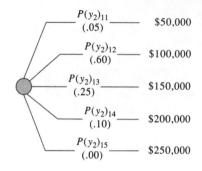

$EV(y_2)_1 = (.05)(50,000)$
$\quad + (.60)(100,000) + (.25)(150,000)$
$\quad + (.10)(200,000) + (.00)(250,000)$
$\quad = \$120,000$

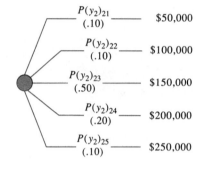

$EV(y_2)_2 = (.10)(50,000)$
$\quad + (.10)(100,000) + (.50)(150,000)$
$\quad + (.20)(200,000) + (.10)(250,000)$
$\quad = \$155,000$

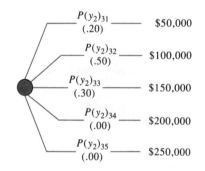

$EV(y_2)_3 = (.20)(50,000)$
$\quad + (.50)(100,000) + (.30)(150,000)$
$\quad + (.00)(200,000) + (.00)(250,000)$
$\quad = \$105,000$

Note: ◯ a_1 = Upper Fillmore home;   ⬤ a_2 = 4-unit Marina apartment;   ⬤ a_3 = Civic Center townhouse.

Attribute constraint value: $(y_2)_i \leq \$200,000$

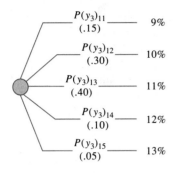

$$EV(y_3)_1 = (.15)(9) + (.30)(10) \\ + (.40)(11) + (.10)(12) + (.05)(13) \\ = 10.6\%$$

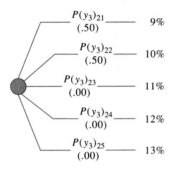

$$EV(y_3)_2 = (.50)(9) + (.50)(10) \\ + (.00)(11i) + (.00)(12) + (.00)(13) \\ = 9.5\%$$

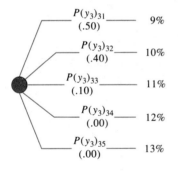

$$EV(y_3)_3 = (.50)(9) + (.40)(10) \\ + (.10)(11) + (.00)(12) + (.00)(13) \\ = 9.6\%$$

Note: ⬤ a_1 = Upper Fillmore home; ⬤ a_2 = 4-unit Marina apartment; ⬤ a_3 = Civic Center townhouse.

Attribute constraint value: $(y_3)_i \leq 12\%$

Step D. For those alternatives without constraint violations, convert the array (k branches) of performance values developed in step B into their corresponding utile values using the utility curves generated earlier in step A [step 7 of the standard MAUM procedure (Section 3.3)]. Do *not* convert the expected value of each attribute calculated in step C into a utility value!

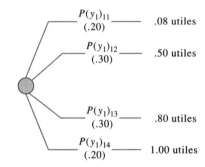

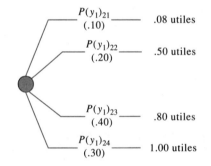

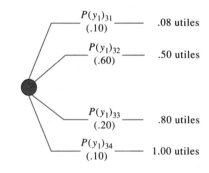

FIGURE 3-24

Expected (Unweighted) Utility, *EU* (y_1)$_{lk}$, of Rate-of-Return Attribute, (y_1)$_{lk}$.

$$EU(y_1)_1 = (.20)(.08) + (.30)(.50)$$
$$+ (.30)(.80) + (.20)(1.00)$$
$$= 606 \text{ utiles}$$

$$EU(y_1)_2 = (.10)(.08) + (.20)(.50)$$
$$+ (.40)(.80) + (.30)(1.00)$$
$$= .728 \text{ utiles}$$

$$EU(y_1)_3 = (.10)(.08) + (.60)(.50)$$
$$+ (.20)(.80) + (.10)(1.00)$$
$$= .568 \text{ utiles}$$

Note:  a_1 = Upper Fillmore home; ● a_2 = 4-unit Marina apartment; ● a_3 = Civic Center townhouse.

We transform the attribute performance values generated in step B (Figure 3-19) into utiles using the utility curves developed in Figures 3-17 through 3-19. These utile values are summarized in Figures 3-24 through 3-26 for each alternative and attribute combination, $(y_j)_i$.

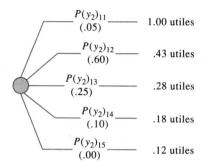

$$EU(y_2)_1 = (.05)(1.00) + (.60)(.43) + (.25)(.28) + (.10)(.18) + (.00)(.12) = .396 \text{ utiles}$$

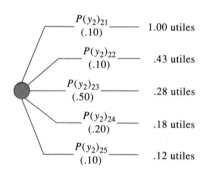

$$EU(y_2)_2 = (.10)(1.00) + (.10)(.43) + (.50)(.28) + (.20)(.18) + (.10)(.12) = .331 \text{ utiles}$$

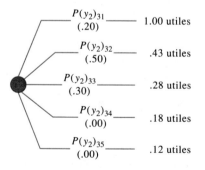

$$EU(y_2)_3 = (.20)(1.00) + (.50)(.43) + (.30)(.28) + (.00)(.18) + (.00)(.12) = .499 \text{ utiles}$$

Note: ⬤ a_1 = Upper Fillmore home;   ⬤ a_2 = 4-unit Marina apartment;   ⬤ a_3 = Civic Center townhouse.

FIGURE 3-26

Expected (Unweighted) Utility of Finance-Rate Attribute, $(y_3)_{ik}$.

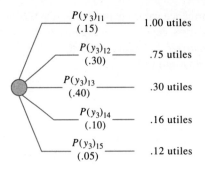

$$EU(y_3)_1 = (.15)(1.00) + (.30)(.75) + (.40)(.30)$$
$$+ (.10)(.16) + (.05)(.12)$$
$$= .517 \text{ utiles}$$

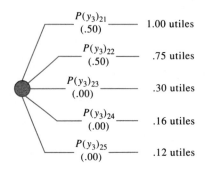

$$EU(y_3)_2 = (.50)(1.00) + (.50)(.75) + (.00)(.30)$$
$$+ (.00)(.16) + (.00)(.12)$$
$$= .875 \text{ utiles}$$

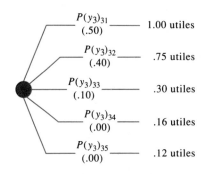

$$EU(y_3)_3 = (.50)(1.00) + (.40)(.75) + (.10)(.30)$$
$$+ (.00)(.16) + (.00)(.12)$$
$$= .830 \text{ utiles}$$

Note: ⬤ a_1 = Upper Fillmore home;   ⬤ a_2 = 4-unit Marina apartment;   ⬤ a_3 = Civic Center townhouse.

Step E. Calculate the expected, unweighted utility value of each attribute, y_j, by multiplying the utility of the various performance level branches found in Figures 3-24 through 3-26, $u(y_j)_{ik}$, by their corresponding probability of occurrence, $P(y_j)_{ik}$, then by summing these products. This step establishes a single measure of expected utility for that single attribute–alternative combination, $EU(y_j)_i$:

$$EU(y_j)_i = \sum_{k=1}^{q} P(y_j)_{ik} \cdot u(y_j)_{ik} \qquad \text{for each } i \, (i = 1, 2, \ldots, m)$$
$$\text{and} \quad (j = 1, 2, \ldots, n)$$

We'll calculate the unweighted, expected utility for the down-payment attribute of the Marina apartment houses, $EU(y_2)_2$, as an illustration of this step:

$$EU(y_2)_2 = (.10)(1.00) + (.10)(.43) + (.50)(.28)$$
$$+ (.20)(.18) + (.10)(.12)$$
$$= .331 \text{ utile}$$

The remainder of the calculations are shown on the right-hand side of Figures 3-24 through 3-26.

Step F. Calculate the composite expected utility of each candidate attribute, $CEU[a_i]$. We obtain this value by multiplying the attribute weights of importance, w_j, times the expected utility values of each attribute (just calculated in step E and displayed in Figures 3-24 through 3-26), $P(y_j)_{ik} \cdot u(y_j)_{ik}$. This relationship is given by

$$CEU[a_i] = \sum_{j=1}^{n} EU(y_j)_i = \sum_{j=1}^{n} \sum_{k=1}^{q} w_j \cdot p(y_j)_{ik} \cdot u(y_j)_{ik}$$
$$\text{for each } i \, (i = 1, 2, \ldots, m)$$

where

$\qquad w_j$ = normalized weight of importance for the jth attribute

$\qquad p(y_j)_{ik}$ = probability of occurrence of kth level of performance for j^{th} attribute and i^{th} alternative, $(y_j)_{ik}$

$\qquad u(y_j)_{ik}$ = utility corresponding to attribute performance $(y_j)_{ik}$

$\qquad EU(y_j)_i$ = expected utility of the jth attribute for the ith alternative,

$$EU(y_j)_i = \sum_{k=1}^{q} P(y_j)_{ik} \cdot u(y_j)_{ik}$$

$\qquad m$ = total number of alternatives

$\qquad n$ = total number of attributes

$\qquad q$ = total number of performance levels for specific attributes

$\qquad CEU[a_i]$ = composite (aggregate) utility of the ith alternative

Let's calculate the expected utility for the Upper Fillmore district single-family home, a_1. First, we determine the expected utility contribution from the rate-of-return attribute component, $(y_1)_1$, by multiplying each branch of the probability distribution for $P(y_1)_{1k}$ times its associated utile value, $u(y_1)_{1k} \cdot EU(y_1)_1$ is, then,

$$EU(y_1)_1 = (.20)(.08) + (.30)(.50) + (.30)(.80) + (.20)(1.00)$$
$$= .606$$

Step A
Perform Steps 1-7 exactly as described in MAUM.

Step B
Estimate array of performance values for attributes, $(y_j)_{ik}$.

Step C
Calculate the expected value of each attribute performance array. Check for constraint violations.

Step D
Convert attribute performance values into utility values.

Step E
Calculate the expected (unweighted) utility value of each attribute, $EU(y_j)_{ik}$.

Step F
Calculate the composite expected utility of each candidate alternative, $CEU[a_i]$.

Step G
Select the alternative with the largest expected composite utility.

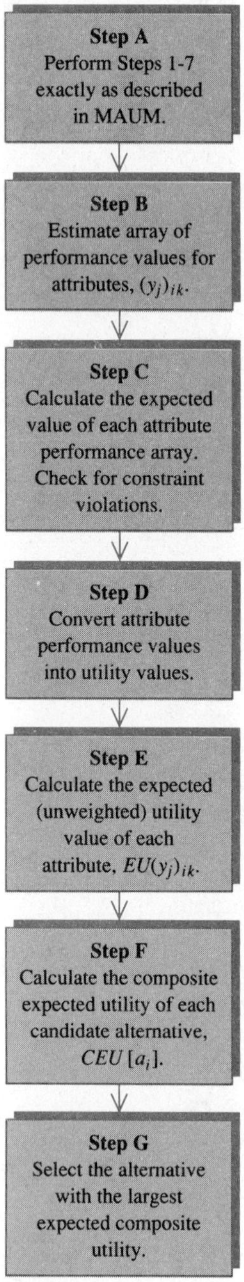

FIGURE 3-27

Flowchart of Stochastic MAUM Process.

The calculation of the remaining two expected utility values for attributes $(y_1)_2$ (down payment) and $(y_1)_3$ (finance rate) are just as easy:

$$EU(y_1)_2 = (.05)(1.00) + (.60)(.43) + (.25)(.28) + (.10)(.18) + (.00)(.12)$$
$$= .396$$
$$EU(y_1)_3 = (.15)(1.00) + (.30)(.75) + (.40)(.30) + (.10)(.16) + (.05)(.12)$$
$$= .517$$

We can now easily find the composite expected utility for this investment alternative by multiplying the expected utility values just calculated, $EU(y_j)_i$, by their associated weight of importance, w_j. So, for a_1,

$$CEU[a_1] = + (.50)(.606) + (.35)(.396) + (.15)(.517)$$
$$= .519 \text{ utile}$$

The composite expected utility for all of the three investment alternatives are calculated as follows:

$$CEU[a_1] = \sum_{j=1}^{n} w_j u_{1j} = (.50)(.606) + (.35)(.396) + (.15)(.513) = .519$$

$$CEU[a_2] = \sum_{j=1}^{n} w_j u_{2j} = (.50)(.728) + (.35)(.331) + (.15)(.810) = .601$$

$$CEU[a_3] = \sum_{j=1}^{n} w_j u_{3j} = (.50)(.568) + (.35)(.499) + (.15)(.765) = .573$$

Step G. Select the optimal strategy (i.e., the strategy with the largest composite expected utility value).

Mr. Trotter can see from these figures that he should select a_2—the four-unit rental property located in the Marina district—because

$$CEU[a_2] > CEU[a_3] > CEU[a_1]$$

An illustration showing the stochastic MAUM process is given in Figure 3-27.

Even though the MAUM and stochastic MAUM techniques are not analytically difficult, the data-organization aspects of these techniques are intricate. Accordingly, it would be judicious to employ appropriate software for these calculations whenever possible. There are a number of inexpensive and exceedingly easy to use software products for conducting standard MAUM-type evaluations.[10] These packages are listed under Microcomputer software for MAUM (below). Unfortunately, no stochastic MAUM software products are available presently.

An example of a microcomputer solution to a study with which we are already familiar is illustrated in the next section.

---

[10]It is also possible to use a spreadsheet software package such as *Lotus 1-2-3*, *Quatro*, or *Excel*, to solve MAUM-type problems. The MAUM mathematics are straightforward and the solution process is highly amenable to a columnar-spreadsheet arrangement.

3.6 MICROCOMPUTER SOLUTIONS TO MAUM PROBLEMS

The *Confidence Factor* software package data entry and solution to the New Orleans low-income housing program discussed earlier in this chapter is presented in Table 3-18. Although this particular program does not (1) eliminate alternatives that have attribute performance values that fall below minimum standard values (constraint violations) or (2) allow for utility curve inputs, it does follow an approximate MAUM process. However, because of these partial departures from the classic MAUM, the final results shown in Table 3-18 are not identical to those provided by the manual solution given earlier in this chapter (although the scores are proportionally similar to the original solution and the rank order retains that of the manual solution). Another MAUM-type software product, *DecisionMap*, is used to solve the job-selection problem presented at the beginning of this chapter (Table 3-19). The order and relative placement of the alternatives is essentially the same as the manual solution. Other software packages that perform MAUM-type analyses are listed on page 110.

TABLE 3-18

MAUM Computer Evaluation of New Orleans Low-Income Housing Program

```
            ---  CONFIDENCE FACTOR™ ---
          PROGRAM:  FIND THE BEST ALTERNATIVE
                FILE NAME: NEW ORLEANS



                  ----  DATA ENTRY ----

        ALTERNATIVES CONSIDERED      DECISION FACTORS (WEIGHTS)
                  A1                       Y5(80)
                  A2                       Y6(50)
                  A3                       Y1(40)
                                           Y4(40)
                                           Y8(25)
                                           Y7(20)
                                           Y2(15)
                                           Y3(10)


                  ---  MATRIX TABLEAU ---

        Decision
        Criteria    Weight        A1    A2    A3
           Y5         80          45    40    10
           Y6         50          25     1    13
           Y1         40           5    10    25
           Y4         40          20    35    45
           Y8         25          13    13    25
           Y7         20          35    25     1
           Y2         15          40    25     1
           Y3         10          25     1    15


                  ---  FINAL RESULTS  ---

        Rank       Alternative   Total Score    Normalized Score
         1             A1           7725               100
         2             A3           6260                81
         3             A2           5060                66
```

Source: The Confidence Factor. Irvine, CA: Simple Software.

TABLE 3-19

**Data Entry and Solution of Fred Kugelman's "Best Job"
Selection Using *DecisionMap* Software Package**

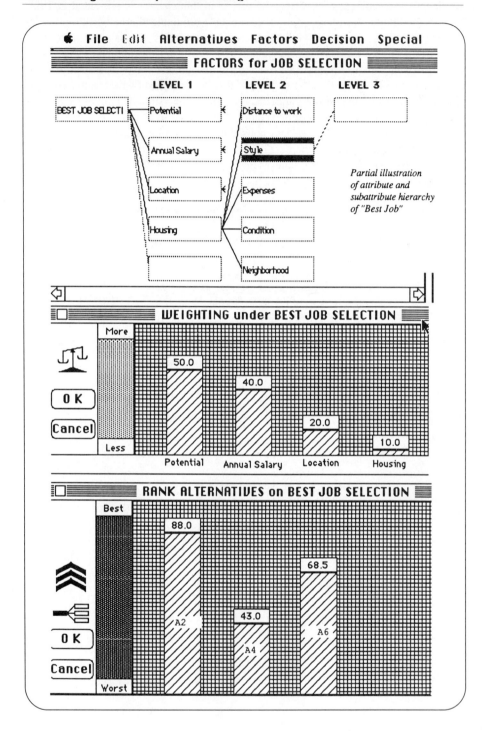

Partial illustration of attribute and subattribute hierarchy of "Best Job"

3.7 SUMMARY AND CONCLUSIONS

Multiattribute utility methods provide the manager with a systematic and reliable means of evaluating multidimensional, often incommensurate, competing alternatives in an internally consistent way. This simple yet elegant methodology incorporates two powerful characteristics not inherent in any other decision-analysis technique:

1. It furnishes a decision maker with a systematic means of evaluating the effectiveness of strategies in terms of dimensioned attributes that are related to a common scale of worth. Therefore, it allows different judges to reach different conclusions *and to see why they differ*.

2. It provides a road map that displays, step by step, the rationale underlying the decision maker's actions. That is, it illuminates the value hierarchy of the decision so that future dialogue about the analysis and the issues can be focused on meaningful points rather than on rhetoric.

3.8 EXERCISES

3-1 A woman is trying to determine the relative importance of seven criteria she wishes to use in selecting (purchasing) a single-family home. She organizes her thoughts and writes the following guidelines regarding the attributes she thinks are important in shaping the ultimate decision: condition of house, availability of garage for automobile and storage, size of living area, location of home, availability of public transportation, size of outdoor area, and sales price. In comparing the relative importance of these attributes she concludes that

1. Outdoor area and garage attributes are of equal importance.
2. Public transportation is 1.5 times as important as outdoor area.
3. Condition of the house is 3 times as important as public transportation.
4. Sales price of the home is 4 times as important as outdoor area.
5. Location is 6 times as important as outdoor area.
6. Public transportation is one-third as important as living area.

ASSIGNMENT

1. Determine the rank order of importance for the seven attributes.
2. Calculate the raw and normalized relative weights of importance for these attributes.

3-2 The woman in Exercise 3-1 assesses the attribute utilities of three different home sites (Table 3-2.1). Calculate the composite utility of the different alternatives and determine which house she should select.

3-3 A law-school faculty panel is trying to determine which student should be the *Law Review* editor for the next academic year. They select and weight three attributes to help them to assess the relative value of the five finalist candidates. The candidate–

TABLE 3-2.1

Utility Assessment Scores for Home-Selection Attribute

Attribute	Utility Score of Home Attributes		
	1	2	3
Condition, y_1	10	5	6
Garage, y_2	3	8	9
Living area, y_3	5	9	8
Location, y_4	6	7	7
Public transportation, y_5	9	5	3
Outdoor area, y_6	5	7	10
Sales price, y_7	8	7	5

attribute scores on a scale of 0 to 10 on the three attributes are shown for each candidate in Table 3-3.1. Which student will ultimately be selected by the panel?

3-4 Informed Sources Associates (ISA) is a Los Angeles consortium of business-management consultants. They are trying to

TABLE 3-3.1

Attribute Utility Scores for Selection of the *Law Review* Editor

Attritube (Weight)	Candidate Student				
	1	2	3	4	5
Classroom performance, y_1 (50)	10	10	9	8	10
Service to law school, y_2 (30)	7	9	9	8	8
Community Service, y_3 (20)	8	7	9	10	7

determine the most attractive microcomputer system to purchase for their immediate needs. Although they realize that they could "mix and match" several different manufacturers' computers, they have decided to purchase only one brand in order to eliminate any concerns over interoffice incompatibility. Most of ISA's work is conducted at the company location, although they are often called on to do on-site managerial training at client locations. These latter functions sometimes require that ISA provide demonstrations using its own microcomputers; therefore, the portability of the computer is important.

Although the initial purchase for ISA will be comparatively small when compared to anticipated purchases in subsequent years, these future larger purchases will be strongly influenced by which system (PC-DOS, Apple-DOS, etc.) is bought now. The candidate systems being considered are (1) IBM, (2) Texas Instruments (TI), (3) Apple Macintosh, (4) Compaq, and (5) Hewlett-Packard (HP). The primary characteristics that are of importance to ISA include system price (y_1), product support (y_2), reliability (y_3), resistance to obsolescence (y_4), and portability (y_5). The relative weights of importance of these attributes are 15, 30, 25, 20, and 10 percent, respectively. For the purpose of this exercise, the hypothetical attribute performance matrix for the various microcomputer systems under consideration is shown in Table 3-4.1.

ISA has also developed a set of utility curves to reflect its relative degree of satisfaction with varying degrees of fulfillment for each of these attributes (Figure 3-4.1).

Finally, let's assume that ISA wishes to observe the following operating constraints: the total cost of the system selected cannot exceed $42,500 and that no candidate system under consideration can have a "poor" rating on any of its attributes.

ASSIGNMENT

1. Using MAUM, tell ISA which system is the best for it to buy based on the specified attributes, weights of importance, constraints, and measures of worth (utility values).

2. Assume you have just learned that ISA has decided to buy IBM. What are some of the issues that this move suggests, assuming that they really do believe in MAUM as an important guide to selecting competing alternatives with multiple criteria?

3-5 Suppose that you have inherited a small fortune. You decide to buy a new car with part of your new wealth. For reasons known only to yourself, you wish to consider the following three cars: (1) a Porsche 928S (a luxury, high-performance sports car costing about $50,000, (2) a Buick Century (a comfortable four-door sedan that sells for about $15,000), and (3) a Honda Civic S (a two-door knockabout that costs about $8000). In addition, pretend the factors you wish to consider in selecting one of these three candidate automobiles—along with their hypothetical relative weights of importance—are provided in Table 3-5.1. Using the utility values provided, determine the best car to purchase. (Assume that there are no attribute constraint values to be considered in this first-cut analysis.)

TABLE 3-4.1

Attribute Performance Matrix for Informed Sources Associates

System, a_i	Attribute Performance, y_j*				
	y_1	y_2	y_3	y_4	y_5
IBM, a_1	$39,000	2	5	5	2
TI, a_2	$31,000	2	3	2	4
Macintosh, a_3	$28,000	5	5	3	4
Compaq, a_4	$30,000	3	4	3	5
HP, a_5	$34,000	3	4	3	5

*A five-point scale of measurement is used for attributes y_2 through y_5, where 1 = poor, 2 = fair, 3 = average, 4 = good, 5 = excellent.

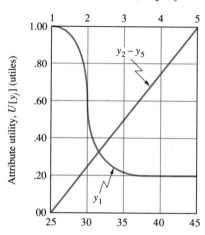

FIGURE 3-4.1

Utility Curve for ISA Microcomputer System Selection.

TABLE 3-5.1

Attribute Utility Scores for (1) Porsche 928S, (2) Buick Century, and (3) Honda Civic S Automobiles

Attribute (Weight)	Automobile-Attribute Value (Utility)		
	1	2	3
Purchase − Resale,* y_1−$1000 (.30)	20 (1)	8 (6)	3 (9)
Reliability,** y_2 (.30)	xlnt (10)	ave (6)	good (8)
Safety,** y_3 (.20)	fair (4)	xlnt (10)	poor (0)
Esthetics,** y_4 (.20)	xlnt (10)	ave (6)	ave (6)

*Purchase price − resale value of car after 3 years.
**Measured on five-point Likert-type scale of excellent, good, average, fair, poor.

TABLE 3-6.1

Attribute Weighting Variations for Selection of *Law Review* Editor

Attribute (Weight)	Weighting Scheme Version 1	2	3
Classroom performance, y_1	75	50	33
Service to law school, y_2	25	25	33
Community Service, y_3	0	25	33

3-6 What would happen to the selection of the *Law Review* editor in Exercise 3-3 if the original attribute weighting scheme changed to the three different scenarios illustrated in Table 3-6.1?

3-7 Assume that you wish to reconsider the original data for Exercise 3-5. What car would you select if the original data were used, but with the following changes?

1. You reassessed the weights of the four attributes as 50, 30, 10, and 10, respectively.
2. You decided against including esthetics as one of the attributes and *proportionately* redistributed that attribute's weight to the three remaining attributes.
3. You wished to include a purchase price minus resale difference maximum value of $12,000.

3-8 A close friend of yours must undergo open-heart surgery. Define, rank, weight, and establish utility curves for the set of attributes that you believe is most important to consider in the selection of the surgeon who will perform this operation. You may also include any attribute constraint values that you think are appropriate.

3-9 For the car-selection problem in Exercise 3-5, define five attributes that would reflect the most important factors you would consider in purchasing an automobile. Try to break down each attribute into several levels of subattributes whenever appropriate (e.g., cost can be broken down into greater detail if expressed with subattributes such as purchase price, operating cost, and resale value; purchase price can be further decomposed into amortized finance costs, dealer or manufacturer rebates, etc.). Weight these attributes and subattributes to reflect their relative importance in your overall decision setting. Take great care to ensure that all attributes are operationally defined and are readily measurable.

3-10 A professional football team is evaluating three quarterbacks who will be available in the upcoming NFL draft. The director of player personnel for the team realizes that the performance capabilities of each athlete are not constant from game to game. Accordingly, he decides to represent the performance of each player's attributes stochastically. He devises an athlete performance matrix for four attributes: (1) arm strength, (2) accuracy passing long, (3) accuracy passing short, and (4) running ability. These attributes, with their associated expected-value constraints, are shown in Table 3-10.1. The stochastic probability distribution matrix is given in Table 3-10.2. Notice that the utility associated with each level of attribute performance—measured on a scale of 0 to 10—is given in parentheses [e.g., the utility associated with a 40-yard arm-strength mean (y_1) is 7 utiles; a short pass accuracy of 25 percent (y_3) is worth 4 utiles].

TABLE 3-10.1

Attribute Set and Weights of Importance for Evaluation of Quarterback Candidates

Attribute, y_j (Weight)	Definition	Constraint, *EV* of y_j
y_1 (.15)	Arm strength: Mean of longest completed pass for each game during season (yards)	≥ 35
y_2 (.35)	Accuracy long: Percentage of completed passes > 30 yards (%)	≥ 33
y_3 (.25)	Accuracy short: Percentage of completed passes ≤ 30 yards (%)	≥ 45
y_4 (.25)	Running ability: Average per yard gain on nonsack carries (yards)	≥ 6

TABLE 3-10.2

Attribute Probability Distributions and Associated Utility Values for Evaluation of Quarterback Candidates

Attribute (Utility)	Probability of Distribution of ith Quarterback for j^{th} Attribute and k^{th} Level of Performance, $P(y_j)_{ik}$		
y_1 *(yards)*	$P(y_1)_{1k}$	$P(y_1)_{2k}$	$P(y_1)_{3k}$
20 (3)	.10	.20	.00
40 (7)	.60	.70	.50
60 (10)	.30	.10	.50
y_2 *(%)*	$P(y_2)_{1k}$	$P(y_2)_{2k}$	$P(y_2)_{3k}$
10 (3)	.05	.10	.20
33 (5)	.60	.30	.40
67 (10)	.35	.60	.40
y_3 *(%)*	$P(y_3)_{1k}$	$P(y_3)_{2k}$	$P(y_3)_{3k}$
25 (4)	.10	.15	.25
50 (8)	.60	.50	.60
75 (10)	.30	.35	.15
y_4 *(yards)*	$P(y_3)_{1k}$	$P(y_3)_{2k}$	$P(y_3)_{3k}$
5 (5)	.70	.80	.50
10 (9)	.20	.10	.30
15 (10)	.10	.10	.20

Note: y_1 = arm strength (yards), y_2 = accuracy long (%), y_3 = accuracy short (%), y_4 = running ability (yards).

ASSIGNMENT

Using the stochastic MAUM process, determine the preferential order in which to draft these three quarterbacks. Eliminate candidates who violate one or more expected-value constraints.

REFERENCES

1. Eckenrode, R. T. "Weighting Multiple Criteria," *Management Science* 12 (No. 3: September–July 1965): 180–192.

2. Edwards, Ward. "How to Use Multiattribute Utility Theory for Social Decision Making," *IEEE Transactions of Systems, Man, and Cybernetics* 7 (1977): 326–340.

3. Edwards, Ward. "Multiattribute Utility Measurement in a Highly Political Context: Evaluating Desegregation Plans in Los Angeles." In Robert Perloff, ed., *Evaluation Intervention: Pros and Cons*. Beverly Hills, CA: Sage, 1979.

4. Edwards, Ward, and J. Robert Newman. *Multiattribute Evaluation*. Beverly Hills, CA: Sage, 1982.

5. Jackson, Barbara B., and Benson P. Shapiro. "New Way to Make Product Line Decisions," *Harvard Business Review* 59 (No. 3: May–June 1979): 139–140.

6. Kamal, Golabi. "Selecting a Portfolio of Solar Energy Projects Using Multiattribute Preference Theory," *Management Science* 27 (1981): 174–189.

7. Keeney, Ralph L., and Detlof von Winterfeldt. "Citizen Evaluation of Energy Systems: An Illustrative Use of the Public Value Forum," paper MC4.4 presented at the joint national meeting of TIMS/ORSA, Boston, 1985.

8. Newman, J. Robert, and Ann Barthelmes Drew. "The Application of Multiattribute Utility Measurement in the Evaluation of an Alternative to Court Adjudication of Disputes," paper presented at the third annual meeting of the Evaluation Research Society, Minneapolis, 1979.

9. Oberstone, Joelee, and J. Robert Newman. "The Application of Decision Analysis to the Selection of Professional Football Players in the Annual National Football League Draft," paper WD06.3 presented at the joint national meeting of TIMS/ORSA, Los Angeles, 1986.

10. Schoemaker, P. J. H., and C. C. Waid. "An experimental Comparison of Different Approaches to Determining Weights in Additive Utility Models," *Management Science* 28 (No. 2: February 1982): 182–196.

11. von Winterfeldt, Detlof. "Value Tree Analysis of a Controversy about Offshore Oil Development," paper MC4.1 presented at the joint national meeting of TIMS/ORSA, Boston, 1985.

12. Weber, Martin, Franz Eisenfuhr, and Detlof von Winterfeldt. "The Effects of Splitting Attributes on Weights in Multiattribute Utility Measurement," *Management Science* 34 (No. 4: April 1988): 431–445.

MICROCOMPUTER SOFTWARE FOR MAUM

1. *The Confidence Factor*, Irvine, CA: Simple Software.

2. *Decision-Analyst*. Ontario, Canada: Executive Software.

3. *DecisionMap*. Honolulu: Softstyle, Inc.

4. *Expert Choice*. McLean, VA: Decision Support Software, Inc.

5. *Lightyear*. Santa Clara, CA: Lightyear.

LINEAR PROGRAMMING: PART 1

PROBLEM FORMULATION AND APPLICATIONS

|4.1| INTRODUCTION

Linear programming (LP) is the most widely used of all the tools of management science. Its purpose is to allocate scarce resources in an attempt to achieve an important organizational objective. Typically, this objective is to maximize profits or to minimize costs. The types of resource limitations include budget allocations, production hours, storage space, and units of raw materials or finished goods. These resources, in turn, must be meticulously assigned to produce a specific mix of "product" that the organization uses to achieve its goal. Usually, this product is some array of goods or services that the organization is in business to provide.

|4.2| APPLICATIONS OF LINEAR PROGRAMMING

Here are a few of the numerous examples of the applications of linear programming:

1. Financial planning of the Central Carolina Bank and Trust Company (Balbirer and Shaw, 1981).
2. Scheduling of network television programs (Horen, 1980).
3. Aircraft maintenance scheduling for Air Canada (Boere, 1977).
4. Fuel management for National Airlines (Darnell and Loflin, 1977).
5. Reduction of travel costs and player fatigue in the National Basketball Association (Bean and Birge, 1980).
6. Matching of supply and demand for the production of heart valves at American Edwards Laboratories (Hilal and Erikson, 1981).
7. Planning of campaign strategies for Senator John V. Tunney in the 1970 California senatorial race (Barkan and Bruno, 1972).
8. Distribution planning of Shell Oil petroleum products (Zener, et al., 1976).
9. Determination of school desegregation assignments for a public school district (Stimson and Thompson, 1972).

"So what's this? I asked for a *hammer*! A hammer! *This* is a crescent wrench! . . . Well, maybe it's a hammer . . . Damn these stone tools."

4.3 BASIC REQUIREMENTS OF LINEAR PROGRAMMING PROBLEMS

As with any management science tool, with LP there are specific ground rules or underlying assumptions that must be observed if the inherent integrity of the methodology is to be maintained. The requirements necessary for using LP are as follows:

1. There is a *single goal*, called the *objective function*, which is to be optimized. Usually, the objective is to maximize profits or to minimize costs.

2. There are *constraints* indicating the scarcity of the available resources that can be used in optimizing the objective function.

3. Both the objective function and all constraint equations can be expressed mathematically as linear relationships (straight line graphs). An example of the standard form of the objective function—which we shall discuss at greater length shortly—is

$$Z = \sum_{i=1}^{m} c_i x_i$$

or

$$Z = c_1 x_1 + c_2 x_2 + \ldots + c_i x_i + \ldots + c_m x_m$$

where each c represents a constant.

4. The amount of each resource must be proportional to the value of the variables in the objective function and constraint equations, and must hold over the entire range of these variables. For example, if the objective function is to minimize the cost of the expression

$$Z = 125x_1 + 75x_2$$

then each and every unit of x_1 must cost \$125, and each and every unit of x_2 must cost \$75. There can be no change in cost per unit over the entire range of x_1 and x_2. If a constraint equation identifying total labor hours available is

$$12x_1 + 8x_2 \leq 110$$

then every unit of x_1 and x_2 will require 12 and 8 hours of time, respectively. This is the property of *proportionality*.

5. The value of the objective function and the amount of resources required for each constraint are equal to the sum of the contribution of the individual variables that comprise them. That is, the whole is simply equal to the sum of individual parts. This characteristic is called *additivity*.

6. The variables in the objective function and constraint equations are assumed to be *divisible* and can, therefore, take on fractional values.

7. All variables must be *nonnegative*. It is not possible to produce negative goods or services. Therefore,

$$x_1, x_2, x_3, \ldots, x_m \geq 0$$

8. The parameters are assumed to be known with *certainty*. Therefore, using the second equation in requirement 4, the per-unit time-consumption rates of 12 hours for each unit of x_1 and 8 hours for each unit of x_2, as well as the total resource level of 110 hours, are assumed to be known without doubt.

Of course, situations will occur that clearly violate some of these requirements. When they do, there are alternative strategies that you can use. Some of them include:

1. If it is not possible or desirable to describe the problem in terms of a single objective, but instead you need multiple goals or objectives, then you can use *goal programming* (Chapter 9).

2. If the problem is not linear, you can employ nonlinear programming methods (NLP). It is important, however, first to see whether approximate methods using LP are satisfactory (LP is far more economical than is NLP).

3. If the problem requires whole number solutions, then the use of some form of *integer programming* (Chapter 7) may be more appropriate. These methods include standard integer, mixed integer, and binary integer.

4. No one can know with certainty the values of the various LP parameters needed to formulate each problem. To account for the sensitivity of such assumptions, *postoptimality analysis* or *sensitivity analysis* (Chapter 6) can be used to answer any "what if" questions (e.g., "What if each labor hour costs $17 instead of $14?" or "What if the budget is $430,000 instead of the $405,000 originally assumed?").

4.4 FORMULATION OF LINEAR PROGRAMMING PROBLEMS

Problem formulation is the first part as well as the most challenging aspect of linear programming. It requires that the manager be able to transform a problem from a text story into a standard mathematical form consisting of (1) the *objective function*, and (2) the *resource constraint equations*. Unfortunately, there is no algorithm to aid you in developing the formulation; you must depend on your ability, experience, and insight. Thus, the formulation process may seem hopeless, but it truly isn't. You will need to spend a considerable amount of time and energy working the many examples that we shall illustrate carefully in this chapter. After this necessary exposure, you will begin to gain confidence about how to approach LP problem formulation. Let's try an example now.

EXAMPLE 4-1   COCA-COLA BOTTLING COMPANY PRODUCT MIX

The soft-drink industry is typical of the majority of businesses that embrace the benefits resulting from the use of linear programming. The following is a hypothetical, introductory illustration of how the problem formulation aspects of linear programming can be used to address a simple product-mix issue that might arise in this industry.

The Coca-Cola Bottling Company manufactures four major brands of cola soft drinks: (1) Classic Coke, (2) New Coke, (3) Diet Coke, and (4) Cherry Coke. It would like to determine the optimal mix of cola types to produce that will result in the largest profits possible.

Assume that the Coca-Cola annual budget for the production of these four products is $80 million, and the annual demand, production costs, and sales revenues associated with each cola type are as illustrated in Table 4-1. In addition, suppose that the managers have decided on two internal policy requirements:

1. At least 35 percent of all production monies expended should be for Diet Coke.

2. The New Coke production level must be no more than one-third that of Classic Coke. Given that the maximum annual production capacity for Coca-Cola is limited to 200 million gallons, determine how many gallons of each of these drinks should be manufactured.

TABLE 4-1

Production Data for Coca-Cola

Cola Type	Annual Demand (10^3 gallons)	Production Costs $(\$/10^3 \text{ gallons})$	Sales Revenues $(\$/10^3 \text{ gallons})$
Classic	75,000	125	240
New	40,000	125	250
Diet	100,000	130	240
Cherry	15,000	135	265

DEVELOPING THE OBJECTIVE FUNCTION EQUATION

The objective function is always a *single equation* that either maximizes something beneficial (e.g., profit, revenue, production level, advertising exposure) or minimizes something undesirable (e.g., cost, labor hours). This equation is constructed from a series of terms called *decision variables* expressed in terms of x. *These decision variables symbolize the quantities of different goods or services that are used in satisfying the objective function.* In business, a significant proportion of objective functions are focused on maximizing profits. Accordingly, the decision variables in these cases would represent the mix of goods or services that an organization offers for sale. In the case of the Coca-Cola production example, the "mix" is the four cola types that the company sells and from which it generates profit. The objective function, in the Coca-Cola case, is to determine that single best mix of the four cola types—in thousands of gallons—that will provide the organization with the largest annual profit possible.

The objective function must be established in a single, linear equation constructed of four decision variables. If we define the quantity of ith type of cola to be ultimately produced as x_i, then these four decision variables are:

x_1: Number of thousands of gallons of Classic Coke produced

x_2: Number of thousands of gallons of New Coke produced

x_3: Number of thousands of gallons of Diet Coke produced

x_4: Number of thousands of gallons of Cherry Coke produced

Now the amount of profits generated from the sale of each cola type can be established. Assume the following: The profit contribution from the sale of each 1000 gallons of Classic Coke is $115 ($240 in revenues less the $125 production cost). The total profit contribution from all sales of Classic Coke is $115x_1$. The $115 represents the Classic Coke per-unit contribution to the objective function and is more formally known as the *objective function coefficient* of x_1. Using the same reasoning, let's write the entire objective function equation, which will always be notationally represented by Z. So, the objective function is:

goal is to make something beneficial as large as possible

profit contribution per 1000 gallons of New Coke

profit contribution per 1000 gallons of Cherry Coke

$$\text{Maximize } Z = 115x_1 + 125x_2 + 110x_3 + 130x_4$$

profit contribution per 1000 gallons of Classic Coke

profit contribution per 1000 gallons of Diet Coke

Observe that the term "maximize" precedes the equation. Objective function statements are always preceded by the intent of the goal: make something desirable as big as possible or make something undesirable as small as possible. Either maximize (or max) or minimize (or min) always should be written at the beginning of each objective function equation.

It is important to note that the actual quantity of the four different cola types to manufacture (x_1, x_2, x_3, and x_4) are, at present, unresolved. We can't determine these values until we bring into play the different resources available for production of these products (e.g., it is easy to understand that the objective function must be influenced by the budget, or by the demand for the products). Nevertheless, what is known at this time is that the profit will grow by $115 for each 1000 gallons of Classic Coke produced, $125 for each 1000 gallons of New Coke produced, and so on.

The *standard form* of an objective function is

$$\text{Maximize } Z = c_1 x_1 + c_2 x_2 + \ldots + c_i x_i + \ldots + c_m x_m$$

Although it is not absolutely necessary to do so, at times it may be more convenient to express this equation in the "shorthand" (summation) standard form:

$$\text{Maximize } Z = \sum_{i=1}^{m} c_i x_i$$

where

x_i = amount of the ith decision variable selected, where there are m total variables being considered (in the Coca-Cola example, $m = 4$ different cola types); also, $x_i \geq 0$ (i.e., decision variables may never be negative; it is not possible to produce a negative amount of a particular cola type)

c_i = per-unit contribution rate (or consumption rate) of the ith activity variable to the objective function, where there are m variables being considered (in the Coca-Cola example, the c_i values are the dollar profit contributions per 1000 gallons of the ith cola type produced)

Z = the objective function being optimized (in this case, total profit)

The summation form becomes more and more important as the number of decision variables and constraint equations increases. In addition, it is the "form of choice" used in professional journals.

Next, let's take a turn at formulating the resource constraint equations.

DEVELOPING THE RESOURCE CONSTRAINT EQUATIONS

All organizations are faced with limited resources. The level to which the objective function can be satisfied is directly limited by these constraints. The scarcity of personnel, money, time, and equipment, and limiting organizational policies, impose ceilings on our ultimate level of attainment.

The resource constraint equations comprise (1) x_i, the decision variables used in the objective function, and (2) a_{ij}, the per-unit contribution of the ith decision variable, x_i, in the jth constraint equation with resource limit, b_j. Each b_j is also referred to as the right-hand-side (RHS) constant associated with the jth constraint.

For our example, we know that we are constrained by the $80 million production budget provided by Coca-Cola. Further, there are demand constraints that set an upper production limit of how much of each cola type should be produced (see Table 4-1,

column 2). Finally, Coca-Cola made several managerial policy statements regarding how it wished to apportion resources between its different products. So we know that we must formulate three different types of resource constraint equations. Each constraint must be described in terms of the appropriate decision variables, constraint coefficients, and resource limits.

For the budget limit of $80 million, we form the constraint equation by determining the per-unit consumption rate of each cola type. That is, multiplying the cost per 1000 gallons of each cola, a_{ij}, times the amount of that cola type ultimately produced, x_i, yields the amount of money spent—out of all monies expended—on that particular cola. For example, the money spent on producing 1000 gallons of Classic Coke is the per-1000-gallons production cost ($125) times the total quantity of Classic Coke produced, x_1. So, the budget constraint equation is

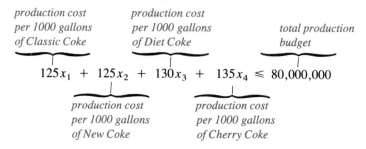

Notice that this relationship is expressed as an inequality. There is no requirement that all the money be spent. It is even conceivable that, based on the rate at which the other resources are exhausted, some funds could be left over (e.g., if the production capacity of 200 million gallons is consumed or if the annual demand is met for all four cola types prior to the budget running out).

The total production capacity is easy to formulate. Since each x_i represents the production level for the ith cola type (in thousands of gallons), then the total quantity of cola produced may not exceed the 200-million-gallon production capacity:

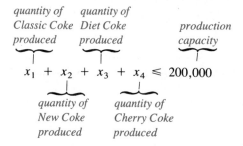

The potential sales volume for each of the cola types, based on forecast demand, is

$$x_1 \leq 75,000$$
$$x_2 \leq 40,000$$
$$x_3 \leq 100,000$$
$$x_4 \leq 15,000$$

It is typical for forecast values to represent ceiling or maximum production values: a greater-than or equal-to ($\geq$) relationship would fail to define a range of feasible values (open-ended).

The final group of constraints centers on the two managerial policy requirements. These relationships can be represented by the following equations:

Policy 1: At least 35 percent of all production monies expended should be for Diet Cola:

$$130\,x_3 \geqslant .35\,(125x_1 \; + \; 125x_2 \; + \; 130x_3 \; + \; 135x_4)$$

Look at the RHS value of this constraint equation. Notice that the 35 percent is not multiplied by the total budget of $80 million; the constraint called for "monies expended." Since it is possible that not all the budget allocation will be expended (as discussed earlier), the monies expended is written, appropriately, as

$$\text{Monies expended} \; = \; 125x_1 \; + \; 125x_2 \; + \; 130x_3 \; + \; 135x_4$$

This constraint form will accommodate either an exhaustive or a partial budget expenditure. In addition, this relationship can be equivalently expressed as a ratio; that is,

$$\frac{130x_3}{125\,x_1 \; + \; 125\,x_2 \; + \; 130x_3 \; + \; 135x_4} \geqslant .35$$

Policy 2: The New Coke production level must be no more than one-third that of Classic Coke.

$$x_2 \leqslant .33\,x_1$$

or

$$\frac{x_2}{x_1} \leqslant .33$$

It is also important to note, for reasons similar to those explained in the constraint for policy 1, that *it would be incorrect* for the RHS value to use the maximum production level for Classic Coke:

$$x_2 \leqslant .33(75,000)$$

This relationship *presupposes* that the maximum quantity of New Coke possible will, in fact, be produced. It may be convenient to make such an assumption; however, to do so is inappropriate: It is not possible to know this information during the formulation phase. One last comment about the two policy constraints: Whenever a constraint relationship is expressed as a ratio (or the equivalent), it is essential to "clear out" the fraction and to collect like terms so that the equation takes on a linear form. For the two policy constraints, this process is as follows:

| *Policy 1:* Multiply the .35 by each term in the RHS parentheses. Next move these RHS variables over to the left-hand side (LHS) of the equation, making sure to change the signs of these coefficients. The RHS value is now zero and the relationship ($\geqslant$) remains unchanged. The correct, and "software-compatible," form of this constraint is

$$-43.75x_1 \; - \; 43.75x_2 \; + \; 84.5x_3 \; - \; 47.25x_4 \geqslant 0$$

| *Policy 2:* Multiply the .33 by the x_1 variable on the RHS. Bring it back to the LHS after changing its sign from "+" to "−." Keep the same relationship ($\leqslant$). The correct constraint form is

$$-.33\,x_1 \; + \; x_2 \leqslant 0$$

Let's summarize the completed formulation for the Coca-Cola production example.

OBJECTIVE FUNCTION

Maximize $Z = 115x_1 + 125x_2 + 110x_3 + 130x_4$

SUBJECT TO

■ *Budget (dollars)*

$$125x_1 + 125x_2 + 130x_3 + 135x_4 \leq 80,000,000$$

■ *Production capacity (10^3 gallons of cola)*

$$x_1 + x_2 + x_3 + x_4 \leq 200,000$$

■ *Demand (forecast sales in 10^3 gallons of cola)*

$$x_1 \leq 75,000$$
$$x_2 \leq 40,000$$
$$x_3 \leq 100,000$$
$$x_4 \leq 15,000$$

■ *Policy 1*

$$-43.75x_1 - 43.75x_2 + 84.5x_3 - 47.25x_4 \geq 0$$

■ *Policy 2*

$$-.33x_1 + x_2 \leq 0$$

As we suggested earlier in this chapter, it may be advantageous sometimes to explore the resource constraint equations in a more concise, standardized form. If so, a typical constraint might look like the following (note that the presentation of three potential sign relationships suggests that these equations will vary according to the types of constraint being addressed. We'll call this the standard form of an *LP problem*:

$$\sum_{i=1}^{m} a_{ij}x_i \begin{pmatrix} \leq \\ = \\ \geq \end{pmatrix} b_j \qquad \text{for each } j\,(j = 1, 2, \ldots, n)$$

where

a_{ij} = per unit contribution of the ith decision variable to the jth resource constraint (in our case, $m = 5$ decision variables and $n = 8$ constraint equations)

b_j = total amount of resources available for the jth constraint

$\begin{pmatrix} \leq \\ = \\ \geq \end{pmatrix}$ = the three types of constraint forms that the resource constraint equations must satisfy; ($\leq$) means that the LHS of the equation is equal to or less than the value of the RHS; ($=$) means that both sides of the equations are equal; ($\geq$) means that the LHS of the equation is equal to or greater than the RHS.

Even though the summation notation form is not essential to LP problem formulation and solution, you should learn it so that you can understand journal articles that use it. For this reason, we shall include summation notation as a supplement to each LP prob-

lem formulation. To sharpen your problem formulation skills, we'll develop several more examples. Be sure that you pay special attention to how the decision variable, x_i, is defined, with its per-unit contribution, in (1) optimizing the objective function, and (2) fulfilling or depleting each resource constraint.

EXAMPLE 4-2 CHICAGO SHOPPING MALL PRODUCT MIX

Suppose that Basil Tweed, one of Chicago's many award-winning architects, has been hired by a successful developer to design a new shopping mall for the Chicago business district. Tweed is preparing the final proposal to present to the Chicago Town Council for building approval of his futuristic mall plans (the mall will be adjacent to the outdoor Picasso sculpture). The mall will have 850,000 square feet of usable space for shops of three different sizes: (1) small specialty (e.g., See's Candy, Swenson's Ice Cream, Bally Shoes); (2) intermediate (e.g., Computerland, Gelson's Market, Wherehouse Records, Footlocker Athletic Shoes); and large department stores (e.g., I. Magnin, Saks Fifth Avenue). The average size for these three different types of stores is 300, 1500, and 75,000 square feet, respectively. The average amortized developer's cost associated with each of these store sizes is $20,000, $60,000, and $800,000 per year, respectively. (These are the amortized construction costs associated with only the "shell" of each store, which includes floor, walls, and ceiling; electrical, water, and gas utility outlets; and a centralized air-conditioning hookup. All other structural modifications and furnishings are the responsibility of the individual leasing store.) Further, Tweed estimates that the annual lease revenues from each of the three different-size stores will yield approximately $25,000, $80,000, and $1,250,000, respectively. The annual amortized operating budget for this project is $35 million. A summary of these data is presented in Table 4-2.

The city fathers hope upon hope that Basil Tweed, architect of the Ear, Nose and Throat Clinic, won't be bidding on the proposed new Proctology Clinic.

ASSIGNMENT

If the developer wants to limit the number of department stores in the project to no more than six, wants at least one-third of the space allocated to all stores to be for the specialty shop type, wants no more than 25 percent of all revenues generated to come from the medium-sized stores, and wants to maximize annual lease profits, what is the problem formulation that will help her to determine the best mix of store sizes to lease (assume that there is a strong market for all store spaces)?

TABLE 4-2

Chicago Mall Data

Store Type	Size (ft^2)	Amortized Building Costs ($/yr)	Revenues ($/year)
Small	300	20,000	25,000
Medium	1,500	60,000	80,000
Large	75,000	800,000	1,250,000
TOTALS	*850,000	**35,000,000	

* = total space available. ** = total budget.

SOLUTION

The objective function is

Maximize annual lease profits, $Z = (25{,}000 - 20{,}000)x_1 + (80{,}000 - 60{,}000)x_2 + (1{,}250{,}000 - 800{,}000)x_3$

$= 5000x_1 + 20{,}000x_2 + 450{,}000x_3$

or

$$\text{Max } Z = \sum_{i=1}^{3} (r_i - c_i)x_i = \sum_{i=1}^{3} p_i x_i$$

where

r_i = revenues associated with the ith size store

c_i = development costs associated with i^{th} size store

p_i = profit associated with i^{th} size store

x_i = number of ith size stores ultimately developed and leased

SUBJECT TO

■ *Budget*

$$20{,}000x_1 + 60{,}000x_2 + 800{,}000x_3 \leq 35{,}000{,}000$$

or

$$\sum_{i=1}^{3} c_i x_i \leq B$$

where

B = total development budget

■ *Space*

$$300x_1 + 1500x_2 + 75{,}000x_3 \leq 850{,}000$$

or

$$\sum_{i=1}^{3} s_i x_i \leq S$$

where

s_i = space of ith size store

S = total space available for all stores

■ *Policy 1*

$$x_3 \leq 6$$

■ *Policy 2*

$$\frac{300x_1}{300x_1 + 1500x_2 + 75{,}000x_3} \geq .33$$

$$200x_1 - 500x_2 - 25{,}000x_3 \geq 0$$

or

$$\frac{s_1 x_1}{\sum\limits_{i=1}^{3} s_i x_i} \leqslant .33$$

■ *Policy 3*

$$\frac{80,000 x_2}{25,000 x_1 + 80,000 x_2 + 1,250,000 x_3} \leqslant .25$$

$$-6250 x_1 + 60,000 x_2 - 312,500 x_3 \leqslant 0$$

or

$$\frac{r_2 x_2}{\sum\limits_{i=1}^{3} r_i x_i} \leqslant .25$$

EXAMPLE 4-3 THE GERMAN CAR DEALER PRODUCT MIX

An auto sales agency specializes in three types of foreign cars: Porsche, BMW, and Mercedes Benz. For this example, we'll assume that each Porsche, BMW, and Mercedes costs the agency an average of $27,000, $20,000, and $32,500, respectively (in this problem, we shall always refer to these three autos in the same order) and that the average sales price for each car is $36,000, $26,000, and $45,000. The estimated demand for each is described in the following statement provided by the general manager, Rolfe:

The agency can almost easily sell at least 40 Porsches and 30 BMWs, but has had a maximum demand for only 6 Mercedes per month.

The maximum number of units available from the distributors to the agency each month are 25, 35, and 8 cars, respectively. The agency's policy is to always have a minimum of 12 Porsches, 12 BMWs, and 4 Mercedes in stock at the beginning of each month. The monthly budget for the car purchases is $800,000. The amount of showroom floor space each type of auto takes up is 120, 115, and 148 square feet. There is a total of 5000 square feet of floor space available. Finally, the average salesperson hours invested per sale is 28, 22, and 30; there is a total of 1100 salesperson hours available per month.

ASSIGNMENT

1. Formulate this problem so that the dealer can ultimately determine the optimal number of units of each type of automobile to purchase each month, so that he can maximize profits (assume the dealer can sell every car he purchases each month, so there is no carryover inventory).

2. Reformulate the problem to reflect that the dealer is considering adding the Audi line to his business. Assume that the pertinent data concerning this new automobile line are as follows: the wholesale costs are $18,000 per unit, the sales price is $25,000 per unit, each car uses 130 square feet of space, no more than 15 units are available each month, and an average of 33 hours of sales time is required per cus-

tomer purchase[1] and Audi would require the dealer to place a minimum monthly purchase of at least 3 units.

SOLUTION

1. The objective function, as stated in the problem, is to maximize profit. This goal is realized through the sale of the three types of autos the dealer offers. So, the profits are equal to the number of autos of each type sold times the per-unit profit the dealer can realize for each. That is, for x_i denoting the number of ith type cars to purchase each month, we calculate the following.

OBJECTIVE FUNCTION

$$\begin{aligned} \text{Maximize profits, } Z &= (36{,}000 - 27{,}000)x_1 + (26{,}000 - 20{,}000)x_2 \\ &\quad + (45{,}000 - 32{,}500)x_3 \\ &= 9000x_1 + 6000x_2 + 12{,}500x_3 \end{aligned}$$

The constraints mentioned include availability, demand, budget, space, and inventory policy. These can be expressed as follows.

SUBJECT TO

- *Availability* $x_1 \leq 25, x_2 \leq 35, x_3 \leq 8$
- *Demand* $x_3 \leq 6$
- *Budget* $27{,}000x_1 + 20{,}000x_2 + 32{,}500x_3 \leq 800{,}000$
- *Space* $120x_1 + 115x_2 + 148x_3 \leq 5000$
- *Inventory* $x_1 \geq 12, x_2 \geq 12, x_3 \geq 4$
- *Sales hours* $28x_1 + 22x_2 + 30x_3 \leq 1100$

Notice that the "demand" constraint did not include those of the Porsches or BMWs because the latter are open-ended statements. Including them might serve only to constrain unduly or to suboptimize the problem. For example, if the dealer could always sell at least 30 or even 300 BMWs every month, would it make sense to enter the constraint $x_2 \geq 30$ or $x_2 \geq 300$? Certainly not! The car dealer's objective is to *maximize profits*. Maximum profits can be realized only when the optimal mix of the *entire* product line is realized, not when sales from a portion of the product line are maximized.

2. Now let's examine the formulation that considers the addition of a potential fourth member to the product mix: Audi. The revised hypothetical formulation—with the accommodations for the Audi set in boldface—is as follows.

OBJECTIVE FUNCTION

$$\begin{aligned} \text{Maximize profits, } Z &= (36{,}000 - 27{,}000)x_1 + (26{,}000 - 20{,}000)x_2 \\ &\quad + (45{,}000 - 32{,}500)x_3 + \mathbf{(25{,}000 - 18{,}000)x_4} \\ &= 9000x_1 + 6000x_2 + 12{,}500x_3 + \mathbf{7000x_4} \end{aligned}$$

SUBJECT TO

- *Availability* $x_1 \leq 25, x_2 \leq 35, x_3 \leq 8, \mathbf{x_4 \leq 15}$
- *Demand* $x_3 \leq 6$
- *Budget* $27{,}000x_1 + 20{,}000x_2 + 32{,}500x_3 + \mathbf{18{,}000x_4} \leq 800{,}000$

[1]Although Audi would require, as do the other manufacturers, some minimum number of units to be purchased each month, the dealer does not wish to consider this constraint now. He first wants to formulate the problem to see if Audi can "win a place" in his product mix of automobiles on its own merits rather than external contractual obligations.

- *Space* $120x_1 + 115x_2 + 148x_3 + \mathbf{130x_4} \leq 5000$
- *Inventory* $x_1 \geq 12,\ x_2 \geq 12,\ x_3 \geq 4$
- *Sales hours* $28x_1 + 22x_2 + 30x_3 + \mathbf{33x_4} \leq 1100$

All the examples we have studied so far have something in common: The decision variables are all of the single-period variety, x_i. That is, the mix of goods or services described by the decision variable can be effectively represented by a single subscript. Sometimes, however, the complexity of an LP problem can be represented more explicitly by a multiple-subscript decision variable. Linear programming problems that are represented more effectively by multiple-subscript decision variables are discussed in the next section.

4.5 | FORMULATION OF MULTIPLE-SUBSCRIPT LP PROBLEMS

If an LP problem has decision variables that are best described by several characteristics, such as a physician with a specific specialty of training treating a patient with a given illness or injury type, the use of multiple-subscript decision variables, x_{ij}, is helpful in tying together these characteristics.[2] Single-subscript labeling of the decision variables—although possible—would be unclear to anyone attempting to assess the formulation or computer output of a particular problem, unless you provided a "directory" of what each single subscript meant.

To understand more clearly the bridge between single and multiple subscripting, let's take a single-characteristic problem with which we are already familiar and add a bit more to it. You will then see why it is sometimes to your advantage to incorporate multiple-subscript notation.

EXAMPLE 4-4 COCA-COLA QUARTERLY PRODUCTION SCHEDULE

Assume that Coca-Cola managers think that it is impossible to portray accurately the seasonal fluctuations of their products using a 1-year plan. As an example, Coca-Cola has found that during some times of the year, it has been unable to meet demand because short-term production limits are exceeded that are not considered by simplified single-period, 1-year plans. Accordingly, the company has decided that the year should be broken into four quarters, so that it is possible to design a production schedule for the four colas to reflect these seasonal variations and to gain a better understanding of why and when they are likely to experience problems. The quarterly forecast sales (demand) is provided in Table 4-3.[3] Assume that the production costs and sales revenues are unchanged, and the two policy constraints can be viewed across the entire year—not on a per-quarter basis. Formulate this problem using the following decision variable notation: x_{ij} = number of gallons (in 1000-gallon multiples) of the ith cola type to be produced during the jth quarter [e.g., x_{32} = number of gallons (in 1000-gallon multiples) of Diet Coke to be produced during the second (April–June) quarter].

---

[2] Actually, the multiple characteristic is presented more definitively by $x_{i,j}$ so that when either i or j (or both) exceeds 9, there is no confusion about whether x_{112} means $x_{1,12}$ or $x_{11,2}$. Also, the term *multiple period* does not necessarily mean that the problem must span different time periods.

[3] The quarterly forecast demand does not represent contracted sales agreements; it is an estimate compiled by the company marketing department on the likely maximum quantity of cola to be consumed by quarter.

TABLE 4-3

Quarterly Forecast Demand for Coca-Cola

Cola Type	Jan–Mar (Q1)	Apr–June (Q2)	July–Sept (Q3)	Oct–Dec (Q4)
Classic	12,000	15,000	32,000	16,000
New	8,000	10,000	16,000	6,000
Diet	20,000	23,000	36,000	21,000
Cherry	3,000	4,000	5,000	3,000
PRODUCTION CAPACITY	50,000	50,000	50,000	50,000

SOLUTION

The intent of the objective function is still to maximize profit. This time, however, the relationship must pinpoint a schedule by identifying the quantity of each cola type to be produced during each of the four quarters. Since it is inappropriate to anticipate even a portion of the solution, it is essential to account for every possible production combination.

OBJECTIVE FUNCTION

Maximize profits,
$$Z = 115(x_{11} + x_{12} + x_{13} + x_{14}) + 125(x_{21} + x_{22} + x_{23} + x_{24})$$
$$+ 110(x_{31} + x_{32} + x_{33} + x_{34}) + 130(x_{41} + x_{42} + x_{43} + x_{44})$$

where the terms represent, respectively: profit contribution of Classic Coke × quantity of Classic Coke produced during four quarters; profit contribution of New Coke × quantity of New Coke produced during four quarters; profit contribution of Diet Coke × quantity of Diet Coke produced during four quarters; profit contribution of Cherry Coke × quantity of Cherry Coke produced during four quarters.

Notice that the profit contribution of each cola type is constant with respect to time; it is not affected by the quarter in which it is produced—only by the cola type. Therefore, the profit-contribution term only has a single subscript, p_i (not p_{ij}).

SUBJECT TO

■ *Budget*

$$125 (x_{11} + x_{12} + x_{13} + x_{14}) + 125(x_{21} + x_{22} + x_{23} + x_{24})$$
$$+ 130(x_{31} + x_{32} + x_{33} + x_{34})$$
$$+ 135(x_{41} + x_{42} + x_{43} + x_{44})$$
$$\leq 80,000,000$$

The budget is an aggregate amount and covers all four quarters and all four cola types. It is possible to have the annual budget segmented into quarterly limits and also to have separate budgets for each type of cola. That is not the case in this example.

■ Quarterly production capacity/supply (10^3 gallons)

$$\text{Quarter 1} \quad x_{11} + x_{21} + x_{31} + x_{41} \leq 50,000$$
$$\text{Quarter 2} \quad x_{12} + x_{22} + x_{32} + x_{42} \leq 50,000$$
$$\text{Quarter 3} \quad x_{13} + x_{23} + x_{33} + x_{43} \leq 50,000$$
$$\text{Quarter 4} \quad x_{14} + x_{24} + x_{34} + x_{44} \leq 50,000$$

- Forecast sales/demand (10^3 gallons)

Classic Coke	$x_{11} \leq 12{,}000;\ x_{12} \leq 15{,}000;\ x_{13} \leq 32{,}000;\ x_{14} \leq 16{,}000$	
New Coke	$x_{21} \leq 8{,}000;\ x_{22} \leq 10{,}000;\ x_{23} \leq 16{,}000;\ x_{24} \leq 6{,}000$	
Diet Coke	$x_{31} \leq 20{,}000;\ x_{32} \leq 23{,}000;\ x_{33} \leq 36{,}000;\ x_{34} \leq 21{,}000$	
Cherry Coke	$x_{41} \leq 3{,}000;\ x_{42} \leq 4{,}000;\ x_{43} \leq 5{,}000;\ x_{44} \leq 3{,}000$	

The way the problem is presently restricted, forecast sales cannot be exceeded for any cola type–quarter combination.

- *Policy 1*

$$
\begin{aligned}
&-43.75\ (x_{11} + x_{12} + x_{13} + x_{14}) \\
&-\ 43.75\ (x_{21} + x_{22} + x_{23} + x_{24}) \\
&+\ 84.50\ (x_{31} + x_{32} + x_{33} + x_{34}) \\
&-\ 47.25\ (x_{41} + x_{42} + x_{43} + x_{44}) \quad \geq 0
\end{aligned}
$$

- *Policy 2*

$$
-.33\ (x_{11} + x_{12} + x_{13} + x_{14}) + (x_{21} + x_{22} + x_{23} + x_{24}) \leq 0
$$

The standard formulation for this example is presented next (optional).

OBJECTIVE FUNCTION

$$
\text{Max}\, Z = \sum_{i=1}^{m} \sum_{j=1}^{n} p_i x_{ij}
$$

SUBJECT TO

- *Budget*

$$
\sum_{i=1}^{m} \sum_{j=1}^{n} c_i x_{ij} \leq B
$$

- *Production capacity (supply)*

$$
\sum_{i=1}^{m} x_{ij} \leq s_j \qquad \text{for each quarter},\, j\,(j = 1, 2, 3, 4)
$$

- *Forecast sales (demand)*

$$
x_{ij} \leq d_{ij} \qquad
\begin{aligned}
&\text{for each cola type},\, i\,(i = 1, 2, 3, 4) \\
&\text{and for each quarter},\, j\,(j = 1, 2, 3, 4)
\end{aligned}
$$

- *Policy 1*

$$
\frac{\displaystyle\sum_{j=1}^{n} c_3 x_{3j}}{\displaystyle\sum_{i=1}^{m} \sum_{j=1}^{n} c_i x_{ij}} \geq .35
$$

- *Policy 2*

$$
\frac{\displaystyle\sum_{j=1}^{n} c_2 x_{2j}}{\displaystyle\sum_{j=1}^{n} c_1 x_{1j}} \leq .33
$$

where

p_i = profit margin of ith cola type

d_{ij} = demand (10^3 gallons) of ith cola type to be produced during j^{th} quarter

c_i = per-unit cost of producing 1000 gallons of ith cola type

B = annual budget ($80 million)

s_j = production capacity (10^3 gallons) for all colas during j^{th} quarter

m = number of different types of colas (m = 4 types)

n = number of different production periods (n = 4 quarters)

CONTRASTING FORMULATIONS OF SINGLE- AND MULTIPLE-SUBSCRIPT LP PROBLEMS

Although it is possible to formulate the entire Coca-Cola example using a single subscript, *our ability to interpret this simplified form is poor*. The decision variables for the double subscripts (x_{ij} = number of gallons, in 1000-gallon multiples, of the ith cola type to be produced during the jth quarter) and for the corresponding single subscripts (x_1 = number of gallons, in 1000-gallon multiples, of the ith cola type to be produced during a specific year) are, in an abbreviated comparison,

x_{ij}	x_i
x_{11}	x_1
x_{12}	x_2
x_{13}	x_3
.	.
.	.
.	.
x_{33}	x_{11}
x_{34}	x_{12}
.	.
.	.
.	.

You can see that the double-subscripted decision variables are *definitively labeled*: x_{33} denotes the quantity of Diet Coke (i = 3) produced during the third quarter (j = 3), whereas the denotation of its counterpart single-subscript decision variable, x_{11}, is unclear (i.e., what does the "11" represent?). The only way the analyst can determine what x_{11} is is to have a directory that catalogs what each subscript means. *Single-characteristic formats cannot be interpreted directly*. And, of course, the more complex the events that characterize the problem you wish to portray, the more helpful multiple-characteristic subscripting can be. For example, suppose you wanted to break down the production scheduling of the colas more finely than we did in this example, not only by the type of cola and the quarter in which each will be produced, but also whether the production was conducted on regular or overtime shifts. The notation would use three subscripts, x_{ijk}, which would represent the quantity of the ith cola type produced during the jth quarter by the kth shift (or some other arrangement of assigning i, j, and k to the three events that define the activity variable). Let's do a few more of these multiple-subscript problem formulations.

TABLE 4-4

Taste Standards for Has Beans Coffee Company

Coffee Criteria	Coffee Blend		
	Café du Monde	*Gold Coast*	*Standard*
Strength	≤8.0	≤7.0	≥9.0
Acidity	≤3.5	≤4.0	≤5.0
Caffeine	≤2.8	≤2.2	≤2.4
Liquoring value	≥7.0	≥6.0	≥5.0
Hardness	≤2.5	≤3.0	≤7.8
Aroma	≥7.0	≥5.0	≥4.0
Body	≥7.0	≥6.0	≥7.0

EXAMPLE 4-5   THE HAS BEANS COFFEE COMPANY BLENDING PROBLEM[4]

One of the most common uses of linear programming is blending problems, such as are faced by the gasoline, pharmaceutical, nutrition, food, and perfume industries. It is also no coincidence that the use of the multiple-subscript formulation notation is of particular value to blending problems. Here is such an example.

Imagine that the Has Beans Coffee Company of Tucson, Arizona, imports, blends, and roasts green coffees for wholesale distribution throughout the southwestern United States. The company produces three primary blends of coffee under the following brand names: Café du Monde (luxury coffee sold primarily to quality hotels and restaurants), Gold Coast (medium-grade coffee sold to supermarkets; high-volume sales brand), and Standard (inexpensive grade sold to discount outlets). The average wholesale per-pound price for each of these coffees (in order of presentation) is $5.95, $4.25, and $3.00, respectively.

Has Beans uses established, highly specialized coffee-industry taste criteria that it believes accurately reflect the general quality of a coffee blend. These criteria are (1) strength, (2) acidity, (3) caffeine, (4) liquoring value, (5) hardness, (6) aroma, and (7) body. Specific standards have been developed using these criteria for each of the three types of coffee Has Beans produces. It is of considerable importance, therefore, that Has Beans' quality-control staff ensure that the three blends are maintained within the limits suggested by the production values in Table 4-4.

At the beginning of each month, the Has Beans marketing and sales department staff forecast the demand for the three blends of coffees for 2 months from the present date. The company requires this 2-month lead time to receive and blend the appropriate mix of the green coffees from Central America, South America, and Africa. For example, green coffees that are to be roasted on July 1 must be ordered by May 1. It is, coincidentally, May 1 today, and the sales department has just completed its July sales forecast, shown in Table 4-5. It is company policy to attempt to meet these demand levels. However, under no condition does Has Beans ever "overproduce" a forecast volume for their product: Once the green beans are roasted, they become a perishable commodity—and an overstock of perishable goods is something the company wishes to avoid. Each of the green coffees Has Beans uses in blending its product mix varies in price, availability, and taste characteristics, as shown in Table 4-6.

[4]This study has been adapted from Thomas H. Naylor and Eugene T. Byrne, *Linear Programming: Methods and Cases* (Belmont, CA: Wadsworth, 1963), pp. 129–136.

As soon as he saw his boss's coffee kick over, Howard's sense of corporate responsibility kicked in.

Reprinted with special permission of Cowles Syndicate, Inc.

TABLE 4-5

Sales Forecast for July Demand for Has Beans Coffee Company

Blend	Forecast Demand (lbs)
	July
Café du Monde	140,000
Gold Coast	380,000
Standard	250,000

TABLE 4-6

Green Coffee Price, Availability, and Taste Standards for Has Beans Coffee Company

Green Coffees Available	Cost ($/lb)	Available Supply (lbs)	Taste Standards						
			Strength Index	*Acidity pH*	*Percent Caffeine*	*Liquoring Value*	*Hardness Index*	*Aroma Index*	*Body Index*
Brazil	1.65	275,000	6	4.0	1.8	6	2	7	7
Colombia	2.50	500,000	8	3.0	3.0	9	1	7	9
Ghana	2.55	140,000	10	3.1	2.9	7	4	10	9

ASSIGNMENT

Has Beans' July budget is $1,800,000. Formulate this problem so that Has Beans can maximize profits during July. (*Hint*: Let x_{ij} = pounds of ith type of green coffee used to make the jth blend of coffee product.)

SOLUTION

OBJECTIVE FUNCTION

$$\text{Maximize profits, } Z = 4.30x_{11} + 2.60x_{12} + 1.35x_{13} + 3.45x_{21} + 1.75x_{22}$$
$$+ .50x_{23} + 3.40x_{31} + 1.70x_{32} + .45x_{33}$$

$$\text{Max profits, } Z = \sum_{i=1}^{m}\sum_{j=1}^{n}(r_{ij} - c_{ij})x_{ij} = \sum_{i=1}^{m}\sum_{j=1}^{n}p_{ij}x_{ij}$$

where

r_{ij} = revenues (wholesale price/pound) of ith green coffee used in j^{th} blend product

c_{ij} = wholesale cost/pound of ith green coffee used in j^{th} blend product

p_{ij} = gross profit/pound of ith green coffee used in j^{th} blend product, $r_{ij} - c_{ij}$

m = number of different green coffees used ($m = 3$)

n = number of different blends of coffee products sold by Has Beans ($n = 3$)

SUBJECT TO

There are seven different taste standards used in the coffee industry. Has Beans achieves the desired blend of the final product by combining the raw materials (green coffees) in a particular manner. The strength criterion for the Café du Monde blend will be used as an example of this process. The desired strength of Café du Monde is to be equal to or less than an index of 8.0. Clearly, Has Beans must use "some" quantity of the Brazilian coffee or "all" Colombian to meet this taste standard (i.e., the Colombian coffee is equal to this strength and the African green coffee exceeds this value). So, the blending formula for the strength index is

$$\frac{\begin{array}{l}\text{Strength index of Brazilian green coffee} \cdot \text{quantity of Brazilian green coffee used in final blend} \\ + \text{ strength index of Colombian green coffee} \cdot \text{quantity of Colombian green coffee used in final blend} \\ + \text{ strength indes of Ghanan green coffee} \cdot \text{quantity of Ghanan green coffee used in final blend}\end{array}}{\begin{array}{l}\text{Total quantity of all green coffee beans used for Café du Monde blend (i.e., total pounds} \\ \text{of Brazilian, Colombian, and Ghanan green coffees purchased for Café du Monde blend)}\end{array}} \leq \text{Desired strength index}$$

So

$$\frac{6x_{11} + 8x_{21} + 10x_{31}}{x_{11} + x_{21} + x_{31}} \leq 8.0$$

or

$$6x_{11} + 8x_{21} + 10x_{31} \leq 8.0x_{11} + x_{21} + x_{31}$$

We can determine the coffee-quality-index constraints using this common blending method and the last equation form.

STRENGTH

- *Café du Monde* $6x_{11} + 8x_{21} + 10x_{31} \leq 8.0\,(x_{11} + x_{21} + x_{31})$
- *Gold Coast* $6x_{12} + 8x_{22} + 10x_{32} \leq 7.0\,(x_{12} + x_{22} + x_{32})$
- *Standard* $6x_{13} + 8x_{23} + 10x_{33} \geq 9.0\,(x_{13} + x_{23} + x_{33})$

ACIDITY

- *Café du Monde* $4.0x_{11} + 3.0x_{21} + 3.1x_{31} \leq 3.5\,(x_{11} + x_{21} + x_{31})$
- *Gold Coast* $4.0x_{12} + 3.0x_{22} + 3.1x_{32} \leq 4.0\,(x_{12} + x_{22} + x_{32})$
- *Standard* $4.0x_{13} + 3.0x_{23} + 3.1x_{33} \leq 5.0\,(x_{13} + x_{23} + x_{33})$

PERCENT CAFFEINE

- *Café du Monde* $1.8x_{11} + 3.0x_{21} + 2.9x_{31} \leq 2.8\,(x_{11} + x_{21} + x_{31})$
- *Gold Coast* $1.8x_{12} + 3.0x_{22} + 2.9x_{32} \leq 2.2\,(x_{12} + x_{22} + x_{32})$
- *Standard* $1.8x_{13} + 3.0x_{23} + 2.9x_{33} \leq 2.4\,(x_{13} + x_{23} + x_{33})$

LIQUORING VALUE

- *Café du Monde* $6x_{11} + 9x_{21} + 7x_{31} \geq 7\,(x_{11} + x_{21} + x_{31})$
- *Gold Coast* $6x_{12} + 9x_{22} + 7x_{32} \geq 6\,(x_{12} + x_{22} + x_{32})$
- *Standard* $6x_{13} + 9x_{23} + 7x_{33} \geq 5\,(x_{13} + x_{23} + x_{33})$

HARDNESS INDEX

- *Café du Monde* $2x_{11} + 1x_{21} + 4x_{31} \leq 2.5\,(x_{11} + x_{21} + x_{31})$
- *Gold Coast* $2x_{12} + 1x_{22} + 4x_{32} \leq 3.0\,(x_{12} + x_{22} + x_{32})$
- *Standard* $2x_{13} + 1x_{23} + 4x_{33} \leq 7.8\,(x_{13} + x_{23} + x_{33})$

AROMA INDEX

- *Café du Monde* $7x_{11} + 7x_{21} + 10x_{31} \geq 7\,(x_{11} + x_{21} + x_{31})$
- *Gold Coast* $7x_{12} + 7x_{22} + 10x_{32} \geq 5\,(x_{12} + x_{22} + x_{32})$
- *Standard* $7x_{13} + 7x_{23} + 10x_{33} \geq 4\,(x_{13} + x_{23} + x_{33})$

BODY INDEX

- *Café du Monde* $7x_{11} + 9x_{21} + 9x_{31} \geq 7\,(x_{11} + x_{21} + x_{31})$
- *Gold Coast* $7x_{12} + 9x_{22} + 9x_{32} \geq 6\,(x_{12} + x_{22} + x_{32})$
- *Standard* $7x_{13} + 9x_{23} + 9x_{33} \geq 7\,(x_{13} + x_{23} + x_{33})$

or, for *each* quality index constraint

$$\sum_{i=1}^{m} a_i x_{ij} \begin{pmatrix} \leq \\ = \\ \geq \end{pmatrix} Q_j \sum_{i=1}^{m} x_{ij} \qquad \text{for each } j\,(\,j = 1, 2, 3)$$

where

a_i = taste index value associated with i^{th} green coffee

Q_j = desired taste quality index for j^{th} blend coffee

BUDGET

$$1.65(x_{11} + x_{12} + x_{13}) + 2.50(x_{21} + x_{22} + x_{23})$$
$$+ 2.55(x_{31} + x_{32} + x_{33}) \leq 1{,}800{,}000$$

or

$$\sum_{i=1}^{m} \sum_{j=1}^{n} c_{ij}x_{ij} \leq B$$

where

B = budget (dollars)

SUPPLY

- *Brazil* $x_{11} + x_{12} + x_{13} \leq 275{,}000$
- *Colombia* $x_{21} + x_{22} + x_{23} \leq 500{,}000$
- *Ghana* $x_{31} + x_{32} + x_{33} \leq 140{,}000$

or

$$\sum_{j=1}^{n} x_{ij} \leq S_i \qquad \text{for each } i \, (i = 1, 2, 3)$$

where

S_i = supply of ith green coffee available for purchase (pounds)

DEMAND

- *Café du Monde* $x_{11} + x_{21} + x_{31} \leq 140{,}000$
- *Gold Coast* $x_{12} + x_{22} + x_{32} \leq 380{,}000$
- *Standard* $x_{13} + x_{23} + x_{33} \leq 250{,}000$

or

$$\sum_{i=1}^{m} x_{ij} \leq D_j \qquad \text{for each } j \, (j = 1, 2, 3)$$

where

D_j = demand for j^{th} coffee blend (pounds)

EXAMPLE 4-6 THE DISTRICT ATTORNEY CASE-ASSIGNMENT PROBLEM

The district attorney (DA) of a major metropolitan city wishes to assign five of her deputy DAs (DDAs) to a number of important trial cases now on the court calendar. There are five different types of cases: (1) murder, (2) rape, (3) kidnapping, (4) armed robbery, and (5) burglary (all case data will be presented in this order throughout this problem). The DA realizes that some of her DDAs are better at prosecuting certain types of cases than they are at prosecuting others. Using past trial data as an empirical guide, the DA develops a probability matrix for conviction obtained by the DDAs by

case type, as shown in Table 4-7. She is also aware that, based on outstanding commitments, each DDA has a limited number of hours that can be spent in the preparation and actual courtroom prosecution of potential cases. Her staff prepares a breakdown of the total number of hours each DDA has available for the remainder of the fiscal year (Table 4-8) and also develops estimates of the average time necessary for a DDA to prepare and try a specific case type (Table 4-9). The total number of cases on the court calendar is shown in Table 4-10, with the average total trial costs per case for the DA's office shown opposite each case type. The DA realizes that the judges' availability to try the cases is also a limiting consideration. She discovers that there is a total of 7300 judge-hours available for the cases on the calendar. She asks her staff to estimate the average preparation and trial time required by a judge per case type, using empirical data from past trials (Table 4-11). The DA wishes to obtain as many convictions as possible during this fiscal year. She realizes that she clearly discriminates the *type* of conviction obtained, so she prepares a list of the case types and of their relative worth to her (Table 4-12). Further, she gives instructions to her staff regarding the minimum number of case types to be tried in order to satisfy public pressure (Table 4-13).

ASSIGNMENT

The DA's total budget for the upcoming fiscal year is $3,450,983.00. What is the optimum mix of DDA case-type assignments to make if we wish to maximize the expected worth of convictions for the DA? Use double-subscript notation and formulate this problem showing the objective function and all constraint equations. (*Hint*: Let x_{ij} be equal to the number of ith-type cases assigned to the jth DDA.)

SOLUTION

The objective function is to maximize the DA's expected worth (utility) for convictions, Z. It seems clear that the likelihood for a conviction is a relationship between the specific DDA and the case to which he or she is assigned. So, if the decision variable, x_{ij}, is defined as the number of ith-type cases ultimately assigned to the jth DDA, then the objective function coefficients must include both the probability of conviction and

TABLE 4-7

Probability of Conviction Matrix

DDA No.	Case Type				
	1	*2*	*3*	*4*	*5*
1	.8	.3	.5	.9	.3
2	.5	.5	.5	.8	.8
3	.5	.5	.6	.6	.9
4	.7	.4	.6	.9	.4
5	.3	.7	.7	.5	.8

TABLE 4-8

Prosecutor Availability

DDA No.	Time (Hours)
1	1600
2	1800
3	1900
4	1200
5	1500

TABLE 4-9

Average Trial and Preparation Time Required per Case for DDAs

Case Type	Preparation Time (Hours)	Trial Time (Hours)
1	120	120
2	40	80
3	24	40
4	60	80
5	16	16

TABLE 4-10

Total Number of Cases on Court Calendar and Average Trial Costs

Case Type	No.	Average Costs ($)
1	31	85,600
2	16	60,300
3	13	75,800
4	25	33,500
5	41	18,900

TABLE 4-11

Judge's Average per Case Trial and Preparation Time

Case Type	Preparation Time (Hours)	Trial Time (Hours)
1	20	120
2	20	80
3	4	40
4	8	80
5	2	16

TABLE 4-12

DAs Relative Worth Conviction Scores

Case Type	DAs "Worth" Score
1	100
2	90
3	60
4	50
5	10

TABLE 4-13

Minimum Number of Cases to Be Heard

Case Type	No.
1	10
2	10
3	5
4	10
5	N/A

the utility of that conviction to the DA. Consequently, using the data from Tables 4-7 and 4-12, we can develop the objective function.

OBJECTIVE FUNCTION

$$\text{Maximize } Z = 100(.8x_{11} + .5x_{12} + .5x_{13} + .7x_{14} + .3x_{15})$$
$$+ \cdots + 10(.3x_{51} + .7x_{52} + \cdots + .8x_{55})$$

or

$$\text{Maximize } Z = \sum_{i=1}^{m} \sum_{j=1}^{n} u_i p_{ij} x_{ij}$$

where

u_i = DA's utility for a conviction of the ith-type case where there are m different types of cases being tried (in this example, $m = 5$).

p_{ij} = probability of a conviction on an ith-type case assigned to the jth DDA (in this example, $n = 5$).

x_{ij} = number of ith-type case ultimately assigned to the jth DDA.

We must accomplish this goal subject to the restrictions of available resources. First, the budget constraint equation can be formed from the expense–per case-type information contained in Table 4-10 and the budget statement:

$$85,600(x_{11} + x_{12} + x_{13} + x_{14} + x_{15})$$
$$+ 60,300(x_{21} + x_{22} + x_{23} + x_{24} + x_{25})$$
$$+ \ldots + 18,900(x_{51} + x_{52} + \ldots + x_{55}) \le 3,450,983$$

or

$$\sum_{i=1}^{m} \sum_{j=1}^{n} a_i x_{ij} \le B \qquad \text{for } i = 1, 2, \ldots, m \quad \text{and} \quad j = 1, 2, \ldots, n$$

where

a_i = average trial cost of the ith type case (Table 4-8)

x_{ij} = number of ith type cases assigned to the jth DDA

B = total budget available to DA's office ($3,450,983)

The limitations regarding the amount of time that each DDA has available are found in Tables 4-8 and 4-9.

$$\begin{aligned}
DDA\ 1: \quad & 240x_{11} + 120x_{21} + 64x_{31} + 140x_{41} + 32x_{51} \le 1600 \\
DDA\ 2: \quad & 240x_{12} + 120x_{22} + 64x_{32} + 140x_{42} + 32x_{52} \le 1800
\end{aligned}$$

$$\cdot \quad \cdot \quad \cdot \quad \cdot \quad \cdot \quad \cdot \quad \cdot \quad \cdot \quad \cdot \quad \cdot \quad \cdot \quad \cdot \quad \cdot$$

$$DDA\ 5: \quad 240x_{15} + 120x_{25} + 64x_{35} + 140x_{45} + 32x_{55} \le 1500$$

or

$$\sum_{i=1}^{5} a_i x_{ij} \le b_j \qquad \text{for each } j\ (j = 1, 2, \ldots, 5)$$

where

a_i = per unit amount of time required for each DDA to try each ith-type case (the sum of the preparation and trial time given in Table 4-9)

b_j = total amount of uncommitted DDA time available (Table 4-8)

Next, the judges' times are similarly calculated from the per case-type preparation time shown in Table 4-11 and from the stated limit for total judge hours available.

$$140[x_{11} + x_{12} + x_{13} + x_{14} + x_{15}] + 100[x_{21} + x_{22} + x_{23} + x_{24} + x_{25}] + \ldots + 18[x_{51} + x_{52} + x_{53} + x_{54} + x_{55}] \leq 7300$$

or

$$\sum_{i=1}^{5} \sum_{j=1}^{5} \alpha_i x_{ij} \leq \Omega$$

where

α_i = judge time required to try i^{th}-type case (Table 4-11)

Ω = total number of judge-hours available (7300)

The availability of cases to be tried and the policy constraints (public pressure) can be dealt with individually or together using Tables 4-10 and 4-13. The policy constraints are, then,

No. murders to be tried	$x_{11} + x_{12} + x_{13} + x_{14} + x_{15} \geq 10$
No. rapes to be tried	$x_{21} + x_{22} + x_{23} + x_{24} + x_{25} \geq 10$

. . . .

No. burglaries to be tried $x_{51} + x_{52} + x_{53} + x_{54} + x_{55} \geq 0$

or

$$\sum_{j=1}^{5} x_{ij} \geq d_i \qquad \text{for each } i \, (i = 1, 2, \ldots, 5)$$

where

d_i = minimum number of ith-type cases that must be tried to satisfy public pressure (Table 4-13)

The availability constraints are (number of different cases on the court calendar):

No. murders to be tried	$x_{11} + x_{12} + x_{13} + x_{14} + x_{15} \leq 31$
No. rapes to be tried	$x_{21} + x_{22} + x_{23} + x_{24} + x_{25} \leq 16$

. . . .

No. burglaries to be tried $x_{51} + x_{52} + x_{53} + x_{54} + x_{55} \leq 41$

or

$$\sum_{j=1}^{5} x_{ij} \leq \Delta_i \qquad \text{for each } i \, (i = 1, 2, \ldots, 5)$$

where

$$\Delta_i = \text{maximum number of } i^{\text{th}}\text{-type cases that can be tried as limited by availability (Table 4-10)}$$

It sometimes is easier to state common constraints—such as these last two constraint sets—together (although they usually must be separated for computer input). That is,

$$10 \leq x_{11} + x_{12} + x_{13} + x_{14} + x_{15} \leq 31$$
$$10 \leq x_{21} + x_{22} + x_{23} + x_{24} + x_{25} \leq 16$$
$$5 \leq x_{31} + x_{32} + x_{33} + x_{34} + x_{35} \leq 13$$
$$10 \leq x_{41} + x_{42} + x_{43} + x_{44} + x_{45} \leq 25$$
$$0 \leq x_{51} + x_{52} + x_{53} + x_{54} + x_{55} \leq 41$$

$$d_i \leq \sum_{j=1}^{5} x_{ij} \leq \Delta_i \qquad \text{for each } i \, (i = 1, 2, \ldots, 5)$$

EXAMPLE 4-7 THE OAKLAND SCHOOL DISTRICT DESEGREGATION PROBLEM

There have been numerous journal articles describing how linear programming has been used to help school districts comply with federal desegregation laws (e.g., Stimson, et al., 1974). A comparatively simple illustration of how LP problem formulation can be employed to achieve racially balanced school populations is presented next.

We shall pretend that one of the many subdistricts in the Oakland Community School District covers three high schools in five neighborhood areas (Figure 4-1). The capacities of each of its three high schools are shown in Table 4-14. The five neighborhoods have very different ethnic mixes (described as minority and nonminority proportions), as shown in Table 4-15. The average distance to each of the three high schools, from the approximate center of each neighborhood, is shown in Table 4-16. A court-ordered desegregation plan has specified that each high school cannot exceed the maximum nor fall below the minimum minority enrollment proportions, as shown in Table 4-17. In addition, no student may be bused more than 10 miles or longer than 25 minutes for a one-way trip (Tables 4-16 and 4-18).

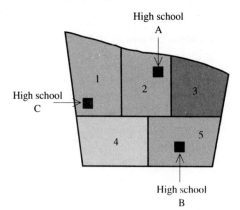

TABLE 4-14

High School Capacities

School	Capacity
A	1000
B	1800
C	1600

TABLE 4-15

Neighborhood and Student Ethnic Mix

Neighborhood	Minority	Nonminority	Totals
1	50	450	500
2	300	500	800
3	870	30	900
4	200	600	800
5	600	400	1000
TOTALS	2020	1980	4000

TABLE 4-16

Average Distance Between Each Neighborhood and High School (Miles)

	Neighborhood				
School	*1*	*2*	*3*	*4*	*5*
A	8	0	4	10	7
B	14	6	8	6	1
C	3	9	15	7	13

TABLE 4-18

Average One-Way Travel Time Between Neighborhoods and Schools (Minutes)

	Neighborhood				
School	*1*	*2*	*3*	*4*	*5*
A	20	0	10	28	18
B	35	15	20	15	3
C	8	26	38	18	32

TABLE 4-17

High School Minority Proportions

	Minority Proportions	
School	*Minimum*	*Maximum*
A	25	55
B	50	70
C	15	30

All students from each neighborhood must be assigned to a high school. Devise a busing plan that will meet these desegregation requirements while minimizing the total number of miles over which students are bused (one way) to school.

SOLUTION

The decision variable for this problem must relate several important characteristics, because we are not merely interested in transporting students to schools. More specifically, we have to know what kind of students (minority or nonminority), from where they are being bused (neighborhood), and to where they are going (to which school they are assigned). So there are three essential properties that we need to identify for each student. The decision variable for such a problem must, therefore, have three subscripts. So, let x_{ijk} represent the number of students residing in the ith neighborhood who are assigned and bused to the jth high school and who are of the kth ethnicity.[5] Now let's use this important information in the problem formulation. The objective function is to minimize the number of one-way student-bused miles:

OBJECTIVE FUNCTION

Minimize one-way student mileage, $Z = 8(x_{111} + x_{112}) + 14(x_{121} + x_{122})$
$$+ 3(x_{131} + x_{132}) + \cdots + 13(x_{531} + x_{532})$$

or

$$\text{Minimize } Z = \sum_{i=1}^{5} \sum_{j=1}^{3} \sum_{k=1}^{2} d_{ij} x_{ijk}$$

[5]The assignment of i, j, and k is usually arbitrary. For the Oakland School example, any arrangement would have been acceptable (e.g., x_{ijk} = number of ith ethnicity students living in jth neighborhood assigned to kth high school, or number of students assigned to ith high school of jth ethnicity living in kth neighborhood).

where

x_{ijk} = number of kth ethnicity students residing in i^{th} neighborhood who are assigned and bused to j^{th} high school.

d_{ij} = number of miles between the ith neighborhood and the jth high school.

The constraint equations are as follows.

SUBJECT TO

■ *Student Assignments*

$$x_{111} + x_{121} + x_{131} = 50$$
$$x_{211} + x_{221} + x_{231} = 300$$

} *minority students*

$$\cdot \quad \cdot \quad \cdot \quad \cdot \quad \cdot \quad \cdot \quad \cdot$$

$$x_{511} + x_{521} + x_{531} = 600$$

$$x_{112} + x_{122} + x_{132} = 450$$
$$x_{212} + x_{222} + x_{232} = 500$$

} *nonminority students*

$$\cdot \quad \cdot \quad \cdot \quad \cdot \quad \cdot \quad \cdot \quad \cdot \quad \cdot$$

$$x_{512} + x_{522} + x_{532} = 400$$

or

$$\sum_{j=1}^{3} x_{ij1} = \chi_{i1} \quad \text{for each } i \, (i = 1, 2, \ldots, 5)$$

$$\sum_{j=1}^{3} x_{ij2} = \chi_{i2} \quad \text{for each } i \, (i = 1, 2, \ldots, 5)$$

where

χ_{i1} = total number of minority students residing in i^{th} neighborhood

χ_{i2} = total number of nonminority students residing in i^{th} neighborhood

■ *School Capacity*

High School A $\quad x_{111} + x_{112} + x_{211} + x_{212} + \cdots + x_{512} \leq 1000$

High School B $\quad x_{121} + x_{122} + x_{221} + x_{222} + \cdots + x_{522} \leq 1800$

High School C $\quad x_{131} + x_{132} + x_{231} + x_{232} + \cdots + x_{532} \leq 1600$

or

$$\sum_{i=1}^{5} \sum_{k=1}^{2} x_{ij1} \leq C_j \quad \text{for each } j \, (j = 1, 2, 3)$$

where

C_j = total capacity of the jth high school

■ Ethnic Balance

High School A

$$.55 \geq \frac{x_{111} + x_{211} + x_{311} + x_{411} + x_{511}}{x_{111} + x_{112} + x_{211} + x_{212} + \cdots + x_{512}} \geq .25$$

or, breaking this relationship into two separate equations and reducing,

$$.75x_{111} - .25x_{112} + .75x_{211} - .25x_{212} + \cdots + .75x_{511} - .25x_{512} \geq 0$$

and

$$.45x_{111} - .55x_{112} + .45x_{211} - .55x_{212} + \cdots + .45x_{511} - .55x_{512} \leq 0$$

Performing the same operations for the remaining two schools, we obtain results for the other two schools.

High School B

$$.50x_{121} - .50x_{122} + .50x_{221} - .50x_{222} + \cdots + .50x_{521} - .50x_{522} \geq 0$$

and

$$.30x_{121} - .70x_{122} + .30x_{221} - .70x_{222} + \cdots + .30x_{521} - .70x_{522} \leq 0$$

High School C

$$.85x_{131} - .15x_{132} + .85x_{231} - .15x_{232} + \cdots + .70x_{531} - .30x_{532} \geq 0$$

and

$$.70x_{131} - .30x_{132} + .70x_{231} - .30x_{232} + \cdots + .70x_{531} - .30x_{532} \leq 0$$

The summation notation for the lower limit of this constraint is

$$\sum_{i=1}^{5} x_{ij1} - [\Pi_j]_{\min} \sum_{i=1}^{5} \sum_{k=1}^{2} x_{ijk} \geq 0 \qquad \text{for each } j \, (j = 1, 2, 3)$$

and the upper-limit bound is

$$\sum_{i=1}^{5} x_{ij1} - [\Pi_j]_{\max} \sum_{i=1}^{5} \sum_{k=1}^{2} x_{ijk} \leq 0 \qquad \text{for each } j \, (j = 1, 2, 3)$$

where

$[\pi_j]_{\max} =$ upper minority proportion
$[\pi_j]_{\min} =$ lower minority proportion

DISTANCE

$$x_{121}, x_{122}, x_{331}, x_{332}, x_{531}, x_{532} = 0$$

for

$$d_{ij} - 10 \geq 0 \qquad \text{for all } i \text{ and } j$$

where

$d_{ij} =$ one-way distance (in miles) between i^{th} neighborhood and j^{th} high school

$$x_{121}, x_{122}, x_{231}, x_{232}, x_{331}, x_{332}, x_{431}, x_{411}, x_{531}, x_{412} = 0$$

for

$$t_{ij} - 25 \geqslant 0 \qquad \text{for all } i \text{ and } j$$

where

$t_{ij} =$ one-way travel time (in minutes) between the ith neighborhood and the jth high school

4.6 MICROCOMPUTER SOFTWARE FOR LINEAR PROGRAMMING

There is a huge selection of different linear-programming software packages available for the microcomputer. Among the small sampling listed here are packages that specialize solely in LP (e.g., *LP83*, *FLP*, *LP88*, *LINDO/PC*, *LP/80*, *ALPAL* and *Big ALPAL*, and *What's Best*) and other packages that include a few to over a dozen other software modules in addition to the LP module (e.g., *Microsolve*, *The Confidence Factor*, *Quantitative Systems for Business*, and *Storm*).

1. *ALPAL*. Santa Barbara, CA: Kinko's Academic Courseware Exchange.
2. *Big ALPAL*. Santa Barbara, CA: Kinko's Academic Courseware Exchange.
3. *The Confidence Factor*. Irvine, CA: Simple Software.
4. *FLP*. Annapolis, MD: Bid & Awards.
5. *LINDO/PC*. Palo Alto, CA: Scientific Press.
6. *LP88*. Alexandria, VA: Eastern Software Products.
7. *LP83*. San Marino, CA: Sunset Software.
8. *LP/80*. Austin, TX: Decision Science Software.
9. *Microsolve*. Oakland, CA: Holden-Day.
10. *Quantitative Systems for Business*. Englewood Cliffs, NJ: Prentice-Hall, 1988.
11. *Storm*. Oakland, CA: Holden-Day.
12. *What's Best*. Oakland, CA: Holden-Day.

4.7 MICROCOMPUTER SOFTWARE SOLUTIONS TO LINEAR PROGRAMMING PROBLEMS

As we mentioned, there is a wide selection of microcomputer linear programming software that can solve the problem formulations on which we have concentrated in this chapter. The particular software package that we shall use to illustrate the data entry for and solution to a problem is *Quantitative Systems for Business* (*QSB*, Chang and Sullivan, 1988, Version 3.0). Let's use *QSB* to determine the optimum mix of automobiles for the German car dealer study (Example 4-3). The spreadsheet data-entry format used in *QSB* is illustrated in Table 4-19. Look how nearly identical the data entry is to the way in which we formulated the problem in Section 4.4. The only nonsubstantive difference is that you never use commas when entering numbers on the computer. Also,

TABLE 4-19

Spreadsheet Data Entry for German Car Dealer
Example Using QSB Linear Programming Module

```
                    Input Data of The Problem GERMAN CAR      Page   1

  Max   +9000.00X1   +6000.00X2   +12500.0X3
  Subject to
  (1)   +120.000X1   +115.000X2   +148.000X3   ≤ +5000.00
  (2)   +27000.0X1   +20000.0X2   +32500.0X3   ≤  +800000
  (3)   +1.00000X1   +.000000X2   +.000000X3   ≤ +25.0000
  (4)   +.000000X1   +1.00000X2   +.000000X3   ≤ +35.0000
  (5)   +.000000X1   +.000000X2   +1.00000X3   ≤ +8.00000
  (6)   +.000000X1   +.000000X2   +1.00000X3   ≤ +6.00000
  (7)   +1.00000X1   +.000000X2   +.000000X3   ≥ +12.0000
  (8)   +.000000X1   +1.00000X2   +.000000X3   ≥ +12.0000
  (9)   +.000000X1   +.000000X2   +1.00000X3   ≥ +6.00000
  (10)  +28.0000X1   +22.0000X2   +30.0000X3   ≤ +1100.00
```

although it doesn't occur in this problem, large numbers may be entered in exponential form (e.g., the number 345,000,000 can be entered as 3.45E8—the E8 means that you move the present decimal point in the 3.45 eight places to the right for the whole number).

The solution to this problem is shown in Table 4-20. The optimal mix for the three decision variables can be seen in the column "Variables, Names" for X1, X2, and X3, and the adjacent values appear in the "Solution" column. The optimal mix of cars for the example is (viewing the fractional values as a monthly average) about 13.5 Porsches, 12 BMWs, and 6 Mercedes. The objective function value, seen on the bottom line of the table, suggests that this optimal mix will provide the dealer with a gross profit of $268,667 per month. There is much more information contained in the printout. However, because these other important details require significant preparation and explanation, we'll defer examining them until later chapters.

TABLE 4-20

Solution to the German Car Dealer Example Using QSB Linear Programming Module

```
                    Summarized Results for GERMAN CAR      Page : 1
```

Variables No. Names	Solution	Opportunity Cost	Variables No. Names	Solution	Opportunity Cost
1 X1	+13.518518	0	9 S6	0	+1666.6666
2 X2	+12.000000	0	10 S7	+1.5185188	0
3 X3	+6.0000000	0	11 A7	0	0
4 S1	+1109.7776	0	12 S8	0	+666.66650
5 S2	0	+.33333334	13 A8	0	−666.66650
6 S3	+11.481482	0	14 S9	0	0
7 S4	+23.000000	0	15 A9	0	0
8 S5	+2.0000000	0	16 S10	+277.48145	0

```
              Maximum value of the OBJ = 268666.7   Iters. = 4
```

4.8 | SUMMARY

The first step in solving linear programming problems is to formulate the analytical statements that "breathe life" into the problem. This process can be viewed as more of an art than a technical skill: proficiency comes only with considerable practice. Even when the problem is formulated accurately, the complexities of the equations that constitute the objective function and resource constraints *defy* manual solution. So, in real life, we must input these formulations on the computer and determine the solution—the optimum mix of goods or services—to our problem (up to this point, we have no idea what the actual answers are!). However, an intermediate operation must be examined before the formulation is solved by a computer. This operation requires that you understand conceptually the mathematical solution process used by the computer called the *simplex method*. This important step will allow you to understand and interpret the computer solution output. In the next chapter, we will quickly develop an overview and sound comprehension of this powerful solution process through the use of simplified algorithms and pictorial examples.

4.9 | EXERCISES

4-1 Years ago, when the German car dealer (Example 4-3) first began his business, he carried only two types of automobiles: Porsche and BMW. Assume that each Porsche and BMW costs the dealer an average of $17,000 and $12,000, respectively (this problem will always refer to these two autos in the same order) and that the average sales price for each car is $23,000 and $16,000. The maximum number of units available from the distributors to the dealer each month is 10 and 20, respectively. The distributors also have a minimum-purchase policy that requires the dealer always to buy three Porsches and three BMWs at the beginning of each month if he wishes to retain his dealership. The monthly budget for the car purchases is $225,000. The amount of showroom floor space each type of auto occupies is 108 and 106 square feet. There is a total of 1400 square feet of floor space available. Finally, the average number of salesperson hours resulting in a sale of a vehicle is 30 and 20. The agency has a total of 300 salesperson hours per month allocated for showroom sales.

ASSIGNMENT

Formulate this problem so that the dealer can determine the optimal number of units of each type of automobile to purchase each month so that he can maximize his profits (assume that he can sell every car he purchases each month, so there is no carryover inventory).

4-2 Accurate finance, production, and operation figures are a closely guarded secret in any competitive industry. Personal computer manufacturers, in particular, do not release such data. Let's suppose, for the sake of conjecture, that we have access to Apple Computers' figures. Further, let's imagine the following scenario: John Sculley, chief executive officer (CEO) of Apple Computers, would like to generate as much profit as possible for his Cupertino, California, company. His biggest money makers at this time are the Macintosh II and the Macintosh SE (always given in this order). The company has set aside a $280-million budget and 2 million labor hours for production and assembly of these two computer models. A brief description of these two products is provided in Table 4-2.1. Sculley would like to determine the optimal mix of these two models that will provide him with the maximum profit possible. Formulate the LP model for this problem given the following information:

1. The unit production costs associated with each unit is $1500 and $800.
2. The projected demand over the next year for each product is 100,000 and 200,000 units.

TABLE 4-2.1

Product Description of Macintosh Lines

Product	Description
Macintosh II	1- to 8-megabyte RAM; color graphics capability; Motorola 68020 microprocessor chip with 68881 math coprocessor. Suggested dealer price of $3500.
Macintosh SE	One floppy-disk 800-kilobyte double-sided drive plus 20-megabyte internal hard disk; Motorola 68000 microprocessor chip. Suggested dealer price of $2200.

---

3. The unit production and assembly labor hours required is 10 and 8 hours.

(*Hint*: Let x_i = number of ith model Macintosh units manufactured (and sold).

4-3 Suppose that the investment firm of Merrill, Lynch, Pierce, Fenner, and Smith (MLPF&S) has been asked by an important client to investigate the best way to distribute $8,750,000 available for investment. In particular, the client has informed MLPF&S that only four investment options are to be considered: (1) IBM, (2) Phillips Oil, (3) Tiffany Diamond Mines, and (4) New Zealand Real Estate. More specifically, the investor wants neither to exceed an average risk of 19 percent, nor to commit beyond an average investment duration of 3.75 years. Finally, he wants at least 60 percent of his total investment dollars to be in the combination of stocks and oil, but no less than 10 percent of the total investment to be invested in each of the four options.

Merrill, Lynch, Pierce, Fenner, & Smith & Mick Jagger.

ASSIGNMENT

Using the hypothetical information shown in Table 4-3.1, what is the exact amount of money he should invest in each option so that the maximum annual return (in dollars) is realized? (*Hint*: Formulate the problem using x_i = total amount of dollars invested in the ith option.)

4-4 A St. Paul, Minnesota, land developer wishes to build three different types of housing units in a particular tract. These include (1) single-family, four-bedroom homes selling for $185,000, (2) single-family, three-bedroom homes selling for $135,000, and (3) two-bedroom condominiums selling for $80,000. The amounts of land, developer's building costs, construction time, and estimated minimum customer demands per housing unit are shown in Table 4-4.1. The developer has a total budget of $15,800,000, 1.35 million square feet of land on which to build, and 233,000 hours of construction time available. There is also a city planning department requirement that at least 15 percent of the housing units that are built be the two-bedroom condominiums.

ASSIGNMENT

With these limitations in mind, what is the best mix of housing units for the developer to build if we assume that demand is great enough to ensure that all units can be sold?

4-5 Imagine that Trans World Airlines (TWA) would like to promote a new travel offer being made for flights between Los Angeles and New York City over the next month. The different

TABLE 4-3.1

MLPF&S Investment-Portfolio Data

Investment, x_i	Annual Return (%)	Risk (%)	Average Terms (Years)
IBM, x_1	12	8	1
Phillips Oil, x_2	17	15	3
Tiffany Diamond Mines, x_3	24	21	5
New Zealand Real Estate, x_4	28	20	4

TABLE 4-4.1

St. Paul Land Developer Data

Housing Type	Land Area (ft^2)	Building Cost ($)	Construction Time (Hours)	Customer Demand (No. Housing Units)
4 BR	10,000	115,000	950	120
3 BR	7,000	90,000	900	180
2 BR	4,000	65,000	600	60

TABLE 4-5.1

TWA Advertising Campaign Media Outlet Data

Media Outlet	Cost per Exposure	Number of Exposures Available	Number of Exposures Available
"Tonight Show"	$180,000/min.	21,400,000	24
"60 Minutes"	$100,000/min.	11,850,000	10
Newsweek	$75,000/pg.	6,875,000	36
NY Times	$4,500/pg.	4,180,000	60
LA Times	$3,000/pg.	2,490,000	85

media outlets that their advertising agency is considering using are

- The Tonight Show (NBC-TV)
- 60 Minutes (CBS-TV)
- *Newsweek* Magazine
- The *New York Times* Sunday Edition
- The *Los Angeles Times* Sunday Edition

The ad agency knows that the costs for advertising vary greatly among the different media outlets, as does the number of potential travelers that each outlet will reach. There are also different numbers of exposure slots available for each of these media outlets. For the purposes of this exercise, assume that the data shown in Table 4-5.1 are correct. TWA wants as many people as possible to see this month-long ad campaign, but does not want to exceed its $4,750,000 advertising budget (the agency fees are paid out of a separate accoount). Further assume that it does not want more than 50 percent of the expendi-

tures associated with the Tonight Show, or less than 10 percent of all expenditures allocated to the two newspapers.

ASSIGNMENT

You have just been appointed head of the advertising agency. How would you formulate the problem? What is your objective? What are the resource constraints?

4-6 Let's assume now that the initial focus of balancing the product mix for the Macintosh SE and Macintosh II models is no longer sufficient for the CEO of Apple Computers, John Sculley (refer to Exercise 4-2). Instead, Mr. Sculley wants a more comprehensive product-mix study—one that takes into account all four of the microcomputer lines: (1) Macintosh II, (2) Macintosh SE, (3) Macintosh Plus, and (4) the Apple IIGS. Assume that the average revenue generated from each of these models, the present fiscal-year sales-forecast estimates, and the production and assembly times required to produce each unit are accurately portrayed by the data provided in Table 4-6.1.

Assume the following scenario: The total production and assembly costs associated with each model is (in order of their original presentation in this case) $1500, $800, $700, and $400, respectively. The total production and assembly time available for this year is 4,392,600 hours. Mr. Sculley wants to make sure that the optimum mix of computer models is selected, but he has a few policy restrictions that must be observed. First, there must be at least some of each unit manufactured; he believes that to "cancel out" one (or more) of the lines simply because the line is not as productive as other models will create enough ill-will among those Apple customers who have already purchased units (as well as generate enough of a detrimental image with potential new buyers) to offset any enhancement of revenues. Therefore, at least 10,000 of each model type must be produced. Next, Sculley wants the number of Macintosh II and Macintosh SE to comprise at least 65 percent of the total of all units produced for this fiscal year. Also, Sculley wants no more than 10 percent of the total number of production hours used to generate all units finally manufactured to be allocated to the Apple IIGS line. Assume that Apple's total production and assembly budget is $345 million.

TABLE 4-6.1

Sales, Assembly, and Production Data for Apple Computers

Model	Average Revenue ($/Unit)	Expected Sales (No. of Units)	Production and Assembly Time (Hours/ Unit)
Macintosh II	3500	100,000	10
Macintosh SE	2000	200,000	8
Macintosh Plus	1200	50,000	8
Apple IIGS	700	150,000	4

ASSIGNMENT

Formulate this problem, showing the objective function and all constraint equations.

4-7 It has been a few years since the German car dealer started his business (Example 4-3). The dealership has continued to grow. It still specializes in selling three types of foreign cars: Porsche, BMW, and Mercedes Benz. Each Porsche, BMW, and Mercedes now costs the agency an average of $31,000, $25,000, and $39,000, respectively (this problem will always refer to these three autos in the same order), and the average sales price for each car is now $40,000, $31,000, and $51,000. The maximum number of cars available from the distributors to the agency each month is now 14, 15, and 10, respectively. The distributors also have minimum-purchase policies that require the dealer to buy at least 12 Porsches, 12 BMWs, and 4 Mercedes at the beginning of each month if he wishes to retain his dealership. The monthly budget for the new car purchases has grown to $1 million. The average number of salesperson hours expended in selling each auto is 28, 20, and 26. The amount of showroom floor space each type of auto consumes is 120, 115, and 148 square feet. There is a total of 6000 square feet of storage and showroom floor space available in the expanded facility. Finally, there are 1500 salesperson hours dedicated each month to be spent on car sales.

ASSIGNMENT

Formulate this problem so that the dealer can determine the optimal number of units of each type of automobile to purchase each month so that he can maximize his profits (assume he can sell every car he purchases each month, so there is no carryover inventory).

4-8 A neighborhood health center (NHC) offers ambulatory-care treatment for four types of complaints: (1) hypertension, (2) sickle-cell anemia, (3) alcohol or other drug addiction, and (4) prenatal care. It wants to provide complete treatment programs to as many patients as possible within certain operating limitations for the following year. These programs include physician's time, treatment costs, minimum patient load requirements (per funding-agency contract stipulations), and maximum patient load potential (as suggested by neighborhood population estimates). In addition, it is known from previous work that only a fraction of the patients will stay in their specific treatment program until completion. A summary of these data is shown in Table 4-8.1.

The total annual budget for the NHC is $885,495, and the total amount of physicians' time available is 19,400 hours. Further, funding-agency policy dictates that the combined costs of the hypertension and alcohol/drug addiction components cannot exceed more than 60 percent of the total monies expended; the expenditures on sickle-cell anemia treatments must be at least 15 percent of all monies spent; and prenatal care cannot use more than 20 percent of the total amount of physicians' time allocated. What is the optimum mix of treatment programs to provide?

4-9 Once again, let us imagine the following hypothetical situation: John Sculley, the company's CEO, has spent considerable time rethinking Apple Computers' production and assembly problem. He feels uneasy about the results obtained in Exercise 4-6. In particular, he is uncomfortable about now having a sense of how much of each model should be manufactured *over time*. That is, the solution gives him only the *total* numbers of model types to generate during the year, but no sense of *schedule*. Without any feel for how the manufacturing should be "timed," Sculley is worried about likely inventory problems: (1) lost sales from stockouts occurring when demand is high and inventory is low, and (2) large storage costs arising when inventory levels are high and demand is low (although inventory costs are not part of this problem). Sculley is convinced that the earlier problem formulation must be refined; he wants production scheduled by quarters. The distributions of projected sales and labor hours available for the year are shown in Tables 4-9.1 and 4-9.2. All other resource data and operating constraints are the same as in Exercise 4-6 (notice that even the labor hours and expected sales figures are the same).

ASSIGNMENT

1. Formulate this problem, showing the objective function and all constraint equations, so that it is possible to determine the optimum production schedule for each of the four Apple models. (*Hint*: Let x_{ij} be the number of ith model computers produced and sold in the jth quarter.)

2. What happens to your formulation if it is not possible to assume that the models can be sold instantaneously? Express this effect in terms of a new decision variable.

4-10 Suppose that the neighborhood health center in Exercise 4-8 needs to assess 3 years of operation, instead of a single year. Data breakdowns similar to those shown in Exercise 4-8 would have to be provided for each of the 3 years. If we had the same goal—that of maximizing the total number of completed treatments—and the same kinds of constraints (with budget and physician time breakdowns by year), then the data might look like those shown in Table 4-10.1. Reformulate the problem so that it is possible to find not only the total number of specific treatment programs that are provided but also *when* they are provided. (*Hint*: Use multiple-subscript notation.)

4-11 Bert Tuna Company has five regional warehouses in Oakland, Dallas, Chicago, Memphis, and Buffalo, and four primary distribution centers in Denver, Atlanta, Detroit, and Trenton. The company is spending a small fortune on trucking their warehouse goods to the various distribution centers, which, in turn, supply the markets with the retail goods. Bert Tuna Company managers want to reexamine their routing assignments. In particular, they wish to assess which warehouses have responsibility for supplying the particular distribution center with goods.

The average per-ton trucking costs associated with the transfer of goods between each of the five warehouses and the four distribution centers are shown in Table 4-11.1. Also included

TABLE 4-8.1

Neighborhood Health Center Resource Limits

Illness Type	Average Treatment Costs ($)	Average Physician's Time (Hours)	Probability of Complete Treatment	Potential Treatment Population (1000)
Hypertension	360	6	.60	1460
Sickle-cell anemia	1480	25	.85	835
Alcohol or other drug addiction	125	12	.30	2900
Prenatal care	250	14	.90	1760

TABLE 4-9.1

Quarterly Sales Forecast for Apple Computers

Model No.	Expected Sales by Quarter			
	1	*2*	*3*	*4*
Macintosh II	25,000	17,000	20,000	38,000
Macintosh SE	70,000	40,000	50,000	90,000
Macintosh Plus	12,500	12,500	12,500	12,500
Apple IIGS	42,000	18,000	30,000	60,000

TABLE 4-9.2

Per-Quarter Production and Assembly Hours Available for Apple Computers

Quarter	Labor Hours
1	1,350,800
2	874,600
3	967,200
4	1,200,000

TABLE 4-10.1

Neighborhood Health Center 3-Year Resource Allocations

Year	Annual Budget ($)	Physician's Time (Hours)
1	885,495	19,400
2	518,594	13,065
3	756,480	16,850

This pretty much confirms all the talk about slipping morale down at the Bert Tuna Co.

in this table are the warehouse supply capacities and the distribution center regional demands.

ASSIGNMENT

Given that management policy dictates that no shipments may be made between the Oakland warehouse and the Trenton distribution center, what are the optimum routing assignments between warehouses and distribution centers that will result in the minimum transportation costs? Formulate the problem showing all constraint equations and the objective function.

4-12 A genetic-engineering company located in Brisbane, California, has been so successful in the marketing of one of its patents that it has decided to open an office in New York City to manage the distribution and sales of its product. It is faced with the task of filling a number of technical and administrative positions. In particular, the personnel department staff know it will cost them approximately $1000 to recruit an employee for each administrative position, and $1500 to recruit an employee for each technical position, on the average. Further, because of labor-market shortages in both categories, the costs for recruit-

TABLE 4-12.1

Recruitment Costs for Minority and Nonminority Men and Women by Type of Position

Classification	Average Recruitment Costs/Position	
	Administrative	Technical
Nonminority men	$1000	$1500
Nonminority women	$1250	$1800
Minority men	$1400	$2100
Minority women	$1700	$2600

ing minority group members and women are even greater than these average baseline figures. The average costs for hiring people in these various personnel categories are shown in Table 4-12.1. The company has specific operating requirements that it must observe:

1. No more than 55 percent of the new hires should be men.
2. At least 35 percent of all recruitment monies ultimately spent should be for minority new hires.
3. Minorities should make up at least 35 percent of all new hires.
4. At least three minority women should be selected for the technical positions.
5. At least two minority men should be selected for the technical positions.
6. The recruiting budget for the entire operation is $100,000.

ASSIGNMENT

The company desires to hire the maximum number of new people possible. Formulate this problem for computer solution. Let x_{ijk} denote the number of people hired of ith ethnicity ($i = 1$, minority, and $i = 2$, nonminority); jth gender ($j = 1$, female, and $j = 2$, male); and kth position ($k = 1$, administrative, and $k = 2$, technical).

4-13 Tire manufacturers represent one of the industries that must be particularly concerned about production scheduling. The dramatic fluctuation in regional demand due to changes in seasonal driving conditions makes the need for a carefully planned production schedule crucial. Imagine, as an example,

TABLE 4-11.1

Trucking Costs and Supply–Demand Capacities of the Bert Tuna Company Distribution Network

Warehouses	Distribution Centers				Supply
	Denver	Atlanta	Detroit	Trenton	
Oakland	$ 35	$ 50	$ 55	$ 60	60,000
Dallas	20	25	35	50	40,000
Chicago	25	45	15	20	50,000
Memphis	50	15	45	40	25,000
Buffalo	55	45	25	10	25,000
DEMAND (tons)	35,000	45,000	40,000	80,000	200,000

TABLE 4-13.1

Michelin Tire Company Contracted Sales Figures by Month of Delivery and by Type of Tire

| Month | Type of Tire | | | |
	Economy Nylon	Medium Rayon	Premium Steel	High-Speed Steel
January	8,000	19,000	4,000	7,000
February	7,000	19,000	15,000	7,000
March	6,000	18,000	17,000	7,000

TABLE 4-13.2

Michelin Tire Company Monthly Production Hours Available by Shift and by Month of Manufacture

| Month | Shift | |
	Day	Night
January	110,000	100,000
February	130,000	120,000
March	115,000	116,000

the following hypothetical scenario regarding the Michelin Tire Company. It produces four specialty tires for its sports car line: (1) the economy nylon radial, (2) the medium-priced rayon radial, (3) the premium steel-belted radial, and (4) the top-of-the-line high-speed steel-belted radial. The competition between Michelin and its rivals (PIrelli, Dunlop, etc.) has become much keener in the last several years and, accordingly, Michelin is very concerned about not over- or underproducing its product. In particular, Michelin must determine the number of each type of tire to produce for the first quarter (January–March) of the next calendar year.

Since it has two shifts that have different hourly salary costs, Michelin must determine the best distribution of production between these shifts. Further, it is under contract to deliver specified amounts of specific tire types for each of the 3 months of the quarter being analyzed.

The sales units for delivery for the four types of tires for each of the 3 months of the quarter are shown in Table 4-13.1. The production capacities, in hours, for each of the two shifts over this 3-month period are shown in Table 4-13.2.

Note that the time to produce each tire may vary. In fact, it takes, 4, 5, 5, and 7 hours to produce each unit of economy, medium, premium, and top premium tire, respectively. The labor costs of production for the day and night shifts are $15 and $18 per hour, respectively. Furthermore, the company pays an additional $4 per tire per month to store any tire that is not delivered in the same month it is manufactured (regardless of tire type).

ASSIGNMENT

1. Formulate this problem so that Michelin can determine what optimal production schedule will minimize the system costs during this quarter.

2. What additional information must you add to the formulation if Michelin managers insist that storage costs cannot exceed 12 percent of the total system costs?

4-14 As a continuation of the hypothetical situation in Example 4-1, suppose that the Coca-Cola Bottling Company produces four soft drinks for the cola market: (1) Classic Coke, (2) New Coke, (3) Diet Coke, and (4) Cherry Coke. Nationally, and in California in particular, competition between Coca-Cola and its rivals (Pepsi-Cola, Royal Crown Cola, etc.) has become much keener over the last several years. Accordingly, Coca-Cola has its own inhouse management science department to help determine the best production strategy. In particular, Coca-Cola must determine the quantity of each type of cola to produce for the first quarter of the year (January–March) for its California operations.

Coca-Cola has three California bottling plants (in San Francisco, Los Angeles, and San Diego). Even though the employee salary structures are almost identical, these bottling plants have different operating costs due to the property-value differentials associated with each site. So, even though the labor cost to produce the different Cokes is the same, there are different profit margins associated with producing the Coke products at each site due to variations in the principle, interest, and tax structure. The forecast sales units for the four colas for each of the 3 months of the quarter are shown in Table 4-14.1.

The company must pay $.20 per gallon per month to store any soft drink that is not delivered in the same month it is manufactured, regardless of cola type or bottling-plant location. The average production cost is $2.50 per gallon, irrespective of Coke type or site (this value does *not* take storage costs into consideration). The profit generated per gallon for each type of Coke is given in Table 4-14.2, along with the production operating budgets (in millions of dollars) for each bottling plant. The production capacities for each of the three plants over this 3-month period are shown in Table 4-14.3.

ASSIGNMENT

Coca-Cola wishes to determine the exact production schedule to use that will maximize gross profits during the first quarter. Using the decision variable notation format of $x_{ijkl} = i^{th}$ plant's production level (gallons) of jth type coke during k^{th} month of production for sale in l^{th} month, *formulate* the answers to the following seven questions (do not use any calculations):

TABLE 4-14.1

Coca-Cola Forecast Sales Figures (1000 gallons) by Month of Delivery and by Cola Type

	Forecast Sales (1000 gallons)			
Month	*Classic Coke*	*New Coke*	*Diet Coke*	*Cherry Coke*
January	800	900	2000	2000
February	1300	900	2000	7000
March	2000	1300	2600	8000

TABLE 4-14.2

Per Gallon Profit Margin ($/gallon) by Type of Cola and by Bottling Plant Location

	Location		
Type of Coke	*SF*	*LA*	*SD*
Classic Coke	1.18	1.21	1.25
New Coke	1.24	1.25	1.41
Diet Coke	.91	1.22	1.38
Cherry Coke	1.01	1.04	1.08
OPERATING BUDGET (10^6)	12.85	17.50	10.00

TABLE 4-14.3

Monthly Production Available (1000 gallons) by Month of Manufacture for California Coca-Cola Bottling Plants

	Location		
Month	*SF*	*LA*	*SD*
January	1500	2100	1000
February	1750	1800	900
March	2200	2050	950

1. How much profit does the San Francisco plant make in the production of New Coke over the quarter?

2. How many gallons of Diet Coke will be produced in the San Diego plant during February?

3. How much of the Los Angeles bottling site budget is consumed in the production of the four-product mix during the quarter?

4. How many gallons of the four different Coke types are bottled by the San Francisco plant during the month of March (include the RHS information)?

5. If Coca-Cola said, "No Cherry Coke can be produced in San Francisco during the month of January," how would you write this (these) policy constraint(s)?

6. Write the constraint(s) that represent(s) the production quantity required to meet demand (forecast sales) for New Coke during the month of January.

7. How would you, as the manager formulating the policy constraint in question 5, suggest that that constraint be used in the objective function?

4-15 For the purpose of illustration only, suppose that a county supervisor is trying to determine the optimal way to provide emergency ambulance services to three of the lowest income regions in Los Angeles: (1) southeast LA (Compton, Watts, Willowbrook, etc.), central LA (downtown business district), and northeast LA (Boyle Heights, Silverlake, etc.). Also, let's assume that there are three ambulance services available: (1) Schaefer, (2) Goodhew, and (3) Medevac. Further, assume that there are three hospitals that can provide emergency service: (1) Martin Luther King (MLK); (2) University of Southern California County General (USCCG); and

TABLE 4-15.1

Hospital Emergency Facility Capacities

Hospital	No. Patients/Day
MLK	75
USCCG	175
DF	35

TABLE 4-15.2

Average Response Times (minutes) by Ambulance, Region, and Hospital

		Hospital		
Ambulance Company	Region	*MLK*	*USCCG*	*DF*
Schaefer	SE	25	45	41
	Central	15	25	38
	NE	55	20	40
Goodhew	SE	28	35	40
	Central	42	21	32
	NE	45	26	40
Medivac	SE	25	30	28
	Central	35	28	27
	NE	48	25	32

(3) Daniel Freeman (DF). (Although the ambulance companies and hospitals really exist, the following example is hypothetical.) The emergency facility capacities of these hospitals can provide service to certain numbers of patients on a daily basis, as shown in Table 4-15.1. The average response times for the ambulance services to patient emergency calls from each of the three regions in Los Angeles to each of the three hospitals in the system (round-trip time from receipt of call to arrival at hospital) are shown in Table 4-15.2. The average charges to the county by the ambulance–hospital combination that provides patient service is shown in Table 4-15.3.

The supervisor's primary concern is to provide these emergency services to the largest number of people possible. However, she is faced with other serious limitations. The county has an average daily budget of $43,750 to spend on these services. In addition, the county has developed guidelines regarding the minimum allowable performance requirements in transporting patients to the hospital emergency facilities: The *overall* average transportation time must be no longer than 55 minutes. Further, no ambulance service is to receive less than 15 percent of the patient assignments, and no hospital is to receive less than 10 percent of the patient treatments.

ASSIGNMENT

Formulate this problem using x_{ijk} = number of patients calling from the ith region who are carried by the jth ambulance company to the emergency room of the kth hospital.

TABLE 4-15.3

Average Ambulance Charges for Trips to Specific Regions and Hospitals ($/patient)

Ambulance Company	Region	Hospital		
		MLK	USCCG	DF
Schaefer	SE	150	165	145
	Central	170	180	160
	NE	130	150	110
Goodhew	SE	135	155	175
	Central	160	190	195
	NE	125	140	155
Medivac	SE	140	145	150
	Central	155	170	180
	NE	110	135	140

REFERENCES

1. Balbirer, Sheldon, and David Shaw. An Application of Linear Programming to Bank Financial Planning. *Interfaces* 11, no. 5 (October 1981): 77–82.

2. Barkan, Joel D., and James E. Bruno. Operations Research in Planning Political Campaign Strategies. *Operations Research* 20, no. 5 (September–October 1972): 925–41.

3. Bean, James C., and John R. Birge. Reducing Travelling Costs and Player Fatigue in the National Basketball Association. *Interfaces* 10, no. 3 (June 1980): 98–102.

4. Bean, James C., et al. Selecting Tenants in a Shopping Mall. *Interfaces* 18, no. 2 (March–April 1988): 1–9.

5. Boere, N. J. Air Canada Saves with Aircraft Maintenance Scheduling. *Interfaces* 7, no. 4 (May 1977): 1–13.

6. Darnell, D. Wayne, and Caraolyn Loflin. National Airlines Fuel Management and Allocation Model. *Interfaces* 7, no. 2 (February 1977): 1–16.

7. Hilal, Said S., and Warren Erikson. Matching Supplies to Save Lives: Linear Programming the Production of Heart Valves. *Interface* 11, no. 6 (December 1981): 48–56.

8. Horen, Jeffrey. Scheduling of Network Television Programs. *Management Science* 26, no. 4 (April 1980): 354–70.

9. Stimson, David H., and Ronald Thompson. Linear Programming and Educational Administration. *Socio-Economic Planning Science* 8 (1974).

10. Zeirer, T. K., W. A. Mitchel, and T. R. White. Practical Applications of Linear Programming to Shell's Distribution Problems. *Interfaces* 6, no. 4 (August 1976): 13–26.

CHAPTER 5

LINEAR PROGRAMMING: PART 2

THE SIMPLEX METHOD

|5.1| INTRODUCTION

In 1947, George Dantzig developed the analytical technique used for solving linear programming problems called the *simplex method*. It is a highly structured process that progresses iteratively—within the feasible space formed by the family of resource constraint equations—from one solution to another, continually improving the objective function until the optimal solution is found. Got it? Very unlikely. One would probably have greater success attempting to explain the subtleties of an Ingmar Bergman film to a five-year old than understanding the preceding description of this very challenging concept, so let's enhance it with an illustrative problem.

EXAMPLE 5.1   THE DENTAL OFFICE STUDY

A dentist employs a hygienist and a dental assistant. She provides two types of services: general dentistry and periodontics (minor cases only). She is interested in managing her office such that she can obtain the maximum profit possible while still providing high-quality services; under no circumstances would she use shortcut procedures or inferior materials. Her records reveal empirical data regarding the amount of time required to provide her services, as shown in Table 5-1. She suspects these data can be used to improve her daily operations. In addition, the dentist, hygienist, and dental assistant do not wish to work more than an average of 10, 8, and 8 hours per day, respectively, for a 5-day workweek. The dentist, on the average, receives $85 profit for each periodontics case, and $50 profit for each general dentistry case.

"The camera shot from inside the room is of Ingrid, looking out the window at Thule, who is in the yard. The room is very sparsely furnished and a clock is ticking in the background. And get this, the only motion is the curtains billowing slightly in the breeze. For 5 minutes that's all we see but it seems like forever because what I think Bergman's trying to tell us here . . . "

© R. Guindon

TABLE 5-1

Time-Constraint Coefficients for the Dental Office

Type of Service Provided, x_i	Average Number of Hours Required per Service		
	Dentist	*Hygienist*	*Dental Assistant*
Periodontics, x_1	1.00	1.00	.50
General, x_2	.75	.27	.75

"Great checkup! Have some candy."

What is the optimal mix of services to provide assuming the demand for the dentist's services are great enough for her to fill her daily schedule? The formulation of this problem is as follows:

OBJECTIVE FUNCTION

Maximize profits, $Z = 85x_1 + 50x_2$

SUBJECT TO

- *Dentist labor hours* $1.00x_1 + .75x_2 \leq 10$
- *Hygienist labor hours* $1.00x_1 + .27x_2 \leq 8$
- *Dental assistant labor hours* $.50x_1 + .75x_2 \leq 8$

It would be easy to solve this problem algebraically. That, unfortunately, is not the purpose of this chapter; rather, we wish to grasp how LP problems are solved by the simplex method. There is another approach, however, that facilitates this understanding painlessly. We shall use a pictorial approach called the *graphical method*. This visual orientation to the simplex method gives you a "gentle introduction" and useful overview of this cornerstone process of linear programming. The graphical method mimics the analytical solution process of the simplex method. We shall examine exactly how the simplex method mathematically approaches LP problems, but only after we use the graphical approach to gain a sound grasp of the basic simplex operation.

5.2 | GRAPHICAL METHODS OF LINEAR PROGRAMMING

The graphical method is not a realistic way of solving LP problems because it is limited to situations of two or, at most, three variables. Real-world problems typically consist of anywhere from a dozen to thousands of variables. The technique is tremendously useful, however, because it performs pictorially many of the same operations that the simplex method does algebraically: It is a kind of visual aid to gaining early insight into the more intimidating analytical approach of the simplex procedure, which we shall examine later.

The graphical approach consists of the following steps:

Step 1. Formulate the problem, defining the objective function and all resource-constraint equations.

Step 2. Assume that each constraint equation formulated in step 1 is an equality, even if it is not. Individually plot each constraint by setting one of the two variables equal to zero and solving for the remaining variable. Repeat this process setting the other variable equal to zero and solving for the value of the remaining variable. This step will provide you with two points for each equation that you can connect by a straight line.

Step 3. Identify the *feasible region*–the space that contains all possible solutions to the problem (i.e., simultaneously satisfies all the constraints). The feasible region envelope, in a simplified sense, is formed by the intersection of the constraint-equation lines. More precisely, the feasible region is dependent on whether the objective function is for maximization or minimization and what the individual relationships of each resource-constraint equation are. The three different types of constraint relationship, illustrated previously in the various formulations of Chapter 4, are[1]

[1]The importance of the constraint relationships in defining an acceptable (feasible) solution in the simplex process is examined in significant detail in Section 5.3.

1. Less than or equal to, LTE (i.e., $\leq$)
2. Greater than or equal to, GTE (i.e., $\geq$)
3. Equal to, E (i.e., $=$)

If the problem is to maximize the objective function, the feasible region is usually the space created "underneath" the lines or toward the origin, because the constraints are usually of the LTE type. If it is a minimization problem, this region is usually "above" the lines or away from the origin, because the constraints are typically GTE. However, a more exacting test for determining whether you are in the feasible region is to select a point on either side of a constraint forming the supposed feasible area. Substitute the values of x_1 and x_2 back into the constraint to see whether the relationship is violated. If it is not, you have defined the feasible region.

Step 4. Determine the x,y coordinates for each "corner" or vertex of the feasible region. The optimal solution will typically be found at one of these locations.[2]

Step 5. Evaluate the objective function by substituting these coordinate values, one corner at a time, into the Z-equation. The optimal solution is the one that best satisfies this equation.[3]

We'll use the dental office problem (Example 5.1) to illustrate this graphical solution process.

Step 1. This step has already been completed.

Step 2. The coordinates for the three resource-constraint equations are shown in Table 5-2: The straight lines connecting the pairs of points for these three constraint equations are shown in Figure 5-1.

Step 3. Since the problem goal is maximizing something desirable, the feasible region, shown in Figure 5-2, is found underneath the envelope formed by the intersecting lines of the three constraints. Since the constraints are of the LTE-type, the feasible region must be located underneath the line in the direction of the origin. Any point within this space will provide a feasible, although not necessarily optimal, solution. That is, any point that lies within these boundaries defines a specific combination of the total number of periodontal services (x_1) and general dentistry services (x_2) that is feasible—that will not violate any of the three constraint equations. It is unlikely, however, that it will be the optimal solution if the point is picked capriciously.

Step 4. There are five vertices (corners) in the feasible region. The coordinates are illustrated in Table 5-3. *Note*: We can find the corner coordinates by simultaneously solving the constraint equations that form the intersection (usually

[2]In *extremely* rare circumstances, a problem may exist in which the slopes of the objective function and the edge of the feasible region that contains the optimal combination of variables are equal. For this situation, there will be an infinite combination of optimal solution points that lie along this edge.

[3]There is an alternative method to finding the optimal solution point. Simply guess a value of Z, then draw the objective function line the same way you do for a constraint. It doesn't matter that this line probably will not be optimal—or even close to optimal. The important aspect of this process is to *get the slope of the objective function line established*. Next, keeping this exact slope of Z, move the line until it is just tangent to (1) the corner farthest from the origin if it is a maximization problem, or (2) the corner closest to the origin if it is a minimization problem. You could also algebraically assume different values of Z—called *isoprofit lines*—that would move you toward this optimal point. Once this corner is identified, determine the coordinate values and solve for Z. Because the graphical method of solving for Z requires you to eyeball the data—unless you use drafting equipment—it is not used often.

TABLE 5-2

Resource-Constraint Coordinates for the Dental Office

Constraint No.	$P(0,x_2)$	$P(x_1,0)$
1	(0, 13.33)	(10, 0)
2	(0, 30)	(8, 0)
3	(0, 10.67)	(16, 0)

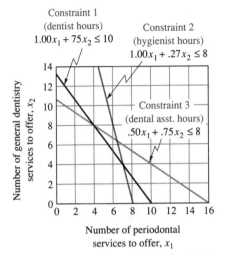

FIGURE 5-1

Constraint Equations for the Dental Office

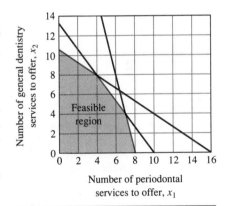

FIGURE 5-2

Feasible Region for the Dental Office

TABLE 5-3

Feasible Region Coordinates for the Dental Office

Vertex No.	$P(x_1, x_2)$
1	$P_1(0, 0)$
2	$P_2(0, 10.67)$
3	$P_3(4, .8)$
4	$P_4(6, 9, 4.2)$
5	$P_5(8, 0)$

TABLE 5-4

Objective Function Profit Values Corresponding to Vertice Values for the Dental Office

Coordinate	Profit
P_1	$0
P_2	$533
P_3	$740
P_4	$797
P_5	$680

there are only two). For example, P_3 results from the intersection of constraint equations 1 and 3. These equations are

$$x_1 + .75x_2 = 10$$
$$.5x_1 + .75x_2 = 8$$

Now we can eliminate x_2 and solve for x_1 by multiplying constraint equation 3 by -1 and adding the two remaining equations. This gives

$$.5x_1 = 2$$
$$x_1 = 4$$

Next, we substitute this value of x_1 into either of the two original equations (let's select constraint equation 1) and solve for the remaining unknown, x_2:

$$4 + .75x_2 = 10$$
$$.75x_2 = 6$$
$$x_2 = 8$$

The corner formed by the intersection of constraint equations 1 and 3, P_3, is

$$P_3(x_1, x_2) = 4, 8$$

Step 5. Finally, we substitute each set of coordinate values into the objective function equation and solve for the dentist's profit (Figure 5-3). These values are shown in Table 5-4.

The optimal value of $797 in profit is achieved by offering 6.88 periodontal services and 4.17 general dentistry treatments per day. Of course, it is not possible to offer fractional treatments on a given day; however, these values may be viewed as what the dentist would like to provide over a broad period of time—a type of long-term *average* service mix.

5.3 THE SIMPLEX METHOD

Although the graphical method can address only very simplified, two-variable LP problems, the simplex method does not suffer from such limitations. Simplex is a powerful, general purpose solution method for solving LP problems. A brief, reasonably pain-free description of how the simplex method works is presented next.

FIGURE 5-3

Feasibility Region Vertices, Isoprofit Lines, and Optimal Mix for the Dental Office

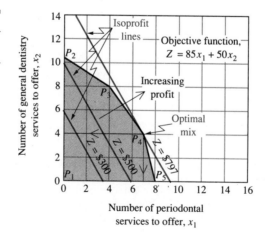

Descriptive Overview

Linear programming problems typically are constructed of more variables (n) than equations (m). We find a basic solution by setting the $n-m$ variables equal to zero and solving the m constraint equation set for the remaining m variables. The m variables making up each of these sets are defined as *basic variables* (i.e., the variables included in the present solution: the *basis*). The $n-m$ variables set equal to zero are *nonbasic variables* (i.e., the variables *not* in the present solution). You may ask yourself, *Which m* variables should be used? or *Which n−m* variables should be set equal to zero? After all, there are a lot of combinations of m variables to select out of the original set of n. In fact, there are exactly

$$C_m^n = \frac{n!}{m!(n-m)!}$$

combinations. So, for a moderate problem of, say, 30 variables and 20 constraints, the number of possible combinations is

$$C_{20}^{30} = \frac{30!}{20!(10)!} \quad \frac{30 \cdot 29 \cdot 28 \cdot \cdots \cdot 2 \cdot 1}{10 \cdot 9 \cdot 8 \cdot \cdots \cdot 2 \cdot 1} = 20{,}030{,}010$$

This identity represents the maximum number of possible basic solution combinations that an algebraic approach would be faced with in searching for the optimal solution. An impractical feat, to say the least! Fortunately, the simplex method isn't your ordinary, run-of-the-mill procedure: It discriminates. Simplex examines only those basic solutions that (1) consist of exactly m variables, and (2) satisfy all constraints, including the nonnegativity condition. A solution set of m variables that satisfies these conditions is called a *basic feasible solution*. Not only does simplex reserve its energy for examining basic feasible solution points—it also knows where to find them. Simplex knows that basic solutions lie at only the extreme points of the feasible region (i.e., the corners or vertices). Therefore, simplex searches only these points of a feasible region, knowing that one of them will contain the optimal solution for the problem.

Simplex uses the origin for its starting point. Even though the origin is not optimal, it represents a convenient location of a basic feasible solution that simplex can use to launch its search for the optimal solution. From the origin, simplex sequentially examines only those adjacent vertices whose objective function value provides an improvement over the previous point. Because of this highly selective search capability, simplex will ultimately assess only a small portion of the total number of basic feasible solution vertices.

The formal procedure for establishing this initial starting point for both maximization and minimization problems is discussed later in this chapter. However, before we can use simplex to solve an LP problem, we must adjust the original formulation equations. The procedure for making these specific modifications is discussed next.

Transforming Inequalities into Equations: Slack, Surplus, and Artificial Variables

Simplex can operate only on a system of *equations*, rather than on the *inequalities* that typically make up LP formulations. Therefore, the first task is to convert each inequality into an equation.

The transformation of inequalities into equalities involves three different conversions: (1) less than or equal to, LTE ($\leq$); (2) greater than or equal to, GTE ($\geq$); and (3) equal to, E ($=$). The general rules for these conversions are discussed next.

Less than or Equal to, LTE ($\leq$) The constraint of the dentist labor hours used in the dental office study (Example 5.1) is

$$1.00x_1 + .75x_2 \leq 10$$

We can easily convert it to an equality by adding an additional variable, called a *slack variable*, s_1.

$$1.00x_1 + .75x_2 + 1s_1 = 10$$

The purpose of the slack variable, s_1, is to account for any *unused resources*. Since the sum of $1.00x_1 + .75x_2$ is not to exceed 10, it is possible that it could also fall short of this limit. If, in fact, this sum were equal to 7, then s_1 would represent the three unused units. The slack variable, s_1, can take on any value between zero and the value of the RHS constraint, and can ultimately appear in the optimal solution.[4]

Greater than or Equal to, GTE ($\geq$) We can convert a GTE inequality into an equation by adding a special type of dummy variable, called an *artificial variable*, and subtracting a slack variable. This negative slack variable is often referred to as a *surplus variable* and, except for the sign, it is treated in the same way as is the slack variable. Unlike the slack variable, the artificial variable is never part of the optimal solution; it is always assigned a large positive objective function coefficient value in minimization problems (M) or a large negative objective function coefficient value in maximization problems ($-M$). This assignment procedure is called the *big M* method. Because of the large values assigned to M, it is always "kicked out" of the optimal solution. The purpose of the artificial variable is not as obvious as is that of the slack or surplus variables. Let it suffice for now to say that it is used solely to provide the simplex process with an initial, feasible starting point at the origin. A detailed examination of the role of the artificial variable is presented later in this chapter. Let's look at the process of transforming GTE constraint equations.

Suppose, for example, that the earlier constraint was written as

$$1.00x_1 + .75x_2 \geq 10$$

We could convert it quickly to an equality by adding in an artificial variable, A_1, and by subtracting the surplus variable, s_1. The conversion is

$$1.00x_1 + .75x_2 + 1A_1 - 1s_1 = 10$$

So, in this conversion, the artificial variable gets simplex rolling and the surplus variable allows the value of $1.00x_1 + .75x_2$ to exceed 10, if necessary.

Equal to, E ($=$) Surprisingly, it is not possible to use an equality constraint "as is" in the simplex tableau, even though this relationship is already an equation! Since the simplex method is an iterative process, it is not clear to the computer what initial values should be assigned to these equation variables. So, it is necessary always to add in an artificial variable, A_i. Suppose that we have the constraint equation

$$1.00x_1 + .75x_2 = 10$$

The transformation is accomplished by

$$1.00x_1 + .75x_2 + 1A_1 = 10$$

---

[4]If a constraint has a decision variable with a negative coefficient, then, as long as the RHS value is ≥ 0, the slack variable can have a value that *exceeds* the RHS value.

If we transform the dentist office study (Example 5.1) from its original inequalities to simplex-ready equations, we have the following:

SUBJECT TO

$$1.00x_1 + .75x_2 + 1s_1 = 10$$
$$1.00x_1 + .27x_2 + 1s_2 = 8$$
$$.50x_1 + .75x_2 + 1s_3 = 8$$

Although these new slack variables add more variables to the overall problem, they have objective-function coefficients of zero. Therefore, they do not contribute to the objective-function value.

OBJECTIVE FUNCTION

$$\text{Maximize } Z = 85x_1 + 50x_2 + 0s_1 + 0s_2 + 0s_3$$

Now we have transformed the original set of inequalities to a system of equations that can be readily solved by the simplex method (algorithm).

5.4 THE MAXIMIZATION SIMPLEX ALGORITHM

The simplex method organizes the formulated problem into a tabular design called a *simplex tableau*. Although simplex is a tedious, sometimes lengthy procedure to use manually (it is not mathematically difficult), it is the only way for you to increase your understanding of the intricacies of the LP solution method. The simplex algorithm for maximization problems is presented next.[5]

The large amount of detail introduced in the dozen steps of the simplex algorithm that follows can be developed more easily through the use of an example. Let's illuminate this method by applying it to the dental office study (Example 5.1) so that you can *see* how these pieces fit together as we go along.

The Dental Study, Continued

Step 1. Formulate the LP problem with constraints of the LTE type.

OBJECTIVE FUNCTION

$$\text{Maximize profits, } Z = 85x_1 + 50x_2$$

SUBJECT TO

- *Dentist labor hours* $1.00x_1 + .75x_2 \leq 10$
- *Hygienist labor hours* $1.00x_1 + .27x_2 \leq 8$
- *Dental assistant labor hours* $.50x_1 + .75x_2 \leq 8$

Step 2. Rewrite the formulation of step 1 (1) by adding slack variables to each resource constraint with unit coefficients, and (2) by including slack variables in the objective function with zero coefficients (i.e., slack variables do not contribute to the objective function value). The formulation is as follows:

[5]Since most constraints of a maximization problem are of the LTE variety, for the purpose of introductory simplicity we shall address only slack variables now. Later, we shall deal with managing surplus and artificial variables.

TABLE 5-5

Initial Simplex Maximization Tableau Design for the Dental Office

c_b	Basic variables	Decision variables		Slack variables			RHS
		c_j					
		85	50	0	0	0	
		x_1	x_2	s_1	s_2	s_3	b_i
0	s_1	1	.75	1	0	0	10
0	s_2	1	.27	0	1	0	8
0	s_3	.50	.75	0	0	1	8
	z_j	0	0	0	0	0	0
	$c_j - z_j$	85	50	0	0	0	

OBJECTIVE FUNCTION

$$\text{Maximize } Z = 85x_1 + 50x_2 + 0s_1 + 0s_2 + 0s_3$$

SUBJECT TO

$$1.00x_1 + .75x_2 + 1s_1 = 10$$
$$1.00x_1 + .27x_2 + 1s_2 = 8$$
$$.50x_1 + .75x_2 + 1s_3 = 8$$

Step 3. Design and fill in the simplex tableau. The objective function coefficients comprise the c_j row, whereas each remaining row in the body of the tableau represents the resource constraint coefficients. The b_i (RHS) values are the resource levels available for each constraint. We find the initial basic feasible solution variables by scanning the columns of the constraint coefficients in the tableau under the decision and slack variable headings (tableau body). We select only those variables with a single +1 coefficient; the remainder of the column values are all zero. This step forces the starting point for the simplex process to begin at the origin.

The only variables that satisfy the initial basic feasible solution tableau with a single, nonzero coefficient of +1 in their respective c_j columns are s_1, s_2, and s_3 (all other coefficient values in each of these columns are zero). The initial simplex tableau for the dental office study (Example 5.1) is shown in Table 5-5. Starting the initial tableau with the set of slack variables as the basis provides us with an initial basic solution. It is, of course, non-optimal, since the slack variables contribute nothing to our objective function. Having s_1, s_2, and s_3 as our basic variables simply means that we have 10, 8, and 8 hours of unused dentist, hygienist, and dental assistant time contributing absolutely nothing toward profit! We have, however, gotten the simplex solution process rolling with an initial feasible, yet nonoptimal, solution.

Step 4. Compute z_j—the amount of profit that will be lost for each unit of x_j brought into the solution—for all decision and slack variables. We find this value by summing the products of the coefficients in the c_b column—the objective

function coefficients of the basic (solution) variables—and multiplying this value by the coefficients in each variable column. That is,

$$z_j = \sum_{i=1}^{m} c_b a_{ij} \qquad \text{for each } j \, (j = 1, 2, \ldots, n)$$

where

a_{ij} = per unit contribution (or consumption) rate of the ith constraint equation and the jth variable

The computations for the basis variables are

$$[z_j]_{x_1} = (0)(1.00) + (0)(1.00) + (0)(.50) = 0$$
$$[z_j]_{x_2} = (0)(.75) + (0)(.27) + (0)(.75) = 0$$
$$[z_j]_{s_1} = (0)(1) + (0)(0) + (0)(0) = 0$$
$$[z_j]_{s_2} = (0)(0) + (0)(0) + (0)(0) = 0$$
$$[z_j]_{s_2} = (0)(0) + (0)(0) + (0)(0) = 0$$

These z_j values represent the decrease in the objective function value—the amount of profit lost from Z—that will occur when we introduce one unit of the jth variable (both slack and decision) into the solution. It is clear why the z_j values for the slack variables are zero—they have a zero per-unit contribution rate to the objective function. But why are these values for x_1 and x_2 zero? Because neither x_1 nor x_2 is in the initial tableau basic solution; we can give up only what is already in the solution.

Step 5. For each tableau column under both the decision and slack variables, calculate $c_j - z_j$. The $c_j - z_j$ term represents the gain (c_j) minus the loss (z_j), or the *opportunity cost* of each additional unit of decision variable, x_j, brought into the solution (i.e., the per-unit increase in the value of the objective function for every unit of x_j added into the solution). If $c_j - z_j \leq 0$ for all columns, stop; you cannot improve the present solution (i.e., you have found the optimal solution). If $c_j - z_j > 0$ for one or more columns, continue to step 6.

$$[c_j - z_j]_{x_1} = 85 - 0 = 85$$
$$[c_j - z_j]_{x_2} = 50 - 0 = 50$$
$$[c_j - z_j]_{s_1} = 0 - 0 = 0$$
$$[c_j - z_j]_{s_2} = 0 - 0 = 0$$
$$[c_j - z_j]_{s_3} = 0 - 0 = 0$$

The $c_j - z_j$ value represents the opportunity cost associated with the jth variable. It is the amount of improvement in the objective function value associated with the introduction of one unit of the jth variable. Since the $c_j - z_j \leq 0$ check for optimality has not been met for all columns, we are going to improve our present situation by identifying two key elements: (1) the nonbasic variable that will provide the largest improvement to our present objective function value (zero), and (2) the basic variable that must be replaced for this improvement to happen. Let's go to step 6.

Step 6. Find the *entering variable* (pivot column). This column has the *maximum positive value of $c_j - z_j$*. It represents the decision variable with the largest

		Decision variables		Slack variables				
	c_j	85	50	0	0	0		
c_b	Basic variables	x_1	x_2	s_1	s_2	s_3	RHS b_i	Ratio
0	s_1	1	.75	1	0	0	10	10/1 = 10
0	s_2	1†	.27	0	1	0	8	8/1 = 8**
0	s_3	.50	.75	0	0	1	8	8/.50 = 16
	z_j	0	0	0	0	0	0§	
	$c_j - z_j$	85*	50	0	0	0		

Pivot element → Pivot row → Objective function value → Pivot column

* Largest positive $c_j - z_j$ value; x_1 is entering variable (i.e., pivot column).

** Smallest positive ratio; s_2 is departing variable (i.e., pivot row).

† Pivot element, 1, at intersection of pivot row and column (i.e., intersectional element).

§ Objective function value, $Z = 0$.

per-unit contribution to the objective function. It is called the entering variable because it will replace one of the basic variables that is now in the solution. If two columns are tied with the same maximum positive $c_j - z_j$ value, arbitrarily select one.

The maximum positive $c_j - z_j$ value, 85, is associated with the x_1 column. This step identifies the variable that will provide the most rapid improvement in the objective function value. So x_1 will replace one of the existing basic variables now in the initial tableau solution. The next step will identify which variable to replace.

Step 7. Find the *departing variable* (pivot row). This row has the *minimum positive ratio*, which we find by dividing the b_i (RHS) constant of each constraint row by the corresponding element in the pivot column. That is,

$$Departing\ variable\ (pivot\ row) = \frac{RHS\ element,\ b_i}{[pivot\ column\ element]_{min}} \geqslant 0$$

This step identifies the departing variable—the variable presently in the basis that is going to be replaced. If there is a tie for the minimum ratio, you may arbitrarily select one.[6]

We find the minimum positive ratio for each row by dividing each of the RHS constants by the corresponding element in the pivot column. This ratio identifies the resource constraint that is limiting the ultimate number of units of the new entering variable, x_1, that can be introduced into the solution: For each unit of x_1 brought into the solution, 1 unit of s_1 (unused dentist hours), 1 unit of s_2 (unused hygienist hours), and .50 unit of s_3 (unused dental assistant hours) will have to given up (exchange rate). There are only 10, 8,

[6]Keep in mind that a minimum positive ratio is valid. In fact, a zero ratio value is a guaranteed minimal value.

and 8 slack hours available for the dentist, hygienist, and dental assistant, respectively. Therefore, the ratios formed by dividing the available resources by the exchange rate associated with the entering variable, x_1, tell us *whose time will run out first*—in this case, the hygienist's. So, the hygienist slack time (s_2) limits the number of periodontal treatments provided, x_1, to 8. Consequently, the first swap of variables will be the 8 hours of s_2 currently in the initial basic solution for eight periodontal treatments, x_1. You can anticipate an improvement resulting from this exchange because you are removing unused resources—which are worthless—in trade for real services that will generate profit. The results are as follows:

ROW NO.	b_i (RHS) VALUE	PIVOT COLUMN ELEMENT	RHS RATIO (b_i/PIVOT COLUMN ELEMENT)	
1	10	1	$10/1 = 10$	
2	8	1	$8/1 = 8$	← *minimum ratio*
3	8	.50	$8/.50 = 16$	

Step 8. Identify the *pivot element—the element at the intersection of the entering and departing variables*. The pivot element in the tableau body at the intersection of the entering column, x_1, and departing row, s_2, is 1.00. The complete initial tableau is presented in Table 5-6.

Step 9. Construct a new solution tableau using the same structure as that in the initial tableau, except replace the departing variable corresponding to the pivot row by the incoming variable that heads the pivot column. Adjust the contribution value, c_b, accordingly.

The tableau 2 design will consist of a solution mix (basic variables) of s_1, x_1, and s_3. Next, we'll calculate the new rows that will replace the data of the initial tableau.

Step 10. Replace the departing variable row (pivot row). We do this by dividing the constraint coefficient of the pivot element into each coefficient of the *original* pivot row (including the pivot element itself). Record these values in the new tableau.

$$\text{Elements of new entering row} = \frac{\text{elements of old row}}{\text{pivot element}}$$

Replace the departing variable row 2 (pivot row). We find the new pivot row by dividing each element of the old row by pivot element. The row is

$$\text{New row 2} = \frac{\text{old row 2}}{\text{pivot element}}$$

$$= \frac{1}{1} \quad \frac{.27}{1} \quad \frac{1}{1} \quad \frac{1}{1} \quad \frac{0}{1} \quad \frac{8}{1}$$

$$= 1 \quad .27 \quad 0 \quad 1 \quad 0 \quad 8$$

The new row is the same as the old row, because the pivot element was 1. You will see in the next iteration that this is not always the case.

Step 11. Replace all nonpivot row elements by applying the following relationship:

New row elements	=	(elements of row to be replaced)	−	[(pivot element)	(corresponding elements in replacement row)]

TABLE 5-7

Completed Simplex Maximization Tableau 2 for the Dental Office

		Decision variables		Slack variables				
	c_j	85	50	0	0	0		
c_b	Basic variables	x_1	x_2	s_1	s_2	s_3	RHS b_i	Ratio
0	s_1	0	.48†	1	-1	0	2	2/.48 = 4.17**
85	x_1	1	.27	0	1	0	8	8/.27 = 29.63
0	s_3	0	.615	0	-.50	0	4	4/.615 = 6.50
	z_j	85	22.95	0	85	0	680§	
	$c_j - z_j$	0	27.05*	0	-85	0		

Pivot element → (at s_1, x_2 = .48†)

Pivot row → (first data row)

Pivot column ↑ (x_2 column)

* Largest positive $c_j - z_j$ value; x_2 is entering variable (i.e., pivot column).

** Smallest positive ratio; s_1 is departing variable (i.e., pivot row).

† Pivot element, .48, at intersection of pivot row and column (i.e., intersectional element).

§ Objective function value, $Z = 680$.

TABLE 5-8

Optimal Solution: Simplex Maximization Tableau 3 for the Dental Office

		Decision variables		Slack variables			
	c_j	85	50	0	0	0	
c_b	Basic variables	x_1	x_2	s_1	s_2	s_3	RHS b_i
50	x_2	0	1	2.08	-2.08	0	4.17
85	x_1	1	0	-.56	1.56	0	6.88
0	s_3	0	0	1.28	.78	1	1.44
	z_j	85	50	56.35	28.65	0	792.7
	$c_j - z_j$	0	0	-56.35	-28.65	0	

* Since all $c_j - z_j$ values ≤ 0, the solution is optimal.

Record these revised row values in the new tableau.

The new rows for the nonpivot row elements are

New row 1 = (1 .75 1 0 0 10) − (1)(1 .27 0 1 0 8)
= 0 .48 1 −1 0 2

New row 3 = (.50 .75 0 0 1 8) − (.50)(1 .27 0 1 0 8)
= 0 .61 0 −.50 1 4

Step 12. Using the new tableau data, recalculate the z_j values and $c_j - z_j$ values. If $c_j - z_j \leq 0$ for all values in the $c_j - z_j$ row, stop. You have found the optimal solution. If $c_j - z_j > 0$ for any column, repeat steps 6 through 12.

The z_j values and $c_j - z_j$ values as recalculated for tableau 2 are shown in Table 5-7. The results suggest that the office should provide eight periodontal treatments and no general dentistry treatments. This mix will generate a daily profit of about $680. Although this is a significant improvement over the initial tableau findings, the $c_j - z_j$ row continues to have positive elements: There is still an opportunity for improvement. Accordingly, we perform a second iteration by repeating steps 6 through 12. Tableau 3 is presented in Table 5-8.

Since the $c_j - z_j$ row has no positive values, we have found the optimal solution: An average treatment mix of 6.88 periodontal and 4.17 general dentistry cases per day will result in a maximum profit possible of $792.71. Although there were 1.44 units of s_3 in the solution, this basic variable did not contribute to the objective function value (i.e., the 1.44 hours of unused dental assistant time, s_3, make no contribution to the profit).

Let's go over this problem again to make sure that the simplex solution process makes sense to you.

1. In the initial tableau (Table 5-5), the three slack variables form the basis. The profit of this mix is, of course, zero: Slack variables do not contribute to the objective function—they are merely unused resources. However, they do provide an immediate feasible basis for the initial tableau. To see how to improve the present objective function, examine the $c_j - z_j$ row. You can see that the $85 value of x_1—the number of periodontal treatments provided—is greater than the $c_j - z_j$ values for any other variable. We can therefore improve the objective function value (which is now zero) by $85 if we bring one unit of x_1 into the solution.

2. In the second tableau (Table 5-7), 8 units of x_1 are brought into the solution with this first iteration. The total contribution to the objective function is equal to the product of the per-unit contribution of x_1 times the change in the number of units of x_1 between the initial and second tableau. Since there were no periodontal treatments (x_1) offered in the initial tableau, the total contribution to the objective function by x_1 is 85 times the eight new periodontal treatments (x_1) introduced, or

($85 profit/periodontal treatment)(8 periodontal treatments) = $680 profit

However, for these eight periodontal treatments to be added to the dentist's business, something had to be given up. From the x_1 column, you can see that, for each unit of x_1 added to the basis, 1.00 units of s_1, 1.00 units of s_2, and 0.50 units of s_3 will be lost (exchanged). Since, in the first iteration between the initial and second tableau, 8 units of x_1 are added, s_1 decreased from 10 to 2 units, all units of s_2 were sacrificed, and s_3 decreased from 8 to 4 units. However, all those commodities "given up" were simply unused (slack) resources. Since the per-unit contribution to the objective function of any slack resource is zero, their loss had no impact. In other words, we gained the eight periodontal treatments "for free." The new objective function value, Z, is now

Z = 0 + (8)(85) = $680

The largest positive $c_j - z_j$ value belongs to x_2—$27.05/unit. This means that the net contribution, $c_j - z_j$, to the objective function for every additional general dentistry treatment offered, x_2, is $27.05. But, once again, for each unit of x_2 brought into the basis, it is necessary to give up .48 units of s_1, .27 units of x_1, and .615 units of s_3 (see the x_2 column).

3. The third tableau (Table 5-8) shows that 4.17 units (general dentistry treatments) are added to the solution basis. This addition resulted in s_1 decreasing 2.00 units (from 2 to 0), x_1 decreasing 1.13 units (from 8 to 6.87), and s_3 dropping 2.54 units (from 4 to 1.44). Therefore, it is necessary to give up the 2 units of s_1 (.48 × 4.17), 1.12 units of x_1 (.27 × 4.17), and 2.56 units of s_3 (.615 × 4.17). The net effect on the objective function was simply the additional 4.17 units of x_2 added to the solution at \$50.00/unit less the 1.12 units of x_1 lost at \$85/unit (once again, the change in the slack variable values in the solution has no impact on the objective function value). The new objective function is, then

$$Z = 680 + (4.17)(50) - (1.12)(85) = \$792$$

Since all $c_j - z_j \leq 0$, we have found the optimal solution (i.e., introduction of any nonbasic variables will only decrease the present objective function value).

5.5 | MINIMIZATION SIMPLEX ALGORITHM

The solution of minimization simplex problems can be approached in two different ways: (1) convert the minimization problem into a maximization problem by multiplying the objective function coefficients by -1 and changing the process from minimize to maximize (nothing needs to be adjusted in the constraint equations), or (2) simply run the problem as a minimization simplex. If the latter procedure is selected, the maximization algorithm can be used almost intact, with only two alterations:

1. The optimality test (step 5) is changed so that solution process is found when all $c_j - z_j$ values are *nonnegative* $(c_j - z_j \geq 0)$. If not, the solution process must continue.

2. The entering variable (step 6) is based on the *largest negative value of* $c_j - z_j$. This revision ensures that the value of the objective function is lowered rather than raised.

A brief description of this latter approach follows, using a revision of the dental office example.

EXAMPLE 5.2   THE DENTAL OFFICE REVISITED: SIMPLEX MINIMIZATION PROCEDURE

The simplex method for a minimization LP requires the addition of artificial variables, represented by A, to the GTE ($\geq$) and E ($=$) constraints (discussed earlier in this chapter). The sole purpose of these artificial variables is to trick the simplex method into using the origin as a starting point and to ensure that a basic feasible solution exists at this vertex *even though the actual feasible region may be displaced away from this location*. Here is how this illusion is created.

The initial simplex tableau enters only those basic variables with a $+1$ constraint coefficient. Therefore, only artificial variables and slack variables are selected; surplus variables associated with GTE type constraints have -1 coefficients and are therefore never in the initial solution. Since only the artificial variables and surplus variables form the basis of the initial tableau, *all decision variables are nonbasic and may be assumed to have values of zero*. Therefore, the initial basic solution is forced to use the

origin for the starting point. It is important, however, that, somewhere between the initial and optimal solution iteration, these artificial variables be kicked out of the basis. After all, they are only dummy variables and contribute nothing real to the objective function. We accomplish this artificial variable purge by assigning a large positive value, M, to the objective function coefficients of each artificial variable in a minimization problem. This big M assignment ensures that no artificial variables will be in the basis of the optimal solution.[7]

If an artificial variable does manage to survive through to the final iteration, this survival suggests that either (1) an infeasible solution exists, or (2) if the *value* of the artificial variable is zero, a degeneracy problem—an endless cycling loop that does not move toward solution—may exist. These special problems are discussed later in this chapter. Now let's develop the simplex minimization algorithm similar to the process used to "choreograph" the maximization algorithm.

The dentist in the original problem at the beginning of this chapter has decided to reformulate her operations so that her business's operating costs are minimized. The per-treatment costs associated with the periodontal (x_1) and general dentistry (x_2) services are $50 and $30, respectively. The time required to provide the two basic types of dental services are not of primary concern to the dentist now: she will hire people who have skills she needs after she sees what mix of services she should offer. In addition, the dentist decides that she wishes

1. To make a profit of at least $1000 per day
2. To provide a maximum of 25 periodontal treatments per day
3. To provide a maximum of 10 general dentistry treatments per day
4. To provide a minimum of five periodontal treatments per day
5. To provide a minimum of five periodontal treatments per day

The dentist's per-treatment profits are the same as those in the original study for the two types of services she offers.

Formulate the new problem. The algorithm for simplex minimization problems follows.

Step 1. Formulate the LP problem with constraints of types LTE, E, and GTE. The formulation for this problem is now as follows:

OBJECTIVE FUNCTION

$$\text{Minimize costs, } Z = 50x_1 + 30x_2$$

SUBJECT TO

- Profit, $85x_1 + 50x_2 \geq 1000$
- Maximum number of periodontal treatments, $x_1 \leq 25$
- Maximum number of general dentistry treatments, $x_2 \leq 10$
- Minimum number of periodontal treatments, $x_1 \geq 5$
- Minimum number of general dentistry treatments, $x_2 \geq 5$

Step 2. Rewrite the formulation of step 1 by introducing the appropriate slack, surplus, and artificial variables.

---

[7]Degenerate conditions are discussed in Section 5.6; the result is that, instead of iterating toward the optimal solution, we cycle—similar to a turntable stylus becoming stuck on one track of a record—and thus loop without resolution.

Transforming these inequalities into the appropriate equations that can be managed by the simplex method yields the following formulation.

OBJECTIVE FUNCTION

Minimize costs, $Z = 50x_1 + 20x_2 + 0s_1 + 0s_2 + 0s_3 + 0s_4 + 0s_5 + MA_1 + MA_2$

SUBJECT TO

- Profit, $85x_1 + 50x_2 - 1s_1 + 1A_1 = 1000$
- Maximum number of periodontal treatments, $x_1 + 1s_2 = 25$
- Maximum number of general denistry treatments, $x_2 + 1s_3 = 10$
- Minimum number of periodontal treatments, $x_1 - 1s_4 + 1A_2 = 5$
- Minimum number of general dentistry treatments, $x_2 - 1s_5 + 1A_3 = 5$

Step 3. Design and fill in the simplex tableau. It will be identical to that of the standard maximization simplex tableau, except that it will now include *surplus variables* and *artificial variables*. We still find the initial basic feasible solution variables by scanning the *columns* of the constraint coefficients in the tableau body. *Select only those variables with a single $+1$ coefficient; the remainder of values are all zero.*

The initial simplex tableau is shown in Table 5-9. Keep in mind that the initial basic solution includes only those column variables with a single $+1$ constraint coefficient (all others are zero). This requirement guarantees that only artificial and slack variables can be in the initial basis. The initial set of basic variables contains A_1, s_2, s_3, A_2, and A_3.

Step 4. Compute z_j for each decision, slack, surplus, and artificial variable. The computations for the basis variables are

$$[z_j]_{x_1} = (M)(85) + (0)(1) + (0)(0) + (M)(1) + (M)(0) = 86M$$
$$[z_j]_{x_2} = (M)(50) + (0)(0) + (0)(1) + (M)(0) + (M)(1) = 51M$$
$$[z_j]_{s_1} = (M)(-1) + (0)(0) + (0)(0) + (M)(0) + (M)(0) = -M$$
$$[z_j]_{s_4} = (M)(0) + (0)(0) + (0)(0) + (M)(-1) + (M)(0) = -M$$
$$[z_j]_{s_5} = (M)(0) + (0)(0) + (0)(0) + (M)(0) + (M)(-1) = -M$$
$$[z_j]_{A_1} = (M)(1) + (0)(0) + (0)(0) + (M)(0) + (M)(0) = M$$
$$[z_j]_{s_2} = (M)(0) + (0)(1) + (0)(0) + (M)(0) + (M)(0) = 0$$
$$[z_j]_{s_3} = (M)(0) + (0)(0) + (0)(1) + (M)(0) + (M)(0) = 0$$
$$[z_j]_{A_2} = (M)(0) + (0)(0) + (0)(1) + (M)(1) + (M)(0) = M$$
$$[z_j]_{A_3} = (M)(0) + (0)(0) + (0)(0) + (M)(0) + (M)(1) = M$$

These values are placed in the z_j row of the tableau (Table 5-10).

Step 5. Fill in the simplex tableau exactly as in the maximization version. Calculate the $c_j - z_j$ values and check to see whether the optimal solution has been reached (i.e., all $c_j - z_j \geq 0$). If it has been, stop. If, however, one or more values are < 0, go to step 6.

We calculate the $c_j - z_j$ values and place them in the last row of the initial tableau (Table 5-11):

TABLE 5-9

Initial Simplex Minimization Tableau
for the Dental Office

c_b	Basic variables	Decision variables		Artificial, slack, and surplus variables								RHS b_i	Ratio
c_j		50	30	0	0	0	M	0	0	M	M		
		x_1	x_2	s_1	s_4	s_5	A_1	s_2	s_3	A_2	A_3		
M	A_1	85	50	–1	0	0	1	0	0	0	0	1000	
0	s_2	1	0	0	0	0	0	1	0	0	0	25	
0	s_3	0	1	0	0	0	0	0	1	0	0	10	
M	A_2	1	0	0	–1	0	0	0	0	1	0	5	
M	A_3	0	1	0	0	–1	0	0	0	0	1	10	
	z_j												
	$c_j - z_j$												

* The initial basic feasible solution (basis) will consist of those column variables with a single +1 coefficient (i.e., A_1, s_2, s_3, A_2, and A_3); all other values are zero.

c_b	Basic variables	Decision variables		Artificial, slack, and surplus variables								RHS b_i	Ratio
c_j		50	30	0	0	0	M	0	0	M	M		
		x_1	x_2	s_1	s_4	s_5	A_1	s_2	s_3	A_2	A_3		
M	A_1	85	50	–1	0	0	1	0	0	0	0	1000	
0	s_2	1	0	0	0	0	0	1	0	0	0	25	
0	s_3	0	1	0	0	0	0	0	1	0	0	10	
M	A_2	1	0	0	–1	0	0	0	0	1	0	5	
M	A_3	0	1	0	0	–1	0	0	0	0	1	10	
	z_j	$86M$	$51M$	$-M$	$-M$	$-M$	M	0	0	M	M	$1015M$	
	$c_j - z_j$												

$$[c_j - z_j]_{x_1} = 50 - 86M$$
$$[c_j - z_j]_{x_2} = 30 - 51M$$
$$[c_j - z_j]_{s_1} = 0 - (-M) = M$$
$$[c_j - z_j]_{s_4} = 0 - (-M) = M$$
$$[c_j - z_j]_{s_5} = 0 - (-M) = M$$
$$[c_j - z_j]_{A_1} = M - M = 0$$
$$[c_j - z_j]_{s_2} = 0 - 0 = 0$$
$$[c_j - z_j]_{s_3} = 0 - 0 = 0$$
$$[c_j - z_j]_{A_2} = M - M = 0$$
$$[c_j - z_j]_{A_3} = M - M = 0$$

Since the $c_j - z_j$ values for x_1 and x_2 are negative, the present solution is clearly suboptimal. Continue to step 6.

		Decision variables		Artificial, slack, and surplus variables									
	c_j	50	30	0	0	0	M	0	0	M	M	**RHS** b_i	**Ratio**
c_b	Basic variables	x_1	x_2	s_1	s_4	s_5	A_1	s_2	s_3	A_2	A_3		
M	A_1	85	50	−1	0	0	1	0	0	0	0	1000	
0	s_2	1	0	0	0	0	0	1	0	0	0	25	
0	s_3	0	1	0	0	0	0	0	1	0	0	10	
M	A_2	1	0	0	−1	0	0	0	0	1	0	5	
M	A_3	0	1	0	0	−1	0	0	0	0	1	10	
	z_j	86M	51M	−M	−M	−M	M	0	0	M	M	*1015M*	
	$c_j - z_j$	50 − 86M	30 − 51M	M	M	M	0	0	0	0	0		

* The $c_j - z_j$ values are calculated and examined to see whether the optimal solution has been found (i.e., if all $c_j - z_j \geq 0$). Since there are negative $c_j - z_j$ values associated with x_1, 50 − 86M, and x_2, 30 − 51M, the initial tableau is suboptimal.

Step 6. Find the entering variable (pivot column). This column will have *maximum negative* value of $c_j - z_j$. It represents the variable with the largest per-unit *decrease* to the objective function.

The $c_j - z_j$ row of Table 5-11 reveals that the largest negative value of 50 − 86M is associated with the x_1 column. Therefore, the entering variable for the next tableau iteration will be x_1.

Step 7. Find the departing variable (pivot row). The departing row has the *minimum positive ratio*, which we find by dividing the b_i (RHS) constant of each constraint row by the corresponding element in the pivot column. This step is identical to its counterpart in the maximization simplex process.

ROW NO.	b_i VALUE	PIVOT COLUMN ELEMENT	RHS RATIO (b_i/PIVOT COLUMN ELEMENT)	
1	1000	85	1000/85 = 11.76	
2	25	1	25/1 = 25	
3	10	0	10/0 = ∞	
4	5	1	5/1 = 5	← *minimum ratio*
5	10	0	10/0 = ∞	

The smallest positive ratio of 5 is associated with the departing variable (pivot row): A_2. Therefore, the variable in the present basis that is going to be replaced with x_1 is A_2.

Step 8. Identify the pivot element. The pivot element is the element at the intersection of the entering and departing variables. The intersection of the incoming variable column of x_1 and departing variable row A_2 is the cell value of 1. The completed initial tableau is shown in Table 5-12; it illustrates (1) the intersection (pivot) element, (2) the pivot column, and (3) the pivot row, as well as the present objective function value.

Steps 9, 10, 11, and 12. These steps are identical to their counterparts in the maximization simplex process. We prepare tableau 2 by replacing departing

c_b	Basic variables	Decision variables		Artificial, slack, and surplus variables								RHS b_i	Ratio
	c_j	50	30	0	0	0	M	0	0	M	M		
		x_1	x_2	s_1	s_4	s_5	A_1	s_2	s_3	A_2	A_3		
M	A_1	85	50	−1	0	0	1	0	0	0	0	1000	1000/85 = 11.76
0	s_2	1	0	0	0	0	0	1	0	0	0	25	25/1 = 25
0	s_3	0	1	0	0	0	0	0	1	0	0	10	10/0 = ∞
M	A_2	1	0	0	−1	0	0	0	0	1	0	5	5/1 = 5
M	A_3	0	1	0	0	−1	0	0	0	0	1	10	10/0 = ∞
	z_j	86M	51M	−M	−M	−M	M	0	0	M	M	1015M	
	$c_j − z_j$	50 − 86M	30 − 51M	M	M	M	0	0	0	0	0		

Pivot element — Pivot row — Pivot column

* The departing variable (pivot row) has the minimum positive ratio, which we find by dividing the RHS constant of each constraint by the corresponding element in the pivot column. The departing variable is, in this case, A_2, which has the minimum positive ratio of 5. The pivot element (i.e., the intersection of the pivot row and pivot column) is 1.

TABLE 5-12

Initial Simplex Minimization Tableau 1 for the Dental Office

variable, A_2, with the new entering variable, x_1, and the new contribution value, c_b, of 50 replaces the old value of (big) M. Let's calculate the new entering row 4 elements as an example:

$$\textbf{Elements of new entering row 4} = \frac{\textbf{elements of old row 4}}{\textbf{pivot element}}$$

$$= \frac{1}{1}\ \frac{0}{1}\ \frac{0}{1}\ \frac{-1}{1}\ \frac{0}{1}\ \frac{0}{1}\ \frac{0}{1}\ \frac{0}{1}\ \frac{1}{1}\ \frac{0}{1}\ \frac{5}{1}$$

$$= 1\ 0\ 0\ -1\ 0\ 0\ 0\ 0\ 1\ 0\ 5$$

We can find the new, nonpivot row element values of a tableau from the following relationship:

$$\begin{matrix} \text{New row} \\ \text{elements} \end{matrix} = \begin{pmatrix} \text{elements of row} \\ \text{to be replaced} \end{pmatrix} - \begin{pmatrix} \text{pivot element} \end{pmatrix} \cdot \begin{pmatrix} \text{corresponding} \\ \text{elements in} \\ \text{replacement row} \end{pmatrix}$$

The new nonpivot rows for tableau 2 are, then,

New row 1 = (85 50 −1 0 0 1 0 0 0 0 1000) − [(85)(1 0 0 −1 0 0 0 0 1 0 5)]
= 1 0 0 −1 0 0 0 0 1 0 5

New row 2 = (1 0 0 0 0 0 1 0 0 0 25) − [(1) (1 0 0 −1 0 0 0 0 1 0 5)]
= 0 0 0 1 0 0 1 0 −1 0 20

New row 3 = (0 1 0 0 0 0 0 1 0 0 10) − [(0) (1 0 0 −1 0 0 0 0 1 0 5)]
= 0 1 0 0 0 0 0 1 0 0 10

New row 5 = (0 1 0 0 −1 0 0 0 0 1 5) − [(0) (1 0 0 −1 0 0 0 0 1 0 5)]
= 0 1 0 0 −1 0 0 0 0 1 5

Pivot element	c_b	Basic variables	Decision variables x_1 (50)	x_2 (30)	s_1 (0)	s_4 (0)	s_5 (0)	A_1 (M)	s_2 (0)	s_3 (0)	A_2 (M)	A_3 (M)	RHS b_i	Ratio	
	M	A_1	0	50	−1	85†	0	1	0	−85	0	0	575	575/85 = 6.76	← Pivot row
	0	s_2	0	0	0	1	0	0	1	0	−1	0	20	20/1 = 20	
	0	s_3	0	1	0	0	0	0	0	1	0	0	10	10/0 = ∞	
	50	x_1	1	0	0	−1	0	0	0	0	1	0	5	5/−1 = −5**	
	M	A_3	0	1	0	0	−1	0	0	0	0	1	5	10/0 = ∞	
		z_j	50	$51M$	$-M$	$85M - 50$	$-M$	M	0	0	$50 - 85M$	M	$580M + 250$§		
		$c_j - z_j$	0	$30 - 51M$	M	$50 - 85M$*	M	0	0	0	$85M - 50$	0			

Pivot column

TABLE 5-13

Simplex Minimization Tableau 2 for the Dental Office

* Largest negative $c_j - z_j$ value; s_4 is entering variable (i.e., pivot column).
** Smallest positive ratio; A_1 is departing variable (i.e., pivot row).
† Intersection (pivot) element, 85 (i.e., intersection of pivot row and pivot column).
§ Objective function value, $580M + 250$.

These new rows are placed in tableau 2, and the z_j and $c_j - z_j$ values are calculated (Table 5-13). Since negative $c_j - z_j$ values are still present, the optimal solution has not yet been found. The largest negative $c_j - z_j$ value is assocated with the s_4 column. The smallest nonnegative ratio value is associated with the first row (A_1). This means that the departing and entering variables will be A_1 and s_4, respectively, for tableau 3. The work to accomplish the remaining iterations will be left to the reader. The results of these iterations are shown in Tables 5-14 and 5-15 for tableau 3 and tableau 4, respectively. The final tableau shows that the minimum daily costs of $591 will be occurred when the dental office offers (an average of) 8.8 periodontic and five general dentistry services.

5.6 SPECIAL PROBLEMS IN LINEAR PROGRAMMING THAT DO NOT RESULT IN UNIQUE, OPTIMAL, OR EXPECTED SOLUTIONS

Typically, the solution of an LP problem will result in a single, optimal outcome. However, there are a few special situations where this does not occur—and they are usually the result of someone's poor judgment. These cases include

1. Unbounded problems

2. Inconsistent problems

3. Degenerate problems

c_b	Basic variables	Decision variables		Artificial, slack, and surplus variables								RHS b_i	Ratio
	c_j	50	30	0	0	0	M	0	0	M	M		
		x_1	x_2	s_1	s_4	s_5	A_1	s_2	s_3	A_2	A_3		
0	s_4	0	.59	−.01	1	0	.01	0	0	−1	0	6.7	6.7/.59 = 11.36
0	s_2	0	−.59	.01	0	0	−.01	1	0	0	0	13	13/.59 = 22.03
0	s_3	0	1	0	0	0	0	0	1	0	0	10	10/1 = 10
50	x_1	1	.59	−.01	0	0	.01	0	0	0	0	11	11/.59 = 18.64
M	A_3	0	1†	0	0	−1	0	0	0	0	1	5	5/1 = 5**
	z_j	50	$M+12$	−.5	0	−M	.5	0	0	0	M	$5M+550$§	
	$c_j - z_j$	0	$18-M$*	.5	0	M	$M-.5$	0	0	M	0		

Pivot element → (pivot column x_2, pivot row A_3)

Pivot column

* Largest negative $c_j - z_j$ value; x_2 is entering variable (i.e., pivot column).
** Smallest positive ratio; A_3 is departing variable (i.e., pivot row).
† Intersection (pivot) element, 1 (i.e., intersection of pivot row and pivot column).
§ Objective function value, $5M + 550$.

TABLE 5-14

Simplex Minimization Tableau 3 for the Dental Office

c_b	Basic variables	Decision variables		Artificial, slack, and surplus variables								RHS b_i
	c_j	50	30	0	0	0	M	0	0	M	M	
		x_1	x_2	s_1	s_4	s_5	A_1	s_2	s_3	A_2	A_3	
0	s_4	0	0	−.01	1	.59	.01	0	0	−1	−.59	3.8
0	s_2	0	0	.01	0	−.59	−.01	1	0	0	−.59	16
0	s_3	0	0	0	0	1	0	0	1	0	1	5
50	x_1	1	0	−.01	0	.59	.01	0	0	0	.59	8.8
30	x_2	0	1	0	0	−1	0	0	0	0	−1	5
	z_j	50	30	−.5	0	0	.5	0	0	0	0	591
	$c_j - z_j$	0	0	.5	0	0	$M-.5$	0	0	M	M	

* Since all $c_j - z_j$ values ≥ 0, the solution is optimal.

TABLE 5-15

Optimal Simplex Minimization Tableau 4 for the Dental Office

Unbounded Problems

Sometimes, an error in the formulation of the problem results in an objective function increasing without limit. This situation can occur if, in the formulation of the constraint equations, the feasible region is unbounded. Figure 5-4 represents an unbounded maximization problem. You can also detect an unbounded problem in the simplex solution process. Suppose you have just chosen the entering variable during one of the

FIGURE 5-4

Example of an Unbounded Feasible Region of Maximization Problem

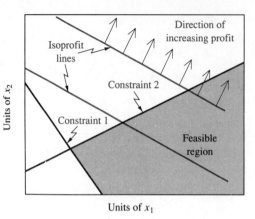

Profit can increase without bound. Something is clearly wrong here. There is probably an error in the formulation of the problem.

iterations. If, in calculating the minimum positive ratio in order to determine the departing variable, you find that *no entries in the pivot column are positive*, no positive ratio can be formed. The problem is then identified as unbounded.

Inconsistent Problems

The constraints are in conflict with each other. Therefore, no feasible solution is possible. There probably is an error in the problem formulation.

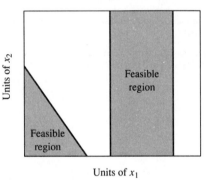

FIGURE 5-5

Example of an Inconsistent (Argumentative) LP Problem

It is also possible to formulate your LP problem such that there are two or more constraints that violate each other (argumentative constraints). A simple graphical illustration of this situation is provided in Figure 5-5. You will not be able to rely on graphical methods to pinpoint the problem, however, since typical LP formulation consists of many more than two or three decision variables. Instead, the best detector for this type of error is the simplex method. When optimality has been reached, all values in the $c_j - z_j$ row are either zero or negative for a maximization problem, or zero or positive for a minimization problem. However, an artificial variable will be nestled in among the other basic solution variables; this variable may be sufficient evidence to indicate that the optimal solution is not feasible. On the other hand, if the value of the artificial variable is zero, this may indicate a degenerate vertex.

Degenerate Problems

The term *degenerate* is not in reference to your Uncle Ralph who is never found without his raincoat, but rather to a basic feasible solution that has "too much traffic running through it" (i.e., too many constraints intersect at this vertex). In a degenerate solution, at least one basic variable has a zero value. In the simplex method, degeneracy can result when a tie occurs between potential departing variables in the basis. Theoretically, this tie can cause the degenerate, zero-value basic variable to be removed from the solution, only to be returned during a later iteration without improvement. The result is a potentially endless looping or cycling. In practice, however, techniques have been established that virtually eliminate the occurrence of cycling. The following formulation contains a degenerate condition.

OBJECTIVE FUNCTION

Minimize $Z = 50x_1 + 15x_2$

SUBJECT TO

$$10x_1 + 20x_2 \geq 100$$
$$30x_1 + 50x_2 \geq 300$$

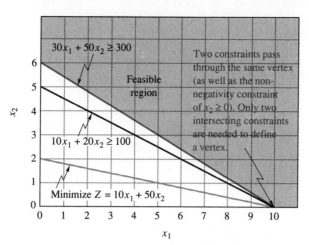

FIGURE 5-6

Example of Degenerate Vertex Condition

An illustration of this degenerate phenomenon is shown in Figure 5-6. Unlike the unbounded and inconsistent problems just discussed, you can find an optimal solution with degeneracy.

5.7 SIMPLEX MICROCOMPUTER APPLICATIONS

Now, let's examine how the computer solves a familiar LP problem. The hypothetical Coca-Cola product mix Example 4-1 (Section 4.4) had the following model formulation:

OBJECTIVE FUNCTION

$$\text{Maximize } Z = 115x_1 + 125x_2 + 110x_3 + 130x_4$$

SUBJECT TO

- Budget (dollars)

$$125x_1 + 125x_2 + 130x_3 + 135x_4 \leq 80{,}000{,}000$$

- Production capacity (10^3 gallons of cola)

$$x_1 + x_2 + x_3 + x_4 + \leq 200{,}000$$

- Demand (forecast sales in 10^3 gallons of cola)

$$x_1 \leq 75{,}000$$
$$x_2 \leq 40{,}000$$
$$x_3 \leq 100{,}000$$
$$x_4 \leq 15{,}000$$

- Policy 1

$$-43.75x_1 - 43.75x_2 + 84.5x_3 - 47.25x_4 \geq 0$$

- Policy 2

$$-.33x_1 + x_2 \leq 0$$

TABLE 5-16

Spreadsheet Data Entry for Coca-Cola Product Mix Example 4-1 Using the QSB Linear Programming Module

```
           Max        115.000X1   +125.000X2   +110.000X3   +1300.000X4
           Subject to

           (1)        +125.000X1   +125.000X2   +130.000X3   +135.000X4
                      ≤ +8.0E+07

           (2)        +1.00000X1   +1.00000X2   +1.00000X3   +1.00000X4
                      ≤ +200000

           (3)        +1.00000X1   +.000000X2   +.000000X3   +.000000X4
                      ≤ +75000.0

           (4)        +.000000X1   +1.00000X2   +.000000X3   +.000000X4
                      ≤ +40000.0

           (5)        +.000000X1   +.000000X2   +1.00000X3   +.000000X4
                      ≤ +100000

           (6)        +.000000X1   +.000000X2   +.000000X3   +1.00000X4
                      ≤ +15000.0

           (7)        -43.7500X1   -43.7500X2   +84.5000X3   -47,25000X4
                      ≥ +.000000

           (8)        -.330000X1   +1.00000X2   +.000000X3   +.000000X4
                      ≤ +.000000
```

It is important to notice that the formulation does *not* include (or need) slack, surplus, or artificial variables. *In fact, it is never necessary to include anything other than the decision variables in the computer input*; the remaining variables are always added automatically by the LP software package. Table 5-16 illustrates how the original formulation information is transferred to the data-entry spreadsheet of the computer program—virtually intact.

During the data-entry process, almost all microcomputer software packages will thoroughly prompt you for such information as the objective function coefficients, constraint equation coefficients, the type of constraint equation you are inputting (LTE, E, or GTE), as well as the RHS value. In addition, you will also be asked whether you would like to change any of the input data, whether you would like to have all of the tableaus or just the final tableau printed out, and so on. Almost all LP software are reasonably user friendly.

The output for (solution to) the Coca-Cola product mix Example 4-1 is shown in Table 5-17. This solution section reveals the following findings:

1. The optimal mix of colas to produce (in units of 1000 gallons, rounded to the nearest whole unit) is 75,000 units of Classic Coke (X1), 24,750 units of New Coke (X2), 85,250 units of Diet Coke (X3), and 15,000 units of Cherry Coke (X4).

2. The expected profit from such a mix is $23,046,250 (2.304625E + 07).

TABLE 5-17

Solution to the Coca-Cola Product Mix Example 4-1 Using QSB Linear Programming Software Module

Summarized Results for EX4-1				Page : 1			
Variables		Solution	Opportunity Costs	Variables		Solution	Opportunity Costs
No.	Names			No.	Names		
1	X1	+75000.00	0	7	S3	0	+9.95000884
2	X2	+24750.00	0	8	S4	+15249.99	0
3	X3	+85249.99	0	9	S5	+14750.00	0
4	X4	+14999.99	0	10	S6	0	+19.9999999
5	S1	+5442375	0	11	S7	+2130812	0
6	S2	0	+109.999999	12	S8	0	+15.0000000
Maximum value of the OBJ = 2.304625E+07				Iters. = 5			

3. The solution also provides the amount of slack or surplus resources associated with each constraint (e.g., S1 refers to constraint 1, S2 refers to constraint 2, etc.). So, for example, the budget slack value, S1 (under the "names" column), shows a solution value of $54,423,752. This value represents the amount of money that remains unused out of the original $80 million budget in constraint 1. The production capacity of constraint 2 reveals that there is zero slack remaining—all 200,000 units of production are consumed. The reason that so much budget money remains unspent is that there are no more hours available for production. The 75,000 units of Classic Coke (constraint 3) is completely satisfied; the slack value for S3 is zero. However, the sales forecast for New Coke of 40,000 units is only partially met: the slack value for constraint 4 (S4) is 15,250 units—the difference between the quantity of New Coke that is, in fact, produced (24,750) and the sales forecast. The interpretation of the remainder of the slack variables is left to the reader.

This brief look at the computer solution has barely scratched the surface of the vast amount of crucial managerial information that is available for interpretation. For example, we have made no attempt to examine such vital issues as these:

1. Exactly how much could the present $115 profit contribution of Classic Coke decrease before it would be wise to remove some of the 75,000 units presently in production?

2. How much of an increase in the present $125 profit margin of New Coke would the company have to realize before it would want to add more than the 24,750 units it presently produces?

3. For which resources (if any) would it be worthwhile to try to get more (and to what limit)?

4. For which resources would it be financially beneficial to try to get less (and to what limit)?

5. What is the existing marginal value of each resource?

6. What is the associated cost of any constraint that might be viewed as arbitrary (e.g., policy constraints 1 and 2)?

All these questions are aimed at probing the influence that the parameter values we have assumed for each of our variables—objective function coefficients, resource constraint coefficients, and RHS values—have on the optimal solution.

| 5.8 | SUMMARY

The graphical method can be used to solve only very simplified LP problems; its use is primarily illustrative. On the other hand, the simplex method can be used to solve large, real-world LP problems using computers. Accordingly, the detailed examination of the simplex method provided in this chapter was intended to give you a foundational grasp of how the method actually works—not to prepare you to perform manual solutions. Now that you understand how the various decision variables compete with one another over the assignment of available, limited resources, the stage is set for us to deal with those issues that surface *after* we have found the optimal solution. In this next setting, we shall examine exactly how sensitive our optimal solution is to changes we may wish to make to the parameters used to formulate the original problem (e.g., objective function coefficients, resource levels). This critical part of linear programming is called *postoptimality* or *sensitivity analysis*.

5.9 EXERCISES

5-1 Solve the two-variable German car dealer Exercise 4-1 using graphical methods. Illustrate the feasible region, identify the vertices coordinates of this region, and calculate the objective function value.

5-2 Graphically display and solve the two-variable Apple Computer Exercise 4-2. Illustrate the feasible region and solve for the vertices coordinates. What is the optimal mix and the resulting objective function value?

5-3 *Design* the initial simplex tableau for Exercise 5-1, ignoring the availability and minimum-purchase-quantity constraints, which will result in only three resource constraints (i.e., budget, space, and salesperson hours). Do not solve.

5-4 *Design* the initial simplex tableau for Exercise 5-2. Do not solve.

5-5 Use the simplex method to calculate the following information about tableau 2 from Exercise 5-3:

1. What is the incoming variable?
2. What is the departing variable?
3. What is the intersection element?
4. What is the objective function value in the initial tableau?

5-6 Use the simplex method to calculate the following information about tableau 2 from Exercise 5-4:

1. What is the incoming variable?
2. What is the departing variable?
3. What is the intersection element?
4. What is the objective function value in the initial tableau?

5-7 Suppose that a Chrysler Corporation Jeep dealer in Indianapolis is trying to determine the most attractive mix of models to offer in his sales department on a month-to-month basis using a $185,000 budget. The primary models to be sold include the Cherokee station wagon, the Wrangler 4×4 two door, and the Comanche pickup truck (models are always given in this order). For the purpose of this exercise, assume that the three models provide the dealer with $3500, $2600, and $2000 of gross profit. Further, the dealer's wholesale cost for each unit is $12,600, $9100, and $7800. Assume the dealer can sell all the Jeeps he purchases each month. Design the initial simplex tableau and answer the following questions:

1. What is the incoming variable?
2. What is the departing variable?
3. What is the intersection element?

Design tableau 2.

5-8 Suppose that the Chrysler Corporation dealer of Exercise 5-7 realizes that he has not taken into consideration the fact that the agency only has 1560 square feet of space to display and store the cars, and that each vehicle requires 140, 135, and 130 square feet of space. Further, each car sold will require an aver-

age of approximately 23, 15, and 18 salesperson hours. Finally, the maximum number of units that the dealer can purchase from Chrysler is 10, 10, and 5 units. There is a total of 680 salesperson hours available each month; all other information discussed in Exercise 5-6 remains the same. Reformulate the problem and design the initial simplex tableau. Answer the following questions:

1. What is the departing variable?
2. What is the new entering variable?
3. What is the pivot element?

Design tableau 2.

5-9 Use the simplex method to solve for the optimal mix of services and objective function value of the three-variable version of the German car dealer study (Example 4-3).

5-10 The computer printout shown in Table 5-10.1 represents the formulation and final tableau solution of the hypothetical TWA advertising problem of Exercise 4-5. Determine the following information regarding this solution:

1. How many units of advertising ultimately were placed with each media outlet? What do you call this specific combination of advertisements?
2. What total number of exposures are expected to be gained from this advertising campaign?
3. How much money was spent on each media outlet? How many exposures will each outlet provide? What is the ratio of exposures to dollars spent on each outlet?
4. Do you think that there is a relationship between the ratio in part 3 and the actual dollars spent on that media? Explain your answer.

Design the initial simplex tableau.

5-11 Answer the following questions regarding the initial simplex tableau design of the Coca-Cola product mix in Example 4-1:

1. How many decision variables are present?
2. How many slack variables are present?
3. How many surplus variables are present?
4. How many artificial variables are present?
5. What is the column order for each decision variable and for each slack, surplus, and artificial variable (i.e., x_1 = column 1, x_2 = column 2, etc.).
6. What variables form the initial basis? Explain your answer.

5-12 Answer the following questions regarding the initial simplex tableau design of the Chicago mall product-mix in Example 4-2:

1. How many decision variables are present?
2. How many slack variables are present?
3. How many surplus variables are present?
4. How many artificial variables are present?

TABLE 5-10.1

Optimal Solution for TWA Media Advertising, Using *Microsolve*
(Paul Jensen, Holden-Day Publishing)

```
                          CONSTRAINT MATRIX

OBJMAX/      2.14E+07X1  +  1.185E+07X2  +  6875000X3   +  4180000X4
C1           180000X1    +  100000X2     +  75000X3     +  4500X4      +
             3000X5      <=4750000
C2           1X1         <=24
C3           1X2         <=10
C4           1X3         <=36
C5           1X4         <=60
C6           1X5         <=85
C7           90000X1     -  50000X2      -  37500X3     -  2250X4      -
             1500X5      <=0
C8        -  1800X1      -  10000X2      -  7500X3      +  4050X4      +
             2700X5      >=0


                        OPTIMAL SOLUTION

             VAR.            NAME           VALUE
              1              X1             13.19444
              2              X2             10
              3              X3             11.33333
              4              X4             60
              5              X5             85
              6              SLK-1          0
              7              SLK-2          10.80556
              8              SLK-3          0
              9              SLK-4          24.66667
             10              SLK-5          0
             11              SLK-6          0
             12              SLK-7          0
             13              SLK-8          49999.97
             14              ART-8          0

             OBJECTIVE = 9.412278E+08
```

5. What is the column order for each decision variable and for each slack, surplus, and artificial variable (i.e., x_1 = column 1, x_2 = column 2, etc.).

6. What variables form the initial basis? Explain your answer.

5-13 Design the initial simplex tableau for Exercise 5-11. Determine the answers to the following questions (show all supporting calculations):

1. What is the incoming variable?
2. What is the departing variable?
3. What is the intersection element?
4. What is the objective function value in the initial tableau?

5-14 Design the initial simplex tableau for Exercise 5-12. Determine the answers to the following questions (show all supporting calculations):

1. What is the incoming variable?
2. What is the departing variable?
3. What is the intersection element?
4. What is the objective function value in the initial tableau?

CHAPTER 6

LINEAR PROGRAMMING: PART 3

THE DUAL AND SENSITIVITY ANALYSIS

6.1 INTRODUCTION

In Chapters 4 and 5, we have concentrated on helping you to formulate and then find the optimal solution of a linear programming (LP) problem through the use of a computer. These two important steps are still not sufficient to complete your fundamental understanding of this crucially important resource-allocation tool.

First, it is very important to know that every LP problem can be illustrated in two distinctly different forms: the *primal*—the approach to which you have been consistently exposed until now—and the *dual*. The advantage of the dual form is that it provides the manager with an alternative perspective to the problem reflected by the resource *shadow prices*. These shadow prices will suggest which resource levels it may be wise to try to change. Also, in many instances, either the primal or dual form of the problem will provide a more efficient solution procedure. This increased efficiency can result in significant decreases in computer solution time and associated costs.

Second, before you can "trust" the solution of any LP problem, *you must determine to what degree it is affected by changes in the assumed parameter values used in the formulation*. Although LP is a deterministic tool—you are assumed to know the values of the objective function coefficients, constraint coefficients, and amounts of resources available (right-hand-side (RHS) values of each constraint) with certainty—realistically, we know that human error in the form of imperfect information is always present. In addition, even if the formulation data used in the analysis were sound at a specific point in time, the accuracy of these parameter estimates tends to be vulnerable to changes in technology, resource availability, market demand, labor costs, and so on. Because of these frailties in human judgment and the likelihood that even accurate information will "fade" with time, it is important to carry the LP analysis through an additional step. This final procedure is commonly referred to as *postoptimality* or *sensitivity analysis*. This procedure, just like all other sensitivity analyses, will help you to determine just how delicate or resilient the optimal solution is to variations in the original parameter inputs. Sensitivity analysis can tell you how much the problem parameters can be varied before the current optimal solution changes.

The specific areas of sensitivity analysis that we shall examine carefully in this chapter include (1) right-hand-side (RHS) ranging—changing the current level of available resources; (2) objective function (OF) coefficient ranging—changing the per-unit contribution of the decision variables in the objective function; (3) adding a new variable—adding another decision variable/product to the original mix; (4) changing the

constraint coefficients—changing the rate at which a particular decision variable consumes/contributes to a given resource level; (5) adding new constraints; and (6) deleting "soft" constraints.

6.2 | THE DUAL FORMULATION AND SHADOW PRICES

Both the dual and the primary forms of an LP problem will yield exactly the same optimal solution. The dual form, however, provides us with a diametrically opposite perspective of our problem, as well as with added insight. Instead of directing its energies toward the allocation of limited resources to, say, maximize profits like the primal, the dual is concerned with finding the most economic use of its resources that results in minimum system costs. This economic orientation provides assessments that are typically expressed in terms of the *marginal rate of return* or *shadow price* associated with each resource (constraint) in the particular LP problem addressed. From this mirror-image or counterpart configuration, we shall be able to extract knowledge from a different view and to gain an even more intimate understanding of the problem. There is even a computational advantage in some uses of the dual form, which can provide faster computer solution times.

It has already been established that the solution of either the primal or dual form of a given problem will provide exactly the same information. So what are these contrasting insights that the dual form provides? To compare these two formulation formats, we are going (1) to provide both visual and verbal algorithms to aid you in conceptualizing the important transpositional process between them, (2) to discuss the computational advantages to consider in determining which form to use, and (3) to compare the elements of each form through the use of a common LP problem.

The Primal and Dual Problem Formulation

For illustrative purposes, let's employ the hypothetical German car dealer study (Example 4.3) to examine the technique of transposing the dual from the primal form. The primal form of this problem is, once again, as follows:

OBJECTIVE FUNCTION

$$\text{Maximize profit, } Z = 9000x_1 + 6000x_2 + 12{,}500x_3$$

SUBJECT TO

- Space $\quad\quad\quad\quad 120x_1 + 115x_2 + 148x_3 \leq 5000$
- Budget $\quad\quad\quad\quad 27{,}000x_1 + 20{,}000x_2 + 32{,}500x_3 \leq 800{,}000$
- Mfg. Availability $\quad x_1 \leq 25, \ x_2 \leq 35, \ x_3 \leq 8$
- Demand $\quad\quad\quad\quad x_3 \leq 6$
- Inventory Policy $\quad x_1 \geq 12, \ x_2 \geq 12, \ x_3 \geq 4$
- Sales Hours $\quad\quad\quad 28x_1 + 22x_2 + 30x_3 \leq 1100$

The *primal canonical form*—a maximization problem formulation consisting of only $\leq$ resource constraints and all nonnegative variables—for this type of maximization problem is as follows:

OBJECTIVE FUNCTION

$$\text{Max } Z = c_1x_1 + c_2x_2 + \cdots + c_jx_j + \cdots + c_nx_n$$

SUBJECT TO

$$a_{11}x_1 + a_{12}x_2 + \cdots + a_{1j}x_j + \cdots + a_{1n}x_n \leq b_1$$
$$a_{21}x_1 + a_{22}x_2 + \cdots + a_{2j}x_j + \cdots + a_{2n}x_n \leq b_2$$
$$\vdots \qquad\qquad \vdots$$
$$a_{m1}x_1 + a_{m2}x_2 + \cdots + a_{mj}x_j + \cdots + a_{mn}x_n \leq b_m$$

The corresponding *dual canonical form*—a minimization problem formulation consisting entirely of $\geq$ resource constraints and all nonnegative variables—is as follows:

OBJECTIVE FUNCTION

$$\text{Min } Z = b_1y_1 + b_2y_2 + \ldots + b_iy_i + \ldots + b_my_m$$

SUBJECT TO

$$a_{11}y_1 + a_{21}y_2 + \cdots + a_{i1}y_i + \cdots + a_{m1}y_m \geq c_1$$
$$a_{12}y_1 + a_{22}y_2 + \cdots + a_{i2}y_i + \cdots + a_{m2}y_m \geq c_2$$
$$\vdots \qquad\qquad \vdots$$
$$a_{1n}y_1 + a_{2n}y_2 + \cdots + a_{in}y_i + \cdots + a_{mn}y_m \geq c_n$$

The information from these two forms provides us with the dual form of Example 4.3.

OBJECTIVE FUNCTION

$$\text{Min } Z = 5000y_1 + 800{,}000y_2 + 25y_3 + 35y_4 + 8y_5$$
$$+ 6y_6 - 12y_7 - 12y_8 - 4y_9 + 1100y_{10}$$

SUBJECT TO

$$120y_1 + 27{,}000y_2 + y_3 + 0y_4 + 0y_5 + 0y_6$$
$$- y_7 + 0y_8 + 0y_9 + 28y_{10} \geq 9000$$

$$115y_1 + 2000y_2 + 0y_3 + y_4 + 0y_5 + 0y_6$$
$$+ 0y_7 - y_8 + 0y_9 + 22y_{10} \geq 6000$$

$$148y_1 + 32{,}500y_2 + 0y_3 + 0y_4 + y_5 + y_6$$
$$+ 0y_7 + 0y_8 - y_9 + 30y_{10} \geq 12{,}500$$

Do you see the symmetrical relationship between the primal and dual forms? The five-step algorithm used for converting the original nine-constraint primal into the three-constraint dual is explained below.

Step 1. Convert the optimization intention of the problem. That is, if the primal is a maximization, change it to a minimization, and vice versa.

Step 2. If the problem is to maximize, make sure that all constraints have $\leq$ signs. If some are $\geq$, multiply the entire constraint through by $a - 1$. If the problem is to minimize, all constraints must be $\geq$. If not, multiply through by -1 for those constraints that have a $\leq$ relationship.

For either maximization or minimization cases, an equality constraint must be handled differently. Split all equality constraints into two inequalities (call

them "nonidentical twins"): one "≤" and the other "≥." So, an equality of, say, $60x_1 + 54x_2 + 140x_3 = 2105$ is expressed as

$$60x_1 + 54x_2 + 140x_3 \leq 2105$$
$$60x_1 + 54x_2 + 140x_3 \geq 2105$$

Now, if the problem is to maximize, multiply the "≥" twin by -1; if it is to minimize, multiply the "≤" twin by -1. The results of this procedure are as follows:

TYPE OF PROBLEM	TWIN EQUATIONS
Maximization	$60x_1 + 54x_2 + 140x_3 \leq 2105$
	$-60x_1 - 54x_2 - 140x_3 \leq -2105$
Minimization	$-60x_1 - 54x_2 - 140x_3 \geq -2105$
	$60x_1 + 54x_2 + 140x_3 \geq 2105$

Step 3. Convert each of the jth primal RHS values, b_j, into the ith decision-variable coefficient in the dual objective function, y_i (e.g., the RHS values of primal constraints 1 through 9 become the objective coefficients of dual decision variables y_1 through y_9).

Step 4. Convert the jth column resource-constraint coefficients of the primal into the jth row resource-constraint coefficient of the dual (e.g., the three coefficient values in constraint 1 of the primal—120, 115, and 148—become the column values of the three constraints for the first dual decision variable, y_1; the coefficient values of constraint 2—27,000, 20,000, and 32,500—become the column values of the three constraints for the second dual decision variable, y_2, etc.).

Step 5. Convert each primal objective function coefficient, c_j, into the RHS value for the jth dual constraint (e.g., the OF coefficients x_1 through x_3 of the primal become the RHS values of dual constraints 1 through 3, respectively).

A pictorial description of this transformation procedure is shown in Figure 6-1. Now that you have the tools to slip between these two formulation arrangements, a question may arise: So what? Why bother with this transformation process if, ultimately, both the dual and primal forms provide the same optimal solution? The compelling motive is that one form usually provides an improved computational efficiency over the other, depending on the number of constraints and decision variables constituting the particular problem. Although the computational efficiency is usually not a critical issue in small LP problem formulations, larger moderate to "industrial strength" (in size) applications can experience significant cost savings by taking advantage of the appropriate form of an LP model. The larger the problem, the greater the potential saving. The selection of the most efficient form to employ is discussed next.

Determining Which Standard Form to Use

Typically, a computer can solve an LP problem formulation more quickly when the number of constraint equations is minimized. Remember that the simplex solution process, described in Chapter 5, sets $n-m$ constraints (where n = number of constraint equations and m = number of decision variables) equal to zero so that it can solve a square $m \times m$ matrix. So, the computer solution time for a given formulation is propor-

FIGURE 6-1

Primal—Dual Transformation

The relationship signs of the primal constraints become the objective function signs in the dual (i.e., $\leq \to$ "+", $\geq \to$ "−")

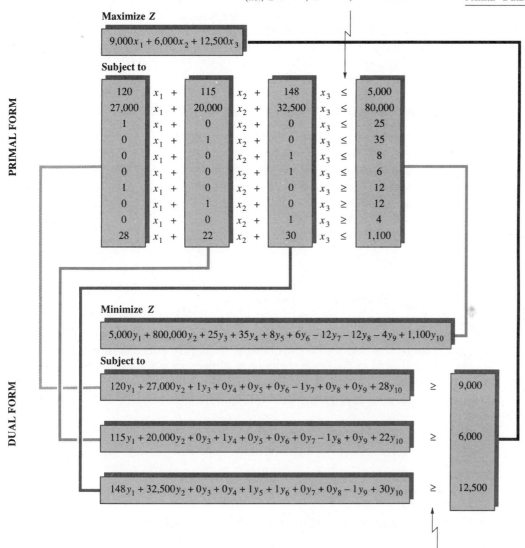

The relationship signs of the dual constraints are GTE ($\geq$) because the objective function is a minimization

tional (not equal) to m^2n.[1] Therefore, it can be extremely advantageous for the manager ultimately to select the form (primal or dual) that minimizes the number of constraint equations. This preference remains consistent even though this optimal form will increase the number of decision variables in each constraint equation. The type of constraint—whether it is LTE, GTE, or an equality—is a secondary consideration (e.g., LTE constraints generally require the least computational time, since they require only slack variables, whereas GTE constraints require both surplus and artificial variables,

[1]Linus Schrage, *Linear Programming Models with LINDO*, (Palo Alto, CA: The Scientific Press, 1981), pp. 28–29.

and E constraints require artificial variables). Now let's compare the solution times and the number of iterations required for the primal and dual form of several examples discussed in earlier chapters. The results, using a common LP software package, are illustrated in Table 6-1. These findings consistently show that we can obtain the fastest solutions by selecting the form that *minimizes the number of rows* in the model. When time is of the essence, it is important to determine which solution form—primal or dual—minimizes the number of rows.

Comparison of Primal and Dual Form Elements

To understand what additional insight the dual can provide, we shall compare the *common components* of the problem formulation.

1. *Objective function decision variables.* Unlike the primal, the dual is not concerned with the maximization of profit. Instead, the dual concentrates on the efficient use of our scarce resources. In effect, the dual views the problem as one of determining the value of additional resources to the German car dealer. It does this by finding the marginal value or shadow prices—represented by y_1 through y_9—of the resources. Thus, y_1 is the amount that the dealer would be willing to pay for each additional square foot of floor space, y_2 is the value to the dealer for each additional dollar of budget, and so on. Logically, only scarce resources—resources that are "used up"—will have nonzero shadow prices.

2. *Resource constraints.* The primal is concerned with making sure that the level of available resources for each constraint is not violated. Conversely, the dual views the need to have the marginal value of the required resources for each product be at least equal to the profit contribution of that product. The first constraint in the primal,

$$120x_1 + 115x_2 + 148x_3 \leq 5000$$

TABLE 6-1

Solution Efficiency Comparisons of Several Primal and Dual LP Formulations

Problem	Form* (P/D)	Number of Rows (Number of constraints)	Number of Columns (Number of decision variables)	Number of Iterations to Solution	Elapsed Time (Seconds)
1. German car dealer,	P	7	2	3	4
Exercise 4-1	D	2	7	2	2
2. German car dealer,	P	10	3	5	4
Exercise 4-6	D	3	10	3	3
3. District attorney study,	P	17	25	20	35
Example 4.6	D	25	17	36	105
4. Ambulance problem,	P	13	27	21	25
Exercise 4-12	D	27	13	39	66
5. Coca-Cola production	P	24	72	34	170
schedule, Exercise 4-11	D	72	24	117	585

*P = primal formulation; D = dual formulation.

ensures that, no matter how many of each of the three types of cars are ultimately purchased by the dealer for sale, the available space to store these cars is not violated. The first dual constraint,

$$120y_1 + 27{,}000y_2 + y_3 + 0y_4 + 0y_5 + 0y_6 - y_7 + 0y_8$$
$$+ 0y_9 + 28y_{10} \geq 9000$$

examines the Porsche-related costs associated with the different resources in contrast to what it actually contributes to the business. That is, the amount of space required for each Porsche (120 square feet) times the shadow price of one square foot of space (y_1) plus the amount of budget consumed for each Porsche ($27,000) times the shadow price of each budget dollar (y_2) plus the monthly per-unit shadow price of manufacturer availability (y_3), minus the per-unit monthly inventory shadow price (y_7) plus the average number of sales hours required to sell one Porsche (28) times the shadow price of one hour of salesperson time (y_{10}) *must be at least equal to $9000*: the profit contribution of a Porsche (the remaining zero coefficient decision variables address the other non-Porsche related products). All other constraint equations for both the dual and primal form are interpreted in exactly the same manner.

|6.3| SHADOW PRICE

The *dual solution* variable values, y_i, represent the marginal return or the *shadow prices* associated with each RHS value of the resource constraints in the primal solution. Shadow prices typically reflect how much change will be caused in the primal objective function value by a corresponding one unit change in the RHS value. For Example 4.3, the primal shadow prices reveal the following points.

1. An additional $1666.67 in *gross profit* is achieved if one additional unit of resource constraint 6—in this case, 1 extra unit of Mercedes—can be sold over the present limit of six (Table 6-2). Therefore, the $1666.67 shadow price represents a maximum *premium* that the dealer would be willing to spend for an additional Mercedes (for a limited quantity) in order to be able to sell more than the current sales level of six Mercedes per month. Notice that this value is identical to the value of the dual solution for the maximum number of Mercedes that could be sold monthly, y_6 (Table 6-3).

2. The shadow price associated with the budget (primal constraint 2) suggests that you can increase gross profits by $0.33 for a limited amount of additional budget beyond the original $800,000 allotted. Thus, the dealer would be willing to add a limited number of dollars to the budget so long as he did not have to pay a premium in excess of $0.33 per dollar. The corresponding dual solution variable value, y_2, reflects the same information.

3. The final improvement of $666.67 gross profit occurs for each one unit *less* of BMW the dealer would be required to carry in inventory under the present requirement of a 12-unit *minimum*—constraint 8. Again, the dealer would be willing to spend up to $666.67 for each unit reduction in the current required minimum inventory of 12 BMWs. The dual solution variable value for y_8 makes the same point.

All other constraints in the primal have an associated resource surplus and, therefore, a zero shadow price. (Predictably, the corresponding solution variable values in the dual also have zero values.) This means that a limited number of additional units of re-

TABLE 6-2

Formulation and Solution to Primal Formulation of German Car Dealer Study

Source: W. Erikson & D. Hall, *Computer Models for Management Science*. Version 2. Reading, MA: Addison-Wesley, 1986.

```
               COMPUTER MODELS FOR MANAGEMENT SCIENCE
                 -=*=- INFORMATION ENTERED -=*=-

     NUMBER OF VARIABLES                          : 3
     NUMBER OF <= CONSTRAINTS                      : 6
     NUMBER OF = CONSTRAINTS                       : 0
     NUMBER OF >= CONSTRAINTS                      : 3

     MAX = 9000 X1 + 6000 X2 + 12500 X3

     SUBJECT TO:
           120 X1  +    115 X2  +    148 X3   <= 5000
         27000 X1  +  20000 X2  +  32500 X3   <= 800000
             1 X1  +      0 X2  +      0 X3   <= 25
             0 X1  +      1 X2  +      0 X3   <= 35
             0 X1  +      0 X2  +      1 X3   <= 8
             0 X1  +      0 X2  +      1 X3   <= 6
             1 X1  +      0 X2  +      0 X3   >= 12
             0 X1  +      1 X2  +      0 X3   >= 12
             0 X1  +      0 X2  +      1 X3   >= 4

                    -=* =- RESULTS -=* =-

                          VARIABLE        ORIGINAL
            VARIABLE        VALUE         COEFFICIENT
              X1          13.519             9000
              X2          12                 6000
              X3           6                12500
     CONSTRAINT   ORIGINAL          SLACK OR     SHADOW
     NUMBER       RIGHT-HAND VALUE  SURPLUS      PRICE
       1              5000          1109.778        0
       2            800000             0           .333
       3                25            11.481         0
       4                35            23             0
       5                 8             2             0
       6                 6             0          1666.667
       7                12             1.519         0
       8                12             0           666.667
       9                 4             2             0
      10              1100           277.481         0
          OBJECTIVE FUNCTION VALUE:       268666.656
```

sources allocated to these constraints will have no effect on the present solution of either the primal or dual objective function. Further, *the shadow price also reflects the marginal rate of change in the objective function caused by changes in the quantity of one or more of the members in the present optimal mix.* (We shall discuss this concept in considerable detail later in this chapter.)

Determining Whether a Nonzero Shadow Price Suggests an Increase or a Decrease in an Existing Resource Level The interpretation of the BMW minimum inventory shadow price raises an important concern. Most LP software packages will provide shadow price, marginal value, or opportunity cost information (all these terms are essentially identical). However, not all of these programs will help you to distinguish explicitly whether the shadow price represents a potential *improvement* or *degradation* of the objective function value because only magnitude values are provided. To know whether it makes sense to *increase* or *decrease* the particular resource level (constraint) in question, you must know one piece of information: Is the specific scarce resource in question a GTE or LTE constraint? The simple rule you can follow

```
                COMPUTER MODELS FOR MANAGEMENT SCIENCE
                    -=*=- INFORMATION ENTERED -=*=-

             NUMBER OF VARIABLES        :     9
             NUMBER OF <= CONSTRAINTS   :     0
             NUMBER OF = CONSTRAINTS    :     0
             NUMBER OF >= CONSTRAINTS   :     3

       MIN = 5000 Y1 + 800000 Y2 + 25 Y3 + 35 Y4 + 8Y5 + 6 Y6 - 12
              Y7 - 12 Y8 - 4 Y9
       SUBJECT TO:
          120   Y1 +  27000   Y2  +  1  Y3   +  0  Y4  +
            0   Y5 +      0    Y6  -  1  Y7   +  0  Y8  +
            0   Y9 ≥  9000

          115   Y1 +  20000   Y2  +  0  Y3   +  1  Y4  +
            0   Y5 +      0    Y6  +  0  Y7   -  1  Y8  +
            0   Y9 ≥  6000

          148   Y1 +  32500   Y2  +  0  Y3   +  0  Y4  +
            1   Y5 +      1    Y6  +  0  Y7   +  0  Y8  -
            1   Y9 ≥  12500

                    -=* =- RESULTS -=* =-

                       VARIABLE        ORIGINAL
          VARIABLE      VALUE        COEFFICIENT
             Y1          0.             5000.
             Y2           .333        800000.
             Y3          0.               25.
             Y4          0.               35.
             Y5          0.                8.
             Y6       1666.667            6.
             Y7          0.               12.
             Y8        666.667           12.
             Y9          0.                4.

    CONSTRAINT       ORIGINAL      SLACK OR      SHADOW
    NUMBER        RIGHT-HAND VALUE  SURPLUS      PRICE
       1              9000            0         13.519
       2              6000            0         12
       3             12500            0          6

        OBJECTIVE FUNCTION VALUE:            268666.656
```

TABLE 6-3

Formulation and Solution to Dual Formulation of German Car Dealer Study

Source: W. Erikson & D. Hall, *Computer Models for Management Science*. Version 2. Reading, MA: Addison-Wesley, 1986.

for *improving* the optimal objective function value when only a magnitude value (positive value) of the shadow price is provided is shown in Table 6-4. Whether the problem is a maximization or minimization type is irrelevant! Only the type of constraint is important. Decreasing a GTE-type constraint or increasing an LTE-type constraint can only serve to further enhance the optimal solution.

Determining Whether Nonzero Shadow Prices Justify Additional Resources Although the shadow price of a particular scarce (depleted) resource identifies a potential way of improving an existing optimal solution, it does not guarantee that that approach will work; shadow prices cannot address the *real costs* associated with actually changing the amount of a given resource level (RHS value). For example, the shadow price for the budget in the primal suggested that an additional dollar of budget would add $.33 to the objective function. However, in most situations like this, there is an expense involved in obtaining additional units of resource. In this particular case, the money might have to be borrowed at an annual rate of 18 percent. Or, possibly, the car dealer could be in such a poor economic position that no financial institution

TABLE 6-4

Simple Rule for Determining Whether RHS Value Should Be Increased or Decreased in Order to Improve* the Objective Function Value

Type of Constraint	Resource Level
≤	Increase level
≥	Decrease level

*An improvement is represented by a decrease in a minimization objective function value or by an increase in a maximization objective function value.

would provide loan money at any rate! *The point here is that shadow prices cannot deal with the situation-specific costs of obtaining more scarce resources: These are real-world problems that can be approached only under actual circumstances.*

6.4 SENSITIVITY ANALYSIS: INTERPRETING THE COMPUTER SOLUTION

The primal solution of our German car dealer problem, disregarding the noninteger solution outcome (obviously, it is not possible to sell fractional numbers of cars), is shown in Table 6-2. The resulting objective function value for the optimum product mix of 13.519 Porsches, 12 BMWs, and 6 Mercedes Benz was $268,666.66 in anticipated gross profit. However, what happens if the estimates of the numerous parameters we gave the computer turn out to be different? What happens to our profit? Does it go up or down? And what about the present mix of cars? Does it stay the same, or change, or what? Obviously, we need to know just how sensitive our input information is. In particular, it is essential to be able to understand such issues as the following:

1. Of which resources, if any, should we try to get more? Are there any resources that we should decrease? In either case, by how much should the resource levels be changed?

2. By how much can the per-unit profit contributions of the different cars change before the present optimal mix changes? What happens to the value of the objective function?

3. Does it make sense to consider adding another make of foreign car to our present mix? If for the sake of argument, the dealer adds Audi to his line of cars, will that enhance the existing profits or undercut the present line sold? How will it affect the resources available?

4. What happens if the distributor increases the dealer's cost on Porsches? How does that affect the optimal mix? What is the new profit? On the other hand, what happens if the BMW distributor decreases the cost to the dealer to promote larger volume sales? What happens to the mix then?

Now let's examine each one of these issues by carefully studying the hypothetical sensitivity analysis portion of the solution in Table 6-5.

Right-Hand-Side (RHS) Constraint Ranging

You have already learned that exhausted resources—those constraints with nonzero shadow prices—may possess the potential to provide further improvement of the present optimal solution. In addition, you know how to determine whether it is necessary to increase or decrease the present resource level to achieve that improvement. But it is *not* reasonable to assume that you can change the resource level *without limit* and continue to achieve the same constant rate of change in the objective function. It is therefore extremely important for the manager to know the range over which he can change the RHS value of a constraint and still have the shadow price for that resource remain valid. Now, how are the RHS ranging limits for a specific resource established? By the removal or addition of some amount (as yet undetermined) of one of the other remaining decision variables (not yet defined) presently in the optimal mix. Although this may

TABLE 6-5

Sensitivity Analysis of German Car Dealer Study

Source: W. Erikson & D. Hall, *Computer Models for Management Science*. Version 2. Reading, MA: Addison-Wesley, 1986.

sound hopeless, it is really quite simple. The process requires only that we use a little common sense. Let's illustrate this logical process by determining the RHS limits associated with the one of the exhausted resources—the budget (constraint 2).

The current budget has a shadow price of $0.333 (for every dollar of change in budget experienced, there will be an associated 33.3-cent change in the current objective function value of $268,666.67). It is important for the manager to determine—especially if changes in the budget are anticipated—the range over which the shadow price will remain valid. So, the questions you must ask yourself are: (1) "If I get more budget money, which member of my existing product mix would it make sense to increase and by how much?" and (2) "If I have my present budget reduced, which of my present products must be reduced and by how much?" Let's tackle the more pleasant situation first.

If the budget is increased, it would be reasonable to select the product that best improves the objective function *per dollar of budget*. For the three makes of cars, the marginal rate of contribution to profits per dollar of budget is

AUTO	PROFIT/BUDGET MARGINAL RETURN
Porsche	$9000/27,000 = 0.333$
BMW	$6000/20,000 = 0.300$
Mercedes	$12,500/32,500 = 0.385$

It is clear that Mercedes would be the most attractive addition if more budget monies were made available. However, we cannot introduce more Mercedes into the solution, because the maximum number that can be sold is already in the solution (constraint 6): $x_1 = 6$. The next most attractive addition is, therefore, Porsche. You know now that an

unspecified number of Porsches will be added from the quantity already in the solution, as long as there are no other resource constraint violations.

If the budget is decreased, it would be reasonable to remove some of the product that least depreciates the objective function *per dollar of budget*. If you used the same marginal values of profit/budget just discussed, you would select BMW: That car will have the least impact on the objective function per dollar of budget reduction. However, BMW is constrained by inventory constraint 8: a minimum of 12 BMWs must be carried. Since this is exactly the number of BMWs in the present solution, the manager cannot purchase fewer units (unless there is a shift in policy at some later point in time). The next most attractive product to reduce is Porsche. *You have now established that varying numbers of Porsche will be added and subtracted from the number presently in the solution to accommodate changes in the budget.* (Note that the fact that the same product is affected by either increases or decreases in the resource constraint under examination is only a coincidence; frequently, different products will be involved with additions and reductions of a RHS level.)

The constraints that pertain to the Porsche are (1) storage space (constraint 1), (2) manufacturer availability (constraint 3), and (3) inventory policy (constraint 7). The surplus values associated with each of these constraints, as originally presented in Table 6-2, are

CONSTRAINT	SURPLUS
2, Space (ft^2)	1109.778
3, Mfg. Avail.	11.481
7, Inventory	1.519

The storage space and the manufacturer availability surpluses both focus on the upper limit of the number of Porsches that could be added to the present optimal solution if the budget were increased. *However, the more stringent of these two constraints will establish the upper limit value.* The minimum inventory will determine the number of Porsches that can be removed from the present optimal solution. Now let's determine what the upper limit and lower RHS limits are by finding the exact number of units of Porsche that can be added or subtracted from the present solution. These calculations follow.

Constraint	Surplus	Per-Unit Rate Contribution/Consumption	Change Allowed
Space (ft^2)	1109.778	1109.778/120	9.248
Mfg. Avail.	11.481	11.481/1	11.481
Inventory	1.519	1.519/1	1.519

You can quickly see that the limiting constraint for the upper limit is storage space. Although manufacturer availability allows the dealer to add a maximum of 11.481 units of Porsche, the storage area is the tighter of the two constraints: Only 9.248 units of Porsche may be added before you run out of space. As identified earlier, the minimum-inventory constraint limits the maximum reduction of Porsches to 1.519 units. Now we are ready to specify the exact upper and lower RHS ranging values for the budget. The upper limit is established by the extra budget required to purchase the additional 9.248 units of Porsche. That is,

$$\begin{pmatrix} \text{Upper RHS value} \\ \text{for budget} \end{pmatrix} = \text{original value} + \begin{pmatrix} \text{Number units of} \\ \text{Porsche added} \end{pmatrix} \begin{pmatrix} \text{Per-unit budget} \\ \text{consumption rate} \\ \text{of Porsche} \end{pmatrix}$$

Upper RHS value for budget $= 800{,}000 + (9.248)(27{,}000)$

$$= 800{,}000 + 249{,}700$$
$$= 1{,}049{,}700$$

The lower limit, as determined by the minimum inventory, is

$$\begin{array}{l}\text{Lower RHS value} \\ \text{for budget}\end{array} = \text{original value} - \left(\begin{array}{c}\text{Number units of} \\ \text{Porsche added}\end{array}\right)\left(\begin{array}{c}\text{Per-unit budget} \\ \text{consumption rate} \\ \text{of Porsche}\end{array}\right)$$

$$= 800{,}000 - (1.519)(27{,}000)$$
$$= 800{,}000 - 41{,}000$$
$$= 759{,}000$$

The rate of change in the objective function value will remain at 33.3 cents per dollar so long as the budget level is kept between $759,000 and $1,049,700. To make sure that you understand how these RHS ranging limits are determined, let's do it again for another constraint with a nonzero shadow price.

There is a shadow price of $1666.67 associated with the maximum demand of Mercedes (constraint 6). That is, for each unit of Mercedes added to or subtracted from the present demand of six, there will be a corresponding change in the objective function value of $1666.67. The RHS ranging limits for constraint 6, reproduced from Table 6-5, are

CONSTRAINT NUMBER	LOWER LIMIT	ORIGINAL VALUE	UPPER LIMIT
6	4	6	7.262

However, let's pretend that we don't know the information regarding the shadow price and the RHS ranging limits. How can we determine these values? To find the maximum number (upper limit) of Mercedes you can have in the solution, you are, in essence, purchasing more units of x_3. To be able to make this purchase, however, you must raise the additional budget monies. Since, in sensitivity analysis, only one variable at a time may be changed, you cannot increase the present budget level while varying the number of Mercedes in the solution. The budget is fixed at $800,000. So, the only way to raise the additional monies needed to purchase more Mercedes is to "trade in" some portion of one of the other makes of automobiles in the solution. Since you cannot decrease the number of BMWs in the solution—you are already at the minimum value of 12 required for the minimum inventory—you must trade in some number of Porsches. Further, there is a minimum inventory limit of 12 Porsches (constraint 7), so the maximum decrease in the number of Porsches that can occur is 1.519 units at $27,000 per unit. This will raise a total of $(1.519)(27{,}000) = \$41{,}000$ of additional budget—the maximum number of Mercedes that can be purchased is fixed by this amount. How many Mercedes can be purchased for $41,000? Since the unit price for Mercedes is $32,500, the number of additional Mercedes units that can be purchased is

$$41{,}000/32{,}500 = 1.262$$

The upper limit of Mercedes is, therefore,

Upper limit $=$ **original value** $+$ **additional purchases**
$$= 6 + 1.262 = 7.262$$

You can establish the lower limit for Mercedes only by "trading in" some of the existing units of Mercedes presently in the solution and by purchasing more of one of the other automobiles. But the minimum number of Mercedes that the dealer wishes to carry is four (constraint 9). Therefore, if the dealer removes two units of Mercedes, the amount of budget that he frees up is $(2)(32,500) = \$65,000$. But which additional units of the remaining two makes of automobile will be purchased? (Remember, the objective function is to maximize profit within the established constraint set.) The make with the highest marginal rate of return per dollar of budget will be selected. These values are

AUTO	PROFIT/BUDGET MARGINAL RETURN
Porsche	$9000/27,000 = 0.333$
BMW	$6000/20,000 = 0.300$

So, the number of Porsches added to the present solution as a result of decreasing the Mercedes line to its lower limit is

$$65,000/27,000 = 2.407$$

If the values for the RHS ranging limits for Mercedes have already been established, why was this last calculation made? Because we need to establish the shadow price associated with these limits.

The shadow price—any shadow price—is simply the change in objective function value per unit of change of the resource in question. Since this shadow price is good across the entire RHS range of Mercedes, it is necessary to calculate it at only one of the limits. So, for the upper limit, 1.262 Mercedes are going to be added to the solution at the expense of giving up 1.519 Porsches. The net effect on the objective function is

$$
\begin{aligned}
Z &= 800,000 - \text{lost profit of 1.519 fewer Porsches} \\
&\quad + \text{added profit of 1.262 more Mercedes} \\
&= 800,000 - (1.519)(9000) + (1.262)(12,500) \\
&= 800,000 - 13,671 + 15,775 \\
&= 802,104
\end{aligned}
$$

The introduction of 1.262 new Mercedes increase the objective function value by $2104. This gives us a shadow price of $2104/1.262 = \$1666.67$ for the maximum demand of Mercedes. Even though it is unnecessary, let's check the shadow price at the lower limit of the RHS range. The new objective function value for the decrease in two units of Mercedes and the corresponding addition of 2.407 Porsches is

$$
\begin{aligned}
Z &= 800,000 - \text{profit loss from reduction of 2 Mercedes} \\
&\quad + \text{profit gain from additional 2.407 Porsches} \\
&= 800,000 - (2)(12,500) + (2.407)(9000) \\
&= 800,000 - 25,000 + 21,663 = 800,000 - 3337 \\
&= 796,663
\end{aligned}
$$

So, the net effect is to decrease the objective function value by $3337 for the two units of Mercedes given up. The shadow price for the lower limit is, unsurprisingly, $3337/2 = 1667.50$ (the 17-cent variation from 1666.67 is merely due to the rounding error). Therefore, a shadow price of $1666.67 is good between the upper and lower limits of 7.262 and four Mercedes, respectively. The determination of the RHS values for any other constraint of interest—including those with zero shadow prices—is accomplished in a similar manner.

Objective Function Coefficient Ranging

Table 6-4 also illustrates that the profit contributions of the three cars to the objective function can vary by different amounts before the basic mix of the current solution will be changed. For example,

1. Porsche, x_1, can decrease its per-unit contribution to profit by \$900 (to a lower limit of \$8100) or increase its per-unit contribution to profit by \$1384.62 (to an upper limit of \$10,384.62) before the current product mix of 13.519 cars in the solution changes.

2. BMW, x_2, can decrease by \$6000 (to a lower limit of \$0) or undergo an increase of \$666.67 (to an upper limit of \$6666.67) before the present number of 12 units in the solution changes.

3. Mercedes Benz can increase without limit, or decrease by approximately \$1667, its present profit contribution before the present six units in the solution is changed.

Now, let's see why these limits make sense.

First, let's address the "no-limit" values associated with the lower limit of BMW and the upper limit of Mercedes. The reason that BMW could decrease to, essentially, a zero profit contribution is that it is already at its lower limit of 12 inventory units (constraint 9). Therefore, the number in the solution cannot be decreased any further, *regardless* of how little it may contribute to the objective function. The "no limit" for the Mercedes is because the maximum number that can be sold—6 units—is the number presently in the solution. Increasing the profit contribution for Mercedes will not increase the demand! Therefore, even if you could get considerably more than the \$12,500 per unit presently achieved, there would be no one else to purchase additional units. A summary of the rationale of the objective function limits associated with the three cars is presented in Table 6-6.

Adding a New Variable

Sometimes, you may want to consider adding a new variable to an existing LP formulation. Will this variable (some good or service) enhance your optimal solution, or will it hinder the original function? Suppose the German car dealer has been experiencing personnel problems among his sales force, particularly in the area of company loyalty.

TABLE 6-6

Rationale of Objective Function Ranging Limits for the German Car Dealer Study

	Upper Limit	Reason for Limits — Lower Limit
Porsche, x_1	Above \$10,384.62, Porsche becomes more attractive than Mercedes. Therefore, more Porsches will be brought into the solution at the expense of fewer units of Mercedes (to a minimum limit of 4 Mercedes).	Below \$8100.00, BMW becomes more attractive than Porsche; therefore, more BMWs will be introduced at this point at the expense of fewer Porsches.
BMW, x_2	When the profit margin of BMW increases above \$6666.67, its marginal rate of return becomes greater than that of Porsche. At this point, more BMWs are brought into the solution, while some of the Porsches are taken out of the solution.	No fewer than the present number of 12 BMWs can be in the solution due to constraint 9. Therefore, there is no lower limit for BMW.
Mercedes, x_3	There is no upper limit for Mercedes because of constraint 6 ($x_3 \leq 6$).	If the profit contribution falls below \$10,833.33, Porsche becomes more attractive than Mercedes. At that lower limit, some of the Mercedes currently in the solution will be removed, and more Porsches will be introduced.

Aaron continues to be overwhelmed by the difference between his position in life and that of his General Manager Norman Flicky.

In fact, one of his salesmen, Howard Grant, has even been accused of suggesting that prospective buyers check out other dealerships that might give him a better deal! In order to stem these serious conditions, the dealer hires Norman Flicky, a seasoned veteran of retail auto sales, to serve as his new general manager. Flicky is, in fact, renowned for his ability to build unflinching loyalty—some would even suggest a mysterious kind of subservience to managerial authority—among his salespeople. One of Flicky's first moves in his new position is to consider the expansion of the German car dealer's product line. In particular, Flicky wants to consider the addition of the Audi automobile to the lineup. How can we use sensitivity analysis to assess the impact of adding a new product into our present mix? More importantly, how can we determine if this addition is wise? Unfortunately, this kind of consideration is not part of the standard sensitivity analysis software package. However, it is not necessary to re-solve the problem. Instead, we can use the shadow prices that represent the marginal value of each scarce resource to calculate the opportunity cost of introducing the Audi. These shadow prices can be multiplied by the amount of each resource required to provide one Audi. The sum of these costs gives us the amount of profit that we must forfeit to add the Audi line. If this value, given by Z_j, is less than the profit contribution, C_j, then the addition is profitable. For our example, the following amount of resources would be expended for each Audi offered: 130 square feet of space and \$17,000 of the available budget. If the Audi's per-unit profit contribution is \$5500, what is the effect of adding it to the present line? We can answer this question easily by calculating the $C_j - Z_j$ value. That is,

$$C_j - Z_j = 5500 - (.333)(17,000) + (1666.67)(0) + (-666.67)(0)$$
$$= 5500 - 5667$$
$$= -\$167$$

Notice that you are merely multiplying the shadow prices associated with the affected constraint by the amount of resources that each unit of this new product would consume (only constraints 2, 7, and 8 have nonzero shadow prices—all other constraints have surplus resources associated with them). The dealer must pay \$17,000 per unit, which must be removed from the budget (constraint 2); adding the Audi has no effect on the optimal number of Mercedes to be sold (constraint 7); and BMW does not have its minimum inventory policy violated (constraint 8). So, unless the Audi would contribute more than \$5667 per unit—which it does not according to our hypothetical example—you will decrease profit by adding it to your product line. Since the Audi does not provide an improvement over the present optimal solution, adding the car to the agency line is not a profitable strategy. The computer formulation and solution are shown in Table 6-7; the sensitivity analysis is shown in Table 6-8. Indeed, no units of Audi are brought into the optimal solution. On further examination of the objective coefficient ranging of Audi (x_4), you can see that the upper limit requires a profit contribution of \$5666.67 before units of this make of car can be introduced into the optimal solution.

Changing the Constraint Coefficients

A change in one of the resource constraint coefficients is a most difficult kind of variation to assess from the perspective of sensitivity analysis—and it is really beyond the intended scope of this book. Generally, the impact this kind of change has on the objective function depends on whether we have a maximization or minimization problem and whether the specific constraint with which the coefficient is associated is an LTE, a GTE, or an equality. In addition, whether the constraint is binding (exhausted) or non-

```
              COMPUTER MODELS FOR MANAGEMENT SCIENCE
                  -=*=- INFORMATION ENTERED -=*=-

                   NUMBER OF VARIABLES      : 4
                   NUMBER OF <= CONSTRAINTS : 9
                   NUMBER OF = CONSTRAINTS  : 0
                   NUMBER OF >= CONSTRAINTS : 2

   MAX = 9000 X1 + 6000 X2 + 12500 X3  + 5500 X4
   SUBJECT TO:
        120  X1  +    115  X2  +    148 X3   +    130 X4  <= 5000
      27000  X1  +  20000  X2  +  32500 X3   +  17000 X4  <= 800000
          1  X1  +      0  X2  +      0 X3   +      0 X4  <= 25
          0  X1  +      0  X2  +      0 X3   +      0 X4  <= 35
          0  X1  +      0  X2  +      1 X3   +      0 X4  <= 8
          0  X1  +      0  X2  +      0 X3   +      1 X4  <= 15
          0  X1  +      0  X2  +      1 X3   +      0 X4  <= 6
          1  X1  +      0  X2  +      0 X3   +      0 X4  >= 12
          0  X1  +      1  X2  +      0 X3   +      0 X4  >= 12
          0  X1  +      0  X2  +      1X3    +      0 X4  >= 4
         28  X1  +     22  X2  +     30 X3   +     33 X4  <= 1100

                    -=* =- RESULTS -=* =-

                         VARIABLE     ORIGINAL
             VARIABLE      VALUE      COEFFICIENT
               X1         13.519         9000.
               X2         12.            6000.
               X3          6.           12500.
               X4          0.            5500.

     CONSTRAINT      ORIGINAL           SLACK OR        SHADOW
     NUMBER       RIGHT-HAND VALUE      SURPLUS         PRICE
        1              5000             1109.778          0
        2            800000                0              .333
        3                25             11.481            0
        4                35             23                0
        5                 8              2                0
        6                15             15                0
        7                 6              0             1666.667
        8                12              1.519            0
        9                12              0              666.667
       10                 4              2                0
       11              1100            277.480            0

          OBJECTIVE FUNCTION VALUE:  268666.656
```

TABLE 6-7

Formulation and Solution of German Car Dealer Study Considering Addition of Audi Car Line

Source: W. Erikson & D. Hall, *Computer Models for Management Science*. Version 2. Reading, MA: Addison-Wesley, 1986.

binding (slack or surplus resources remain) will also influence the ultimate effect on the objective function. Of course, we can evaluate this influence simply by reformulating the original problem with the appropriate change in the constraint coefficient and solving it on the computer as a new case run (commonly referred to as the "brute-force technique").

Adding New Constraints

The addition of new constraints to the original problem is similar in effect to the changing of the constraint coefficient just discussed: The calculation procedure is a tedious one. The simplest way to address this consideration is to use the same approach—reformulate the problem with the new constraint and solve it with the aid of a computer. Sup-

TABLE 6-8

**Sensitivity Analysis of German
Car Dealer Study Considering
Addition of Audi Car Line**

Source: W. Erikson & D. Hall, *Computer Models for
Management Science.* Version 2. Reading, MA: Addison-Wesley, 1986.

```
                -- SENSITIVITY ANALYSIS --

             OBJECTIVE FUNCTION COEFFICIENTS

                   LOWER      ORIGINAL        UPPER
      VARIABLE     LIMIT      COEFFICIENT     LIMIT
        X1        8735.294    9000          10384.615
        X2     NO LIMIT       6000           6666.667
        X3       10833.333   12500         NO LIMIT
        X4     NO LIMIT       5500           5666.667

               RIGHT-HAND-SIDE VALUES

      CONSTRAINT  LOWER      ORIGINAL        UPPER
      NUMBER      LIMIT      VALUE           LIMIT
        1        3890.222    5000          NO LIMIT
        2       759000      800000          1049700
        3          13.519    25           NO LIMIT
        4          12        35           NO LIMIT
        5           6         8           NO LIMIT
        6      NO LIMIT      15           NO LIMIT
        7           4         6               7.262
        8      NO LIMIT      12              13.519
        9           0        12              14.05
       10      NO LIMIT       4               6
       11         822.520   1100          NO LIMIT

         -------  END OF ANALYSIS  -------
```

pose that the German car dealer wishes to include the fact that his shop can provide
about 180 hours of warranty maintenance per month for the three-car product mix he
sells. Further, he estimates that each Porsche, BMW, and Mercedes sold will require an
average 5.8, 6.3, and 5.2 hours, respectively, of this type of maintenance. The impact
of the addition of the constraint equation representing the maintenance hours to the
original problem is illustrated in the microcomputer solution and sensitivity analysis
provided in Table 6-9. When the additional maintenance constraint is added to the
problem formulation, the objective function decreases from $268,666.66 to
$260,586.20, and the optimal product mix changes to 12.621 Porsches (from 13.519),
12 BMWs (no change), and 6 Mercedes Benz (no change). Also examine the significant changes that occur in the objective function coefficient ranging, RHS constraint
ranging, and shadow prices. A more detailed description of how to resolve the simplex
tableau manually when adding a new constraint can be found in Markland.[2]

Deleting "Soft" Constraints: The Cost of Making Policy

Sometimes, problem formulations include policy constraints that can be described as
political or, more euphemistically, managerial prerogatives. In these cases, policy constraints may be considered to be nonessential components. More important than their
being superfluous, they can be very costly. It is usually enlightening for management to
see just how expensive these policies are in terms of impact on the objective function.
You can show the expense simply by resolving the original problem after eliminating
these types of constraints from the formulation. In this way, management has an oppor-

[2]Robert E. Markland, *Topics in Management Science* (New York: Wiley, 1989). pp. 160–162.

```
            COMPUTER MODELS FOR MANAGEMENT SCIENCE
              -=*=- INFORMATION ENTERED -=*=-

                   NUMBER OF VARIABLES      : 3
                   NUMBER OF <= CONSTRAINTS : 7
                   NUMBER OF = CONSTRAINTS  : 0
                   NUMBER OF >= CONSTRAINTS : 3

    MAX = 9000 X1 + 6000 X2 + 12500 X3
    SUBJECT TO:
        120  X1  +    115 X2  +      148 X3  <= 5000
      27000  X1  +  20000 X2  +    32500 X3  <= 800000
          1  X1  +      0 X2  +        0 X3  <= 25
          0  X1  +      0 X2  +        0 X3  <= 35
          0  X1  +      0 X2  +        1 X3  <= 8
          0  X1  +      0 X2  +        1 X3  <= 6
          1  X1  +      0 X2  +        0 X3  >= 12
          0  X1  +      1 X2  +        0 X3  >= 12
          0  X1  +      0 X2  +        1 X3  >= 4
        5.8 X1  +    6.3   X2  + 5.2 X3  <= 180

                    -=* =- RESULTS -=* =-

                         VARIABLE   ORIGINAL
            VARIABLE      VALUE      COEFFICIENT
               X1         12.621        9000.
               X2         12.           6000.
               X3          6.          12500.

    CONSTRAINT     ORIGINAL           SLACK OR        SHADOW
    NUMBER       RIGHT-HAND VALUE     SURPLUS         PRICE
        1             5000            1217.517           0
        2           800000           24241.430           0
        3               25              12.379           0
        4               35              23                0
        5                8               2                0
        6                6               0          1666.667
        7               12                .621           0
        8               12               0          3775.862
        9                4               2                0
       10              180               0          1551.724

         OBJECTIVE FUNCTION VALUE:        260586.20

                 -- SENSITIVITY ANALYSIS --

               OBJECTIVE FUNCTION COEFFICIENTS

                 LOWER       ORIGINAL        UPPER
    VARIABLE     LIMIT       COEFFICIENT     LIMIT
       X1        5523.810      9000        13942.309
       X2      NO LIMIT        6000         9775.862
       X3        8068.965     12500        NO LIMIT

                RIGHT-HAND-SIDE VALUES

    CONSTRAINT  LOWER       ORIGINAL         UPPER
    NUMBER      LIMIT       VALUE            LIMIT
        1       3890.222     5000          NO LIMIT
        2       759000     800000            104970
        3         12.621       25          NO LIMIT
        4         12           35          NO LIMIT
        5          6            8          NO LIMIT
        6          4            6             6.692
        7       NO LIMIT       12            12.621
        8          9.401       12            12.571
        9       NO LIMIT        4             6
       10        176.400      180           185.207

             ------ END OF ANALYSIS -------
```

TABLE 6-9

Formulation and Solution of German Car Dealer Study with Added Labor-Hours Constraint

Source: W. Erikson & D. Hall, *Computer Models for Management Science*. Version 2. Reading, MA: Addison-Wesley, 1986.

tunity to reconsider the inclusion of such elements. As an example, let's assume that the three inventory policy constraints (constraints 7, 8, and 9) of the original German car dealer example are internal policy constraints of the agency, rather than a minimum purchase set by the three different manufacturers. The solution and sensitivity analysis of these new conditions are illustrated in Tables 6-10 and 6-11, respectively. These tables show that the optimum mix of cars, as well as the value of the objective function, have changed. The new mix of 22.407 Porsches, 0 BMWs, and 6 Mercedes results in an anticipated profit of $276,666.67. The cost of the inventory policy constraints is $8000 per month ($276,666.67 − $268,666.66) or approximately $100,000 per year. Managers may or may not view this expense as a necessary one, but at least now they will have the information on which to base an intelligent decision. Just to play it safe, let's try one more sensitivity analysis interpretation.

EXAMPLE 6.1   THE SAN FRANCISCO SOLID WASTE DISPOSAL PROGRAM

Every city in the country is faced with the increasingly difficult problem of how to manage the disposal of its solid waste. The backyard incinerators of the past are no longer acceptable because we have recognized the health hazards of air pollution. (London, England, has even gone so far as to outlaw the use of residential fireplaces due to concern for both air pollution and fire safety!) Determining how to keep the costs of waste disposal within reason while matching up processing-site capacities with area pickup demands is a considerable task. For purposes of illustration, let's assume that the city of San Francisco, California, wishes to study this particular problem area for three of its neighborhood areas.

Let us, once again, assume for the purpose of illustration that the city of San Francisco has three solid-waste disposal sites for processing refuse. There are six refuse-collection areas, in the Sunset, Richmond, and Haight-Ashbury district neighborhoods, that use these dumps. The cost associated with the disposal of the trash has two components: (1) the processing cost of the incinerator at each of the three disposal sites, and (2) the transportation costs associated with pickup and removal of the refuse from the six collection areas to each disposal site. Each collection area generates a weekly tonnage of refuse (demand), and each disposal site has a weekly (supply) capacity for processing this refuse. These hypothetical data are illustrated in Table 6-12.

"Polyester waste dumps will last as long as the pyramids. I hope the discount stores are happy."

```
        COMPUTER MODELS FOR MANAGEMENT SCIENCE
         -=*=- INFORMATION ENTERED -=*=-

              NUMBER OF VARIABLES      : 3
              NUMBER OF <= CONSTRAINTS : 6
              NUMBER OF = CONSTRAINTS  : 0
              NUMBER OF >= CONSTRAINTS : 0

 MAX = 9000 X1 + 6000 X2 + 12500 X3
 SUBJECT TO:
        120 X1 +     115 X2 +      148 X3   <= 5000
      27000 X1 +   20000 X2 +    32500 X3   <= 800000
          1 X1 +       0 X2 +        0 X3   <= 25
          0 X1 +       0 X2 +        0 X3   <= 35
          0 X1 +       0 X2 +        1 X3   <= 8
          0 X1 +       0 X2 +        1 X3   <= 6


             -=* =- RESULTS -=* =-

                       VARIABLE     ORIGINAL
           VARIABLE     VALUE      COEFFICIENT
             X1         22.407        9000.
             X2          0.           6000.
             X3          6.          12500.

   CONSTRAINT    ORIGINAL          SLACK OR       SHADOW
    NUMBER    RIGHT-HAND VALUE     SURPLUS        PRICE
       1           5000           1423.111          0
       2         800000              0             .333
       3             25             11.481           0
       4             35             23               0
       5              8              2               0
       6              6              0           1666.667

       OBJECTIVE FUNCTION VALUE:         276666.67
```

TABLE 6-10

Formulation and Solution to the German Car Dealer Study after Elimination of Minimum Inventory Constraints 7, 8, and 9

Source: W. Erikson & D. Hall, *Computer Models for Management Science*. Version 2. Reading, MA: Addison-Wesley, 1986.

```
            -- SENSITIVITY ANALYSIS --


            OBJECTIVE FUNCTION COEFFICIENTS

                   LOWER      ORIGINAL        UPPER
        VARIABLE   LIMIT     COEFFICIENT      LIMIT
          X1        8100        9000         10384.615
          X2     NO LIMIT       6000          6666.667
          X3     10833.333     12500         NO LIMIT


              RIGHT-HAND-SIDE VALUES

   CONSTRAINT  LOWER      ORIGINAL        UPPER
    NUMBER     LIMIT       VALUE          LIMIT
       1     3576.889      5000          NO LIMIT
       2     195000      800000           104970
       3      22.407        25           NO LIMIT
       4        0           35           NO LIMIT
       5        6            8           NO LIMIT
       6      3.846          6              8.
       7     807.408       1100          NO LIMIT

       ------ END OF ANALYSIS -------
```

TABLE 6-11

Sensitivity Analysis of German Car Dealer Study after Elimination of Minimum Inventory Constraints 7, 8, and 9

Source: W. Erikson & D. Hall, *Computer Models for Management Science*. Version 2. Reading, MA: Addison-Wesley, 1986.

TABLE 6-12

Transportation and Processing Costs Associated with the San Francisco Neighborhood Solid-Waste Disposal Program

		Disposal Site 1	Disposal Site 2	Disposal Site 3		
	1	$ 80	$ 50	$ 70	700	
Refuse	2	$ 85	$125	$ 45	500	**Area Refuse**
Collection	3	$100	$ 80	$ 80	1100	**Generation**
Area	4	$ 65	$ 55	$ 70	635	(Tons/Week)
	5	$ 75	$ 70	$ 45	1025	
	6	$ 75	$ 40	$ 85	450	
Site Capacity (Tons/Week)		1900	1600	2100	5600/4410	TOTALS (Tons/Week)
Site Processing Costs ($/Ton)		40	75	65		

The manager of the solid-waste disposal program wants to be able to determine some detailed operating characteristics of her program. Specifically, she wishes to find out

1. What assignments will be made between the specific neighborhood refuse collection areas and individual disposal sites?

2. What are the total system operating costs, including both the transportation and processing costs?

3. How much unused resources remain?

4. Which scarce resources suggest a potential for improving the present assignment by reducing the overall system operating costs?

5. How much can the specific operating costs for each assignment change before it makes sense to change the present optimal mix?

6. To what percentage of full capacity is each of the sites used?

7. What happens to the overall system costs if a high-rise office building is built in refuse collection area 2, which will triple the present solid-waste demand from that neighborhood? She is told that the building owners will be willing to subsidize the city with $2500 per week. Is this amount acceptable?

SOLUTION

The objective is to minimize the overall system costs, which will include both the transportation and processing costs.

OBJECTIVE FUNCTION

Minimize system costs, $Z = 120x_{11} + 125x_{12} + 135x_{13} + 125x_{21} + 200x_{22} + \cdots + 150x_{63}$

or

$$\text{Minimize } Z = \sum_{i=1}^{m} \sum_{j=1}^{n} c_{ij}x_{ij}$$

SUBJECT TO

- *Constraints 1–6*

Area Refuse	$x_{11} + x_{12} + x_{13} = 700$
Generation	$x_{21} + x_{22} + x_{23} = 500$

$$\cdot \qquad \cdot$$
$$\cdot \qquad \cdot$$
$$\cdot \qquad \cdot$$

$$x_{61} + x_{62} + x_{63} = 450$$

or

$$\sum_{j=1}^{n} x_{ij} = \chi_i \qquad \text{for each } i \ (i = 1, 2, \ldots, 6)$$

- *Constraints 7–9*

Disposal	$x_{11} + x_{21} + x_{31} + x_{41} + x_{51} + x_{61} \leq 1900$
Site	$x_{12} + x_{22} + x_{32} + x_{42} + x_{52} + x_{62} \leq 1600$
Capacity	$x_{13} + x_{23} + x_{33} + x_{43} + x_{53} + x_{63} \leq 2100$

or

$$\sum_{i=1}^{m} x_{ij} \leq \chi_j \qquad \text{for each } j \ (j = 1, 2, 3)$$

This computer formulation is given in Table 6-13.

```
          COMPUTER MODELS FOR MANAGEMENT SCIENCE
             -=*=- INFORMATION ENTERED -=*=-

              NUMBER OF VARIABLES       : 18
              NUMBER OF <= CONSTRAINTS  : 3
              NUMBER OF = CONSTRAINTS   : 6
              NUMBER OF >= CONSTRAINTS  : 0

MAX = 120 X11 +  125 X12 +  135 X13 +  125 X21 +  200 X22 +  110 X23
+ 140 X31 +  155 X32 +  145 X33 +  105 X41 +  130 X42 +  135 X43
+ 115 X51 +  145 X52 +  110 X53 +  115 X61 +  115 X62 +  150 X63

SUBJECT TO:
X11  +  X12  +  X13  =    700
X21  +  X22  +  X23  =    500
X31  +  X32  +  X33  =   1100
X41  +  X42  +  X43  =    635
X51  +  X52  +  X53  =   1025
X61  +  X62  +  X63  =    450
X11  +  X21  +  X31  +  X41  +  X51  +  X61  ≤  1900
X12  +  X22  +  X32  +  X42  +  X52  +  X62  ≤  1600
X13  +  X23  +  X33  +  X43  +  X53  +  X63  ≤  2100
```

TABLE 6-13

Formulation of San Francisco Solid-Waste Disposal Program

Source: W. Erikson & D. Hall, *Computer Models for Management Science*. Version 2. Reading, MA: Addison-Wesley, 1986.

TABLE 6-14

Solution to San Francisco
Solid-Waste Disposal Program

Source: W. Erikson & D. Hall, *Computer Models for Management Science*. Version 2. Reading, MA: Addison-Wesley, 1986.

```
-=* =- RESULTS -=* =-

                   VARIABLE        ORIGINAL
     VARIABLE      VALUE           COEFFICIENT
       X11         165.            120.
       X12         535.            125.
       X13           0.            135.
       X21           0.            125.
       X22           0.            200.
       X23         500.            110.
       X31        1100.            140.
       X32           0.            155.
       X33           0.            145.
       X41         635.            105.
       X42           0.            130.
       X43           0.            135.
       X51           0.            115.
       X52           0.            145.
       X53        1025.            110.
       X61           0.            115.
       X62         450.            115.
       X63           0.            150.


   CONSTRAINT    ORIGINAL            SLACK OR       SHADOW
   NUMBER        RIGHT-HAND VALUE    SURPLUS        PRICE
       1            700                0            125
       2            500                0            110
       3           1100                0            145
       4            635                0            110
       5           1025                0            110
       6            450                0            115
       7           1900                0              5
       8           1600              615              0
       9           2100              575              0

        OBJECTIVE FUNCTION VALUE:        526850
```

ANSWERS

1. The solution shows that there are seven different combinations of refuse collection areas—represented by nonzero variable values—and disposal site assignments (Table 6-14).

2. The optimum routing patterns and usage rates of each site that will result in a minimum system cost of $526,850 per week.

3. Constraints 1 through 6 show that all of the refuse from each neighborhood area was collected (the slack/surplus values are all zero for the six collection sites). Since the capacity for processing the refuse was greater than the supply (the sites could process up to 5600 tons per week, whereas the neighborhoods only generated 4410 tons per week), two of the disposal sites did not operate at full capacity. Specifically, sites 2 and 3 had 615 and 575 tons per week of processing capacity that were unused (slack values).

4. The *shadow prices* shown in Table 6-14 illustrate that potential savings in system costs might occur with the *reduction* of resource levels (refuse generation) associated with each neighborhood (constraints 1–6) and the *addition* of resources to disposal site 1 (constraint 7). So, for example, for each ton of refuse generation *reduced* at neighborhood area 3, there would be a corresponding drop in the overall

system cost of $145 (see the shadow price associated with constraint 3). Conversely, each additional ton of refuse generated in this neighborhood would increase system costs by the same amount. The $145 shadow price is valid between a lower limit of 565 tons and an upper limit of 1265 tons (RHS ranging limits for constraint 3, Table 6-15).

5. The upper and lower limits for the *objective function ranging* provide the manager with estimates of how much the present processing costs associated with specific neighborhood area–site assignments can vary before the amount of refuse presently being processed is changed. For example, the present optimal solution processes all 1025 tons of refuse from neighborhood refuse collection area 5 at site 3 (x_{53}). However, if the costs for this processing increases from its present value of $110 per ton to any amount exceeding $120 per ton, at least some of the 1025 tons presently in the solution will be sent to a different site for processing. Also notice that there is no lower cost limit that would result in the reassignment of any portion of the x_{53} refuse to another site if the cost decreased below its present value of $110 per ton. This should make perfect sense to you: If this assignment is being made at a specific cost,

TABLE 6-15

Sensitivity Analysis of San Francisco Solid-Waste Disposal Program

Source: W. Erikson & D. Hall, *Computer Models for Management Science*. Version 2. Reading, MA: Addison-Wesley, 1986.

```
                -- SENSITIVITY ANALYSIS --


              OBJECTIVE FUNCTION COEFFICIENTS

                 LOWER      ORIGINAL        UPPER
      VARIABLE   LIMIT      COEFFICIENT     LIMIT
        X11      110.        120.           125.
        X12      120.        125.           135.
        X13      125.        135.        NO LIMIT
        X21      105.        125.        NO LIMIT
        X22      110.        200.        NO LIMIT
        X23   NO LIMIT       110.           130.
        X31   NO LIMIT       140.           150.
        X32      145.        155.        NO LIMIT
        X33      145.        145.        NO LIMIT
        X41   NO LIMIT       105.           125.
        X42      110.        130.        NO LIMIT
        X43      110.        135.        NO LIMIT
        X51      105.        115.        NO LIMIT
        X52      110.        145.        NO LIMIT
        X53   NO LIMIT       110.           120.
        X61      110.        115.        NO LIMIT
        X62        0.        115.           120.
        X63      115.        150.        NO LIMIT


                RIGHT-HAND-SIDE VALUES

     CONSTRAINT  LOWER    ORIGINAL          UPPER
     NUMBER      LIMIT    VALUE             LIMIT
        1        165.      700.            1315.
        2          0.      500.            1075.
        3        565.     1100.            1265.
        4        100.      635.             800.
        5          0.     1025.            1600.
        6          0.      450.            1065.
        7       1735.     1900.            2435.
        8        985.     1600.         NO LIMIT
        9       1525.     2100.         NO LIMIT


          ------- END OF ANALYSIS --------
```

the reduction of that cost would only enhance that assignment. The other objective coefficient ranges can be interpreted by the same technique.

6. The present percentages of full capacity usage (in tons per week) of the three sites are:

SITE	CAPACITY	PRESENT USAGE	UTILIZATION %
1	1900	1900	100
2	1600	985	62
3	2100	1525	73

7. Table 6-16 shows that a 10 percent increase in refuse collection area 2 (from 500 to 550 tons per week) will increase the total system costs to $532,350. This represents a $5500 increase due to the additional demand caused by the high-rise office building. The $2500 offer from the building owners leaves the city with a $3000 per week shortage—an arrangement likely to be unacceptable.

6.5 JUST IN CASE: "WHAT TO DO IN A POWER FAILURE," OR USING THE OPTIMAL SIMPLEX TABLEAU TO CONDUCT SENSITIVITY ANALYSIS

Although not the preferred approach, the optimal simplex tableau can be used to determine the objective function coefficient and RHS-value ranging limits of an LP formulation. Clearly, the risk of error in combination with the time-consuming manual number crunching needed to execute the simplex tableau sensitivity analysis makes this procedure a poor substitute for a computer solution. However, it is possible that a time may come when you need to have a sensitivity analysis of a linear-programming problem and the only information available to you is the final simplex tableau.[3] Use of

[3]It is also possible that a time will come when Sylvester Stallone will do *The Merchant of Venice* on Broadway.

TABLE 6-16

Solution to San Francisco Solid-Waste Disposal Program with 10 Percent Increase in Demand for Refuse Area 2

Source: W. Erikson & D. Hall, *Computer Models for Management Science*. Version 2. Reading, MA: Addison-Wesley, 1986.

```
           -=* =- RESULTS -=* =-

                    VARIABLE     ORIGINAL
     VARIABLE        VALUE      COEFFICIENT
       X11           165.          120.
       X12           535.          125.
       X13            0.           135.
       X21            0.           125.
       X22            0.           200.
       X23           550.          110.
       X31          1100.          140.
       X32            0.           155.
       X33            0.           145.
       X41           635.          105.
       X42            0.           130.
       X43            0.           135.
       X51            0.           115.
       X52            0.           145.
       X53          1025.          110.
       X61            0.           115.
       X62           450.          115.
       X63            0.           150.


     OBJECTIVE FUNCTION VALUE:      532350
```

the simplex tableau to conduct sensitivity analysis should be limited to such a rare instance.

The algorithms presented in this section are adaptations of those developed earlier by Turban and Meredith.[4]

Objective Function Coefficient Ranging

The quantity of each basic decision variable in the optimal mix remains unchanged as long as the objective function coefficient ranging limits associated with each basic decision variable are not exceeded. To determine the objective function coefficient ranging limits for any *basic decision variable* in the optimal tableau, take these steps:

Step 1. Copy the $c_j - z_j$ row

Step 2. Copy the basic decision variable row elements across the same columns as those that correspond to the $c_j - z_j$ row copied in step 1.

Step 3. Divide each $c_j - z_j$ row entry, *for the nonbasic variables only*, by the associated variable a_{ij} from the basic decision variable row selected in step 2.

Step 4. The *smallest positive number* found in step 3 identifies the amount by which the basic decision variable objective function value can be increased before the present optimal solution changes. If there are no positive values, there is no limit (i.e., +infinity).

Step 5. The least negative number (smallest absolute value) indicates by how much the basic decision variable objective function coefficient can be decreased before the present optimal solution changes. If there are no negative values, there is no limit (i.e., −infinity).

Step 6. Repeat steps 1 through 5 for the remaining basic decision variables. The general relationship for the objective function ranging for *basic decision variables* is given by

$$\text{(Upper limit)}_{OF} = \min \quad c_b + \frac{c_j - z_j}{a_{ij}} \quad \text{for all } a_{ij} < 0$$

$$\text{(Lower limit)}_{OF} = \max \quad c_b + \frac{c_j - z_j}{a_{ij}} \quad \text{for all } a_{ij} > 0$$

The objective function coefficient of *nonbasic decision variables*, c_j, will have to change to a new value, $c_j{}^*$, in the optimal tableau in order to be brought into the solution. The general relationship for nonbasic decision variables is given by

$$c_j{}^* \geq z_j$$

This represents the objective function upper limit for a maximization problem. There is no lower limit since any value less than the original objective function coefficient, c_j— which wasn't good enough to bring the nonbasic variable into solution—will make the decision variable, x_j, even less desirable. Therefore, the lower limit for such a nonbasic variable is minus infinity.

As an example, let's look at the two-variable dental office study (Example 5.1) using graphical methods. The optimal simplex tableau is shown in Table 6-17.

[4]Efraim Turban and Jack R. Meredity, *Fundamentals of Management Science*, 3d ed. (Plano, TX: Business Publications, 1985), pp. 223–232.

TABLE 6-17

Optimal Solution:* Simplex Maximization Tableau 3 for Dental Office Study

c(j)		85	50	0	0	0	
	Basic						RHS
c(B)	Variables	x_1	x_2	s_1	s_2	s_3	b(i)
50	x_2	0	1	2.08	−2.08	0	4.17
85	x_1	1	0	−.56	1.56	0	6.88
0	s_3	0	0	−1.28	.78	1	1.44
	z(j)	85	50	56.35	28.65	0	**792.71**
	c(j) −z(j)	0	0	−56.35	−28.65	0	

*Since all $c_j - z_j$ values ≤ 0, this solution is optimal.

As an example, let's look at the two-variable dental office study (Example 5.1) using graphical methods. The optimal simplex tableau is shown in Table 6-17.

Step 1. The $c_j - z_j$ row is

0	0	−56.35	−28.65	0

Step 2. The row elements for basic variable x_2 are

0	1	2.08	−2.08	0

Step 3. Divide each $c_j - z_j$ row entry, *for the nonbasic variables only*, by the associated variable a_{ij} from the basic variable row selected in step 2.

	x_1	x_2	s_1	s_2	s_3
$\dfrac{c_j - z_j}{a_{ij}}$	0	0	−56.35	−28.65	0
	0	1	2.08	−2.08	0
$\dfrac{c_j - z_j}{a_{ij}}$	—	0	−27.09	13.77	—

Step 4. The *smallest positive number* found in step 3 is 13.77 (in fact, it is the only positive value). Therefore, the upper limit is

$$(\text{Upper limit})_{OF} = 50 + 13.77 = 63.77$$

Step 5. The least negative number (smallest absolute value) indicates by how much the objective function coefficient can be decreased before the present optimal solution changes. If there are no negative values, there is no limit (i.e., −infinity).

$$(\text{Lower limit})_{OF} = 50 - 27.09 = 22.91$$

Step 6. The objective function coefficient rangings for the remaining basic variables are found by repeating steps 1 through 5.

There are no nonbasic decision variables.

RHS Value Ranging

The shadow price for any constraint in the optimal tableau remains unchanged within the upper and lower RHS-value ranging limits. These limits may be found for any constraint by using the following procedure:

Step 1. List the quantity column of the optimal tableau (i.e., the number of units of each variable in the final solution).

Step 2. List the substitution ratios, a_{ij}, of the resource constraint whose RHS range is being analyzed.

Step 3. Divide the b_i values by the substitution ratio values, b_i/a_{ij}.

Step 4. Identify the least negative and smallest positive result.

Step 5. The *least negative value* found in step 4 is the largest amount by which the present resource level, b_i, can be increased without changing the present shadow price; it is the RHS upper limit.

Step 6. The *least positive value* found in step 4 indicates the largest amount by which the present resource level, b_i, can be decreased without changing the present shadow price; it is the RHS lower limit.

The general relationships are:

$$(\text{Upper limit})_{\text{RHS}} = \text{original } b_i \text{ value } + \text{ smallest negative ratio of } \frac{b_i}{a_{ij}}$$

$$(\text{Lower limit})_{\text{RHS}} = \text{original } b_i \text{ value } - \text{ smallest positive ratio of } \frac{b_i}{a_{ij}}$$

For the dentist hours (constraint 1), the RHS ranging limits are as follows:

Step 1. The RHS (b_i) column of the optimal tableau is

RHS, b_i
4.17
4.17
6.88
1.44

Step 2. The substitution ratios, a_{ij}, for the dentist's hours (constraint 1) are:

s_1
  2.08
 −.56
−1.28

Step 3. Divide the b_i values by the substitution ratio values, a_{ij}:

b_i/s_1
   $4.17/2.08 = 2.00$
   $6.88/−.56 = −12.29$
  $1.44/−1.28 = −1.125$

Step 4. Identify the smallest negative and smallest positive result:

   Smallest negative $= −1.125$
   Smallest positive $= 2.00$

Step 5. The least negative value found in step 4 is the largest amount by which the present resource level, b_i, can be increased without changing the present shadow price; it is the RHS upper limit.

$$(\text{Upper limit})_{\text{RHS}} = 10 + 1.125 = 11.125$$

Step 6. The least positive value found in step 4 indicates the largest amount by which the present resource level, b_i, can be decreased without changing the present shadow price; it is the RHS lower limit.

$$(\text{Lower limit})_{\text{RHS}} = 10 - 2 = 8$$

6.6 SUMMARY

You have reached the point in our study of linear programming methods where you can translate complex problem statements into a language that can be understood and solved by a computer. In addition, you can now accurately interpret and use these results to make intelligent managerial decisions regarding the allocation of limited resources. You have gained an important skill, since almost every type of organization faces problems that require these management science techniques. Few texts, however, concentrate on developing your ability to read the scenarios, complete with ambiguities, that you will face in your everyday work. This text does. If you continue to find excuses to apply this powerful tool, your skills in this area will continue to grow.

Although linear programming is the most widely used management science tool in business, there are several other important linear resource allocation methods that deserve attention. Some of these tools are specialized versions of the LP model (integer, transportation, and assignment methods), several are related but have quite a different focus (goal programming and the GP-MAUM model), and one may be viewed as LP's countermodel (de novo programming). The next three chapters will address these useful linear resource allocation methods.

6.7 EXERCISES

6-1 Formulate the dual problem of the hypothetical Apple Computers product mix study introduced in Exercise 4-6. The primal version is shown in Table 6-1.1.

6-2 The primal formulation of the hypothetical TWA advertising study (Exercise 4-5) is shown in Table 6-2.1. Transform this version into the dual form.

6-3 Determine whether it would be more advantageous—from a solution-efficiency perspective—to use the primal or dual forms in Exercises 6-1 and 6-2. Defend your selections.

6-4 The primal formulation of the district attorney case-assignment study (Example 4.6) is shown in Table 6-4.1. Construct the dual version and determine which form will allow the most efficient computer solution.

6-5 The computer solution for the St. Paul land developer introduced in Exercise 4-4 is shown in Table 6-5.1. Answer the following questions regarding this information:

1. What is the optimal mix of homes?
2. What is the developer's gross profit?
3. What sales price would the developer have to be able to get for his two-bedroom condominiums before he could increase the present number in the solution?
4. Using the appropriate constraint numbers for identification, of which resource levels would it be foolish to attempt to get more? Why?
5. The number 13,260.865 appears only once in the computer solution. Explain what this number represents and under what conditions it is valid.

```
                    MICROSOLVE/OPERATIONS RESEARCH
                         REVISED EDITION IBM-PC
                            STUDENT VERSION
CONSTRAINT MATRIX

OBJMAX/      + 2000 X1   + 1200 X2   + 500 X3    + 300 X4
CON1/        + 10 X1     + 8 X2      + 8 X3      + 4 X4      <= 4392600
CON2/        + 1500 X1   + 800 X2    + 700 X3    + 400 X4    <= 345000000
CON3/        + 1 X1      <=   100000
CON4/        + 1 X2      <=   200000
CON5/        + 1 X3      <=    50000
CON6/        + 1 X4      <=   150000
CON7/        + 1 X1      >=    10000
CON8/        + 1 X2      >=    10000
CON9/        + 1 X3      >=    10000
CON10/       + 1 X4      >=    10000
CON11/       + .35 X1    + .35 X2    - .65 X3    + .35 X4    >=  0
CON12/       - 1.00 X1   - .80 X2    - .80 X3    + 3.6 X4    <=  0
```

```
                -=*=-  INFORMATION ENTERED  -=*=-

              NUMBER OF VARIABLES         :  5
              NUMBER OF <= CONSTRAINTS     :  7
              NUMBER OF  = CONSTRAINTS     :  0
              NUMBER OF >= CONSTRAINTS     :  1

MAX  =        21400 X1 +11850 X2 + 6875 X3 + 4180 X4 + 2490 X5
SUBJECT TO:
  180000 X1  +  100000 X2  +   75000 X3  + 4500 X4 + 3000 X5
<= 4750000
        1 X1  +       0 X2  +       0 X3  +    0 X4 +    0 X5 <= 24
        0 X1  +       1 X2  +       0 X3  +    0 X4 +    0 X5 <= 10
        0 X1  +       0 X2  +       1 X3  +    0 X4 +    0 X5 <= 36
        0 X1  +       0 X2  +       0 X3  +    1 X4 +    0 X5 <= 60
        0 X1  +       0 X2  +       0 X3  +    0 X4 +    1 X5 <= 85
    90000 X1  -    0000 X2  -   37500 X3  - 2250 X4 - 1500 X5 <= 0

   -18000 X1  -   10000 X2  -    7500 X3  + 4050 X4 + 2700 X5 >= 0
```

TABLE 6-1.1

Primal Formulation of Apple Computer Production Mix Exercise 4-6

Source: Paul Jensen, *Microsolve*.

TABLE 6-2.1

Primal Formulation of TWA Advertising Exercise 4-5

Source: W. Erikson & D. Hall, *Computer Models for Management Science*. Version 2. Reading, MA: Addison-Wesley, 1986.

6. Why is there no limit associated with the objective function coefficient upper value of X1?

6-6 The computer solution to and sensitivity analysis of the Apple Computer's product mix study (Exercise 4-6) are shown in Tables 6-6.1 and 6-6.2, respectively. Answer the following questions regarding this information:

1. What is the present optimal mix of computer products that Apple will produce? What can you determine about the "desirability" of the individual models based on only these numbers? (*Hint*: Use your knowledge of the other constraints.)

2. What percent profit will Apple make on its investment?

3. How would you interpret the RHS ranging for the budget?

4. What increase in sales price would Apple need to get for the Apple IIGS line to justify manufacturing more than are presently in production? Explain your answer.

5. What amount of production and assembly hours are unused? If the average worker consumes 2000 hours per year from this resource, how many full-time-equivalent (FTE) production and assembly workers does this represent? If you were the production manager, what would you suggest to top management regarding changes in the P & A (production and assembly) labor force? Explain your answer.

6. The Jensen software package (Microsolve) exhibits a negative number in the RHS ranging values. What does this negative number mean?

7. The Jensen software package used to solve this problem also exhibits negative dual-solution values. What do you guess this negative value means in terms of the shadow price?

6-7 Illustrate how the RHS ranging values for the minimum BMW inventory of 12 units (constraint 7) discussed in the German car

TABLE 6-4.1

Formulation of the District Attorney Study

Source: W. Erikson & D. Hall, *Computer Models for Management Science*. Version 2. Reading, MA: Addison-Wesley, 1986.

```
              -=*=-  INFORMATION ENTERED  -=*=-

            NUMBER OF VARIABLES       : 25
            NUMBER OF <= CONSTRAINTS   : 12
            NUMBER OF  = CONSTRAINTS   : 0
            NUMBER OF >= CONSTRAINTS   : 4

   MAX Z =  80 X11  +   50 X12  +   50 X13  +   70 X14  +   30 X15
         +   27 X21  +   45 X22  +   45 X23  +   36 X24  +   63 X25
         +   30 X31  +   30 X32  +   36 X33  +   36 X34  +   42 X35
         +   45 X41  +   40 X42  +   30 X43  +   45 X44  +   25 X45
         +    3 X51  +    8 X52  +    9 X53  +    4 X54  +    8 X55

SUBJECT TO:

85600 X11  +  85600 X12  +  85600 X13  +  85600 X14  +  85600 X15
+  60300 X21  +  60300 X22  +  60300 X23  +  60300 X24  +  60300 X25
+  75800 X31  +  75800 X32  +  75800 X33  +  75800 X34  +  75800 X35
+  33500 X41  +  33500 X42  +  33500 X43 +  33500 X44  +  33500 X45
+  18900 X51 +  18900 X52  +  18900  X53  +  18900 X54  +  18900 X55
<= 3450983


240 X11  +     0 X12  +     0 X13  +    0 X14  +    0 X15 +
120 X21  +     0 X22  +     0 X23  +    0 X24  +    0 X25 +
 64 X31  +     0 X32  +     0 X33  +    0 X34  +    0 X35 +
140 X41  +     0 X42  +     0 X43  +    0 X44  +    0 X45 +
 32 X51  +     0 X52  +     0 X53  +    0 X54  +    0 X55  <= 1600

0 X11  +   240 X12  +   0 X13  +    0 X14  +    0 X15  +
0 X21  +   120 X22  +   0 X23  +    0 X24  +    0 X25  +
0 X31  +    64 X32  +   0 X33  +    0 X34  +    0 X35  +
0 X41  +   140 X42  +   0 X43  +    0 X44  +    0 X45  +
0 X51  +    32 X52  +   0 X53  +    0 X54  +    0 X55  <= 1800

0 X11  +     0 X12  +   240 X13  +   0 X14  +    0 X15  +
0 X21  +     0 X22  +   120 X23  +   0 X24  +    0 X25  +
0 X31  +     0 X32  + -  64 X33  +   0 X34  +    0 X35  +
0 X41  +     0 X42  +   140 X43  +   0 X44  +    0 X45  +
0 X51  +     0 X52  +    32 X53  +   0 X54  +    0 X55  <= 1900

0 X11  +     0 X12  +     0 X13  +  240 X14  +    0 X15  +
0 X21  +     0 X22  +     0 X23  +  120 X24  +    0 X25  +
0 X31  +     0 X32  +     0 X33  +   64 X34  +    0 X35  +
0 X41  +     0 X42  +     0 X43  +  140 X44  +    0 X45  +
0 X51  +     0 X52  +     0 X53  +   32 X54  +    0 X55  <= 1200

0 X11  +     0 X12  +     0 X13  +    0 X14  +  240 X15  +
0 X21  +     0 X22  +     0 X23  +    0 X24  +  120 X25  +
0 X31  +     0 X32  +     0 X33  +    0 X34  +   64 X35  +
0 X41  +     0 X42  +     0 X43  +    0 X44  +  140 X45  +
0 X51  +     0 X52  +     0 X53  +    0 X54  +   32 X55  <= 1500

140 X11  +   140 X12  +   140 X13  +   140 X14  +   140 X15  +
100 X21  +   100 X22  +   100 X23  +   100 X24  +   100 X25  +
 44 X31  +    44 X32  +    44 X33  +    44 X34  +    44 X35  +
 88 X41  +    88 X42  +    88 X43  +    88 X44  +    88 X45  +
 18 X51  +    18 X52  +    18 X53  +    18 X54  +    18 X55  <= 7300
```

```
1 X11  +  1 X12  +  1 X13  +  1 X14  +  1 X15  +
0 X21  +  0 X22  +  0 X23  +  0 X24  +  0 X25  +
0 X31  +  0 X32  +  0 X33  +  0 X34  +  0 X35  +
0 X41  +  0 X42  +  0 X43  +  0 X44  +  0 X45  +
0 X51  +  0 X52  +  0 X53  +  0 X54  +  0 X55  <= 31

0 X11  +  0 X12  +  0 X13  +  0 X14  +  0 X15  +
1 X21  +  1 X22  +  1 X23  +  1 X24  +  1 X25  +
0 X31  +  0 X32  +  0 X33  +  0 X34  +  0 X35  +
0 X41  +  0 X42  +  0 X43  +  0 X44  +  0 X45  +
0 X51  +  0 X52  +  0 X53  +  0 X54  +  0 X55  <= 16

0 X11  +  0 X12  +  0 X13  +  0 X14  +  0 X15  +
0 X21  +  0 X22  +  0 X23  +  0 X24  +  0 X25  +
1 X31  +  1 X32  +  1 X33  +  1 X34  +  1 X35  +
0 X41  +  0 X42  +  0 X43  +  0 X44  +  0 X45  +
0 X51  +  0 X52  +  0 X53  +  0 X54  +  0 X55  <= 13

0 X11  +  0 X12  +  0 X13  +  0 X14  +  0 X15  +
0 X21  +  0 X22  +  0 X23  +  0 X24  +  0 X25  +
0 X31  +  0 X32  +  0 X33  +  0 X34  +  0 X35  +
1 X41  +  1 X42  +  1 X43  +  1 X44  +  1 X45  +
0 X51  +  0 X52  +  0 X53  +  0 X54  +  0 X55  <= 25

0 X11  +  0 X12  +  0 X13  +  0 X14  +  0 X15  +
0 X21  +  0 X22  +  0 X23  +  0 X24  +  0 X25  +
0 X31  +  0 X32  +  0 X33  +  0 X34  +  0 X35  +
0 X41  +  0 X42  +  0 X43  +  0 X44  +  0 X45  +
1 X51  +  1 X52  +  1 X53  +  1 X54  +  1 X55  <= 41

1 X11  +  1 X12  +  1 X13  +  1 X14  +  1 X15  +
0 X21  +  0 X22  +  0 X23  +  0 X24  +  0 X25  +
0 X31  +  0 X32  +  0 X33  +  0 X34  +  0 X35  +
0 X41  +  0 X42  +  0 X43  +  0 X44  +  0 X45  +
0 X51  +  0 X52  +  0 X53  +  0 X54  +  0 X55  >= 10

0 X11  +  0 X12  +  0 X13  +  0 X14  +  0 X15  +
1 X21  +  1 X22  +  1 X23  +  1 X24  +  1 X25  +
0 X31  +  0 X32  +  0 X33  +  0 X34  +  0 X35  +
0 X41  +  0 X42  +  0 X43  +  0 X44  +  0 X45  +
0 X51  +  0 X52  +  0 X53  +  0 X54  +  0 X55  >= 10

0 X11  +  0 X12  +  0 X13  +  0 X14  +  0 X15  +
0 X21  +  0 X22  +  0 X23  +  0 X24  +  0 X25  +
1 X31  +  1 X32  +  1 X33  +  1 X34  +  1 X35  +
0 X41  +  0 X42  +  0 X43  +  0 X44  +  0 X45  +
0 X51  +  0 X52  +  0 X53  +  0 X54  +  0 X55  >= 5

0 X11  +  0 X12  +  0 X13  +  0 X14  +  0 X15  +
0 X21  +  0 X22  +  0 X23  +  0 X24  +  0 X25  +
0 X31  +  0 X32  +  0 X33  +  0 X34  +  0 X35  +
1 X41  +  1 X42  +  1 X43  +  1 X44  +  1 X45  +
0 X51  +  0 X52  +  0 X53  +  0 X54  +  0 X55  >= 10
```

TABLE 6-5.1

**Formulation and Solution of the
Land Developer Study**

Source: W. Erikson & D. Hall, *Computer Models for
Management Science*. Version 2. Reading, MA: Addison-Wesley, 1986.

```
C O M P U T E R   M O D E L S   F O R   M A N A G E M E N T   S C I E N C E

                    -=*=-  INFORMATION ENTERED  -=*=-
          NUMBER OF VARIABLES           :    3
          NUMBER OF <= CONSTRAINTS      :    6
          NUMBER OF  = CONSTRAINTS      :    0
          NUMBER OF >= CONSTRAINTS      :    1

          MAX Z =       70000    X1 +45000   X2 +15000   X3
          SUBJECT TO:
              115000    X1 +90000   X2 +65000   X3        <=15800000
               10000    X1 + 7000   X2 + 4000   X3        <= 1350000
                 950    X1 +  900   X2 +  600   X3        <=  233000
                   1    X1 +    0   X2 +    0   X3        <=     120
                   0    X1 +    1   X2 +    0   X3        <=     180
                   0    X1 +    0   X2 +    1   X3        <=      60
            -   .15    X1 -  .15   X2 +  .85   X3        >=       0

                        -=*=-   RESULTS  -=*=-
                         VARIABLE        ORIGINAL        COEFFICIENT
          VARIABLE        VALUE         COEFFICIENT      SENSITIVITY
            X1             120            70000              0
            X2             6.145          45000              0
            X3            22.261          15000              0
          CONSTRAINT      ORIGINAL        SLACK OR          SHADOW
          NUMBER       RIGHT-HAND VALUE    SURPLUS          PRICE
            1           15800000             0               .443
            2            1350000          17941.863           0
            3             233000         100113.047           0
            4              120               0            13260.865
            5              180             173.855            0
            6               60              37.739            0
            7                0               0            18260.869

          OBJECTIVE FUNCTION VALUE:        9010435

                      -- SENSITIVITY ANALYSIS --
                     OBJECTIVE FUNCTION COEFFICIENTS
                          LOWER          ORIGINAL          UPPER
          VARIABLE        LIMIT         COEFFICIENT        LIMIT
            X1          56739.133         70000          NO LIMIT
            X2          20769.23          45000          55639.531
            X3          NO LIMIT          15000          32500

                         RIGHT-HAND-SIDE VALUES
          CONSTRAINT      LOWER          ORIGINAL          UPPER
          NUMBER          LIMIT           VALUE            LIMIT
            1           15176470         15800000        16036257
            2          1332058.125       1350000         NO LIMIT
            3          132886.953         233000         NO LIMIT
            4               0              120             124.93
            5             6.145            180            NO LIMIT
            6            22.261             60            NO LIMIT
            7        -   16.289             0              8.154
```

TABLE 6-6.1

Solution of Apple Computer Product Mix

Source: Paul Jensen, *Microsolve*.

```
                PRIMAL SIMPLEX ALGORITHM
                   OPTIMUM SOLUTION
          BASIC SOLUTION -    PHASE 2  -  ITER. 14
               VAR.       NAME       VALUE
                1         X1         100000
                2         X2         200000
                3         X3          10000
                4         X4          70000
                5         SLK-1      143260
                6         SLK-2           0
                7         SLK-3           0
                8         SLK-4       40000
                9         SLK-5       80000
               10         SLK-6       60000
               11         SLK-7       53000
               12         SLK-8       16000


            OBJECTIVE   =   4.66000E+08
```

TABLE 6-6.2

Sensitivity Analysis of Apple Computer Product Mix

Source: Paul Jensen, *Microsolve*.

```
                                    SIMPLE RANGING FOR
          DUAL SOLUTION             RIGHT HAND SIDE OF CONSTRAINTS

                                              LOWER      UPPER
    ROW   NAME    VALUE        RHS             RANGE      RANGE
     1    CON1     .75         3.45E+08        ----       ----
     2    CON2      0          4392600         ----       ----
     3    CON3    875.0000      100000         98896.55   116000
     4    CON4    600.0000      200000         198000     230000
     5    CON5      0            50000         10000       ----
     6    CON6      0           150000         70000       ----
     7    CON7      0            10000         ----       100000
     8    CON8      0            10000         ----       200000
     9    CON9    -25.000        10000         7746.48    44285.71
    10    CON10     0            10000         ----       70000
    11    CON11     0                0         ----       53000
    12    CON12     0                0         -16000      ----


                    OBJ.      LOWER      UPPER
          VAR.      COEF.     RANGE      RANGE

           X1       2000      1125       ----
           X2       1200      600        ----
           X3       500       ----       525
           X4       300       285.71     533.33
```

dealer study in Section 6.2 were established (for your convenience, the RHS ranging values for this study are reproduced in Table 6-7.1). Further, prove that a shadow price of $666.67 is, indeed, correct and that it is relevant only for *reductions* in the minimum inventory requirement.

6-8 The solution and sensitivity analysis for the district attorney study (Example 4.6) are shown in Tables 6-8.1 and 6-8.2. Using these tables, make the following managerial assessments:

1. Currently, each of the five deputy DAs has a limited amount of time to prepare and conduct the various types of trials. If you could increase these limits for any one of these deputy DAs, which one would you choose? Explain your choice.

2. How many murder cases will *not* be tried?

3. Which deputy DA prosecutes the largest number of cases? How many and which type(s) of cases does he or she prosecute?

4. Which deputy DA works the fewest number of cases? How many and which type(s) of cases does he or she work?

5. Which deputy DA prosecutes the largest number of different case types? How many of each type does he or she prosecute?

6. What is the value of the objective function and how would you describe its meaning?

7. The DA believes that she can get an additional $25,000 in budget. What effect would this have on the objective function value? Explain your answer.

8. The DA is currently trying to get more rape cases assigned to the court calendar. The cases are still in a preliminary stage of development. Can you tell her how many more rape cases she

should attempt to get ready for the court calendar if the present marginal value for this case type does not change?

9. The DA is concerned about the assignment of rape cases to deputy DA 5. She knows that this deputy DA's probability for conviction on this case type is about .70 (see Table 4.5 in Chapter 4). However, she also knows that this value has some uncertainty associated with it. Therefore, she would like to determine the amount that this probability value can change before she would either assign more or fewer of this type of case to this deputy DA. Tell her the amount of variation that would cause these new assignments to be made. Show all work.

TABLE 6-7.1

Right-Hand-Side (RHS) Ranging of German Car Dealer Study

Constraint Number	Right-Hand-Side Values		
	Lower Limit	Original Value	Upper Limit
1	3890.222	5000	No Limit
2	759000	800000	1049700
3	13.519	25	No Limit
4	12	35	No Limit
5	6	8	No Limit
6	4	6	7.262
7	No Limit	12	13.519
8	0	12	14.05
9	No Limit	4	6
10	822.522	1100	No Limit

Source: W. Erikson & D. Hall, *Computer Models for Management Science*. Version 2. Reading, MA: Addison-Wesley, 1986.

TABLE 6-8.1

Solution of District Attorney Study

Source: W. Erikson & D. Hall, *Computer Models for Management Science*. Version 2. Reading, MA: Addison-Wesley, 1986.

```
              -=*=-  RESULTS  -=*=-


                   VARIABLE           ORIGINAL
      VARIABLE       VALUE           COEFFICIENT

         X11         6.667              80.
         X12         0.                 50.
         X13         2.862              50.
         X14          .472              70.
         X15         0.                 30.
         X21         0.                 27.
         X22         0.                 45.
         X23         3.5                45.
         X24         0.                 36.
         X25        12.5                63.
         X31         0.                 30.
         X32         0.                 30.
         X33        12.393              36.
         X34         0.                 36.
         X35         0.                 42.
         X41         0.                 45.
         X42        12.857              40.
         X43         0.                 30.
         X44         7.763              45.
         X45         0.                 25.
         X51         0.                  3.
         X52         0.                  8.
         X53         0.                  9.
         X54         0.                  4.
         X55         0.                  8.
```

CONSTRAINT NUMBER	ORIGINAL RHS VALUE	SLACK OR SURPLUS	SHADOW PRICE
1	3450983.	0.	.001
2	1600.	0.	.364
3	1800.	0.	.204
4	1900.	0.	.156
5	1200.	0.	.239
6	1500.	0.	.306
7	7300.	1940.117	0.
8	31.	21.	0.
9	16.	0.	5.587
10	13.	.607	0.
11	25.	4.38	0.
12	41.	41.	0.
13	10.	0.	16.813
14	10.	6.	0.
15	5.	7.393	0.
16	10.	10.62	0.

```
OBJECTIVE FUNCTION VALUE:         3097.545
```

TABLE 6-8.2

Sensitivity Analysis of District Attorney Study

Source: W. Erikson & D. Hall, *Computer Models for Management Science*. Version 2. Reading, MA: Addison-Wesley, 1986.

```
           --  SENSITIVITY ANALYSIS  --

         OBJECTIVE FUNCTION COEFFICIENTS
```

VARIABLE	LOWER LIMIT	ORIGINAL COEFFICIENT	UPPER LIMIT
X11	70.	80.	NO LIMIT
X12	NO LIMIT	50.	61.429
X13	44.286	50.	61.429
X14	58.571	70.	75.714
X15	NO LIMIT	30.	86.
X21	NO LIMIT	27.	70.
X22	NO LIMIT	45.	50.714
X23	39.413	45.	51.75
X24	NO LIMIT	36.	55.
X25	56.25	63.	NO LIMIT
X31	NO LIMIT	30.	49.333
X32	NO LIMIT	30.	39.048
X33	32.4	3.6	46.698
X34	NO LIMIT	36.	41.333
X35	NO LIMIT	42.	45.6
X41	NO LIMIT	45.	62.5
X42	33.333	40.	NO LIMIT
X43	NO LIMIT	30.	33.333
X44	41.667	45.	51.667
X45	NO LIMIT	25.	54.333
X51	NO LIMIT	3.	18.145
X52	NO LIMIT	8.	13.002
X53	NO LIMIT	9.	11.478
X54	NO LIMIT	4.	14.145
X55	NO LIMIT	8.	16.278

```
              RIGHT-HAND-SIDE VALUES
```

CONSTRAINT NUMBER	LOWER LIMIT	ORIGINAL VALUE	UPPER LIMIT
1	3059340.5	3450983.	3483127.
2	1446.616	1600.	1690.302
3	1646.616	1800.	2246.961
4	1746.616	1900.	1990.302
5	1046.616	1200.	1646.961
6	1346.616	1500.	1590.302
7	5359.883	7300.	NO LIMIT
8	10.	31.	NO LIMIT
9	14.838	16.	23.933
10	12.393	13.	NO LIMIT
11	20.62	25.	NO LIMIT
12	0.	41.	NO LIMIT
13	9.462	10.	15.171
14	NO LIMIT	10.	16.
15	NO LIMIT	5.	12.393
16	NO LIMIT	10.	20.62

```
----------  E N D   O F   A N A L Y S I S  ----------
```

6-9 Use the formulation of the hypothetical Oakland school district desegregation study (Example 4.7) to obtain the optimal solution and associated sensitivity analysis using a microcomputer package of your choice. Answer the following questions:

1. What is the total number of student miles traveled (one-way) that represents the optimal solution to this study?

2. What are the specific student-to-school assignments that constitute this optimal solution in terms of (a) the neighborhood representation at each school, and (b) the student ethnicity proportion for each school.

3. Explain the meaning of the objective function ranging coefficients associated with this particular problem.

4. Would it make sense to attempt to decrease or increase the present capacity of any of the three schools if that were possible? If so, which school(s) would you change, and by how much?

5. What possible changes in the individual neighborhood student populations would potentially affect the present objective function value? By what amount can these changes occur? Explain your answer in detail.

6. What is the optimal solution if the time and distance constraints are eliminated?

7. What is the optimal solution if the present ethnicity-porportion requirements of the three high schools is relaxed?

8. What is the optimal solution if the time, distance, and the ethnicity proportions of the three high schools are relaxed?

9. Re-solve the problem given that the new objective function is to minimize round-trip system costs, assuming that each student mile traveled costs the district $.60.

References

1. Lapin, Lawrence. *Quantitative Methods for Business Decisions,* 2d ed. New York: Harcourt Brace Jovanovich, 1981.

2. Markland, Robert E. *Topics in Management Science*. New York: Wiley, 1989.

3. Turban, Efraim, and Jack R. Meredith. *Fundamentals of Management Science*, 3d ed, Plano, Texas: Business Publications, 1985.

© 1984 Universal Press Syndicate

Early experiments in transportation

CHAPTER 7

SPECIAL LINEAR RESOURCE-ALLOCATION MODELS

TRANSPORTATION METHOD, ASSIGNMENT METHOD, INTEGER PROGRAMMING, AND DE NOVO PROGRAMMING

7.1 INTRODUCTION

The simplex method provides a general algorithm capable of solving any linear resource-allocation problem; it is a faithful workhorse—"Old Paint." However, there are special problem situations that arise in which the simplex method, although usable, is an inefficient tool to employ. The special models that will be discussed in this chapter include

1. The transportation method (TM)

2. The assignment method (AM)

3. Integer programming (IP)

4. De novo programming

The transportation and assignment methods are two types of LP models—often referred to as network models—that have a particular type of mathematical structure. This special structure facilitates the use of streamlined versions of the general simplex method that can rapidly solve large TM and AM problems. Integer programming does not recognize the assumption of divisibility in the standard LP model. Instead, IP is concerned with solving linear resource-allocation models whose product mix comprises variables that must be in whole number units. In addition to these three models, a fourth model, de novo programming will also be presented. De novo programming provides an alternative perspective to traditional linear programming: it challenges the presumption that linear programming does, in fact, *meaningfully* optimize limited resource allocation problems.

7.2 TRANSPORTATION METHOD (TM)

The transportation method (TM) addresses a special kind of LP problem. It is particularly concerned with, but not limited to, the transportation or distribution of goods, people, or services between sets of origins or sources (supply centers) and destinations (demand centers). Typically, the TM is formulated as a minimization problem in which the objective function is concerned with transportation costs. The standard formulation

of minimizing the system costs of transporting goods from the ith origin to the jth destination is

$$\text{Minimize } Z = \sum_{i=1}^{m} \sum_{j=1}^{n} c_{ij} x_{ij}$$

subject to the allocation of all supply goods

$$\sum_{j=1}^{n} x_{ij} = s_i \qquad \text{for each } i \, (i = 1, 2, \ldots, m)$$

and to the satisfaction of all demand needs

$$\sum_{i=1}^{m} x_{ij} = d_j \qquad \text{for each } j \, (j = 1, 2, \ldots, n)$$

and that the total supply is exactly equal to the total demand,

$$\sum_{i=1}^{m} s_i = \sum_{j=1}^{n} d_j$$

and that the total number of routes that will be allocated shipping assignments is

$$\text{Number assigned routes } = m + n - 1$$

where

Z = total system costs

c_{ij} = cost of transporting one unit of goods from the ith origin to the jth destination

x_{ij} = total number of units of goods transported from the ith origin to the jth destination

s_i = total number of supply units of goods to be shipped from the ith origin

d_j = total number of demand units of goods to be received at the jth destination

m = total number of origins ($i = 1, 2, \ldots, m$)

n = total number of destinations ($j = 1, 2, \ldots, n$)

Of course, the goods shipped cannot take on negative values, so the nonnegativity constraint (which will be part of any transportation software package) is

$$x_{ij} \geq 0 \quad \text{for all } i \text{ and } j$$

Supply and Demand Imbalances

Total supply and demand are rarely equal. However, we need to make only a minor adjustment to handle transportation problems that have unmatched supply and demand. Here are the simple alterations that can be made to handle any imbalance:

1. *Supply exceeds demand.* Add a fictitious (dummy) destination column whose demand is equal to the excess supply quantity to the real set of destinations. Also, assign a zero transportation cost for the cells in that dummy column. Sometimes, the final solution may allocate goods to a cell in this fictitious column. If this occurs, the manager should interpret these units as *unshipped goods*.

2. *Demand exceeds supply.* Merely add a dummy source row whose supply matches the excess demand quantity to the real set of sources. The transportation cost for the cells in the dummy row are given a value of zero. The manager should interpret any units assigned to these cells as *unmet demand*.

Transportation Method Algorithms

The TM uses a streamlined version of the simplex method. Because of this, TM software—when contrasted with a comparable version of simplex LP software—is many times faster, uses less memory, and thereby can solve far larger problems. The TM also has another advantage over the simplex method: It is possible to solve reasonably large transportation problems using *manual* techniques. From a real-world standpoint, this is not necessarily useful—any manual technique will be error-prone and more time consuming than will be one that uses appropriate software. However, examining a few of these manual methods will provide the same type of insight to the TM solution process as did studying the simplex method for the standard LP solution process.

Two of the most widely used manual procedures are Vogel's approximation method (VAM) and the modified distribution method (MODI). The VAM provides feasible solutions that are usually nearly optimal. The MODI takes an initial feasible solution from, for example, the VAM, refines it, and ultimately determines the optimal solution if one exists. These techniques are presented next.

Vogel's Approximation Method (VAM)   Vogel's approximation method can provide optimal or, more likely, near-optimal solutions. VAM is considered a satisfactory technique if the manager or analyst is willing to accept a good approximation of the optimal solution.

VAM's underlying objective is to resist making shipping assignments along the more expensive routes. We shall present the VAM algorithm using the hypothetical San Francisco solid-waste disposal program (Example 6.1). We shall make a single modification to this example to protect illustrative clarity: The policy constraints are eliminated, so that the only resource restrictions are supply and demand. The procedure is as follows.

Step 1. *Design the VAM calculation cost table.* The basic cost matrix is shown in Table 7-1. Since demand exceeds supply by 1190 tons/week, row 7 has been added to the original tableau as a *dummy* refuse collection area.

Step 2. *For each table row, find the minimum cost cell and the next-to-lowest cost cell in that same row.* Calculate the opportunity loss by taking the difference between these two values.

| The difference between the minimum and next-to-minimum cost cells are calculated for each row and the corresponding opportunity loss values are recorded: row 1 = 5; row 2 = 15; row 3 = 5; row 4 = 25; row 5 = 5; row 6 = 5; row 7 = 0. |

Step 3. *Perform for each column in the table the same operation that you did in step 2.*

| The difference between the minimum and next-to-minimum cost cells are calculated for each column and the corresponding opportunity loss values are recorded: column 1 = 105; column 2 = 115; column 3 = 110. |

TABLE 7-1

San Francisco Solid-Waste Disposal Cost Matrix

		To j^{th} Disposal Site (Demand)				
		Site 1	Site 2	Site 3		
	Area 1	$ 120	$ 125	$ 135	700	
From	Area 2	$ 125	$ 200	$ 110	500	*Area Refuse*
i^{th} Refuse	Area 3	$ 140	$ 155	$ 145	1100	*Generation*
Collection	Area 4	$ 105	$ 130	$ 135	635	*(tons/week)*
Area	Area 5	$ 115	$ 145	$ 110	1025	
(Supply)	Area 6	$ 115	$ 115	$ 150	450	
	Area 7*	$ 0	$ 0	$ 0	1190	
		1900	1600	2100	5600	TOTAL

Disposal Site Capacity

(tons/week)

*Area 7 is a dummy site (i.e., it balances the 1190 tons/week of surplus capacity of the disposal sites to process the refuse—5600 tons/week—versus the rate at which the collection areas generate the refuse—4410 tons/week.

Step 4. *Determine the largest potential opportunity loss from among all the rows and columns.* Find the minimum cost cell associated with this row or column. This number is the *critical cell value.* If there is a tie among the opportunity losses, you may arbitrarily select either of the tied cells.

The initial opportunity cost matrix is illustrated in Table 7-2. Iteration 1 shows the maximum opportunity cost of $115/ton is associated with column

TABLE 7-2

Initial VAM Tableau for the San Francisco Solid-Waste Disposal, Illustrating Original Opportunity Cost Values

Column opportunity costs

		105 Site 1		*115* Site 2		*110* Site 3		Demand
5	Area 1	120	**0**	125	**0**	135	**0**	700
15	Area 2	125	**0**	200	**0**	110	**0**	500
5	Area 3	140	**0**	155	**0**	145	**0**	1100
25	Area 4	105	**0**	130	**0**	135	**0**	635
5	Area 5	115	**0**	145	**0**	110	**0**	1025
5	Area 6	115	**0**	115	**0**	150	**0**	450
0	Area 7	0	**0**	0	**0**	0	**0**	1190
	Supply	**1900**		**1600**		**2100**		

(Row opportunity costs — left margin label)

Note: The number in the upper-left corner within each cell represents the per-ton transportation cost of moving refuse between each specific combination of area pickup–disposal site route; the bold-face number in each cell is the amount of tonage allocated to that particular route; the bold-face numbers in the right-hand-side row and bottom column margins represent the demand and supply totals for the refuse areas and disposal sites, respectively; the italic numbers in the top column and the left-hand-side row margins represent the disposal site–collection area opportunity-cost values, respectively.

2. The least-cost cell associated with column 2 is $0 (row 7) and is the critical cell value.

Step 5. *Assign the maximum number of units to the cell selected in step 4.* This number will be the smaller value from among the column-row totals associated with the critical cell value. This step will completely exhaust a row or column or, possibly, both. Omit the exhausted row or column from further calculations.

Allocate the maximum number of supply units—1190—to the minimum cost cell (7,2). This will eliminate row 7 and decrease column 2 from 1600 to 410 tons.

Step 6. *Repeat steps 2 through 5 using the surviving rows and columns until the total supply is depleted.* New column and row opportunity cost values are calculated. The revised opportunity cost matrix is shown in Table 7-3.

During the *second iteration*, the largest opportunity cost is associated with row 4. The least-cost cell in this row at $105 is cell (4,1). Therefore, allocate the maximum number of supply units—635—to the minimum-cost cell (4,1). This will eliminate row 4 and decrease column 1 from 1900 to 1265 tons. The new opportunity costs are generated. The revised opportunity cost matrix is shown in Table 7-4.

TABLE 7-3

VAM Iteration 1 for San Francisco Solid-Waste Disposal

Column opportunity costs

Row opportunity costs		10 Site 1		10 Site 2		0 Site 3		Demand
5	Area 1	120	0	125	0	135	0	700
15	Area 2	125	0	200	0	110	0	500
5	Area 3	140	0	155	0	145	0	1100
0	Area 4	105	0	130	0	135	0	635
5	Area 5	115	0	145	0	110	0	1025
0	Area 6	115	0	115	0	150	0	450
0	Area 7	0	0	0	1190	0	0	0
Supply		**1900**		**410**		**2100**		

Allocate 1190 tons/week to the maximum opportunity cost ($115/ton)—column 2—and minimum transportation cost in this column ($0)—row 7: cell (7, 2). Therefore, row 7 is eliminated and the column 2 capacity is decreased to 410 tons/week.

☐ Note: Eliminated row or column

TABLE 7-4

VAM Iteration 2 for San Francisco Solid-Waste Disposal

Column opportunity costs

Row opportunity costs		0 Site 1		10 Site 2		0 Site 3		Demand
5	Area 1	120	0	125	0	135	0	700
15	Area 2	125	0	200	0	110	0	500
5	Area 3	140	0	155	0	145	0	1100
0	Area 4	105	635	130	0	135	0	0
5	Area 5	115	0	145	0	110	0	1025
0	Area 6	115	0	115	0	150	0	450
0	Area 7	0	0	0	1190	0	0	0
Supply		**1265**		**410**		**2100**		

Allocate 635 tons/week to the maximum opportunity cost ($25/ton)—row 4—and minimum transportation cost in this row ($105)—column 1: cell (4, 1). Accordingly, row 4 is eliminated and the capacity if column 1 is reduced to 1265 tons/week.

☐ Note: Eliminated row or column

The *third iteration* shows that the largest opportunity cost of $15/ton is associated with row 2. The least-cost remaining cell in this row is the $110 of column 3. Therefore, allocate the maximum number of supply units (the minimum value between the row and column totals for that critical cell value)—500—to the minimum-cost cell (2,3). This will eliminate row 2 and decrease column 3 from 2100 to 1600 tons. The revised opportunity cost matrix is shown in Table 7-5.

The largest opportunity cost available in the *fourth iteration* is $25/ton in column 3. The least-cost remaining cell in this column is $110 (row 5). Therefore, allocate the maximum number of supply units—1025—to the minimum-cost cell (5,3). This will eliminate row 5 and decrease column 3 from 1600 to 575 tons. The revised opportunity cost matrix is shown in Table 7-6.

The *fifth iteration* reveals that the largest opportunity cost of $10/ton is associated with columns 2 and 3. Let's arbitrarily select column 2. The least-cost cell in this column is $115 (row 6). Therefore, allocate the maximum number of units possible—410—to the minimum-cost cell (6,2). This will exhaust column 2 and decrease row 6 from 450 to 40 tons. The revised opportunity cost matrix is shown in Table 7-7.

The *sixth iteration* is illustrated in Table 7-8. The largest opportunity cost is found with row 6 at $35/ton. Since the minimum remaining cell in this row

---

TABLE 7-5

VAM Iteration 3 for San Francisco Solid-Waste Disposal

Column opportunity costs

		0 Site 1		0 Site 2		25 Site 3		Demand
5	Area 1	120	0	125	0	135	0	700
0	Area 2	125	0	200	0	110	500	0
5	Area 3	140	0	155	0	145	0	1100
0	Area 4	105	635	130	0	135	0	0
5	Area 5	115	0	145	0	110	0	1025
0	Area 6	115	0	115	0	150	0	450
0	Area 7	0	0	0	1190	0	0	0
	Supply	1265		410		1600		

Row opportunity costs

Allocate 500 tons/week to the maximum opportunity cost ($15/ton)—row 2—and minimum transportation cost in this row ($110)—column 3: cell (2, 3). Accordingly, row 2 is eliminated and the capacity of column 3 is reduced to 1600 tons/week.

☐ Note: Eliminated row or column

TABLE 7-6

VAM Iteration 4 for San Francisco Solid-Waste Disposal

Column opportunity costs

		5 Site 1		10 Site 2		10 Site 3		Demand
5	Area 1	120	0	125	0	135	0	700
0	Area 2	125	0	200	0	110	500	0
5	Area 3	140	0	155	0	145	0	1100
0	Area 4	105	635	130	0	135	0	0
0	Area 5	115	0	145	0	110	1025	0
0	Area 6	115	0	115	410	150	0	450
0	Area 7	0	0	0	1190	0	0	0
	Supply	1265		0		575		

Row opportunity costs

Allocate 1025 tons/week to the maximum opportunity cost ($25/ton)—column 3—and minimum transportation cost in this row ($110)—row 5: cell (5, 3). Accordingly, row 5 is eliminated and the capacity of column 3 is reduced to 575 tons/week.

☐ Note: Eliminated row or column

is (6,1)—at \$115/ton—the remaining 40 tons are assigned to this cell. The total of row 6 is exhausted, while the column 1 total is reduced from 1265 to 1225 tons.

The *seventh and final iteration* is provided in Table 7-9. The maximum opportunity cost is \$20/ton associated with column 1. The minimum remaining cell value in this column is (1,1)—\$120/ton. The remaining 700 tons of row 1 are assigned to cell (1,1). This reduces the column 1 supply from 1225 to 525 tons. The remaining 1100 tons of row 3 can now be assigned implicitly: 525 tons satisfies the remaining supply of column 1, while the residual amount, 575 tons, satisfies column 3. All the allocations have now been made. (It is also important to note that exactly $m + n - 1$ routes were selected.)

The final system cost associated with this transportation routing pattern is

$$\text{Minimize}\, Z = \sum_{i=1}^{m} \sum_{j=1}^{n} c_{ij} x_{ij}$$

$$
\begin{aligned}
\text{Min}\, Z = \; & 120(700) + 110(500) + 140(525) + 145(575) \\
& + 105(635) + 110(1025) + 115(40) \\
& + 115(410) + 0(1190) \\
= \; & \$527{,}050
\end{aligned}
$$

TABLE 7-7

VAM Iteration 5 for San Francisco Solid-Waste Disposal

Column opportunity costs

		5 Site 1		0 Site 2		10 Site 3		Demand
15	Area 1	120	0	125	0	135	0	700
0	Area 2	125	0	200	0	110	500	0
5	Area 3	140	0	155	0	145	0	1100
0	Area 4	105	635	130	0	135	0	0
0	Area 5	115	0	145	0	110	1025	0
35	Area 6	115	0	115	410	150	0	40
0	Area 7	0	0	0	1190	0	0	0
	Supply	1265		0		575		

Row opportunity costs

Allocate 410 tons/week to the maximum opportunity cost (\$10/ton)—either column 2 or 3 (let's arbitrarily select column 2)—and minimum transportation cost in this column (\$115)—row 6: cell (6, 2). Accordingly, column 2 is eliminated and the capacity of row 6 is reduced to 40 tons/week.

▨ Note: Eliminated row or column

TABLE 7-8

VAM Iteration 6 for San Francisco Solid-Waste Disposal

Column opportunity costs

		20 Site 1		0 Site 2		10 Site 3		Demand
15	Area 1	120	0	125	0	135	0	700
0	Area 2	125	0	200	0	110	500	0
5	Area 3	140	0	155	0	145	0	1100
0	Area 4	105	635	130	0	135	0	0
0	Area 5	115	0	145	0	110	1025	0
35	Area 6	115	45	115	410	150	0	0
0	Area 7	0	0	0	1190	0	0	0
	Supply	1225		0		575		

Row opportunity costs

Allocate 40 tons/week to the maximum opportunity cost (\$35/ton)—row 6—and minimum transportation cost in this row (\$115)—column 1: cell (6, 1). Accordingly, row 6 is eliminated and the capacity of column 1 is reduced to 1225 tons/week.

▨ Note: Eliminated row or column

TABLE 7-9

VAM Iteration 7 for San Francisco Solid-Waste Disposal

Row opportunity costs		20 Site 1		0 Site 2		10 Site 3		Demand
15	Area 1	120	**700**	125	0	135	0	0
0	Area 2	125	0	200	0	110	**500**	0
5	Area 3	140	**525**	155	0	145	**575**	0
0	Area 4	105	**635**	130	0	135	0	0
0	Area 5	115	0	145	0	110	**1025**	0
0	Area 6	115	**40**	115	**410**	150	0	0
0	Area 7	0	0	0	**1190**	0	0	0
	Supply		**0**		**0**		**0**	

Allocate 700 tons/week to the maximum opportunity cost ($20/ton)—row 1—and minimum transportation cost in this row ($120)—column 1: cell (1, 1). Accordingly, row 1 is eliminated and the capacity of column 1 is reduced to 525 tons/week. The remaining 1100 tons/week of row 3 is assigned implicity: 525 tons to column 1 and 575 tons/week to column 3. The allocations are now complete.

[ ] Note: Eliminated row or column

Although solutions using the VAM may not always be optimal, they provide answers that are usually nearly so. The next technique uses the results of the VAM solution and determines whether these results are optimal. If the results are nonoptimal, the optimal allocation is found.

Modified Distribution Method (MODI)   Using a feasible solution from, say, a final VAM tableau, the modified distribution (MODI) method will provide an optimal solution—if one exists. If improvement is possible, MODI will identify the amounts of resources and the specific routes in the VAM tableau that must be adjusted. The underlying principles of MODI are discussed next.

MODI knows that, if a solution is both feasible and optimal, the occupied cells ($x_{ij} > 0$) of a transportation tableau will have implied costs that are zero according to the following relationship:

$$c_{ij} = R_i + K_j$$

where

c_{ij} = actual per-unit transportation cost of moving goods between i^{th} origin and j^{th} destination (route ij)

x_{ij} = quantity of goods ultimately allocated to route ij

R_i = row index value; implicit cost of having one more unit of goods at the ith origin (i.e., shadow price; per-unit storage cost)

K_j = column index value; implicit cost of having one more unit of goods at the jth destination (i.e., shadow price; per-unit stockout/shortage cost)

Conversely, if a route is empty (nonbasic), $x_{ij} = 0$, one of two possible conditions must exist:

1. The actual cost of transporting the goods exceeds the implied costs of route ij:

$$c_{ij} > R_i + K_j$$

2. The actual cost of transporting goods exceeds or is equal to the implied cost of goods along route ij:

$$c_{ij} = R_i + K_j$$

and the problem has *multiple optimal solutions*. Although the route is nonbasic in this particular solution, it will become basic in an alternative version.

When $c_{ij} > R_i + K_j$, an opportunity cost (the per unit cost savings of *not* shipping goods along route ij, that is, e_{ij}) is represented by

$$e_{ij} = c_{ij} - (R_i + K_j)$$

Any nonbasic cell with a positive or zero opportunity cost should not be used. If, however, a nonbasic route is found to have a negative opportunity cost, the manager should immediately anticipate that the present solution can be improved.

An illustration of how the MODI method employs these principals in determining an optimal solution to the San Francisco solid-waste disposal program (Example 6.1) follows:

Step 1. Starting with the solution to a transportation problem—using an available method such as VAM—*check to see that there are exactly $m + n - 1$ cells assigned resources.* If there are, go to step 2. If, however, there are *less* than $m + n - 1$ cells allocated goods, *degenerate conditions* exist that must be corrected. A brief description of a corrective procedure for this situation is presented toward the end of this section. Since Example 6.1 has exactly $7 + 3 - 1 = 9$ basic cells (cells allocated resources) in the final VAM tableau (Table 7-9), the solution is feasible: continue to step 2.

Step 2. *Calculate the row and column index values (implied costs), R_i and K_j, respectively, for each nonbasic cell* in Table 7-10. The *sum* of the row and column index values is established by the actual per-unit transportation cost of the basic cells: For *any* cell—basic or nonbasic—in the MODI tableau, the

TABLE 7-10

Final VAM Tableau for San Francisco Solid-Waste Disposal

To j^{th} site

		K_1 Site 1		K_2 Site 2		K_3 Site 3		Supply
R_1	Area 1	120	700	125	0	135	0	700
R_2	Area 2	125	0	200	0	110	500	500
R_3	Area 3	140	525	155	0	145	575	1100
R_4	Area 4	105	635	130	0	135	0	635
R_5	Area 5	115	0	145	0	110	1025	1025
R_6	Area 6	115	40	115	410	150	0	450
R_7	Area 7	0	0	0	1190	0	0	1190
	Demand		1900		1600		2100	

From i^{th} area

implied costs are established by the actual transportation costs of the basic cells:

$$R_i + K_j = (c_{ij})_{\text{basic}}$$

where

$(c_{ij})_{\text{basic}}$ = actual transportation cost associated with basic route ij

The opportunity costs of each *nonbasic cell* are

$$e_{ij} = c_{ij} - (R_i + K_j)$$

where

c_{ij} = actual transportation cost associated with route ij (i.e., regardless of whether the cell is basic or nonbasic)

Remember, since $c_{ij} = (R_i + K_j)$ for a basic cell, the opportunity costs for a basic cell must, in turn, be equal to zero (i.e., $e_{ij} = 0$). This information expedites the calculation of the implied costs for any route—the sum of the row and column index values, R_i and K_j, respectively for the initial MODI tableau. For Example 6.1, there are $m + n - 1$ cells that will ultimately receive allocations in an optimal solution. Therefore, the same number of c_{ij} equations can be formulated and solved for the various row and column index values. So, using Table 7-10, we have the following set of nine equations and 10 unknown variables:

$$c_{11} = R_1 + K_1 = 120 \qquad c_{53} = R_5 + K_3 = 110$$
$$c_{23} = R_2 + K_3 = 110 \qquad c_{61} = R_6 + K_1 = 115$$
$$c_{31} = R_3 + K_1 = 140 \qquad c_{62} = R_6 + K_2 = 115$$
$$c_{33} = R_3 + K_3 = 145 \qquad c_{72} = R_7 + K_2 = 0$$
$$c_{41} = R_4 + K_1 = 105$$

To solve for the seven row and three column index values, we must arbitrarily set one of these variables equal to zero. It is common to let R_1 be equal to zero. If this is done, $K_1 = 120$ and the remaining nine variables can be quickly calculated:

1. Solve for R_3 from the third equation (c_{31}) in the preceding set. That is,

$$R_3 + K_1 = 140$$
$$R_3 + K_1 = 140$$
$$R_3 = 140 - K_1$$
$$R_3 = 140 - 120$$
$$R_3 = 20$$

2. The remaining unknowns are solved just as simply. They are:

$$R_2 = -15 \quad K_2 = 120$$
$$R_3 = 20 \quad K_3 = 125$$
$$R_4 = -15$$
$$R_5 = -15$$
$$R_6 = -5$$
$$R_7 = -120$$

Notice that the index values can be zero, positive, or negative.

Step 3. *Calculate the opportunity costs for shipping goods through each nonbasic cell* in Table 7-10 using

$$e_{ij} = c_{ij} - (R_i + K_j)$$

The opportunity cost for each basic cell is zero, whereas each nonbasic cell must have an opportunity cost that is nonnegative, $e_{ij} \geq 0$. If a nonbasic cell is found to have a negative opportunity cost, this indicates that adding this route to the basic solution can improve the existing solution. The optimal solution is reached only when *all* the $c_{ij} - (R_i + K_j)$ values are either zero or positive.

As an illustration of this procedure, let's calculate the opportunity cost for an arbitrarily selected nonbasic cell, e_{12}:

$$
\begin{aligned}
e_{12} &= c_{12} - (R_1 + K_2) \\
&= 125 - (0 + 120) \\
&= 125 - 120 \\
&= 5
\end{aligned}
$$

As one more illustration, let's find the opportunity cost using cell (6,3):

$$
\begin{aligned}
e_{63} &= c_{63} - (R_6 + K_3) \\
&= 150 - (-5 + 125) \\
&= 150 - 120 \\
&= 30
\end{aligned}
$$

The summary of the remaining opportunity costs of the nonbasic cells is

$e_{12} = 5$	$e_{43} = 25$	$e_{22} = 95$	$e_{63} = 30$
$e_{13} = 10$	$e_{51} = 5$	$e_{32} = 15$	$e_{71} = 0$
$e_{21} = 20$	$e_{52} = 40$	$e_{42} = 25$	$e_{73} = -5$

Step 4. *Construct the initial feasible MODI tableau* (Table 7-11):

1. The row and column index values generated in step 2 are entered in the appropriate tableau margins.
2. Each opportunity cost calculated in step 3 is represented within a circle for each nonbasic cell in the tableau.
3. The actual transportation cost is placed within a small rectangle in the upper-left corner of each cell in the tableau.

Step 5. *Determine the closed path that identifies the routes and specific amounts of goods to be shifted that will further improve the present solution.* First, select the *nonbasic cell* with the most negative opportunity cost value. If there is a tie among two or more of these negative cells, arbitrarily select one. This cell will mark the starting point of the closed path. Mark this cell with a "+" sign. Second, observe the following restrictions to select the remaining cells of the closed path:

■ The closed path must begin and end with the starting-point cell.
■ Only clockwise and either horizontal or vertical moves may be used.

To j^{th} site

	Site 1	Site 2	Site 3	Row index value, R_i
Area 1	120	125 ⑤	135 ⑩	$R_1 = 0$
Area 2	125 ⑳	200 ㉞	110	$R_2 = -15$
Area 3	140	155 ⑮	145	$R_3 = 20$
Area 4	105	130 ㉕	135 ㉕	$R_4 = -15$
Area 5	115 ⑤	145 ㊵	110	$R_5 = -15$
Area 6	115	115	150 ㉚	$R_6 = -5$
Area 7	0 ⓪	0	0 ⑤	$R_7 = -120$
Column index value, K_j	$K_1 = 120$	$K_2 = 125$	$K_3 = 125$	

From i^{th} area

▨ Basic cell in final VAM tableau

ⓔ$_{ij}$ Opportunity cost of nonbasic cells:
$$e_{ij} = c_{ij} - (R_i + K_j)$$

$\boxed{c_{ij}}$ Actual transportation cost of cell: c_{ij}

- The path elements are limited to basic cells *except* for the original cell (starting point), which is always the nonbasic cell with the most negative opportunity cost.
- The sign of each cell in the loop alternates as the cells join the closed path (i.e., the second cell receives a "−" sign, the third cell a "+" sign, etc.
- The closed path will consist of a minimum of four or more even-numbered cells.
- It may be necessary to skip over some basic cells to ensure that the supply and demand constraints are not violated.
- Any column or row in the loop is eliminated (signed off) once it has accumulated the limit of one "+" sign and one "−" sign (i.e., for each "leg"—row and column—in the closed path, there can be only two path members to maintain the resource balance).
- The geometry of the path is not necessarily a simple rectangle or square: it is solely dependent on the ultimate path members.

Using this procedure, let's identify the closed path for Example 6.1:

- The only nonbasic cell that can reduce the shipping costs is c_{73}, with an opportunity cost of −$5 per ton. So, for every unit (ton) of waste sent from area 7 that can be disposed of at site 3, the total system cost will be reduced by $5. A "+" sign is placed in cell (7,3).
- The remaining cells introduced into the loop must be basic cell elements. The clockwise direction of movement requires that the next basic cell be found in a horizontal move (a vertical move at this point would imply that a third move—both horizontal and to the right—would be available; it is not). Therefore, select cell (7,2) as the second path member and place a

"−" sign in it. Row 7 can now be eliminated (signed off) because it contains two cells in the closed path—one with a "+" sign and one with a "−" sign.

- A vertical move is required next. The only remaining basic cell in column 6 is (6,2)—an easy selection! Place a "+" sign in this cell and sign off column 6, which now consists of its limit of two, opposite-sign cell members.
- The fourth move must be horizontal, to basic cell (6,1). Sign off row 6 after marking it with a "−" sign.
- Move 5 must be vertical, to a basic cell. At first glance it may *seem* as though you have a choice between cells (3,1) and (4,1)—actually, you do not. Here's why: You must be able to get back to column 3 on your next-to-last basic cell selection, so that the last move returns you to the starting-point cell (7,3). Notice that cell (4,1) does not have a corresponding basic cell in column 3—cell (4,3) is nonbasic. However, row 3 has two basic cells: (3,1) and (3,3). Therefore, skip over cell (4,1) to cell (3,1) and place a "+" sign in it.
- Move horizontally to basic cell (3,3) and give it a "−" sign.
- Close the path by returning vertically down to cell (7,3).

The closed path consisting of cell elements (7,3), (7,2), (6,2), (6,1), (3,1), and (3,3) is illustrated in Table 7-12. Notice the $0 opportunity cost associated with cell (7,1). This should be the signal that multiple optimal solutions exist for the problem (see Section 7.7, Table 7-27, for an alternative optimal solution).

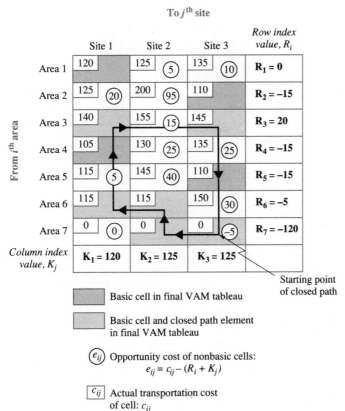

TABLE 7-12

MODI Tableau Identifying Closed Path for San Francisco Solid-Waste Disposal

Step 6. *Determine the amount of goods that needs to be shifted along the closed path.* The signs associated with the cells in the loop indicate the chain reaction that will occur once the amount shipped through cell (7,3) is increased; i.e., cell (7,2) must decrease to maintain the balance of refuse transported along row 7, while cell (6,2) must increase to make up for the loss column 2 will experience when the refuse through cell (7,2) is decreased. A similar effect occurs with cell (6,1): It must undergo a decrease in transported refuse to balance the column increase experienced by the initial addition of refuse moved through cell (6,2). *The exact amount of refuse that can be added to cell (7,3) is equal to the smallest amount of refuse associated with any cell in the closed path that was given a "−" sign* [i.e., cells (7,2), (6,1) and (3,3).] This equality is necessary so that no shipment becomes negative. So, the most that can be routed through cell (7,3) is the 40 tons of refuse limited by cell (6,1). In addition, we must add 40 tons to the other two "+" cells in the loop, and subtract the same value from the three negative loop cells. The new MODI tableau assignment is shown in Table 7-13. In the new solution, x_{73} has entered the solution as a basic variable, whereas x_{61} has left the solution and become a nonbasic variable.

Step 7. *Calculate the new system costs.* From Table 7-13, the sum of transportation costs along the new routing design is

TABLE 7-13

Revised (Second) MODI Tableau Illustrating Adjusted Resource Allocations in the Closed Path for San Francisco Solid-Waste Disposal

$$Z = 120(700) + 110(500) + 140(565) + 145(535) + 105(635)$$
$$+ 110(1025) + 115(450) + 0(1150) + 0(40)$$
$$= \$526{,}850$$

This solution has resulted in a \$200 decrease in total system costs (\$527,050 − 526,850).

Step 8. *Check solution for optimality.* Go back to step 2 and recalculate the row and column index values. Further, generate new opportunity costs (step 3). If there are no negative opportunity costs, stop: You have an optimal solution. If there are some left, continue with step 4.

A recalculation of row and index values for Example 6.1 yields (once again, assume R_1 is equal to zero)

$$R_2 = -15 \qquad K_1 = 120$$
$$R_3 = 20 \qquad K_2 = 125$$
$$R_4 = -15 \qquad K_3 = 125$$
$$R_5 = -15$$
$$R_6 = -10$$
$$R_7 = -125$$

The new opportunity costs, e_{ij}, are recalculated for all nonbasic cells and are shown in Table 7-14. Since all the opportunity cost values are either positive or zero, we have found the optimal solution.

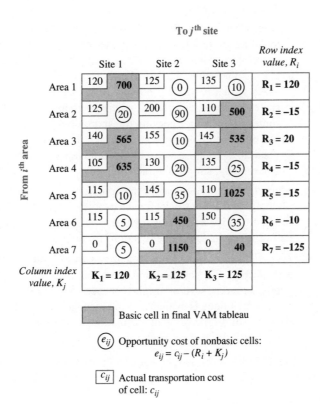

To j^{th} site

From i^{th} area	Site 1	Site 2	Site 3	Row index value, R_i
Area 1	120 · **700**	125 · ⓪	135 · ⑩	$R_1 = 120$
Area 2	125 · ⑳	200 · ⑨⓪	110 · **500**	$R_2 = -15$
Area 3	140 · **565**	155 · ⑩	145 · **535**	$R_3 = 20$
Area 4	105 · **635**	130 · ⑳	135 · ㉕	$R_4 = -15$
Area 5	115 · ⑩	145 · ㉟	110 · **1025**	$R_5 = -15$
Area 6	115 · ⑤	115 · **450**	150 · ㉟	$R_6 = -10$
Area 7	0 · ⑤	0 · **1150**	0 · **40**	$R_7 = -125$
Column index value, K_j	$K_1 = 120$	$K_2 = 125$	$K_3 = 125$	

▨ Basic cell in final VAM tableau

ⓔ$_{ij}$ Opportunity cost of nonbasic cells:
$$e_{ij} = c_{ij} - (R_i + K_j)$$

$\boxed{c_{ij}}$ Actual transportation cost of cell: c_{ij}

TABLE 7-14

Revised (Second) MODI Tableau Illustrating Nonnegative Opportunity Costs for All Nonbasic Cells for San Francisco Solid-Waste Disposal: Optimal Solution

Although the TM example we have used is a minimization problem, the process is identical for a *maximization problem* except for one consideration: Optimality is reached when the opportunity cost values of *all nonbasic cells* are zero or negative.

Difficulties Encountered in Transportation Problems

In Chapter 5, we discussed a few of the special obstacles that may arise when we use linear programming (e.g., unbounded solutions, degeneracy). Transportation-type problems can pose similar difficulties. The more common transportation difficulties encountered include the following:

1. *Degenerate outcomes.* Whenever the number of assigned routes (basic cells) is less than $m + n - 1$, degenerate conditions exist. This malady typically develops either (1) at the initial assignment of goods, or (2) during the iterative solution process. In the first situation, supply of a specific row and demand of a particular column are equal and are allocated to a single route. This step eliminates a row and column simultaneously. In the second case, degeneracy occurs whenever the assignment of goods to a new basic cell depletes the goods in two or more of the old basic cells. In either situation, we correct degeneracy by assigning an infinitesimally small amount of goods, ϵ, to one or more of the empty cells, so that the total number of cells in the solution is ultimately $m + n - 1$. It is important that the assignment of ϵ does not form a loop; this would invalidate the basis.

2. *Restricted route assignments.* Sometimes there are constraints limiting the amount of goods that can be shipped along a particular route. Generally, there are two types:

   ■ There is a specific limit on the maximum level of goods that may be sent along route *ij*, or a required minimum amount of goods that must be sent along route *ij*. These types of constrained upper or lower levels of resource limits are *capacitated* conditions. We can solve capacitated transportation problems by reformulating the problem as an LP one, rewriting the capacitated limitations as resource constraints, and resolving using the simplex method.

   ■ It is also possible, due to either internal or external organizational policy constraints, that absolutely no shipment of goods is allowed along one or more routes. In the latter instance, where no goods may be allocated along a particular route, assign a large per-unit transportation cost value, M, equal to the total supply or demand—whichever is larger. If the transportation-problem goal is to maximize profits, assign a large negative value to the route, $-M$. As an alternative remedy, simply eliminate the cell.

3. *Multiple optimal solutions.* If the opportunity cost of a nonbasic cell is zero, multiple optimal solutions exist for the problem. Alternative solutions are found when the first optimal solution is revised to include the zero-opportunity-cost nonbasic cell. The results (objective function) for both versions will be identical.

4. *Transshipment capacity.* Shipment is always limited between an origin–destination pairing. The standard transportation model does not allow the exchange of goods between several origins or between several destinations. Fortunately, another technique is available to the manager when the exchange of goods among the group of origins or set of destinations is necessary—the transshipment method, which we'll discuss in Chapter 8.

The TM makes the assignment of various amounts of goods along specific routes. Goods from the same origin may be sent to several destinations, or a single destination

may receive allocations from several origins. The linear resource-allocation model that we'll examine next specializes in supply and demand problems in which the assignments are made on a one-to-one basis.

7.3 | ASSIGNMENT METHOD (AM)

The TM addresses a special type of LP problem. Coincidentally, the assignment method (AM) is a special kind of transportation problem in which resources, (e.g., people or equipment) are assigned to tasks on a one-to-one basis. Accordingly, the number of resources and the number of tasks must be equal. The purpose of such an assignment is, typically, to minimize overall system costs, or, if the objective is in terms of some measure of profit, worth, or utility, to maximize overall system "performance." It is important to understand that the district attorney case (Example 4.6) is *not* an AM, because the assignments are not on a one-to-one basis. Instead, each deputy district attorney has the potential for multiple case assignments.

The general AM formulation for assigning the ith person to the jth task is

$$\text{Minimize system costs}, Z = \sum_{i=1}^{n} \sum_{j=1}^{n} c_{ij} x_{ij}$$

or

$$\text{Maximize system utility}, Z = \sum_{i=1}^{n} \sum_{j=1}^{n} u_{ij} x_{ij}$$

subject to the assignment of each person to a task,

$$\sum_{j=1}^{n} x_{ij} = 1 \qquad \text{for each } i \, (i = 1, 2, \ldots, n)$$

and the assignment of each task to a person

$$\sum_{i=1}^{n} x_{ij} = 1 \qquad \text{for each } j \, (j = 1, 2, \ldots, n)$$

Of course, there is no such thing as a negative assignment, so

$x_{ij} \geq 0$ for all i and j

where

Z = system costs to be minimized or the system worth to be maximized

c_{ij} = per unit cost of assigning the ith person (or equipment) to the jth task

u_{ij} = per unit worth of assigning the ith person (or equipment) to the jth task

x_{ij} = assignment of one person to one task ($x_{ij} = 1$ if the person is assigned to the task, or $x_{ij} = 0$ if the person is not assigned)

n = total number of people to be assigned *and* total number of tasks to be fulfilled

The Hungarian Method

Although the use of appropriate microcomputer software for solving real-world AM problems is encouraged in order to minimize human error and computation time, it is possible—even simple—to solve AM problems manually. In fact, the solution process is much less complicated than is that for the TM, as you shall see.

One of the most popular techniques used to solve assignment problems is the Hungarian method. Unlike the VAM algorithm used to solve transportation problems, the Hungarian method provides both a feasible and optimal solution. We'll illustrate the Hungarian algorithm in order to improve your understanding of the solution process used for solving AM problems, although the underlying theory is not presented. For a minimization assignment, the steps of the Hungarian method are as follows:

Step 1. Construct the AM cost tableau illustrating each combination of "person" (row) and "job" (column).

Step 2. Select the least-cost cell in each row and subtract it from all cells in that row, including from itself. This step reveals the best job for an individual person—ignoring the other individuals—and transforms the cost tableau into a *person-opportunity cost tableau*. At least one zero will be present in each row to indicate the zero opportunity cost assignment(s) of that person.

Step 3. Select the least-cost cell in each column—using the person-opportunity cost table established in step 2—and subtract it from all cells in that column. This procedure brings into consideration the opportunity costs related to each job, as well as the person-opportunity costs, and it transforms the data into a *total opportunity cost table*.

Step 4. Draw the minimum number of horizontal and vertical lines through all of the zero-cost cell values until all the zeros are covered in the opportunity cost table. If the number of lines used is less than *n* (the number of rows or columns in the tableau), go to step 5. If it is not, stop. You may now make the optimal assignment:

  ■ Select any row or column with a single zero cell. This represents your first assignment in the set. Eliminate the row and column intersecting at this cell, since both the person associated with the row and the job represented by the column have been satisfied. Continue this procedure until all rows and columns are exhausted.

Step 5. Select the *minimum uncovered cell value* and *subtract* it from all uncovered values in the tableau; *add* this value to any intersection cells where a horizontal and vertical line cross. *Ignore all single covered cells!* Return to step 4.

The Hungarian method is equally applicable to a maximization of worth or profit problem. Take either of these steps:

1. Calculate the opportunity cost based on the differences between the *largest* cells values in each row and column (rather than the smallest cell values).

2. Change the signs on the objective function coefficients.

Further, if there is an imbalance between the number of people and the number of jobs to be matched, simply add the appropriate dummy row or variable to manage the excess (or shortage), using the same procedure as that used in the transportation method.

Let's look at examples of both a minimization and a maximization problem using the AM algorithm.

TABLE 7-15

Risk Index for Assignment of Surgeons to Procedures at St. Eligius Hospital

Surgeon	Coronary-Artery Bypass	Liver Failure	Spleen Removal	Pulmonary Embolism	Abdominal Gunshot	Emergency Lung Biopsy
Auschlander	75	10	30	40	50	60
Morris	75	40	75	30	30	60
Fiscus	70	40	90	20	10	60
Erlich	25	35	30	40	30	40
Craig	5	20	10	40	20	30
Westfall	20	20	20	25	30	20

EXAMPLE 7.1 HOSPITAL ADMINISTRATOR SURGEON ASSIGNMENT

Let's say that the chief of surgery at St. Eligius Hospital in Boston must determine the optimal way to assign physicians to six different types of procedures. Obviously, if there is a cardiac surgeon available to treat a myocardial infarction and a neurosurgeon available to treat a brain injury—and if those were the only emergency procedures to be performed—the assignment would be trivial. However, in our example, there are six procedures that must be conducted in the next few hours, and only six surgeons are available to do them. The Chief of Surgery must immediately decide the best way to assign her staff. She develops a table illustrating the specific combination of procedures, the available physicians, and a subjective index of risk that represents the likely degree of failure of each particular surgeon–procedure assignment. The risk index ranges from 0 to 100, with 0 being lowest (best); it is shown in Table 7-15. The solution to this problem using the Hungarian method follows.

Step 1. Since the chief of surgery wishes to minimize the overall risk in her ultimate set of assignments, construct the cost matrix. This has already been done in Table 7-15.

Step 2. Convert the risk values into a surgeon–opportunity cost table by subtracting the least-risk cell in each row from every cell in the row (including from itself). The surgeon–opportunity cost data are shown in Table 7-16.

Step 3. Transform the surgeon–opportunity cost table into a total opportunity cost table by subtracting the least-risk cell in each column from every cell in the

Reason for Procedure

Surgeon	coronary artery bypass	liver failure	spleen removal	pulmonary embolism	abdominal gunshot	lung biopsy
Auschlander	75 – 10 = 65	10 – 10 = 0	30 – 10 = 20	40 – 10 = 30	50 – 10 = 40	60 – 10 = 50
Morris	75 – 30 = 45	40 – 30 = 10	75 – 30 = 45	30 – 30 = 0	30 – 30 = 0	60 – 30 = 30
Fiscus	70 – 10 = 60	40 – 10 = 30	90 – 10 = 80	20 – 10 = 10	10 – 10 = 0	60 – 10 = 50
Erlich	25 – 25 = 0	35 – 25 = 10	30 – 25 = 5	40 – 25 = 15	30 – 25 = 5	40 – 25 = 15
Craig	5 – 5 = 0	20 – 5 = 15	10 – 5 = 5	40 – 5 = 35	20 – 5 = 15	30 – 5 = 25
Westfall	20 – 20 = 0	20 – 20 = 0	20 – 20 = 0	25 – 20 = 5	30 – 20 = 10	20 – 20 = 0

TABLE 7-16

Row-Reduced Cost Table for Assignment of Surgeons to Procedures at St. Eligius Hospital

TABLE 7-17

Opportunity Cost for Assignment of Surgeons to Procedures at St. Eligius Hospital

Surgeon	coronary artery bypass	liver failure	spleen removal	pulmonary embolism	abdominal gunshot	lung biopsy
Auschlander	65	0	20	30	40	50
Morris	45	10	45	0	0	30
Fiscus	60	30	80	10	0	50
Erlich	0	10	5	15	5	15
Craig	0	15	5	35	15	25
Westfall	0	0	0	5	10	0

column (including from itself). The total opportunity cost data are shown in Table 7-17.

Step 4. The minimum number of straight, horizontal, and vertical lines needed to cover the zeros in the table is 5. Since $n = 6$, the solution is not optimal.

Step 5. The smallest uncovered cell value in the table is 5. Subtract this value from itself and from the other uncovered cells; add this value to any intersectional cells. Make the assignments by first searching the various rows and columns until you find a single zero in either a row or column. The revised optimal solution assignment tableaus for this problem are shown in Tables 7-18 and 7-19. The single zeros occur in cells (1,2), (2,4), (3,5), and (6,6) and represent four of the six assignments. Rows 4 and 5 suggest that there are *multiple*

TABLE 7-18

Revised Total Opportunity Cost (Optimal Solution, Version 1) for Assignment of Surgeons to Procedures at St. Eligius Hospital

Reason for Procedure

Surgeon	coronary artery bypass	liver failure	spleen removal	pulmonary embolism	abdominal gunshot	lung biopsy
Auschlander	65	(0)	20 − 5 = 15	30 − 5 = 25	40	50 − 5 = 45
Morris	45 + 5 = 50	10 + 5 = 15	45	(0)	0 + 5 = 5	30
Fiscus	60	30	80 − 5 = 75	10 − 5 = 5	(0)	50 − 5 = 45
Erlich	0	10	(5 − 5 = 0)	15 − 5 = 10	5	15 − 5 = 10
Craig	(0)	15	5 − 5 = 0	35 − 5 = 30	15	25 − 5 = 20
Westfall	0 + 5 = 5	0 + 5 = 5	0	5	10 + 5 = 15	(0)

▨ Old opportunity lines (5)　　▨ New line after revision (1)

Assignment

Auschlander treats liver failure	10
Morris treats pulmonary embolism	30
Fiscus treats abdominal gunshot	10
Erlich does spleen removal	30
Craig does coronary artery bypass	5
Westfall does lung biopsy	20
	105

Surgeon	coronary artery bypass	liver failure	spleen removal	pulmonary embolism	abdominal gunshot	lung biopsy
Auschlander	65	(0)	20 – 5 = 15	30 – 5 = 25	40	50 – 5 = 45
Morris	45 + 5 = 50	10 + 5 = 15	45	(0)	0 + 5 = 5	30
Fiscus	60	30	80 – 5 = 75	10 – 5 = 5	(0)	50 – 5 = 45
Erlich	(0)	10	5 – 5 = 0	15 – 5 = 10	5	15 – 5 = 10
Craig	0	15	(5 – 5 = 0)	35 – 5 = 30	15	25 – 5 = 20
Westfall	0 + 5 = 5	0 + 5 = 5	0	5	10 + 5 = 15	(0)

■ Old opportunity lines (5)　　　■ New line after revision (1)

TABLE 7-19

Revised Total Opportunity Cost* (Optimal Solution, Version 2) for Assignment of Surgeons to Procedures at St. Eligius Hospital

*The tableau opportunity costs of the cell assignments can vary because there is, typically, more than one way in which the minimum number of lines used to cover the zero cell values during each iteration can be drawn. Accordingly, the cover line pattern ultimately determines which cells remain uncovered, remain covered with a single line, or are intersectional elements—the same characteristic that determines whether a cell is reduced, ignored, or increased by the value of the smallest uncovered value, respectively.

Assignment

Auschlander treats liver failure	10
Morris treats pulmonary embolism	30
Fiscus treats abdominal gunshot	10
Erlich does coronary artery bypass	25
Craig does spleen removal	10
Westfall does lung biopsy	20
	105

optimal solutions to this problem. Specifically, either assignments (4,1) and (5,3) or (4,3) and (5,1) can be made; both combinations will provide identical solutions. The risk scores for the two optimal solutions are

$$\text{Minimize system risk, } Z = \sum_{i=1}^{6} \sum_{j=1}^{6} r_{ij} x_{ij}$$

where

r_{ij} = risk index of assigning the ith surgeon to the jth procedure

$$x_{ij} = \begin{cases} 0 \text{ if } i^{th} \text{ surgeon is not assigned to the } j^{th} \text{ procedure} \\ 1 \text{ if } i^{th} \text{ surgeon is assigned to the } j^{th} \text{ procedure} \end{cases}$$

Version 1

$$Z = r_{12}x_{12} + r_{24}x_{24} + r_{35}x_{35} + r_{41}x_{41} + r_{53}x_{53} + r_{66}x_{66}$$
$$= (10)(1) + (30)(1) + (10)(1) + (25)(1) + (10)(1) + (20)(1)$$
$$= 105$$

Version 2

$$Z = r_{12}x_{12} + r_{24}x_{24} + r_{35}x_{35} + r_{43}x_{43} + r_{51}x_{51} + r_{66}x_{66}$$
$$= (10)(1) + (30)(1) + (10)(1) + (30)(1) + (5)(1) + (20)(1)$$
$$= 105$$

The application of linear programming to the field of athletics is not uncommon. In fact, the Joint National Meetings of the Operations Research Society of America (ORSA) and The Institute of Management Science (TIMS) have a special section on the application of operations research and management science to sports. Let's consider

the potential use of the assignment method to a sports application in which the objective function is to be maximized.

EXAMPLE 7.2 UNITED STATES MEN'S OLYMPIC GYMNASTIC TEAM SELECTION

As a hypothetical application of the assignment method in which the objective is to maximize the value of the objective function, let's explore the following ficticious scenario. The coach of the men's gymnastic team for the 1984 Olympics wished to determine the most powerful assignment of his athletes to the five different events in this sport. (Although each gymnast can and will compete in a number of events, the coach wanted to determine the single most outstanding event assignment—the *primary* event assignment.) He was convinced that, if these assignments were made carefully, he could maximize not only the likelihood of winning the individual gold medals in each event, but also that of winning the prestigious overall team championship. His gymnasts were (1) Bart Connors, (2) Mitch Gaylord, (3) Peter Vidmar, (4) Jim Hartung, and (5) Tim Daggett. The events were (1) floor exercise, (2) parallel bars, (3) rings, (4) pommel horse, and (5) high bar. The coach assessed the history of mean scores for each gymnast in each of the five events as shown in Table 7-20. Without the special-purpose AM algorithm, this problem would have to be formulated as a standard LP problem:

$$\text{Maximize } Z = 9.65x_{11} + 9.50x_{12} + 9.45x_{13} + \cdots + 9.55x_{54} + 9.55x_{55}$$

SUBJECT TO

Each gymnast will have a single, best event:

$$x_{11} + x_{12} + x_{13} + x_{14} + x_{15} = 1$$
$$x_{21} + x_{22} + x_{23} + x_{24} + x_{25} = 1$$
$$\cdot \qquad\qquad\qquad \cdot$$
$$\cdot \qquad\qquad\qquad \cdot$$
$$\cdot \qquad\qquad\qquad \cdot$$
$$x_{51} + x_{52} + x_{53} + x_{54} + x_{55} = 1$$

Each event will be performed by only one gymnast:

$$x_{11} + x_{21} + x_{31} + x_{41} + x_{51} = 1$$
$$x_{12} + x_{22} + x_{32} + x_{42} + x_{52} = 1$$
$$\cdot \qquad\qquad\qquad \cdot$$
$$\cdot \qquad\qquad\qquad \cdot$$
$$\cdot \qquad\qquad\qquad \cdot$$
$$x_{15} + x_{25} + x_{35} + x_{45} + x_{55} = 1$$

Step 1. Select the maximum mean scores in each row. Subtract all values in this row from this maximum cell value (remember to include the subtraction of this maximum value from itself as part of this procedure). This will give you the person-opportunity worth (profit) associated with each gymnast (i.e., this step focuses solely on the best event assignment for that gymnast, while disregarding the other gymnasts). The results of these calculations are shown in Table 7-21.

TABLE 7-20

Initial Mean Event Score Tableau for Primary Event Assignments of United States Men's Olympic Gymnastic Team

	Gymnastic Event				
Gymnast	Floor exercise	Parallel bars	Rings	Pommel horse	High bar
Bart Conners	9.65	9.50	9.45	9.55	9.55
Mitch Gaylord	9.40	9.50	9.60	9.55	9.50
Peter Vidmar	9.55	9.55	9.55	9.60	9.55
Jim Hartung	9.65	9.35	9.65	9.45	9.40
Tim Daggett	9.35	9.50	9.60	9.55	9.55

TABLE 7-21

Gymnast Opportunity Cost Tableau for Primary Event Assignment of United States Men's Olympic Gymnastics Team

		Event				
	Gymnast	floor exercise	parallel bars	rings	pommel horse	high bar
	Bart Conners	9.65 − 9.65 = 0	9.65 − 9.50 = .15	9.65 − 9.45 = .20	9.65 − 9.55 = .10	9.65 − 9.55 = .10
	Mitch Gaylord	9.60 − 9.40 = .20	9.60 − 9.50 = .10	9.60 − 9.60 = 0	9.60 − 9.55 = .05	9.60 − 9.50 = .10
	Peter Vidmar	9.60 − 9.55 = .05	9.60 − 9.55 = .05	9.60 − 9.55 = .05	9.60 − 9.60 = 0	9.60 − 9.55 = .05
	Jim Hartung	9.65 − 9.65 = 0	9.65 − 9.35 = .30	9.65 − 9.65 = 0	9.65 − 9.45 = .20	9.65 − 9.60 = .05
	Tim Daggett	9.60 − 9.35 = .25	9.60 − 9.50 = .10	9.60 − 9.60 = 0	9.60 − 9.55 = .05	9.60 − 9.55 = .05

		Event				
	Gymnast	floor exercise	parallel bars	rings	pommel horse	high bar
	Bart Conners	0	.15 − .05 = .10	.20	.10	.10 − .05 = .05
	Mitch Gaylord	.20	.10 − .05 = .05	0	.05	.10 − .05 = .05
	Peter Vidmar	.05	.05 − .05 = 0	.05	0	.05 − .05 = 0
	Jim Hartung	0	.30 − .05 = .25	0	.20	.05 − .05 = 0
	Tim Daggett	.25	.10 − .05 = .05	0	.05	.05 − .05 = 0

TABLE 7-22

Total Opportunity Cost Tableau for Primary Event Assignment of United States Men's Olympic Gymnastics Team

Step 2. Calculate the total opportunity cost associated with each event by subtracting the smallest cell value from itself and from each remaining nonzero cell value in that column. This step determines the most attractive gymnast assignment for an individual event, while disregarding the other events (Table 7-22).

Step 3. Draw the minimal number of horizontal and vertical lines through all the zero-loss cells. Since this can be accomplished with four lines (less than *n* lines), the solution is suboptimal.

Step 4. Select the smallest value not covered by a single line and subtract it from all other *uncovered* values except those cells located at an intersection of a horizontal and vertical line; add the minimum uncovered cell value to these intersectional values. The smallest uncovered value is .05. The new, revised tableau is shown in Table 7-23. Since five lines are now required to cover all zero-value cells, an optimal solution has been found. The best assignment of gymnast to event is based on the options as dictated by the zero-cell values in the tableau of Table 7-24. Due to the similarity of scores from the various gymnast-event combinations, there are multiple optimal assignments possible. Three such assignments are shown in Table 7-25. The composite worth of any optimal arrangement will, of course, be identical. The maximum worth of any of these optimal assignments sums to 47.95 utiles.

TABLE 7-23

Revised Total Opportunity Cost Tableau for Primary Event Assignment of United States Men's Olympic Gymnastics Team

	Event				
Gymnast	floor exercise	parallel bars	rings	pommel horse	high bar
Bart Conners	0	.10 − .05 = .05	.20	.10 − .05 = .05	.05
Mitch Gaylord	.20	.05 − .05 = 0	0	.05 − .05 = 0	.05
Peter Vidmar	.05 + .05 = .10	0	.05 + .05 = .10	0	0 + .05 = .05
Jim Hartung	0	.25 − .05 = .20	0	.20 − .05 = .15	0
Tim Daggett	.25	.05 − .05 = 0	0	.05 − .05 = 0	0

TABLE 7-24

Possible Primary Event Assignment of United States Men's Olympic Gymnastics Team

	Event				
Gymnast	floor exercise	parallel bars	rings	pommel horse	high bar
Bart Conners	floor exercise				
Mitch Gaylord		parallel bars	rings	pommel horse	
Peter Vidmar		parallel bars		pommel horse	
Jim Hartung	floor exercise		rings		high bar
Tim Daggett		parallel bars	rings	pommel horse	high bar

Gymnast	Solution 1	Solution 2	Solution 3
Bart Conners	floor exercise	floor exercise	floor exercise
Mitch Gaylord	rings	parallel bars	pommel horse
Peter Vidmar	parallel bars	pommel horse	parallel bars
Jim Hartung	high bar	high bar	rings
Tim Daggett	pommel horse	rings	high bar

TABLE 7-25

Three Possible Optimal Primary Event Assignments of United States Men's Olympic Gymnastics Team (Multiple Optimal Solutions)

7.4 | INTEGER PROGRAMMING (IP)

Up to now, we have been assuming that the decision variables constituting LP problems could assume fractional values. However, in real terms, it is simply not possible to build 12.33 medium-sized stores for a shopping mall, or to assign a deputy district attorney 3.67 murder cases, or to treat 4.2 dental patients per day. In fact, the majority of all LP problems require that the solution comprise *integer* decision variables.

There is only one basic difference between integer (IP) and linear programming (LP) problems: IP has decision variables that are *not divisible*. As a result, ordinary LP solution methods—such as the simplex method—will only coincidentally provide integer solutions. Moreover, the LP solution to a problem characterized by integer decision variables will almost certainly be more optimistic than would the optimal IP solution, thereby providing a false sense of security. Even though it is possible to round off a simplex solution as an approximation of an IP solution, there is no guarantee that that solution will be either optimal or feasible.

Typically, IP problems require mathematical algorithms more complex than is the simplex algorithm used for LP problems. As a result, the time needed to solve a problem as an integer solution may be significantly longer than that for a simplex solution.

Although formulation procedures are essentially the same for IP and LP problems, there are special types of managerial problems whose constraints can be accurately portrayed by only special types of integer variables. We'll discuss this special area of formulation technique later in this section.

Types of Integer Programming (IP) Problems

There are three basic categories of IP problems.

1. *General, pure, or all-integer IP* problems have decision variables that must all have integer values. In fact, most of the LP problem formulations covered earlier were really general IP problems. These included the St. Paul land developer (Exercise 4-4), neighborhood health center (Exercise 4-8), and foreign car dealer case studies (Exercises 4-1 and 4-7), to mention just a few. All the decision variables in these case studies must be whole numbers. A formulation example of a simplified all-integer model is

$$\text{Max } Z = 85x_1 + 50x_2$$

$$x_1 + x_2 \leq 10$$
$$x_1 + .27x_2 \leq 8$$
$$.50x_1 + .75x_2 \leq 10$$

x_1, x_2 integers

2. *The binary, or "0–1," IP* problem has decision variables that are either zero or one. This is particularly applicable when the problem addresses "go–no-go," "yes–no," or "either–or" situations. Examples of these cases typically occur in one-person-for one-task assignments or in alternative site, project, or investment opportunity selections. The *men's Olympic gymnastic team selection* (Example 7.2) is an example of a 0–1 IP problem. A formulation example of a simplified 0–1 integer model is

$$\text{Max } Z = 85x_1 + 50x_2$$

SUBJECT TO

$$x_1 + x_2 \leq 10$$
$$x_1 + .27x_. \leq 8$$
$$.50x_1 + .75x_2 \leq 10$$

x_1, x_2-0 or 1

3. *Mixed integer IP* problems are those with some—but not all—integer decision variables. The solutions of these problems will have various combinations of continuous and integer variables. Depending on the particular problem, the integer variables can be either 0–1 or just general integers. A formulation example of a simplified mixed integer problem is

$$\text{Max } Z = 85x_1 + 50x_2$$

SUBJECT TO

$$x_1 + x_2 \leq 10$$
$$x_1 + .27x_2 \leq 8$$
$$.50x_1 + .75x_2 \leq 10$$
$$x_1 \geq 0$$

x_2 integer

Special Integer Programming (IP) Formulation Procedures

Even though the formulation procedures we studied in Chapter 4 are generally true for IP problems, there are special circumstances that require the incorporation of new kinds of constraint forms that can be addressed only by integer variables. The following example illustrates these special types of constraints.

EXAMPLE 7.3   PEPSI-COLA BOTTLING COMPANY SITE SELECTION

American businesses often find it advantageous to market their products and services internationally. Although foreign marketing was a relatively rare occurrence only a few years ago, the recent growth of multinational organizations has been dramatic.

One of the most aggressive industries in the international business community is the cola soft-drink manufacturers. The leaders in this field have, for many years, exported their goods to such nontraditional markets as Asia, Africa, East Europe, and the Middle East. Let's consider a possible situation in which one of the cola manufacturers is trying to determine the optimal location of a new facility in France.

Suppose that the Pepsi-Cola Bottling Company is studying the potential location of new manufacturing facilities that will serve five sales regions in southern and central France. The five cities being considered are Marseille, Toulouse, Lyon, Grenoble, and Limoges (Figure 7-1). The ultimate selection will be based on the location that will provide the minimum combination of fixed and transportation costs needed to operate and maintain the new plant (labor and utility expenses can vary significantly among the five sites under examination). Pepsi-Cola is presently interested in developing only one new site, although it may decide to expand dramatically in the near future. Let's use the following notation in formulating this problem:

x_{ij}: Amount of product shipped from i^{th} plant site to j^{th} demand region

c_{ij}: Per-unit transportation costs between i^{th} plant site and j^{th} demand region

d_j: Level of demand in j^{th} region

f_i: Fixed cost of operating and maintaining i^{th} plant site

y_i: 1 if i^{th} plant site is opened; 0 otherwise

The various costs for the potential sites are shown in Table 7-26. The formulation is

$$\text{Min } Z = c_{11}x_{11} + c_{12}x_{12} + c_{13}x_{13} + \cdots + c_{54}x_{54} + c_{55}x_{55}$$
$$+ f_1 y_1 + f_2 y_2 + \cdots + f_5 y_5$$
$$= 15x_{11} + 25x_{12} + 18x_{13} + \cdots + 31x_{45} + 40x_{55}$$
$$+ 2000y_1 + 1500y_2 + \cdots + 1200y_3$$

or

$$\text{Min } Z = \sum_{i=1}^{m} \sum_{j=1}^{n} c_{ij}x_{ij} + \sum_{i=1}^{m} f_i y_i$$

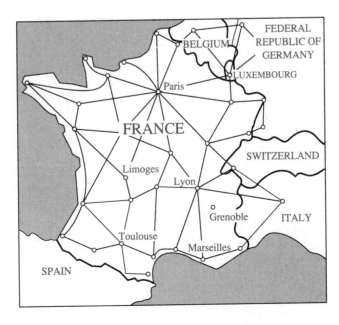

FIGURE 7-1

Potential Pepsi-Cola Bottling Company Locations for Southern and Central France

TABLE 7-26

Site Locations in France for Pepsi-Cola

Site, i	Fixed Costs, f_i	Transportation Costs, c_{ij}				
		1	2	3	4	5
1 Marseille	2000	15	25	18	37	35
2 Toulon	1500	24	25	19	20	40
3 Lyon	1800	30	15	25	24	25
4 Grenoble	2400	35	20	30	15	12
5 Limoges	1200	20	30	30	31	40
	Demand, d_j	15,000	8000	35,000	18,000	6000

SUBJECT TO

Area demand

$$x_{11} + x_{21} + x_{31} + x_{41} + x_{51} = 15{,}000$$
$$x_{12} + x_{22} + x_{32} + x_{42} + x_{52} = 8000$$
$$\vdots \qquad\qquad\qquad\qquad \vdots$$
$$x_{15} + x_{25} + x_{35} + x_{45} + x_{55} = 6000$$

or

$$\sum_{i=1}^{m} x_{ij} = d_j \qquad \text{for each } j\,(\,j = 1, 2, \ldots , 5)$$

Constraints that keep ith plant closed unless $y_i = 1$

$$x_{11} + x_{12} + x_{13} + x_{14} + x_{15} \leq My_1$$
$$x_{21} + x_{22} + x_{23} + x_{24} + x_{25} \leq My_2$$
$$\vdots \qquad\qquad\qquad\qquad \vdots$$
$$x_{51} + x_{52} + x_{53} + x_{54} + x_{55} \leq My_5$$

or

$$\sum_{j=1}^{n} x_{ij} \leq My_i \qquad \text{for each } i\,(i = 1, 2, \ldots , 5)$$

Develop only one site $\qquad y_1 + y_2 + y_3 + y_4 + y_5 = 1$

or

$$\sum_{i=1}^{\beta} y_i = \beta - K$$

where

β = number of potential new sites to be evaluated

K = number of potential new sites ultimately *not* selected

y_i = 0 or 1

$x_{ij} \geq 0$ for all i and j

The purpose of the last constraint set is to ensure that plants not selected remain "closed" and that the one ultimately chosen remains "open." The integer variables on

the right-hand side of these equations play the key role in this process. For those sites *not* ultimately selected, y_i is set equal to zero and the equation drops out; no shipments of goods can be made from any site when the y_i term is zero. Further, the fixed cost associated with these sites, f_i, will also drop out of the objective function because it has a y_i coefficient of zero. However, for the site ultimately selected, y_i is equal to 1. Accordingly, its fixed costs are included in the objective function. The M value—an arbitrarily large number—provides sufficient amounts of supply to ensure that the demands from all areas are satisfied (let M be equal to, say, twice the total demand).

There are many additional constraint variations integer variables that are possible other than the situation just discussed. To introduce more of them, let's present different types of constraint versions of the baseline study.

Selecting K out of β Constraints   As suggested in the original study, Pepsi-Cola may decide to develop more than one site. Suppose, then, that two out of the five sites are to be developed, rather than the single site. This would be represented by

$$\sum_{i=1}^{\beta} y_i = \beta - K$$

$$\sum_{i=1}^{5} y_i = 5 - 3$$

and

$$y_1 + y_2 + y_3 + y_4 + y_5 = 2$$

Or, suppose that at least three sites are to be developed. Then

$$y_1 + y_2 + y_3 + y_4 + y_5 \geq 3$$

All these constraints assume that y_i is a 0 or 1 variable.

If–Then Constraints   Some problems will have constraints that are *mutually dependent*. That is, the development of one site may be tied to the ultimate decision on another site or sites. For example, suppose that Pepsi-Cola decides to develop two sites. However, Marseilles cannot be selected unless Lyon is also chosen. This constraint can be written as

$$y_1 - y_3 \leq 0$$

It would have been incorrect to have written that $y_1 - y_3 = 0$, because that would have implied that either *both* sites must be selected or both must not be selected. That was not the case. Lyon can be chosen without consideration of the decision made on Marseilles. It is even possible that *multiple* if–then constraints could exist. For example, suppose that Grenoble would be selected only if both Marseilles and Lyon were chosen also. This constraint would look like

$$y_1 + y_3 - 2y_4 \geq 0$$

For the Grenoble site to be selected ($y_4 = 1$), both Marseilles ($y_1 = 1$) and Lyon ($y_3 = 1$) must also be selected. If *either* Marseilles or Lyon (but not both) were selected, y_4 would have to be equal to 0 for the preceding equation to be satisfied.

The formulations just presented represent some of the more practical applications of using integer variable constraints; there are many other possible formulation pos-

sibilities not covered in this text. Be aware that there are significant practical limitations in using integer variable constraint formulations: The computational complexity is far more difficult than is that of the standard LP formulations. This complexity often results in computer solution times that are orders of magnitude longer than that required by the simplex algorithm—even for relatively small problems. For large formulation, integer-programming solutions can be prohibitively expensive due to the extensive solution time required.

Integer Programming Algorithms

Two of the algorithms that are used to solve IP problems are: (1) the cutting-plane method and (2) the branch and bound method. We'll discuss each one briefly.

Gomory Cutting-Plane Method   The cutting-plane method, first developed by Gomory in the late 1950s, initially ignores the integer requirements and solves the problem using the simplex method. If the solution comprises all-integer decision variables (highly unlikely), it is viewed as optimal. If there are noninteger decision variables in the solution, new constraints—called *Gomory cuts*—are added to the problem. These new constraints form a cutting plane that reduces the size of the set of feasible solutions. This cutting plane slices away noninteger solutions: No integer solutions are lost. After each cut, an optimal solution is examined to see whether all noninteger decision variables have been removed. Ultimately, after enough cuts, a feasibility region providing only integer decision variables in the solution remains. Unfortunately, the cutting-plane method does not iterate toward the optimal solution in a logical manner like the simplex method. Instead, it trudges along, attempting nearly every possible slice imaginable in search of the optimal, integer solution. Because of this, problems with as few as 10 variables and only five or six constraints may require ten of thousands of iterations. The inherent slowness of this technique prompted the development of other integer solution methods that were not as cumbersome or time consuming. The branch and bound method, discussed next, is an example of such an algorithm.

Branch and Bound Method   The single most widely used procedure for solving IP problems is the branch and bound method. Unlike the cutting-plane method, branch and bound uses a systematic, intelligent search technique that greatly reduces the possible number of combinations of solutions to a manageable number for small problems. We can illustrate this process effectively by borrowing from the graphic illustrations of the dental office problem (Example 5.1). The original feasibility region was for a solution that does not require integer answers. Since an integer solution is necessary, the only true feasible area is represented by the *integer points* within the original shaded area (Figure 7-2). Therefore, it is necessary to devise a method that will help the manager to restructure this region so that only an integer solution is possible. Here is how the branch and bound method complies with these needs for the dentist office example (i.e., maximization problem):

Step 1. *Establish the upper bound* in the set of all possible solutions by using the standard simplex solution method to solve the problem. Ignore the integer requirements. This describes the initial node 1.

> | For the Dentist Office Example, the optimal solution consisted of 6.875 (rounded earlier to 6.9) periodontal and 4.167 (rounded earlier to 4.2) general dentistry treatments per day, providing the dentist with a daily profit of $792.71 ($797 earlier). |

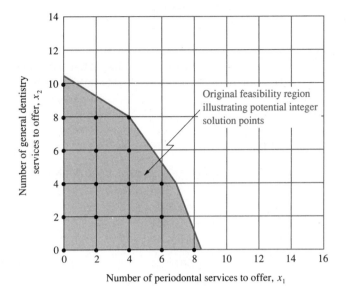

NODE 1

Max $Z = 85x_1 + 50x_2$ *Solution*

Subject to $x_1 + .75x_2 \leq 10$ Max $Z = \$792.71$

$\qquad\qquad x_1 + .27x_2 \leq 8$ $x_1 = 6.875$

$\qquad\quad .5x_1 + .75x_2 \leq 8$ $x_2 = 4.167$

Step 2. *Examine the upper-bound solution.* If all basic variables are integers, stop; you have found the optimal solution. If the basic variables are not all integers, the upper bound is not feasible; go to step 3.

| Because the optimal decision variables are noninteger, we must continue to step 3. The upper bound is not feasible. |

Step 3. *Find the feasible lower bound.* Branch the set of noninteger solution values into two subproblems by introducing two mutually exclusive constraints that are needed to satisfy the integer requirement of each solution variable. Select one noninteger solution (basic) variable at a time *starting with the one with the largest fractional value*. The two mutually exclusive constraints introduced for the selected noninteger variable, x_i, with a solution value of $x_i = b_i + \Delta_i$ (where $b_i =$ the integer portion of the ith noninteger variable, and Δ_i = the fractional portion of the noninteger variable) are

$x_i \geq b_i$

$x_i \leq b_i + 1$

For each subproblem, there will be an *upper-bound* solution and a *lower-bound* solution. The *best noninteger solution* is the upper bound, whereas the *best integer solution* found in any subproblem is the lower bound. Any subsets that have upper bounds that are inferior to the prevailing lower bound are terminated. The eliminated subset is referred to as *fathomed*. The optimum

integer solution is found when it is as least as good as any upper-bound solution for any other subset. If such an optimal integer solution does not exist, continue the branching process from each feasible, noninteger solution node until each subproblem is exhausted.

| Begin with x_1, since it has a larger fractional value than does x_2. Round x_1 up and down to provide the first two subproblems: Let $x_1 \leq 6$ and $x_1 \geq 7$.

NODE 2

$\text{Max } Z = 85x_1 + 50x_2$

$\begin{aligned}\text{Subject to } \quad x_1 + .75x_2 &\leq 10 \\ x_1 + .27x_2 &\leq 8 \\ .5x_1 + .75x_2 &\leq 8 \\ x_1 &\leq 6\end{aligned}$

$\begin{aligned}\textit{Solution} \quad Z &= \$776.67 \\ x_1 &= 6 \\ x_2 &= 5.333\end{aligned}$

NODE 3

$\text{Max } Z = 85x_1 + 50x_2$

$\begin{aligned}\text{Subject to } \quad x_1 + x_2 &\leq 10 \\ x_1 + .27x_2 &\leq 8 \\ .5x_1 + .75x_2 &\leq 8 \\ x_1 &\leq 7\end{aligned}$

$\begin{aligned}\textit{Solution } Z &= \$780.19 \\ x_1 &= 7 \\ x_2 &= 3.704\end{aligned}$

Neither solution provides an all-integer set of basic variables; therefore, neither a feasible nor an optimal solution has been found. However, the solutions provide new upper bounds. Branching is continued from both nodes 2 and 3. First, node 2 is split into two branches: $x_2 \leq 5$ (node 4) and $x_2 \geq 6$ (node 5):

NODE 4

$\text{Max } Z = 85x_1 + 50x_2$

$\begin{aligned}\text{Subject to } \quad x_1 + .75x_2 &\leq 10 \\ x_1 + .27x_2 &\leq 8 \\ .5x_1 + .75x_2 &\leq 8 \\ x_1 &\leq 6 \\ x_2 &\leq 5\end{aligned}$

$\begin{aligned}\textit{Solution } Z &= \$760 \\ x_1 &= 6 \\ x_2 &= 5\end{aligned}$

NODE 5

$\text{Max } Z = 85x_1 + 50x_2$

$\begin{aligned}\text{Subject to } \quad x_1 + x_2 &\leq 10 \\ x_1 + .27x_2 &\leq 8 \\ .5x_1 + .75x_2 &\leq 8 \\ x_1 &\leq 6 \\ x_2 &\leq 6\end{aligned}$

$\begin{aligned}\textit{Solution } Z &= \$767.50 \\ x_1 &= 5.50 \\ x_2 &= 6\end{aligned}$

Node 4 provides an optimal (all-integer) lower-bound solution and is terminated. Node 5 results in another upper-bound, noninteger solution; further branching from node 5 will be continued shortly, since that node has a noninteger decision variable value *and* its objective function value (\$767.50) exceeds that of the lower bound found in node 4 (\$760)—it has the *potential* of providing an optimal integer solution with an objective function value greater than \$760. First, however, branching will continue from node 3 with nodes 6 ($x_2 \leq 3$) and 7 ($x_2 \geq 4$):

NODE 6

$\text{Max } Z = 85x_1 + 50x_2$

Subject to
$$x_1 + .75x_2 \leq 10$$
$$x_1 + .27x_2 \leq 8$$
$$.5x_1 + .75x_2 \leq 8$$
$$x_1 \leq 7$$
$$x_2 \leq 3$$

Solution $Z = \$745$
$$x_1 = 7$$
$$x_2 = 3$$

NODE 7

$\text{Max } Z = 85x_1 + 50x_2$

Subject to
$$x_1 + x_2 \leq 10$$
$$x_1 + .27x_2 \leq 8$$
$$.5x_1 + .75x_2 \leq 8$$
$$x_1 \geq 7$$
$$x_2 \geq .4$$

Solution infeasible

Node 6 provides an optimal, lower-bound integer solution ($745). However, since the objective function value of node 6 is less than that of an existing lower-bound value (node 4, $Z = \$760$), it is terminated. Node 7 results in an infeasible solution; it too is concluded.

Now let's go back to node 5. Branching the noninteger solution portion ($x_1 = 5.50$) into two subproblems, node 8 ($x_1 \leq 5$) and node 9 ($x_1 \geq 6$) divulges

NODE 8

$\text{Max } Z = 85x_1 + 50x_2$

Subject to
$$x_1 + .75x_2 \leq 10$$
$$x_1 + .27x_2 \leq 8$$
$$.5x_1 + .75x_2 \leq 8$$
$$x_1 \leq 5$$
$$x_2 = 6$$

Solution $Z = \$725$
$$x_1 = 5$$
$$x_2 = 6$$

NODE 9

$\text{Max } Z = 85x_1 + 50x_2$

Subject to
$$x_1 + x_2 \leq 10$$
$$x_1 + .27x_2 \leq 8$$
$$.5x_1 + .75x_2 \leq 8$$
$$x_1 \leq 6$$
$$x_2 = 6$$

Solution infeasible

Node 8 provides an optimal, integer solution ($725)—albeit not as attractive as that provided by node 4—and is terminated. Node 9 results in an infeasible solution and is also terminated. This exhausts all of the possible solutions from the branch and bound method. Since node 4 provided the superior lower-bound solution, the optimal solution to the dental office example is $x_1 = 6$, $x_2 = 5$, and $Z = \$760$. An illustration of the entire branch and bound process is shown in Figure 7-3.

Limitations of Integer Programming

Even though the majority of linear resource-allocation problems require one of the three basic forms of integer programming, the complexity of the solution process for moderate to large problems makes the real-world application of IP very limited (even the two-variable dental office example required nine separate solution sets!): The number of iterations in searching for the optimal outcome may be astronomical. In response to the impracticality of such situations, we make a common tradeoff between solution efficiency and solution accuracy by rounding off noninteger solutions when the magnitudes of the decision variable values are sufficiently large enough to absorb such inaccuracies of expedience.

FIGURE 7-3

Branch and Bound Tree for the Dental Office Study

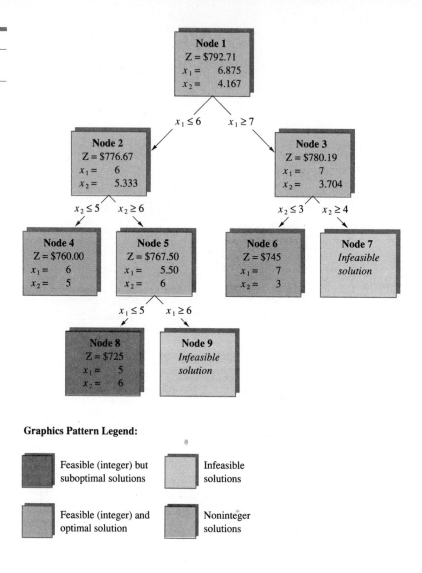

Graphics Pattern Legend:

Feasible (integer) but suboptimal solutions

Infeasible solutions

Feasible (integer) and optimal solution

Noninteger solutions

|7.5| DE NOVO PROGRAMMING

In 1981, Milan Zeleny wrote a journal article on de novo programming.[1] Although the de Novo model is a linear-programming model, it approaches allocation of scarce resources from a different perspective. Zeleny presented the argument that LP myopically concentrates on fine-tuning the optimization of a *given* system instead of questioning how this existing system came into being; he charged that these narrow presumptions used in formulating the typical LP problem produce *necessarily* nonoptimal results. Zeleny argued that instead of focusing on what choice of product mix will satisfy resource constraints (e.g., available work force, production capacities, warehouse limitations, raw materials, market potentials, budget) while optimizing a given figure of merit such as profit, we should address these significant concerns: Given a figure of merit such as profit, how much and what kinds of resources should be ac-

[1]"On the Squandering of Resources and Profits via Linear Programming," *Interfaces* 11, No. 5:(October 1981): pp. 101–107.

quired, within affordable limits, to design an optimal system of constraints? Although the arguments against Zeleny's paper generally revolved around the theme that Zeleny was simply overstating the perception of the intrinsic versus controllable resources, it may be of considerable value to examine this philosophically different perspective on linear programming.

The general de novo programming model is

$$\text{Maximize } Z = c_1 x_1 + c_2 x_2 + \cdots + c_m x_m$$

or

$$\text{Maximize } Z = \sum_{i=1}^{m} c_i x_i$$

SUBJECT TO

$$a_{11} x_1 + a_{21} x_2 + \cdots + a_{m2} x_m - b_1 = 0$$
$$a_{12} x_1 + a_{22} x_2 + \cdots + a_{m2} x_m - b_2 = 0$$

$$\vdots \qquad\qquad\qquad \vdots$$

$$a_{1n} x_1 + a_{2n} x_2 + \cdots + a_{mn2} x_m - b_n = 0$$
$$p_1 b_1 + p_2 b_2 + \cdots + p_j b_j + \cdots + p_n b_n = W$$

or

$$\sum_{i=1}^{m} a_{ij} x_i - b_j = 0 \qquad \text{for each } j\,(\,j = 1, 2, \ldots, n)$$

and

$$\sum_{j=1}^{n} p_j b_j = W$$

where

b_j = the quantity of the jth resource available

p_j = the per-unit cost of the jth resource

$p_j b_j$ = the total value of the jth resource

W = the amount of budget available for the purchase of resources

De novo programming adds m new variables—a b_j variable is added to each resource equation—and one new constraint (marginal costs) to the formulation. The standard simplex algorithm is all that is needed to solve de novo formulations. Only $m + 1$ variables could constitute the solution, even if the constraints would be satisfied as inequalities ($\leq$) rather than as equalities ($=$). It is very probable that this type of constraint-relaxed formulation will result in a single product under optimal conditions, rather than in the typical LP multiple-product mix—there are no limits on forecast sales, availability of resources, production capacity, space, and so on. So, de novo programming will select as much of the best product as the prevailing budget level al-

lows. More constraints would have to be added to have a greater variety of products in the optimal mix.

As an illustration, we'll reformulate the four-product Apple Computers hypothetical problem (Exercise 4-6) as a de novo model. The policy constraints, along with the minimum production and maximum projected sales levels, have been omitted for clarity.

$$\text{Max } Z = 2000x_1 + 1200x_2 + 500x_3 + 300x_4$$

SUBJECT TO

- P&A hours: $10x_1 + 8x_2 + 8x_3 + 4x_4 - b_1 = 0$
- minimum production:

Macintosh II:	$x_1 - b_2 = 0$
Macintosh SE:	$x_2 - b_3 = 0$
Macintosh Plus:	$x_3 - b_4 = 0$
Apple IIGS:	$x_4 - b_5 = 0$

- budget: $\qquad 1500x_1 + 800x_2 + 700x_3 + 400x_4 - b_6 = 0$
- marginal values: $\quad 15b_1 + 1500b_2 + 800b_3 + 700b_4 + 400b_5$
  $$+ 1.10b_6 = 345{,}000{,}000$$

The formulation for de novo programming produces a "tight" system design—all slack variables are zero (i.e., there are no underutilized resources).

The risk of actually operating a system under such conditions is acknowledged by Zeleny. He even suggests that some safety levels of spare or additional resources are desirable. However, these safety buffers should be added a posteriori to the optimally designed system; they should not be a capricious outcome of the mathematical properties of a system's model (e.g., safety reserves can be determined either as experimental percentages of the actual usage or as distinct managerial policy operators; the budget limitation, W, can be relaxed, and the system can be analyzed for a series of alternative budgets—W_1, W_2, etc.).

| 7.6 | SUMMARY

This chapter has presented four types of linear resource-allocation models that do not follow the strict requirements of the traditional LP problem. The transportation method can be solved by a heuristic—Vogel's approximation method (VAM), which usually provides near-optimal solutions. The MODI method does find the optimal solution to a TM problem—if one exists—and is used as a refining, follow-on procedure to VAM. The problem of degeneracy in the transportation model is a more significant concern than it was in the simplex method. However, we can easily avert or correct degenerate conditions by making sure that there are always $m + n - 1$ basic cells in the transportation tableau.

The assignment method is a special kind of transportation problem. The Hungarian method, another heuristic technique, is a simple procedure that determines the optimal assignments of m people to m tasks.

Integer programming addresses those resource-allocation problems that require whole-number outcomes. The types of IP models examined include all-integer, mixed-integer, and binary-integer ones. There are, however, significant difficulties in apply-

ing IP to moderate to large problems, because the mathematical process required to solve this type of problem is not efficient. As a result, LP solutions are often rounded off as an approximation of an integer solution.

De novo programming presents a philosophical countermodel to typical LP method practices. It challenges the very notion that LP does, in fact, meaningfully optimize, and it makes the argument that, instead, LP is wasteful of resources, ignorant of productivity, and unconcerned about profit. It offers, instead, a model that, in order to optimize a given figure of merit, determines what kind of and how much resources should be purchased, so that the resulting system is the best possible under the constraints and circumstances of the problem setting.

7.7 MICROCOMPUTER SOLUTIONS OF TRANSPORTATION METHOD, ASSIGNMENT METHODS, AND INTEGER PROGRAMMING PROBLEMS

The microcomputer solutions to the San Francisco solid-waste disposal program (Example 6.1, Transportation Method), St. Eligius Hospital problem (Example 7.1, Assignment Method), and the de novo version of the Apple Computer problem (Exercise 4-6; using the original budget of $345,000,000) are shown in Tables 7-27 through 7-29, respectively. The microcomputer solution to the solid-waste disposal example is represented in Table 7-27. Notice that the objective function is the same as the example illustrated in Section 7.3; however, the basic cells and resource levels are different than the earlier version. This represents the another version of the multiple optimal solutions possible in this particular transportation problem. Table 7-28 illustrates one of the two multiple optimal solutions to the St. Eligius surgeon assignment (although the printout says that there are multiple solutions). The de novo solution to the Apple Computer exercise employs a marginal cost constraint (constraint 7) that assumes a per unit resource cost for production and assembly hours of $15/hour and a budget coefficient of 1.10 (10 percent interest rate for each dollar of additional budget monies). Further, the de novo solution illustrates the likely outcome with this method if there are very few constraints: Multiple production lines will be "boiled down" to one or two products (e.g., the 203,090 Macintosh 512Es that will be manufactured will account for all of the P&A hours and budget needed to run the "new" single product line of computers).

```
                  Summary of Results for SFSWMS          Page:   1
   From  To Shipment Cost  Opp.Ct.: From To Shipment  Cost   Opp.Ct.:
   ----------------------------------------------------------------------
   S1    D1  165.00 120.00     0     S4   D3     0    135.00  25.00
   S1    D2  535.00 125.00     0     S5   D1     0    115.00  10.00
   S1    D3     0   135.00  10.00    S5   D2     0    145.00  35.00
   S2    D1     0   125.00  20.00    S5   D3 1025.00 110.00    0
   S2    D2     0   200.00  90.00    S6   D1     0    115.00   5.00
   S2    D3  500.00 110.00     0     S6   D2  450.00 115.00    0
   S3    D1 1100.00 140.00     0     S6   D3     0    150.00  35.00
   S3    D2     0   155.00  10.00    Dummy D1    0      0      5.00
   S3    D3     0   145.00     0     Dummy D2  615.00   0      0
   S4    D1  635.00 105.00     0     Dummy D3  575.00   0      0
   S4    D2     0   130.00  20.00
   ----------------------------------------------------------------------
   Minimum value of OBJ = 526850 (multiple sols.) Iterations = 2
   ----------------------------------------------------------------------
```

TABLE 7-27

Transportation Method Solution to San Francisco Solid-Waste Disposal Program

Source: Quantitative Systems for Business Version 3.0, Chang & Sullivan. Prentice-Hall, 1986, Englewood Cliffs, NJ. 07632.

TABLE 7-28

Assignment of Surgeons to Procedures at St. Eligius Hospital

Source: Quantitative Systems for Business Version 3.0, Chang & Sullivan.

```
Input Data of The Problem STELIGIUS (Cost/Profit Coefficients)    Page 1
                                   Tasks
   Objects    T1:bypass T2:liver T3:spleen T4:emboli T5:abdom T6:lung
  01: Auschl    75.00    10.00    30.00    40.00    50.00    60.00
  02: Morris    75.00    40.00    75.00    30.00    30.00    60.00
  03: Fiscus    70.00    40.00    90.00    20.00    10.00    60.00
  04: Erlich    25.00    35.00    30.00    40.00    30.00    40.00
  05: Craig      5.00    20.00    10.00    40.00    20.00    30.00
  06: Westfa    20.00    20.00    20.00    25.00    30.00    20.00


              Final tableau   (Total iterations = 2)
          :Ob\Tk    T1     T2    T3     T4    T5     T6    Cov.Ln:
          :01     70.00    0    20.00 30.00 40.00 50.00
          :02     50.00 10.00 45.00    0     0    30.00   ←
          :03     65.00 30.00 80.00 10.00    0    50.00
          :04       0    5.00    0   10.00 10.00 10.00
          :05       0   10.00    0   30.00 10.00 20.00
          :06     5.00    0     0    5.00 10.00    0
          :Cov.Ln ↑      ↑     ↑     ↑     ↑


              Summary of Assignments for STELIGIUS

   Object  Task  Cost\Prof.:  Object  Task  Cost\Prof.:
     01     T2      10.00        04     T1      25.00
     02     T4      30.00        05     T3      10.00
     03     T5      10.00        06     T6      20.00
        Minimum value of OBJ = 105   Total iterations = 2
```

TABLE 7-29

De Novo Programming Solution and Sensitivity Analysis of Apple Computer Product Mix

Source: Big Alpal, Version 2.0, 1986. Philadelphia: Drexel University, Kinko Software.

```
                        SOLUTION
                        Z*   =   581374722.84
                        x1*  =   305986.70
                        x2*  =   0.00
                        x3*  =   0.00
                        x4*  =   0.00
                        b1*  =   2600886.92
                        b2*  =   305986.70
                        b3*  =   0.00
                        b4*  =   0.00
                        b5*  =   0.00
                        b6*  =   305986696.23
```

RIGHT HAND SIDE RANGING

Constraint name	Current value	Lower limit	Upper limit	Shadow price
labor hrs	0.00	- Infinity	+ Infinity	25.28
min prod x1	0.00	-345000.00	+ Infinity	1685.14
min prod x2	0.00	0.00	+ Infinity	1241.46
min prod x3	0.00	0.00	+ Infinity	342.23
min prod x4	0.00	0.00	+ Infinity	592.78
budget	0.00	- Infinity	+ Infinity	0.00
marginal values	345000000.00	- Infinity	+ Infinity	1.69

CONTRIBUTION RANGING

Variable name	Current value	Lower limit	Upper limit
x1	1900.00	1871.10	+ Infinity
x2	1450.00	- Infinity	1472.39
x3	595.00	- Infinity	1432.37
x4	795.00	- Infinity	876.27
b1	0.00	- Infinity	13.47
b2	0.00	-28.90	+ Infinity
b3	0.00	- Infinity	22.39
b4	0.00	- Infinity	837.37
b5	0.00	- Infinity	81.27
b6	0.00	-0.90	+ Infinity

7-1 Assume that Delta Airlines has recently been granted permission to start service along several new intercontinental routes. However, to be able to offer this expanded service, Delta must purchase a number of new aircraft from among the Boeing 757, Lockheed L1011, European Air Bus, and Douglas DC-10 models. Further imagine the following hypothetical conditions:

1. The budget for new aircraft purchases and associated maintenance costs (labor and mechanic salaries) is estimated at about $245,000,000.

2. Maintenance capacity for the existing fleet of aircraft is already at the limit; new aircraft purchases must be accompanied by the hiring of new maintenance personnel. The total number of technician maintenance hours associated with new plane purchases is limited to a total of 27,000 hours.

3. Each new plane will have a specific purchase price, provide a certain amount of after-taxes profit per year, and require a specific number of annual maintenance hours and associated increase in salary for new mechanic hires, as shown in Table 7-1.1. Assume that if Delta has decided that it will not purchase both L1011s and DC-10s. Formulate this problem and determine the optimal mix of new purchases for maximizing after-tax profit.

7-2 The managers of the Bert Tuna Company (Exercise 4-8) have decided to allow only specific shipping routes to be used. Specifically, these are the requirements:

1. Trenton must receive goods from at least two of the following three warehouses: Chicago, Memphis, and Buffalo.

2. Memphis cannot ship goods to both Denver and Trenton.

3. Denver cannot receive goods from both Memphis and Buffalo.

4. If Detroit receives goods from Oakland, it cannot also receive goods from Memphis.

Use a combination of standard and 0–1 integer programming techniques to formulate this problem.

7-3 The manager of the German car dealer study (Example 4.3) has reconsidered his original problem formulation. He now feels that de novo programming will provide him with a more realistic perspective of how his business should really be run. After all, the building lease for his business will soon expire; there is no absolute need to carry all three makes of car; and so on. The only hard constraint that he cannot ignore is the monthly $800,000 budget. Reformulate this problem using de novo programming and solve for the optimal mix of car(s) to carry as well as the appropriate amount of resources needed to conduct business.

7-4 The manager of the San Francisco solid-waste disposal program (Example 6.1) is faced with the decision to reduce the present number of disposal sites from three to two sites. To meet demand with this new arrangement, he must increase the processing capacity at the two sites that are ultimately retained. The costs associated with streamlining and enlarging existing capacities at each of the three sites—as well as the individual enlargement limits—are shown in Table 7-4.1. Assume that all other elements of the problem remain the same. Reformulate this example as an integer programming problem and determine the two sites that should ultimately be chosen.

7-5 The German car dealer (Example 4.3) wishes to consider offering a broader variety of automobiles. More specifically, he would like to examine the possibility of carrying Alfa Romeo Milano, Maserati BiTurbo, and Audi in addition to his present three-car line of Porsche, BMW, and Mercedes Benz. The unit costs, sales prices, and other resource considerations associated with these automobiles are shown in Table 7-5.1. The monthly budget available for automobile purchases by the agency has now grown to $1,375,400.

ASSIGNMENT

Formulate this exercise as an integer programming problem, assuming that

1. The maximum number of different automobile lines that the dealer wishes to carry is five.

2. The minimum number of different automobile lines that the dealer wishes to carry is two.

TABLE 7-1.1

Resource Requirements for Different Airplane Configurations

Aircraft Type	Purchase Price ($1000)	After-Tax Profit	Annual Maintenance for Each New Airplane	
			Labor Hours	Mechanic Salaries
Boeing 757	$6000	$376,000	800	$270,000
Lockheed L1011	$5250	$329,000	1000	$225,000
Air Bus	$8500	$525,000	580	$300,000
Douglas DC-10	$3275	$208,000	1200	$200,000

TABLE 7-4.1

Cost Matrix for Enlargement of Two of the Facilities for the San Francisco Solid-Waste Disposal Program

| | | | Destination | | | |
| | | | To Disposal Site | | | |
			1	2	3	Area Refuse Generation (Tons/Week)
		1	$ 120	$ 125	$ 135	700
	From	2	$ 125	$ 200	$ 110	500
Origin	Refuse	3	$ 140	$ 155	$ 145	1100
	Collection	4	$ 105	$ 130	$ 135	635
	Area	5	$ 115	$ 145	$ 110	1025
		6	$ 115	$ 115	$ 150	450
		7	$ 0	$ 0	$ 0	1190
	Present Site Disposal Capacity (Tons/Week)		1900	1600	2100	5600
	Enlarged Capacity (tons)		3500	3100	3000	
	Capacity Cost Increase Per Ton ($1,000,000)		3.25	2.42	3.88	

TABLE 7-5.1

Resource Requirements for Five Candidate Automobile Makes for German Car Dealer

Parameter	Automobile Make					
	Porsche	BMW	Mercedes	Audi	Alfa Romeo	Maserati
Unit Cost ($)	27,000	20,000	32,500	18,000	12,000	23,000
Sales Price ($)	36,000	26,000	45,000	23,000	17,500	31,000
Space (ft²)	120	115	148	130	120	130
Min. Quant. (#)	12	12	4	3	3	2
Max. Quant. (#)	25	35	8	15	12	10

TABLE 7-6.1

Effectiveness Index for Various Media Outlets and Advertising Agencies for *Sports Illustrated*

Agency	Media			
	Television	Radio	Newspapers	Direct Marketing
1. FC&B	86	75	63	45
2. JWT	78	80	85	55
3. O&M	75	83	78	67
4. Megamedia	85	85	75	71

3. No more than two of the Porsche, Alfa Romeo, and Maserati lines can be carried.

4. If BMW is carried, Audi may not be included.

5. If Porsche is included, Mercedes must also be included.

7-6 Imagine that *Sports Illustrated* (*SI*) magazine wishes to conduct a new advertising campaign to increase its subscriber population. *SI* has decided to advertise in four types of media outlets: (1) television, (2) radio, (3) newspapers (business sections), and (4) direct marketing (mailers). Further, *SI* wishes to use four different agencies to conduct four separate advertising programs: (1) Foote, Cone, and Belding, (2) J. Walter Thompson,

(3) Olgilvy and Mather, and (4) Megamedia. To make the assignments effectively, *SI* has subjectively assessed the overall effectiveness of each agency to conduct each of the four media campaigns. These hypothetical evaluations are shown in Table 7-6.1. Use the assignment method to determine the specific assignment profile that will maximize the overall system effectiveness index.

7-7 Let's assume that after a 4-month training program the four representatives of the United States' men's 014×100-meter relay team were assessed to see how well each raced in the four possible race position assignments (i.e., "leg" assignments). The dif-

C.E.O. Brad Shocker believes his very touch transmits competence and energy to his people.

ferent legs in the race demand very different skills. It is, therefore, crucial to ensure that the final assignments are made, taking into consideration all the strengths and weaknesses of each runner. A brief description of the race follows:

1. The first leg ("start leg") starts out in the middle of the first curve and terminates toward the end of the first straightaway.

2. The second leg ("curve leg") receives the baton from the start leg at the end of the first straightaway and accelerates around a 180-degree curve.

3. The third leg receives the baton at the top of the second straightaway and accelerates about halfway through the second turn, where he passes the baton to the anchor leg.

4. The fourth leg ("anchor leg") receives the baton as he accelerates to full speed through the last portion of the second turn and into the second and final straightaway.

For the purpose of this exercise assume that the average times for the four men running the four different leg assignments are shown in Table 7-7.1.

TABLE 7-7.1

United States Men's Olympic Track and Field Team;
4 × 100 Meters Relay Mean Time Trials (Seconds)

Runner	1st 100	2nd 100	3rd 100	4th 100
Carl Lewis	10.21	9.95	9.65	9.23
Dennis Mitchell	10.32	10.16	9.59	9.31
Calvin Smith	10.18	9.88	9.63	9.26
Albert Robinson	10.39	10.07	9.49	9.30

ASSIGNMENT

Use these average times to determine the following:

1. What is the optimal assignment of runner and 100-meter leg?

2. What is the estimated finish time for the race?

3. How does the time (from part 2) compare with the existing world record of 37.94 seconds?

7-8 Suppose that the responsibility of surgeon assignments in Example 7-1 is now the responsibility of Brad Shocker, C.E.O. and chairman of the board of directors at St. Eligius. Now, instead of assigning one surgeon to one case, the policy is to allow one surgeon to perform up to two cases. This means, of course, that some surgeons may not be used. The times required to treat and follow up each case have been estimated at (1) coronary artery bypass, 10 hours; (2) liver failure, 20 hours; (3) spleen removal, 8 hours; (4) pulmonary embolism, 15 hours; (5) abdominal gunshot, 20 hours; (6) lung biopsy, 12 hours. The amount of uncommitted time that each of the six surgeons has available is (1) Auschlander, 29 hours; (2) Morris, 30 hours; (3) Fiscus, 30 hours; (4) Erlich, 20 hours; (5) Craig, 15 hours; (6) Westfall, 20 hours.

ASSIGNMENT

1. Assume that the original risk-index information remains unchanged. Reformulate this example as an integer programming problem.

2. Using an appropriate software package, determine the optimal assignment. Which surgeons are used and what services do they provide?

Microcomputer Software for the Transportation Method, Assignment Method, and Integer Programming

A few of the many transportation, assignment, and integer software packages available for the microcomputer are listed here. The following notation will denote which types of algorithms are included on each software product: T = transportation method; A = assignment method; I_1 = all integer; I_2 = mixed integer; I_3 = 0–1). The de novo programming method can be used with any standard LP package.

1. *AMPS*. Commack, NY: Micro Vision; I_2.

2. *Computer Models for Management Science*. Reading, MA: Addison-Wesley; T-A.

3. *Management Science Models and the Microcomputer*. New York, NY: Macmillan; T, A, I_1, I_2, I_3.

4. *Micro Manager*. Madison, WI: Wm. C. Porown; T, A, I_1.

5. *Microsolve*. Oakland, CA: Holden-Day; T, A, I_1, I_3.

6. *MIP83*. San Marino, CA: Sunset Software; I_2.

7. *MP7-MIPROG*. Wilmette, IL: SCI Computing; I_2.

8. *Programs for Quantitative Analysis in Management*. Newton, MA: Allyn and Bacon; T, A.

9. *Storm*. Oakland, CA: Holden-Day; T, A.

10. *TSA88*. Alexandria, VA: Eastern Software; T.

References

1. Booler, J. M. P. The Solution of a Railway Locomotive Scheduling Problem. *Operations Research* 31, no. 10 (1980).

2. Capettini, Robert and Howard Toole. Designing Leveraged Leases: A Mixed Integer Linear Programming Approach. *Financial Management* (Autumn 1981), 15–23.

3. Horen, Jeffrey H. Scheduling of Network Television Programs. *Management Science* 26, no. 4 (April 1980).

4. Kolesar, Peter. Testing for Vision Loss in Glaucoma Suspects. *Management Science* 26, no. 5 (May 1980).

5. Marsten, Roy E., Michael R. Muller, and Christine L. Killion. Crew Planning at Flying Tiger: A Successful Application of Integer Programming. *Management Science* 25, no. 12 (December 1979).

6. Ruth, R. Jean. A Mixed Integer Programming Model for Regional Planning of a Hospital Inpatient Service. *Management Science* 27, no. 5 (May 1981).

7. Shapiro, Monroe. Scheduling Crewmen for Recurrent Training. *Interfaces* 11, no. 3 (June 1981).

8. Wilson, J. M. The Scheduling of Magistrates to Courts. *Operations Research* 32, no. 2 (1981).

9. Zeleny, Milan. On the Squandering of Resources and Profits via Linear Programming. *Interfaces* 11, no. 5 (October 1981).

10. ———. Multicriterion Design of High-Productivity Systems: Extensions and Applications. In *Proceedings of the Sixth International Conference on Multicriteria Decision Making*. Cleveland, OH: Case Western Reserve University, June 1984.

11. Zierer, T. K., W. A. Mitchell, and T. R. White. Practical Applications of Linear Programming to Shell's Distribution Problems. *Interfaces* 6, no. 4 (August 1976).

CHAPTER 8

LINEAR DISTRIBUTION NETWORKS

SHORTEST-ROUTE, MINIMAL-SPANNING-TREE, MAXIMAL-FLOW, AND TRANSSHIPMENT MODELS

8.1 INTRODUCTION

Linear distribution networks (LDNs) form a special and widely used subgroup of linear resource-allocation models. LDN models address situations where the primary interest is in determining a least cost, least time, or least distance way of moving or distributing goods (vehicles, people, oil, raw materials, etc.) or information (technical services, financial data, consumer marketing data, etc.) among different locations. In this sense, the term "network" can be viewed as a type of logistic web that geographically connects removed locations. The four LDN models examined in this chapter are:

1. Shortest route (SR)
2. Minimal spanning tree (MST)
3. Maximal flow (MF)
4. Transshipment (TSS)

Unlike some traditional LP problems concerned with distribution, network models have *special purpose algorithms* that are unparalleled in terms of the size of the problem they can address as well as their solution-speed prowess. The simplex method is a comparatively *inefficient* technique for solving large-scale network models. In view of this shortcoming, the emphasis of this chapter will be the special purpose algorithms and appropriate software associated with each type of LDN model; LP formulation techniques will be used to provide supplemental insight and clarity to specific problems as needed.

This chapter will address network models, which concentrate on linear distribution systems; later, in Chapter 13, several different network methods specializing in *schedule management* will be presented. They are the program evaluation and review technique (PERT) and critical path method (CPM).

8.2 APPLICATIONS OF NETWORK ANALYSIS

The ease of use and highly efficient solution process that characterize the special purpose LDN algorithms contribute heavily to the popularity of these methods. Consequently, there is a wealth of real-world applications of these useful techniques. A few LDN examples are these:

- The Alaskan pipeline uses maximal flow type methods to accommodate the appropriate amount of oil flow between connecting segments linking the various oil fields, pumping stations, refineries, and storage facilities throughout the United States.
- Westinghouse cable sequences daily service appointments using a minimal spanning tree model.
- Delta Airlines, which flies thousands of routes, uses transshipment and maximal flow models to determine the most effective way to provide service to its customers.
- The borough of Manhattan uses a traffic-light–timing system that is designed to facilitate a high volume flow of automobiles throughout burrough intersections that is based on specific street capacities and artery demand (maximal-flow model).
- Emergency vehicles in Boston are dispatched to accident victims according to the shortest (quickest) route available.
- Porsche uses a transshipment model to determine the specific distribution routes for delivering its automobiles throughout the European and North American market place such as to minimize overall system delivery costs.

Numerous illustrations of how to use each of the four LDN models will be presented throughout the remainder of this chapter.

8.3 THE JARGON OF LDN ANALYSIS

An LDN can be effectively represented by graphical illustration. A hypothetical, seven-city LDN is shown in Figure 8-1. This LDN "snapshot" consists of three basic LDN elements:

1. Nodes
2. Arcs (or branches)
3. Arc flow

Let's use Figure 8-1 to demonstrate the role that these three elements play in portraying an LDN problem:

1. The *nodes* in an LDN are illustrated as numbered circles that represent locations, such as a set of cities, branches of a specific business, or electrical outlet locations within the same building. The cities are identified by the following node-numbering system: 1 = San Francisco, 2 = Chicago, 3 = Minneapolis, 4 = New Orleans, 5 = Washington, D.C., 6 = New York City, 7 = Boston.

2. The arrows that connect pairs of nodes are called *arcs*. For example, the arc connecting San Francisco and New York City is 1-6.

3. Each arc is defined by the numbers of the nodes it connects. The arc connecting nodes 1 and 3 (San Francisco–Minneapolis) is arc 1-3.

4. The actual quantity of goods or information being sent from starting node i and ending at node j is denoted by x_{ij} and is called the *arc flow*. The arc flow (quantity) of goods or information that is to be moved along arc 1-6 (San Francisco–New York) is x_{16} units.

5. The movement along any arc may or may not be restricted to a single direction: If the flow along an arc is limited to one direction, that arc is a *directed arc*; an arc without a single direction flow restriction is an *undirected arc*. The flows between all nodes in Figure 8-1 are directed, with the exception of the undirected flow be-

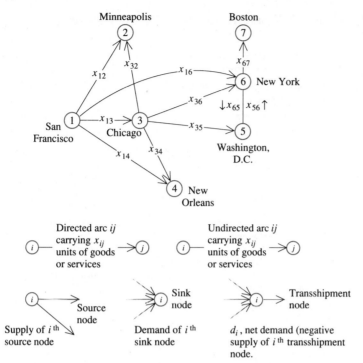

tween nodes 5 and 6: the movement of goods or services between New York and Washington, D.C., may occur in either direction.

6. A given arc may restrict the quantity of goods or information that can be shipped or transmitted. When the flow along an arc is limited, that arc is a *capacitated arc*.

7. Sometimes, there are specific combinations of connective nodes and arcs that represent special network elements. For example, any sequence of arcs connecting two nodes is called a *path* or *chain*. The arcs connecting San Francisco–Chicago–Washington, D.C.–New York–Boston (1-3-5-6-7) represents a path (or chain) between nodes 1 and 7. When the path consists of directed arcs (with defined flow capacities) between nodes, it is called a *directed path* or *directed chain*. A path that begins and ends with the same node is called a *loop*.

8. There are three types of nodes in a LDN: (1) source nodes, (2) sink nodes, and (3) transshipment nodes. A node that has only outgoing arcs is called a *source node*. If all arcs associated with a particular node end with that node, the node is called a *sink node*. When a specific node has both incoming and outgoing arcs—is both "receiving" and "shipping"—it is a *transshipment node*. Examples of each of the three different types of nodes represented in Figure 8-1 are source node 1; sink nodes 2,4, and 7; and transshipment nodes 3,5, and 6.

The shortest route, minimal spanning tree, and maximal flow models that will be presented in this chapter, along with the transportation and assignment models of Chapter 6, are all special versions of the generalized capacitated-flow LDN model. Enough talk. It's time to examine the kinds of management problems that four popular network models commonly address: (1) *shortest route*, (2) *minimal spanning tree*, (3) *maximal flow*, and (4) *transshipment* problems.

8.4 | THE SHORTEST ROUTE (SR) MODEL

Shortest route problems help the manager to find either the quickest, shortest, or least expensive way of moving through an LDN from an origin to any or all of the other nodes. Accordingly, view the term "shortest" to be interchangeable with "least cost" or "least time," depending on the particular problem being examined. The coefficients along the arcs are always assumed to be nonnegative commodities, such as distance, time, or travel costs. Further, the arcs for shortest route problems are often *non-directed*—movement usually can be in any direction.

To find the shortest route, it is always necessary to realize that only one arc from each node may be selected. So, if x_{ij} *represents the selection or rejection of a specific arc between origin i and destination j*, then following relationship must be true:

$$x_{ij} = \begin{cases} 1 \text{ if the path between } i^{th} \text{ and } j^{th} \text{ locations (nodes) is selected;} \\ 0 \text{ otherwise} \end{cases}$$

This statement says that, once we select a specific arc from the ith location, no other arc starting with that same origin can occur. Also, if we call the cost of moving one unit of goods or information between nodes i and j, c_{ij}, the per-unit cost of using this arc is c_{ij}. That is, if the arc is selected, the "cost" is

$$c_{ij}x_{ij} = c_{ij}(1) = c_{ij}$$

If it is not selected, the cost is

$$c_{ij}x_{ij} = c_{ij}(0) = 0$$

So, the process of determining the shortest arc will consist of either selecting an arc beginning with location i and ending with destination j ($x_{ij} = 1$) and incurring a cost of c_{ij} or of not selecting this arc ($x_{ij} = 0$) and incurring a cost of 0. In addition, the shortest-route model cannot have flow into the source node (origin node) or out of the sink node (destination node). For this reason, the model always has a constraint structure with a supply of one unit at the origin node and a demand of one unit at the terminal (end) node. All intermediate nodes must have a net demand of zero units.

Shortest route problems can be solved by either a 0–1 integer programming model formulation or a more efficient, specially tailored algorithm.[1] Although the standard formulation method is more cumbersome than are specialized network methods, it may be helpful to continue to connect the *formulation* interrelationship among different types of LP family problems, so that the many similarities among these techniques will be clear. Both techniques are described next.[2]

Standard LP Formulation of the Shortest Route (SR) Problem

The following example is intended to simplify our understanding and application of this 0–1 formulation technique to SR problems.

"This 'Bottled in 1835' is written in ball-point pen."

[1]The general LP formulation of the shortest route model is presented in Charles M. Harvey, *Operations Research: An Introduction to Linear Optimization and Decision Analysis* (New York: Elsevier North Holland, 1979).

[2]Dijkstra's algorithm provides a more rigorous treatment of the shortest route model, although it is a little more intricate than desired for this text (see Dreyfus, [reference]).

EXAMPLE 8.1 ROBERT MONDAVI WINERY SALES REPRESENTATIVE STUDY

The vineyards of northern California are viewed by many people as comparable to those in France. Wine growers in both regions also have in common the necessity of maintaining sales networks to supply their distributors. Let us pose a hypothetical problem using an imaginary sales representative from the prestigious Robert Mondavi Winery in St. Helena, California. She is responsible for providing service to distributors in the greater San Francisco region. After reading Tom Peters' book *In Search of Excellence*, she wholeheartedly agrees that one of the greatest shortcomings of business is in failing to provide customers with outstanding service after the sale is made.[3] To improve her availability to her clients, she thinks it is imperative to determine the quickest (least time) routes from her office-home in St. Helena to any of her nine distributors in the region that spreads as far south as San Jose. The various routes she might employ are not so few that the optimal paths are obvious. For example, it is not clear to her at this point whether she should travel through San Francisco or whether the route through the East Bay (Vallejo, Berkeley, Oakland, etc.) would yield the shortest travel times to, say, Fremont or San Jose. The highway routes for the sales representative extend between St. Helena in the north to San Jose in the south; they are shown in Figure 8-2. The standard LP formulation is as follows:

OBJECTIVE FUNCTION

$$\text{Minimize } Z = 30x_{12} + 24x_{13} + 30x_{25} + 30x_{34} + 23x_{46} + 11x_{56}$$
$$+ 22x_{59} + 12x_{67} + 36x_{78} + 10x_{79} + 24x_{8,10}$$
$$+ 66x_{9,10}$$

SUBJECT TO

1. *St. Helena* $x_{12} + x_{13} = 1$
2. *Santa Rosa* $x_{25} - x_{12} = 0$
3. *Napa* $x_{34} - x_{13} = 0$
4. *Vallejo* $x_{46} - x_{34} = 0$
5. *San Rafael* $x_{56} + x_{59} - x_{25} = 0$
6. *Berkeley* $x_{67} - (x_{46} + x_{56}) = 0$
7. *Oakland* $x_{78} + x_{79} - (x_{67} + x_{79}) = 0$
8. *Fremont* $x_{8,10} - x_{78} = 0$
9. *San Francisco* $x_{79} + x_{9,10} - (x_{59} + x_{79}) = 0$
10. *San Jose* $x_{8,10} + x_{9,10} = 1$

$$x_{ij} = \begin{cases} 1 \text{ if route (arc) } ij \text{ is selected} \\ 0 \text{ otherwise} \end{cases}$$

Although the standard formulation of the shortest route problem is a bit cumbersome, it nevertheless can be done with reasonable ease for this small problem. However, the formulation does not solve the problem. The results can be obtained with the aid of a 0–1 integer programming software package.

[3]Thomas Peters and Robert Waterman, Jr., *In Search of Excellence* (New York: Harper & Row, 1982).

FIGURE 8-2

Average Intradistributor Highway Travel Time for Mondavi Winery Sales Representative, San Francisco Region Territory

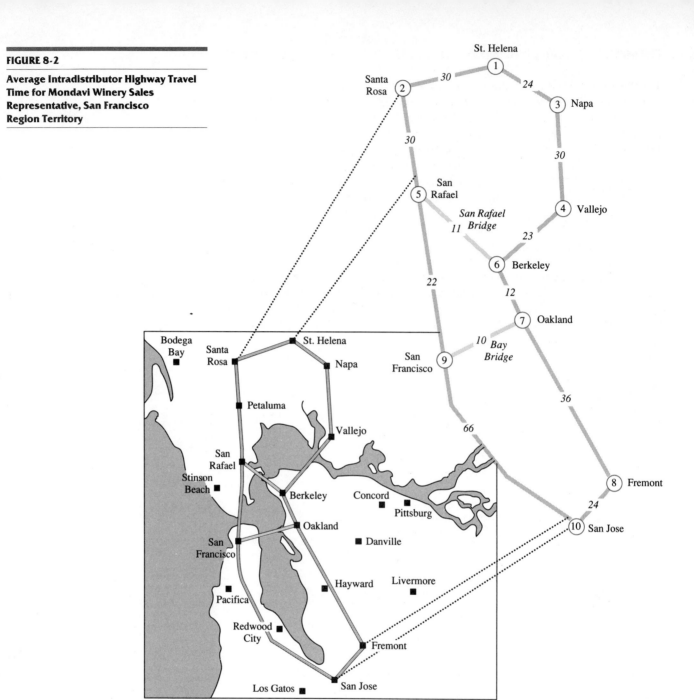

Special Purpose Shortest Route Algorithm

Although standard LP problem formulation techniques are possible, the special method shortest path LDN algorithm will facilitate the manual solution of moderate-sized SP problems. The SP algorithm employs a *labeling* and then a *backtracking* procedure to determine (1) the shortest (or least expensive or quickest) path between the origin and all other nodes. We'll illustrate the procedure using the hypothetical Mondavi Winery example.

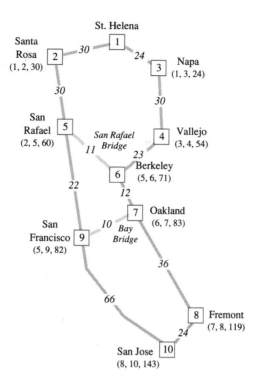

The permanent label values are shown in Figure 8-7, along with alternative, inferior route calculations.

Step 5. Once the permanent label process is complete, it is easy to determine the fastest route between the origin node and any other node. Here's how it works. Backtrack from any "final destination" of interest using the predecessor node indicated in the permanent label. Continue this process all the way back to the beginning node.

| Assume, in our particular example, that the sales representative wants to find the quickest path between St. Helena (node 1) and San Jose (node 10). The predecessor node label of node 10 reads (8,10,143): It is clear that we must *backtrack* to node 8. At node 8, we see that the label is (7,8,119), and that the predecessor node is 7. Continuing this straightforward process identifies the least time, 143-minute path between St. Helena and San Jose as nodes 1-2-5-6-7-8-10. Specifically, the route begins in St. Helena and progresses to San Rafael. From San Rafael it crosses over to the East Bay to Berkeley, then to Oakland, to Fremont, and finally to San Jose. |

The illustration of the backtrack procedure for the Robert Mondavi Winery sales representative formulation is shown in Figure 8-8. This same procedure can be used to find the optimal path between the origin and *any* of the other retail distributors (e.g., the shortest route between St. Helena and San Francisco is 82 miles and follows the backtrack path of 9-5-2-1; that between St. Helena and Berkeley is 71 miles and is along the 6-5-2-1 route).

The SR method can also be effectively used to analyze *equipment-replacement* problems, as illustrated in this next example.

FIGURE 8-8

Shortest Route (Minimum Travel Time) Backtracking Procedure for Mondavi Sales Representative

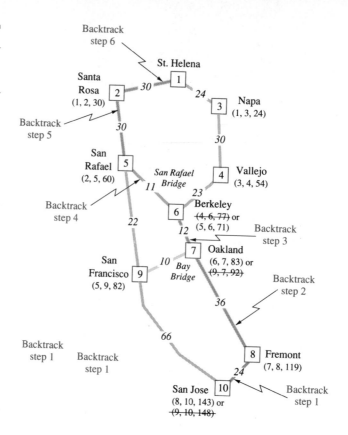

EXAMPLE 8.2 NATIONAL CAR RENTAL AUTOMOBILE FLEET PURCHASE–RESALE PLAN

"I only got halfway there and it ran out of gas!"

The replacement of aging machinery or perishable goods is a significant concern to thousands of businesses. The car-rental market provides a particularly illustrative example. We shall consider how a business may thoughtfully determine the optimal timing for the replacement of aging rental automobiles.

Suppose that one of the National Car Rental agencies is trying to determine the least expensive approach to buying and maintaining a fleet of rental automobiles over a 4-year planning period. National must decide whether it should purchase new cars and (1) keep and maintain them over the 4-year period, or (2) trade them in frequently (e.g., every year) for new models. In the former scenario, National will incur a one-time, high capital expenditure, and will incur increasing maintenance costs and significant depreciation over the 4 years. In the latter option, National will annually experience high capital outlays, but will have significantly lower maintenance expenses and equipment depreciation. Assume that the total costs of associated with purchasing a new car at the beginning of the ith year and keeping it until the beginning of the jth year is c_{ij}. This cost estimate assumes that National may decide to sell its used automobiles and to buy new ones during this 4-year period (imagine, for simplicity, that any transaction—sale and purchase—must occur only at the beginning of each year). The total costs experienced between the time of purchase and time of resale for the National Car Rental fleet may now be expressed as

$$(c_{ij})_{total} = (c_i)_{purchase} + (c_{ij})_{maintenance} - (c_j)_{resale}$$

where

$(c_i)_{\text{purchase}}$ = cost of purchase of automobile at the beginning of the ith year

$(c_j)_{\text{resale}}$ = revenues from sale of automobile at the beginning of the jth year

$(c_{ij})_{\text{maintenance}}$ = maintenance costs of automobile from the beginning of the ith year of purchase to the beginning of the jth year of resale

$(c_{ij})_{\text{total}}$ = total costs of automobile from the beginning of the ith year of purchase to the beginning of the jth year of resale

An illustration of numerous combinations of purchase and resale alternatives for the 4-year plan of operation is shown in Figure 8-9. The nodes represent points in time when the automobiles are purchased or resold. The average purchase price (assuming a 3 percent annual inflation rate), estimated annual maintenance costs, estimated resale value, and *arc cost* for automobiles between new (beginning of year 1) and 4 years of age (beginning of year 5) are shown in Table 8-1.

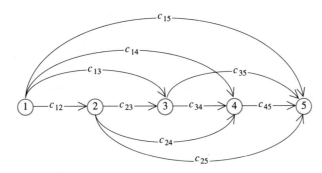

FIGURE 8-9

Expected New Car Expenses Over 4-Year Period for National Car Rental; Equipment-Replacement Application of Shortest Route Method

TABLE 8-1

New Car Purchase Price, Annual Maintenance Expenses, Resale Value, and Arc Costs Over 4-Year Period for National Car Rental

Beginning of Year Automobile Purchased/Sold	Purchase Price of Automobile, c_i, ($)	Annual Maintenance Expense, c_{ij} ($)	Resale Value, c_j, ($)
1	11,000	1500	9000
2	11,330	2000	5000
3	11,670	4000	3000
4	12,020	7000	1500
5	12,380	10,000	1000

$c_{12} = 11{,}000 + 1500 - 9000 = \$3500$

$c_{23} = 11{,}330 + 1500 - 9000 = \$3830$

$c_{34} = 11{,}670 + 1500 - 9000 = \$4170$

$c_{45} = 12{,}020 + 1500 - 9000 = \$4520$

$c_{13} = 11{,}000 + (1500 + 2000) - 5000 = \$9500$

$c_{24} = 11{,}330 + (1500 + 2000) - 5000 = \$9830$

$c_{35} = 11{,}670 + (1500 + 2000) - 5000 = \$10{,}170$

$c_{14} = 11{,}000 + (1500 + 2000 + 4000) - 3000 = \$15{,}500$

$c_{25} = 11{,}330 + (1500 + 2000 + 4000) - 3000 = \$15{,}830$

$c_{15} = 11{,}000 + (1500 + 2000 + 4000 + 7000) - 1500 = \$24{,}000$

The arc cost represents the total costs incurred over the variety of options of buying and reselling cars over the 4-year period: It is the sum of the costs of the variety of alternative paths that connect nodes 1 (beginning of year 1) and 5 (end of year 4/beginning of year 5). We'll examine two equipment-replacement plans.

Option 1. Suppose that National Car Rental is considering purchasing new automobiles at the beginning of the first year and trading them in for new automobiles at the end of the second year (beginning of year 3). The second group of cars will be traded in at the end of the fourth year. The per-unit costs of this program are as follows:

c_1:   Cost of initial purchase of car at beginning of year $i = 1$: \$11,000

c_3:   Cost of initial purchase of car at beginning of year $i = 3$: \$11,670

c_{13}:   Maintenance costs from initial purchase of new car at beginning of year $i = 1$ to resale of car at beginning of year $j = 3$: \$1500 + \$2000 = \$3500

c_{35}:   Maintenance costs from initial purchase of new car at beginning of year $i = 3$ to resale of car at beginning of year $j = 5$: \$1500 + \$2000 = \$3500

c_3:   Resale value of car at beginning of year $j = 3$ (2 years old): \$3000 ($j = 3$)

c_5:   Resale value of car at beginning of year $j = 5$ (2 years old): \$3000 ($j = 5$)

The total costs are

$$(c_{ij})_{\text{total}} = (c_1 + c_3)_{\text{purchase}} + (c_{13} + c_{35})_{\text{maintenance}}$$
$$- (c_3 + c_5)_{\text{resale}}$$
$$= (11,000 + 11,670) + (3500$$
$$+ 3500) - (3000 + 3000)$$
$$= 22,670 + 7000 - 6000$$
$$= \$23,670$$

The maintenance costs reflect the fact that, in both purchase–resale situations of this option, the car is kept for 2 years. Therefore, both c_{13} and c_{35} reflect the same maintenance costs (i.e., $1500 + 2000 = \$3500$).

Option 2. Suppose that National Car Rental is considering purchasing all new cars at the beginning of the first year ($i = 1$) and keeping them throughout the 4 years ($j = 5$). The per-unit costs for this option are:

$$(c_{ij})_{\text{total}} = (c_1)_{\text{purchase}} + (c_{12} + c_{23} + c_{34} + c_{45})_{\text{maintenance}}$$
$$- (c_5)_{\text{resale}}$$
$$= (11,000) + (1500 + 2000 + 4000 + 7000)$$
$$- (1000)$$
$$= 11,000 + 14,500 - 1000$$
$$= \$24,500$$

There are a surprising number of different combinations of purchase and resale alternatives for even a modest problem, such as the National Car Rental one. Finding the single policy that provides the lowest cost by inspection may not be a simple task. Fortunately, we can employ the SR algorithm to solve directly for the optimal (least cost)

path quickly and without concern for computational error. Regardless, when the network has a moderate to large number of nodes, it is risky to attempt manual solution—with or without the SR algorithm. The use of appropriate computer software is highly advised if not essential.

8.5 MINIMAL SPANNING TREE (MST) METHOD

The purpose of the minimal spanning tree (MST) method is to connect *every* node in a network while minimizing the total distance, the cost, or the time of the connected arcs. The MST model is commonly used in highway and street design and in the layout of communication networks.

Special Purpose MST Network Algorithm

The most popular technique that solves such a MST problem is called the *greedy algorithm* because each step of the process selects the largest improvement possible. The two forms of the MST algorithm—tabular and graphical—are presented next.

Tabular MST Method   For small to moderate problems, the three-step tabular algorithm used for solving MST problems develops simply:

Step 1. Design a matrix listing travel times (or costs or distances) between every possible combination of node locations. Leave blank any cells that represent an origin-location combination that is not possible (e.g., the hypothetical Mondavi Winery Example 8.1 illustrated in the shortest route algorithm that the sales representative cannot proceed directly between Berkeley and San Jose).

Step 2. Arbitrarily begin with any origin (row) node. Define this node as *connected* and mark the row with a star, check mark, arrow, or whatever. Eliminate the column number corresponding with this row (i.e., $j = i$ is crossed out). Search the connected node row for the least time destination; the column containing this time indicates the new connected node. Break any ties arbitrarily. Circle this value and eliminate the corresponding destination column. This step forms the first connected path: A segment of one arc and two nodes is now formed.

Step 3. Continue to repeat step 2 until all nodes have been connected. Remember to look for the smallest value in *all* rows that are "marked" when searching for the next connected node. The minimum spanning tree is defined by the connected (circled) nodes. It will require $n - 1$ (n is the total number of nodes in the network) iterations to complete this process.

There may be some special situations in which there will be more than a single optimal spanning tree. In all situations, however, the total number of connecting segments will be $n - 1$. Further, there are also some spanning tree problems in which the arcs have capacities or limits that can be sent along the various paths. This type of problem will be discussed in the transshipment model later in this chapter. Now let's apply the MST method to the hypothetical Robert Mondavi Winery sales representative problem (Example 8.1).

EXAMPLE 8.3 ROBERT MONDAVI WINERY SALES REPRESENTATIVE STUDY REVISITED

In addition to finding the quickest routes between her home and her nine distributors, assume the San Francisco region sales representative of Robert Mondavi Winery has another concern: It is sometimes important for her nine retail distributors to be able to reach her promptly to report low stock levels (or unanticipated stockouts), to place new orders, to request the latest price changes, to obtain new products information, to report breakage or order discrepancies, and so on. In order to be highly responsive to these types needs, the sales representative is studying the idea of setting up a microcomputer-based communication system between each retail distributor and herself; each distributor will purchase its own microcomputer, and Mondavi will install and maintain the interconnecting communications network. To design a cost-effective system, she wishes to determine the minimum mileage required to interconnect everyone (i.e., the telephone company will base charges proportional to line distances). She decides to apply the MST algorithm so that she can find the single interconnecting path to all her distributors that will result in the smallest number of miles.

Step 1. The distance matrix for the 10 nodes (St. Helena office and the nine retail distributors in her region) is shown in Table 8-2.

Step 2. Begin by arbitrarily selecting St. Helena (node 1) in row 1 as the first connected node. Mark row 1 with "*iteration 1* →" to indicate its selection and eliminate the cells in column 1 from further consideration. The shortest distance in row 1 is the 20 miles associated with the node 3 destination (Napa). Circle the 20-mile value, mark row 3, and cancel the remaining (uncircled) cells in column 3. Nodes 1 and 3 are the first connected arc, as shown in Table 8-3.

Step 3. Repeat step 2 until all remaining unconnected nodes have been examined and either have been added to the spanning tree or eliminated from further consid-

---

TABLE 8-2

Intradistributor Distance Matrix for Mondavi Sales Representative

j^{th} destination city (node j)

i	1	2	3	4	5	6	7	8	9	10
1		25	20							
2	25				25					
3	20			25						
4		25				19				
5		25				9		18		
6				19	9		10			
7						10		30	6	
8							30			20
9					18		6			55
10								20	55	

i^{th} origin city (node i)

Nodes: 1 = St. Helena, 2 = Santa Rosa, 3 = Napa, 4 = Vallejo, 5 = San Rafael, 6 = Berkeley, 7 = Oakland, 8 = Fremont, 9 = San Francisco, 10 = San Jose.

TABLE 8-3

Intradistributor Distance Matrix for Mondavi Sales Representative; Minimal Spanning Tree, Iteration 1

*j*th destination city (node *j*)

i	1	2	3	4	5	6	7	8	9	10
Iteration 1 → 1		25	(20)							
2	25				25					
3	20			25						
4			25			19				
5		25				9		18		
6				19	9		10			
7						10		30	6	
8							30			20
9					18		6			55
10								20	55	

Initial node 1 selected; shortest unconnected node is 3 (20 miles). First arc of 1-3 established. Next element to be connected is node 3.

Nodes: 1 = St. Helena, 2 = Santa Rosa, 3 = Napa, 4 = Vallejo, 5 = San Rafael, 6 = Berkeley, 7 = Oakland, 8 = Fremont, 9 = San Francisco, 10 = San Jose.

eration. The remaining iterations used in determining each of the segments in the Robert Mondavi Winery minimal spanning tree example follow:

Segment 1. Iteration 1—discussed in steps 1 through 3—has already completed the first 20-mile arc between nodes 1 (St. Helena) and 3 (Napa).

Segment 2. Iteration 2 searches the noncanceled column values in rows 1 and 3 for the shortest distance. The closest unconnected node reveals a tie between distances in columns 2 and 4 (25 miles). Column 4 is arbitrarily chosen. Arc 3-4 (Napa–Vallejo) is the second connected segment in the network. Cross out the remaining (uncircled) cells in column 4 and go to the third iteration in row 4 (Table 8-4).

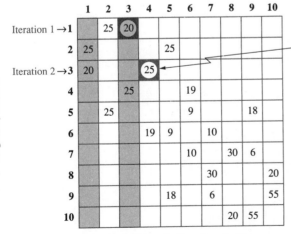

*j*th destination city (node *j*)

i	1	2	3	4	5	6	7	8	9	10
Iteration 1 → 1		25	(20)							
2	25				25					
Iteration 2 → 3	20			(25)						
4			25			19				
5		25				9		18		
6				19	9		10			
7						10		30	6	
8							30			20
9					18		6			55
10								20	55	

Searching rows 1 and 3 for the shortest unconnected node reveals a tie between distances in column 2 and 4 (25 miles). Column 4 is arbitrarily selected. Arc 3-4 becomes the second connected segment in the network; cancel column 4.

TABLE 8-4

Intradistributor Distance Matrix for Mondavi Sales Representative; Minimal Spanning Tree, Iteration 2

Nodes: 1 = St. Helena, 2 = Santa Rosa, 3 = Napa, 4 = Vallejo, 5 = San Rafael, 6 = Berkeley, 7 = Oakland, 8 = Fremont, 9 = San Francisco, 10 = San Jose.

TABLE 8-5

Intradistributor Distance Matrix for Mondavi Sales Representative; Minimal Spanning Tree, Iteration 3

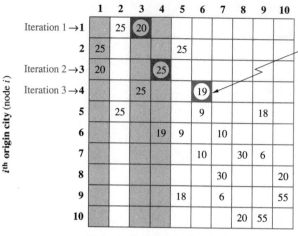

Searching rows 1, 3, and 4 for the shortest unconnected node shows the column 6 distance of 19 miles as the next node to be connected. Arc 4-6 becomes the third connected segment in the network. Cross off column 6.

Nodes: 1 = St. Helena, 2 = Santa Rosa, 3 = Napa, 4 = Vallejo, 5 = San Rafael, 6 = Berkeley, 7 = Oakland, 8 = Fremont, 9 = San Francisco, 10 = San Jose.

Segment 3. Iteration 3 examines rows 1,3, and 4 for the shortest unconnected node. Column 6 contains the minimal value of 19 miles and represents the next node to be connected. Arc 4-6 is formed as the third connected segment in the network. Go to row 6 for the next iteration and eliminate the uncircled cells in column 6 (Table 8-5).

Segment 4. Using rows 1,2,3, and 6, the shortest unconnected node—9 miles—is found in column 5. Arc 6-5 becomes segment 4 in the network. Cross off the uncircled cells in column 5 and add row 5 to the eligible group of origin nodes that will contain the next unconnected segment of the network (Table 8-6).

TABLE 8-6

Intradistributor Distance Matrix for Mondavi Sales Representative; Minimal Spanning Tree, Iteration 4

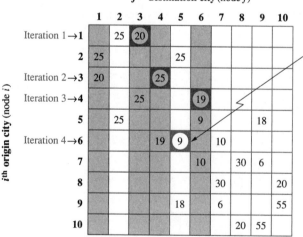

Searching rows 1, 3, 4, and 6 for the shortest unconnected node shows the column 5 distance of 9 miles as the next node to be connected. Arc 6-5 becomes the fourth connected segment in the network. Cross off column 5.

Nodes: 1 = St. Helena, 2 = Santa Rosa, 3 = Napa, 4 = Vallejo, 5 = San Rafael, 6 = Berkeley, 7 = Oakland, 8 = Fremont, 9 = San Francisco, 10 = San Jose.

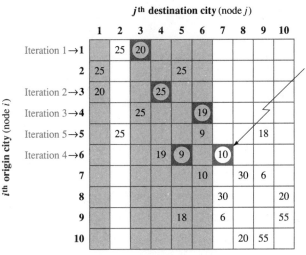

TABLE 8-7

Intradistributor Distance Matrix for Mondavi Sales Representative; Minimal Spanning Tree, Iteration 5

Searching rows 1, 3, 4, 5, and 6 for the shortest unconnected node reveals the column 7 distance of 10 miles as the next node to be connected. Arc 6-7 becomes the fifth connected segment in the network. Cross off column 7.

Nodes: 1 = St. Helena, 2 = Santa Rosa, 3 = Napa,
4 = Vallejo, 5 = San Rafael, 6 = Berkeley, 7 = Oakland,
8 = Fremont, 9 = San Francisco, 10 = San Jose.

Segment 5. Rows 1,3,4,5, and 6 are examined for the shortest unconnected node. Column 7 contains a distance of 10 miles and is connected to the network: arc 6-7 becomes the fifth connected segment. Cross off the remaining, uncircled cells in column 7 (Table 8-7).

Segments 6–9 The remaining iterations for the 164-mile minimal spanning tree are presented in Table 8-8.

Graphical MST Method

The iterative, three-step process for a graphical MST algorithm is presented next. We'll reexamine the Robert Mondavi Winery sales representative problem that we discussed

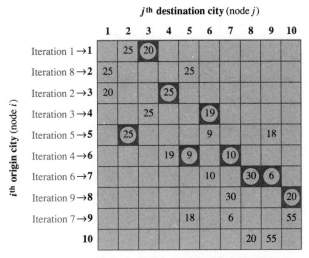

TABLE 8-8

Intradistributor Distance Matrix for Mondavi Sales Representative; Minimal Spanning Tree, Iterations 1–9

Nodes: 1 = St. Helena, 2 = Santa Rosa, 3 = Napa,
4 = Vallejo, 5 = San Rafael, 6 = Berkeley, 7 = Oakland,
8 = Fremont, 9 = San Francisco, 10 = San Jose.

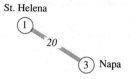

FIGURE 8-10

Minimal Spanning Tree Graphical Algorithm for Mondavi Sales Representative; Segment 1

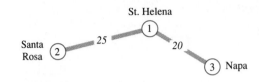

FIGURE 8-11

Minimal Spanning Tree Graphical Algorithm for Mondavi Sales Representative; Segment 2

using the tabular format algorithm. The graphical method is, arguably, even simpler than is the tabular format. The graphical algorithm follows.

Step 1. As in the tabular method, *arbitrarily select a starting node.* Select the shortest travel time arc directly connected to the starting node. This step identifies the first *connected* two-node arc in the network. The remaining nodes are, as in the tabular method, unconnected.

> *Connect node 1.* The unconnected node closest to the connected node is node 3. Arc 1-3 is 20 miles long (Figure 8-10).

Step 2. *Search for and select the shortest distance between any unconnected nodes directly tied to either node in the first connected arc found in step 1.* This step forms the second segment of the network.

> *Connect node 3.* Node 2 is the closest unconnected node to node 1. Arc 1-2 is 25 miles long (Figure 8-11).

Step 3. *Continue step 2 until all nodes are connected. Never connect new nodes that bring you back to an earlier connected node.* As in the tabular method, $n - 1$ interations will be required.

A summary of the MST connected segments is shown in Figure 8-12. Have you noticed that the solutions suggested by the two MST algorithms are different? Although the optimal solution value of 164 miles is the same for both the tabular and graphical methods, one segment is different in each: The tabular method used segment 3-4, whereas the graphical method picked 2-5 (both are 25 miles long). There is no mistake; multiple optimal solutions exist.

8.6 │ MAXIMUM FLOW (MF) MODEL

As the name implies, the maximum flow model determines the maximal amount of flow that can pass through a network between one origin node and one final destination (sink) node during a specified time period. In many instances, the amount of flow that can be facilitated is even more important than is the cost of the transmission (i.e., the value of the delivered "good" simply outweighs the associated "shipping" costs). It addresses such broad concerns as the flow of oil and gas; the transmission of money; the movement of people through buildings, airports, or department-store aisles; the flow of automobile traffic along freeways; the movement of packages, parcels, and letters; and the exchange of information within a communications network. The flow can be either

MST Segment	Distance
1-2	25
1-3	20
2-5	25
4-6	19
5-6	9
6-7	10
7-8	30
7-9	6
8-10	20
	164 miles

directed or nondirected. In addition, the quantity of flow either can be identical (symmetrical) or can differ (asymmetrical) between any two nodes.

Both the standard LP formulation as well as the special purpose network algorithm will be presented for the maximum flow model.[5]

Standard LP Formulation of the Maximum Flow Problem

One of the most common applications of the maximal flow model is solving problems of transporting gas and oil. Let's look at an example to illustrate this special LDN method.

EXAMPLE 8.4   OKLAHOMA CRUDE PIPELINE STUDY

The Oklahoma Crude Company (Exercise 1-10) is concerned with piping oil between its fields outside of Tulsa to its refinery in Minneapolis using a network of existing pipelines. These various pipeline segments were built during different time periods, follow dramatically disparate contours due to elevation differentials in the territory they span (as well as dramatically unequal climate variations), and have differing levels of oil-flow capacity. The oil-flow network, and the associated capacity restrictions for each arc (in barrels per minute), is shown in Figure 8-13. The formulation for this maximal flow problem follows.

[5]The Ford-Fulkerson method [L. Ford and D. Fulkerson, *Flows in Networks* (Princeton, N.J.: Princeton University Press, 1962)], although more intricate than desired for the intended nature of this text, provides a more rigorous treatment of the maximal flow mode. The general LP formulation of the maximal flow model is presented in Harvey M. Wagner, *Principles of Operations Research: With Application to Managerial Decisions* (Englewood Cliffs, N.J.: Prentice-Hall, 1969).

FIGURE 8-13

Maximal Flow Oklahoma Crude Pipeline Network Capacities

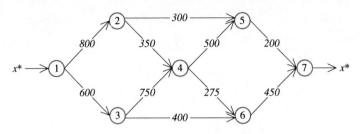

x^* = flowrate to be maximized

OBJECTIVE FUNCTION

Maximize flow rate, $Z = \Omega$

SUBJECT TO

$$x_{12} + x_{13} = \Omega$$
$$x_{12} - x_{24} - x_{25} = 0$$
$$x_{13} - x_{34} - x_{36} = 0$$
$$x_{24} + x_{34} - x_{45} - x_{46} = 0$$
$$x_{25} + x_{45} - x_{57} = 0$$
$$x_{36} + x_{46} - x_{67} = 0$$
$$x_{57} + x_{67} = \Omega$$
$$x_{12} \leq 800, x_{13} \leq 600, x_{24} \leq 350, x_{25} \leq 300, x_{34} \leq 750,$$
$$x_{36} \leq 400, x_{45} \leq 500, x_{46} \leq 275, x_{57} \leq 200, x_{67} \leq 450$$
$$x_{ij} \geq 0 \quad \text{for all } i \text{ and } j$$

You may have already guessed that this formulation does not lend itself to a standard LP solution because the unknown flowrate appears *both* in the objective function and as the right-hand-side value for the beginning and ending nodes. We can easily alleviate this difficulty, however, by introducing a dummy arc that *closes* the network between the ending and beginning network—a sort of feedback arc (Figure 8-14). The new objective function maximizes the flow rate over this dummy arc (7, 1) and, at the same time, makes it possible to remove Ω from the right-hand-side values of the initial and final node constraints as well as the objective function. The formulation for this *circular network* follows.

FIGURE 8-14

Maximal Flow Oklahoma Crude Pipeline Network Capacities

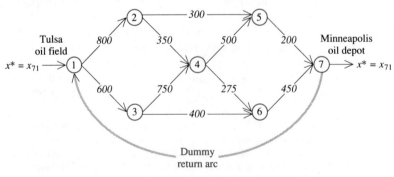

x^* = flowrate to be maximized = x_{71}

OBJECTIVE FUNCTION

Maximize flow rate, $Z = x_{71}$

SUBJECT TO

$x_{71} - x_{12} - x_{13} = 0$

$x_{12} - x_{24} - x_{25} = 0$

$x_{13} - x_{34} - x_{36} = 0$

$x_{24} + x_{34} - x_{45} - x_{46} = 0$

$x_{25} + x_{45} - x_{57} = 0$

$x_{36} + x_{46} - x_{67} = 0$

$x_{57} + x_{67} - x_{71} = 0$

$x_{12} \leq 800, x_{13} \leq 600, x_{24} \leq 350, x_{25} \leq 300, x_{34} \leq 750,$

$x_{36} \leq 400, x_{45} \leq 500, x_{46} \leq 275, x_{57} \leq 200, x_{67} \leq 450,$

$x_{ij} \geq 0$ for all i and j

Special Purpose Maximum Flow Algorithm   Once a maximum flow network is identified (Figure 8-13), it is not difficult to use an iterative procedure to determine the maximal flow limit. Here is the process (*again*, with a three-step algorithm!):

Step 1. *Examine the network for a continuous path between the source node to the sink node with positive flow capacity* (eliminate from consideration any path with one or more arcs with zero flow capacity). If no such path exists, stop. The net flows already provided represent the maximal flow possible. If there is a continuous path, go to step 2.

Step 2. *Search this path for the smallest flow capacity, c_{ij}^*; decrease the flow along all segments of this path by c_{ij}^*.*

Step 3. *Return to step 1 and continue the procedure until no paths with positive flow capacity exist* (every continuous path between the source and sink nodes will have at least one zero flow-capacity value).

This process allows the manager to make an arbitrary selection regarding which path to examine initially for positive flow capacity (step 1). However, the final optimal solution will be consistent regardless of which starting point is selected. Now let's apply this algorithm to the Oklahoma Crude Study (Example 8.4).

Step 1. Arbitrarily choose path 1-3-6-7.

Step 2. The minimal flow, c_{ij}^*, along this path is 400 barrels per minute (BPM). The new capacity is found by subtracting c_{ij}^* from each arc in this path.

BRANCH	ORIGINAL CAPACITY	NEW CAPACITY
1-3	600	200
3-6	400	0
6-7	450	50

The oil pipeline network flow capacity is now 400 barrels per minute (bpm; Figure 8-15).

Step 3. Next, select branch 1-2-5-7. The minimal flow, c_{ij}^*, along this path is 200 bpm. The new capacity along this branch is, then,

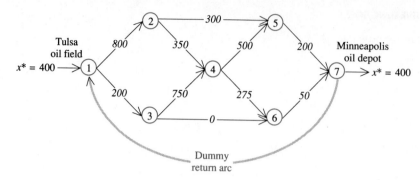

x^* = flowrate to be maximized = x_{71}

BRANCH	ORIGINAL CAPACITY	NEW CAPACITY
1-2	800	600
2-5	300	100
5-7	200	0

The oil-pipeline network revision is shown in Figure 8-16. The maximal flow possible at this point has increased to 600 BPM. This process is repeated for one of the remaining branches without a zero arc. In this iteration, we will examine 1-3-4-6-7. (We could have just as easily used path 1-2-4-6-7; however, our choice will make no difference to the final result.)

BRANCH	ORIGINAL CAPACITY	NEW CAPACITY
1-3	200	150
3-4	750	700
4-6	275	225
6-7	50	0

At this point, all remaining continuous paths between the source and sink nodes have at least one arc with zero capacity (Figure 8-17). We have, therefore, determined that the maximal flow possible in our network is 650 BPM.

Let's look at another example of the maximal flow method: airline route assignments.

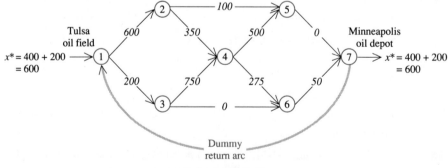

x^* = flowrate to be maximized = x_{71}

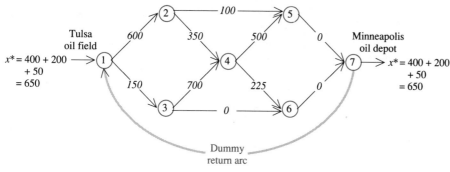

$x^* = $ flowrate to be maximized $= x_{71}$

EXAMPLE 8.5   AMERICAN AIRLINES WESTERN CORRIDOR
DAILY FLIGHT ASSIGNMENTS

In 1987, American Airlines took over a number of new, short distance air routes when
it purchased Air Cal. A simplified, hypothetical version of this flight network is illustrated in Figure 8-18. For illustrative purposes only, imagine that, after careful examination of the existing schedule, American discovered consistently overbooked flights
along some of these inherited routes, and other routes that were experiencing large va-
cancy rates. American decided to study the passenger demand for its entire western corridor of flights. The findings showed the likely number of flights that each one-way
route could support, as detailed in Table 8-9.

ASSIGNMENT

Using the maximum flow algorithm, determine how many connecting flights American
Airlines should opt to provide between each potential pair of cities.

SOLUTION

The solution process of the maximum number of one-way flights possible using the
maximum flow algorithm is summarized in Table 8-10.

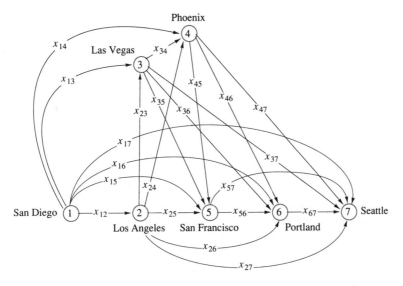

FIGURE 8-18

Daily Flight Routes for American Airlines

TABLE 8-9

American Airlines Forecast of Maximum Number of Daily Connecting Flights for Western Region

Branch	Originating City, i	Destination City, j	No. of Daily Flights, i–j
1-2	San Diego	Los Angeles	10
1-3	San Diego	Las Vegas	3
1-4	San Diego	Phoenix	1
1-5	San Diego	San Francisco	5
1-6	San Diego	Portland	2
1-7	San Diego	Seattle	3
2-4	Los Angeles	Phoenix	3
2-5	Los Angeles	San Francisco	16
2-6	Los Angeles	Portland	3
2-7	Los Angeles	Seattle	5
3-4	Las Vegas	Phoenix	5
3-5	Las Vegas	San Francisco	5
3-6	Las Vegas	Portland	1
3-7	Las Vegas	Seattle	2
4-5	Phoenix	San Francisco	2
4-6	Phoenix	Portland	1
4-7	Phoenix	Seattle	1
5-6	San Francisco	Portland	2
5-7	San Francisco	Seattle	2
6-7	Portland	Seattle	8

TABLE 8-10

Maximum Flow Flight Schedule for American Airlines Western Corridor

Step No.	Path Selected	Maximum Flow Branch	No. of Flights
1	1-2-5-6-7	5-6	2
2	1-2-5-7	5-7	2
3	1-2-5-3-4-6-7	4-6	1
4	1-2-5-3-4-7	4-7	1
5	1-2-5-3-6-7	3-6	1
6	1-2-5-3-7	5-3	1
7	1-2-5-4-3-7	3-7	1
8	1-2-6-7	1-2	1
9	1-3-4-5-2-6-7	2-6	2
10	1-3-4-5-2-7	1-3	1
11	1-4-2-7	1-4	1
12	1-5-2-7	2-7	3
13	1-6-7	6-7	1
14	1-7	1-7	3

8.7 | TRANSSHIPMENT PROBLEMS

If you don't look closely, you can mistake a transshipment problem for a common transportation problem: Both methods facilitate the search for the cheapest way of transporting goods between a set of origins (supply locations) and a set of destinations (demand locations). Transshipment problems are, in fact, a special kind of transportation problem. However, unlike the standard transportation model, transshipment mod-

els can address problems in which there is an exchange of goods or information among specific origins or among specific destinations in which goods are shipped *through* one city to another—not merely between one pair of supply-demand locations. Because goods or information can be distributed through several locations, transshipment problems can have sites that only send, only receive, or both send and receive. Therefore, each location (node) must be carefully defined as either a supply node (send only), sink node (receive only), or transshipment node (both send and receive). Based on this categorization, the flow of goods or information from, to, or through a node can be carefully balanced. These important relationships defined by flow-balance equations are lucidly illustrated by Shogan (reference 11) and presented next.

Flow-Balance Equations   The *general flow-balance equation* for any type of node is

(node's supply) $=$ (flow on arcs out of the node) $-$ (flow on arcs into the node)

Because of this general relationship, it is not difficult to see three points.

1. *The flow-balance equation for a supply node is*

$$\binom{\text{Net supply}}{\text{of node}}_{\text{supply node}} = \binom{\text{flow of goods out}}{\text{of supply node}} - \binom{\text{flow of goods into}}{\text{supply node}}$$

However, *the second term on the right-hand-side of the equation is zero*, because there is no flow of goods into a supply node. Therefore the flow-balance equation for a supply node is

(Net supply of node) $_{\text{supply node}}=$ (flow of goods out of supply node)

2. *The flow-balance equation for a sink node is*

$$\binom{\text{Net supply}}{\text{of node}}_{\text{sink node}} = \binom{\text{flow of goods out}}{\text{of sink node}} - \binom{\text{flow of goods into}}{\text{sink node}}$$

Since a sink node only receives goods or information, you can think of it as negative supply (demand only) node. Accordingly, *the first term on the right-hand-side of the equation is zero*, because there is no outflow of goods from a sink node. The revised flow-balance equation for a sink node is

(Net supply of node)$_{\text{sink node}}$ $=$ $-$(flow of goods into sink node)

3. *The flow-balance equation for a transshipment node is*

$$\binom{\text{Net supply}}{\text{of node}}_{\substack{\text{transshipment}\\\text{node}}} = \binom{\text{flow of goods out of}}{\text{transshipment node}} - \binom{\text{flow of goods into}}{\text{transshipment node}}$$

Transshipment nodes receive and send goods. The net supply to a transshipment node can be zero (the flow of goods into and out of a transshipment node can be equal):

(Net supply of node)$_{\text{transshipment}}$ $= 0$

If, however, a transshipment node saves a portion of the goods received, then the amount of flow out of the node will be less than that into the node. In this case, the flow-balance equation is

$$\binom{\text{Net supply}}{\text{of node)}}_{\substack{\text{transshipment}\\\text{node}}} = \binom{\text{flow of goods out of}}{\text{transshipment node}} - \binom{\text{flow of goods into}}{\text{transshipment node}} \leq 0$$

This gives a transshipment node the possibility to receive goods and to send either all or part of them to another node. *If it does not send all of the goods received, the transshipment node is said to have a demand or a negative supply.* The demand (negative supply) for a transshipment node that keeps part of a shipment is

$$
\begin{pmatrix} \text{Net supply} \\ \text{of node} \end{pmatrix}_{\substack{\text{transshipment} \\ \text{node}}} = \begin{pmatrix} \text{flow of goods out of} \\ \text{transshipment node} \end{pmatrix} - \begin{pmatrix} \text{flow of goods into} \\ \text{transshipment node} \end{pmatrix} = - \begin{pmatrix} \text{demand} \\ \text{of node} \end{pmatrix}_{\substack{\text{transshipment} \\ \text{node}}}
$$

The generalized formulation of the transshipment model is presented in the References (see Harvey, 1969; Winston, 1987; and Budnick, et al., 1988). Let's illuminate the transshipment model with an LDN problem examining the possible worldwide distribution network of a new microcomputer company, NeXT Computer Corporation.

EXAMPLE 8.6   INTERNATIONAL DISTRIBUTION SYSTEM FOR NeXT COMPUTER CORPORATION

Steven Jobs, cofounder of the Apple Corporation, was ousted in a much publicized corporate power struggle. Since his departure from Apple, Jobs has founded a new company—NeXT Computer Corporation—that is developing a microcomputer product that industry gurus anticipate will be a show stopper. The rest of the scenario that follows is conjecture, but it is certainly not implausible.

To increase his chances for success, Jobs knows that he must have a well-planned distribution network to sell his computers. After opening his headquarters in Palo Alto, California, Jobs establishes manufacturing facilities in Taiwan and Seoul along with an East Coast headquarters in Pittsburgh. Just prior to the unveiling of his new microcomputer in the summer of 1988, Jobs selected key cities throughout Western Europe, South America, and Australia to complement his Palo Alto and Pittsburgh headquarters and to serve as his international distribution centers (an Asian distribution center is planned in the very near future). These international distribution centers include Montreal, Paris, Buenos Aires, and Sydney. Jobs plans for the computers to be entirely manufactured in Taiwan and Seoul. From these two locations, specific numbers of these products will be shipped to each of the regional distribution points for allocation to selected retail sales outlets over the next 3 years. An illustration of the NeXT LDN for this 3-year time period is shown in Figure 8-19. The shipping direction restrictions associated with each route are shown by the direction of the arrowhead: Those routes without arrows signify bidirectional shipping as needed (e.g., computers may be exchanged only between Taiwan and Seoul or between Palo Alto and Pittsburgh). The per-unit distribution costs associated with the various routes, the manufacturing capacities, and the demand of the distribution centers are given in Table 8-11. The darkened cells of the table indicate that no shipping is available along this particular route (this is consistent with the distribution network illustrated in Figure 8-19). In addition to the shipping charges, each route may have restrictions regarding the maximum and minimum volume of goods that can be moved during the next 3 years: an upper limit may be based on the number of carriers and their physical capacities, whereas a minimum quantity might reflect a contractual guarantee to ensure an "availability" commitment from each carrier. The upper and lower limits associated with the shipping restrictions of the distribution network are provided in Table 8-12. Using the information provided in Tables 8-11 and 8-12, we can develop the standard LP formulation of the NeXT distribution capacitated network. Assume that x_{ij} is the number of units (in

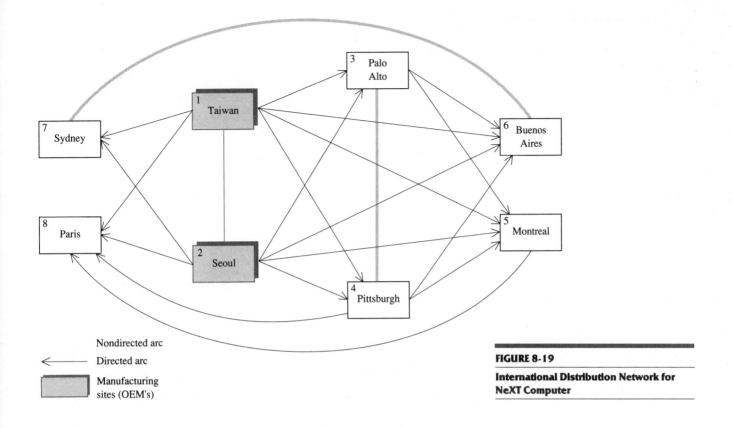

Nondirected arc

← Directed arc

Manufacturing
sites (OEM's)

FIGURE 8-19

International Distribution Network for NeXT Computer

thousands) of NeXT microcomputers shipped between the ith city and the jth city, and Z is the total network distribution costs for each thousand units.

OBJECTIVE FUNCTION

Minimize network distribution costs,

$$
\begin{aligned}
Z = {} & 12x_{12} + 35x_{13} + 50x_{14} + 80x_{15} + \\
& 85x_{16} + 100x_{17} + 90x_{18} \\
& + 11x_{21} + 37x_{23} + 53x_{24} + 78x_{25} + 90x_{26} \\
& 98x_{27} + 88x_{28} + 10x_{34} + 35x_{35} + 49x_{36} + 10x_{43} + 28x_{45} \\
& + 45x_{46} + 41x_{48} + 32x_{58} + 30x_{67} + 28x_{76}
\end{aligned}
$$

SUBJECT TO

Flow-balance equations:

Taiwan:	$x_{12} + x_{13} + x_{14} + x_{15} + x_{16} + x_{17} + x_{18} - x_{21} = 250$
Seoul:	$x_{21} + x_{23} + x_{24} + x_{25} + x_{26} + x_{27} + x_{28} - x_{12} = 480$
Palo Alto:	$x_{34} + x_{35} + x_{36} - (x_{13} + x_{23} + x_{43}) = -200$
Pittsburgh:	$x_{43} + x_{45} + x_{46} + x_{48} - (x_{14} + x_{24} + x_{34}) = -200$
Montreal:	$x_{58} - (x_{15} + x_{25} + x_{35} + x_{45}) = -100$
Buenos Aires:	$x_{67} - (x_{16} + x_{26} + x_{36} + x_{46} + x_{76}) = -30$
Sydney:	$x_{76} - (x_{17} + x_{27} + x_{67}) = -50$
Paris:	$x_{18} + x_{28} + x_{48} + x_{58} = -150$

TABLE 8-11

International Distribution Network Transportation Costs, and Annual Supply and Demand Capacities, for NeXT Computer

	Annual production capacity (1000)
Taiwan	280
Seoul	450
	730

	Annual regional distribution center demand (1000)
Palo Alto	200
Pittsburgh	200
Montreal	100
Buenos Aires	30
Sydney	50
Paris	150
	730

jth destination city

ith origin city	Taiwan	Seoul	Palo Alto	Pittsburgh	Montreal	Buenos Aires	Sydney	Paris
Taiwan		12	35	50	80	85	100	90
Seoul	11		37	53	78	90	98	88
Palo Alto				10	35	49		
Pittsburgh			10		28	45		41
Montreal								32
Buenos Aires							30	
Sydney						28		
Paris								

c_{ij}	Per-unit distribution costs along arc ij		Goods may not be shipped along this ij arc.

Transportation costs between
ith origin city and jth destination city (arc ij)

Upper- and lower-bound flow constraints:

Seoul: $0 \leq x_{21} \leq 225, 50 \leq x_{23} \leq 175, 50 \leq x_{24} \leq 9999,$
$0 \leq x_{15} \leq 65, 10 \leq x_{16} \leq 9999, 10 \leq x_{17} \leq 9999,$
$30 \leq x_{18} \leq 9999$

Palo Alto: $0 \leq x_{34} \leq 9999, 10 \leq x_{35} \leq 9999, 0 \leq x_{36} \leq 9999$

Pittsburgh: $0 \leq x_{43} \leq 9999, 10 \leq x_{45} \leq 9999, 0 \leq x_{46} \leq 9999,$
$10 \leq x_{48} \leq 9999$

Montreal: $0 \leq x_{58} \leq 9999$

Buenos Aires: $0 \leq x_{67} \leq 9999$

Sydney: $0 \leq x_{76} \leq 9999$

	Taiwan	Seoul	Palo Alto	Pittsburgh	Montreal	Buenos Aires	Sydney	Paris
Taiwan		140/*	150/50	150/50	40/5	*/5	*/5	*/10
Seoul	225/*		175/50	*/50	65/*	*/10	*/10	*/30
Palo Alto				*/*	*/10	*/*		
Pittsburgh			*/*		*/10	*/*		*/10
Montreal								*/*
Buenos Aires							*/*	
Sydney						*/*		
Paris								

Upper and lower bounds for quantity of goods shipped along arc ij, upper bound/lower bound (1000s of units of microcomputers)
*No Limit

TABLE 8-12

International Distribution Network Showing Upper/Lower Arc Capacities for NeXT Computer

Be aware that some of these upper- and lower-bound constraints are superfluous. For example, the nonnegativity constraints require all x_{ij} decision variables to be ≥ 0. Therefore, when a lower-bound constraint is zero, it provides redundant information. In addition, upper-bound constraints of 9999 are so far beyond actual resource limits that they, too, become extraneous.[6]

8.8 MICROCOMPUTER SOLUTIONS TO LINEAR DISTRIBUTION NETWORK PROBLEMS

There is a dramatic contrast between the significant time and energy spent on formulating and solving an LDN problem using standard LP procedures versus the small effort involved in achieving the same end results using specialty algorithm software. You might even feel guilty about how easy it is to set up and solve an LDN problem using a good software package. The only information you will need to provide is a list identifying the arrangement of the network's nodes and arcs; the supply or demand for each node; any upper or lower capacities of an arc; and the distance, time, or costs associated with each unit of flow across each arc.

The data entry and solutions to the National Car Rental shortest-route problem (Example 8.2), the Robert Mondavi Winery sales representative minimum spanning tree problem (Example 8.1), the Oklahoma Crude Pipeline maximum flow problem (Example 8.4) and NeXT Computer Corporation international distribution network capacitated transshipment problem (Example 8.6) are illustrated in Tables 8-13 through 8-16, respectively.

[6]There is nothing magic about the selection of the upper-bound value of 9999. It would be adequate simply to set the cost of any forbidden route equal to a *big M*–type value, as discussed in Chapters 5 and 6.

TABLE 8-13

Shortest Route Data Entry and Final Solution for National Car Rental Equipment Replacement Problem

Source: Chang & Sullivan. Quantitative Systems for Business Version 3.0. Englewood Cliffs, NJ: Prentice-Hall, 1986.

```
                Input Data of the Problem SR.CAR     Page 1

   Branch        Branch        Start        End        Distance
   Number        Name          Node         Node
      1         <C12    >      <1   >       <2   >    < 3500.000>
      2         <C23    >      <2   >       <3   >    < 3830.000>
      3         <C34    >      <3   >       <4   >    < 4170.000>
      4         <C45    >      <4   >       <5   >    < 4520.000>
      1         <C13    >      <1   >       <3   >    < 9500.000>
      1         <C14    >      <1   >       <4   >    < 3500.000>
      1         <C15    >      <1   >       <5   >    <15500.000>
      1         <C35    >      <3   >       <5   >    <24000.000>
      1         <C24    >      <2   >       <4   >    <10170.000>
      1         <C25    >      <2   >       <5   >    <15830.000>


          The Final Shortest Routes for SR.CAR        Page 1

     Node    Distance     Shortest Route from Node 1

       2       3500       1-2 (C12)
       3       7330       1-2-3 (C12-C23)
       4      11500       1-2-3-4 (C12-C23-C34)
       5      16020       1-2-3-4-5 (C12-C23-C34-C45)
```

TABLE 8-14

Minimal Spanning Tree Data Entry and Solution to Mondavi Sales Representative Problem

Source: Chang & Sullivan. Quantitative Systems for Business Version 3.0. Englewood Cliffs, NJ: Prentice-Hall, 1986.

```
        NET Model Entry for MSTREE.MONDAVI          Page 1

   Branch        Branch        Start        End        Distance
   Number        Name          Node         Node
      1         <        >     <1   >      <2   >   <   30.000>
      2         <        >     <1   >      <3   >   <   24.000>
      3         <        >     <2   >      <5   >   <   30.000>
      4         <        >     <3   >      <4   >   <   30.000>
      5         <        >     <4   >      <6   >   <   23.000>
      6         <        >     <5   >      <6   >   <   11.000>
      7         <        >     <5   >      <9   >   <   22.000>
      8         <        >     <6   >      <7   >   <   12.000>
      9         <        >     <7   >      <8   >   <   36.000>
     10         <        >     <7   >      <9   >   <   10.000>
     11         <        >     <8   >      <10  >   <   24.000>
     12         <        >     <9   >      <10  >   <   66.000>


   The Final Minimal Spanning Tree for MSTREE.MONDAVI    Page 1

            Branch on the Tree          Distance
               1-2  (B1)                   25
               1-3  (B2)                   20
               2-5  (B3)                   25
               5-6  (B6)                    9
               4-6  (B5)                   19
               6-7  (B8)                   10
               7-8  (B9)                   30
               7-9  (B10)                   6
               8-10 (B11)                  20

             Total distance = 164
```

```
          Input Data of the Problem MF.OKLA    Page 1

  Branch       Branch        Start     End     Flow Capacity    Flow Capacity
  Number       Name          Node      Node    From Start Node  From End Node
    1       <B1    >      <1  >     <2  >    < 800.000>       < 800.000>
    2       <B2    >      <1  >     <3  >    < 600.000>       < 600.000>
    3       <B3    >      <2  >     <4  >    < 350.000>       < 350.000>
    4       <B4    >      <2  >     <5  >    < 300.000>       < 300.000>
    5       <B5    >      <3  >     <4  >    < 750.000>       < 750.000>
    6       <B6    >      <3  >     <6  >    < 400.000>       < 400.000>
    7       <B7    >      <4  >     <5  >    < 500.000>       < 500.000>
    8       <B8    >      <4  >     <6  >    < 275.000>       < 275.000>
    9       <B9    >      <5  >     <7  >    < 200.000>       < 200.000>
   10       <B10   >      <6  >     <7  >    < 450.000>       < 450.000>



          The Final Flow for MF.OKLA        Page 1

              Branch            Net Flow
              1-2  (B1)            650
              2-4  (B3)            350
              2-5  (B4)            300
              3-6  (B6)            175
              4-6  (B8)            275
              4-3  (B5)            175
              5-7  (B9)            200
              5-4  (B7)            100
              6-7  (B10)           450

          Maximal total flow = 650
```

TABLE 8-15

Maximal Total Flow Data Entry and Solution to Oklahoma Crude Problem

Source: Chang & Sullivan. Quantitative Systems for Business Version 3.0. Englewood Cliffs, NJ: Prentice-Hall, 1986.

Right Hand Side Ranging

Constraint name	Current value	Lower limit	Upper limit	Shadow price
Taiwan supply	280.00	255.00	280.00	-85.00
Seoul supply	450.00	350.00	450.00	-88.00
Palo Alto	200.00	200.00	225.00	45.00
Pittsburg	200.00	200.00	225.00	35.00
Montreal	100.00	100.00	125.00	10.00
Buenos Aires	30.00	30.00	55.00	0.00
Sydney	50.00	50.00	150.00	-10.00
Paris	150.00	150.00	+ Infinity	0.00
x12 max	140.00	0.00	+ Infinity	0.00
x12 min	0.00	0.00	25.00	-15.00
x13 max	150.00	90.00	190.00	5.00
x13 min	50.00	- Infinity	150.00	0.00
x14 max	150.00	90.00	+ Infinity	0.00
x14 min	50.00	- Infinity	90.00	0.00
x15 max	40.00	5.00	+ Infinity	+ Infinity
x15 min	5.00	0.00	40.00	40.00
x16 max	730.00	20.00	+ Infinity	0.00
x16 min	5.00	- Infinity	20.00	0.00
x17 max	730.00	5.00	+ Infinity	0.00
x17 min	5.00	0.00	30.00	-5.00
x18 max	730.00	10.00	+ Infinity	0.00
x18 min	10.00	0.00	35.00	-5.00
x21 max	225.00	0.00	+ Infinity	0.00

TABLE 8-16

Solution of International Distribution Network for NeXT Computers Capacitated Transshipment Example (Part 1/4)

Source: Big ALPAL, John Burton, Version 1.0. Philadelphia: Drexel University, 1987.

Right hand side ranging (continued)

Constraint name	Current value	Lower limit	Upper limit	Shadow price
x21 min	0.00	0.00	40.00	-8.00
x23 max	175.00	150.00	215.00	6.00
x23 min	50.00	- Infinity	175.00	0.00
x24 max	730.00	50.00	+ Infinity	0.00
x24 min	50.00	25.00	90.00	-0.00
x25 max	65.00	40.00	+ Infinity	0.00
x25 min	0.00	- Infinity	40.00	0.00
x26 max	730.00	10.00	+ Infinity	0.00
x26 min	10.00	0.00	25.00	-2.00
x27 max	730.00	45.00	+ Infinity	0.00
x27 min	10.00	- Infinity	45.00	0.00
x28 max	730.00	130.00	+ Infinity	0.00
x28 min	30.00	- Infinity	130.00	0.00
x34 max	730.00	80.00	+ Infinity	0.00
x34 min	0.00	- Infinity	80.00	0.00
x35 max	730.00	45.00	+ Infinity	0.00
x35 min	10.00	- Infinity	45.00	0.00
x36 max	730.00	0.00	+ Infinity	-4.00
x36 min	0.00	0.00	15.00	0.00
x43 max	730.00	0.00	+ Infinity	-20.00
x43 min	0.00	0.00	650.00	0.00
x45 max	730.00	10.00	+ Infinity	-3.00
x45 min	10.00	0.00	45.00	0.00
x46 max	730.00	0.00	+ Infinity	-10.00
x46 min	0.00	0.00	15.00	0.00
x48 max	730.00	10.00	+ Infinity	-6.00
x48 min	10.00	0.00	35.00	0.00
x58 max	730.00	0.00	+ Infinity	0.00
x58 min	0.00	0.00	25.00	-22.00
x67 max	730.00	0.00	+ Infinity	0.00
x67 min	0.00	0.00	25.00	-20.00
x76 max	730.00	0.00	+ Infinity	0.00
x76 min	0.00	0.00	730.00	-28.00

Contribution Ranging

Variable name	Current value	Lower limit	Upper limit
x12	12.00	-3.00	+ Infinity
x13	35.00	- Infinity	40.00
x14	50.00	48.00	55.00
x15	80.00	75.00	+ Infinity
x16	85.00	65.00	87.00
x17	100.00	95.00	+ Infinity
x18	90.00	85.00	+ Infinity
x21	11.00	3.00	+ Infinity
x23	37.00	- Infinity	43.00
x24	53.00	53.00	+ Infinity
x25	78.00	73.00	78.00
x26	90.00	88.00	+ Infinity
x27	98.00	- Infinity	103.00
x28	88.00	- Infinity	93.00
x34	10.00	7.00	10.00
x35	35.00	35.00	38.00
x36	49.00	45.00	+ Infinity
x43	10.00	-10.00	+ Infinity
x45	28.00	25.00	+ Infinity
x46	45.00	35.00	+ Infinity
x48	41.00	35.00	+ Infinity
x58	32.00	10.00	+ Infinity
x67	30.00	10.00	+ Infinity
x76	28.00	0.00	+ Infinity

8.9 SUMMARY

In this chapter, we've examined some of the most widely used LDN models that can provide a manager with tools that can, for a given network, determine (1) the shortest distance between any two locations (shortest-route model), (2) the specific family of paths that will interconnect all locations while minimizing the total number of miles traveled (minimal spanning tree model), (3) the largest amount of flow between an origin and destination (maximal flow model), and (4) the least expensive way of distributing goods between one or more origins and numerous destination points that have specific supply, demand, and route restrictions (transshipment model).

Most of these network models can be easily formulated using standard LP formulation methods. However, the actual solution of these types of distribution models is more efficient if managed by special purpose algorithms. These special algorithms can rapidly solve very large network problems of, say, thousand of nodes and arcs. Although it would be also possible to solve these same problems using the simplex algorithm, the formulations would be very tedious and the solutions would be excessively time consuming and expensive. As a general rule, standard LP formulation approaches to network distribution models should be limited to problems of no more than 20 nodes.

8.10 EXERCISES

8-1 Suppose that the Robert Mondavi Winery sales representative (Example 8.3) is being relocated to an office that the company managers think will be more centrally located than is her home in St. Helena. She has been relocated to Berkeley. Determine, using the appropriate algorithms,

1. What is her new shortest route?
2. What is the new minimal spanning tree?

8-2 The Robert Mondavi Winery sales representative (Exercise 8-1) is just settling into her new Berkeley digs when she gets a telephone call from her boss. Imagine that she is told that, due to low sales, the Fremont distributor is being dropped. For now, Mondavi has no new distributor to fill in the void. Determine, using the appropriate algorithm,

1. What is her new shortest route?
2. What is the new minimal spanning tree?

8-3 Pretend that the San Francisco 49er football team employs scouts who are assigned to specific geographic regions throughout the United States for the purpose of evaluating college football players. These evaluations are critical in helping the 49ers to determine which players they would like to select in the annual National Football League draft. Suppose that one of their scouts who lives in Sacramento is assigned to assess the players at six major universities: Stanford, University of California at Berkeley, Oregon, Oregon State, Washington, and Washington State. The automobile traveling time between the scout's home (node 1) and the six schools is illustrated in Figure 8-3.1. When the scout leaves on a trip, he wants to minimize the total time he must drive between the various schools. Determine for him what is the quickest route for traveling between his home and all six schools. Also determine the specific individual paths that provide the quickest interconnecting network.

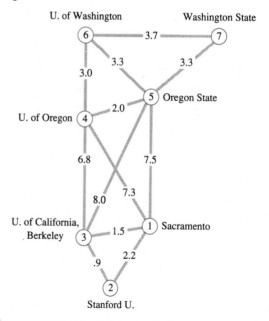

FIGURE 8-3.1

Travel Times (Hours) for San Francisco 49ers Scouting Territory

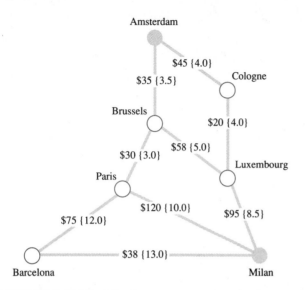

FIGURE 8-4.1

First-Class Eurorail Expense (U.S. Dollars) and Travel Times (Hours) Between Various European Cities

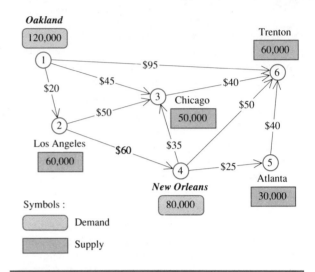

FIGURE 8-5.1

Bert Tuna Company Transshipment Network

8-4 Find the least expensive and fastest route(s) for traveling between Amsterdam and Milan on a first-class Eurorail ticket on the railroad network shown in Figure 8-4.1.

8-5 The Bert Tuna Company (Exercise 4-11) has been revised to reflect changes in the distribution system as well as a revision of the basic philosophy of direct shipping between all warehouses and distribution centers. These primary changes are as follows:

1. Four of the original five warehouses have been shut down, a new warehouse has been opened, and the capacity of the single remaining warehouse has been increased significantly.
2. Three of the four distribution centers have been relocated.
3. The routes between warehouses and distribution centers are not necessarily direct—or even possible. In fact, it is often necessary to route goods *through* intermediate locations in order to reach the final destination. The trucking costs associated with the *allowable* routes between the two warehouses and four distribution centers are presented in Table 8-5.1 and in Figure 8-5.1.

ASSIGNMENT

1. Formulate the problem as a standard LP model.
2. Using the transshipment model and an appropriate microcomputer software package, solve for the specific amounts assigned to each route and the minimum total system transportation costs to be expected.

8-6 *Microcomputer Currents* is a California-based, free, bimonthly magazine. The magazine primarily contains review articles about the latest hardware and software products for the business community. For illustrative purposes only, assume the following scenario to be true.

The magazine does not employ centralized publishing. Instead, the magazine is published in northern California (San Francisco) and southern California (Los Angeles) regions where it carries local dealer ads, user-group announcements, and so on.

In Los Angeles, the magazine must be printed and rapidly transported to six distribution centers (there are actually seven

TABLE 8-5.1

Transportation Costs and Supply-Demand Capacities of the Bert Tuna Company Distribution Network

	To: City				
From: City	*Los Angeles*	*Chicago*	*Atlanta*	*Trenton*	Supply (tons)
Oakland*	$20	$45	—	$95	120,000
New Orleans*	—	$35	$25	$50	80,000
Los Angeles	—	$50	—	—	
Chicago	—	—	—	$40	
Atlanta	—	—	—	$40	
Demand (tons)	60,000	50,000	30,000	60,000	200,000

*Warehouse locations.

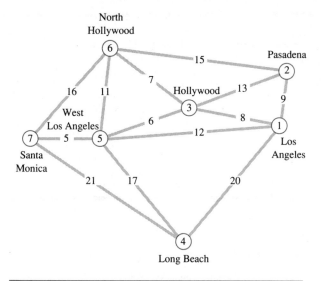

FIGURE 8-6.1

Distribution Network for *Microcomputer Currents*

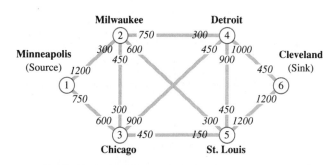

FIGURE 8-7.1

Exxon Pipeline Flow Network

distribution centers—one is at the printing facility). The distribution network is shown in Figure 8-6.1.

ASSIGNMENT

1. Formulate the problem as a standard LP model.

2. Determine the optimal delivery route to all distribution centers for *Microcomputer Currents* using the appropriate software package.

8-7 Assume that the pipeline network illustrated in Figure 8-7.1 is Exxon's Midwest installation. Find the maximal flow from the source (Minneapolis) to the sink (Cleveland) given that the flow capacity from node i to node j represents the identification convention used along branch (i, j) nearest node i.

8-8 Assume that the National Car Rental agency (Example 8.2) wants to determine which of two new policies it is considering is the least expensive for its 4-year plan. The managers have new data concerning the purchase price of used automobiles: cars 1, 2, 3, and 4 years old can be bought for $9500, $5500, $3500, and $1800, respectively. Using these new data (as well as the original data), calculate the costs of the following two policies and tell the managers which one is the most cost effective:

■ *Policy 1*: Purchase cars that are all 2 years old and keep them for 2 years. Resell them at the 2-year mark (when they are 4 years old) and repurchase more 2-year-old cars. The second group of cars are kept 2 additional years to complete the balance of the 4-year plan.

■ *Policy 2*: Purchase cars that are 1 year old. Keep these cars 2 years (until they are 3 years old). Trade them in on cars that are, once again, 1 year old. Keep the second group of cars 2 years, completing the 4-year cycle.

8-9 Suppose that Apple Computer is studying the best way of distributing their microcomputers to five distribution centers throughout Western Europe. The company uses two ports of entry: Le Havre on the French coast, and Amsterdam. The various monthly supply, demand, and distribution costs (dollars/unit) associated with the two ports of entry (Le Havre and Amsterdam) and the five distribution centers in London, Paris, Berlin, Rome, and Brussels are shown in Figure 8-9.1 and Table 8-9.1.

ASSIGNMENT

1. Formulate this problem using standard LP procedures.

2. Using an appropriate LP software package, determine the exact quantity of computers sent to and from each of the seven European cities as well as the total system distribution costs.

8-10 Using all the information available on the NeXT Computers LDN (Example 8.6, including the formulation of the capacitated network), use appropriate microcomputer software to determine the following information for Mr. Jobs:

1. By how much must the present per-unit distribution costs change in order (1) to increase the present total number of computers sent from the Seoul and Taiwan production centers, and (2) to decrease the present total number of computers sent from the Seoul and Taiwan production centers?

2. By how much must the present per-unit distribution costs decrease in order to increase the present number of computers sent from Taiwan to Paris?

3. There is currently an interchange of goods sent from Palo Alto to the Pittsburgh headquarters. What increase in the per-unit shipping cost between these two locations would force NeXT to reduce the quantity presently shipped?

TABLE 8-9.1

Apple Computer's Shipping Costs per Unit (Microcomputer) between European Ports of Entry and Distribution Centers

Origin City	Destination City Paris	Brussels	London	Berlin	Rome	Supply (tons)
Le Havre	$12	$16	$19	—	—	71,000
Amsterdam	—	12	14	—	—	30,000
Paris	—	12	—	32	38	—
Brussels	—	—	—	20	—	—
London	—	—	—	—	—	—
Berlin	—	—	—	—	40	—
Rome	—	—	—	—	—	—
Demand (tons)	35,000	14,000	25,000	18,000	9000	101,000

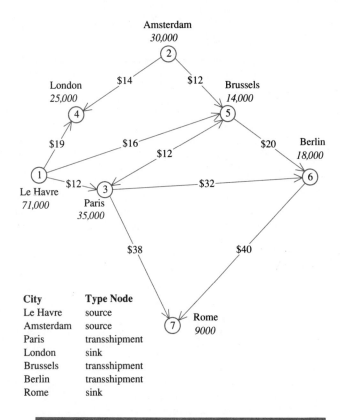

City	Type Node
Le Havre	source
Amsterdam	source
Paris	transshipment
London	sink
Brussels	transshipment
Berlin	transshipment
Rome	sink

FIGURE 8-9.1

Distribution Network for Apple Computer

4. Steven Jobs believes that he may be able to overcome the capacity restrictions in his distribution network by finding alternative shipping outlets that will provide additional shipping capacity for his product and at the same time, will not require minimum quantities of goods to ship. If he is correct, what percent savings in distribution costs would he realize over the 3-year period? (*Hint*: Reformulate and solve the problem after dropping all capacitated routing limitations.)

References

1. Belford. Racially Balancing Schools. *Operations Research* 20 (1972), 619–28.

2. Bodin, Lawrence D. A Computer-Assisted System for the Routing and Scheduling of Street Sweepers. *Operations Research* 26, no. 4 (1978), 525–37.

3. Boldyreff. Maximum Flow Through a Railroad Network. *Operations Research* 3 (1955), 443–65.

4. Budnick, Frank S., Dennis McLeavey, and Richard Mojena. *Principles of Operations Research for Management*. Irwin, 1988.

5. Denardo, Eric V. Shortest-Route Methods: Reaching, Pruning, and Buckets. *Operations Research* 27, no. 1 (1979), 161–86.

6. Ford, L., and D. Fulkerson. *Flows in Networks*. Princeton, NJ: Princeton University Press, 1962.

7. Francis, Richard L. Distance Constraints for Tree Network Multifacility Location Problems. *Operations Research* 26, no. 4 (1978), 570 796.

8. Garcia-Diaz, Alberto. An Investment Staging Model for a Bridge Replacement Problem. *Operations Research* 28, no. 3 (1980), 736–53.

9. Glover, Fred. An Integrated Production, Distribution, and Inventory Planning System. *Interfaces* 9, no. 5 (1979), 21–35.

10. Harrison, H. A Planning System for Facilities and Resources in Distribution Networks. *Interfaces* 9, no. 2 (1979), 6–22.

11. Harvey, Charles M. *Principles of Operations Research: With Application to Managerial Decisions*. Englewood Cliffs, NJ: Prentice-Hall, 1969.

12. Peters, Thomas, and Robert Waterman, Jr. *In Search of Excellence*. New York: Harper & Row, 1982.

13. Segal. Telephone Operator Scheduling. *Operations Research* 22 (1974), 808–23.

14. Shogan, Andrew W. *Management Science*. Englewood Cliffs, NJ: Prentice-Hall, 1988.

15. Srinivasan, V. Network Models for Estimating Brand-Specific Effects in Multi-Attribute Marketing Models. *Management Science* 25, no. 1 (1979), 11–21.

16. Wagner, Harvey M. *Principles of Operations Research: With Application to Managerial Decisions*. Englewood Cliffs, NJ: Prentice-Hall, 1969.

17. Winston, Wayne L. *Operations Research: Applications and Algorithms*. Duxbury Press, 1987.

Microcomputer Software for Network Models

LDN (network analysis) software is plentiful. A few of the available, usually inexpensive software packages that can be used to analyze shortest-route, minimal spanning tree, maximal-flow, and transshipment problems are listed here. If your needs are such that features such as color graphics are important (color *is* helpful in these types of analyses), you probably will be faced with purchasing the professional or industrial specialty packages that cost from $1000 up. These are the relatively inexpensive software products.

1. *Computer Models for Management Science* Version 2. Erikson & Hall. Reading, MA: Addison-Wesley, 1986.
2. *Management Science and the Microcomputer*. Burns & Austin. New York, NY: Macmillan, 1985.
3. *Microcomputer Models for Management Decision-Making*. Dennis & Dennis. St. Paul, MN: West, 1986.
4. *Micro Manager*. Lee & Shim. Dubuque, IA: Wm. C. Brown, 1986.
5. *NETSOLVE*. Columbia, MD: DISTINCT Management Consultants, 1986.
6. *Quantitative Systems for Business* Version 3. Chang & Sullivan. Englewood Cliffs, NJ: Prentice-Hall, 1986.

CHAPTER 9

GOAL PROGRAMMING

MULTIPLE-OBJECTIVE RESOURCE-ALLOCATION METHODS

| 9.1 | INTRODUCTION

Linear programming can be used only for problems that are characterized by a single objective consisting of decision variables that are measurable in a common dimension. However, it is not unusual for an organization to have an agenda comprising numerous objectives. It is quite common, in fact, for these objectives (or goals) to be multidimensional and conflicting. For example, suppose IBM wanted to achieve sales revenues of $200 million on its IBM OS/2 model computers over the next fiscal year and, at the same time, not to exceed 1,300,000 hours of manufacturing effort. Of course, the lower the production effort, the fewer the units produced and the less likely that the sales goal will be achieved. In addition, these two goals are dimensionally nonequivalent: Dollars and hours are incommensurate. In situations similar to this one, LP will simply not work.

Fortunately, a relatively new technique has been developed for analyzing resource-allocation problems characterized by multiple, conflicting, and incommensurate goals. It is appropriately called goal programming (GP), and is a variation of linear programming (LP). The first important applications of GP took place in the early 1970s, although the theoretical model development occurred earlier. Since then, the number of real-world uses of this tool has grown steadily. These are a few of the impressively broad array of GP applications:

1. Allocating human resources and policy determination for the Federal Drug and Food Administration (Jones and Kuck, 1982).
2. Research and development funds allocation at the Lord Corporation (Salvia and Ludwig, 1979).
3. Formulating blood rotation policies for the American Red Cross (Kendall and Lee, 1980).
4. Agricultural planning in Egypt (Bazarra and Borzahev, 1981).
5. Planning officer accession in the United States Navy (Pares, et al., 1980).
6. Multicriteria school busing (Lee and Moore, 1977).
7. Planning and budgeting in the crippled children's sector (Drake and Joiner, 1981).

9.2 OVERVIEW OF GOAL PROGRAMMING (GP)

Because GP must often deal with not only multiple objectives but also goals that are contradictory and incommensurate, it does not optimize: it suffices. Simply stated, GP does the best it can. Each situation is viewed not as a problem that is to be optimized, but rather as a situation that must be managed *as best as possible*. Here's how GP works.

1. The organization, instead of limiting itself to a single goal, decides on a list of specific, operationally defined goals that it wishes to achieve. The list is arranged from the most important goal to the goal with the lowest *priority*. This arrangement is often referred to as the *priority structure*. Unlike in LP, where the single goal becomes the objective function portion of the problem formulation, the GP goals do not. Instead, they ultimately form the set of *goal constraints*. An abbreviated set of goal constraint statements might look like this:

   Priority 1 (P_1): Achieve a sales revenue quota of $21,500 for the week.

   Priority 2 (P_2): Limit production hours to 1700 for the week.

   Priority 3 (P_3): Make the proportion of managerial-to-nonmanagerial overtime hours for the week at least 25 percent, if possible.

2. Since GP uses a sufficing approach, it is likely that each goal will not be achieved exactly. If this is the case, then it is also likely that the final results will deviate from what we had ideally hoped for. The quantity by which each goal is missed—either underachieved or overachieved—is referred to as the *deviational variable*. Because the analyst cannot know, prior to the solution, whether the miss will be high or low, *both* possibilities must be taken into account. Therefore, both an overachievement (d_i^+) and underachievement (d_i^-) deviational variable must be included with each goal statement (constraint). It is important to understand that, for each particular goal, only d_i^- or d_i^+ can ultimately occur; a goal cannot experience both an overachieved and underachieved outcome simultaneously (it is possible, however, for both deviational variables to be zero if the goal is achieved exactly). These deviational variables may be thought of as similar to the slack and surplus variables that are included in the resource constraints of the LP problem formulations. Because of this, all goal constraints are written as equalities. Suppose, for example, that a company sells two products—x_1 and x_2—and that the unit profit from them is $8 and $11, respectively. If its first priority, P_1, is to achieve a profit of $45,000, the goal constraint statement will look like this:

$$8x_1 + 11x_2 + d_1^- - d_1^+ = 45,000$$

   where the negative d_i^+ is the quantity by which the $45,000 profit goal is exceeded and the positive d_i^- represents the quantity by which the $45,000 profit goal falls short. So, if the GP solution resulted in a profit of (1) $48,000, d_i^+ takes on a value of $3000, while the $d_i^- = 0$; (2) $40,000, $d_i^+ = 0$ and $d_i^- = $5000; and (3) $45,000, both $d_i^+ = 0$, and $d_i^- = 0$.

3. In GP, not all resource limitations need be expressed as goal constraints. Instead, it is also possible that a GP will have *both* goal constraints and resource constraints, with the latter being written and treated identically to the form used in LP problem formulations.

4. Although LP problems have objective functions that can be either maximized or minimized, all GP objective function formulations have a common structure: *Minimize the sum of the relevant goal deviations* within the preemptive priority structure established for the problem. Only those deviational variables that are viewed as *harmful* to the minimization process are considered *relevant* and appropriate for inclusion in the objective function. For example, if one of the goal constraints is to minimize the overachievement of the budget, you would *not* typically include the underachievement deviational variable, d_i^-, since that variable certainly could not be viewed as detrimental. It is simple to know which deviational variables to include solely on the basis of the type of goal constraint statement, we are addressing—LTE ($\leq$), E ($=$), or GTE ($\geq$). Table 9-1 provides a simple set of guidelines to use in determining which deviations should be included in the objective function.

5. Priority factors and (sometimes) differential weights of importance are also assigned to each deviational variable in the objective function. The weights of importance, although optional, can discriminate only between those deviational variables *within the same priority level*. Unless a differential treatment is specified, unit weight values (1.0) are assumed (illustrations of this technique are depicted later in Examples 9.1, 9.2, and 9.4). The priority factors serve as a safeguard that a goal can be improved only *as long as it does not detract from the degree of fulfillment of any higher-ranked goal*.

Now let's see how to formulate applications using two distinctly different GP models: (1) preemptive goal programming and (2) archimedean (nonpreemptive) goal programming.

TABLE 9-1

Guideline Criteria for Determining Relevant Deviational Variables

If the constraint is of the type,	include the following deviational variable(s) in the objective function
$\leq$	d_i^+
$=$	d_i^+, d_i^-
$\geq$	d_i^-

9.3 THE STANDARD (PREEMPTIVE) GP MODEL FORMULATION

The standard GP problem formulation follows this form.

OBJECTIVE FUNCTION

$$\text{Minimize } Z = \sum_{k=1}^{K} P_k \sum_{i=1}^{m} (w_{i,k}^+ d_i^+ + w_{i,k}^- d_i^-)$$

SUBJECT TO

Goal constraints:

$$\sum_{j=1}^{n} a_{ij}x_j + d_i^- - d_i^+ = b_i \qquad \text{for } i = 1, 2, \ldots, m$$

Resource constraints:

$$\sum_{j=1}^{n} a_{ij}x_j \begin{pmatrix} \leq \\ = \\ \geq \end{pmatrix} b_i \qquad \text{for } i = m+1, \ldots, m+p$$

$$x_j, d_i^+, d_i^- \geq 0 \qquad \text{for } j = 1, 2, \ldots, n \quad \text{and} \quad i = 1, 2, \ldots, m$$

where

P_k = priority level of the kth goal constraint, (i.e., P_1 is the highest priority factor, P_2 is the second highest priority factor, etc.)

$w^+_{i,k}$ = the relative weight of importance of the overachievement variable, d_i^+, in the kth priority level

$w^-_{i,k}$ = the relative weight of importance of the underachievement variable, d_i^-, in the kth priority level

m = number of goal constraints

p = number of resource constraints

n = number of decision variables

K = number of priority levels

The weights of importance ($w^-_{i,k}$, $w^+_{i,k}$) are used only when there exist two undesirable deviations for the same goal. Since the priority factors (P_k) are preemptive—higher goals must be satisfied as completely as possible before lower goals are addressed—there is no interaction or tradeoff between goal constraints and, therefore, weights have no effect outside of the specific goal to which they are applied.[1] Although P_k are not variables or parameters (no numerical values are assigned to them), the mathematical relationship among them may be expressed as

$$P_k >>> P_{k+1}$$

This means that P_k is so much more important than P_{k+1} that there is no number, c, by which you could multiply the lower-ranked priority factor to increase its rank; that is,

$$P_k >>> cP_{k+1}$$

The use of these parameters in formulating a GP problem is similar to that for the techniques you have already learned in formulating LP problems. To take advantage of this natural connection, we'll first formulate a problem as an LP one. Next, the necessary modifications to convert it into a GP problem will be conducted. Once this is accomplished, the contrast as well as the bridge between the two methods becomes clear.

EXAMPLE 9.1   THE DENTAL CARE FACILITY AS AN LP PROBLEM

A public dental care facility offers specialized types of treatments to patients. These services include pedodontics, periodontics, oral surgery, orthodontics, endodontics, prosthodontics, and general dentistry. Although the patients may have personal payment capacities, insurance programs, or public subsidization payment benefits, these monies usually are not enough to cover the cost to the facility in providing their services. The average costs, c_j, and treatment time, t_j, per treatment type, x_j, which must be absorbed by the facility are shown in Table 9-2. The total facility operating budget averages $7875 per day and there are 100 dentist-hours available. The number of pedodontic and general dentistry cases cannot exceed one-third of all cases treated, and

"You'll have to sit up!"

[1]The preemptive weighting scheme is also referred to as *lexicographical ordering*. In lexicographical ordering, a multiple attribute alternative, a_1, dominates another alternative, a_2, if and only if the first nonzero attribute of $a_1 - a_2$ is positive. So, if the performance vector of, say, a four-attribute alternative, a_1 is (3,0,0,1) and the performance vector of another four-attribute alternative, a_2 is (2,7,5,6), a_1 is considered to lexicographically dominate a_2. It makes no difference that a_1 is inferior to a_2 in all but the first attribute performance area; the first attribute performance (goal) that distinguishes one alternative from another determines the dominance [Milan Zeleny, *Multiple Criteria Decision Making* (New York: McGraw-Hill, 1982), 295].

TABLE 9-2

Dental Care Facility Associated Costs and Labor Expenditures for Each Service Offered

Type of Dental Treatment, x_i	Average Facility Cost per Treatment, c_i	Average Treatment Time, t_i, hours
Pedodontic, x_1	$ 45	.33
Periodontic, x_2	$ 50	1.00
Oral surgery, x_3	$185	1.25
Orthodontic, x_4	$ 60	.50
Endodontic, x_5	$ 80	.75
Prosthodontic, x_6	$105	.50
General dentistry, x_7	$ 35	.50

if orthodontic cases must comprise at least 10 percent of the cases treated. Formulate this problem given that the goal of the clinic is to maximize the number of cases treated daily.

SOLUTION

OBJECTIVE FUNCTION

Maximize $Z = x_1 + x_2 + x_3 + \cdots + x_7$

SUBJECT TO

- *Budget*: $45x_1 + 50x_2 + 185x_3 + \cdots + 35x_7 \leq 7875$
- *Dentist hours*: $33x_1 + 1.00x_2 + 125x_3 + \cdots + .50x_7 \leq 100$
- *Policy 1*: $x_1 + x_7 \leq .33(x_1 + x_2 + x_3 + \cdots + x_7)$

or, collecting like terms,

$$.67x_1 - .33x_2 - .33x_3 - .33x_4 - .33x_5 - .33x_6 + .67x_7 \leq 0$$

- *Policy 2*: $x_4 \geq .10(x_1 + x_2 + x_3 + \cdots + x_7)$

or,

$$-.10x_1 - .10x_2 - .10x_3 + .90x_4 - .10x_5 - .10x_6 - .10x_7 \geq 0$$

Now, let's look at the problem again, but this time we'll restate the situation with a few differences. Suppose that the clinic director is uncomfortable about trying to achieve the single objective of maximizing the number of treatments the clinic provides. Instead, assume that she thinks that the situation is more complex than that: There are a number of goals that would be beneficial to strive for instead of just one, and there is a definite priority among these goals. The restated problem follows.

EXAMPLE 9.2   THE DENTAL CARE FACILITY AS A GP PROBLEM

Instead of wanting to maximize the number of cases treated each day, suppose the clinic director establishes a specific number of cases that she would like to treat. Let's say that she wishes to treat 90 patients daily. Further, in order of importance, she also establishes additional organizational goals (ranked from most important to least important):

1. Minimize the underachievement of the treatment goal of 90 patients.
2. Avoid expenditures exceeding $7875 per day.
3. Minimize the overachievement of policy 2.
4. Achieve, as closely as possible, policy 1.

Apart from these goal constraints, the only other concern of the director is to make sure that the 100 hours of dentists' time available each week is not exceeded.

SOLUTION

The objective function relies on the form of the goal constraint equations and is usually easier to develop at the end of the formulation. The constraint equations are as shown here.

SUBJECT TO

Goal Constraints

1. $x_1 + x_2 + x_3 + \cdots + x_7 + d_1^- - d_1^+ = 90$
2. $45x_1 + 50x_2 + 185x_3 + \cdots + 35x_7 + d_2^- - d_2^+ = 7875$
3. $.67x_1 - .33x_2 - .33x_3 - \cdots + .67x_7 + d_3^- - d_3^+ = .10$
4. $-.10x_1 - .10x_2 - .10x_3 + .90x_4 - \cdots - .10x_7 + d_4^- - d_4^+ = .33$

Resource Constraint

$$.33x_1 + 1.00x_2 + 1.25x_3 + \cdots + .50x_7 \leq 100$$

Also, as in LP problem formulation, all variables in a GP formulation must be real (nonnegative). Therefore,

$$x_1, x_2, x_3, x_4, x_5, x_6, x_7, d_1^-, d_1^+, d_2^-, d_2^+, d_3^-, d_3^+, d_4^-, d_4^+ \geq 0$$

It will rarely be necessary, however, for you to include the nonnegativity constraints in the problem formulation, since all software packages will have them built-in. The objective function can now be expressed as

$$\text{Minimize } Z = P_1 d_1^- + P_2 d_2^+ + P_3 d_3^+ + P_4 (d_4^- + d_4^+)$$

The meaning of this relationship is illustrated best by Figure 9-1.

Since the top-priority goal is concerned with only the underachievement of the number of treated patients, d_1^+ is not included; only d_1^- is of concern. Further, since we are worried only about *exceeding* the budget, d_2^+ is the only deviational variable

FIGURE 9-1

Objective Function Rationale for the Dental Clinic

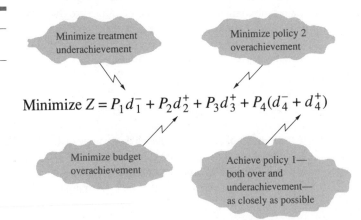

representing the second-ranked goal. Policy 2 is similar to the budget goal. However, since we are trying to achieve policy 1 *exactly*, *both* deviational variables are included. As mentioned earlier, it would even be possible to express differential weights of importance for deviational variables of the same priority, such as in policy 1. For example, if the manager thought that the overachievement of policy 1 was 2.5 times as damaging as was the underachievement of it, the objective function would be written as

$$\text{Minimize } Z = P_1 d_1^- + P_2 d_2^+ + P_3 d_3^+ + 4 P_4 d_4^- + 2.5 P_4 d_4^+$$

Let's continue now with several more examples of GP problem formulations to solidify the technique. We'll place a continuing emphasis on problems that we initially formulated in the LP chapters, so that the distinction between the two methods is made clear and the transition is simplified.

EXAMPLE 9.3   CHICAGO SHOPPING MALL STUDY REVISITED: BASIL REFLECTS

Award-winning architect Basil Tweed, in rethinking his earlier position (Example 4.2), is feeling a tad edgy, even uncomfortable, with the notion that the name of the game is simply profit. In fact, he's very close to convinced that the intense diversity of opinion of the individuals on the Chicago City Council may result in the council's viewing his suggestions regarding the optimal mix of store sizes as too narrow. Tweed is positive that his final proposal must have multiple objectives to reflect the complexity of the project (as well as to patronize as many of the board members as possible). He quickly reformulates the problem to reflect the following goal and resource constraint sets.

SUBJECT TO

Goal Constraints

   Priority 1: Minimize the overachievement of the \$35,000,000 budget.

   $$20,000x_1 + 60,000x_2 + 800,000x_3 + d_1^- - d_1^+ = 35,000,000$$

   Priority 2: Minimize the underachievement of an amortized annual profit of \$3,500,000 per year.

   $$5000x_1 + 20,000x_2 + 450,000x_3 + d_2^- - d_2^+ = 3,500,000$$

   Priority 3: Minimize the overachievement of the 850,000 square feet of mall space.

   $$300x_1 + 1500x_2 + 75,000x_3 + d_3^- - d_3^+ = 850,000$$

Resource Constraints

   Policy 1:
   $$x_3 \leqslant 6$$
   Policy 2:
   $$200x_1 - 500x_2 - 25,000x_3 \geqslant 0$$
   Policy 3:
   $$-6250x_1 + 60,000x_2 - 312,500x_3 \leqslant 0$$

OBJECTIVE FUNCTION

   $$\text{Minimize } Z = P_1 d_1^+ + P_2 d_2^- + P_3 d_3^+$$

Tweed examines his formulation to make sure he understands it. The policy constraints are the same as before regarding the policy restrictions on the maximum or

minimum number of different size stores, and so on. However, the goal set has changed. If he interprets it correctly, the solution will be concerned primarily with not overrunning the $35,000,000 budget: That is its top priority since only d_1^+ is present in the objective function ($d_1^- = 0$ because it is not something that you have to worry about; it is not harmful). Once this is done, the solution will try to make as much profit as possible, but only if it does not reduce the earlier level of achievement with the budget (d_2^- is included in the objective function because only the underachievement of profits is of concern). Next, the solution will try to keep the square footage under the 850,000 available; however, not if that compromises either of the two higher goal constraints, and so on. "Yeah, that's the ticket," Tweed muses, confident in his proposal reevaluation.

EXAMPLE 9.4 THE TRANSWORLD AIRLINES MEDIA ADVERTISING STUDY

The TWA hypothetical advertising problem (refer to Exercise 4-5) was initially concerned with determining the optimal media mix to use in advertising the New York to Los Angeles route. A reconsideration by TWA managers of their earlier position has led to a revision of their intent. TWA now wishes to achieve, as best as possible, the following set of ranked goals:

1. Minimize the underachievement of 50,000,000 exposures.
2. Avoid exceeding the $4,750,000 advertising budget.
3. Minimize the overachievement of the Tonight Show policy constraint.
4. Try to achieve, as closely as possible, the newspaper advertising policy constraint.

The total number of advertising slots available for each media outlet remains the same. They are

$$x_1 \leq 24, x_2 \leq 10, x_3 \leq 36, x_4 \leq 60, x_5 \leq 85$$

SOLUTION

Goal Constraints

1. *Exposures*

$$21,400,000x_1 + 11,850,000x_2 + 6,875,000x_3 + 4,180,000x_4 \\ + 2,490,000x_5 + d_1^- - d_1^+ = 50,000,000$$

2. *Budget*

$$180,000x_1 + 100,000x_2 + 75,000x_3 + 4500x_4 \\ + 3000x_5 + d_2^- - d_2^+ = 4,750,000$$

3. *Tonight Show Policy 1*

$$90,000x_1 - 50,000x_2 - 37,500x_3 - 2250x_4 \\ - 1500x_5 + d_3^- - d_3^+ = 0$$

4. *Newspaper Policy 2*

$$-18,000x_1 - 10,000x_2 - 7500x_3 + 4050x_4 + 2700x_5 + d_4^- \\ - d_4^+ = 0$$

Resource Constraints

$$x_1 \leq 24, x_2 \leq 10, x_3 \leq 36, x_4 \leq 60, x_5 \leq 85$$

OBJECTIVE FUNCTION

$$\text{Minimize } Z = P_1 d_1^- + P_2 d_2^+ + P_3 d_3^+ + P_4 (d_4^+ + d_4^-)$$

Since there was no information suggesting that there were different "costs" associated with underachieving versus overachieving policy 2 (goal constraint 4), no differential weighting was employed in the objective function: underachieving and overachieving are assumed equal in impact.

EXAMPLE 9.5 COMPUTERCITY

Suppose that the owner of Computercity, a small, fictitious, personal-computer retail sales outlet in Sausalito, California, wishes to consider the best way to run his store. It is a small business and he has little help, so he is concerned about operating his business both efficiently and effectively. He would like to make enough money to be able to live comfortably and he doesn't mind working hard. However, he does not wish to be a slave to his business. His primary source of income is through the sales of two brands of computers: the Apple Macintosh and the IBM-PC. For the purposes of this example, assume the following: The average contribution to gross profit is about $900 and $1200 for each Macintosh and IBM-PC sold, respectively. Further, each unit costs him approximately $1600 and $2200, respectively. The owner, in looking over monthly sales and maintenance records, also notices that there seems to be a strong, positive correlation between the number of hours he works and the number of sales made (hardly a revelation): approximately 30 and 45 hours per month are spent on the sale, warrantee maintenance (nonrevenue generating), and familiarization with new software for each Macintosh and IBM-PC unit, respectively. (Although he has part-time help, it is essentially his responsibility to do most of the work.) Both Apple and IBM require Computercity to purchase a minimum of two units per month if it is to remain an authorized dealer.

After considerable thought, the owner decides that it is of primary importance to be an authorized dealer of the Apple and IBM microcomputer lines. It is, therefore, essential to satisfy the minimum monthly purchase quantity of each manufacturer. Accordingly, these two goals are given the same priority and are placed in the first and second position of the rank set. The next two most important considerations are that he would like to generate about $9000 in monthly gross profits and also stay close to his $13,000 monthly budget allotment. However, these goals are so close in relative importance to him that he is almost indifferent about which one is the most important. He finally decides to rank the budget and gross profits as the third- and fourth-ranked goals, respectively. Finally, after he estimates the fifth-ranked goal—the amount of time he is willing to work each month—to be about 180 hours, he formulates his goal hierarchy:

Priority 1 (P_1): Satisfy the minimum monthly manufacturer purchase requirement of two units each of the Macintosh and the IBM-PC.

Priority 2 (P_2): Stay within the monthly budget of $13,000.

Priority 3 (P_3): Achieve at least $9000 in monthly gross profits.

Priority 4 (P_4): Do not work more than 180 hours per month.

Based on the hierarchy of his priorities, what is the most satisfactory solution? Assume x_1 and x_2 are the average number of units of Macintosh and IBM-PC computer units Computercity purchases each month for sale, respectively.

SOLUTION

We find the problem formulation by first defining the goal constraints (no resource constraints were mentioned). They are as follows.

1. $x_1 + d_1^- - d_1^+ = 2$
2. $x_2 + d_2^- - d_2^+ = 2$
3. $1600x_1 + 2200x_2 + d_3^- - d_3^+ = 13,000$
4. $900x_1 + 1200x_2 + d_4^- - d_4^+ = 9000$
5. $30x_1 + 45x_2 + d_5^- - d_5^+ = 180$

OBJECTIVE FUNCTION

$$\text{Min } Z = P_1[d_1^- + d_2^-] + P_2d_3^+ + P_3d_4^- + P_4d_5^+$$

EXAMPLE 9.6   SOLID-WASTE DISPOSAL STUDY

Suppose that Pasadena, California, has five garbage collection districts and three incinerator-dump sites for processing the waste. As in the similar San Francisco solid-waste disposal study (Example 6.1), there are operating costs for each incinerator and transportation costs for each district-to-incinerator route combination. Also, each district generates different amounts of solid waste and each incinerator has its own capacity (the maximum amount of waste it can process each week). These hypothetical data are shown in Table 9-3.

The city wishes to keep weekly transportation costs under $2,200,000, determine the optimum responsibility pattern for getting the solid waste between the five collection districts and the three incinerator sites for the following set of ranked goals:

1. Do not exceed the $2,200,000 budget.
2. Minimize the overachievement of demand made on incinerator sites 1 and 3.
3. Minimize the overachievement of demand made on incinerator site 2.
4. Minimize underachievement of supply from all five collection districts.

SOLUTION

If we assume that x_{ij} is the number of tons of solid waste collected at the ith district and processed at the jth disposal site, then we can write the goal constraint equations as follows.

Budget, P_1:
$$110x_{11} + 60x_{12} + \cdots + 90x_{52} + 55x_{53} + d_1^- - d_1^+ = 2,200,000$$
Policy 1, P_2:
$$x_{11} + x_{21} + \cdots + x_{51} + d_2^- - d_2^+ = 1500$$
$$x_{13} + x_{23} + \cdots + x_{53} + d_3^- - d_3^+ = 1600$$
Policy 2, P_3:
$$x_{12} + x_{22} + \cdots + x_{52} + d_4^- - d_4^+ = 600$$
Policy 3, P_4:
$$x_{11} + x_{12} + x_{13} + d_5^- - d_5^+ = 175$$
$$x_{21} + x_{22} + x_{23} + d_6^- - d_6^+ = 450$$
$$\vdots \qquad\qquad \vdots$$
$$x_{51} + x_{52} + x_{53} + d_9^- - d_9^+ = 800$$

TABLE 9-3

**Transportation Costs per Ton of Solid Waste
between the ith Collection District and the jth Incinerator Site**

Collection District, i	Incinerator-to-Dump Site Costs, $c(ij)$—($/ton)			Tons of Waste Generated Weekly
	1	2	3	
1	110.	60.	85.	175.
2	85.	75.	105.	450.
3	100.	50.	75.	1100.
4	95.	75.	95.	500.
5	80.	90.	55.	800.
WEEKLY SITE CAPACITY(TONS)	1500.	600.	1600.	3700./3025.

Since there are no resource constraints, the objective function can be solved for immediately. It is expressed as

$$\text{Minimize } Z = P_1 d_1^+ + P_2(d_2^+ + d_3^+) + P_3 d_4^+ \\ + P_4(d_5^- + d_6^- + d_7^- + d_8^- + d_9^-)$$

Notice that deviational variables 2 and 3 have the same priority factor, P_2, and that deviational variables 5 through 9 also share the same priority factor, P_4. So, if you want to show that any deviational variable of the same priority is more important than are any of the others at that rank, simply incorporate the differential weighting method used in the previous GP cases. It would be necessary, of course, to define the relative "costs" of the different deviational variables, so that the differential weighting used in the objective function would be clearly understood.

Now that we have examined several examples of how to formulate GP problems, let's see how these models are solved. Although the processes used in solving goal programming problems are very similar to those for the simplex method, there are distinguishing features that reflect the inherent differences between LP and GP. First, the graphical solution process will be used to provide visual insight into the differences between these two resource-allocation techniques.

9.4 THE GRAPHICAL SOLUTION METHOD FOR GOAL PROGRAMMING

As was the case in linear programming, the use of a graphical solution method only serves the purpose of illustration: the two-variable problems are far too simplistic to represent any realistic situation you might encounter in an actual problem setting. Instead, computer solutions will always be preferred. It can be of considerable value, however, to use the graphical method to gain a more intimate level of understanding of the GP solution process.

The steps used to solve a GP problem graphically after formulation follow.

Step 1. *Plot all resource-constraint equations.* These constraints must be satisfied even though they do not contribute to the objective function. If the GP formulation has no resource constraints, the feasible region is the first (nonnegative) quadrant; that is, $x_1 \geq 0$ and $x_2 \geq 0$.

Step 2. *Plot all goal constraint equations* by setting the deviational variables of each equal to zero.

Step 3. *In order of priority* (i.e., $P_1, P_2, P_3 \ldots, P_K$) *determine the feasible region by setting the objective function deviational variable(s) equal to zero.* Repeat this process for each descending goal constraint at every priority level *as long as the degree of achievement of higher-priority goals is not reduced.* (The optimal solution will always lie somewhere along the perimeter of the feasible region for the variable case.)

Step 4. *For any unsatisfied goals* (those that do not help to form the feasible region), *determine the degree to which the present level of under- or overachievement may be improved* by moving the goal, in a parallel manner, until it just touches the nearest point on the edge of the feasible region. As usual, proceed from higher to lower ranked goals. This point of tangency will identify the optimal solution.

Let's illustrate this process using the fictitious *Computercity* problem (Example 9.5). The problem formulation developed was as follows.

OBJECTIVE FUNCTION

$$\text{Min } Z = P_1[d_1^- + d_2^-] + P_2 d_3^+ + P_3 d_4^- + P_4 d_5^+$$

SUBJECT TO

Priority 1

Goal constraint 1: $x_1 + d_1^- - d_1^+ = 2$
Goal constraint 2: $x_2 + d_2^- - d_2^+ = 2$

Priority 2

Goal constraint 3: $1600x_1 + 2200x_2 + d_3^- - d_3^+ = 13{,}000$

Priority 3

Goal constraint 4: $900x_1 + 1200x_2 + d_4^- - d_4^+ = 9{,}000$

Priority 4

Goal constraint 5: $30x_1 + 45x_2 + d_5^- - d_5^+ = 180$

Step 1. Since there are no resource constraints in the original formulation, the feasible region will be located in the first quadrant.

Step 2. The five goal constraints are plotted in Figure 9-2.

Step 3. Initiate the construction of the feasible region by plotting the first two goal constraints comprising priority 1 (minimum inventory goals for the two computer brands). Set their relevant deviational variables equal to zero (i.e., $d_1^- = 0$ and $d_2^- = 0$). The shaded region provides the first subdivision of our feasible quadrant (Figure 9-3). Next, plot the second highest priority goal, constraint 3 (budget availability), and set the relevant deviational variable, d_3^+, equal to zero. This step minimizes the budget overachievement. The new, shaded triangular feasible region formed by the two highest priorities is shown in Figure 9-4. The first three goal constraints represented by priorities 1 and 2 have been achieved exactly (i.e., $d_1^-, d_2^-, d_3^+ = 0$).

The third priority (goal constraint 4) is the gross revenues goal constraint. The relevant deviational variable associated with this goal is d_4^-. However,

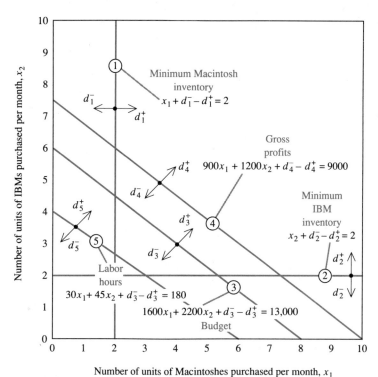

FIGURE 9-2

Computercity Goal Constraint Equations

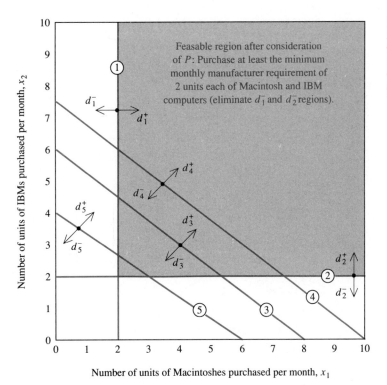

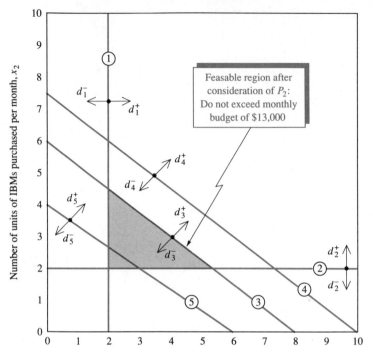

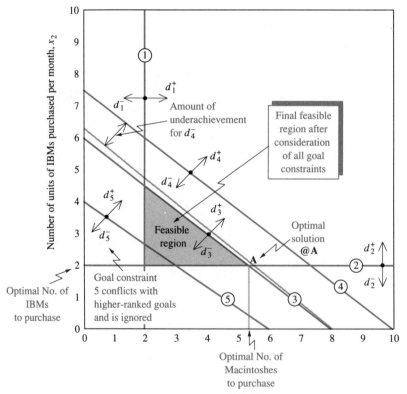

attempting to minimize the underachievement by this goal by setting d_4^- equal to zero would reduce the degree of achievement the higher-ranked budget goal constraint 3 (i.e., d_3^+). The feasible region remains the same as in Figure 9-4. Similarly, it is also not possible to minimize the amount of overachievement of the owner's labor hours for the relevant deviational variable of the fourth and last priority, d_5^+, because it is found to conflict with d_4^-. Accordingly, it too must be bypassed. The final feasible region remains the triangular area described by P_1 and P_2.

We find the optimal point in the feasible region by determining the amounts by which the third and fourth priority goal constraints may be *partially* satisfied without causing conflict with the higher-ranked goal constraints. Since P_3 is more important than P_4, we can reduce d_4^- until the gross revenues (dashed) line—$900x_1 + 1200x_2 + d_4^- - d_4^+ = 9000$—just touches the budget line—$1600x_1 + 2200x_2 + d_3^- - d_3^+ = 13,000$. This occurs at point **A** in Figure 9-5. The coordinates at this point are $x_1 = 2$ and $x_2 = 5.375$. Next, examine the labor hours goal—$30x_1 + 45x_2 + d_5^- - d_5^+ = 180$. To reduce the overachievement of this constraint, d_5^+, we reduce the gross profits goal; therefore, it is not possible to improve the fourth priority. We find the final results by substituting the optimal values of $x_1 = 2$ and $x_2 = 5.375$ into each of the goal constraint equations:

PRIORITY	GOAL NO.	RHS VALUE	d_i^+	d_i^-
P_1	1	2.	3.375	0.
	2	2.	0.	0.
P_2	3	13,000.	0.	0.
P_3	4	9,000.	0.	1765.5
P_4	5	180.	71.25	0.

The following section will focus on the algebraic solution process for these more likely, complex problems.

9.5 THE MODIFIED SIMPLEX METHOD FOR GOAL PROGRAMMING

As in linear programming, after you have learned how to formulate a GP problem accurately, it is very useful to understand how these problems must be ultimately solved. The technique used to solve goal-programming problems employ the *modified simplex method*. The modified simplex method employs an iterative tableau solution process very similar—although not identical—to that described for linear programming in Chapter 5. This modified GP simplex algorithm, which we shall describe, has been largely influenced by the work of K. Roscoe Davis and Patrick G. McKeown (1984, see References) and Sang Lee (1972, see References). Let's use the Computercity problem (Example 9.5) to illustrate the method.

Step 1. *Formulate the problem and construct the initial modified simplex tableau.* This tableau will look very similar to the standard simplex minimization tableau. There are, however, a few differences.

| The modified initial simplex tableau for this formulation is shown in Table 9-4. |

c_j			0	0	P_1	P_1	0	P_3	0	0	0	P_2	0	P_4
c_b	Basic Variables	RHS Values Solution	x_1	x_2	d_1^-	d_2^-	d_3^-	d_4^-	d_5^-	d_1^+	d_2^+	d_3^+	d_4^+	d_5^+
P_1	d_1^-	2	1	0	1	0	0	0	0	-1	0	0	0	0
P_1	d_2^-	2	0	1	0	1	0	0	0	0	-1	0	0	0
0	d_3^-	13000	1600	2200	0	0	1	0	0	0	0	-1	0	0
P_3	d_4^-	9000	900	1200	0	0	0	1	0	0	0	0	-1	0
0	d_5^-	180	30	45	0	0	0	0	1	0	0	0	0	-1
$z_j - c_j$	P_4	0	0	0	0	0	0	0	0	0	0	0	0	-1
	P_3	9000	900	1200	0	0	0	0	0	0	0	0	-1	0
	P_2	0	0	0	0	0	0	0	0	0	0	-1	0	0
	P_1	4	1	1	0	0	0	0	0	-1	-1	0	0	0

TABLE 9-4

Initial Modified GP Simplex Tableau for Computercity Example

The primary variations are as follows.

■ Every GP problem will be a minimization problem. Therefore, instead of multiplying the objective function by -1, multiply $c_j - z_j$ by -1 and compute $z_j - c_j$ so that we can use the standard simplex method.

■ The z_j row is eliminated—it serves only to clutter the GP simplex tableau calculations.

■ The objective function for all GP problems is expressed by goal priorities (and associated differential weights, if any). Therefore, the customary unit contribution rates, c_b and c_j, are replaced by these priorities (and weights).

■ The last rows of the tableau will be a *matrix* of $z_j - c_j$ rows)—one *for each priority level*. This is necessary because the preemptive priority weights are in *multidimensional* units of measure (i.e., units of computers, dollars, and hours). These priorities are arranged from the lowest (top $z_j - c_j$ row) to the highest (bottom $z_j - c_j$ row); this arrangement will allow us to determine the entering variable from the bottom of the tableau. The $z_j - c_j$ values for each column are calculated the same as before in the standard simplex tableau.

■ The variables of the problem are listed across the top of the tableau as before, with the decision variables (x_i) first. The negative deviational variables (d_i^-) come next, followed by the positive deviational variables (d_i^+). The associated priority (and weights) for these variables are seen at the very top row of the tableau.

■ The negative deviational variables for each constraint will constitute the basic feasible solution for the initial tableau. They serve the same purpose as the slack variables in providing an initial feasible simplex tableau solution.

Step 2. The iterative solution process always begins with the highest unattained priority. Therefore, *begin by initially setting* $k = 1$; k is a pointer that represents the $z_j - c_j$ row associated with the P_k priority row.[2] Check the right-

[2]See Roscoe K. Davis and Patrick G. McKeown, *Quantitative Models for Management* (Boston: Kent, 1984, p. 374). It is crucial to remember that the highest priority is P_1; a lower priority will have a higher k-index value.

hand-side (RHS) solution column of the P_k priority row for optimality. If the value is zero, that goal has been attained (satisfied). Skip to step 6. If a zero value does not exist, go to step 3.

| The initial tableau shows the following values:

P_4 0

P_3 9000

P_2 0

P_1 4

You can see immediately that the highest unsatisfied priority, P_1, is still four units short of its goal. It is therefore necessary to go to step 3. |

Step 3. The new entering nonbasic variable column will have the largest positive $z_j - c_j$ row value coefficient for priority P_k and, in addition, *will not have any negative coefficients associated with it at a lower priority.* If there is a tie between two different variable columns with coefficients of equal value, go to the next lower, unsatisfied priority level for the tied columns and select the nonbasic variable column with the greatest positive coefficient. If there is no positive coefficient in the P_k row that satisfies the necessary conditions, skip to step 6; otherwise, go to step 4.

| Since the highest-priority goal solution is not zero ($P_1 = 4$), search the P_1 row for the largest positive row value *associated with a nonbasic variable column*. Table 9-4 reveals that there are two identical positive values of 1 in the x_1 and x_2 columns. To break this tie, examine the next highest *unsatisfied* priority level, P_2. Since this goal priority is completely satisfied (0), we must look at the next-highest goal, P_3. Inspection of the P_3 priority shows that there is a greater value (1200) in the x_2 column than that in the x_1 column (900). Therefore, select x_2 as the entering variable. |

Step 4. *Find the departing variable* exactly as you did in the *minimization* simplex tableau. Select the row with the minimum, nonnegative ratio formed by dividing the solution value by the positive coefficient in the entering column. These calculations are shown in Table 9-5.

| The departing variable is, then, d_2^-. The initial tableau illustrating the entering column and departing row is shown in Table 9-6. |

TABLE 9-5

Calculations for Identifying the Departing Row in Initial Tableau

Row	Solution	÷	Coefficient	=	Quotient
d_1^-	2	÷	0	=	∞
d_2^-	2	÷	1	=	2.00
d_3^-	13,000	÷	2200	=	5.91
d_4^-	9000	÷	1200	=	7.50
d_5^-	180	÷	45	=	4.00

c_j			0	0	P_1	P_1	0	P_3	0	0	0	P_2	0	P_4
c_b	Basic Variables	RHS Values Solution	x_1	x_2	d_1^-	d_2^-	d_3^-	d_4^-	d_5^-	d_1^+	d_2^+	d_3^+	d_4^+	d_5^+
P_1	d_1^-	2	1	0	1	0	0	0	0	-1	0	0	0	0
P_1	d_2^-	2	0	1	0	1	0	0	0	0	-1	0	0	0
0	d_3^-	13000	1600	2200	0	0	1	0	0	0	0	-1	0	0
P_3	d_4^-	9000	900	1200	0	0	0	1	0	0	0	0	-1	0
0	d_5^-	180	30	45	0	0	0	0	1	0	0	0	0	-1
	P_4	0	0	0	0	0	0	0	0	0	0	0	0	-1
$z_j - c_j$	P_3	9000	900	1200	0	0	0	0	0	0	0	0	-1	0
	P_2	0	0	0	0	0	0	0	0	0	0	-1	0	0
	P_1	4	1	1	0	0	0	0	0	-1	-1	0	0	0

Departing row → (P_1, d_2^-)

Entering column ↑ (x_2)

TABLE 9-6

Initial Modified GP Simplex Tableau Illustrating Entering Column and Departing Row Variables for Computercity Example

Step 5. *Develop the new tableau* using the same procedures as in the LP simplex method to revise the exchange coefficients in the body of the tableau. Recalculate the $z_j - c_j$ row values:

$$\begin{pmatrix} \text{new row} \\ \text{elements} \end{pmatrix} = \begin{pmatrix} \text{elements of row} \\ \text{to be replaced} \end{pmatrix} - \left[(\text{pivot element}) \cdot \begin{pmatrix} \text{corresponding} \\ \text{elements in} \\ \text{replacement row} \end{pmatrix} \right]$$

As an example, let's calculate the new row for, say, d_3^-. First, the new entering row for x_2 (replacing d_2^-) is found from

New row value = old row value ÷ pivot element

Therefore, since the pivot element is 1, the new row is unchanged:

New row value = (2 0 1 0 1 0 0 0 0 −1 0 0 0)

The new row for d_3^- is, then,

New row 3 (d_3^-) = (13000 1600 2200 0 0 1 0 0 0 0 −1 0 0 0)
               − [(2200) (2 0 1 0 1 0 0 0 0 −1 0 0 0)]
          = 8600 1600 0 0 −2200 0 0 0 0 2200 0 0 0

Repeat this calculational process for all the rows in the new tableau.

Step 6. *Check for optimality* by examining the next lower priority level, P_{k+1}. If the new $k + 1$ value exceeds the value of the total number of priority levels in the problem formulation, K, stop; you have found the optimal solution. If, however, $k + 1 \leqslant K$, then return to step 2 and reexamine the $z_j - c_j$ row for P_{k+1}.

For the sake of brevity, let's skip ahead five iterations to the final, optimal tableau (Table 9-7). The optimum solution suggests that the manager purchase 5.375 IBMs and two Macintoshes (on the average) each month. Computercity's goal attainment is shown in Table 9-8.

c_b	c_j Basic Variables	RHS Values Solution	0 x_1	0 x_2	P_1 d_1^-	P_1 d_2^-	0 d_3^-	P_3 d_4^-	0 d_5^-	0 d_1^+	0 d_2^+	P_2 d_3^+	0 d_4^+	P_4 d_5^+
0	x_1	5.375	1	0	0	−1.375	.001	0	0	−1	1.375	−.001	0	0
0	x_2	2	0	1	0	1	0	0	0	0	−1	0	0	0
P_4	d_5^+	71.25	0	0	3.75	.019	0	−1	0	−3.75	−.019	0	1	0
P_3	d_4^-	1762.5	0	0	0	37.5	−.563	1	0	0	−37.5	.563	−1	0
0	d_1^+	3.375	0	0	−1	−1.375	.001	0	0	1	−1.375	−.001	0	0
$z_j - c_j$	P_4	71.25	0	0	3.75	.019	0	−1	0	−3.75	−.019	0	0	−1
	P_3	1762.5	0	0	0	37.5	−.563	0	0	0	−37.5	.563	−1	0
	P_2	0	0	0	0	0	0	0	0	0	0	−1	0	0
	P_1	0	0	0	−1	−1	0	0	0	−1	−1	0	0	0

9.6 | NONPREEMPTIVE GOAL PROGRAMMING: THE ARCHIMEDEAN GP MODEL

TABLE 9-7

Final Modified GP Simplex Tableau for Computercity Example

The priority structure of the standard, preemptive goal-programming (GP) model assumes that higher-ranked goals are *infinitely* more important than are goals ranked somewhat lower. This ordinal structure thus ensures that a higher-ranked goal will always be satisfied as completely as possible before the next-lower-ranked goal is even addressed. Further, any goal that reduces, however slightly, the level of fulfillment of a higher goal will be completely bypassed. But what of those cases where a manager views several goals to be of nearly the same value? How can one assume that resources will be allocated to both goals even where those goals may be in conflict? One way to accomplish the possibility of goal tradeoffs is to ignore preemptive GP models. More specifically, there are several nonpreemptive GP models that allow the manager to remove the preemptive priority coefficients and to replace them with additive weights of importance.

Two of the nonpreemptive GP models are: archimedean goal programming and multigoal programming. These variations of the standard goal programming model differ only in the way the objective function is formulated: the goal and resource constraints

TABLE 9-8

Computercity's Goal Attainment

Priority	Row	RHS Value	d_i^+	d_i^-
P_1	1	2	3.375	0
	2	2	0.	0
P_2	3	13,000	0.	0
P_3	4	9000	0.	1765.5
P_4	5	180	71.25	0

have identical form. *Multigoal programming* does not identify goal weights and does not provide aggregate results that give the manager with a measure of worth. Because of this limitation—as well as several other complicating characteristics—multigoal programming falls outside of this text's intended area of coverage.[3] Contrary to multigoal programming, *archimedean goal programming* has considerable simplicity and is easy to understand. These attractive qualities make a brief discussion of the archimedean model worthwhile.

The objective function of the archimedean GP model is:

$$\text{Minimize } Z = \sum_{i=1}^{m} (w_i^+ d_i^+ + w_i^- d_i^-)^{\psi}$$

where

ψ = power to which the weighted deviations are raised; ψ can take on any values, but usually $\psi = 1, 2,$ or ∞[4]

w_i = relative weight of importance (interval scale) of the ith goal constraint

For expediency, assume a linear archimedean model ($\psi = 1$). Now the model may be presented as

$$\text{Minimize } Z \sum_{i=1}^{m} (w_i^+ d_i^+ + w_i^- d_i^-)$$

Now the manager must establish the relative weights of importance of the different "per-unit" goal deviation values. The final product of this evaluation will be a summed product value of weight times deviation value. It will have no *intrinsic* meaning. Nevertheless, it will provide a means for allowing an interplay or tradeoff between goal constraints. Further, these weights are not indelible; differences of opinion between managers can be resolved by healthy communication; weights reflecting a happy medium can ultimately be achieved by even the most dissimilar groups. An application of the archimedean GP model to the Chicago shopping mall problem (see Example 4.2) is illustrated next.

EXAMPLE 9.7 THE CHICAGO SHOPPING MALL STUDY REVISITED (AGAIN): AN ARCHIMEDEAN GP APPLICATION

Once again, Basil Tweed is not sleeping well these days. It is just a few hours before he is to make his presentation to the Chicago City Council on his plans for the proposed new mall. This time, Tweed is worried that the preemptive nature of the GP model he used earlier may tend to ignore the importance of lower-ranked goals. Sure, it's crucial to not exceed budget, but to do so with such limited regard for the importance of the other goals makes him squirm. This time, he decides he is going to use the archimedean GP model, which will allow some interplay among goals—tradeoff is important to him. So he completely replaces the ordinal priority system established earlier with ar-

---

[3]The objective of multigoal programming is to minimize the objective function

$$\text{Minimize } [f_1(d_1^-, d_1^+), f_2(d_2^-, d_2^+), \ldots, f_n(d_n^-, d_n^+)]$$

This procedure involves the identification of all nondominated solutions—which is not necessarily a simple procedure. Since no weighting is given to the multiple goal set, the final product does not provide the manager with aggregate findings. Finally, multigoal programming is comparatively obscure in business applications.

[4]See Milan Zeleny, *Multiple Criteria Decision Making* (New York: McGraw-Hill, 1982, p. 300).

chimedean interval-level relative weights of importance. The weights of importance are subjectively established for each "harmful" deviational variable (those in the objective function only): each \$1 million of budget overrun, d_1^+, is equivalent to a weight of 10; each \$1 million of profit shortfall, d_2^-, is given a weight of 70; each 1000 square feet of space over the limit of 850,000 square feet, d_3^+, will be equivalent to a weighting value of 1. The formulation of the archimedean model (assuming the same resource constraints as before) follows.

SUBJECT TO

GOAL CONSTRAINTS (NO PRIORITY SYSTEM)

Goal 1: Minimize the overachievement of the \$35,000,000 budget.

$$20,000x_1 + 60,000x_2 + 800,000x_3 + d_1^- - d_1^+ = 35,000,000$$

Goal 2: Minimize the underachievement of an amortized annual profit of \$3,500,000 per year.

$$5,000x_1 + 20,000x_2 + 450,000x_3 + d_2^- - d_2^+ = 3,500,000$$

Goal 3: Minimize the overachievement of the 850,000 square feet of mall space.

$$300x_1 + 1500x_2 + 75,000x_3 + d_3^- - d_3^+ = 850,000$$

RESOURCE CONSTRAINTS

Policy 1

$$x_3 \leq 6$$

Policy 2

$$200x_1 - 500x_2 - 25,000x_3 \geq 0$$

Policy 3

$$-6250x_1 + 60,000x_2 - 312,500x_3 \leq 0$$

OBJECTIVE FUNCTION

$$\text{Minimize } Z = w_1^+ d_1^+ + w_2^- d_2^- + w_3^+ d_3^+ = 10d_1^+ + 70d_2^- + d_3^+$$

"Of course," he says, "I may have a tough time explaining to the council exactly how I came up with these weights of importance. Then again, if they want to change them, they can."

9.7 GP SENSITIVITY ANALYSIS

There may be occasions when, on examination of the computer results, you find that all goal constraints have been exactly achieved; that is, the deviational variables are all zero. Although you may think that this is a time for celebration, it is not. Under such circumstances, the total achievement of the goal set is more than likely a strong indication that the goals were not demanding enough—your target setting was unambitious! You can raise your expectations of one or more of your higher-ranked goals without hurting the performance of the remaining goals for the resources you have available.

Unlike in LP, in a preemptive GP problem there is no built-in set of parameters that is automatically "ranged" for you, no dual form that provides you with shadow prices,

no associated opportunity costs. For this reason, five primary issues must be addressed anew for each GP problem:

1. What is the impact of various goal constraint hierarchical arrangements on the optimal solution? The variety of different arrangements that are possible in ordering the preemptive goal constraints makes the priority structure the foremost feature.

2. What is the right-hand-side ranging sensitivity of the goal constraint target values, b_i? At what point does a change in this value cause a change in the present optimal solution?

3. In a preemptive GP problem, how much can the relative weights of a specific priority level change before the present optimal solution is shifted?

4. If we relax the priority structure, what are the possible tradeoffs among archimedean goal constraints; for example, what happens to the solution if we decrease slightly the weight of a more highly regarded goal in an attempt to increase the level of satisfaction of a less important goal?

5. What is the tradeoff among the different deviational variable values of the competing goals?

9.8 CONCLUSIONS

Goal programming is a powerful and useful tool when multiple, conflicting, incommensurate objectives describe the resource allocation setting with which you must deal. If, however, the preemptive attributes and incommensurate results of the standard (preemptive) GP model are unacceptable, a nonpreemptive (archimedean) GP model may be the preferable technique to select. Archimedean GP can simplify the arguable interpretation of the incommensurate, ordinal results and the *likely meaning* of the various objective function solutions that typically arise from different goal-set arrangements. Instead, the archimedean GP model will allow the manager to improve his thinking regarding the relative importance of each goal beyond merely ranking them. Instead, the *implied* value structure of the ordinal outcome assessments is replaced with one that is both explicit and parametric (interval). Although it will not make the assessment any less subjective, it will provide a more *internally* consistent framework for making such judgments. Because of this, archimedean GP can illuminate the value hierarchy of the manager so that future dialogue regarding the analysis can be focused on meaningful differences rather than on rhetoric.

9.9 GP MICROCOMPUTER SOFTWARE: HOW TO SOLVE GP PROBLEMS WITH AND WITHOUT IT

Compared to the plethora of programs available for linear programming, the availability of GP microcomputer software can best be described as sparse. Fortunately, however, there are several packages available that you can use.

Goal Programming Microcomputer Software

1. James Ignizio, *Microsolve/Goal Programming Via Multiplex-1*. Version 1, 1983. Oakland, CA: Holden Day.

2. Sang Lee and Yung Shim, *Micro Manager*. Dubuque, IA: Brown, 1986.

Using LP Software to Solve Goal Programming Problems

If you do not have access to a GP software package, you can use a standard simplex LP package to solve a preemptive problem (archimedean GP problems are solved with LP packages anyway, since there is no lexicographic structure to the goal constraints). Let's illustrate how to formulate a preemptive GP problem so as to facilitate the use of a standard LP package. We'll return to the Chicago shopping mall problem (Example 9.3) for this purpose.

Initially, the objective function is designed to minimize the deviation of the highest-priority goal (budget overruns):

$$\text{Minimize } Z = d_1^+$$

SUBJECT TO

$$20{,}000x_1 + 60{,}000x_2 + 800{,}000x_3 + d_1^- - d_1^+ = 35{,}000{,}000$$
$$5000x_1 + 20{,}000x_2 + 450{,}000x_3 + d_2^- - d_2^+ = 3{,}500{,}000$$
$$300x_1 + 1500x_2 + 75{,}000x_3 + d_3^- - d_3^+ = 850{,}000$$
$$x_3 \leqslant 6$$
$$200x_1 - 500x_2 - 25{,}000x_3 \geqslant 0$$
$$-6250x_1 + 60{,}000x_2 - 312{,}500x_3 \geqslant 0$$
$$d_1^+ = 0$$

Do you see how the top-ranked goal was protected from change? We simply added $d_1^+ = 0$ as a new resource constraint in the second iteration. The second-iteration solution may or may not be able to satisfy goal 2 completely. Regardless, continue the process through all goal levels using the same approach. Let us arbitrarily assume that, say, $d_2^- = \$565{,}000$ (i.e., the annual profits attainable are $\$3{,}500{,}000 - 565{,}000 = \$2{,}935{,}000$). The third iteration would then be

$$\text{Minimize } Z = d_3^+$$

SUBJECT TO

$$20{,}000x_1 + 60{,}000x_2 + 800{,}000x_3 + d_1^- - d_1^+ = 35{,}000{,}000$$
$$5000x_1 + 20{,}000x_2 + 450{,}000x_3 + d_2^- - d_2^+ = 3{,}500{,}000$$
$$300x_1 + 1500x_2 + 75{,}000x_3 + d_3^- - d_3^+ = 850{,}000$$
$$x_3 \leqslant 6$$
$$200x_1 - 500x_2 - 25{,}000x_3 \geqslant 0$$
$$-6250x_1 + 60{,}000x_2 - 312{,}500x_3 \geqslant 0$$
$$d_1^+ = 0$$
$$d_2^- \leqslant 565{,}000$$

Once solved, we protect the value of each deviational variable by adding it to the resource-constraint set prior to the next solution iteration.

You can solve archimedean GP problems easily by treating them as though they were an LP formulation: Since the goal constraints are nonpreemptive and the objective function coefficients are interval-level (parametric) data, an everyday LP software package will work smoothly.

9.10 | EXERCISES

9-1 Assume that the German car dealer (Example 4-3) finds that the single objective approach that he had used to determine optimal resource allocation is no longer attractive to him. Instead, he now wishes to use a multiple-objective approach. The three priorities for his business are

1. Generate monthly profits of at least $180,000.
2. Stay within the budget of $800,000.
3. Do not exceed the 1100 monthly salesperson-hours for car sales.

All other resource constraints remain the same.

ASSIGNMENT

1. Formulate this problem so that you can solve it using goal programming (assume the dealer can sell every car that he purchases each month, so that there is no carryover inventory).
2. Use a standard, preemptive goal programming software package and determine the optimal mix of goods that minimizes the sum of the goal deviations.

9-2 The German car dealer in Exercise 9-1 realizes that any goal may be either under- or overachieved. Most goals, he reasons, have only one undesirable non–bull's eye outcome. For example, he thinks that it's no problem—in fact, it's a windfall—if he makes more than the $180,000 in monthly profit. Similarly, it's terrific if he comes in under budget (spends less than $800,000), and so on. However, underachieving salesperson-hours may not be desirable: he may have to fire some of his sales personnel—a possibly undesirable action if his business continues to grow as rapidly as in the past (not to mention the effect on company morale). Accordingly, the dealer decides to weight both the under- and overachievement outcomes associated with the third goal constraint. Specifically, he thinks that it is about 1.5 times as bad to overshoot salesperson-hours as undershoot them.

ASSIGNMENT

1. Reformulate the objective function of Exercise 9-1 to reflect this dealer's new perspective.
2. Use a standard preemptive goal programming software package and determine the optional mix of goods that minimize the sum of the goal deviations.

9-3 The German car dealer wishes to reexamine the GP formulation conducted in Exercise 9-1. Specifically, although the goal priority arrangement is fine, he is not so sure that he views monthly profits as *infinitely* more important than the other goals. He assigns the following weights of importance to the three goals: monthly profits (50), budget (35), salesperson-hours (15) and $\Psi = 1.0$. All other information stays the same as in Exercise 9-1.

ASSIGNMENT

1. Reformulate the problem as an archimedean GP formulation.
2. Solve using a standard LP software package.

9-4 Contrast the differences among the results of Exercises 9-1, 9-2, and 9-3.

9-5 Assume that the management staff at Apple Computers, on reexamination of the hypothetical problem setting given in Exercise 4-6, has revised its approach to include the following prioritized list of goals:

The overachievement of the maximum production level is viewed as being more harmful to the corporation than is the underachievement of this same goal. More specifically, these overachievement deviations are weighted as 5, 4, 3, and 1.75 times as harmful as are underachievements for the Macintosh II, Macintosh SE, Macintosh Plus, and Apple IIGS models, respectively. All other considerations of the case are identical to those in the original problem.

ASSIGNMENT

1. Formulate the problem as a GP.
2. Solve using a GP software package.
3. Solve using an LP package.

9-6 Reformulate Exercise 9-5 as an archimedean GP problem using weights of 80, 30, 15, and 10 for priorities 1, 2, 3, and 4, respectively. Use a standard LP package to solve it.

9-7 Imagine that the investment firm of E. F. Hutton has taken over the portfolio of the client introduced in Exercise 4-3 (originally with MLPF & S). Hutton is reexamining the client's $8.75 million investment portfolio. In particular, this investor has told the new firm that he has a number of different, possibly conflicting goals regarding the four investment options being considered: IBM stock, Phillips Oil, Tiffany Diamond Mines, and New Zealand Real Estate Corporation. For the purpose of this exercise, the investor's hypothetical goal priorities are

1. Do not exceed the investment portfolio budget.
2. Do not exceed an average risk of 19 percent.
3. Stay within an average investment duration of 3.75 years.
4. Achieve a rate of return of no less than 17.0 percent.
5. Ensure that 60 percent of the total investment dollars are in a combination of stocks and oil and, of equal importance, that no less than 10 percent of the total investment is allocated to each of the four options.

E. F. Hutton trying to get a word in at home.

TABLE 9-7.1

Investment Portfolio Data for E. F. Hutton

Investment, x_i	Annual Return (%)	Annual Risk (%)	Term (yrs)
IBM stock, x_1	12	8	1
Phillips Oil, x_2	17	15	3
Tiffany Diamond Mines, x_3	24	21	5
New Zealand Real Estate, x_4	28	20	4

tion because they think that a set of multiple objectives comes closer to representing their actual situation than does a single goal. As a result, they have established the following organizational goals hierarchy:

1. At least 45 percent of the new hires should be women.
2. Minorities should make up at least 35 percent of all new hires.
3. At least three minority women should be selected for the technical positions.
4. At least two minority men should be selected for the technical positions.
5. The budget overrun should be minimized.
6. The total number of administrative hires should be 40 and the total number of technical hires should be 17.

They consider it to be three times as bad to underhire the total number of technical positions (i.e., hire less than 17 people for these positions) as it is to overhire them (i.e., hire more than 17 people). Use the following notation: x_{ijk} is the number of people hired of the ith ethnicity ($i = 1$, minority; $i = 2$, nonminority); jth gender ($j = 1$, female, $j = 2$, male); and kth position ($k = 1$, administrative; $k = 2$, technical).

ASSIGNMENT

1. Formulate as a preemptive GP problem.
2. Solve using a GP standard software package.
3. Reformulate as an archimedean GP problem and solve using either a GP or an LP software package. Assume that the relative weights of importance of the goals are (1) 25, (2) 20, (3) 15, (4) 15, (5) 15, (6) 10.

ASSIGNMENT

1. Using the information shown in Table 9-7.1, reformulate the original LP problem as a GP problem.
2. Determine the optimal investment strategy based on these multiple goals by solving the problem with an LP software package.

9-8 The simplicity of the single objective of minimizing system transportation costs is no longer acceptable to Bert Tuna Company managers (Exercise 4-11). Instead they think that it is important to achieve the following agenda of objectives (in order of preference):

1. Keep system transportation costs under $5,000,000 per month.
2. Achieve, as closely as possible, the demands of Trenton and Detroit. It is, however, twice as undesirable to underachieve these goals as it is to overachieve them.
3. Achieve, as closely as possible, the supply capacity of Memphis.

All other aspects of the problem are the same as in the original study.

ASSIGNMENT

1. Formulate the problem as a standard GP problem.
2. Solve using a GP software package.
3. Reformulate the problem as a nonpreemptive (archimedean) GP one using the following weights of importance: transportation costs (70), Trenton and Detroit demands (20), and Memphis supply.

9-9 The managers of the genetic engineering company originally examined in Exercise 4-12 wish to reexamine the original situa-

References

1. Bazaraa, Mokhtar, and Aziz Bouzaher. "A Linear Goal Programming Model for Developing Economies and an Illustration from the Agricultural Sector in Egypt." *Management Science* 27, (No. 4: April 1981).

2. Bres, E. S., D. Burns, A. Charnes, and W. W. Cooper. "A Goal Programming Model for Planning Officer Accessions." *Management Science* 26 (No. 8: August 1980).

3. Davis, K. Roscoe, and Patrick G. McKeown. *Quantitative Models for Management*. Boston: Kent, 1984.

4. Edwards, Ward, Detlof von Winterfeldt, and David L. Moody. "Simplicity in Decision Analysis: An Example and a Discussion." In *Decision Making: Descriptive, Normative, and Prescriptive Interactions*. Cambridge, MA: Harvard Business School, 1983.

5. Ignizio, James P. *Linear Programming in Single and Multiple-Objective Systems*. Englewood Cliffs, NJ: Prentice-Hall, 1982.

6. Joiner, Carl, and Albert Drake. "Planning and Budgeting in the Crippled Children's Sector through Goal Programming." *American Journal of Public Health* 71 (No. 9: September 1981).

7. Jones, Lawrence, and N. K. Kwak. "A Goal Programming Model for Allocating Human Resources for the Good Laboratory Practice Regulations." *Decision Sciences* 13 (1982).

8. Kendall, Kenneth, and Sang Lee. "Formulating Blood Rotation Policies with Multiple Objectives." *Management Science* 26 (No. 11: November 1980.)

9. Lee, Sang. "Goal Programming for Decision Analysis." In (Au: editor(s)?) Philadelphia: Auerbach, 1972.

10. Lee, Sang, and Laurence Moore. "Multi-Criteria School Busing Models." *Management Science* 23 (No. 7: March 1977).

11. Lee, Sang, and Jung P. Shim. Micro Manager Software. Dubuque, IA: William C. Brown, 1985.

12. Salvia, Anthony, and William Ludwig. "An Application of Goal Programming at Lord Corporation." *Interfaces* 9 (No. 4: August 1979).

13. Zeleny, Milan. *Multiple Criteria Decision Making*. New York: McGraw-Hill, 1982.

CHAPTER 10

MARKOV ANALYSIS

AN ANALYTICAL TECHNIQUE FOR STUDYING HOW
MARKETS, PEOPLE, OR GOODS CHANGE OVER TIME

|10.1| INTRODUCTION

Markov analysis (MA) provides a way to study how the conditions of a system—usually people or goods—change over time. More concisely, it forecasts the behavior of *things*. The two most common areas of application are

1. *Consumer purchasing behavior* (brand switching or brand loyalty)
2. *Optimum policy formulations* for maintenance, usage, and replacement of people or goods

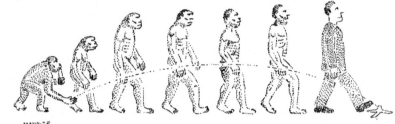

© 1980 Robin Mankoff.

Typically, the conditions that undergo change are classified into specific categories or states. It is of considerable importance to know that the periods are not necessarily always time-related. In Markov analysis, a period can also be event-oriented. The transition from one state to another over defined periods has many common illustrations, including the following:

System	Type of Change	Period(s)
▪ Newspaper subscribers	Continue subscription or switch to another periodical	Daily, weekly, monthly, etc.
▪ Hospital patients	Health status (critical, fair, satisfactory, etc.)	Hourly, daily, etc.
▪ Department-store charge charge accounts	Credit status (on time, delinquent, bad debt ratings, etc.)	Monthly, quarterly, etc.
▪ College students	Class status (freshman, sophomore, etc.)	Quarterly, semester, annual, etc.
▪ Blood plasma	Age of unit ("shelf life")	Weeks, months, etc.
▪ Commercial aircraft	Operating status (operating, down for minor repairs, down for major overhaul, etc.)	Flight hours, mileage, number of flights, daily, weekly, etc.

| 10.2 | APPLICATIONS OF MARKOV ANALYSIS

Following are actual examples of the application of this sophisticated technique. (Complete references are provided at the end of this chapter.)

1. Modeling the movement of coronary patients within a hospital (Kao, 1974).

2. Predicting the damage of dynamic goods inventory (Anderson, 1982).

3. Determining the average life of newspaper subscriptions (Deming and Glasser, 1968).

4. Assessing affirmative-action policies on improving the economic equality between blacks and whites (Oliver and Glick, 1982).

5. Determining the order of viral DNA/RNA sequences (Garden, 1980).

6. Performing human resources valuations (Sadan and Auerbach, 1974).

7. Establishing optimum doctoral-candidate admission policies by determining student flow through a university department (Bessent and Bessant, 1980).

8. Determining how many New York City fire companies to dispatch initially (Swersey, 1982).

9. Determining realistic hiring practices and evaluation methods for meeting affirmative action goals at Stanford University (Hopkins, 1980).

10. Evaluating the cost effectiveness of a specialized resocialization program for geriatric patients at Napa State Hospital (Meredith, 1973).

11. Forecasting market shares of alternative home-heating units in the United States (Ezzati, 1974).

Without much difficulty, you can see that MA is a type of forecasting tool. It is also important to understand that this tool is *descriptive* in nature: Its intent is to describe the behavior of the system, rather than to provide a *normative* analysis (to optimize), as did linear programming. It is also referred to as a *stochastic* tool, because the change that occurs over time is probabilistic and is dependent on only the conditions of the preceding time period. In the following section, we shall clarify the underlying assumptions associated with MA.

| 10.3 | FIRST-ORDER MARKOV ANALYSIS

This chapter will concentrate on first-order Markov models only. In such models, the probability of being in a particular state depends on only the state of the previous period. Second-order Markov models assume that the probability of changing to a particular state in the next period will depend on solely the states occupied during the preceding two periods. Similarly, n^{th} order Markov models assume that the probability of being in particular states in the future period hinges entirely on the states occupied during the n previous periods. The higher-order models require a much more time-consuming and expensive data-collection process, as well as complex mathematical techniques. Fortunately, however, first-order MA can adequately analyze about 70 percent of the problems typically encountered.

As there are with any of the management-science tools, there are four basic assumptions that we must observe when using first-order MA:

1. *Constant-sized population.* The total population (people or goods) of the Markov system remains constant over the time period of the analysis. This means that the system must be either reasonably stable—there must be no great fluctuation in the number of participants—or that the analyst must make the projections over appropriately short time periods.

2. *Fixed number of states.* The number of states remains constant. No new states are introduced and no states initially in the analysis are either changed or eliminated. This means, for example, that if we are studying the market flow of automobile purchasers who buy Porsche, BMW, and Mercedes Benz, we will not introduce new auto brands into the picture, and none of the original brands will drop out.

3. *Stochastic-state conditions.* The states occur in an uncertain environment requiring estimates of their chances of happening. This means, reflecting on the foreign car market, that it is possible to establish only the *likelihood* of a consumer buying one of the specific brands of automobiles; that is, MA is stochastic, not deterministic.

4. *Fixed duration transition periods.* The transition periods—the periods of time over which the projection or forecast takes place—are of equal duration. So, if the problem is being examined over 1-month time increments, this duration cannot be changed to 1 week or 1 year. The forecast period remains constant.

It seems to be wise, at this point, to mention that the mathematical procedures used in this chapter—matrix algebra—may be either new to you or a vague memory. Regardless, if you wish to have a more broad review of matrix algebra than this chapter provides, read Appendix B. If you are comfortable with basic matrix manipulations, skip it.

Now let's put Markov analysis to work. We'll apply it to an example to illustrate the kinds of useful managerial information that it can provide. A familiar subject will be used to highlight the first application: television advertising.

EXAMPLE 10.1   THE TV NETWORK ADVERTISING MARKET STUDY

The three major television networks—ABC, CBS, and NBC—are continually involved in a heated competition for the billions of dollars spent on program advertising. Since a highly rated show can command considerably more dollars per minute for advertising spots than can one with just average ratings, the name of the game is to obtain high Nielsen ratings (synonymous with high market shares). Let us imagine the following hypothetical setting.

During the last month, the ABC, CBS, and NBC market shares for Thursday evenings at 9:00 P.M. averaged 38, 24, and 28 percent, respectively, and the following data regarding viewer behavior patterns were found by the Nielsen poll from their 1300 "family members."

- ABC retained 83.3 percent of its viewers while losing 6.3 percent to CBS and 10.4 to NBC.
- CBS retained 85.7 percent of its viewers, but lost 8.3 percent to ABC and 6.0 percent to NBC.
- NBC lost 13.2 percent of its viewers to CBS and 7.4 percent to ABC while keeping 79.4 percent.

Although it would be difficult to make intelligent deductions from this information intuitively, MA can reduce these data into potentially valuable insights regarding what

the short- and long-term future holds in store for the competing networks. For example, MA can indicate:

1. The probability that a viewer will stay with the specific network program or will change to one of the other competitors over time (transition probabilities)

2. The percentage of the market share that the specific network program will "own" over time for both the short (transient) and long term (steady-state or equilibrium)

10.4 THE TRANSITION PROBABILITY MATRIX, P

The information regarding the television market viewer behavior of the previous section can be used to develop a primary component of MA called the *transition probability matrix*, **P**. The **P** is shown in Table 10-1. From a quick scan of this matrix you can see, for example, that the probability of a viewer who presently favors CBS (state 2) becoming an NBC viewer (state 3) in the next period, p_{23}, is .060. Also notice that the sum of the probabilities for any *row* is 1.00. This should make sense to you, since the only possible transitions between the present and next time period occur when a viewer either stays with the present network ($i = j$)—called the *probability of retention*—or switches to another network ($i \neq j$)—called the *probability of change*. So, for any row i,

$$p_{i1} + p_{i2} + \cdots + p_{in} = 1.00$$

or

$$\sum_{j=1}^{n} p_{ij} = 1.00$$

A more general form of the **P** is shown in Table 10-2. In that table, π_i is the ith state of the present period, and π_j is the jth state of the next period.

Another way to represent the market transition probabilities pictorially is to use a *Markov map*. This map, although not as analytically convenient as the **P**, illustrates essentially the same information. The Markov map of the TV programming problem is shown in Figure 10-1.

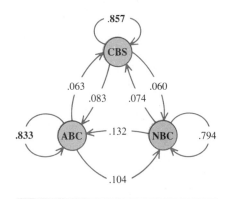

FIGURE 10-1

Markov Map of the Television Network Market Study

TABLE 10-1

Television Network Transition Probability Matrix, *P*, for the Thursday, 9:00 P.M. Time Slot

		Viewer's State in Next Period, j		
		State 1 (ABC)	State 2 (CBS)	State 3 (NBC)
	State 1 (ABC)	.833	.063	.104
Viewer's State in Present Period, *i*	State 2 (CBS)	.083	.857	.060
	State 3 (NBC)	.132	.074	.794

TABLE 10-2

General Form of the Transition Probability Matrix, P

		To State in the Next Period, j				
		π_1	π_2	π_j	π_n	
From State in the Present Period, i	π_1	p_{11}	p_{12}	p_{1j}	p_{1n}	$= \mathbf{P}$
	π_2	p_{21}	p_{22}	p_{2j}	p_{2n}	
	π_i	p_{i1}	p_{i2}	$\boldsymbol{p_{ij}}$	p_{in}	
	π_n	p_{n1}	p_{n2}	p_{nj}	p_{nn}	

10.5 | INDEPENDENT STATE (TRANSIENT) PROBABILITIES

It is often of interest to determine the probability of the system being in a particular state, i, at some particular time period, t (note that the initial condition is undefined— only the final period, t, is of importance). This is analogous to being able to forecast the future market share of a given competitor at some point in time. The term used to denote this probability is $\pi_i(t)$, and it is called the *transient probability* (not to be confused with the transition probability, p_{ij}, discussed earlier) or *state probability*. For our TV network example, the initial (present) market shares ($t = 0$) are

$$\pi_1(0) = .380 = \text{ABC's initial market share}$$
$$\pi_2(0) = .340 = \text{CBS's initial market share}$$
$$\pi_3(0) = .280 = \text{NBC's initial market share}$$

Since it is possible to occupy only one of the possible states during any given time period, the sum of all π_i values for any t^{th} period must be equal to one. The general expression is

$$\pi_1(t) + \pi_2(t) + \cdots + \pi_n(t) = 1.00$$

or

$$\sum_{i=1}^{n} \pi_i(t) = 1.00 \qquad \text{for each } i \, (i = 1, 2, \ldots, n)$$

for every period t, where n is the total number of different states and t is the number of transition periods being examined. It also follows that the *probability distribution* of the system (people or goods) being in any state, i, and in any given time period, t, can be written in a general form:

$$\Pi(t) = [\pi_1(t), \pi_2(t), \ldots, \pi_n(t)]$$

This distribution of n possible states is written in a mathematically operational form referred to as a *row vector*. For the TV network example, the probability distribution (in row-vector form) for the initial period ($t = 0$) is given by

$$\Pi(0) = [\pi_1(0), \pi_2(0), \pi_3(0)] = [.380, .340, 280]$$

The next logical step is to determine the state probabilities for the following time period (let's arbitrarily call it the $t + 1$ time period, and call our present time period t). We ac-

complish this by multiplying the probability distribution (row vector) of the present period, t, by the transition probability matrix, $\mathbf{P}$. That is,

$$\Pi(\text{next period}) = \Pi(\text{present period}) \, \mathbf{P}$$

or

$$\Pi(t + 1) = \Pi(t) \, \mathbf{P}$$

In expanded form, the expression looks like

$$[\pi_1(t + 1), \pi_2(t + 1), \ldots, \pi_n(t + 1)]$$

$$= [\pi_1(t), \pi_2(t), \ldots, \pi_n(t)] \begin{bmatrix} p_{11} & p_{12} & \cdots & p_{1n} \\ p_{21} & p_{22} & \cdots & p_{2n} \\ \cdots & \cdots & \cdots & \cdots \\ p_{n1} & p_{n2} & \cdots & p_{nn} \end{bmatrix}$$

Now let's illustrate how we can apply these relationships to our TV network example. The state probabilities (market shares) of the next time period (next week's Nielsen ratings) can be found from

$$[\pi_1(1), \pi_2(1), \pi_3(1)] = [\pi_1(0), \pi_2(0), \pi_3(0)] \begin{bmatrix} p_{11} & p_{12} & p_{13} \\ p_{21} & p_{22} & p_{23} \\ p_{31} & p_{32} & p_{33} \end{bmatrix}$$

This relationship can be broken down to focus on the next-period market share (state probability) of each specific network by the following method:

$$\pi_1(1) = \text{ABC's market share after one transition period}$$

$$\pi_1(1) = [\pi_1(0), \pi_2(0), \pi_3(0)] \begin{bmatrix} p_{11} \\ p_{21} \\ p_{31} \end{bmatrix} = \pi_1(0)p_{11} + \pi_2(0)p_{21} + \pi_3(0)p_{31}$$

We solve for CBS's and NBC's next-period market shares in the identical manner. That is,

$$\pi_2(1) = [\pi_1(0), \pi_2(0), \pi_3(0)] \begin{bmatrix} p_{12} \\ p_{22} \\ p_{32} \end{bmatrix} = \pi_1(0)p_{12} + \pi_2(0)p_{22} + \pi_3(0)p_{32}$$

$$\pi_3(1) = [\pi_1(0), \pi_2(0), \pi_3(0)] \begin{bmatrix} p_{13} \\ p_{23} \\ p_{33} \end{bmatrix} = \pi_1(0)p_{13} + \pi_2(0)p_{23} + \pi_3(0)p_{33}$$

$$\pi_1(1) = (.380)(.833) + (.340)(.083) + (.280)(.132) = .382$$
$$\pi_2(1) = (.380)(.063) + (.340)(.857) + (.280)(.074) = .336$$
$$\pi_3(1) = (.380)(.104) + (.340)(.060) + (.280)(.794) = .282$$

Solving directly for these market shares gives us

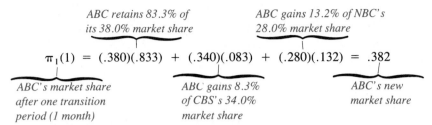

$$\pi_1(1) = (.380)(.833) + (.340)(.083) + (.280)(.132) = .382$$

ABC's market share after one transition period (1 month)   *ABC gains 8.3% of CBS's 34.0% market share*   *ABC's new market share*

ABC retains 83.3% of its 38.0% market share   *ABC gains 13.2% of NBC's 28.0% market share*

The same reasoning gives us CBS's and NBC's market shares:

$$\pi_2(1) = (.380)(.063) + (.340)(.857) + (.280)(.074) = .336$$
$$\pi_3(1) = (.380)(.104) + (.340)(.060) + (.280)(.794) = .282$$

The general expression for calculating future state probabilities after one transition period for n possible states assuming we start in some initial period t is

$$\pi_1(t+1) = \pi_1(t)\,p_{11} + \pi_2(t)\,p_{21} + \cdots + \pi_n(t)\,p_{n1}$$
$$\pi_2(t+1) = \pi_1(t)\,p_{12} + \pi_2(t)\,p_{22} + \cdots + \pi_n(t)\,p_{n2}$$
$$\vdots \qquad\qquad\qquad\qquad \vdots$$
$$\pi_n(t+1) = \pi_1(t)\,p_{1n} + \pi_2(t)\,p_{2n} + \cdots + \pi_n(t)\,p_{nn}$$

Another way to view the interrelationship between the state and transition probabilities is to use probability-tree diagrams. For the TV network problem, the tree diagram is shown in Figure 10-2. You can see that the decision tree become an increasingly awkward approach for an MA application if the number of transitions exceeds three or four periods (i.e., the tree quickly becomes a forest).

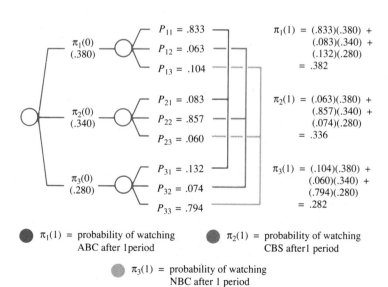

FIGURE 10-2

Probability-Tree Diagram of State Probabilities for the Television Network Study

It is also possible to forecast state probabilities for more than one transition period at a time. That is, if

$$\Pi(\text{next period}) = \Pi(\text{present period})\, \mathbf{P}$$

then

$$\Pi(1) = \Pi(0)\, \mathbf{P}$$
$$\Pi(2) = \Pi(1)\, \mathbf{P}$$

Similar logic leads us to a general form of being able to forecast state probabilities for t time periods into the future. It is

$$\Pi(t) = \Pi(0)\, \mathbf{P}^t$$

This equation requires that, in addition to knowing the initial state probabilities, you are also able to raise the $\mathbf{P}$ to the tth power. Here is an illustration of the algebra necessary to solve for a two-period projection:

$$\mathbf{P}^2 = \begin{bmatrix} \begin{matrix}(.833)(.833)\\ +\,(.063)(.083)\\ +\,(.104)(.132)\end{matrix} & \begin{matrix}(.833)(.063)\\ +\,(.063)(.857)\\ +\,(.104)(.074)\end{matrix} & \begin{matrix}(.833)(.104)\\ +\,(.063)(.060)\\ +\,(.104)(.794)\end{matrix} \\ \begin{matrix}(.083)(.833)\\ +\,(.857)(.083)\\ +\,(.060)(.132)\end{matrix} & \begin{matrix}(.083)(.063)\\ +\,(.857)(.857)\\ +\,(.060)(.074)\end{matrix} & \begin{matrix}(.083)(.104)\\ +\,(.857)(.060)\\ +\,(.060)(.794)\end{matrix} \\ \begin{matrix}(.132)(.833)\\ +\,(.074)(.083)\\ +\,(.794)(.132)\end{matrix} & \begin{matrix}(.132)(.063)\\ +\,(.074)(.857)\\ +\,(.794)(.074)\end{matrix} & \begin{matrix}(.132)(.104)\\ +\,(.074)(.060)\\ +\,(.794)(.794)\end{matrix} \end{bmatrix}$$

$$= \begin{bmatrix} .713 & .114 & .173 \\ .148 & .744 & .108 \\ .221 & .130 & .649 \end{bmatrix}$$

This type of calculation, as you can see, can be very tedious and error-prone when conducted manually. Can you imagine the even more bizarre matrices that would result when t is 3, 4, 5, and so on? An alternative to this power-raising approach is simply to stick with the one-period-at-a-time method for as many periods as your analysis requires. It really doesn't take much more time and is considerably easier to accomplish. Of course, the ideal way is simply to use an MA microcomputer software package for complex problems such as these.

10.6 | CONDITIONAL (TRANSIENT) STATE PROBABILITIES

Although the independent state probabilities discussed in the last section are typically of greater interest, there may be situations in which it is desirable to determine the state probabilities when an initial condition has been specified. We may, for example, want to know the likelihood that a viewer who was originally watching the NBC (state 3) program, will switch to the CBS (state 2) program during the same time slot after 2 weeks. The general notation for such a problem can be represented by the expression $\pi_{ij}(t)$, where

$\pi_{ij}(t)$ = probability of being in state j, given some initial state i, after t transition periods

This means that, for the situation just mentioned, the probability that a TV viewer, originally with NBC, will switch to CBS after two transition periods is given by $\pi_{32}(2)$. The logic of the mathematics needed for this type of calculation can be first illustrated with a probability tree (Figure 10-3). The ease of this type of calculation diminishes rapidly with increases in the number of transition periods used in the study, as was the case in the earlier use of decision trees. Of course, computer solutions are readily available to almost any analyst after the problem has been formulated (which is the *real* work!).

There is, however, another analytical method for solving for $\pi_{ij}(t)$ values; it involves these two steps:

1. Raise the **P** to the tth power.

2. Select the value in the **P** matrix whose row number corresponds to the initial state, i, and whose column number is that of the final state, j.

Using our TV network example again, we can determine the value of, say, $\pi_{32}(2)$. Following the guidelines, we merely:

1. Square ($t=2$) the **P**. Since this operation has already been completed earlier in this section, we'll simply reproduce the results.

$$\mathbf{P}^2 = \begin{bmatrix} .713 & .114 & .173 \\ .148 & .744 & .108 \\ .221 & .130 & .649 \end{bmatrix}$$

The analytical solution is given by

$$\begin{aligned}
\pi_{32}(2) &= p_{32}p_{12} + p_{32}p_{22} + p_{33}p_{32} \\
&= (.132)(.063) + (.074)(.857) + (.794)(.074) \\
&= .130
\end{aligned}$$

2. Since $i = 3$ and $j = 2$, the desired $\pi_{ij}(t)$ corresponds to the third row and the second column. That is,

$$\pi_{ij}(t) = \pi_{32}(2) = .130$$

So we now have two different methods for calculating conditional probabilities: (1) decision trees and (2) the matrix-power-raising approach. Both become messy as t increases; however, with the aid of a microcomputer, the second method is far more flexible.

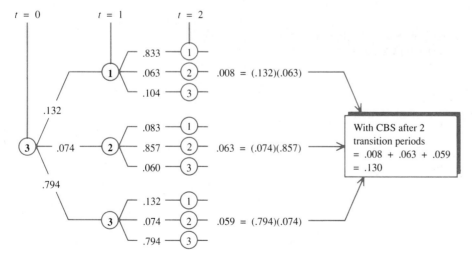

FIGURE 10-3

Probability-Tree Diagram of Conditional State Probability of TV Viewers Who Watch NBC (State 3) After Two Transition Periods Given that They Watched NBC Originally, $\pi_{33}(2)$

10.7 STEADY-STATE (EQUILIBRIUM) PROBABILITIES

At some future point in time, the state probabilities will stabilize.

$$\mathbf{P} = \begin{bmatrix} p_{11} & p_{12} & \cdots & p_{1n} \\ p_{21} & p_{22} & \cdots & p_{2n} \\ \cdots & \cdots & & \cdots \\ p_{n1} & p_{n2} & \cdots & p_{nn} \end{bmatrix}$$

and the equations for the steady-state probabilities are found from

$$\Pi = [\pi_1, \pi_2, \ldots, \pi_n] \cdot \mathbf{P}$$

Using the same matrix multiplication methods as we have illustrated in the last two sections, it is possible to derive n simultaneous linear equations that can be solved for these steady-state conditions. More specifically,

$$\pi_1(p_{11} - 1) + \pi_2 p_{21} + \cdots + \pi_n p_{n1} = 0$$
$$\pi_1 p_{12} + \pi_2(p_{22} - 1) + \cdots + \pi_n p_{n2} = 0$$
$$\vdots \qquad\qquad \vdots$$
$$\pi_1 p_{1n} + \pi_2 p_{2n} + \cdots + \pi_n(p_{nn} - 1) = 0$$

There is also one additional equation that comes from the requirement that the sum of the state probabilities at any period, including that of equilibrium, be equal to one. Then

$$\pi_1 + \pi_2 + \cdots + \pi_n = 1$$

The addition of this latter equation results in one more equation than there are unknown variables (state probabilities). Since algebraic solution requires that the number of equations and the number of unknown variables be equal, it is necessary to eliminate, arbitrarily, one of these equations. However, it would not be a good idea to eliminate the last equation developed, because that one is the only *independent* equation in the entire set. Without it, it would be impossible to solve for the unknown variables in the matrix. Of course, it is also important to make sure that the equilibrium equations are always "polished" by collecting like terms—regardless of whether you are going to solve them manually or by computer. So, for the general case, the equilibrium equations will look like

$$\pi_1(p_{11} - 1) + \pi_2 p_{21} + \cdots + \pi_n p_{n1} = 0$$
$$\pi_1 p_{12} + \pi_2(p_{22} - 1) + \cdots + \pi_n p_{n2} = 0$$
$$\vdots \qquad\qquad \vdots$$
$$\pi_1 p_{1n} + \pi_2 p_{2n} + \cdots + \pi_n(p_{nn} - 1) = 0$$
$$\pi_1 + \pi_2 + \cdots + \pi_n = 1$$

For the TV network example, these steady-state equations can be easily formed from the **P**:

$$\pi_1(.833 - 1) + \pi_2(.083) + \pi_3(.132) = 0$$
$$\pi_1(.063) + \pi_2(.857 - 1) + \pi_3(.074) = 0$$
$$\pi_1(.104) + \pi_2(.060) + \pi_3(.794 - 1) = 0$$
$$\pi_1 + \pi_2 + \pi_3 = 1.00$$

Collecting like terms in the first three equations of the preceding set yields

$$-.167\pi_1 + .083\pi_2 + .132\pi_3 = 0$$
$$.063\pi_1 - .143\pi_2 + .074\pi_3 = 0$$
$$.104\pi_1 + .060\pi_2 - .206\pi_3 = 0$$
$$\pi_1 + \pi_2 + \pi_3 = 1.00$$

There are several ways to solve these equations. You can use algebraic substitution methods or determinant solutions (matrix algebra), or you can call on computer software. The last approach is usually the most sound, since the various manual methods are tedious, error-prone, and usually more expensive. You have already done the real work by formulating the set of equations.

10.8 | ADDITIONAL ILLUSTRATIONS OF MARKOV ANALYSIS

Now that the basic techniques of MA have been illustrated, let's get more experience by running through a few more practical examples.

EXAMPLE 10.2 THE BLOOMINGDALE'S DEPARTMENT STORE ACCOUNTS RECEIVABLE STUDY

Department stores typically offer credit accounts to their customers. These businesses must monitor carefully how promptly their credit customers resolve debts so that the proportion of accounts that ultimately become "bad debts" can be minimized. Imagine, then, that the director of accounting at the famous Manhattan department store, Bloomingdale's, wishes to examine his customer credit accounts to address a major concern—anticipating the percentage of accounts that become bad debts. More specifically, Bloomingdale's has defined three categories (states) of accounts: (1) pay on time, π_1; (2) delinquent, π_2; and (3) bad debt, π_3. In examining a random sample of 1000 accounts, suppose Howie Dexter, the assistant accounting auditor, discovers the following customer credit behavior patterns over the past month:

■ There are 200 people who pay on time, 500 who are delinquent (30–60 days past their payment due date), and 300 who are considered bad debts (over 60 days past their payment due date).

■ Ninety percent of those people who paid on time continued to do so, whereas 13 percent of those with delinquent accounts and 2 percent of those with bad-debt accounts improved their credit ratings to the pay-on-time category.

Howie Dexter would be just another face at the office were it not for the attack ferret he keeps chained to his desk.

- Seventy-two percent of the delinquent accounts remain delinquent, whereas 10 percent of the pay-on-time and 11 percent of the bad-debt accounts change to the delinquent category.
- Eighty-seven percent of the bad debt accounts remain so, whereas none of the pay-on-time and 15 percent of the delinquent account customers change to bad debts.

Using these data, generate the **P** and then estimate: (1) how these customers will be distributed among the three credit classifications 2 months from now, and (2) what the steady-state conditions will be.

SOLUTION

From the information given in the problem statement, we can write the state probabilities for the initial period ($t=0$) as

$$\pi_1(0) = .200$$
$$\pi_2(0) = .500$$
$$\pi_3(0) = .300$$

where $\pi_1(t)$, $\pi_2(t)$, $\pi_3(t)$ are the probabilities of an account being classified as pay on time, delinquent, or bad debt during time period, t, respectively.

Next, we can generate **P** from the customer behavior data given in the problem statement. Now we can calculate the proportion of customers in each credit classification two transition periods into the future: $\pi_1(2)$, $\pi_2(2)$, and $\pi_3(2)$. It was suggested earlier that the easiest way to calculate future conditions manually is to progress by one transition period at a time, in lieu of raising the **P** to the tth power. So, for our problem, the distribution for the pay-on-time rating 1 month from now is

$$[\pi_1(1), \pi_2(1), \pi_3(1)] = [\pi_1(0), \pi_2(0), \pi_3(0)] \ \mathbf{P}$$

$$\pi_1(1) = [\pi_1(0), \pi_2(0), \pi_3(0)] \begin{bmatrix} p_{11} \\ p_{21} \\ p_{31} \end{bmatrix} = \pi_1(0)p_{11} + \pi_2(0)p_{21} + \pi_3(0)p_{31}$$

$$\pi_1(1) = (.200)(.900) + (.500)(.130) + (.300)(.020)$$
$$= .180 + .065 + .006 = .251$$

Similarly, for the delinquent and bad-debt groups, we find

$$\pi_2(1) = \pi_1(0)\, p_{12} + \pi_2(0)\, p_{22} + \pi_3(0)\, p_{32}$$
$$= (.200)(.100) + (.500)(.720) + (.300)(.110) = .413$$

and

$$\pi_3(1) = (.200)(.000) + (.500)(.150) + (.300)(.870) = .336$$

Repeating this process for the second transition period, we find that the distribution of credit ratings is

$$\pi_1(2) = [\pi_1(1), \pi_2(1), \pi_3(1)] \begin{bmatrix} p_{11} \\ p_{21} \\ p_{31} \end{bmatrix}$$

$$= (.251)(.900) + (.413)(.130) + (.336)(.020) = .287$$
$$\pi_2(2) = (.251)(.000) + (.413)(.720) + (.336)(.110) = .359$$
$$\pi_3(2) = (.251)(.000) + (.413)(.150) + (.336)(.870) = .354$$

TABLE 10-3

Bloomingdale's Transition Probability Matrix for Customer Credit Ratings

		To Next State, j		
		π_1	π_2	π_3
From Initial State, i	π_1	.900	.100	.000
	π_2	.130	.720	.150
	π_3	.020	.110	.870

We can find the steady-state conditions directly from the columns of the **P**. That is,

$$\pi_1 = .900\pi_1 + .130\pi_2 + .020\pi_3$$
$$\pi_2 = .100\pi_1 + .720\pi_2 + .110\pi_3$$
$$\pi_3 = .000\pi_1 + .150\pi_2 + .870\pi_3$$

We also know that, at equilibrium, as in any other period, the sum of the proportions of customers in each credit rating must be equal to unity.

$$\pi_1 + \pi_2 + \pi_3 = 1.00$$

Collecting like terms for the equations, we formulate the information in readily solvable relationships that will yield the steady-state conditions.

$$-.100\pi_1 + .130\pi_2 + .020\pi_3 = 0$$
$$.100\pi_1 - .280\pi_2 + .110\pi_3 = 0$$
$$.000\pi_1 + .150\pi_2 - .130\pi_3 = 0$$
$$\pi_1 + \pi_2 + \pi_3 = 1.00$$

The resulting steady-state conditions for our problem are

$$\pi_1 = .416$$
$$\pi_2 = .271$$
$$\pi_3 = .313$$

Bloomingdale's may conclude that, although the majority of its customers are good bill payers, over 30 percent of their accounts (31.3 percent) fall in the bad-debt category. If these results were actual rather than hypothetical, Bloomingdale's would rapidly revise the criteria used to determine whether a customer is eligible for a credit account.

EXAMPLE 10.3 THE COLA SOFT-DRINK MARKET "BRAND LOYALTY" STUDY

The competition between the major cola manufacturers is legendary in advertising circles. The media have even dubbed the battle for market share the "cola wars." The following fictitious example shows how Markov analysis can be used to provide forecasting insight for this high-visibility market.

Suppose that Coca-Cola, Pepsi-Cola, Royal Crown, and Shasta have 28, 32, 22, and 18 percent of today's across-the-counter sales of the cola soft-drink market in the United States. The market behavior during the past year is described by the following hypothetical information. Estimate the new market shares for next year and also determine what ultimate steady-state conditions will result if the market patterns remain essentially unchanged (formulate the equilibrium equations for computer solution):

■ Coca-Cola lost 15, 8, and 17 percent of its customers to Pepsi-Cola, Royal Crown, and Shasta, respectively, while retaining 60 percent of its own customers.
■ Pepsi-Cola retained 70 percent of its market while losing 10, 15, and 5 percent to Coca-Cola, Royal Crown, and Shasta, respectively.
■ Royal Crown retained 90 percent of its customers while losing 3, 6, and 1 percent to Coca-Cola, Pepsi-Cola, and Shasta, respectively.
■ Shasta lost 10, 10, and 5 percent of its market to Coca-Cola, Pepsi-Cola, and Royal Crown, respectively, while keeping 75 percent of its customers.

SOLUTION

The individuals or goods in this problem are those people who make up the cola-buying market. The states in this problem are the different cola brands—Coca-Cola (state 1), Pepsi-Cola (state 2), Royal Crown (state 3), and Shasta (state 4). The time period is given as 1 year. Figure 10-4 illustrates the problem in the form of a Markov map. The Markov transition probability matrix, $\mathbf{P}$, can also be illustrated in tabular form, as shown in Table 10-4. The calculations of the market shares for next year will use the following initial-period market shares of

$$\pi_1(0) = .280$$
$$\pi_2(0) = .320$$
$$\pi_3(0) = .220$$
$$\pi_4(0) = .180$$

Coca-Cola's market share 1 year from the present is

$$\begin{aligned}\pi_1(1) &= \pi_1(0)p_{11} + \pi_2(0)p_{21} + \pi_3(0)p_{31} + \pi_4(0)p_{41}\\ &= (.280)(.600) + (.320)(.100) + (.220)(.030) + (.180)(.100)\\ &= .225\end{aligned}$$

Using similar methods we find that the Pepsi-Cola, Royal Crown, and Shasta market shares for next year are, respectively

$$\begin{aligned}\pi_2(1) &= \pi_1(0)p_{12} + \pi_2(0)p_{22} + \pi_3(0)p_{32} + \pi_4(0)p_{42}\\ &= (.280)(.150) + (.320)(.700) + (.220)(.060) + (.180)(.100)\\ &= .297\end{aligned}$$

$$\begin{aligned}\pi_3(1) &= \pi_1(0)p_{13} + \pi_2(0)p_{23} + \pi_3(0)p_{33} + \pi_4(0)p_{43}\\ &= (.280)(.080) + (.320)(.150) + (.220)(.900) + (.180)(.050)\\ &= .277\end{aligned}$$

$$\begin{aligned}\pi_4(1) &= \pi_1(0)p_{14} + \pi_2(0)p_{24} + \pi_3(0)p_{34} + \pi_4(0)p_{44}\\ &= (.280)(.170) + (.320)(.050) + (.220)(.010) + (.180)(.750)\\ &= .201\end{aligned}$$

TABLE 10-4

Transition Probability Matrix of the Cola Soft-Drink Market

		Buyer State in Next Period, j			
		π_1	π_2	π_3	π_4
Buyer	π_1	.600	.150	.080	.170
State in	π_2	.100	.700	.150	.050
Present	π_3	.030	.060	.900	.010
Period, i	π_4	.100	.100	.050	.750

FIGURE 10-4

Markov Map of the Cola Soft-Drink Market

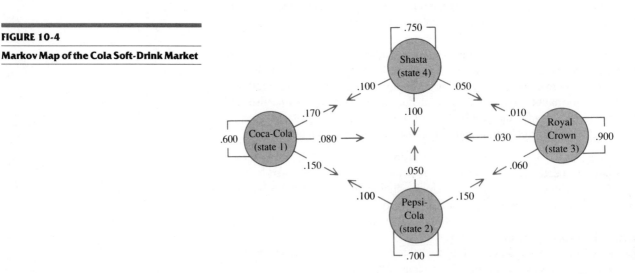

The steady-state conditions, found from the columns of $\mathbf{P}$, as well as the sum of the market shares equation are as follows. Since there are more equations than unknowns, we have an excess of equations, and the equation for state 4 has been arbitrarily omitted.

$$\pi_1 = .600\pi_1 + .100\pi_2 + .030\pi_3 + .100\pi_4$$
$$\pi_2 = .150\pi_1 + .700\pi_2 + .060\pi_3 + .100\pi_4$$
$$\pi_3 = .080\pi_1 + .150\pi_2 + .900\pi_3 + .050\pi_4$$

and

$$\pi_1 + \pi_2 + \pi_3 + \pi_4 = 1.00$$

Collecting the like terms yields the formulated information necessary to determine the steady-state market shares:

$$-.400\pi_1 + .100\pi_2 + .030\pi_3 + .100\pi_4 = 0$$
$$.150\pi_1 - .300\pi_2 + .060\pi_3 + .100\pi_4 = 0$$
$$.080\pi_1 + .150\pi_2 - .100\pi_3 + .050\pi_4 = 0$$
$$\pi_1 + \pi_2 + \pi_3 + \pi_4 = 1.00$$

Remember that there is an excess equation and that you may arbitrarily eliminate any one of those constructed from the columns of the $\mathbf{P}$. The remaining equations, including the sum of the market shares equation, can then be solved. The computer solution, which was not requested in this problem, is

$$\pi_1 = .138$$
$$\pi_2 = .208$$
$$\pi_3 = .501$$
$$\pi_4 = .153$$

10.9 ABSORBING STATES

When, in moving from one state to another, it is not possible to leave the latest state, that state is considered to be *absorbing* (or a *sink* condition). There are numerous examples, such as hospital patients dying, a student graduating, or a unit of machinery becoming irreversibly damaged or worn. The method used to study absorbing states allows the analyst to determine important system characteristics, such as

1. The average number of transition periods that the system will occupy each nonabsorbing state before it is absorbed
2. The number of transition periods that it takes the system to become absorbed
3. The probability of moving from each nonabsorbing state into each absorbing state

The mathematics needed to perform these types of operations are even more tedious than the ones previously explored. For this reason, it is especially important to consider the use of appropriate software as the only sensible approach. However, just for the sake of illustration, let's look at a simplified absorbing-state example.

EXAMPLE 10.4 THE CAREER LIFE EXPECTANCY OF A PROFESSIONAL BASEBALL PLAYER

Suppose we wish to examine the progress of professional baseball players during their careers. Assume that the system is described by four possible states:

STATE NO.	DESCRIPTION
1	Playing minor league baseball, π_1
2	Playing major league baseball, π_2
3	Retired, π_3
4	Released unconditionally without being signed by any other professional baseball organization, π_4

TABLE 10-5

Baseball Player Transition Probability Matrix

	π_1	π_2	π_3	π_4
π_1	.600	.200	.100	.100
π_2	.100	.800	.050	.050
π_3	.000	.000	1.000	.000
π_4	.000	.000	.000	1.000

Of course, this set of states implies several simplifying assumptions, including the possibility that a released player could, conceivably, sign with another club—in either the major or the minor leagues. However, since this happens very rarely, this likelihood is assumed to be, essentially, zero. The transition probabilities for this system are shown in Table 10-5. Efraim Turbin and Jack R. Meredith (1985, see Reference) use an excellent and easy-to-follow six-step process for solving absorbing-state problems. This useful process is illustrated in the following sections.

Mean Time in Each Nonabsorbing State

You can see that states 3 and 4 are the absorbing states: once you enter either one, there is no way out (there is a probability of zero for moving from either state 3 or 4 to any other state). The following process will allow you to calculate *the average time that the system is in each nonabsorbing state before being absorbed.*

Step 1. Eliminate the *rows* of each absorbing state. So, for our baseball example

$$
\begin{array}{c}
 \\
\pi_1 \\
\pi_2
\end{array}
\begin{array}{cccc}
\pi_1 & \pi_2 & \pi_3 & \pi_4 \\
\left[\begin{array}{cccc}
.600 & .200 & .100 & .100 \\
.100 & .800 & .050 & .050
\end{array}\right]
\end{array}
$$

Step 2. Arrange the *columns* into separate groups of absorbing and nonabsorbing states.

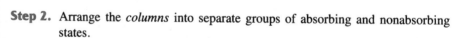

ABSORBING STATES (A)	NONABSORBING STATES (N)
$\begin{bmatrix} .100 & .100 \\ .050 & .050 \end{bmatrix}$	$\begin{bmatrix} .600 & .200 \\ .100 & .800 \end{bmatrix}$

The columns can be expressed as separate matrices. The absorbing matrix, **A**, is

$$
\mathbf{A} = \begin{bmatrix} .100 & .100 \\ .050 & .050 \end{bmatrix}
$$

"Excuse me, sir . . . you'll have to cover your shirt, it's distracting the pitcher."

Dan Piraro

The nonabsorbing matrix, $\mathbf{N}$, is given by

$$\mathbf{N} = \begin{bmatrix} .600 & .200 \\ .100 & .800 \end{bmatrix}$$

You might find it of interest to know that the nonabsorbing matrix, $\mathbf{N}$, will always be a square matrix. This importance of this property becomes apparent in Step 3.

Step 3. Calculate the *fundamental matrix*, $\mathbf{F}$, given by the relationship

$$\mathbf{F} = (\mathbf{I} - \mathbf{N})^{-1}$$

where $\mathbf{I}$ is an *identity matrix* given by (for a 2×2 problem)

$$\mathbf{I} = \begin{bmatrix} 1 & 0 \\ 0 & 1 \end{bmatrix}$$

and the minus one superscript indicates the inverse of the $\mathbf{I} - \mathbf{N}$ matrix (identity matrices are characterized by elements that are all zeros except for an upper-left to lower-right diagonal of all ones). For our example,

$$\mathbf{F} = \begin{bmatrix} 1 & 0 \\ 0 & 1 \end{bmatrix} - \begin{bmatrix} .600 & .200 \\ .100 & .800 \end{bmatrix}^{-1} = \begin{bmatrix} .400 & -.200 \\ -.100 & .200 \end{bmatrix}^{-1}$$

The inverse of any square 2×2 matrix, denoted by, say, μ, is solved by the following relationship

$$\mu = \begin{bmatrix} \mu_{11} & \mu_{12} \\ \mu_{21} & \mu_{22} \end{bmatrix}$$

$$\mu^{-1} = \begin{bmatrix} \mu_{22}/d & -\mu_{12}/d \\ -\mu_{21}/d & \mu_{11}/d \end{bmatrix}$$

where $d = \mu_{11}\mu_{22} - \mu_{21}\mu_{12}$, which is the determinant of the 2×2 matrix. So, for our example,

$$\mathbf{F} = \begin{bmatrix} .400 & -.200 \\ -.100 & .200 \end{bmatrix}^{-1} = \begin{bmatrix} .200/d & .200/d \\ .100/d & .400/d \end{bmatrix}$$

and d is

$$d = (.200)(.400) - (.100)(.200) = .060$$

Then,

$$\mathbf{F} = \begin{bmatrix} .200/.060 & .200/.060 \\ .100/.060 & .400/.060 \end{bmatrix} = \begin{bmatrix} 3.33 & 3.33 \\ 1.67 & 6.67 \end{bmatrix}$$

The cell values in the fundamental matrix, $\mathbf{F}$, represent the average number of periods (in our example, years or seasons would be the appropriate time period) a baseball player will be in each nonabsorbing state until finally being absorbed into either π_3 or π_4. For example, if a player is in the minor leagues, π_1, then he (or she, someday) will spend, on the average, 3.33 years in the

minor leagues (π_1) and 3.33 years in the major leagues (π_2) prior to either retiring from baseball or being unconditionally released (states π_3 and π_4, respectively). If the player starts out in the major leagues, π_2, then he will spend, on average, 1.67 years in the minors and 6.67 years in the majors prior to being absorbed into either state 3 or 4 (π_3 or π_4).

Step 4. *Calculate the mean total time prior to being absorbed.* This step tells you the total amount of time spent in each nonabsorbing state and absorbing state. We easily calculated it by summing the *row* cell values for each initial state. If the player starts in the minors, π_1, it will take about 6.67 seasons until he either retires (π_3) or is released (π_4). If the player is initially in the major leagues, it will take about 8.33 seasons prior to his either retiring or being released.

Step 5. *Calculate the probability of moving between a nonabsorbing and absorbing state.* Solve the matrix, **B**, given by the relationship

$$\mathbf{B} = \mathbf{FA}$$

Then

$$
\mathbf{B} = \overset{\mathbf{F}}{\begin{bmatrix} 3.33 & 3.33 \\ 1.67 & 1.67 \end{bmatrix}} \overset{\mathbf{A}}{\begin{bmatrix} .100 & .100 \\ .050 & .050 \end{bmatrix}}
$$

$$
\mathbf{B} = \begin{bmatrix} (3.33)(.100) + (3.33)(.100) \\ + (3.33)(.050) + (3.33)(.050) \\ (1.67)(.100) + (1.67)(.100) \\ + (6.67)(.050) + (6.67)(.050) \end{bmatrix} = \begin{array}{c|cc} & \pi_3 & \pi_4 \\ \hline \pi_1 & .500 & .500 \\ \pi_2 & .500 & .500 \end{array}
$$

Thus, if a player is initially in the minor leagues (π_1), there is a .500 chance that he will ultimately retire (be absorbed into π_3) and a .500 chance that he will be released (be absorbed into π_4). Similar chances exist for the player who is initially in the major leagues. The row probabilities in this matrix will always sum to 1.00 (it is only coincidental that the column probabilities also sum to unity).

Step 6. *Calculate the final proportion (or number) in each absorbing state.* The proportion of players in each of the absorbing states can be calculated using the information found in step 5. If, among the 675 players presently active in the major leagues, only 145 had begun their careers in the majors, then

1. The expected total number of players who will retire is

Total in π_3 is $= (530)(.500) + (145)(.500) = 337.5$ retired

2. The expected total number of players who will be released is

Total in π_4 is $= (145)(.500) + (530)(.500) = 337.5$ released

As a closing comment, remember that the matrix algebra necessary to solve absorbing-state MA problems that have absorbing *or* nonabsorbing matrices larger than 2×2 results in significant computational complications. *Use Markov analysis software instead!* The amount of time needed for a microcomputer to solve a 20×20 matrix is usually less than 1 minute.

EXAMPLE 10.5 THE XEROX CORPORATION MANAGEMENT PERSONNEL PLANNING PROGRAM

No matter how wonderful a working environment a company may provide for its employees, people will change jobs. Regardless of the reason for an employee's leaving, finding the right replacement is expensive for the organization. It is not unusual for companies to pay significant fees to professional managerial-placement businesses for aid in finding the right person for the vacant position. This significant problem of filling vacancies can be minimized, however, if the company studies how its personnel changes over time, using historical information. As an illustrative example, suppose that one of the Xerox Corporation's regional offices was interested in understanding the change in status of managerial employees. With this information in hand, it would be possible to plan more accurately the personnel requirements with respect to future hiring and, when necessary, layoff operations.

The personnel manager, Mr. Bangsiding, is particularly concerned with more reliable forecasting methods since it is his department that has to manage the brunt of personnel problems created by significant, unanticipated turnover. Particularly, there is a great deal of pressure on the rapid recruitment and hiring of replacement personnel—some of whom do not work out—and it is Bangsiding's department that has to deal with these problem employees. Assume that the following hypothetical information was gathered from the company files:

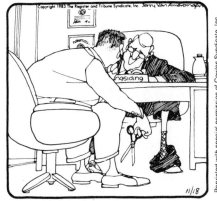

Mr. Bangsiding felt (and wrongly so) that a little man-to-man chat would be enough to stop Bob's practical joking.

- The possible states that a manager can occupy are beginning management (π_1), middle management (π_2), top management (π_3), corporation-initiated employee termination (i.e., fired or laid off), π_4, and employee-initiated termination (i.e., quit or retired), π_5.

- Over the past year, 60 percent of those in beginning management remained at that level, 15 percent were promoted to middle management, 10 percent experienced company-initiated terminations, and 15 percent self-initiated their termination. Of those who started the year in middle-management positions, 75 percent remained at that level, 5 percent were demoted to lower management, 10 percent were promoted to top management positions, 2 percent experienced company-initiated terminations, and 8 percent self-initiated their termination. Eighty percent of the personnel in top management remained at that level, 5 percent were demoted to middle management, 12 percent were terminated by the company, and 3 percent initiated their departure from the company. Regardless of whether any termination was company or employee initiated, the terminated employees did not rejoin the organization (at least not over the near-term future).

- At the beginning of the year, 60, 30, and 10 percent of the management employees were at the beginning, middle, and top levels of management. There are a total of 2700 employees classified in these three managerial states (levels).

ASSIGNMENT

What kind of MA calculations are appropriate for this problem? Is it similar to either the Bloomingdale (Example 10.2) or Cola market (Example 10.3) cases? Why or why not?

SOLUTION

In examining the given information, it is clear that, although we have states conditions similar to the Bloomingdale case (there is little similarity to the Cola market case), there is a major difference: In the Xerox problem, we have *two absorbing states*. Therefore, calculating the characteristics that typify absorbing states, in addition to the transient

TABLE 10-6

Transition Probability Matrix of Xerox Managerial Personnel Planning Program

		π_1	π_2	π_3	π_4	π_5
	π_1	.600	.150	.000	.100	.150
	π_2	.050	.750	.100	.020	.080
P =	π_3	.000	.050	.800	.120	.030
	π_4	.000	.000	.000	1.000	.000
	π_5	.000	.000	.000	.000	1.000

and steady-state information associated with the more general MA problem, will be of primary importance in understanding how to guide the company personnel-planning program. Using the six-step process discussed earlier, it is possible to generate these important criteria.

From the information given in the problem statement, we can form the **P**, shown in Table 10-6.

Steps 1 and 2. Eliminate the absorbing-state rows (4 and 5) and arrange the columns into absorbing (**A**) and nonabsorbing (**N**) groups.

$$
\begin{array}{c c}
 & \begin{array}{ccccc} \pi_4 & \pi_5 & \pi_1 & \pi_2 & \pi_3 \end{array} \\
\begin{array}{c} \pi_1 \\ \pi_2 \\ \pi_3 \end{array} &
\left[\begin{array}{ccccc}
.100 & .150 & .600 & .150 & .000 \\
.020 & .080 & .050 & .750 & .100 \\
.120 & .030 & .000 & .050 & .800
\end{array} \right] \\
 & \begin{array}{cc} \quad\;\; \mathbf{A} \qquad\qquad\quad \mathbf{N} \end{array}
\end{array}
$$

Step 3. Calculate the fundamental matrix, **F**. Once again, it is important to use a computer to complete the inverse-matrix operation.

$$
\mathbf{F} = \begin{bmatrix} 1 & 0 & 0 \\ 0 & 1 & 0 \\ 0 & 0 & 1 \end{bmatrix} - \begin{bmatrix} .600 & .150 & .000 \\ .050 & .750 & .100 \\ .000 & .050 & .800 \end{bmatrix}^{-1} = \begin{bmatrix} .400 & -.150 & .000 \\ -.050 & .250 & -.100 \\ .000 & -.050 & .200 \end{bmatrix}^{-1}
$$

	π_1	π_2	π_3
π_1	2.73	1.82	.91
F = π_2	.61	4.85	2.42
π_3	.15	1.21	5.61

The cell values indicate that, if you start in beginning management, you will spend, on the average, 2.73 years at that level, 1.82 years in middle management, and 0.91 years in top management prior to being absorbed into either form of termination with the corporation. Similar assessments can be made for starting initially in middle- and top-management positions.

Step 4. The total number of periods (years) it will take to be absorbed for any initial state is simply the cell sum for that state. The total number of years a person will spend at Xerox prior to being absorbed into either state 4 or 5 is 5.46,

7.88, and 6.97 years for beginning, middle, and top-level managers, respectively.

Step 5. The probability of moving between each nonabsorbing to an absorbing state is found from the solution of the **B** matrix, which is

$$\mathbf{B} = \mathbf{FA}$$

$$\mathbf{B} = \begin{bmatrix} 2.73 & 1.82 & .91 \\ .61 & 4.85 & 2.42 \\ .15 & 1.21 & 5.61 \end{bmatrix} \begin{bmatrix} .100 & .150 \\ .020 & .080 \\ .120 & .030 \end{bmatrix}$$

$$\mathbf{B} = \begin{array}{c c c} & \pi_4 & \pi_5 \\ \pi_1 & .42 & .58 \\ \pi_2 & .46 & .54 \\ \pi_3 & .71 & .29 \end{array}$$

This shows that, the higher a person's initial managerial level, the more likely that the termination will be corporation initiated. For example, the probability that an employee will be absorbed into π_4 increases from .42—if she starts in π_1—to a value of .71, if she is initially π_3. Conversely, the chances that the termination will be employee initiated decreases as the employee's initial managerial level increases—from a probability of .58 for employees who start in π_1 to only .29 for those who begin their tenure in π_3.

We can, of course, also employ transient analysis to see what these behavior patterns mean in the short term with respect to various managerial levels becoming either under- or overpopulated and to the overall affects to the company as reflected by, say, turnover rate. When we do this analysis, we obtain the following results:

1. The total number of managers in all three categories would decrease from 2700 to 1791 employees in only 2 years!

2. The percent in each managerial category would experience the following changes:

MANAGERIAL CATEGORY	PERCENT AT BEGINNING OF YEAR		
	1	2	3
1	.600	.300	.100
2	.466	.398	.137
3	.362	.456	.181

From this small amount of information, we can see that not only is the turnover rate for this particular office alarmingly high, but also the general trend of losing such a large percentage of the beginning managers is resulting in a top-heavy managerial structure. It is obvious that this condition would require a recruitment and retention program aimed at maintaining a more stable beginning managerial environment unless the company wishes to change drastically the initial 60–30–10 profile for its three levels of management.

EXAMPLE 10.6   THE RENTAL CAR AGENCY MAINTENANCE POLICY STUDY

For car-rental agencies, vehicle maintenance is a much larger headache than it is for the average private driver. It is not unusual for a single rental car to have been driven heavily by a number of different people of widely varying driving skills during a single

week. Now, suppose that a car-rental agency makes detailed, weekly inspections of its cars, in addition to the safety inspection each car receives when it is turned in from a customer. At the time of the detailed inspection, each car is classified as being in one of five operating conditions (states):

State 1: Excellent condition; like new

State 2: Good condition

State 3: Satisfactory condition; some minor problems

State 4: Fair to poor condition; running, but serious problems

State 5: Car not running

The type of repair, repair costs (labor and parts), and vehicle repair time associated with these five conditions is

STATE NO.	TYPE OF REPAIR	REPAIR COSTS ($)	REPAIR TIME (WEEKS)
1	none	0	0.00
2	none	0	0.00
3	tuneup	75	0.07
4	minor overhaul	250	0.50
5	major overhaul	450	0.90

At present, the agency policy (policy 1) is to repair any car that is in state 3, 4, or 5. The agency is also considering two alternative policies posed by one of their managers who believes that the present maintenance philosophy might be too expensive:

■ *Policy 2*: Repair cars that are in *either* state 4 or state 5.
■ *Policy 3*: Repair only those cars that are in state 5.

The average revenue generated by each operational rental car is $140 per week. The car-rental agency maintenance logs indicate that the weekly performance characteristics—in the form of a transition probability matrix, **P**—for the existing maintenance policy 1 are as shown in Table 10-7. However, if alternative policies are employed, the new **P** would look like those shown in Tables 10-8 and 10-9 for policy 2 and policy 3, respectively (based on maintenance logs of other car-rental agencies using similar policies).

TABLE 10-7

Transition Probability Matrix for Existing Rental-Car Agency Maintenance Policy 1

		Next Week				
		1	2	3	4	5
	1	.000	.600	.200	.100	.100
Present	2	.000	.300	.400	.200	.100
Week	3	1.000	.000	.000	.000	.000
	4	1.000	.000	.000	.000	.000
	5	1.000	.000	.000	.000	.000

TABLE 10-8

Transition Probability Matrix for Proposed Rental-Car Agency Maintenance Policy 2

		Next Week				
		1	2	3	4	5
	1	.000	.600	.200	.100	.100
Present	2	.000	.300	.400	.200	.100
Week	3	.000	.000	.400	.400	.200
	4	1.000	.000	.000	.000	.000
	5	1.000	.000	.000	.000	.000

TABLE 10-9

Transition Probability Matrix for Proposed Rental-Car Agency Maintenance Policy 3

		Next Week				
		1	2	3	4	5
	1	.000	.600	.200	.100	.100
Present	2	.000	.300	.400	.200	.100
Week	3	.000	.000	.400	.400	.200
	4	.000	.000	.000	.500	.500
	5	1.000	.000	.000	.000	.000

ASSIGNMENT

1. Do the probabilities whose values are 1.000 represent absorbing states in this case? Explain your answer.

2. Determine which of the three maintenance policies results in the lowest expected weekly costs. Show all of your work.

SOLUTION

1. Absorbing states represent conditions from which there is no escape. Obviously, since the cars can always be repaired regardless of their state of operation, the 1.000 values do not represent absorbing states.

2. The only information we will need is the steady-state condition for each of the three different policies which are being compared. The microcomputer solutions for these three policies are shown in Table 10-10:

TABLE 10-10

Steady-State Conditions for the Three Proposed Rental-Car Agency Maintenance Policies

Equilibrium Value	Policy		
	1	2	3
π_1	.350	.270	.200
π_2	.300	.230	.170
π_3	.190	.240	.180
π_4	.100	.170	.250
π_5	.060	.100	.200

The costs associated with each maintenance policy comprise two components: (1) the expected repair costs, and (2) the expected costs of the lost revenues due to the "down time" or unavailability of the car. The "optimum" maintenance policy will be the one with the lowest expected total costs. That is,

$$
\begin{array}{l}
\text{Expected total costs} \\
\text{for } j^{th} \text{ policy}
\end{array}
=
\left(
\begin{array}{c}
\text{expected weekly} \\
\text{maintenance costs} \\
\text{for } i^{th} \text{ repair state}
\end{array}
\right)
+
\left(
\begin{array}{c}
\text{expected lost revenues} \\
\text{associated with "down time"} \\
\text{of } i^{th} \text{ repair state}
\end{array}
\right)
$$

$$
EC_j = \sum_{i=1}^{n} \pi_i [M_i] + [Rt_i]
$$

where

EC_j = expected total costs associated with the jth maintenance policy
$(j = 1,2,3)$

M_i = maintenance cost associated with the ith steady state $(i = 1,2, \ldots ,5)$

π_i = proportion of cars in the ith steady state

t_i = amount of down time associated with i^{th} steady state (weeks)

R = average revenue generated by each car (\$140/week)

The expected costs for maintaining each car on a weekly basis for policy 1 are

$$
\begin{aligned}
EC_1 &= \pi_3 [M_3 + 140t_3] + \pi_4 [M_4 + 140t_4] + \pi_5 [M_5 + 140t_5] \\
&= (.19)[75 + (140)(.07)] + (.10)[296.67] + (.06)[576] \\
&= \$80.34/\text{car/week}
\end{aligned}
$$

For policy 2, the expected maintenance costs are

$$
\begin{aligned}
EC_2 &= \pi_4 [M_4 + 140t_4] + \pi_5 [M_5 + 140t_5] \\
&= (.17)[250 + (140)(.33)] + (.10)[450.67 + (.140)(.90)] \\
&= (.17)[296.67] + (.10)[576] \\
&= \$108.03/\text{car/week}
\end{aligned}
$$

For maintenance policy 3, the expected costs are

$$
\begin{aligned}
EC_1 &= \pi_5 [M_5 + 140Rt_5] \\
&= (.20)[450 + (140)(.90)] \\
&= (.20)[576] \\
&= \$115.20/\text{car/week}
\end{aligned}
$$

The least-cost maintenance policy for the car-rental agency is the present repair policy—policy 1. The greater responsiveness of this policy dramatically reduces the number of cars operating in the three repair states. Sometimes, as in the case of the two proposed reduced-repair-state policies, less costs more.

10.10 MICROCOMPUTER SOFTWARE SOLUTIONS TO MARKOV ANALYSIS PROBLEMS

We'll use Markov analysis microcomputer software packages such as *QSB* (Chang and Sullivan) and *Computer Models for Management Science* (Erikson and Hall), which have particularly friendly user interfaces, to illustrate the simplicity in solving some of the problems used in this chapter. As an example, the data entry and solution to the Cola Soft-Drink Market problem (Example 10.3) are shown in Table 10-11, using *CMMS*. We've also used this same software package to analyze an absorbing-state problem—the Xerox personnel-planning program (Example 10.5). The data entry and solution are shown in Table 10-12. The only adjustment that is required to use *CMMS* for absorbing-state problems is to rearrange the original transition probability matrix so that the absorbing states form an identity matrix in the upper-left corner (a matrix with all zeroes and ones, where the ones are all on a diagonal that goes from the upper-left corner to the lower-right corner). The *QSB* software is used to solve for the career life

```
        COMPUTER MODELS FOR MANAGEMENT SCIENCE
                    MARKOV MODELS
            -=*=-  INFORMATION ENTERED -=*=-

              TOTAL NUMBER OF STATES    : 4
              NUMBER OF ABSORBING STATES: 0
-------------------------------------------------------------------
                  TRANSITION TABLE
MARKET SHARE PROBABILITIES
STATES  1     2     3     4              STATES  SHARE
   1   0.600 0.150 0.080 0.170             1     0.280
   2   0.100 0.700 0.150 0.050             2     0.320
   3   0.030 0.060 0.900 0.010             3     0.220
   4   0.100 0.100 0.050 0.750             4     0.180

          MARKET SHARE ANALYZED FOR 3 PERIODS

                -=*=-  RESULTS -=*=-
                        MARKET SHARE AT THE BEGINNING OF
                                 EACH PERIOD
STEADY STATE PROBABILITIES                  STATE
0.130  0.216  0.504 0.150    PERIOD   1     2     3     4
                               1    0.280 0.320 0.220 0.180
                               2    0.225 0.297 0.277 0.201
                               3    0.193 0.279 0.322 0.206
                               4    0.174 0.264 0.358 0.205

        ---------  END OF ANALYSIS  ------------
```

TABLE 10-11

Computer Solution for Cola Soft-Drink Market Study

Source: Erickson & Hall, *Computer Models for Management Science*. Version 1.0. Englewood Cliffs, NJ: Prentice-Hall.

```
        COMPUTER MODELS FOR MANAGEMENT SCIENCE
                    MARKOV MODELS
            -=*=-  INFORMATION ENTERED -=*=-

              TOTAL NUMBER OF STATES    : 5
              NUMBER OF ABSORBING STATES: 2
-------------------------------------------------------------------
               T R A N S I T I O N   T A B L E
        STATES   1     2     3     4     5
           1   1.000 0.000 0.000 0.000 0.000
           2   0.000 1.000 0.000 0.000 0.000
           3   0.100 0.150 0.600 0.150 0.000
           4   0.020 0.080 0.050 0.750 0.100
           5   0.120 0.030 0.000 0.050 0.800
                    -=*=- RESULTS -=*=-
         TIME TO ABSORPTION  TIME TO ABSORPTION  CONDITIONAL PROBABILITIES
STATES       BY STATE             TIME                 BY STATE
   3    2.727 1.818 0.909         5.4545            0.418  0.582
   4    0.606 4.848 2.424         7.8788            0.448  0.552
   5    0.152 1.212 5.606         6.9697            0.712  0.288
```

TABLE 10-12

Xerox Corporation Management Planning Program Study

Source: Erickson & Hall, *Computer Models for Management Science*. Version 1.0. Englewood Cliffs, NJ: Prentice-Hall.

expectancy of a professional baseball player (Example 10.4) and the rental-car maintenance policy (Example 10.6) studies in Tables 10-13 and 10-14.

|10.11| SUMMARY

Unlike almost any other management science tool, MA can address problems that both are uncertain and change over time. However, it is a demanding and difficult method to use. The primary reason for this difficulty is that the expense involved in collecting the

TABLE 10-13

Life Expectancy of a Professional Baseball Player Study

Source: Chang and Sullivan, *QSB* (Version 3.0). Version 1.0. Englewood Cliffs, NJ: Prentice-Hall.

```
Input Data Describing Your Problem  BASEBL(Transition Probability Matrix) Pg1
   From    To
   S1      S1:  0.6000  S2:  0.2000  S3:  0.1000  S4:  0.1000
   S2      S1:  0.1000  S2:  0.8000  S3:  0.0500  S4:  0.0500
   S3      S1:  0.0000  S2:  0.0000  S3:  1.0000  S4:  0.0000
   S4      S1:  0.0000  S2:  0.0000  S3:  0.0000  S4:  1.0000


              Final Iteration -- Total Iterations = 80

         S1:  0.0000  S2:  0.0000  S3:  0.5000  S4:  0.5000


                   Recurrent Period for Each State

         S1:  0.0000  S2:  0.0000  S3:  2.0000  S4:  2.0000
```

accurate information needed to define the market behavior in terms of "brand loyalty" considerations is often prohibitive. Further, in the case of brand switching, attempting to model the change of human needs, desires, and even shifts in fashion can result in disastrous outcomes. In contrast, the application of Markov analysis to policy-formulation problems does not pose the same degree of difficulty.

At this point, it is both timely and necessary to supplement and even refine some of the earlier information about MA. For example:

1. The standard MA is usually first-order. However, if the system of interest exhibits significant behavioral fluctuations in moving between states, it is inappropriate to continue to assume that only one time period is needed to provide information that is sufficient to determine future behavior. An example of this could be a new product market in which there is activity among a number of near-equal competitors— say, the computer games market of the late seventies and early eighties. A possible remedy is to incorporate n th-order Markov methods (and appropriate software), which are more sensitive to these larger variations.

2. The number of states is to remain constant. It is not uncommon, however, for brand-switching problems to have new competitors that enter a growing market and to have competitors who are eliminated from a market that is leveling off or shrinking. This variation occurs in settings that are similar to those in concern 1. The same remedial considerations may apply.

3. The quantity or value of goods purchased by any two customers are likely to be unequal. Therefore, customers have varying values in the marketplace that first-order Markov methods cannot reflect.

4. First-order Markov models assume that there is a purchase of transaction in every period. This may not be the case: it is not uncommon for no transaction to occur. In such situations, a "no-transaction" state can be added to the model.

5. In some situations, there may be a large number of state conditions; however, the number of *significant* states could be only three or four, with the remainder of minor states capable of being grouped into a single additional state called "other." An example of this situation could be a product in which the top three competitors control 90 percent of the market, while the remaining 4 to 10 lesser competitors share the remaining 10 percent. It may even be possible to decrease a large number of states into a fraction of the original set by dividing the states into *similar* subgroups, and then by examining these clusters separately. Clearly, the number of automobile

```
Input Data Describing Your Problem AVIS10-7(Transition Probability Matrix) Pg1
  From      To
  S1        S1:  0.0000  S2:  0.6000  S3:  0.2000  S4:  0.1000  S5:  0.1000
  S2        S1:  0.0000  S2:  0.3000  S3:  0.4000  S4:  0.2000  S5:  0.1000
  S3        S1:  1.0000  S2:  0.0000  S3:  0.0000  S4:  0.0000  S5:  0.0000
  S4        S1:  1.0000  S2:  0.0000  S3:  0.0000  S4:  0.0000  S5:  0.0000
  S5        S1:  1.0000  S2:  0.0000  S3:  0.0000  S4:  0.0000  S5:  0.0000

                  Final Iteration -- Total Iterations = 22
            S1:  0.3500  S2:  0.3000  S3:  0.1900  S4:  0.0950  S5:  0.0650

                     Recurrent Period for Each State
            S1:  2.86    S2:  3.33    S3:  5.26    S4:  10.33   S5: 15.38


Input Data Describing Your Problem AVIS10-8(Transition Probability Matrix) Pg2
  From      To
  S1        S1:  0.0000  S2:  0.6000  S3:  0.2000  S4:  0.1000  S5:  0.1000
  S2        S1:  0.0000  S2:  0.3000  S3:  0.4000  S4:  0.2000  S5:  0.1000
  S3        S1:  0.0000  S2:  0.0000  S3:  0.4000  S4:  0.4000  S5:  0.2000
  S4        S1:  1.0000  S2:  0.0000  S3:  0.0000  S4:  0.0000  S5:  0.0000
  S5        S1:  1.0000  S2:  0.0000  S3:  0.0000  S4:  0.0000  S5:  0.0000

                  Final Iteration -- Total Iterations = 18
            S1:  0.2658  S2:  0.2278  S3:  0.2405  S4:  0.1684  S5:  0.0975

                     Recurrent Period for Each State
            S1:  3.76    S2:  4.39    S3:  4.16    S4:  5.94    S5: 10.26


Input Data Describing Your Problem AVIS10-9(Transition Probability Matrix) Pg3
  From      To
  S1        S1:  0.0000  S2:  0.6000  S3:  0.2000  S4:  0.1000  S5:  0.1000
  S2        S1:  0.0000  S2:  0.3000  S3:  0.4000  S4:  0.2000  S5:  0.1000
  S3        S1:  0.0000  S2:  0.0000  S3:  0.4000  S4:  0.4000  S5:  0.2000
  S4        S1:  0.0000  S2:  0.0000  S3:  0.0000  S4:  0.5000  S5:  0.5000
  S5        S1:  1.0000  S2:  0.0000  S3:  0.0000  S4:  0.0000  S5:  0.0000

                  Final Iteration -- Total Iterations = 19
            S1:  0.1989  S2:  0.1705  S3:  0.1799  S4:  0.2519  S5:  0.1989

                     Recurrent Period for Each State
            S1:  5.03    S2:  5.87    S3:  5.56    S4:  3.97    S5:  5.03
```

manufacturers is great; however, individual manufacturers of similar types of autos could be partitioned, and the competition with that "specialty" market examined. An illustration of this situation is the many people who typically buy the same *kind* of car at each purchase, even though the manufacturer may change from one purchase to another—say, Toyota, Nissan, Mazda (small foreign cars). So why worry about analyzing interaction between this type of buyer and autos such as those produced by Buick, Chevrolet, or Pontiac? Of course, this type of similification may bring with it the perils of the assumption being inappropriate in some special instances; in the long term, however, the partitioning approach is effective. The moral of this story, then, is that you should reassess each analysis on the basis of its specific and unique criteria, rather than trying to stretch a generalization to the breaking point.

TABLE 10-14

Data Entry and Solution for Rental-Car Maintenance Policy

Source: Chang and Sullivan, *QSB* (Version 3.0). Englewood Cliffs, NJ: Prentice-Hall.

6. Predictive analytical tools become less and less effective the further into the future that we attempt to push them. As suggested earlier, this is particularly true of marketing-application and brand-loyalty problems, but is less of a limitation in policy-formulation applications.

7. The quality of the data collected necessary to accomplish MA will ultimately determine the accuracy of your predictions (sound familiar?). So, be sure you are thoughtful in defining state conditions and developing the transition probabilities. Use your common sense in examining whether the time frame over which you collect your data is *representative* of the activity or if it has *atypical events* occurring that probably will not be repeated. Examples of this situation might include collecting data during such nonrepresentative occurrences as a labor strike, depression, war, or food shortage. Trying to make forecasts for the future when these anomaly situations are present would be foolish.

When you understand these important considerations, you will become capable of exercising one of two important steps:

1. Make the necessary adjustments, which will allow you to make appropriate use of Markov analysis.

2. Determine that such adjustments are not possible, and approach the problem with a different (non-Markovian) method.

10.12 EXERCISES

10-1 Assume the three most popular European luxury sedan automobiles in the American market are the Mercedes 500, the Jaguar XJ6, and the BMW 633i. The market shares among these three are .41, .27, and .32, respectively. Assume that the sales trends of these three autos over the past year have followed the pattern illustrated in the transition probability matrix, **P**, in Table 10-1.1. The table uses state notation: π_1 = Mercedes 500, π_2 = Jaguar XJ6, π_3 = BMW 633i.

ASSIGNMENT

1. If the market-purchase dynamics and the economic considerations stay essentially unchanged, what will the new market shares be 1, 2, and 3 years from now?
2. What would the steady-state (equilibrium) conditions be?
3. If the market sales for these luxury sedans are about $415 million per year and if the industry profit margin is about 10 percent, what will the annual sales be for each of the manufacturers for the 3 years discussed in part 1?

TABLE 10-1.1

European Luxury Sedan Transition Matrix

		Next Period		
		π_1	π_2	π_3
Present	π_1	.800	.100	.100
Period	π_2	.100	.700	.200
	π_3	.050	.100	.850

10-2 For illustration only, let's pretend that the present personal-computer market shares for primary manufacturers of microcomputers are IBM (45.2 percent), Apple (29.4 percent), Compaq (12.3 percent), and the remainder of the market, "others" (13.1 percent). The total market sales for last year were $10.753 billion. The market-sales behavior over the previous year is described by the following hypothetical dynamics (we use the following state notation: π_1 = IBM, π_2 = Apple, π_3 = Compaq, and π_4 = others):

■ IBM retains 90 percent of its original clients while losing 3 percent to Apple and 1 percent to others.
■ Apple loses nothing to Compaq and 13 percent to others while retaining 85 percent of its original clients.
■ Compaq retains 75 percent of its original clients while losing 15 percent to IBM and nothing to Apple.
■ The other computer manufacturers lose 20 percent to IBM, 5 percent to Compaq, and 10 percent to Apple.

Assume that the market sales will increase 10 percent each of the next 5 years and that the average market profit margin will be 13 percent.

ASSIGNMENT

What will the change in gross profit for Compaq for each of the next 2 years be?

10-3 Suppose that data from the Bureau of Labor Statistics (BLS) suggest that in a population of 83,000,000 people in the United States work force on June 1 of this year, 15 percent are unemployed, 22 percent are part-time employees, 47 per-

cent are full-time employees, and 16 percent are retired. Between May 1 and June 1, the following employment patterns were observed:

■ Ninety percent of the unemployed remained unemployed, 6 percent found part-time jobs, and 4 percent found full-time work.

■ Of the partially employed force, 10 percent retired, 35 percent found full-time jobs, and 15 percent lost their jobs.

■ Seventy percent of the fully employed retained their job status, while 10 percent lost their jobs and 10 percent retired.

■ Of those who were retired, essentially none took full-time positions, 2 percent found part-time work, and 98 percent remained in retirement.

ASSIGNMENT

Using these data, answer the following questions:

1. What will the total number of partially employed people be on August 1 if the population remains constant?
2. What are the equilibrium equations that we would need to determine steady-state conditions? (Formulate only; no solution required.)
3. How would changes in the June 1 employment data affect the steady-state conditions? For example, what would be the result if the unemployed were 5 percent instead of 15 percent (with appropriate accompanying changes in the other employment statuses)? Be *very* brief.

10-4 Assume that three prestigious companies, Gucci, Fendi, and Louis Vuitton, are engaged in ongoing head-to-head competition for the high end of the luxury luggage market, share 38, 17, and 45 percent, respectively. Buying behavior over the past year indicates that

■ Gucci retained 71 percent of its current clients while gaining 4 and 15 percent of Fendi's and Louis Vuitton's market, respectively.

■ During the same period, Louis Vuitton gained 20 and 12 percent of Gucci's and Fendi's market, respectively.

■ Fendi retained 84 percent of its customers while gaining 5 percent from Louis Vuitton.

Assume that the market purchasing patterns remain consistent with these data.

ASSIGNMENT

1. Illustrate the transition probability matrix, **P**.
2. What will the market shares for these two competitors be 2 years from present?
3. What is the probability that a customer who initially purchased Gucci will stay loyal to that brand during the next year?

10-5 Real-estate buying patterns in the greater San Francisco area reveal the information in Table 10-5.1. Assume that the total population of the region does not change significantly over the next 5 years.

TABLE 10-5.1

Transition Matrix for San Francisco Region Real-Estate Home-Purchasing Market

		Next Purchase			
		San Francisco	East Bay	Peninsula	Marin County
	San Francisco	.820	.080	.050	.050
Present	East Bay	.001	.950	.001	.003
Purchase	Peninsula	.040	.050	.910	.000
	Marin County	.050	.000	.000	.950

Note: San Francisco = City of San Francisco; East Bay = Oakland, Berkeley, Fremont, etc.; Peninsula = Burlingame, San Mateo, Palo Alto, San Jose, etc.; Marin County = Sausalito, Mill Valley, Tiburon, San Rafael, etc.

ASSIGNMENT

1. What will the individual populations for each of the four areas be 1, 3, and 5 years from now if the present populations are approximately 800,000, 1.25 million, 1.50 million, and 500,000 people for San Francisco, East Bay, Peninsula, and Marin County, respectively?
2. What are these figures at equilibrium?
3. What real-world limits probably would make it impossible for the equilibrium figures to become a reality?

10-6 Pretend that on flights between the mainland (primarily San Francisco and Los Angeles) and the Hawaiian Islands, four major airlines capture essentially all of the tourist market (greater than 95 percent of all people who fly between these points). The airlines and their assumed individual market shares are shown in Table 10-6.1. Over the last year (November 1 of last year to October 31 of this year), the consumer behavior was described by the following brand-loyalty patterns:

■ United retained 80 percent of its customers while losing 8 percent to Pan Am and 3 percent to NWO.

■ Pan Am kept 70 percent of its customers while losing 10 percent to United and 17 percent to TWA.

■ TWA lost 5 percent of its customers to NWO, 15 percent to Pan Am, and 13 percent to United.

■ NWO retained 90 percent of its customers while losing 3 percent to TWA and 4 percent to United.

TABLE 10-6.1

Present (November 1) Market Shares for Hawaiian Islands Air Travel

Airline	Market Share (%)
United, π_1	48.0
Pan Am, π_2	21.5
TWA, π_3	19.7
NWO, π_4	10.8

Last year's market sales for these four airlines on this lucrative route were $500 million. The industrywide profit margin on sales averaged 8 percent. Over the past 3 years, market sales have increased about 10 percent per year; however, suppose that recent recessionary trends and the declining hospitality of local Hawaiian residents toward tourists is expected to result in only a 5 percent increase over last year's market for the upcoming year. Accordingly, NWO (Northwest Orient) is considering implementing one of two possible strategies. Neither is expected to change the projected market sales total; however, both possess an opportunity to change NWO's market share in that market.

■ *Strategy 1*. NWO will lower the round-trip fare from $300 (assume this to be their average fare) to $199 per coach ticket. If it does this, reduction in airfare will also result in a proportional decrease in NWO's profit margin. The anticipated market behavior, based on a professional survey, is as follows. United will retain 75 percent of its customers while losing 5 percent to Pan Am and 8 percent to TWA. Pan Am will keep 76 percent of its customers while losing 8 percent to TWA and 8 percent to NWO. TWA will retain 70 percent of its customers while losing 15 percent to NWO and 6 percent to Pan Am. NWO will lose 2, 3, and 5 percent of its customers to United, Pan Am, and TWA, respectively.

■ *Strategy 2*. NWO will increase its average airfare to $375 and will offer more luxurious accommodations (gourmet food, free first-run movies, recliner seats, etc.). The anticipated market behavior is shown in Table 10-6.2. These additional accommodations will cost NWO $535,000 for the year and will increase its profit margin proportionally. The anticipated market behavior is the same as in strategy 1.

ASSIGNMENT

Analyze both hypothetical strategies, as well as the status quo, and determine which of the three is the most attractive approach. What are the equilibrium (steady-state) market shares for all three situations?

10-7 Suppose that Irwin Memorial Blood Bank (IMBB) of San Francisco is concerned with how to most efficiently use its inventory of blood plasma. It typically keeps an inventory of 1000 units. The frozen plasma has a "shelf life" of 6 months. Older units must be thrown out. Because of the recent complications arising over AIDS, the already-severe blood-donor shortage problem makes the use of the available blood even more crucial. Presently, IMBB has a policy of randomly selecting plasma units. IMBB estimates that, with current demand, each unit of plasma has a 25 percent chance of being used during any month and a 75 percent chance of remaining in inventory.

ASSIGNMENT

Because this alternative policy requires considerably more refined record keeping and more sophisticated storage organization, IMBB would like to know the percentage decrease in wasted units of blood plasma that will result if the policy revision is made (assume that the policy of keeping a 1000-unit blood inventory level does not change).

1. Design the transition probability matrix for IMBB.
2. Determine the proportion of blood that will be thrown out using this random selection policy.
3. Assuming that IMBB wants to continue to keep a 1000 unit inventory of blood plasma, how many donors are needed each month?

10-8 Imagine that the national headquarters of Citicorp Bank in New York City has 80 mainframe computers that run continuously (24 hours per day, 7 days per week). These computers are judged to be in four possible operating states during any day of operation: (π_1) operating in excellent condition; (π_2) operating in satisfactory condition but possible near-term problems likely; (π_3) operating in poor condition (up time only 50 percent); (π_4) not operating—major system breakdown. The average maintenance time for a computer operating in poor condition is 12 hours (.50 day), whereas the down time for a major system breakdown is 36 hours (1.50 days). The average cost associated with each hour of down time is $600 per hour, plus $7500 in parts for a computer operating in poor condition (π_3) and $35,000 in parts for computers that experience a major system breakdown (π_4). Presently, Citicorp provides maintenance for computers only if the latter experience a major system breakdown (π_4). The computer operating logs for this existing policy reveal the daily system behavior shown in Table 10-8.1. Citicorp is also considering a new policy for maintaining its

TABLE 10-6.2

Transition Matrix for Airline Market Strategy 2

		Next Period			
		π_1	π_2	π_3	π_4
Present	π_1	.830	.060	.090	.020
Period	π_2	.050	.800	.100	.050
	π_3	.080	.100	.750	.070
	π_4	.100	.100	.100	.700

TABLE 10-8.1

Daily Transition Probability Matrix for Citicorp Mainframe Computer System Using 60-Day Maintenance Schedule

		Next Day			
		π_1	π_2	π_3	π_4
Present	π_1	.850	.050	.090	.010
Day	π_2	.200	.600	.150	.050
	π_3	.800	.000	.190	.010
	π_4	.090	.000	.900	.010

TABLE 10-8.2

Daily Transition Probability Matrix for Citicorp Mainframe Computer System Using 30-Day Maintenance Schedule

		Next Day			
		π_1	π_2	π_3	π_4
Present	π_1	.870	.100	.020	.010
Day	π_2	.100	.750	.100	.050
	π_3	.740	.000	.250	.010
	π_4	.150	.000	.840	.010

TABLE 10-9.2

Transition Probability Matrix for Revised Remy Martin Oak Cognac Crate Maintenance Schedule

		Next Week			
		Rebuilt	Good	Fair	Damaged
	Rebuilt	.000	.750	.200	.050
Present	Good	.000	.600	.300	.100
Week	Fair	1.000	.000	.000	.000
	Damaged	1.000	.000	.000	.000

computer bank that involves maintenance for computers in either state π_3 or π_4. The estimated computer operation for this proposed policy is shown in Table 10-8.2.

ASSIGNMENT

Citicorp would like to know whether the present or proposed maintenance policy should be incorporated based on overall system costs. (*Hint*: Use expected cost to assess the two policies.)

10-9 Assume that the regional distributor of Remy Martin cognac in New York City uses hand-finished oak containers to deliver 12 one-liter bottles of product to local distributors. These containers require monthly maintenance to be used regularly. The specific conditions of these containers can fall into one of four categories: (1) reconditioned; (2) acceptable; (3) damaged but usable; and (4) unusable—damaged beyond use. If the container is damaged beyond use, it is repaired by the carpentry shop during a 1-week turnaround time. The Remy Martin warehouse records indicate the approximate matrix of transition probabilities for the cognac container maintenance process, as shown in Table 10-9.1. It costs about $17.50 to rebuild a crate, and the importer incurs a loss of $15.00 in distribution efficiency each time a crate is found to be damaged beyond use. This efficiency is lost because broken crates slow down the truck-loading process.

The importer is considering a new maintenance policy in an effort to find a less expensive way to preserve the oak crates, specifically, the crates also will be rebuilt whenever they are inspected and are found to be in damaged but usable condition. Although this does not eliminate the chances that a crate will become damaged, it does decrease the likelihood that it will. The new matrix of transition probabilities for this policy is estimated as shown in Table 10-9.2.

ASSIGNMENT

1. Determine the average weekly costs for maintaining the crates and the loss of weekly production efficiency for these two different maintenance policies. Assume that the importer uses approximately 800 crates in his operation.

2. Assume that the present maintenance policy has been in place for several years. What would the monthly maintenance policy costs be for the first 3 months during the transition period if the Remy Martin importer management decided to switch to the new maintenance policy? Plot the results.

3. How many months would it take to reach equilibrium if the new maintenance policy was selected?

10-10 Suppose the car-rental agency has just received updated information concerning repair costs, and it has discovered some interpretive errors concerning the transition matrix data presented in the original study (Example 10.6). The new data concerning repair costs and repair times are shown in Table 10-10.1. The car-rental agency maintenance logs indicate that the weekly performance characteristics for the existing

TABLE 10-9.1

Transition Probability Matrix for Standard Remy Martin Oak Cognac Crate Maintenance Schedule

		Next Week			
		Reconditioned	Acceptable	Damaged but Usable	Unusable
	Reconditioned	.000	.750	.200	.050
Present	Acceptable	.000	.600	.300	.100
Week	Damaged but usable	.000	.000	.400	.600
	Unusable	1.000	.000	.000	.000

TABLE 10-10.1

Rental-Car Agency Revised Repair Type, Repair Costs, and Associated Repair Time (Vehicle "Down Time")

State No.	Type of Repair	Repair Costs ($)	Repair Time (weeks)
1	none	0	0.00
2	none	0	0.00
3	tuneup	100	0.07
4	minor overhaul	400	0.50
5	major overhaul	700	1.25

TABLE 10-10.2

**Transition Probability Matrix for Existing
Rental-Car Agency Maintenance Policy 1**

		Next Week				
		1	*2*	*3*	*4*	*5*
Present	1	.000	.600	.200	.100	.100
Week	2	.000	.300	.400	.200	.100
	3	.980	.000	.020	.000	.000
	4	.900	.000	.000	.100	.000
	5	.850	.000	.000	.000	.150

TABLE 10-10.3

**Transition Probability Matrix for Proposed
Rental-Car Agency Maintenance Policy 2**

		Next Week				
		1	*2*	*3*	*4*	*5*
Present	1	.000	.600	.200	.100	.100
Week	2	.000	.300	.400	.200	.100
	3	.000	.000	.400	.400	.200
	4	.900	.000	.000	.100	.000
	5	.850	.000	.000	.000	.150

TABLE 10-10.4

**Transition Probability Matrix for Proposed
Rental-Car Agency Maintenance Policy 3**

		Next Week				
		1	*2*	*3*	*4*	*5*
Present	1	.000	.600	.200	.100	.100
Week	2	.000	.300	.400	.200	.100
	3	.000	.000	.400	.400	.200
	4	.000	.000	.000	.500	.500
	5	.850	.000	.000	.000	.150

maintenance policy 1 and for the two proposed policies are as shown in Tables 10-10.2 through 10-10.4. Notice that these new, revised transition tables reflect the fact that the repairs are not always perfect—there is less than 100 percent quality control. Accordingly, cars that receive maintenance in each of the three repair states are not always returned to service within the average repair time. The company officials think that this estimate is more realistic than were the original data.

ASSIGNMENT

1. Determine the expected costs associated for each of the three policies. Which policy has the lowest expected cost?

2. Assume that the company wishes to make a minimum expected profit of $50 per car per week. Determine what the average weekly rental charges must be for each car.

References

1. Anderson, Michael Q. "Damage to Finished Goods Inventory in a Dynamic Environment: A Markov Chain Model for the Arts and Crafts Industry." *Computers and Operations Research* 9 (No. 2: 1982): 109–117.

2. Bessent, E. Wailand, and Authella M. Bessant. "Student Flow in a University Department: Results of a Markov Analysis." *Interfaces* 10 (No. 2: April 1980): 52–59.

3. Deming, W. Edwards, and Gerald J. Glasser. "Markovian Analysis of the Life of Newspaper Subscriptions." *Management Science* 14 (No. 6: February 1968): B283–293.

4. Ezzati, Ali. "Forecasting Market Shares of Alternative Home-Heating Units by Markov Process Using Transition Probabilities Estimated from Aggregate Time Series Data." *Management Science* 21 (No. 4: December 1974): 462–472.

5. Garden, Peter W. "Markov Analysis of Viral DNA/RNA Sequences." *Journal of Theoretical Biology* 82 (1980): 679–684.

6. Hopkins, David S. P. "Models for Affirmative Action Planning and Evaluation." *Management Science* 26 (No. 10: April 1980): 994–1006.

7. Kao, Edward P. C. "Modeling the Movement of Coronary Patients within a Hospital by Semi-Markov Processes." *Operations Research* 22 (No. 4: July–August 1974): 683–699.

8. Meredith, Jack. "A Markovian Analysis of a Geriatric Ward." *Management Science* 19 (No. 6: February 1973): 604–612.

9. Oliver, Melvin L., and Mark A. Glick. "An Analysis of the New Orthodoxy on Black Mobility." *Social Problems* 29 (No. 5: June 1982): 511–523.

10. Sadan, Simcha, and Len B. Auerbach. "A Stochastic Model for Human Resources Valuation." *California Management Review* 16 (No. 4: Summer 1974): 24–31.

11. Swersey, Arthur J. "A Markovian Decision Model for Deciding How Many Fire Companies to Dispatch." *Management Science* 28 (No. 4: April 1982): 352–365.

12. Turban, Efraim, and Jack R. Meredith. *Fundamentals of Management Science*. Plana, TX: Business Publications, 1985.

(Au: Re No. 7—one of these names a typo?)

Microcomputer Software for Markov Analysis

Most of the microcomputer software available for Markov analysis is contained in multiple-module management-science products such as those listed here.

1. *Computer Models for Management Science*. Erikson and Owen Hall. Englewood Cliffs, NJ: Prentice-Hall.
2. *Micro Manager*. Sang Lee and Yüng Shim. Dubuque, IA: William C. Brown.
3. *Microsolve*. Paul Jensen. Oakland, CA: Holden-Day.
4. *Quantitative Systems for Business*. Yih-Long Chang and Robert Sullivan. Englewood Cliffs, NJ: Prentice-Hall.

CHAPTER 11

FORECASTING METHODS

11.1 INTRODUCTION

Paul Newman, in the title role of the movie *Hud* said, "Life's the toughest game in town. No matter how well you play it, you never get out of it alive." Forecasting is a little like life. No matter how well you plan and conduct a forecast, you are always going to be wrong. Even *great* forecasters are never *really* right. What makes them great is that they are not *too* wrong. Yet forecasting remains the lifeline of almost every thriving business. How does Chrysler determine the demand and ultimate production level for each of its automobiles? What information does Apple Computers use to determine the most sensible production levels for their product mix of personal computers? You guessed it: forecasting! for managers to do the best they can in forecasting future business environments instead of merely using unguided intuition is essential to surviving each year's carnivorous market competition.

Managers yearn to find better ways to predict the future. The need for accurate forecasts forms the fabric of almost every management decision. Although informal forecasting approaches—such as crystal balls, personal hunches, or horoscopes—may be appealing, they are clearly unacceptable for serious business settings. Managers require sales forecasts to determine production levels and schedules, inventory levels, work-force size and possible multiple shift arrangements, budgets, facility capacity and locations, and the level of advertising and the specific media outlets to use, among many other considerations. It is the *accuracy* of these forecasts that will ultimately determine the degree of success of an organization—whether, in fact, the organization survives.

In the beginning chapters of this textbook we dealt with decision methods, and we argued that every situation must ultimately conclude in a decision (even doing nothing is to select the status quo by default). However, when a decision is made, the selection is made *now*: The business manager makes the selection today with the full knowledge that the actual consequences of the decision will occur in the *future*. That is why people make a considerable attempt to predict accurately the value and likelihood of the future conditions or states of nature. This chapter will explore the different types of forecasting techniques that can be used by managers to anticipate the future.

So much for horoscopes . . .

11.2 | APPLICATIONS OF FORECASTING

The application of forecast models in business are numerous. Here is a small sampling (complete references are provided at the end of this chapter):

1. Forecast averaging in the automotive industry (Koten, 1981).
2. Seasonal-style goods-inventories forecasting (Hertz, 1965).
3. Strategic business forecasting for the aerospace and defense industries (Millett and Randles, 1986).
4. Forecasting nurse staffing requirements by intensity-of-care level (Helmer, 1980).
5. Forecasting cash flows from accounts receivable (Cochrane, 1978).
6. Planning a performing arts series using forecasting (Weinberg, 1978).
7. Forecasting the demand for blood tests (Gardner, 1979).
8. Long-term forecasting in the field of solar energy (Sarin, 1979).

11.3 | DIFFERENT TYPES OF FORECASTING METHODS

There are many different types of forecasting methods, and the types can be further classified according to numerous attributes. One of the more common approaches is to organize these forecasting models according to whether they use *qualitative* or *quantitative* methods of analysis. One such arrangement is shown in Figure 11-1 (Georgoff and Murdick, 1986). A few of the most common qualitative modes are discussed briefly in this chapter; however, *because of the nature of this textbook, quantitative models will receive the primary emphasis*. The array of forecast models introduced will be representative of the most popular kinds used in practice. Even so, many models will end up on the cutting-room floor, for at least one of two reasons: (1) they are beyond the intended scope of this textbook or (2) the shear number of available models necessitates their exclusion—though the choice of which to omit is a subjective one.

In addition to the division of forecast models along the line of qualitative versus quantitative data usage, many other criteria must be taken into account before a manager is ready to make a final selection. These criteria include the following:

1. *Forecast horizon*. How far into the future is the forecast to serve? Is the forecast needed for short-, medium-, or long-range planning? Even though these relative durations are not definitive (they will vary from one organization to another), we can classify them informally: short-range forecasts are typically between 1 week and a few months; medium-range forecasts are between 1 month and 3 years; long-range forecasts usually extend beyond 2 years (Figure 11-2).

2. *Forecast accuracy*. Is the forecast required to provide only gross estimates, or is significant accuracy essential? If a rough approximation is sufficient, *qualitative techniques* may be sufficient. These types of estimates include group-opinion or panel consensus, market research, the Delphi method, and historical analogy. If significant accuracy is required, the use of *quantitative methods* probably will be necessary.

3. *Forecast data availability*. Are there sufficient data available (and are they accessible), or are data essentially nonexistent? When sufficient historical data are available, it is often possible to incorporate quantitative forecasting methods.

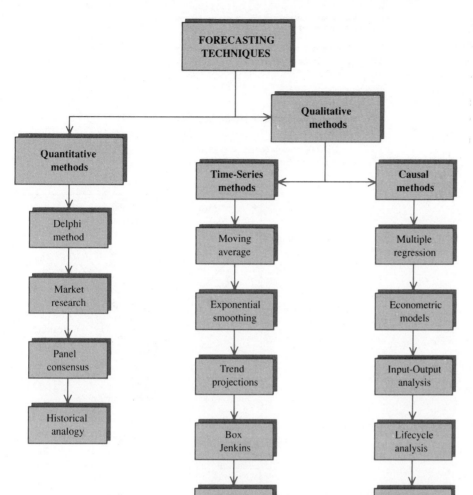

FIGURE 11-1

Typical Classification of
Forecasting Models

FORECASTING
TECHNIQUES

Qualitative
methods

Quantitative
methods

Time-Series
methods

Causal
methods

Delphi
method

Moving
average

Multiple
regression

Market
research

Exponential
smoothing

Econometric
models

Panel
consensus

Trend
projections

Input-Output
analysis

Historical
analogy

Box
Jenkins

Lifecycle
analysis

Bayesian

Simulation

4. *Time to conduct forecast.* How long does the manager have to conduct the forecast? When are the findings needed? Whether the forecast information is required immediately or whether there is sufficient time—say, 1 to 3 months—to conduct the study will significantly influence which of the many forecasting models can be employed.

5. *Forecast funding.* Is there sufficient money to finance the forecast? The smaller the forecasting budget, the more likely that less sophisticated forecasting methods will have to be used. The manager must wrestle with the dilemma of trading off the cost of conducting the forecast with the cost of the forecast inaccuracy (Figure 11-3).

Although there is no absolute way for a manager to proceed in the search for the optimal forecast model, an illustration of one possible approach is presented in Figure 11-4. There is a general rule for the manager to use in determining the selection of forecast method to employ: If adequate data and resources are available, *quantitative methods*

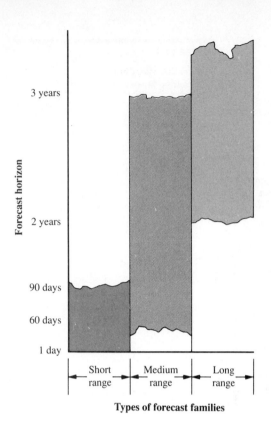

Forecast horizon

3 years

2 years

90 days

60 days

1 day

Short range | Medium range | Long range

Types of forecast families

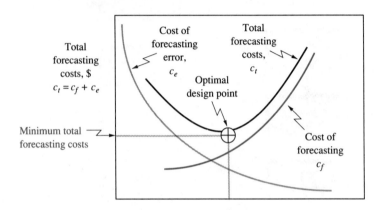

FIGURE 11-2

Illustration of Relationship between Types of Forecasts and Forecast Horizon

FIGURE 11-3

Tradeoff between Forecasting Accuracy and Costs of Forecasting Error Costs

Total forecasting costs, \$
$c_t = c_f + c_e$

Cost of forecasting error, c_e

Total forecasting costs, c_t

Optimal design point

Minimum total forecasting costs

Cost of forecasting c_f

Forecasting accuracy

FIGURE 11-4

Overview of Process for Selecting a Forecast Method

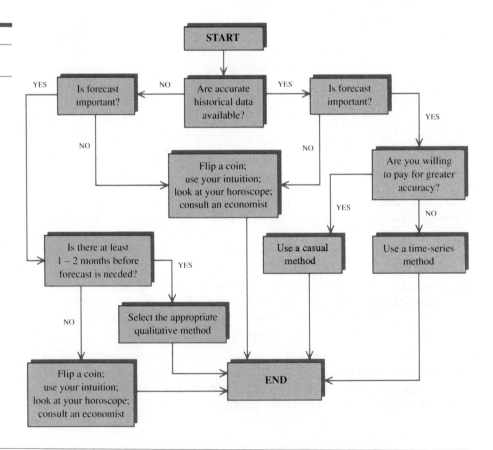

should be employed. Two of the advantages that quantitative forecast methods have over qualitative methods are these:

1. Quantitative findings provide measurable performance values. This makes it possible to uncover important characteristics in the findings that might otherwise be overlooked (e.g., seasonal variation in the data may overshadow a trend, so a continuing decline or growth pattern remains undiscovered).

2. Qualitative data provide impressions or intuition that may be considerably different from the characteristics of the actual problem. Further, it is difficult to debate or even clearly to understand different qualitative selections, since there is often no concrete (measurable) frame of reference. Without quantitative guidelines and findings to restrict them, marketing and sales managers will optimistically forecast tremendous growth while fiscal officers will tend to be conservative and to underestimate future company performance.

Even though there is a clear preference for quantitative forecast methods, qualitative forecasting is indeed used in business. We shall briefly survey three of the more popular qualitative forecast methods in the next section. A broader and more detailed presentation of the large number of qualitative models can be found in a textbook that specializes in forecast methods (Thomopoulos, 1981; Wheelwright et al., 1977; Makridakis and Wheelwright, 1982; Box and Jenkins, 1970; Sullivan and Claycombe, 1977; Spencer et al., 1961).

11.4 QUALITATIVE FORECASTING METHODS

Qualitative forecasting methods typically provide the manager with a more subjective assessment than do quantitative methods. For this reason, they are usually selected only when it is either unnecessary or infeasible to employ quantitative techniques. For example, there may not be enough time, the data may be sparse or unreliable, there may be insufficient money, or there may be no crucial need for a high level of accuracy.[1] There are many qualitative methods; only three of them will be discussed in this section: (1) market research, (2) the Delphi method, and (3) expert-panel opinion.

Market Research

When time and money are not in short supply, market research can often provide sophisticated, accurate forecasts. Although considered a qualitative method of forecasting, market research actually incorporates both intuition and hard data. Prestigious market-research firms are common household names: the Nielsen Company, Arbitron, and Lou Harris.

Market research attempts to extract information from members of the target market population regarding either their opinion of an existing product or service (for purposes of changing or improving it), a proposed new product or service (for purposes of determining what market share the company might hope to capture and, consequently, whether they should in fact produce the product—or offer the service), or merely an idea about a specific product or service that is still in the planning stage (for purposes of incorporating desired characteristics before the concept becomes fixed).

Various media are used to collect market research data, such as telephone surveys, personal interviews, mailed questionnaires, and staged test markets (such as handing

---

[1] An exception to the typically soft findings provided by qualitative forecast models is those obtained with market research—one of the three methods discussed in this section.

out samples of a new or proposed beauty product in specific department stores). The aggregate response to these different data-gathering instruments will ultimately provide information about the consumer demand, and about perceived quality and value of the product.

Usually, sophisticated inferential statistical methods are used to determine whether anticipated relationships among the market population are supportable (significant). Both nonparametric and parametric statistics can be used, depending on the characteristics of the sampled population (size, normality), the level of measurement solicited by the various data-collection instruments, and so on.

Market surveys can be time consuming and extremely expensive to plan, conduct, and evaluate. If done thoughtfully, however, this form of forecasting can provide great accuracy.

Delphi Method

The Delphi method was developed by the Rand Corporation in the late 1950s. Delphi uses a nonconfrontational setting for eliciting expert opinion. Where the traditional round-table approach places manager and subordinate alike in face-to-face contact with one another, Delphi does not. Delphi attempts to minimize the impact of organizational pecking order and dominant personalities by physically separating people, as well as keeping their identities anonymous.

Delphi uses iterative rounds of questionnaires that are distributed among the panel experts—typically by regular mail, electronic mail, or messenger. The findings of each round are organized and redistributed—without identifying any expert by name—along a continuum scale bounded by the extreme responses. Each panel expert is free to see not only her response, but also where it stands along the continuum of all other responses. The panel members are then asked to reconsider their response of the preceding round in light of all the other opinions. Each subsequent round usually results in the more extreme responses moving closer to the majority-opinion cluster. Usually, within three to five rounds of questionnaires, the Delphi method has provided a consensus forecast.

Although the Delphi method need not be expensive, the time needed to conduct the multiple, iterative rounds of responses and feedback can be considerable (especially if the participants are separated by significant distances and the data-collection process is written-and-mailed questionnaires). Further, participant availability from one round to the next may sometimes be delayed due to other commitments.

Expert Panel Opinion

A panel of experts can be organized to develop a forecast. Ongoing, round-table discussions are used to provide each member with an open forum to share his ideas. Dialogue is exchanged and various scenarios are argued until the panel forms a consensus opinion.

The merit of the findings from an expert panel is greatly influenced not only by the knowledge of the experts selected, but also by chemistry of their personalities. Persuasive ability and a powerful personality do not necessarily go hand in hand with insight. Further, political considerations—such as not wanting to alienate other participants—often result in bandwagon effects.

Even though expert-panel approaches can typically be conducted in little time and are relatively inexpensive, the associated accuracy is usually inferior to that of other types of qualitative methods.

TABLE 11-1

Characteristics of Qualitative Forecasting Techniques

| Characteristic | Qualitative Forecasting Model | | |
	Delphi Method	*Market Research*	*Expert Panel Consensus*
Accuracy			
Short term	fair to very good	excellent	poor to fair
Medium term	fair to very good	good	poor to fair
Long term	fair to very good	fair to good	poor
Cost*	$5000	$12,500	$5000
Time required	2 months +	3 months +	2 weeks +

Source: John C. Chambers, et al., "How to Choose the Right Forecasting Technique," *Harvard Business Review* (July–August, 1971): 57–86.

*Cost figures arbitrarily adjusted to reflect inflation.

The various characteristics of these three qualitative forecasting methods are summarized in Table 11-1. Next, we shall examine the other side of the forecasting ledger: quantitative methods. The two types of quantitative forecasting families that will be presented are time series methods and causal methods.

11.5 QUANTITATIVE FORECASTING METHODS: TIME SERIES

A *time series* is simply a collection of measurements sequentially recorded across fixed time periods. The number of pairs of shoes sold by Cole-Haan Shoe Company during each month of the past 2 years, and the Sun Computer Systems sales revenues generated by quarter for each of the last 4 years, represent 24-period and 16-period time series, respectively. A time-series pattern can be more clearly understood if it is broken down into the four components that constitute these forecasting models:[2] (1) trend, (2) seasonal variation, (3) cyclical variation, and (4) random variation. This isolation of these components of the time series is called *decompositional analysis*.

1. *Trend.* The component that reflects the general, long-term direction of the data is called the trend. Possible reasons for a gradual, ongoing type of change are shifts in consumer preferences or taste, changes in the economy, and breakthroughs in the state of the art of relevant technologies. The continuing increase in the cost of living is an example of trend, as is the general increase in the volume of airline customers over the last decade, attributed in part to the popularization of air travel.

2. *Seasonal variation.* Periodic increases or decreases in the data value above and beyond the trend is the seasonal-variation component. Seasonal fluctuations are typically related to particular times of the year, month, or day. Travel-associated industries (airlines, hotels, and so on) peak during holiday and vacation times (summer, Thanksgiving, and Christmas) and dramatically drop during the "off season" (January through May, September, and October). Traffic tends to peak during the morning. Physicians anticipate the "flu season" in the winter, and law-enforcement officers can count on increases in violent crime during the hot summer months.

[2]This approach is similar to the use of control groups in an experiment where it is important to differentiate between the effects of the treatment and extraneous factors.

3. *Cyclic variation.* The oscillation of data about the trend line that can be detected only over extended periods is the cyclic component. The oscillation may not be apparent unless the time series extends over several years. It is virtually impossible to predict the impact of the cyclic component on short-term forecasting. The reasons for the cycle are often inexplicable.

4. *Random variation.* The difference between the actual time series and the forecast we anticipate from the trend, seasonal, and cyclic components is the random component. This type of variation is in the form of isolated fluctuations—also referred as "noise"—and occurs without pattern. Typically, it cannot be anticipated. Random changes are sometimes explainable after they have occurred. Examples include the decrease in overseas passenger travel due to airline travel–related terrorism, such as airline hijackings and airport bombings.

There is no explicit way for the manager to know, with certainty, the most attractive quantitative forecast model to use. It is quite common to try a number of models and to select the one that provides the greatest accuracy. That is exactly what we are going to do in the following sections of this chapter. Five popular time-series forecast models will be applied to a common forecast problem. The accuracy of each model will be measured and compared against the accuracy provided by a benchmark model: To be considered a viable candidate, any model must have greater accuracy than does the benchmark model. Let us begin this process by next establishing ways in which we can measure forecast accuracy (error) and, in addition, forecast bias (consistency).

Forecast Model Accuracy: Error Measurement

Ultimately, the manager will examine the fit of a number of forecast models on the particular time series in question. But which one should the manager select, and what guidelines should she use in selecting it? Picking the optimal forecast model will be greatly influenced by the accuracy that model provides. Although it is possible *visually* to examine a time-series forecast graph or chart, a manager's perceptual assessment will rarely be viewed as concrete. Instead, visual impressions will be judged as subjective, highly suspect, and usually professionally unacceptable. *It is, therefore, essential to use a method that will provide a quantitative evaluation of the forecast accuracy.*

Methods that evaluate model accuracy focus on some measure of the *forecasting error* or *residuals* associated with that model. The error or residual is simply the difference between the actual and forecast values for a given time period. That is,

$$e_t = A_t - F_t$$

where

e_t = forecast error during time period t

A_t = actual variable value during time period t

F_t = forecast variable value during time period t

Among the most common error-measurement indices are

1. Mean absolute deviation (MAD)

2. Mean absolute percentage error (MAPE)

3. Mean square error (MSE)

The MAD is the average of the absolute differences between the forecast and actual values:

$$\text{MAD} = \frac{\sum\limits_{t=1}^{n} |A_t - F_t|}{n}$$

where n = number of time periods during which there is a comparison between actual data and a corresponding forecast value

MAD treats each error component, small or large, equally: It does not address the magnitude of the data being assessed. This can be somewhat of a problem to a manager who is comparing several sets of forecasts. Look at the summary of two hypothetical forecasts illustrated in Table 11-2. A manager may assume that the smaller MAD value of forecast 2 suggests greater accuracy than does the larger value in forecast 1. In truth, the proportion of the MAD to the mean actual value in forecast 1 is only 6 percent, compared to 25 percent for forecast 2. Even though this kind of oversight is unlikely in a comparison between forecast data sets that are as dramatically different as the two exhibited in Table 11-2, it may not be so clear when the proportional (MAD/mean actual value ratio) errors are close. For this reason, the manager may wish to include the MAPE method. The MAPE is the average of the absolute percentage differences between the actual and forecast values, and is essentially identical to MAD except that it normalizes the magnitude of the measurements. The MAPE relationship is given by

$$\text{MAPE} = \frac{\sum\limits_{t=1}^{n} \dfrac{|A_t - F_t|}{A_t}}{n}$$

Even though the MAD and MAPE assessment procedures provide the manager with useful information, both approaches treat error components equally; large and small errors are weighted alike. The mean square error (MSE) method, unlike either MAD or MAPE, penalizes larger errors more severely.

The MSE is the average of the squared error. Many managers prefer the MSE method to either the MAD or MAPE methods because, in fact, one large error may have a much greater influence on the vitality of a business than do numerous small errors. The MSE method is given by

$$\text{MSE} = \frac{\sum\limits_{t=1}^{n} (A_t - F_t)^2}{n}$$

It is important to know that it is not rare for these different error-measurement techniques to yield differing assessments of the accuracy between, say, two forecast methods. For example, it is quite possible that, in one setting, the MAD–MAPE family of assessment methods will give lower values than will the MSE method; in another instance, the reverse outcome may be true. So which of the various assessment methods is best when they yield conflicting findings? The manager must use her judgment after a thorough review of the various evaluative options. *To compare the accuracy of the various forecast models introduced in this chapter from a common frame of reference, we shall use the MSE.*

TABLE 11-2

Comparison of Forecast Accuracy Using the MAD Method for Two Different Sets of Data

Forecast	Mean Actual Value	MAD
1	35,000	2,100
2	1600	400

Monitoring Implemented Forecast Models: Tracking Signal Measurement (Bias)

Once a forecasting model has been selected and implemented, it is possible to monitor and evaluate the forecast errors by measuring (1) the *bias*, and (2) the *tracking signal* of the time series. These two measurements, although they both focus on the accuracy of the forecast, are quite different. Bias indicates whether the forecast, taken as a whole, tends to be high or low, and by how much. It is, therefore, a *summative measurement* of the forecast accuracy. The tracking signal, on the other hand, examines how the forecast is doing on an ongoing basis; it provides a dynamic or *running measurement* of the forecast accuracy. Let's see how both of these accuracy measures are used.

Ideally, a good forecasting model will have errors that tend to alternate high and low in approximately the same magnitude. Accordingly, over the entire forecast, these errors should come close to canceling out. It is essential for a manager to know whether the forecast predictions tend to be typically high or low. If a manager knew not only the amount of error in the forecast but also whether the forecast was consistently underestimating or overestimating, he could build in a correction factor as a hedge against the *bias* direction. The bias of a forecast is measured by

$$\text{Bias} = \frac{\sum_{t=1}^{n} (A_t - F_t)}{n}$$

The ratio between a forecast's bias and MAD is called the *tracking signal*, δ_n. The tracking signal provides the manager with a type of running account of the forecast error; it is given by

$$\delta_n = \frac{\dfrac{\sum_{t=1}^{n} (A_t - F_t)}{n}}{\dfrac{\sum_{t=1}^{n} |A_t - F_t|}{n}}$$

$$= \frac{\dfrac{\sum_{t=1}^{n} (A_t - F_t)}{n}}{\text{MAD}}$$

$$= \frac{\text{Bias}}{\text{MAD}}$$

If the selected forecast model is following the actual data in an unbiased manner, you should anticipate the numerator to be high and low nearly alternately. Also, displacement values should be approximately equal, so they should cancel out each other. This will result in a summed numerator value (and ratio value) of near zero. If the forecast is biased, however, it will tend to read either high or low more often. The tracking signal ratio will then gradually grow either negatively or positively, depending on the direction of the forecast model bias. So, the manager may use the tracking signal as a *warn-*

ing device that indicates when the existing forecasting model needs to be revised. Often, a manager will set the tracking signal value at a specific limit, δ. So long as δ_n is less than or equal to δ, the forecast is operating acceptably. However, if δ_n exceeds δ, the model parameters must be adjusted or a new forecast model must be selected (e.g., hedge the forecast opposite in direction and equal in amount to the bias magnitude).

Lousy, Acceptable, or Terrific: Determining the Goodness of Your Forecast Against the Naive Model

After the error and bias of a particular model has been measured, how can the manager judge the ultimate value of the forecast? Is it an acceptable, poor, or terrific forecast? One of the best ways of assessing the quality of the forecast is to compare it against the *naive model* (also referred to as the *persistence model*). The performance of the naive model will provide the manager with the minimum allowable level of accuracy. Any forecast method must be able to improve on the performance of the naive model if it is to be considered a viable method.

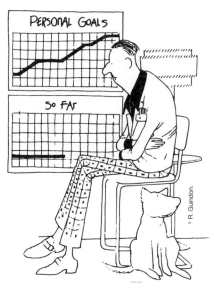

Benchmark Method: The Naive Model The naive model is a theoretical benchmark model that assumes that the value of the forecast in a subsequent period is simply equal to the actual value of the preceding period. It is aptly named. We denote it

$$F_{t+1} = A_t$$

If the particular forecast method is not more accurate than the naive model is, the manager eliminates it from further consideration. However, the search does not end simply because the manager finds a model superior to the benchmark. The naive model is simply a *screening device*: It determines minimal acceptable standards for any candidate forecasting model. The most attractive forecasting model will be the one with the highest accuracy as measured by the error-assessment method preferred by the manager. For the comparisons conducted in this chapter, the MSE values will be used. The lower the MSE, the more accurate the model. (You should, however, feel free to select whatever other accuracy measurement you prefer.)

To assess the various forecast models consistently, we shall use a single forecast problem throughout the chapter (the naive model will be used to establish the baseline standards for forecast performance). Let us now construct a hypothetical set of data so that we can explore some of the most popular forecast models used in business.

EXAMPLE 11.1 SUN BELT AIRLINES TICKET-SALES FORECAST

The airlines industry is one of the most complex forecast environments imaginable. In addition to the seasonal fluctuations of high and low passenger demand—typically corresponding to vacation times and holidays—airlines also have to contend with fluctuations in fuel costs (as influenced by oil prices in the Middle East), the strength of the dollar against foreign currencies (influencing high or low demand for flights abroad), unanticipated weather problems, union strikes, airline mergers or takeovers, ticket price wars, terrorist attacks, and bankruptcies.

Suppose, for illustrative purposes only, that Sun Belt Airlines has collected passenger ticket-sales information regarding the route between New York City and Miami Beach [Kennedy (JFK) and Miami International airports] for each quarter of the 1984 to 1986 calendar years. Assume these figures are depicted by the data shown in Table

TABLE 11-3

Number of Passenger Tickets Sold for Sun Belt Airlines for the Route from New York City to Miami Beach

Quarter	Year	Ticket Sales
1	1984	70,000
2		60,000
3		105,000
4		100,000
5	1985	75,000
6		75,000
7		110,000
8		105,000
9	1986	85,000
10		75,000
11		120,000
12		125,000

11-3. The naive model forecast can now be conducted easily. The results are shown in Table 11-4: MSE = 5.98E08, MAD = 18,636, and the bias = 5,000. We will concentrate on the MSE, since it is the measure of accuracy selected to be used as the basis for the comparisons to follow. Therefore, for any model to be a viable candidate, it must have an MSE value less than that of the naive model.

Time-Series Models   Next, five popular forecast models will be examined. They belong to one of the two families of quantitative forecast models presented in this chapter; they are called *time-series* or *extrapolation models*. The five time-series models that will be studied in this section are (1) simple moving average, (2) weighted moving average, (3) simple exponential smoothing, (4) Holt trend-adjusted exponential smoothing, and (5) multiplicative linear trend–seasonal component decomposition.

Model 1: Simple Moving Average (SMA)

The simple moving average (SMA) method ignores the possible effects of seasonal, cyclical, or random fluctuations by taking the average of the last Δn historical data points. Only if the aforementioned effects do not exist, or are of minor influence, does the SMA method prove to be of value. The SMA is calculated from the following equation:

$$F_t = \frac{\sum_{i=1}^{\Delta n} A_{t-i}}{\Delta n}$$

$$= \frac{A_{t-1} + A_{t-2} + A_{t-3} + \cdots + A_{t-\Delta n+1} + A_{t-\Delta n}}{\Delta n}$$

TABLE 11-4

Naive Model Benchmark Accuracy Measurements for Sun Belt Airlines Ticket Sales Example

Period	Actual Sales	Forecast Sales	Error e_t	Σe_t	Absolute e_t	Absolute % e_t	$e_t^2 (10^6)$	Tracking Signal
1	—	—	—	—	—	—	—	—
2	60,000	70,000	−10,000	−10,000	10,000	16.67	100	−1.00
3	105,000	60,000	45,000	35,000	45,000	42.85	2025	.64
4	100,000	105,000	−5000	30,000	5000	5.00	25	.50
5	75,000	100,000	−25,000	5,000	25,000	33.33	625	.06
6	75,000	75,000	0	5,000	0	0.00	0	.06
7	110,000	75,000	35,000	40,000	35,000	31.82	1225	.33
8	105,000	110,000	−5000	35,000	5000	4.76	25	.28
9	85,000	105,000	−20,000	15,000	20,000	23.53	400	.10
10	75,000	85,000	−10,000	5,000	10,000	13.33	100	.03
11	120,000	75,000	45,000	50,000	45,000	37.50	2025	.25
12	125,000	120,000	5000	55,000	5000	4.00	25	.27
13	—	125,000			205,000	210.40	6575	

MAD = 205,000/11 = 18,636

MAPE = 210.40/11 = 19.13

MSE = 6575/11 = 5.98E08

BIAS = 55,000/11 = 5,000

where

F_t = forecast value for time period t (i.e., the average of the previous Δn observations)

A_{t-i} = actual sales for period $t - i$

Δn = number of past time periods used in the averaging process

For the Sun Belt Airlines data, the first SMA for a four-quarter time period interval ($\Delta n = 4$) is for the fifth quarter (first quarter 1985), F_5:

$$F_5 = \frac{\sum_{i=1}^{4} A_{5-i}}{4}$$

The SMA may now be calculated for every succeeding quarter. F_5 is computed as follows:

$$F_6 = \frac{A_4 + A_3 + A_2 + A_1}{4}$$
$$= \frac{100,000 + 105,000 + 60,000 + 70,000}{4}$$
$$= 83,750$$

Two- and four-quarter SMAs are summarized for the Sun Belt Airlines data in Table 11-5 and in Figure 11-5, including the bias and MAD as well as the MSE error measurement. (No tracking signal value is calculated for moving-average–type models. The tracking error value, which is accumulated over the duration of the forecast, could be biased toward longer forecast periods and is, therefore, not used for moving-average models.)

TABLE 11-5

Sun Belt Airlines Data Sales Forecast Using 2- and 4-Month Simple Moving Averages

Quarter	Year	Actual Ticket Sales	Forecast Ticket Sales 2 month	4 month
1	1984	70,000	—	—
2		60,000	—	—
3		105,000	65,000	—
4		100,000	82,500	—
5	1985	75,000	102,500	83,750
6		75,000	87,500	85,000
7		110,000	75,000	88,750
8		105,000	92,500	90,000
9	1986	85,000	107,500	91,250
10		75,000	95,000	93,750
11		120,000	80,000	93,750
12		125,000	97,500	96,250
13	1987	—	122,500	101,250

2 month:	4 month:
MAD = 25,500	MAD = 16,880
MSE = 7.46E08	MSE = 3.45E08
Bias = −9,000	Bias = −5,938

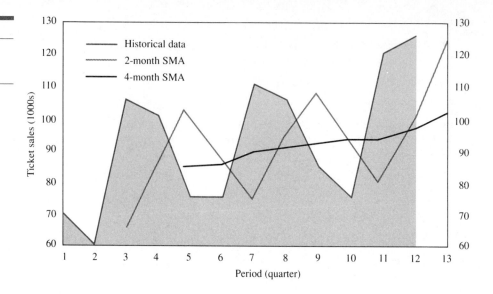

Although the selection of the number of time periods over which you wish to average your data is arbitrary, larger Δn values will provide smoother forecast data: The longer time periods tend to distribute seasonal patterns, cycles, and random-error variations more uniformly across each observation. There is a practical limit, however, to the length of the moving-average forecast period. As the length of this period approaches that of the actual time series, the forecast value approaches the mean of the empirical data—a constant value. Notice that the MSE value is more than halved when the forecast periods are increased from two to four.

At first, it may seem strange that forecasts are made for the actual values of past time periods. Why worry about outcomes that are already known and documented? *These historical data provide a frame of reference against which the manager may examine how well any particular forecast technique works*. The comparison of actual to forecast values also allows the manager to examine the error and bias associated with the various models introduced in this chapter.

When compared against the naive model, only the four-period SMA has greater accuracy. The two-period SMA yields error levels considerably higher than those of the naive model and is, therefore, eliminated from further consideration.

Model 2: Weighted Moving Average (WMA)   Experience shows us that a forecast sometimes can be improved when more recent data are given greater weight. The weighted moving average (WMA) using Δn past time periods is given by

$$F_t = \frac{\sum_{i=1}^{\Delta n} W_{t-i} A_{t-i}}{\sum_{i=1}^{\Delta n} W_{t-i}}$$

where W_{t-i} = proportional weight assigned to time period $t - i$

However, the denominator of this expression must sum to 1.00. That is,

$$\sum_{i=1}^{\Delta n} W_{t-i} = 1$$

Accordingly, the forecast value for the weighted moving average becomes

$$F_t = \sum_{i=1}^{\Delta n} W_{t-i} A_{t-i}$$

To calculate, say, a four-quarter WMA for the Sun Belt Airlines data, we must first determine the weighting profile for the four quarters. Let us assume that we arbitrarily select a weighting scheme of 60–25–10–5, starting with the most recent through the fourth-removed quarter. The WMA for the fifth quarter, F_5, is then

$$F_5 = (.60)(100,000) + (.25)(105,000) + (.10)(60,000) + (.05)(70,000)$$
$$= 95,750$$

The WMA for these data using two- and four-quarter periods is shown in Table 11-6 and in Figure 11-6. The WMA is an expedient forecasting method to use: It is a simple,

TABLE 11-6

Sun Belt Airlines Data Sales Forecast Using 2- and 4-Month Weighted Moving Averages

Quarter	Year	Actual Ticket Sales	Forecast Ticket Sales 2 month	4 month
1	1984	70,000	—	—
2		60,000	—	—
3		105,000	64,000	—
4		100,000	87,000	—
5	1985	75,000	102,000	95,750
6		75,000	85,000	83,500
7		110,000	75,000	79,000
8		105,000	96,000	97,250
9	1986	85,000	107,000	101,750
10		75,000	93,000	92,000
11		120,000	79,000	82,250
12		125,000	102,000	104,500
13	1987	—	123,000	116,750

2 month:
MAD = 23,900
MSE = 7.00E08
BIAS = −0.36

4 month:
MAD = 20,000
MSE = 4.92E08
BIAS = −0.21

Note: Weighting schemes for 2- and 4-month moving averages are 60–40 and 60–25–10–5, respectively.

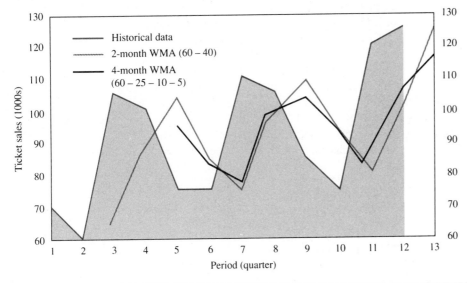

FIGURE 11-6

Sun Belt Airlines Sales Forecast Using 2- and 4-Month Weighted Moving Average (WMA) Method

quick, and inexpensive method to employ when the behavior of the data is uncomplicated, the forecasting horizon is short, and the accuracy required is undemanding. However, the only way to determine the optimal forecast period and weighting scheme is to experiment. Unfortunately, the number of possible combinations of weighting schemes and forecast periods is huge—a serious drawback to using this technique. In addition, the number of historical data required for moving average-type forecasts is also large: Real-world applications employ at least 12 periods or more (Levin, Rubin, and Stinson, 1986).

As in the earlier forecast using the SMA models, only the four-period WMA has greater accuracy than does the naive model. Once again, the two-period model yields error levels considerably higher than does the naive model and should be eliminated from further consideration.

Model 3: Simple Exponential Smoothing (SES)   Another method that attempts to account for seasonal, cyclical, or random variations in chronological data is the family of *exponential smoothing* forecast models. The most simple algebraic form of this type of forecasting model, called *simple exponential smoothing* (SES), is

$$F_t = F_{t-1} + \alpha (A_{t-1} - F_{t-1})$$
$$= F_{t-1} + \alpha e_{t-1}$$

where

$$F_{t-1} = \text{forecast value of variable in period } t - 1$$
$$A_{t-1} = \text{actual value of variable in period } t - 1$$
$$\alpha = \text{smoothing constant}$$
$$e_{t-1} = A_{t-1} - F_{t-1}, \text{forecasting error in period } t - 1$$

The value of the smoothing constant, α, selected is arbitrary but must range between 0 and 1. The trial-and-error process of selecting α will depend on how sensitive the model is to random fluctuations. The impact of α and random fluctuation can be seen more illustratively from the initial SES equation:

$$F_t = F_{t-1} + \alpha (A_{t-1} - F_{t-1})$$

Any new forecast for period t, F_t, is simply the value of the earlier forecast period, F_{t-1}, plus some fraction of the earlier period forecast error, $\alpha (A_{t-1} - F_{t-1})$. The size of this correction fraction is determined by the value of α selected: The larger the α-values, the more rapid the adjustment. *Time series with little random variation would be best modeled by using larger smoothing constants. However, when the fluctuation of the data is primarily random, the manager does not want the forecast to react too quickly, and thus to overreact; smaller α-values would be more appropriate.* Ultimately, the manager should be aware that, if values of α larger than .5 are required to gain the level of predictive accuracy desired, it is possible that a better forecasting model exists (Baker and Kropp, 1985, p. 369).

Using the data of Table 11-3, let's forecast ticket sales for period 2 by arbitrarily selecting an α-value of .1 and assuming that the first-period forecast value, F_1, is equal to the actual sales observed during that same time period, A_1. That is, $F_1 = A_1 = 70,000$. The forecast sales for period 2 is, then,

$$F_2 = F_1 + \alpha (A_1 - F_1)$$
$$= 70,000 + (.10)(70,000 - 70,000)$$
$$= 70,000 + 0$$
$$= 70,000 \text{ passengers}$$

Now let's proceed by forecasting the sales for period 3:

$$F_3 = F_2 + \alpha(A_2 - F_2)$$
$$= 70,000 + (.10)(60,000 - 70,000)$$
$$= 70,000 + -1,000$$
$$= 69,000 \text{ passengers}$$

The impact of α-values of .1, .5, and .9 on the passenger ticket sales forecast for Sun Belt Airlines assuming a first-period ticket-sales forecast of 70,000 is presented in Table 11-7 and in Figure 11-7. A plot of the MSE reveals that the optimal smoothing-constant value for minimizing error occurs at approximately $\alpha = 0.4$ (Figure 11-8). We

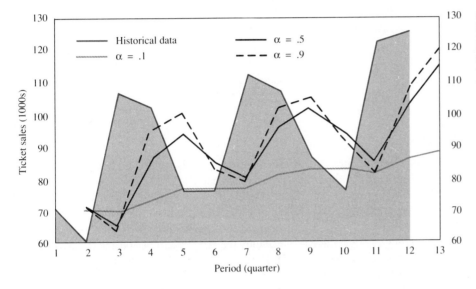

FIGURE 11-7

Forecasts Using Simple Exponential Smoothing for Sun Belt Airlines Ticket Sales Data

TABLE 11-7

Number of Passenger Tickets Sold for Sun Belt Airlines Route From New York City (La Guardia and JFK Airports) to Miami Beach, Using Simple Exponential Smoothing

Period	Actual Ticket Sales	Forecast Ticket Sales $\alpha = .1$	Error	$\alpha = .5$	Error	$\alpha = .9$	Error
1	70,000	—	—	—	—	—	—
2	60,000	70,000	10,000	70,000	10,000	70,000	10,000
3	105,000	69,000	−36,000	65,000	−40,000	63,000	−42,000
4	100,000	72,600	−27,400	85,000	−15,000	92,400	−7,600
5	75,000	75,340	340	92,500	17,500	97,720	22,720
6	75,000	75,306	306	83,750	8,750	81,816	6,816
7	110,000	75,275	−34,725	79,375	−30,625	77,045	−32,955
8	105,000	78,748	−26,252	94,688	−10,313	100,113	−4,887
9	85,000	81,373	3,627	99,844	14,844	103,534	18,534
10	75,000	81,736	6,736	92,422	17,422	90,560	15,560
11	120,000	81,062	−38,938	83,711	−36,289	79,668	−40,332
12	125,000	84,956	−40,044	101,855	−23,145	107,900	−17,100
13	—	88,960	—	113,428	—	119,870	—
$\alpha =$		.1		.5		.9	
MAD $=$		20,397		20,397		18,526	
MSE $=$			6.56E08		5.21E08		5.85E08
Bias $=$			−17,237		−7,396		−5,461

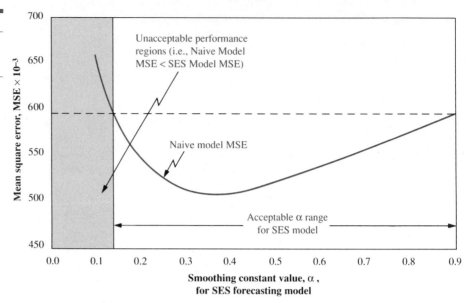

can also see from Figure 11-8 that SES forecast models with a smoothing constant of at least .15 are more accurate than is the naive model.

SES is considered to be an effective forecasting method over a wide variety of time-series problem settings. It is particularly attractive if the time series includes a significant random-error component. Further, SES models require fewer historical data than do the moving-average models, since only the last forecast period and α are needed to initiate the projection. However, SES also has a significant shortcoming: It does not respond well to time-series data that include significant, rapid trend component changes. Accordingly, the SES forecasts will be tend to lag behind this type of time series. Now let's look at one of several exponential smoothing methods that is designed to manage time series that include a significant trend component. It is called the Holt method.

Model 4: Holt Trend-Adjusted Exponential Smoothing The various smoothing methods, such as the moving-average and SES methods that we have examined, can be useful in understanding the overall performance of business data only if there is no significant trend component present in the data. In addition, SES methods are limited to short-term forecasting situations—one period into the future. If the manager wishes to extend her knowledge into the mid-range or long-term forecasting, other more elaborate methods that can accommodate trend will need to be employed. There are numerous trend-adjusting exponential-smoothing forecasting models that are available. The one that will be illustrated now is the Holt method.

The Holt method uncovers the trend component, if it exists, and allows the manager to make forecast predictions any number of time periods into the future. The method works by continuously determining the smoothed forecast value, given by

$$F'_{t+1} = \alpha (F'_t + T_t) + (1 - \alpha) A_t$$

as well as the value of the trend component, given by

$$T_{t+1} = \beta T_t + (1 - \beta) (F'_{t+1} - F'_t)$$

where

F'_{t+1} = smoothed forecast value being calculated for time period $t + 1$

F'_t = smoothed forecast value already calculated for time period t

T_{t+1} = trend-component value already calculated for time period t

A_t = actual value of time series for time period t

α = subjectively selected smoothing constant value ($0 < \alpha < 1$)

β = subjectively selected smoothing constant value ($0 < \beta < 1$)

Smoothed forecast values and trend-component values are calculated for the n time periods for which actual data exist (in the case of Sun Belt Airlines, there are 12 time periods of empirical data). From that point on, the Holt method forecasts into the future for as many time periods as desired, using the following relationship:

$$F_{n+j} = F'_n + jT_n$$

where

F_{n+j} = forecast value being calculated for j time periods into the future

F'_n = smoothed forecast value already calculated for last time period n

T_n = trend-component value already calculated for last time period n

j = number of time periods into the future

n = number of time periods during which there is a comparison between actual data and a corresponding forecast value

To initiate the calculations in the Holt method, we must select values for the smoothing constants, α and β, and assume that $F'_2 = A_2$ and $T_2 = Y_2 - Y_1$. The subsequent values for F'_{t+1} and T'_{t+1} for the remaining time periods of interest ($t+1=3, 4, , \ldots, n$) can then be calculated. Let's use the Sun Belt Airlines example to illustrate this intricate procedure.

Step 1. First, assume that the smoothed forecast value for period 2 is given by

$$F'_2 = A_2 = 60,000$$

Step 2. Next, let the trend component for that time period be equal to the difference between the actual values for periods 2 and 1.

$$T_2 = A_2 - A_1 = 60,000 - 70,000 = -10,000$$

Step 3. Arbitrarily choose values for α and β. If $\alpha = .2$ and $\beta = .1$, the general forecast equations for the smoothed forecast value, F'_{t+1}, and the trend value, T'_{t+1}, can be formulated.

Step 4. Calculate the smoothed forecast value:

$$F'_{t+1} = .2 (F'_t + T_t) + .8 A_t$$

Step 5. Calculate the trend value:

$$T'_{t+1} = .1 T_t + .9 (F'_{t+1} - F'_t)$$

Let's calculate F'_{t+1} and T'_{t+1} for the third quarter ($t + 1 = 3$) in 1984 to make sure that Holt procedure is clear:

$$F'_3 = .2(F'_2 + T_2) + .8 A_3$$
$$= (.2)(60,000 - 10,000) + (.8)(105,000)$$
$$= 10,000 + 84,000$$
$$= 94,000$$

The value for the trend component in the same time period is

$$T_3 = .1 T_2 + .9(F'_3 - F'_2)$$
$$= (.1)(-10,000) + (.9)(94,000 - 60,000)$$
$$= -1,000 + 30,600$$
$$= 29,600$$

The smoothed forecast values and the trend-component values for the 12 time periods of data are shown in Table 11-8. The future forecast values are all calculated using the smoothed forecast value and trend value of the last time period of actual data ($n = 12$):

$$F_{12+j} = F'_{12} + j T_{12}$$
$$= 127,088 + 20,041 j$$

So, for three quarters into the future, F_{15},

$$F_{15} = 127,088 + (20,041)(3) = 187,212$$

TABLE 11-8

Holt Trend Adjusted Exponential Smoothing Forecast for Sun Belt Airlines Ticket Sales for Route from New York City to Miami Beach

Period	Actual Ticket Sales	Smoothed Forecast	Trend	Forecast	Error
1	70,000				
2	60,000	60,000	−10,000		0
3	105,000	94,000	29,600		11,000
4	100,000	104,720	12,608		−4,720
5	75,000	83,466	−17,868		−8,466
6	75,000	73,119	−11,098		1,881
7	110,000	100,404	23,446		9,596
8	105,000	108,770	9,874		−3,770
9	85,000	91,729	−14,350		−6,729
10	75,000	75,476	−16,603		−476
11	120,000	107,883	27,560		12,117
12	125,000	127,088	20,041		−2,088
13				147,130	
14				167,171	
15				187,212	
16				207,254	

Model = Holt TAES
MSE = 4.70E07
MAD = 5341
Bias = 759
$\alpha = .2, \beta = .1$

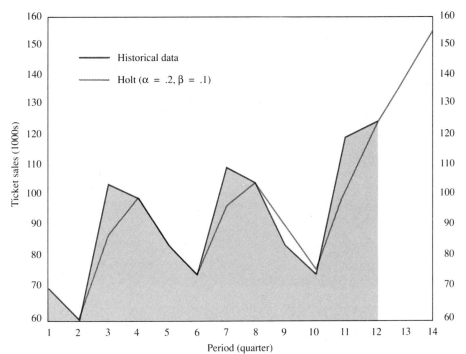

Notice that, unlike the previous methods examined, the Holt forecast values for future time periods change instead of remaining constant. An illustration of these data is shown in Figure 11-9.

Model 5: Multiplicative Decomposition of Linear Trend and Seasonal Component

The overall variation of a specific time series can be described by the four components of variation introduced at the beginning of Section 11.4. If the manager can break down the total variation of each time-series forecast into these four different components, the forecast accuracy can often be improved.

There are numerous versions of the linear time-series model. Some of them view the four components of variation as additive; other versions suggest that the model is multiplicative. Further, the number of components isolated by different decomposition models varies. This section will present a simple, two-component multiplicative model that adjusts for trend and seasonal variations while assuming that cyclic and random variation are negligible. The model follows the relationship

$$F_t = T_t \times S_t$$

where

F_t = forecast associated with time period t

T_t = trend component of time period t

S_t = seasonal component of time period t

Linear Trend Isolation: Least Squares Regression

It is always valuable for the manager to understand the general, long-term direction—or *trend*—of the time series. One of the techniques used to isolate this effect is called *trend projection*. Although

"So, Higgens, the severity of our third-quarter dip comes as a surprise to you, too! . . ."

there are several types of trend projection, this chapter will only examine those time series that have linear or near-linear performance.

Trend projection borrows the least squares regression method from statistics for the purpose of attempting to fit a straight line to a set of time series data. The independent variable is time, and the dependent variable is the measure being forecast. For the Sun Belt Airlines example, the dependent variable is the volume of ticket sales during each quarter. The simple regression equation for forecasting ticket sales during any time period, t, is

$$\hat{Y} = a + bX$$

where

$\hat{Y}$ = forecast value of ticket sales based upon a particular time period, X

a = the Y-axis intercept (when $X=0$)

b = the slope of the regression line; that is, the rate of change in ticket sales per quarter, $\Delta Y/\Delta X$

The equations for solving these values are

$$b = \frac{\sum XY - n\bar{X}\bar{Y}}{\sum X^2 - n\bar{X}^2}$$

and

$$a = \bar{Y} - b\bar{X}$$

To calculate these and subsequent equations, we must organize the sample data in a format similar to that used in Table 11-9. The tabular calculations can be made easier if the

---

TABLE 11-9

Computational Table for Sun Belt Airlines Simple Regression of Time Period (X) and Ticket Sales (Y)

X	Y	XY	X^2	Y^2
1	70	70	1	4900
2	60	120	4	3600
3	105	315	9	11,025
4	100	400	16	10,000
5	75	375	25	5625
6	75	450	36	5625
7	110	770	49	12,100
8	105	840	64	11,025
9	85	765	81	7225
10	75	750	100	5625
11	120	1320	121	14,400
12	125	1500	144	15,625
78	1105	7675	650	106,775

$$\bar{X} = \frac{\sum X}{n} = \frac{78}{12} = 6.50$$

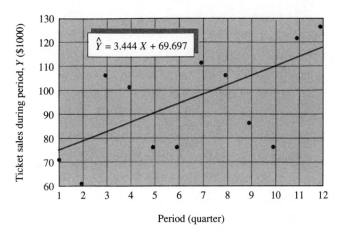

Y-data (volume of ticket sales) are presented in multiples of 1000. The regression equation can now be readily calculated. First, calculate the slope, *b*:

$$b = \frac{\sum XY - n\overline{X}\overline{Y}}{\sum X^2 - n\overline{X}^2}$$

$$= \frac{7675 - (12)(6.5)(92.10)}{650 - (12)(6.5)^2}$$

$$= 3.444$$

Next, we find the *Y*-intercept, *a*:

$$a = \overline{Y} - b\overline{X}$$

$$= 92.10 - (3.444)(6.5)$$

$$= 69.697$$

The single equation that best fits the sample data is, then,[3]

$$\hat{Y} = 3.444 X + 69.697$$

as is illustrated in Figure 11-10. Sun Belt may now use this equation to estimate the most likely level of ticket sales it will generate, *Y*, for a specific time period, *X*. So, for time period 10, the volume of ticket sales should be about 104,000. That is,

$$\hat{Y} = 3.444 (10) + 69.697$$

$$= 34.44 + 69.697$$

$$= 104.137$$

or

$$\hat{Y} = 104{,}137 \text{ tickets}$$

Sun Belt realizes that this value is, of course, just an estimate. The 12 quarters representing Sun Belt's database of ticket sales are far from a perfect fit (Figure 11-10). Be-

---

[3]Notice that the order of the two terms in the prediction equation have been flip-flopped. Reversing the order of the constant and variable terms is not uncommon *after* the values for the model have been developed. Nevertheless, the interpretation of the equation, regardless of the presentation order of the terms, remains unchanged.

cause of this, Sun Belt management wants to know by how much this specific point estimate, Y, might vary. The measure of variability about any point estimate (and the regression line) is called the *standard error of the estimate*, s_e, and is given by

$$s_e = \sqrt{\frac{\sum Y^2 - a \sum Y - b \sum XY}{n-2}}$$

$$= \sqrt{\frac{106.775 - (69.697)(1105) - (3.444)(7675)}{10}}$$

$$= 18.239$$

Now Sun Belt can predict the most probable, best (highest), and worst (lowest) ticket sales volumes that are likely to be generated from a specific advertising investment level by using the following small sample relationship ($n < 30$ quarters) to establish the prediction interval limits, PIL, about the regression line,

$$\text{PIL} = \hat{Y} \pm t_e s_e$$

where

t_e = t-value associated with the standard error of the estimate, which is a function of the desired confidence level and sample size (degrees of freedom)

$\quad = t_{(1-\text{CL})/2, \, df=n-2}$

s_e = standard error

So, a 95 percent level of confidence (CL = .95) and a sample size of 12 (representing the 12 time periods) gives $t_{(1-\text{CL})/2, \, df=n-2} = 2.228$. The variability about $\hat{Y}$ is, then,

$$\text{PIL} = 104.14 \pm t_{.025, 10} \, s_e$$

$$= 104.14 \pm (2.228)(18.24)$$

$$= 104.14 \pm 40.65$$

or

$$63,490 \le \text{PIL} \le 144,790$$

Sun Belt Airlines can be 95 percent certain that a \$100,000 advertising expenditure will help it to sell between a low of 63,490 and a high of 144,790 passenger tickets along the route from New York City to Miami Beach.

Finally, the airlines may also wish to know the sample *degree of association*, $\hat{r}^2$, between the period (X) and ticket sales (Y). That is, how much of the variation in sales is explained by its relationship with the independent variable of ticket sales? This value may be calculated from

$$\hat{r}^2 = \frac{a \sum Y + b \sum XY - n\bar{Y}^2}{\sum Y^2 - n\bar{Y}^2}$$

$$= \frac{(69.697)(1105) + (3.444)(22,785) - (12)(92.10)^2}{106,775 - (12)(92.10)^2}$$

$$= .338$$

It is also possible to calculate the p-value of this relationship from the following statistical test ratio:

$$t_b = \frac{b}{s_b}$$

where

b = regression line slope

s_b = standard error of the regression coefficient (slope)

t_b = t-ratio test statistic that determines whether the value of the slope, b, varies significantly from zero; since this condition would suggest no relationship, a "good" condition will exist when the t-value is large (small p-value)

The standard error of the regression coefficient, s_b, is given by

$$s_b = \frac{s_e}{\sqrt{\sum X^2 - n\bar{X}^2}}$$

This measurement indicates the variability of the slope about its point estimate value, b. The t-value associated with the slope indicates the strength of the relationship between the X and Y variables. In short, the t-value will ultimately indicate whether this relationship is real (statistically significant) or whether Y is not really associated with X. If this latter instance is true, the best predictor of sales would be not the time period, X, but rather the mean of the Y data, $\hat{Y}$. Let's solve for the standard error of the regression coefficient, s_b:

$$s_b = \frac{18.239}{\sqrt{6.50 - (12)(6.50)^2}}$$

$$= 1.525$$

The t-value of the slope, t_b, is

$$t_b = \frac{b}{s_b}$$

$$= \frac{3.444}{1.525} = 2.258$$

We find the p-value by simply calculating the degrees of freedom associated with the sample size of the Sun Belt Airlines database of $n = 12$ periods. That is, $df = n - 2 = 10$. This specific value of df and the t-value just calculated will give us a p-value of between .025 and .05 (using t-distribution tables from any statistics book). The trend analysis microcomputer solution using *Statview 512+* is shown in Table 11-10. The MSE value of the trend projection model, 277.23, suggests considerably higher accuracy than that of the naive model for this particular application.[4]

Seasonal Component Isolation   The previous component isolation method helps the manager to determine what part of the forecast variation is attributable to the trend.

---

[4]The sales data was entered in multiples of $1000. Therefore, the 277.23 mean square of the error is actually "read" as MSE = 277.23E06 or 2.77E08.

Simple Regression X$_1$: QUARTER   Y$_1$: SALES (1000)

Beta Coefficient Table

DF:	R:	R-squared:	Std. Error:	MSE
10	.581	.338	18.239	277.23

Parameter:	Value:	Std. Err.:	Std. Value:	t-Value:	Probability:
INTERCEPT	69.697				
SLOPE	3.444	1.525	.581	2.258	.0475

QUARTER X$_1$	SALES(10^3) Y$_1$	SALES(10^3) Pred. Y$_1$
1	70	73.141
2	60	76.585
3	105	80.029
4	100	83.473
5	75	86.917
6	75	90.361
7	110	93.805
8	105	97.249
9	85	100.693
10	75	104.138
11	120	107.582
12	125	111.026

Reference: *StatView 512+,* ©1986
BrainPower, Inc., Calabasas, CA 91302.

However, the trend line is typically above the data during the first two quarters of each year, and is below those of the last two quarters for the Sun Belt Airlines example. This variational pattern of oscillation about the trend line probably can be attributed to the seasonal effects in the Sun Belt Airlines data: It is no secret that heavy vacation and holiday travel are traditionally associated with the third and fourth quarters of each year. A method that allows the manager to determine the amount of seasonality associated with each quarter is called the *ratio-to-trend method* or *seasonal index*.

The seasonal component for any period, S_t, is given by

$$S_t = \frac{A_t}{\hat{Y}_t}$$

where

S_t = seasonal component for time period t

A_t = actual ticket sales for time period t

$\hat{Y}_t$ = computed value for trend for time period t

For example, the seasonal component for period 3 is

$$\hat{Y}_3 = 3.444X + 69.697$$
$$= (3.444)(3) + 69.697$$
$$= 80.029$$

or

$$\hat{Y}_3 = 80{,}029 \text{ tickets sold}$$

Of course, the actual volume of ticket sales was 105,000. The seasonal index for the third period is, then,

$$S_3 = \frac{A_3}{\hat{Y}_3}$$

$$= \frac{105{,}000}{80{,}029} = 1.312$$

The actual volume of ticket sales in period 3 was over 131 percent of the expected volume based on the linear-trend model. The seasonal components for the 12 periods of ticket sales is given in Table 11-11. Now take the seasonal component values that have been calculated for each of the 12 periods and group them on the basis of quarter. For each of these four quarters, calculate the simple average. The mean seasonal component value for each quarter, S_q is called the *seasonal index*. So, the relationship between the seasonal index of a particular quarter and the different seasonal components (number of years) of data for that quarter is

$$S_q = \frac{\sum_{t=q}^{q+4(n-1)} S_{t(q)}}{N} \qquad \text{for each } q \, (q = 1, 2, 3, 4)$$

where

$\quad S_q$ = mean seasonal index for quarter q

$\quad S_{t(q)}$ = seasonal index component of quarter q during time period t

$\quad n$ = year number associated with quarter q (e.g., $n=1$ for $q=1,2,3,4$; $n=2$ for $q=5,6,7,8$; and so on)

$\quad N$ = total number of years of data (3 years)

TABLE 11-11

Seasonal Component Data by Period for Sun Belt Airlines Ticket Sales Example

Period	Quarter	Forecast Actual	Trend	Seasonal Index
1	1	70	73.141	.957
2	2	60	76.585	.783
3	3	105	80.029	1.312
4	4	100	83.473	1.198
5	1	75	86.917	.863
6	2	75	90.361	.830
7	3	110	93.805	1.173
8	4	105	97.249	1.080
9	1	85	100.693	.844
10	2	75	104.138	.720
11	3	120	107.582	1.115
12	4	125	111.026	1.126

For example, the seasonal index of the first quarter, S_1, is

$$S_1 = \frac{S_{1(1)} + S_{5(1)} + S_{9(1)}}{3}$$

$$= \frac{.957 + .863 + .844}{3}$$

$$= .888$$

The calculations for all 12 periods are shown in Table 11-12. The trend and seasonal variation have now been isolated, and the manager is ready to forecast ticket sales for any period in the future. The process simply consists of multiplying the trend value for the period of interest, Y_t, by the mean quarterly seasonal index value, S_q, to obtain the forecast value in the period of interest. That is,

$$F_t = \hat{Y}_t \times S_q$$

For example, we can find the adjusted forecast value for period 6 by calculating the trend value for that period, Y_6, that is equal to 90.361 (Table 11-10). Since period 6 corresponds to a second-quarter forecast, the seasonal index value, S_2, is .778 (Table 11-12). The forecast value for period 6 is

$$F_6 = \hat{Y}_6 \times S_2$$

$$= (90.361)(.778)$$

$$= 70.301$$

Let's try another forecast for a high-demand quarter, say period 11. The forecast for this period (third quarter) is

$$F_{11} = \hat{Y}_{11} \times S_3$$

$$= (107.582)(1.200)$$

$$= 129.098$$

However, the purpose of any time-series model is to forecast the future. So, suppose you wished to know the ticket-sales demand for time period 13 (first quarter, 1987). The trend value would be

$$\hat{Y}_3 = 3.444X + 69.697$$

$$= (3.444)(13) + 69.697$$

$$= 114.469$$

TABLE 11-12

Seasonal Index by Quarters for Sun Belt Airlines Ticket Sales Example

	Quarter			
Year	*1*	*2*	*3*	*4*
1984	.957	.783	1.312	1.198
1985	.863	.830	1.173	1.080
1986	.844	.720	1.115	1.126
Totals	2.664	2.333	3.600	3.404
Seasonal Index, $S_{t(q)}$	.888	.778	1.200	1.135

Since the first-quarter seasonal index is .888, the forecast for period 13 is

$$F_{13} = \hat{Y}_{13} \times S_1$$
$$= (114.469)(.888)$$
$$= 101.648$$

or

$$F_{13} = 101,648 \text{ tickets}$$

We can see the dramatic improvement in forecast accuracy that we gain by using both the trend and the seasonal indices when we compare the forecast with the actual data (Table 11-13 and Figure 11-11). After accounting for both trend and seasonal compo-

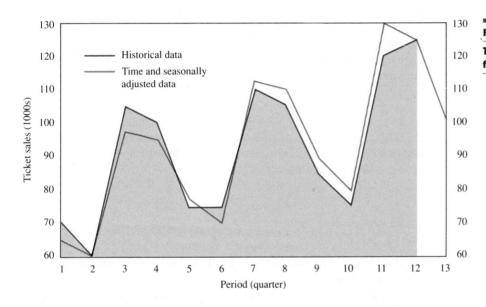

FIGURE 11-11

Trend and Seasonally Adjusted Forecast for Sun Belt Airlines Ticket Sales Data

TABLE 11-13

Trend and Seasonally Adjusted Data for Sun Belt Airlines Ticket Sales Example

Period	Quarter	Actual	Forecast $Y_t \times S_q$	Error, e
1	1	70	64.949	5.051
2	2	60	59.583	.417
3	3	105	96.035	8.965
4	4	100	94.742	5.258
5	1	75	77.182	2.182
6	2	75	70.301	4.699
7	3	110	112.566	2.556
8	4	105	110.378	5.378
9	1	85	89.415	4.415
10	2	75	81.019	6.019
11	3	120	129.098	9.098
12	4	125	126.015	1.015
13	1	—	101.648	

Model = Trend-Seasonal
MSE = 2.80E07
MAD = 4.59E03
Bias = −523

nents, the MSE value from this model dramatically decreases to 27.964: the error component from trend component isolation is cut by a factor of almost 10.[5]

Model 6: Forecast Model Averaging　It is obvious by now that different forecast models generally will provide different forecasts. However, each individual forecast may provide the manager with useful and unique information not available from any other model. Some forecasters therefore *aggregate* results of different forecast models (Chambers, et al., 1971; Plossl, 1973; Makridakis and Winkler, 1983; Bates and Granger, 1969; Koten, 1981; Newbold and Granger, 1974).

The typical averaging method begins with the somewhat arbitrary selection of a number of different forecast models (between two to 16 models have been used for the averaging set).[6]

Forecasts are made regarding a specific problem using the average of the individual model results. *The aggregate results have shown that the accuracy of the combination is typically superior to that of any of the individual models!* Further, this accuracy increases as the number of models used in the averaging set is increased. Of course, the accuracy of combined forecasts depends on both the number of models in the average and the specific models selected. Even the variability (error measurement) associated with the choice of methods, as measured by the MAPE, is reduced as more models are included.[7] The conclusion of this body of forecast model research has been that, if a single satisfactory model cannot be found, it is safer and far more accurate to average the results of a number of forecast models—even those that were individually unacceptable—than to select a single weak model.

11.6　QUANTITATIVE FORECASTING METHODS: CAUSAL

In the previous section, we examined five models that attempted to explain the ticket sales of Sun Belt Airlines over time. *Causal forecasting* methods explore the possible relationship between variables—other than time—to see whether a significant association exists. Although the connection of ticket sales to time is extremely important, there was never any suggestion that merely the passage of time *caused* ticket sales. However, there is a possibility that factors, other than time, may be closely *correlated* with the volume of ticket sales for Sun Belt Airlines. In fact, Sun Belt's managers believe that there is a connection between the amount of its media advertising in the New York City and Miami regions and the subsequent ticket sales for that route: Larger advertising expenditures appear to coincide closely with higher ticket sales within the same time frame. The causal models that will be studied in this section will include are: (1) simple linear regression, and (2) multiple regression.

Model 7: Simple Linear Regression　Even though advertising may not cause the sale of tickets, it is at least an important prerequisite to ticket sales because it makes potential customers aware of the services Sun Belt offers on this particular flight route (frequency of flights, schedule, competitive prices, etc.). Table 11-14 provides infor-

TABLE 11-14

Advertising Costs (X) and Ticket Sales (Y) Data for Sun Belt Airlines Example

Period	Advertising Costs	Ticket Sales
1	50	70
2	60	60
3	75	105
4	75	100
5	105	75
6	100	75
7	100	110
8	105	105
9	125	85
10	125	75
11	140	120
12	150	125

[5]For the same reason as in the trend projection model, the MSE = 27.964E06 or .280E08.

[6]The specific combination of forecast models to include is influenced by the strengths and weaknesses of each model. The thoughtful matching of two or more complimentary techniques can offset the limitations of one model with the strengths of the other (Georgoff and Murdick, 1986).

[7]The MAPE was used instead of the MSE or MAD to compare model accuracy across the different magnitude measurements of variables being forecast.

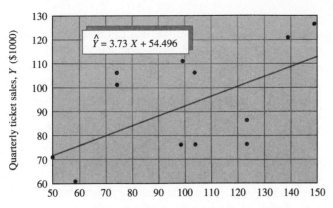

mation regarding the possible association between ticket-sales volume and advertising expenditures. After examining these data, Sun Belt decides to investigate its assumptions by incorporating the least squares regression model (introduced in the trend-projection section) to determine what relationship, if any, exists between ticket sales, *Y*, and advertising costs, *X*. *Note that the least-squares model and simple regression are identical*: only the purpose of the application differs. Simple regression models are not limited to an independent variable of time. Any two variables that are suspected of being associated in some way may be used.

Sun Belt calculates the simple regression equation for estimating ticket sales, *Y*, on the basis of advertising costs, *X*, as

$$\hat{Y} = .373\,X + 54.496$$

where advertising costs is given in $1000 multiples, and *Y* is measured in 1000s of tickets sold (Figure 11-12). Sun Belt may now use this equation to estimate the most likely revenue it will generate, $\hat{Y}$, for a specific advertising expenditure, *X*. So, if it spends $100,000 on advertising during a particular period (and conducts its business with the same effort), the sales volume should be about 92,000 tickets. That is,

$$\hat{Y} = (.373)(100) + 54.496$$
$$= 91.80$$

Sun Belt managers realize that this value is, of course, just an estimate. They wish to know how variable the return on their advertising investment might be, so they decide to solve for the standard error of the estimate, s_e.

$$s_e = \sqrt{\frac{106,775 - (54.496)(1105) - (.373)(115,425)}{10}}$$
$$= 18.789$$

At the 95 percent level of confidence, the prediction interval limit established, PIL, about $\hat{Y}$ is

$$\text{PIL} = 91.80 \pm (2.228)(18.79)$$
$$= 91.80 \pm 41.86$$

or

$$49,940 \leq \text{PIL} \leq 133,660$$

So, the airlines can be 95 percent certain that a $100,000 advertising expenditure will generate revenues between 49,940 and 133,660 ticket sales.

Almost the entire Sun Belt management team was quite pleased with the findings, except for one person. She suggested that, although they may have established a useful association between ticket sales and advertising expenditures, she is not comfortable with the results. She was worried that this relationship is spurious, because she believed that it is normal for both sales and advertising to grow as a business matures. In addition, she suspected that there might still be other independent variables that could help to refine the prediction ability of this regression model. After all, that sales will be somewhere between 49,940 and 133,660 is a prediction far too crude to be of planning value.

To support her suspicions, the manager decided to calculate the sample coefficient of determination, $\hat{r}^2$—something that the rest of the team had overlooked. She found that the proportion of change in ticket sales that was explained by the advertising expenditures was less than three-tenths! That is,

$$\hat{r}^2 = .297$$

Further, just to see whether the model findings were statistically significant, the manager calculated the *p*-value—the probability that the relationship is *not* real, but, rather, was accidental or random—by using exactly the same technique as that in the trend analysis model. First, she found the standard error of the regression coefficient or slope, s_b:

$$s_b = .181$$

Next, she calculated the *t*-value of the slope, t_b, from the ratio of the slope constant, b, and the s_b value just found:

$$t_b = \frac{b}{s_b}$$

$$= \frac{.373}{.181}$$

$$= 2.056$$

Finally, she determined the *p*-value, for *df* = 10:

$$.05 < p\text{-val} < .10$$

The simple regression model microcomputer solution using *Statview 512+* is shown in Table 11-15. In spite of these statistically impressive findings, however, the dissenting manager could reconcile the large chunk of the variability in Y that remained a mystery. She was convinced that the identification of *additional* relevant variables could help to improve dramatically the accuracy of the prediction model. The next section explores the forecasting method used to develop regression models in which there are two or more independent variables.

Model 8: Multiple Regression After considerable thought, the Sun Belt managers agree to explore the argument for additional relevant variables that could help to improve the prediction accuracy of their original simple regression model. They decide that, in addition to advertising expenditures, the average, one-way coach fare during each of the 12 time periods may be a valuable independent variable to include. So, these data are collected, and the second independent variable is added to the relationship

Simple Regression X_1: ADV.COSTS (\$1000) Y_1: SALES (1000)

Beta Coefficient Table

DF:	R:	R-squared:	Std. Error:	MSE
10	.545	.297	18.789	294.190

Parameter:	Value:	Std. Err.:	Std. Value:	t-Value:	Probability:
INTERCEPT	54.496				
SLOPE	.373	.181	.545	2.056	.0668

(Table 11-16). The Sun Belt managers must now use a multiple regression model to help predict the volume of ticket sales, Y, as a function of both advertising costs, X_1, and mean ticket price, X_2. The general estimation equation for the *multiple regression model* is given by the plane

$$\hat{Y} = A + b_1 X_1 + b_2 X_2 + \cdots + b_k X_k$$

where

$$\hat{Y} = \text{value of the dependent variable being forecast}$$

$$a = Y \text{ intercept when all independent variables are zero}$$

$$X_1, X_2, \ldots, X_k = \text{values of independent variables}$$

$$b_1, b_2, b_k = \text{regression coefficients associated with independent variables (the change in } Y \text{ corresponding to a one-unit change in a specific } X_i \text{ independent variable when all other independent variables are held constant)}$$

TABLE 11-16

Data on Ticket Sales, Advertising-Costs, and Mean Ticket Price for Sun Belt Airlines Example

Period	Sales Volume (thousands)	Advertising Costs (\$, thousands)	Mean Ticket Price (\$, hundreds)
1	70	50	1.20
2	60	60	1.40
3	105	75	1.00
4	100	75	1.00
5	75	105	1.00
6	75	100	1.10
7	110	100	.90
8	105	105	.90
9	85	125	1.00
10	75	125	1.00
11	120	140	.80
12	125	150	.80

To solve the regression equation, we must solve the following three equations simultaneously:

$$\sum Y = na + b_1 \sum X_1 + b_2 \sum X_2$$
$$\sum X_1 Y = a \sum X_1 + b_1 \sum X_1^2 + b_2 \sum X_1 X_2$$
$$\sum X_2 Y = a \sum X_2 + b_1 \sum X_1 X_2 + b_2 \sum X_2^2$$

Although it is possible to solve a reasonably small multiple regression problem manually, it is far more sensible to use any one of a number of inexpensive and easy-to-run microcomputer statistical software packages. The multiple regression computer solution printout of these data, using the *Statview 512+* microcomputer package, is illustrated in Table 11-17. We construct the regression plane by using the *parameter* column in the top section of Table 11-17. These values are intercept = 256.688, and regression coefficients $b_1 = -.215$ (advertising expenditures), and $b_2 = -141.706$ (mean ticket price). The regression plane equation is

$$\hat{Y} = 256.688 - .215 X_1 - 141.706 X_2$$

where Y is measured in thousands of tickets sold, X_1 in thousands of advertising dollars spent, and X_2 in hundreds of dollars per ticket. Note that the coefficient of multiple determination, R^2, is .793. Thus, the independent variables explain about 79 percent of the behavior in the regression plane, whereas approximately 21 percent of this performance remains unaccounted for (the addition of the second independent variable, mean ticket price, X_2, increased the original simple regression coefficient of determination, $\hat{r}^2$, from 30 to 79 percent!). The estimated volume of ticket sales can be calculated easily for specific amounts of X_1 and X_2. So, if the advertising costs and mean ticket price were 100,000 and 100, respectively, then the number of tickets sold for that time period would be, approximately, 93,000. That is,

$$\hat{Y} = 256.688 - (.215)(100) - (141.706)(1.00)$$
$$= 93.48$$

or

$$\hat{Y} = 93,480$$

The "Std. Error" term in the middle part of Table 11-17 represents the root mean square error, or the *standard error of the estimate*, for the regression plane, s_e. The s_e value represents the scatter of the sample data about the regression plane, just as the standard error of the estimate provided the measure of variability about the regression line in simple regression. The root MSE is given by

$$s_e = \sqrt{\frac{\sum (Y - \hat{Y})}{n - k - 1}}$$

Notice that the s_e value of 10.738 represents about a 45 percent reduction of the earlier standard error measurements for the simple regression models presented in the last two sections. For a 95 percent level of confidence, the prediction interval limits, PIL, of the regression plane are described by

$$\text{PIL} = \hat{Y} \pm t_{(1 - CL)/2, df} s_e \qquad \text{for } df = n - k - 1$$

TABLE 11-17

StatView 512 + **Multiple Regression Computer Output for Sun Belt Airlines Example***

Source: Yi-Long Chang and Robert Sullivan, *QSB*, Version 3. Englewood Cliffs, NJ: Prentice-Hall, 1988.

Multiple Regression Y$_1$: SALES (1000)   2X variables

Beta Coefficient Table

DF:	R:	R-squared:	Std. Error:	MSE
9	.891	.793	10.738	86.485

Parameter:	Value:	Std. Err.:	Std. Value:	t-Value:	Probability:
INTERCEPT	256.688				
ADV. COSTS	-.215	.164	-.315	1.317	.2203
MEAN TIX COST	-141.706	30.48	-1.112	4.649	.0012

TABLE 11-17a. BETA COEFFICIENTS

Analysis of Variance (ANOVA) Table

Source	DF:	Sum Squares:	Mean Square:	F-test:
NUMERATOR	2	3985.101	1992.551	17.28
DENOMINATOR	9	1037.815	115.313	p=8.0000E-4
TOTAL	12	5022.917		

TABLE 11-17b. ANALYSIS OF VARIANCE TABLE

Multiple Correlation Coefficients

	SALES	ADV. COSTS	MEAN TIX
SALES	1.000	----	----
ADV. COSTS	.545	1.000	----
MEAN TIX	-.868	-.774	1.000

TABLE 11-17c. MULTIPLE CORRELATION MATRIX

where n is the number of sets of measures, and k is the number of independent variables used in the model.[8]

The prediction interval may now be calculated easily. For $n = 12$ and $k = 2$, the corresponding $t_{(1-CL)/2, df}$ value is 2.262. The prediction interval for a 95 percent level of confidence is, then,

$$Y = 93.48 \pm (2.262)(10.738)$$
$$= 93.48 \pm 24.29$$

or

$$69.19 \leq Y \leq 117.77$$

[8]Note, however, that these prediction intervals are only approximate. The *exact* standard error for the prediction, s_p, is given by

(equation 118)

where X_0 is the specific value of X at which we want to predict the value of Y. This will cause s_p to take on a unique value for each corresponding value of X_0. More specifically, s_p will take on larger values the further the X_0 value is from X, because $(X - X_0)^2$ will be large. On the other hand, the closer X_0 is to X, and the larger n is—say, at least 10—the closer s_p will be to s_e. Generally, it is acceptable to approximate the prediction interval with s_e.

So, the high and low estimate for the number of passenger tickets sold with an investment of $100,000 of advertising and an average ticket price of $100 would be between 69,190 and 117,770 for that time period.

Sun Belt now wants to know whether the regression *as a whole* is significant—that's the bottom line. The analysis of variance (ANOVA) *F*-statistic from the middle of Table 11-17 provides this information. The resulting *F*-statistic value is 17.28, with an accompanying *p*-value equal to .0008. This means that the likelihood of the collective effect of the independent variables being insignificant is only one chance in 1250! The contribution of advertising costs and mean ticket price seems to be highly significant in predicting the dependent variable of ticket sales. A further indication of the accuracy of this model can be seen in the MSE value of 86.485 (less than one-third of the error exhibited by the simple regression model).

The *individual effect* of each independent variable reveals that the *p*-values for advertising costs and mean ticket prices are .2203 and .0012, respectively (Table 11-17, top). Although the mean ticket price appears to be quite significant, the advertising costs *p*-value is far too high to make a similar conclusion. A good manager may want to know why the advertising costs, when correlated in the earlier simple regression model against ticket sales, resulted in a *p*-value of .0668 but jumped to .2203 when the second independent variable was added. The reason is that advertising costs and ticket prices are highly correlated. In fact, the correlation between these two variables is $-.774$. The bottom of Table 11-17 shows the correlation matrix for the multiple regression model. The specific type of problem that results when there is a high degree of association between independent variables is called *multicollinearity*. Although there is no agreed-on standard value, generally speaking, correlation values equal to or greater than .7 are viewed as potential problems (i.e., $|\hat{r}| \geq .7$). Advertising costs are increasing while mean ticket prices are decreasing, and vice versa. One likely explanation is that there is a need to advertise more heavily during periods of lower sales; the average ticket price is also lower during this period. During higher-demand periods, when the airlines can command higher ticket prices, the level of advertising is not as intense. Even though the correlation between independent variables distorts the regression coefficient values, the ability to predict *Y* with precision is not affected: The model provides statistically significant forecasting information and the highest accuracy afforded by any of the forecasting models.

11.7 MICROCOMPUTER APPLICATIONS TO FORECAST PROBLEMS

Microcomputer software packages that offer forecast models are plentiful and are extremely easy to use. Time-series models require the barest amount of information imaginable. Simply type in the name of the forecast model you wish to try (moving average, exponential smoothing, regression, etc.), the number of periods the historical data cover, the duration of the forecast periods you wish to use, the number of periods you wish to forecast, and any model particulars (e.g., smoothing constant values). Causal models require only the identification of dependent and independent variable(s) and their values across the number of time periods of historical data that you wish to forecast.

Microcomputer solutions to two of the forecast models presented in this chapter will be illustrated next. First, a sample of the simple exponential smoothing (SES) model for $\alpha = .5$ will be run for the Sun Belt Airlines data using the Chang and Sullivan microcomputer software, *QSB* (Table 11-18). Next, the input and solution to the simple regression model for the Sun Belt Airlines data using *StatView 512 +* is shown in Table

Source: Yi-Long Chang and Robert Sullivan, QSB, Version 3, Prentice-Hall (1988).

TABLE 11-18

Sample Microcomputer Input and Output of Simple Exponential Smoothing Forecast

Single exponential smoothing for EASTERN AIRLINES   Page: 1

Period	Act. Demand	F(t)	T(t)/W(t)	I(t)	Forecast	Error
1	70.00	70.00				
2	60.00	65.00			70.00	10.00
3	105.00	85.00			65.00	-40.00
4	100.00	92.50			85.00	-15.00
5	75.00	83.75			92.50	17.50
6	75.00	79.38			83.75	87.50
7	110.00	94.69			79.38	-30.63
8	105.00	99.84			94.69	-10.31
9	85.00	92.42			99.84	14.84
10	75.00	83.71			92.42	17.42
11	120.00	101.86			83.71	-36.29
12	125.00	113.43			101.86	-23.14
13					113.43	

MAD = 20.353   MSE = 5.21E08   Bias = -7.90   a = 0.500

TABLE 11-19

Simple Regression Solution of Sun Belt Airlines Advertising Costs versus Ticket Sales Using *StatView*+ Microcomputer Program (95 Percent Confidence Interval Illustrated)

Simple Regression X_1: ADV.COSTS ($1000) Y_1: SALES (1000)

DF:	R:	R-squared:	Adj. R-squared:	Std. Error:
11	.545	.297	.227	18.789

Analysis of Variance Table

Source	DF:	Sum Squares:	Mean Square:	F-test:
REGRESSION	1	1492.632	1492.632	4.228
RESIDUAL	10	3530.285	353.029	p=.0668
TOTAL	11	5022.917		

Residual Information Table

SS[e(i)-e(i-1)]:	e>= 0:	e< 0:	DW test:
6759.722	6	6	1.915

Beta Coefficient Table

Parameter:	Value:	Std. Err.:	Std. Value:	t-Value:	Probability:
INTERCEPT	54.496				
SLOPE	.373	.181	.545	2.056	.0668

Confidence Intervals Table

Parameter:	95% Lower:	95% Upper:	99% Lower:	99% Upper:
MEAN(X,Y)	79.997	104.17	74.892	109.274
SLOPE	-.031	.777	-.202	.947

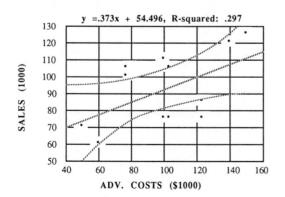

y = .373x + 54.496, R-squared: .297

11-19. The graphic portion of this printout illustrates the 95 percent prediction interval using the exact standard error (notice how the variability of the data is smallest as they approach the mean of the X-data) of the prediction interval, discussed briefly in footnote 8.[9]

11.8 SUMMARY

Even though there are numerous ways to categorize forecast models, the most common arrangement is to view them as either qualitative or quantitative. This chapter was primarily interested in exploring the two families of quantitative forecast models: time series and causal.

There is no simple process for a manager to use in determining the forecast model most likely to be best. However, the accuracy desired from the forecast—in combination with the limited resources available to conduct the forecast—will usually identify at least a few potential candidates. Once the models that are practical to consider for a particular application are tested, error-measurement methods can be used to find the one with the highest accuracy. In addition, it is important to determine whether the model has a bias (tracking error) and to make the necessary, on-the-run accommodating adjustments, if possible.

Finally, combining a number of different forecast models may provide the manager with more accurate results than will any individual model. This approach might be especially attractive if several methods have been tried but have all provided unacceptable levels of forecast accuracy.

[9] In addition, sophisticated statistical data regarding issues not covered in this textbook are also included (e.g., the Durbin–Watson test for autocorrelation/residual analysis).

11.9 EXERCISES

11-1 Apple Computers of Cupertino, California, has experienced meteoric success with their Macintosh series of microcomputers. Although exact sales information is typically kept confidential, in 1987 Apple publicly announced that it had just sold the one-millionth Macintosh. Assume that the sales data (in units of 1000) are shown in Table 11-1.1 represent the approximate history of this innovative microcomputer over its first 24 months of marketing. Determine the following forecast performance characteristics for the naive model:

1. The forecast error, e_t, associated with each period.
2. The mean average deviation, MAD.
3. The mean average percent error, MAPE.
4. The mean square of the error, MSE.
5. The tracking error during each period, δ_n.
6. The bias of the time series.
7. The time-series plot.

| The remainder of problems in this chapter refer to the hypothetical Apple Computer sales data introduced in Exercise 11-1. |

11-2 Calculate a 2-, 4-, and 8-month simple moving average (SMA) for the data.

11-3 Calculate the MSE, bias, and the tracking error, δ_n, for the three forecasts conducted in Exercise 11-2. Provide the following information in light of your findings:

1. Which forecast period gives you the most accurate findings according to MAD, to MAPE, to MSE, to the final tracking error, δ, and to bias?

TABLE 11-1.1

Theoretical Apple Computers Sales Figures for Macintosh Models during First 24 Months of Marketing

Month	Sales Volume (1000)	Month	Sales Volume (1000)	Month	Sales Volume (1000)
1	10	9	35	17	60
2	5	10	40	18	70
3	15	11	25	19	50
4	10	12	45	20	40
5	10	13	25	21	90
6	15	14	30	22	70
7	20	15	60	23	120
8	15	16	40	24	100

2. Which of the three sales projections for the 25-month period?

3. Which of the three SMA forecasts, if any, outperforms the naive model?

4. Illustrate the three SMA time-series forecasts.

11-4 Use a 3-month weighted moving average (WMA) model of 60-30-10 to forecast the 24-month performance of the Apple Computers data. When compared with the naive model,

1. Which model displays greater accuracy with respect to the MSE?

2. Which of the two models has the lowest bias?

3. In general, is there any inconsistency if the answers to parts 1 and 2 are not the same? Explain your answer.

4. Forecast period 25, then plot the entire time series.

11-5 Use the simple exponential smoothing (SES) forecast model to determine the following:

1. The single α-value that provides the minimal MSE (plot your results for three or four values of α).

2. The smoothing constant value, if any, that you must use for the SES model to outperform the naive model, based on MSE.

11-6 Use the Holt model and smoothing constant values of $\alpha = .3$ and $\beta = .2$:

1. Determine the forecast values corresponding to the actual Apple Computer data.

2. Calculate the MAPE and tracking error, and determine whether the model is more accurate and less biased than is the naive model.

3. Generate the twenty-fifth through twenty-eighth period forecast value.

4. Plot the results.

11-7 Assuming that the two-component multiplicative model of trend and season discussed in this chapter is appropriate, isolate the trend component only, and answer the following questions:

1. What is the trend-projection (least squares) equation that allows you to forecast best the sales data, Y, from the period of interest, X?

2. For the period 15, what is the predicted sales forecast? What is the error associated with this period?

3. What measure best describes the variability of the data about the trend projection? What is the value of this measure?

4. Using a prediction interval of 95 percent, what are the upper and lower limits for the forecast of period 15?

5. What percentage of the sales performance is accounted for by the time period?

6. What is the strength of the trend projection model (i.e., the p-value)?

7. Calculate the MSE for this model. Is this model superior to the naive model?

11-8 Isolate the seasonal component of the multiplicative model described in Exercise 11-7. Determine the following pieces of information:

1. Develop a table illustrating the seasonal components for the 24 periods of sales data.

2. Assuming that period 1 corresponds to the first quarter, use the seasonal component information to generate quarterly seasonal indices.

3. Forecast the ticket sales for period 15. What is error associated with this period? Forecast ticket sales for period 30. What is the error associated with this period?

4. Calculate the MSE and bias for the model for combined linear trend and seasonal index.

11-9 Suppose the managers at Apple Computers think that time-series methods are not the best forecasting approach to use. Instead, they suspect that the sales were really associated with the number of new software products arriving in the marketplace. So, they decided to measure the number of different Macintosh software products advertised in some combination of *MacWorld*, *MacUser*, and *Macazine* (i.e., as the number of software products grew, so must their sales have done). They found the data given in Table 11-9.1. Using this new information and the simple regression model, determine Macintosh sales as a function of the number of different software ads placed in the three primary Macintosh monthly magazines mentioned earlier. More specifically, find the following:

1. The simple regression equation that will best forecast sales and number of new ads.

TABLE 11-9.1

Theoretical Apple Computers Sales and Number of Different Software Product Ads for Macintosh during First 24 Months of Marketing

Month	Sales Vol (1000)	No. of Ads	Month	Sales Vol (1000)	No. of Ads	Month	Sales Vol (1000)	No. of Ads
1	10	6	9	35	46	17	60	165
2	5	8	10	40	51	18	70	189
3	15	9	11	25	60	19	50	215
4	10	14	12	45	72	20	40	235
5	10	17	13	25	90	21	90	281
6	15	27	14	30	109	22	70	320
7	20	32	15	60	114	23	120	356
8	15	35	16	40	132	24	100	385

"Well, there's not much here . . ."

COPYRIGHT © 1971 by Gahan Wilson. Reprinted by permission of SIMON & SCHUSTER, INC.

2. For the period 15, the predicted sales forecast, and the error associated with this period.

3. The measure that best describes the variability of the data about the regression line, and the value of this measure.

4. Using a prediction interval of 95 percent, the upper and lower limits for the forecast of period 15.

5. The percentage of the sales performance accounted for by period 15.

6. The strength of the simple regression model in terms of the *p*-value.

7. The MSE for this model. Is this model superior to the naive model? Is it superior to the multiplicative model using linear trends and seasonal components?

11-10 Further thought leads the managers at Apple Computers to believe that not the number of software ads, but also the number of new hardware product ads, related to the sales volume (Table 11-10.1). Use multiple regression techniques and a software package of your choice to answer the following questions:

1. What is the multiple regression plane that can best forecast Macintosh sales?

2. For the period 15, what is the predicted sales forecast? What is the error associated with this period?

3. Has the variability of the multiple regression model been improved with the addition of the second independent variable (i.e., as compared with the simple regression version)? Explain your answer.

4. Using a prediction interval of 95 percent, what are the upper and lower limits for the forecast of period 15?

5. What percentage of the sales performance is accounted for by period 15? Has this value improved over the simple regression model?

6. What is the collective strength of the simple regression model (i.e., *F*-test *p*-value)? Is this value an improvement over the simple regression model?

7. What are the *p*-values associated with the independent variables? Do these values suggest any possible adjustments that Apple might make to their model?

8. Calculate the MSE for this model. Is this model superior to the naive model?

9. Is this model superior to the simple regression model? Explain your answer.

11-11 Average the results from the 8-month, simple moving average (Exercise 11-2) and from the Holt model (Exercise 11-6). Recalculate the MSE and determine whether the combined model represents an improvement over both of the original models.

TABLE 11-10.1

Theoretical Apple Computers Sales (Y) and Number of Different Software (X_1) and Hardware (X_2) Product Ads for Macintosh during First 24 Months of Marketing

Month	Sales Vol (1000)	No. of Ads Soft	No. of Ads Hard	Month	Sales Vol (1000)	No. of Ads Soft	No. of Ads Hard
1	10	6	1	13	25	90	27
2	5	8	1	14	30	109	32
3	15	9	3	15	60	114	38
4	10	14	5	16	40	132	42
5	10	17	5	17	60	165	49
6	15	27	6	18	70	189	55
7	20	32	10	19	50	215	72
8	15	35	11	20	40	235	75
9	35	46	11	21	90	281	78
10	40	51	15	22	70	320	85
11	25	60	19	23	120	356	91
12	45	72	25	24	100	385	106

References

1. Baker, Kenneth R., and Dean H. Kropp. *Management Science: An Introduction to the Use of Decision Models.* New York: Wiley, 1988.

2. Bates, J. M., and C. W. J. Granger. "The Combination of Forecasts." *Operations Research Quarterly* 20 (No. 3: September 1969): 451–468.

3. Box, G. E. P., and G. M. Jenkins. *Time Series Analysis: Forecasting and Control.* Oakland, CA: Holden-Day, 1970.

4. Chambers, John C., Satinder K. Mullick, and Donald D. Smith. "How to Choose the Right Forecasting Technique." *Harvard Business Review* 49 (No. 4: July–August 1971): 57–86.

5. Cocorane, A. Wayne. "The Use of Exponentially Smoothed Transition Matrices to Improve Forecasting of Cash Flows from Accounts Receivable." *Management Science* 24 (No. 7: July 1978): 732–739.

6. Cook, Thomas M., and Robert A. Russell. *Introduction to Management Science*, 3rd ed. Englewood Cliffs, NJ: Prentice-Hall, 1985.

7. Dannenbring, David G., and Martin K. Starr. *Management Science: An Introduction.* New York: McGraw-Hill, 1981.

8. Davis, K. Roscoe, Patrick G. McKeown, and Terry R. Rakes. *Management Science: An Introduction.* Boston: Kent Publishing Company, 1986.

9. Gardner, Everette S., Jr. "Box-Jenkins vs. Multiple Regression: Some Adventures in Forecasting the Demand for Blood Tests." *Interfaces* 9 (No. 4: August 1979): 49–54.

10. Georgoff, David M., and Robert G. Murdick. "Manager's Guide to Forecasting: How to Choose the Best Technique—or Combination of Techniques—to Help Solve Your Particular Forecasting Dilemma." *Harvard Business Review* 64 (No. 1: January–February 1986): 110–120.

11. Helmer, Theodore F. "Forecasting Nurse Staffing Requirements by Intensity-of-Care Level." *Interfaces* 10 (No. 3: June 1980): 50–56.

12. Hertz, David B. "A Forecasting Method for Management of Seasonal-Style Goods Inventories." *Operations Research* 13 (No. ??:(month? 1965): 157–158.

13. Koten, J. "They Say No Two Economists Ever Agree, So Chrysler Tries Averaging Their Opinions." *Wall Street Journal* (November 3, 1981): p. 31.

14. Levin, Richard P., David S. Rubin, and Joel P. Stinson. *Quantitative Approaches to Management*, 6th ed. New York: McGraw-Hill, 1986.

15. Mahmoud, E. "Accuracy in Forecasting." *Journal of Forecasting* 3 (No. 2: April–June 1984): 139–159.

16. Makridakis, Spyros, and Steven C. Wheelwright. *The Handbook of Forecasting: A Manager's Guide.* New York: Wiley, 1982.

17. Makridakis, Spyros, and Robert L. Winkler. "Averages Results." *Management Science* 29 (No. 9: September 1983): 987–996.

18. Millett, Stephen M., and Fred Randles. "Scenarios for Strategic Business Planning: A Case History for Aerospace and Defense Companies." *Interfaces* 16 (No. 6: November–December 1986): 64–72.

19. Newbold, P., and C. W. J. Granger. "Experience with Forecasting Univariate Time Series and the Combination of Forecasts." *Journal of Royal Statistical Society* 137 (Serial A: 1974): 131–165.

20. Plossl, George W. "Getting the Most from Forecasting." *Scientific Management* (Vol. 14, No. 1: First Quarter 1973): 1–15.

21. Sarin, Rakesh K. "An Approach for Long-Term Forecasting with an Application to Solar Electric Energy." *Management Science* 25 (No. 6: June 1979): 543–554.

22. Spencer, Milton H., et al. *Business and Economic Forecasting.* Homewood, IL: Irwin, 1961.

23. Sullivan, William G., and W. Wayne Claycombe. *Fundamentals of Forecasting.* Reston, VA: Reston, 1977.

24. Thomopoulos, Nick T. *Applied Forecasting Methods.* Englewood Cliffs, NJ: Prentice-Hall, 1981.

25. Turbin, Efraim, and Jack R. Meredith. *Fundamentals of Management Science*, 3rd ed. Plano, TX: Business Publications, 1985.

26. Weinberg, Charles B. "ARTS PLAN: A Model-Based System for Use in Planning a Performing Arts Series." *Management Science* 24 (No. 6: June 1978): 654–664.

27. Wheelright, Steven C., et al. *Forecasting Methods for Management*, 2nd ed. New York: Wiley, 1977.

Microcomputer Forecasting Software

There are very few microcomputer software packages that specialize in forecasting. There are, however, numerous inexpensive, multiple-tool software packages that include, among other techniques, a forecast module. A few of these software packages are mentioned here:

1. Microcomputer Models for Management Decision Making, Version 1.2. Terry Dennis and Laurie Dennis. St. Paul, MN: West, 1986.

2. Microcomputer Software for Management Science and Operations Research. Barry Render and Ralph M. Stair, Jr. Boston: Allyn & Bacon, 1986.

3. StatView 512 + . Daniel S. Feldman, Jr., and Jim Gagnon. Calabasas, CA: BrainPower, 1986.

4. Storm: Quantitative Modeling for Decision Support. Hamilton Emmons, A. Dale Flowers, and Kamlesh Mathur. Oakland, CA: Holden-Day, 1986.

Being out of Banana Dreamsicles proves costly to Gerald.

CHAPTER 12

INVENTORY-MANAGEMENT SYSTEMS

| 12.1 | INTRODUCTION

Inventories can be thought of as the amount of usable resources—typically, finished goods—available at a particular point in time. Examples of inventories include room vacancies at the Mark Hopkins Hotel in San Francisco; gasoline and oil supplies at the Standard Oil depot in El Segundo, California; the blood plasma stock at Saint Eligius Hospital in Boston; the cash supply at Chase Manhattan Bank; the soft-shell crab availability at Ralph and Kuckoo's Restaurant in New Orleans; the sprare parts on hand at the Volvo East Coast warehouse in Trenton, New Jersey, and so on.

The level of any inventory—how much resource to have available at any point in time—is a crucial issue. In one extreme setting, an organization can make sure that there will always be enough inventory on hand to meet any level of demand. This strategy probably will please the company's customers, because there will *never* be any instances of stock shortages. Unfortunately, the organization providing this type of stock-rich setting will probably put itself into the financial grave due to the prohibitive holding costs associated with bloated inventories. At the opposite end of the inventory-strategy spectrum, inventory costs can be kept near zero by maintaining correspondingly sparse stock levels. This "it'll be in next week" strategy will, on the other hand, create an assured decline in sales, an increase in ill-will, plummeting market share, and an almost-guaranteed going-out-of-business sign in the window.

The dilemma of the manager is to develop an inventory-management system (IMS) that can tread this delicate balance between excessively high or low stock levels. It is essentially identical to the way you purchase food at a market and then store these goods in the refrigerator, freezer, or kitchen cabinets. Why do you buy more goods than you will immediately consume? Because you wish to minimize the inconvenience of numerous trips to the market, to take advantage of quantity or discount sales, and to hedge against possible price increases or shortages at the market. You are willing to spend extra budget monies—monies that can no longer be used for investments, entertainment, bill paying, and so on—to create your own food inventory as insurance against these drawbacks. You can now survive food shortages at the market, or unexpected guests for dinner. And that is exactly how businesses operate! Businesses will invest significant portions of their annual budget monies in inventory: (1) to have the operational flexibility they will need to manage fluctuations in consumer demand and changes in their (or suppliers') ability to produce (or acquire) these goods; (2) to protect

themselves against potential price increases or as an inflation hedge; (3) to take advantage of discounts made available by large lot purchases; (4) to reduce ordering costs (usually a fixed cost-per-order expense), by making larger replenishment orders and thereby decreasing the total number of orders made per year; (5) to avoid stockouts, shortages, and the resulting sales losses and goodwill of their consumers; (6) to provide itself with greater bargaining power in labor negotiations with employee trade unions and in supplier product-cost mediations; and (7) to have the flexibility to close down portions of its operations for refurbishing equipment, or making major operating changes (facility redesign or relocation).

12.2 APPLICATIONS OF INVENTORY-MANAGEMENT SYSTEMS

A few applications of inventory management techniques follow (complete references are provided at the end of this chapter):

1. Hospital blood bank inventory control (Dumas, 1977).

2. Spare-parts inventory at Devro, Inc., a division of Johnson & Johnson (Flowers, 1978).

3. Parking-policy analysis (Narragon, Dessouky, and Devor, 1974).

4. Hotel overbooking inventory system (Lieberman, 1978).

12.3 OPERATION OF INVENTORY MANAGEMENT SYSTEMS

When an item is stored, it constitutes an *inventory*. The number of units of inventory is called the *inventory level*. The *consumer demand* will result in a corresponding shrinkage of this inventory level. The rate at which the level drops will, of course, depend on the rate of this demand; the higher the demand for the stocked item, the more quickly the level will fall. The pattern of consumer demand can strongly affect the way in which the inventory is depleted. Illustrations of the effect of demand rates and demand patterns on inventory flow are shown in Figures 12-1 through 12-3.

In time, the inventory will reach some minimum level, called the *reorder point* (also referred to as "order launching"), when a new order is placed with the manufacturing–production facility. Some time usually will pass between the point the stock is ordered and when it is received, called the *lead time*. Ideally, the new shipment should arrive exactly at the instant the last inventory unit is exhausted. In actuality, however, it is quite likely that one of two events will instead occur:

1. During the lead time, if the consumer demand is higher than predicted or the lead time is longer than expected, the company may experience a total inventory depletion, called a *stockout*.

2. On the other hand, if the new order arrives early or the consumer demand is lower than anticipated, it is possible to have a *surplus* of stock remaining. An illustration of these events is shown in Figure 12-4.

The next important step is to determine how we can keep system costs at the lowest level possible and still provide an acceptable level of responsiveness to the consumer.

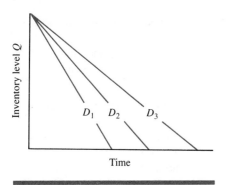

FIGURE 12-1

Constant Demand ($D_1 > D_2 > D_3$)

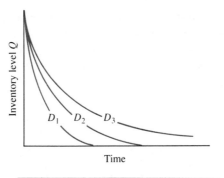

FIGURE 12-2

Decreasing Demand ($D_1 > D_2 > D_3$)

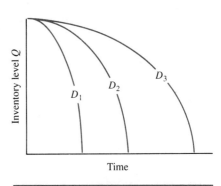

FIGURE 12-3

Increasing Demand ($D_1 > D_2 > D_3$)

|12.4| COSTS OF INVENTORY MANAGEMENT

No matter how simple or sophisticated an IMS may be, there are really only two pieces of information that the manager needs to know: (1) *When* should the inventory be replenished, or an order placed, or a new lot produced? and (2) *How much* should be ordered or produced? Since the IMS does not traditionally approach optimization from a profit or revenues perspective, the answer to these questions will be based on the manager's ability to minimize the total system inventory costs. To see how to accomplish this, we shall describe the three primary types of inventory cost contributions:

1. *Ordering costs* are the expenses incurred with placing and receiving each inventory order. They are considered fixed costs and include salaries for the clerical work of each order, inspection, receiving, and accounting, as well as transportation charges. They are expressed in *dollars per order*.

2. *Holding costs* comprise both direct and indirect costs. They include the opportunity cost (the rate of return the organization might have expected to make if the money

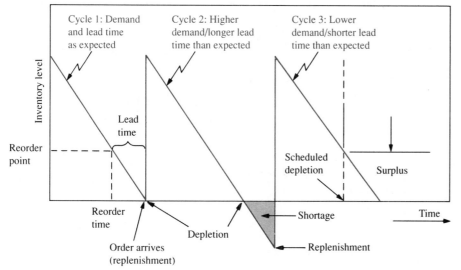

FIGURE 12-4

Stockouts and Surplus as a Result of Variances in Consumer Demand and Lead Time

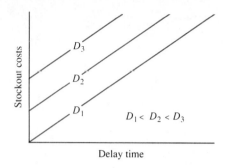

FIGURE 12-5

Effect of Demand Rate on Stockout Costs with Backordering

invested in the inventory were available for other opportunities), warehouse costs (rent, utilities, insurance, taxes, security, etc.), finance costs associated with inventory purchases, and inventory goods deterioration or obsolescence. These costs are summed and expressed either as *dollars per unit of inventory item per year*, or as a *percentage of the value of each inventory item*.

3. *Stockout* (shortage) *costs* occur when the item is out of stock and the consumer demand is unsatisfied. If no backordering (accepting consumer orders for the goods to be filled at a later time) is allowed, then the costs could include the lost sales and consumer ill-will, idle employee labor hours, material deterioration, and so on. These costs are proportional to the amount of shortage experienced during the stockout. If backordering is allowed, a certain proportion of the unsatisfied consumers will be willing to wait. This proportion, and the dollar loss of those consumers who will not wait, will be directly related to shortage quantity and the delay time in filling backorders. These relationships are illustrated in Figures 12-5 and 12-6.

At this point, you should have a reasonably good understanding of the purpose, operation, and cost impact of an IMS. You are going to use all of this information in the next section, in which we shall look at a broad variety of IMS models, in terms of various combinations of operating characteristics and the three cost components.

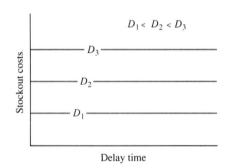

FIGURE 12-6

Effect of Demand Rate on Stockout Costs without Backordering

12.5 MODELS OF INVENTORY-MANAGEMENT SYSTEMS

Basically, there are two kinds of inventory models. If the demand for the product and the lead time needed to replenish the product stock is reasonably predictable, we have a *deterministic model*; we can estimate these key variables with a high level of confidence, regardless of whether they are uniform (constant) or uneven (lumpy). If, however, either the consumer demand or the lead time exhibits significant fluctuation, or if both do, we have a *stochastic model*. The next two sections will examine these two families of IMS models.

12.6 DETERMINISTIC SUPPLY AND DEMAND IMS MODELS

The first group of inventory-control system models discussed will be the deterministic type. They are much easier to model analytically than are the stochastic variety, and can provide quick estimates of inventory-system performance. However, they also suffer from several simple assumptions—a common problem among the deterministic models. The results from these models can be very useful, but only when viewed as rough estimates or approximations. The different deterministic models reviewed are these:

1. Basic EOQ model
2. Lead-time EOQ model
3. Backorders (shortages) EOQ model
4. Economic lot-size EOQ model
5. Quantity discounts EOQ model
6. Resource-constrained EOQ model
7. Multiple Product Production Runs EOQ model

Model 1: Basic Economic Order Quantity (EOQ)

The oldest, most commonly used IMS is the basic economic order quantity (EOQ); the original work was completed in 1915 by General Electric's F. W. Harris. Even though the basic EOQ has numerous operating assumptions that fall short of real-world situations, the model is still popular today. The model's assumptions are

1. The demand, D, is known with certainty and occurs at a constant rate.

2. The lead time, T_L, is known with certainty, and orders can be placed such that the shipment arrives exactly as the inventory level reaches zero. Accordingly, there are never any shortages.

3. The receipt of an order is instantaneous.

4. Order quantities, Q, are constant.

5. Quantity discounts are not allowed.

6. The only cost contributions are the ordering costs, C_O, and holding costs, C_H, and are both constant (shortage costs, C_S, are zero).

Using these assumptions, the inventory flow can be represented as shown in Figure 12-7. Since the objective of almost all inventory models is to minimize total system costs, C_T, the optimal order quantity, Q^*, will be the value that minimizes the sum of ordering and holding costs (Figure 12-8). Notice that the ordering cost decreases as the order quantity increases, because the total number of orders placed per year decreases at the same time; however, larger order quantities force the organization to carry larger inventory levels, resulting in proportionally increased holding costs. The trick is to trade off the ordering and holding costs so that their sum—the total annual costs—is minimized. Although this process can be accomplished by trial and error, it is less than elegant to use that approach—especially when the solution of the optimal order quantity that results in minimum total annual costs is quite simple, and when the identical process can be used for all EOQ-type inventory models.[1] Let's see how it is done.

[1] Since this process is the same for all of the EOQ models studied in this chapter, for the sake of brevity, it will not be repeated. Instead, the optimal parameters of each model will be provided immediately.

$$C_T = C_o + C_H = \left(\frac{D}{Q}\right)c_o + \left(\frac{Q}{2}\right)c_h$$

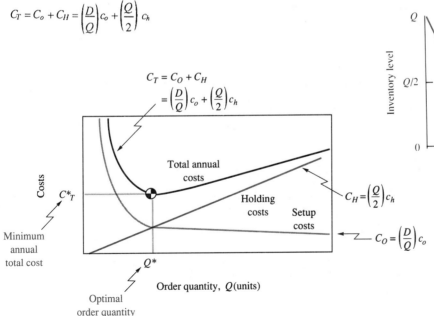

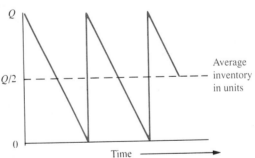

FIGURE 12-7

Inventory Flow for Basic EOQ Model

FIGURE 12-8

Relationship Between Inventory Costs and Order Quantity for Basic EOQ Model

Take the first derivative of the total cost equation with respect to Q and set this result equal to zero (i.e., $dC_\pm/dQ = 0$). Solve this resulting equation for Q. However, it is not yet appropriate to assume that minimal conditions for the order have been found, since the first derivative may yield *either* a maximum or a minimum point. If minimal conditions have been found, the second derivative of total annual costs with respect to Q will be *positive*. The total annual costs for the basic EOQ model are given by

$$C_T = C_O + C_H = \left(\frac{D}{Q}\right)c_o + \left(\frac{Q}{2}\right)c_h$$

where

$$\begin{aligned}
C_T &= \text{total annual inventory costs of basic EOQ (\$)} \\
C_O &= \text{annual ordering costs (\$)} \\
C_H &= \text{annual holding costs (\$)} \\
D &= \text{annual demand for inventory product (units/year)} \\
Q &= \text{order quantity for product (units/order)} \\
c_o &= \text{ordering costs per order (\$/order)} \\
c_h &= \text{holding costs per unit of product (\$/year/unit)}
\end{aligned}$$

The first derivative of this relationship is found and is set equal to zero:

$$\frac{d}{dQ}(C_T) = -\frac{Dc_o}{Q^2} + \frac{c_h}{2} = 0$$

The optimal order quantity, Q^*, is now solved for

$$Q^* = \sqrt{2D\left(\frac{c_o}{c_h}\right)}$$

The second derivative is

$$\frac{d^2}{dQ^2}(C_T) = -\frac{-(Dc_o)2Q}{Q^4}$$

$$= \frac{(Dc_o)2}{Q^3}$$

Since the sign of the second derivative is positive, we can now assume that Q^* is, indeed, the minimal order quantity.

Now we are in a position to calculate the three pieces of information we need to know to operate this model effectively. The three parameters are (1) the optimal order quantity, Q^*; (2) the number of times per year we will need to place new orders, N^* (and the corresponding time between each order, t^*); and (3) the minimum total system cost, C_T^*.

The optimal order quantity has already been found:

$$Q^* = \sqrt{2D\left(\frac{c_o}{c_h}\right)}$$

Using Q^*, the optimal number of orders per year is easy to calculate:

$$N^* = \frac{365D}{Q^*}$$

where

N^* = optimal number of annual orders (orders/year)

The time between each of these orders is

$$t^* = \frac{365}{N^*}$$

where

t^* = optimal order time (days)

The total system cost, C_T, for these optimal conditions is

$$C_T^* = C_O + C_H = \left(\frac{D}{Q^*}\right)c_o + \left(\frac{Q^*}{2}\right)c_h$$

where

C_O = total annual ordering costs ($/year)

C_H = total annual holding costs ($/unit)

Now let's illustrate the use of these relationships with several hypothetical examples.

EXAMPLE 12.1   MUNI TRANSPORTATION DISTRICT TIRES

Suppose that the MUNI Transportation District of San Francisco needs 5000 tires per year for its fleet of buses. The ordering costs are $250 per order, and the holding costs average $40 per tire per year. What is the optimal order quantity the district should select, how many orders per year will have to be placed, and what is the total cost of this inventory system?

Given D = 5000 tires/year

c_o = $250/order

c_h = $40/year

Solution

The optimal order quantity is

$$Q^* = \sqrt{2D\left(\frac{c_o}{c_h}\right)}$$

$$= \sqrt{(2)(5000)\left(\frac{250}{40}\right)} = 250 \text{ tires/order}$$

The optimal number of orders per year is

$$N^* = \frac{D}{Q^*}$$

$$= \frac{5000}{250} = 20 \text{ orders/year}$$

The time between each order is

$$t^* = \frac{365}{N^*}$$

$$= \frac{365}{20} = 18.25 \text{ days between orders}$$

The minimum total cost is

$$C_T^* = (20)(250) + \left(\frac{250}{2}\right)(40) = \$10,000.00 \text{ per year}$$

EXAMPLE 12.2 CADILLAC SMOG CONTROL VALVES

Pretend that the Eastern Region Parts Warehouse of Cadillac Motor Cars orders 10,000 smog-control valves for its maintenance departments each year. These valves cost $1.00 per unit and $25 per shipment order. The holding cost is estimated at 12.5 percent of the value of the inventory. Define the optimal inventory operating parameters for this organization.

Given $D = 10,000$ units/year

$c_o = \$1.00$/unit

$c_h = .125 \times 1.00 = \$.125$/unit/year

Solution

$$Q^* = \sqrt{(2)(10,000)\left(\frac{1.00}{.125}\right)} = 400 \text{ units/order}$$

$$N^* = \frac{D}{Q^*}$$

$$= \frac{10,000}{400} = 25 \text{ orders/year}$$

$$t^* = \frac{365}{N^*}$$

$$= \frac{365}{25} = 14.60 \text{ days between orders}$$

$$C_T^* = (25)(1.00) + \left(\frac{400}{2}\right)(.125) = \$50.00 \text{ per year}$$

Model 2: Lead Time EOQ

For this variation of the basic model, we relax the assumption of zero lead time. In this case, we assume some finite value of lead time, T_L. As before, we are assuming that lead time is deterministic. There are two possible situations that can occur with respect to lead time now. The lead time can be either less than the optimal cycle time, t^*, or greater than this value. That is, either

$$T_L < t^*$$

or

$$T_L > t^*$$

Several important points should be made in contrasting this model with model 1. First, the optimal reorder point, R^*, must be determined, so that the new order arrives exactly at the start of a new cycle. Next, the optimal order quantity, Q^*, is not affected by lead time, so it will be the same as it would be were we dealing with model 1 conditions. The same holds for N^*, t^*, and C_T^*. If the lead time is less than the cycle time $(T_L < t^*)$, the demand D during this lead time is less than the optimal order quantity because $(T_L \times D) < (t^* \times D)$. For this situation, we must place an order when the inventory level drops to some minimum value, R^*, which is

$$R^* = T_L D$$

This will allow the new order to arrive exactly at the end of the current cycle (Figure 12-9).

Next, consider the situation when the lead time needed is greater than the optimal cycle time $(T_L > t^*)$. The demand for goods during this cycle is now greater than the available stock on hand because $(T_L \times D) > (t^* \times D)$; it is not possible to reorder at an inventory level that will exactly absorb lead-time demand with that same cycle. Lead time, in these cases, is managed by launching orders from previous cycles that arrive during the lead time of the cycle under consideration (Figure 12-10). The demand for

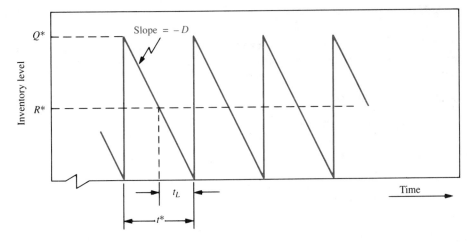

FIGURE 12-9

Inventory Flow Cycle for Lead Times Less Than Optimal Cycle Time ($t_L < t^*$)

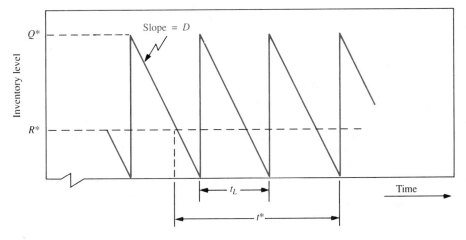

FIGURE 12-10

Inventory Flow Cycle for Lead Times Greater Than Optimal Cycle Time ($t_L > t^*$)

goods that occurs during the lead time in this situation is

$$D = \left(\begin{array}{c}\text{minimum inventory}\\ \text{level}\end{array}\right) + \left(\begin{array}{c}\text{new orders that arrive}\\ \text{during lead time}\end{array}\right)$$

$$T_L D = R^* + \left(\frac{T_L}{t^*}\right) Q^*$$

The minimum inventory level is

$$R^* = T_L D - \left(\frac{T_L}{t^*}\right) Q^*$$

where (T_L/t^*) represents the number of complete cycles during a lead time; it is the integer value of this ratio. This simply means that, when $T_L > t^*$, you will truncate down any fractional value above the value of the integer, (e.g., $1.83 = 1, 4.25 = 4$). Also, in cases when $T_L < t^*$, this method will force any of these values to be equal to zero. Once again, let's look at a few examples to illustrate the use of the lead-time model. First, let's use a case for $T_L < t^*$.

EXAMPLE 12.1 CONTINUED

Let's use the MUNI example of the previous model, but this time assume that the lead time for this system is .020 years (approximately 7 days). The optimal order quantity will be exactly the same as discussed earlier, so

$$Q^* = 250 \text{ tires/order}$$

The minimum inventory level is

$$R^* = T_L D - \left(\frac{T_L}{t^*}\right) Q^*$$

$$= (.02)(5000) - \left(\frac{0.020}{.05}\right)(250)$$

$$= 100 - 0 = 100 \text{ tires}$$

The second term in this expression must be equal to zero, because the T_L/t^* value is less than 1.

EXAMPLE 12.2 CONTINUED

If the lead time for the MUNI example is such that $T_L > t^*$—say, .080 years (about 30 days)—then the optimal reorder point is

$$R^* = (.08)(5000) - \frac{(.080)(250)}{.05}$$

$$= 400 - (1.60)(250)$$
$$\overset{\curvearrowright}{1.00}$$

$$= 400 - 250$$

$$= 150 \text{ tires}$$

Notice that the (T_L/t^*) value of 1.60 became 1, since the equation uses *truncated integer values* only. For both of the examples, every other critical parameter—optimal order quantity, number of orders per year, time between orders, and total system costs—is the same as in the basic EOQ model. Only the lead-time consideration is different.

Model 3: Backorders (Shortages) EOQ

Another variation of the basic model allows shortages to occur. Although orders are taken, they are not filled until a later time. This model is quite realistic if the product that you are selling has a loyal following or is usually in scarce supply. The organization, by delaying the consumer purchase of the item, can order less frequently, resulting in lower inventory levels and ordering costs. However, there is a cost associated with the shortage that reflects ultimate consumer dissatisfaction because of having to wait for an out-of-stock item. This cost component is not readily available and requires considerable skill to estimate. The inventory flow cycle for the backorder model is shown in Figure 12-11. In this model, the primary variables we must determine are the optimal order quantity, Q^*; the maximum allowable shortage, S^*; the maximum inventory level, L^*; the time within a cycle in which there is available stock, t_1; the time within a cycle in which there is a shortage, t_2; and the total minimum system costs, C_1^*. There must also be an estimate of the shortage cost, c_s. The equations that you will need for this model are presented next. The maximum inventory is

$$L^* = Q^* - S^*$$

The optimal order quantity is

$$Q^* = \sqrt{2D\left(\frac{c_o}{c_h}\right)\left(\frac{c_h + c_s}{c_s}\right)}$$

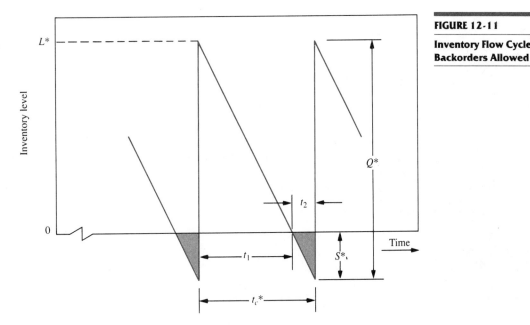

FIGURE 12-11

Inventory Flow Cycle with Backorders Allowed

The maximum allowable shortage is

$$S^* = \sqrt{2D\left(\frac{c_o}{c_h}\right)\left(\frac{c_s}{c_s + c_h}\right)}$$

Finally, the total minimum system cost is

$$C_T^* = \frac{Dc_o}{Q^*} + \frac{(Q^* - S^*)^2 c_h}{2Q^*} + \frac{S^{*2} c_s}{2Q^*}$$

Also, if you want to calculate the number of orders to be placed each year and the time between each of these orders, you will need to use the next set of relationships. First, the amount of time during each cycle that inventory is available is

$$t_1 = \frac{L^*}{D}$$

The amount of time during each cycle that inventory is not available is

$$t_2 = \frac{S^*}{D}$$

The length of each cycle is

$$t^* = t_1 + t_2$$

The number of orders placed is

$$N^* = \frac{365}{t^*}$$

Let's apply these relationships to an example.

EXAMPLE 12.3 TOYS'R'US TEDDY BEARS

Suppose Toys'R'Us has a demand for 50,000 talking teddy bears per year. Each order costs the company $50.00, the per-unit holding cost is $2.00 per year, and the shortage cost is estimated at $4.00 per unit per year. Find the optimal order quantity, maximum shortage level, total number of orders per year, time between each order, time during each cycle that the product is available, time during each cycle the product is not available (stockout), and minimum total system costs.

Given

$$D = 50,000 \text{ units}$$
$$c_o = \$50.00 \text{ per order}$$
$$c_h = \$2.00 \text{ per unit per year}$$
$$c_s = \$4.00 \text{ per unit per year}$$

Solution

The optimal order quantity is

$$Q^* = \sqrt{(2)(50{,}000)\left(\frac{50}{2}\right)\left(\frac{2+4}{4}\right)}$$

$$= 1936 \text{ sets}$$

The maximum shortage allowed is

$$S^* = \sqrt{(2)(50{,}000)\left(\frac{50}{2}\right)\left(\frac{4}{4+2}\right)}$$

$$= 646 \text{ sets}$$

The total number of orders per year is

$$N^* = \frac{D}{Q^*}$$

$$= \frac{50{,}000}{1936} = 25.82 \text{ orders/year}$$

The stockin (t_1) and stockout (t_2) times are

$$t_1 = \frac{(Q^* - S^*)}{D}$$

$$= \frac{(1936 - 646)}{50{,}000} = .0258 \text{ year (9.42 days)}$$

$$t_2 = \frac{S^*}{D}$$

$$= \frac{646}{50{,}000} = .0129 \text{ year (4.72 days)}$$

The total minimum system costs for inventory control are

$$C_T^* = \frac{Dc_o}{Q^*} + \frac{(Q^* - S^*)^2 c_h}{2Q^*} + \frac{S^{*2} c_s}{2Q^*}$$

$$= 1291 + 860 + 431$$

$$= \$2582$$

Model 4: Economic-Lot-Size (ELS) EOQ

When an organization receives inventory over time rather than in an instantaneous batch, a variation of the basic EOQ model is needed. In this model, the product is being sold and replenished at the same time. A graphic representation of the inventory flow profile of this model is shown in Figure 12-12. We can see from this figure that the new inventory is added gradually, so that there is never a stockout; the production rate is tailored to be in concert with the daily demand for the product of interest, although this rate must always exceed the demand if there is to be a buildup after stock depletion. As

FIGURE 12-12

**Inventory Flow Cycle for
Economic Lot-Size Model**

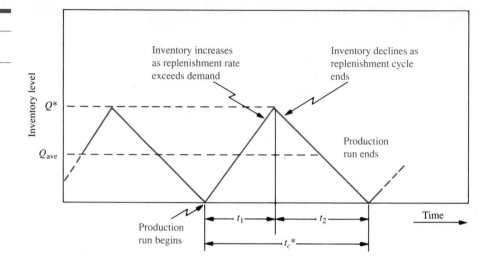

a result of an ongoing replenishment pattern, instead of the traditional ordering cost, there will be a *setup cost*. This is, literally, the cost of setting up the production process that will be producing the goods. It usually includes items such as the salaries for all the people involved in the production process, as well as the administrative, material-goods, and overhead costs. The holding costs associated with this model are the same as those constituting the basic EOQ model. The optimal total cost for the Economic Lot size is given by the following relationship (Figure 12-13).

$$C_T^* = \left(1 - \frac{d}{p}\right)\left(\frac{Q^*}{2}\right)c_h + \left(\frac{D}{Q^*}\right)c_u$$

where

p = uniform production/inventory replenishment rate (units of goods/day)

P = annual production = $250p$ (units of goods/year, assuming a 250-day-per-year operating schedule)

d = uniform demand for goods per time period (units of goods/day)

D = annual demand = $250d$ = (units of goods/year assuming a 250 day per year operating schedule)

C_o = annual setup costs ($)

c_u = setup costs per production run ($)

c_h = annual holding costs ($/year)

The optimal production quantity is given by[2]

$$Q^* = \sqrt{\frac{2d(c_u/c_h)}{1 - (d/p)}}$$

There are other operating parameters in this model that are considerably different from those in the basic model.

1. The production period, t_1, is given by

$$t_1 = \frac{Q^*}{p}$$

[2]For the order quantity to be positive, p must exceed d; otherwise, stockouts will occur.

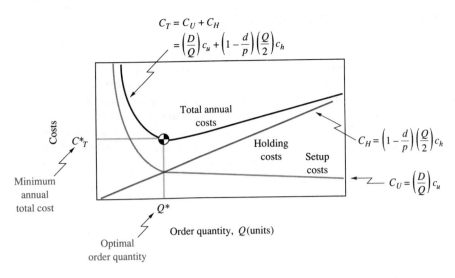

$$C_T = C_U + C_H$$
$$= \left(\frac{D}{Q}\right)c_u + \left(1 - \frac{d}{p}\right)\left(\frac{Q}{2}\right)c_h$$

Total annual costs

C^*_T

Minimum annual total cost

Holding costs

Setup costs

$$C_H = \left(1 - \frac{d}{p}\right)\left(\frac{Q}{2}\right)c_h$$

$$C_U = \left(\frac{D}{Q}\right)c_u$$

Q^*

Order quantity, Q(units)

Optimal order quantity

Costs

2. The maximum inventory level, Q_{max}, is

$$Q_{max} = (p - d)t_1$$
$$= (p - d)\left(\frac{Q^*}{p}\right)$$

3. The average inventory level Q_{ave}, is

$$Q_{ave} = \frac{Q_{max}}{2}$$

4. The annual holding cost, C_H, is

$$C_H = \left(1 - \frac{d}{p}\right)\left(\frac{Q^*}{2}\right)c_h$$

5. The duration of the depletion period, t_2, is

$$t_2 = \frac{Q_{max}}{d}$$

6. The duration of one complete cycle, t^*, for the optimal setting (minimum total system costs) is

$$t^* = t_1 + t_2$$

7. The total number of cycles per year, N^*, is

$$N^* = \frac{D}{Q^*}$$

8. The annual setup cost (production run cost), C_U, is

$$C_U = \left(\frac{D}{Q^*}\right)c_u$$

An example of this model follows.

EXAMPLE 12.4 TIMELESS FURNITURE

A furniture manufacturer, Timeless International, specializes in high-quality reproductions of period pieces of American furniture. This company has an exclusive contract with the Frank Lloyd Wright estate to reproduce the classic Robie Chair, originally designed by the renowned architect in circa 1920. Timeless has an annual demand of 1500 units. The production capacity of the company for this particular product is 2000 units per year furing the 250 days of annual production. The chair has an associated setup cost of $100, whereas the holding costs are estimated at an annual rate of 18 percent. The retail sales price for the chair is $2300 (the company sells directly to retail buyers). What are the optimal inventory parameters for this problem?

GIVEN

P = 2000 chairs/year (or p = 2000/250 = 8 chairs/day)

D = 1500 chairs/year (or d = 1500/250 = 6 chairs/day)

c_u = $100/production run

c_h = (.18)(2300) = $414/chair

SOLUTION

The optimal order size, Q^*, is

$$Q^* = \sqrt{\frac{2D(c_u/c_h)}{1 - (d/p)}}$$

$$= \sqrt{\frac{(2)(1500)(100/414)}{1 - (6/8)}}$$

$$= 53.83 = 54 \text{ chairs/production run}$$

The total system cost, C_T^*, is

$$C_T^* = \left(1 - \frac{d}{p}\right)\left(\frac{Q^*}{2}\right)c_h + \left(\frac{D}{Q^*}\right)c_u$$

$$= \left(1 - \frac{6}{8}\right)\left(\frac{54}{2}\right)(414) + \left(\frac{1500}{54}\right)(100)$$

$$= 2794.50 + 2777.78$$

$$= \$5572.28$$

The length of the production period, t_1, is

$$t_1 = \frac{Q^*}{p}$$

$$= \frac{54}{8} = 6.75 \text{ days/production period}$$

The maximum inventory level is

$$Q_{max} = (p - d)t_1$$

$$= (8 - 6)(6.75) = 13.5 \text{ chairs}$$

The average inventory level is

$$Q_{ave} = \frac{Q_{max}}{2}$$

$$= \frac{13.5}{2} = 6.75 \text{ chairs}$$

The annual holding costs are

$$C_H = \left(1 - \frac{d}{p}\right)\left(\frac{Q^*}{2}\right)c_h$$

$$= \frac{(8 - 6)(54)(414)}{(2)(8)}$$

$$= \$2794.50$$

The length of the shortage (depletion) period is

$$t_2 = \frac{Q_{max}}{d}$$

$$= \frac{13.5}{6} = 2.25 \text{ days}$$

The total number of production run cycles per year is

$$N^* = \frac{D}{Q^*}$$

$$= \frac{1500}{54} = 27.78 \text{ production runs/year}$$

The annual setup costs are

$$C_U = \left(\frac{D}{Q^*}\right)c_u$$

$$= \left(\frac{1500}{54}\right)100$$

$$= \$2777.78$$

There is only one significant difference between the production-run model (PRM) and the basic EOQ model. The PRM is producing as well as receiving stock simultaneously. Because of this, the optimal order size will always be larger for the PRM: since the $[1 - (p/d)]$ value in the denominator is always less than 1. It will act as a multiplying factor on Q^*.

Model 5: Quantity Discounts EOQ

It is not unusual for an organization to be able to purchase large quantities of goods at a discount. There can even be multiple price breaks as the order size increases from one plateau to another. There are also other advantages associated with large purchases, including lower annual ordering costs and lower stockout rates. However, there are also negative considerations. Holding costs will increase as a result of the larger inventory

reflecting the associated deterioration, obsolescence, and greater capital expenditures for purchasing these goods. So, discount buying may not be wise in the instances when the disadvantages of the larger inventories just discussed outweigh the price breaks of the larger quantity purchase. Now let's look at the model parameters.

The analytics of the discount model are almost identical to those of the basic EOQ. The optimal conditions in the discount model pivot around the various plateaus—sometimes referred to as *cutoff points*—of order quantities required to get the different price breaks. The optimal inventory costs for the quantity discounts model are found from

$$C_T^* = \frac{Dc_o}{Q} + \frac{Qc_h}{2} + Dc_d$$

Unfortunately, the minimal inventory cost, C_T^*, cannot be solved explicitly: The discount purchase cost associated with the third term on the right-hand side, c_d, is dependent on order quantity size, D, and this dependency is a *discontinuous* relationship (i.e., c_d is correct only up to the discount quantity, D, under consideration; it "steps down" once the next larger plateau is reached).

The technique for doing this calculation is eloquently described by Efraim Turban and Jack Meredith (pp. 603–607, 1988). It consists of an algorithmic process that will be illustrated in the following fictitious example.

EXAMPLE 12.5   HYATT HOTEL AND MONDAVI WINERY

TABLE 12-1

Discount Price Structure for Robert Mondavi and Hyatt Regency Hotel Example

Quantity	Unit Price
0–4999	$2.75
5000–9999	$2.60
≥ 10,000	$2.50

For illustrative purposes only, let us suppose that the Hyatt Regency Hotel in Chicago buys the majority of its house wine from Robert Mondavi Winery of St. Helena, California. These wines—red, white, and Chablis—have the three-plateau price structure per bottle shown in Table 12-1.

Assume the following: Hyatt sells about 50,000 bottles of these wines per year. The wines cost $50.00 per order, and the holding cost is estimated at 20 percent of the price per unit per year. What is the optimal inventory policy for the restaurant?

GIVEN

$$D = 50,000$$
$$c_o = \$50.00/\text{order}$$
$$c_h = 20\% \text{ bottle/year}$$

SOLUTION

Step 1. Find the order level, Q, for the lowest price level, Q_3.

$$Q_3 = \sqrt{\frac{2Dc_o}{c_h}}$$

$$= \sqrt{\frac{(2)(50,000)(50)}{(.20)(2.50)}}$$

$$= 3163 \text{ bottles}$$

Step 2. Compare Q_3 with the required order level necessary for the restaurant to receive this price break.

Since $Q_3 < 10,000$ units, this discount is not possible. (If, however, Q_3 were greater than 10,000 bottles, the problem would be solved.)

Step 3. Go to the next-best discount plateau, and repeat steps 1 and 2:

$$Q_2 = \sqrt{\frac{(2)(50,000)(50)}{(.20)(2.60)}}$$

$$= 3101 \text{ bottles}$$

Since this value is far less than the required minimum order level for the second plateau (5000 bottles), repeat this step for the only remaining discount price:

$$Q_1 = \sqrt{\frac{(2)(50,000)(50)}{(.20)(2.75)}}$$

$$= 3015 \text{ bottles}$$

Although this value meets the minimum order level for that plateau, the achievement is not rewarding, since this is the lowest discount available.

Step 4. Now calculate the total system cost for each discount point of the prices that gave us unfeasible values in steps 1 and 2 (these were the 5000 and 10,000 minimum-order-level plateaus).

$$C_T^* = \frac{Dc_o}{Q} + \frac{Qc_h}{2} + Dc_d$$

where

c_d = per unit discount cost at a specific plateau

For the third plateau, Q_3, the total system costs are

$$C_{T_3} = \frac{(50,000)(50)}{10,000} + \frac{(10,000)(.20)(2.50)}{2} + (50,000)(2.50)$$

$$= 250 + 2500 + 125,000$$

$$= \$127,750$$

For Q_2, the total costs are

$$C_{T_2} = \frac{(50,000)(50)}{5000} + \frac{(5000)(.20)(2.60)}{2} + (50,000)(2.60)$$

$$= \$131,800$$

Step 5. Calculate the total system cost for the feasible solution plateau:

$$C_{T_1} = \frac{(50,000)(50)}{3015} + \frac{(3015)(.20)(2.75)}{2} + (50,000)(2.75)$$

$$= \$139,158$$

Since it is cheaper to buy 10,000 units per order, it is more prudent to revise our earlier "optimal" order quantity of 3015 bottles. You can see now that the discount-model optimal order level, Q^*, does not necessarily give you the minimum total system cost, as does the basic EOQ model; you must search each price level and separately solve for the total cost in order to ensure optimality. An illustration of the effect of quantity discounts on the relationship between total system costs and order quantity is provided in Figure 12-14. Notice that the cost function is not a continuous relationship but holds only for the specific ranges which correspond to the various price break plateaus.

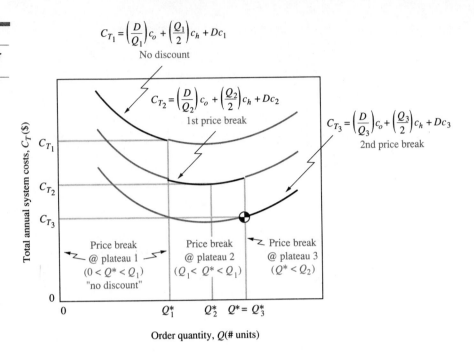

$$C_{T_1} = \left(\frac{D}{Q_1}\right)c_o + \left(\frac{Q_1}{2}\right)c_h + Dc_1$$

No discount

$$C_{T_2} = \left(\frac{D}{Q_2}\right)c_o + \left(\frac{Q_2}{2}\right)c_h + Dc_2$$

1st price break

$$C_{T_3} = \left(\frac{D}{Q_3}\right)c_o + \left(\frac{Q_3}{2}\right)c_h + Dc_3$$

2nd price break

Total annual system costs, C_T (\$)

C_{T_1}

C_{T_2}

C_{T_3}

Price break @ plateau 1 ($0 < Q^* < Q_1$) "no discount"

Price break @ plateau 2 ($Q_1 < Q^* < Q_1$)

Price break @ plateau 3 ($Q^* < Q_2$)

Q_1^* Q_2^* $Q^* = Q_3^*$

Order quantity, Q(# units)

Model 6: Resource-Constrained EOQ

Sometimes, we may find that an inventory system's resource limits—budget, space, and so on—fall short of allowing the system to match the optimal conditions suggested by the analytical model solution. Herbert Moskowitz and Gordon Wright (pp. 594–599, 1979) discuss this important possibility. For example, suppose that the clothing design and manufacturing firm of Perry Ellis, Inc., has a budget for their men's camel-hair overcoat that would limit to 1750 the number of units that could be manufactured. If the solution of the appropriate EOQ model—ignoring the constraint—suggested that the optimal value should be 1500 units, then the optimal value that we would select is 1500 units. However, it is also possible that the optimal order level could exceed our real resource limits. So, if Q^* was, say, 2165 units, our selected "best possible" value would be 1750 units: no larger value is possible. An illustration of this situation is shown in Figure 12-15. The case of dealing with a single inventory item is clearcut. However, when we consider multiple inventory items in competition for the same limited resources, the problem complexity skyrockets. Suppose, for example, you have several items competing for the available storage space (V) in your warehouse. Each item has an annual demand (D), ordering cost (c_o), carrying cost (c_h), stockout cost (if allowed, c_s), and per-unit storage-space allotment (v). Also, the available storage space in the warehouse has a per-unit rental cost, c_v, which is usually based on the maximum inventory level—not just on the proportion used at any time. The total system cost for this model is

$$C_T = \sum_{i=1}^{n} C_i = \sum_{i=1}^{n} \left(\begin{array}{c}\text{ordering cost}\\\text{for } i^{\text{th}} \text{ item}\end{array}\right) + \sum_{i=1}^{n} \left(\begin{array}{c}\text{holding cost}\\\text{for } i^{\text{th}} \text{ item}\end{array}\right) + \sum_{i=1}^{n} \left(\begin{array}{c}\text{warehouse cost}\\\text{for } i^{\text{th}} \text{ item}\end{array}\right)$$

$$= \sum_{i=1}^{n} \left(\frac{c_{o_i} D_i}{Q_i} + \frac{c_{h_i} Q_i}{2} + c_{v_i} v_i Q_i\right)$$

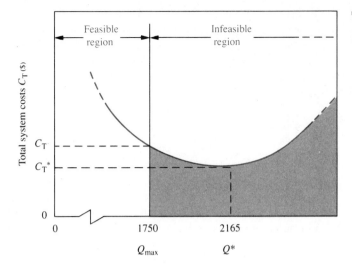

FIGURE 12-15

Relationship between Total System Costs and Order Quantity for a Resource-Constrained EOQ Model

The holding costs in this model do not include any storage component, and the independence of each inventory item is assumed implicitly. The optimal order quantity—ignoring constraints—is

$$Q_i^* \sqrt{\frac{2c_{o_i}D_i}{c_{h_i} + 2y_i c_{v_i}}}$$

The next step is to solve for the EOQ of each separate inventory item, then to check whether the total storage space constraint, V, is exceeded. That is,

$$\sum_{i=1}^{n} v_i Q_i \leq V$$

If the sum of storage space that would be used by all inventory items based on the EOQ model dictates ignoring the space constraints (the left-hand-side value of the equation)—that is, if it does not exceed the total storage space value (right-hand-side value)—then the actual storage space limits are not violated and the solution obtained is acceptable. However, if the EOQ model value is greater than V, you can use an interesting constrained optimization technique called *Lagrange multipliers* (do not panic). To do this, you have to formulate the problem in nearly the identical way as you did for the linear programming minimization problem! In this case, you are minimizing the total cost function subject to the warehouse volume constraint:

$$\text{Min} \sum_{i=1}^{n} C_T = \text{Min} \sum_{i=1}^{n} \left(\frac{c_{o_i}D_i}{Q_i} + \frac{c_{h_i}Q_i}{2} + c_{v_i} v_i Q_i \right)$$

SUBJECT TO

$$\sum_{i=1}^{n} y_i Q_i \leq V$$

After execution of the Lagrange multiplier process, the problem is transposed to an unconstrained optimization. The new function is

$$Q_i = \sqrt{\frac{2c_{o_i}D_i}{c_{h_i} + 2v_i(\lambda + c_{v_i})}}$$

Notice that this Q_i equation is almost identical to the earlier expression for Q_i^*. The multiplier, λ (Langrangian multiplier), in the denominator serves as a type of *rental rate* for space and is in units of dollars per cubic foot. To solve the problem, we need to perform one more step because, in this process, it is necessary to find the value of λ before we can find that of Q_i. This is accomplished by substituting the Q_i equation into the constraint equation for V. Then,

$$\sum_{i=1}^{n} v_i \left[\frac{2c_{o_i}D_i}{c_{h_i} + 2v_i(\lambda + c_{v_i})} \right] = V$$

The values for all the variables except that of λ are given. This makes it necessary to solve implicitly for λ, which we do by finding the value for $\lambda > 0$ that will make the value of the left-hand side of the equation exactly equal to V. Next, we substitute this value back into the equation for Q_i and solve for the optimal order quantity, Q_i^*, for each inventory item. An example, fortunately, follows.

EXAMPLE 12.6 PERRY ELLIS WAREHOUSE SPACE

Suppose that Perry Ellis is concerned about three clothing lines that are competing for warehouse space: (1) men's apparel, (2) women's apparel, and (3) children's apparel. The pertinent inventory parameters of these lines are shown in Table 12-2. If the maximum storage space available for these three clothing lines is 3000 ft^3 and the rental charge for the warehouse is $1.00 per cubic foot per year, what is the minimum inventory system cost?

SOLUTION

Step 1. Solve for Q_1^* for each line:

$$Q_1^* = \sqrt{\frac{2(50)(15,000)}{[2.75 + (2)(1.00)(2.50)]}}$$

$$= 440 \, \text{units}$$

$$Q_2^* = \sqrt{\frac{2(50)(40,000)}{[3.50 + (2)(1.00)(3.00)]}}$$

$$= 649 \, \text{units}$$

$$Q_3^* = \sqrt{\frac{2(50)(5000)}{[1.50 + (2)(1.00)(1.00)]}}$$

$$= 378 \, \text{units}$$

TABLE 12-2

Inventory Parameters for Perry Ellis Multiple Product Line

Parameter	Men's Line (1)	Women's Line (2)	Children's Line (3)
D_i, units/year	15,000.	40,000.	5,000.
c_{o_i}, \$/order	50.	50.	50.
c_{h_i}, \$/unit/year	2.75	3.50	1.50
v_i, ft^3/unit	2.50	3.00	1.00

Step 2. Compare the total storage space required by these optimal order quantities with the real space limits:

$$\sum_{i=1}^{n} v_i Q_i \leq V?$$

$$2.50Q_1^* + 3.00Q_2^* + 1.00Q_3^* \leq 3000?$$

Since the left-hand-side value exceeds our constraint, we do not have a feasible solution.

Step 3. Since $v_i Q_i^* > V$, solve the V equation for λ. This solution requires an iterative trial-and-error process. We know that, if the problem was not constrained ($\lambda = 0$), the optimal space allotment as determined by the EOQ model equations would be acceptable and we could use the 3425 ft³. However, here λ must take on a positive value so that V is reduced to exactly 3000 ft³. Table 12-3 and Figure 12-16 illustrate this iterative process. After some trial-and-error calculations, we find that the value of λ that satisfies this constraint is .48.

Step 4. Substitute $\lambda = .48$ into the Q_i equation and solve for the constrained order quantity values of Q_1^*, Q_2^*, and Q_3^*.

$Q_1^* = 384$ units

$Q_2^* = 568$ units

$Q_3^* = 335$ units

And, as a check,

$$V = (2.50)(384) + (3.00)(568) + (1.00)(335) = 3000 \text{ ft}^3$$

TABLE 12-3

Trial and Error Solution of λ for $V = 3000$ ft³ of Perry Ellis Resource-Constrained EOQ Example

λ	$\sum_{i=1}^{n} v_i \left[\dfrac{2c_{o_i} D_i}{c_{h_i} + 2v_i(\lambda + c_{v_i})} \right] = V$
.00	3425
.10	3322
.25	3183
.40	3061
.50	2987
1.00	2683

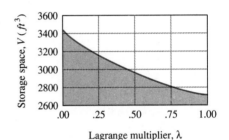

FIGURE 12-16

Iterative Solution of Lagrange Multiplier, λ, Given $V = 3000$ ft³ for Resource-Constrained Perry Ellis Example

Model 7: Multiple Product Production Runs EOQ

When various products must compete for the same manufacturing equipment, it is no longer reasonable to assume independence among these products. Accordingly, it is also no longer possible to solve for the EOQ of each product separately. To manage the conflict that would surely arise if we did not acknowledge the interdependence of each product on the overall manufacturing schedule, we develop a joint production-run routine.

The model for the multiple product production situation is similar to the single product model discussed earlier. For the present model, however, the optimal decision rule is the cycle length that minimizes inventory holding plus setup costs jointly for the entire set of products, N^*. First, the total system cost is given by

$$C_T = N \sum_{i=1}^{n} c_{o_i} + \frac{1}{2N} \sum_{i=1}^{n} \left[c_{h_i} D_i \left(1 - \frac{d_i}{R_i} \right) \right]$$

where N = the common number of production runs annually, and is given by

$$N = \frac{D_i}{Q_i}$$

The optimal number of production cycles, N^*, is

$$N^* = \frac{\sum\limits_{i=1}^{n}\left[c_{h_i}D_i\left(1-\frac{d_i}{R_i}\right)\right]}{2\sum\limits_{i=1}^{n}c_{o_i}}$$

The optimal order size for each product run is

$$Q_i^* = \frac{D_i}{N^*}$$

We find the optimal total system cost by substituting the expression for N^* into the equation for C_T. This gives us the minimal-system-cost relationship, C_T^*:

$$C_T^* = \sqrt{2\sum\limits_{i=1}^{n}c_{o_i}\sum\limits_{i=1}^{n}\left[c_{h_i}D_i\left(1-\frac{d_i}{R_i}\right)\right]}$$

An example follows.

EXAMPLE 12.7   PERRY ELLIS FUR JACKETS

Perry Ellis has three lines of women's imitation fur jackets that it wishes to market for the fall season. The lines must compete for the same manufacturing equipment, so it is absolutely necessary to develop a compatible production schedule that will take into consideration all three items. Suppose that these three lines are fox (1), ranch mink (2), and beaver (3) jackets. Table 12-4 provides the projected production, demand, and cost information for these goods. The demand rate of column 3 assumes that there are 250 production days per year (5 days per week $\times$ 50 weeks per year), which is divided into the annual demand of column 2. The required production time shown in column 5 is the ratio of demand (column 2) to production rate (column 4). As you probably noticed, the total for the production time needed for these three lines of fur jackets is only 225 days—5 weeks short of capacity. So why worry about production capabilities if there is a surplus of available time? Because the 225 days assumes no competition between product lines for the manufacturing resources—which, of course, is not true! Now let's apply the appropriate model equations to determine these optimal parameters. Table 12-5 organizes the inventory data provided in Table 12-4 so that we can easily calculate

TABLE 12-4

Perry Ellis Inventory Data for Fall Line of Women's Fur Jackets

(1)	(2)	(3)	(4)	(5)	(6)	(7)
Item	Annual Demand, D_i (#)	Demand Rate, d_i (#/day)	Production Rate, P_i (#/day)	Required Production Time, t_i (days)	Holding Costs, ch_i ($/unit/yr)	Setup Costs, cs_i ($/run)
1	3000	12	20	150	20	20
2	1000	4	20	50	30	30
3	500	2	20	25	50	30

TABLE 12-5

Perry Ellis Inventory Data for Determining Optimum Joint Production-Run Duration, N^*

(1) Item	(2) d_i/P_i	(3) $1-$col 2	(4) ch_iD_i	(5) col 3 × col 4	(6) cu_i
1	.600	.400	60,000	24,000.	20.
2	.200	.800	30,000	24,000.	30.
3	.100	.900	25,000	22,500.	30.
				70,500	80

TABLE 12-6

Joint Lot Size and Production Adequacy for Perry Ellis Women's Fur Jacket Lines

Product	$Q_i=D_i/N^*$	R_i	Q_i/R_i	D_i	Q_i/D_i
1	143	20	7.15	12	12
2	48	20	2.40	4	12
3	24	20	1.20	2	12
			10.75		

the optimal joint production-run duration. Using the information from Table 12-5 and the relationship for N^*, we find that the optimal production duration for these three inventory items is

$$N^* = \frac{70,500}{(2)(80)}$$

$$= 20.99 \text{ days}$$

The minimum total inventory cost for these three jacket lines, using the equation for C_T^*, is

$$C_T^* = (2)(80)(70,500) = \$3359$$

This means that each of the three products would be produced about 12 times per year in lot sizes of one-twenty-first of the annual demand. The production time required to produce Q_i is shown in Table 12-6 (column 4) and is 10.75 days. Column 6 of this table shows that each lot provides 12 production days of supply, so the joint cycle can accommodate all three product lines.

12.7 LUMPY DEMAND DETERMINISTIC INVENTORY MODELS

Many businesses sell products that have seasonal demand patterns. This results in a lumpy (uneven or nonuniform) demand. When this is the case, managers must choose between changing production rates throughout the year to accommodate demand or absorbing the fluctuation with large inventories. This type of situation is often the rule rather than the exception (constant demand is far more rare an occurrence).

Although lumpy demand methods are considered to fall in the category of deterministic inventory-control systems, the nonuniformity of this predictable demand

TABLE 12-7

Computerland Demand over 10 Weeks

	1	2	3	4	5	6	7	8	9	10
Demand	5	10	15	2	30	15	20	5	20	25

violates the basic assumption of the standard EOQ models. Nevertheless, the same principles used to find the optimal solution for the uniform demand models—such as balancing holding and ordering costs—still provide the basis for determining the optimal parameters for the lumpy demand methods.

Although dynamic programming (Wagner–Whitin algorithm[3]) can be used to optimize lumpy demand problems, the computational complexities are significant. In practice, heuristic approaches are more typically used (and are far more easily understood). A common example will be used to illustrate a number of heuristic methods that David Dannenbring and Martin Starr (pp. 515–523, 1981) discuss comprehensively.

EXAMPLE 12.8   COMPUTERLAND

Assume that Computerland in Santa Monica, California, has a 10-week demand schedule for the IBM PC, as illustrated in Table 12-7. The ordering cost from IBM is $135, and the holding costs are estimated at $10 per unit per week. The beginning inventory is zero. For the sole purpose of contrast, let's first use the standard EOQ model to see its relative effectiveness—in term of total inventory costs—as contrasted with several of the heuristic methods.

Baseline EOQ Lumpy Model

To use the standard EOQ, we will have to restate everything in terms of per period rather than per year. The demand will be based on the average for the 10-week period and the "goodness" of the EOQ model will depend on how far from this average the actual lumpy demand varies. The average demand across the 10-week period is

$$D = \frac{147}{10}$$

$$= 14.7 \text{ units/week}$$

The optimal reorder quantity, Q^*, is

$$Q^* = \frac{(2)(14.7)(135)}{10}$$

$$= 19.92$$

$$= 20 \text{ units/order}$$

Since the basic EOQ does not permit shortages, orders in units of 20 will have to be received at the beginning of any period when demand exceeds the available inventory left

---

[3]M. Wagner and T. M. Whitin, "Dynamic Version of the Economic Lot Size Model," *Management Science*, Vol. 5, No. 1, (1958), pp. 89–96.

TABLE 12-8

EOQ Model Solution for Computerland Example

	Week									
	1	*2*	*3*	*4*	*5*	*6*	*7*	*8*	*9*	*10*
Quantity Received	20	0	20	20	20	20	20	20	0	20

over from the previous period. This process is illustrated in Table 12-8. The first order received would satisfy the demand for weeks 1 and 2, but a new delivery would be required at the beginning of the third week. The reason for this is that the total cumulative demand through and including week 3 is 30 units, so the second order of 20 units is needed. Do you see how this fixed order quantity that the EOQ models use causes severe order–demand mismatches? We are frequently carrying inventory quantities in excess of what demand requires because we are forced to order in constant-sized lots. As a result, we start off by carrying 15 extra units during week 1, then carry 5 extra units during week 2, and continue in a similar way until we end up with 13 extra units during our last week. The total inventory costs for the EOQ is

$$C_T = C_O + C_H$$
$$= (8)(135) + (10)[15 + 5 + 10 + 28 + 18 + 23 + 23 + 28 + 18 + 13]$$
$$= 1080 + 1810$$
$$= \$2890$$

Model 8a: Lot-for-Lot (L4L) Heuristic

The lot-for-lot (L4L) approach requires orders to be received during any period in which a nonzero demand exists. That is, an order is placed in *each* nonzero demand period. As a result, the lot-for-lot method always maximizes ordering costs and minimizes holding costs. Of course, when the inventory system being analyzed has low ordering costs, few nonzero demand periods, and highly variable demand, this approach is quite attractive. The results for this method are shown in Table 12-9. The order quantity is always identical to demand. As a result, the holding costs are zero and the ordering costs are the sole contributor to the total inventory costs, which are

$$C_T = C_O + C_H$$
$$= (10)(135) + 0$$
$$= \$1350$$

This represents a significant improvement over the basic EOQ model approach and illustrates, very clearly, just how inappropriate the constant demand assumption is in some instances.

TABLE 12-9

Lot-for-Lot Order Pattern for Computerland Example

	Week									
	1	*2*	*3*	*4*	*5*	*6*	*7*	*8*	*9*	*10*
Quantity Received	5	10	15	2	30	15	20	5	20	25

Model 8b: Fixed Order Quantity (FOQ) Heuristic

Sometimes, the size of the order must be based on considerations other than those dictated by holding or ordering costs. A few examples are restrictions regarding the minimum allowable order quantity as dictated by the supplier, the size required to achieve discounts, or the size forced on purchases by packaging in specific multiples (gross, barrels, etc.). As an example, suppose that IBM will allow purchases only in units of 30 in a lot. The order pattern would look as shown in Table 12-10. The first order would satisfy the demand of weeks 1, 2, and 3; however, to meet the demand of the fourth week, another lot purchase of 30 computers will have to be made—and the demand is only two units! The total inventory costs are

$$
\begin{aligned}
C_T = C_O &+ C_H \\
&= (5)(135) + (10)[28 + 25 + 15 + 5 + 0 + 28 + 28 + 23 \\
&\qquad + 13 + 23 + 18 + 28 + 3] \\
&= 675 + 1810 \\
&= \$2485
\end{aligned}
$$

Model 8c: Periodic Order Quantity (POQ) Heuristic

The periodic order quantity (POQ) heuristic uses EOQ principles to determine the order timing, but it is more efficient than is the basic EOQ in minimizing the mismatch between order and customer demand. The POQ takes the basic EOQ order quantity, Q^*, and transforms it into an equivalent number of time periods. So, for our example, the order quantity of 20 units is equivalent to 1.36 time periods of average demand. That is,

$$
\begin{aligned}
T_{equiv} &= \frac{Q^*}{D_{av}} \\
&= \frac{20}{14.7} \\
&= 1.36 \text{ weeks}
\end{aligned}
$$

This means that, whenever the demand in a period is greater than the ending inventory from the previous period, an order should be received that is equal to the total demand over the next T_{eq} periods. The value of T_{eq} is always rounded up, so we must set order quantities to equal the demand for each successive pair of weeks. The order pattern is illustrated in Table 12-11. If the average demand was four units per week (instead of the

---

TABLE 12-10

EOQ Order Pattern for Computerland Example

	Week									
	1	*2*	*3*	*4*	*5*	*6*	*7*	*8*	*9*	*10*
Quantity Received	30	0	0	30	30	0	30	0	30	0

TABLE 12-11

POQ Order Pattern for Computerland Example (Average Demand = 14.7 IBM PCs/Week)

	Week									
	1	*2*	*3*	*4*	*5*	*6*	*7*	*8*	*9*	*10*
Quantity Received	15	0	17	0	45	0	25	0	45	0

TABLE 12-12

POQ Order Pattern for Computerland Example (Average Demand = 4 IBM PCs/Week)

	Week									
	1	*2*	*3*	*4*	*5*	*6*	*7*	*8*	*9*	*10*
Quantity Received	62	0	0	0	0	85	0	0	0	0

14.7 units), the quantity received would have to cover 20/4 or 5 weeks at a time. This new schedule would look as shown in Table 12-12. The total inventory costs for these two examples are, respectively,

$$C_T[T_{eq} = 2] = C_O + C_H$$
$$= (5)(135) + (10)[10 + 0 + 2 + 0 + 15 + 0 + 5 + 0$$
$$+ 25 + 0]$$
$$= 675 + 570$$
$$= \$1245$$

$$C_T[T_{eq} = 5] = C_O + C_H$$
$$= (2)(135) + (10)[57 + 47 + 32 + 30 + 0 + 45 + 70$$
$$+ 50 + 45 + 25 + 0]$$
$$= 270 + 4510$$
$$= \$4780$$

This tremendous difference in inventory costs between these two POQ examples illustrates how sensitive the operating parameters are to this heuristic method, and the caution the analyst must exercise in not generalizing about the value of one particular tool: You must investigate the impact on each problem as a unique and individual case.

Model 8d: Part-Period-Balancing (PPB) Heuristic

The part-period-balancing (PPB) method tries to balance holding and ordering costs similarly to the basic EOQ. PPB reviews various order quantity values until it finds the single value that results in the two cost components being as close to equal as possible. The first step in using this model is to consider a specific order quantity, and then to determine whether the holding and ordering costs over the period that this amount will satisfy demand are about equal. As an example, suppose we order just enough computers to cover the first week (5 units). The ordering cost is \$135 and the holding cost is \$0—certainly no balance. If we order enough for the first 2 weeks (15 units), the ordering cost remains at \$135, but the holding cost is \$100 (the 10 units carried over from the first to second week at \$10 per unit per week). We are obviously heading in the right direction—only \$35 dollars apart. Can we improve? If we order enough stock to satisfy the demand for the first 3 weeks (30 units), the ordering cost is \$135 and the holding costs are

$$C_H = (10)[(30 - 5) + (25 - 10) + (15 - 15)] = \$400$$

This shows that the previous order size should be enough to cover the first 2 weeks, since it is for that value (15 units) that the ordering and holding costs are closest to equal (\$35 difference). All other order quantities will result in larger differences. The second order will be received at the beginning of week 3. The amount will be determined similarly to that of the first order. The tabulations for the second-order size are shown in

TABLE 12-13

PPB Second Order Size for Computerland Example

Order Size	Covers Period(s)	C_H	C_O
15	3	0	135
17	3,4	20	135
47	3,4,5	620	135

TABLE 12-14

PPB Third Order Size for Computerland Example

Order Size	Covers Period(s)	C_H	C_O
30	5	0	135
45	5,6	150	135
65	5.6.7	550	135

TABLE 12-15

PPB Fourth Order Size for Computerland Example

Order Size	Covers Period(s)	C_H	C_O
20	7	0	135
25	7,8	50	135
45	7.8.9	450	135

TABLE 12-16

PPB Fifth Order Size for Computerland Example

Order Size	Covers Period(s)	C_H	C_O
20	9	0	135
45	9,10	250	135

Table 12-13. So, the second order of 17 units will arrive at the start of week 3 and will cover demand for weeks 3 and 4. The third order will be received at the beginning of week 5. The calculation for size determination is provided in Table 12-14 and illustrates that 45 units will satisfy demand in weeks 5 and 6. The fourth order consists of 25 units, which covers demand for weeks 7 and 8, for a total inventory cost of $185 and a minimal differential between the holding and ordering costs of $85 (Table 12-15). The minimal differential between holding and ordering costs of $115 results when the 5th and final order of 45 computers is placed to cover weeks 9 and 10 (Table 12-16). The total inventory costs for the entire 10-week period are given in Table 12-17. They are

$$
\begin{aligned}
C_T &= C_O + C_H \\
&= (5)(135) + (10)[10 + 0 + 2 + 0 + 15 + 0 + 5 + 0 + 25 \\
&\quad + 0] \\
&= 675 + 570 \\
&= \$1245
\end{aligned}
$$

Model 8e: Least Unit Cost (LUC) Heuristic

The least unit cost (LUC) heuristic attempts to minimize the average per unit holding and ordering costs to determine the size of each new order. Sometimes, these average costs will first decrease and then increase as the order size is enlarged, so the trick is to carry the calculations for each order-size decision through enough periods for this inflection to occur. These calculations are illustrated in Table 12-18. They show us that we should make seven orders of sizes 15, 15, 32, 15, 20, 25, and 25 units at the beginning of weeks 1, 3, 4, 6, 6, 8, and 10. The total inventory costs for this system would be

$$
C_T = 200 + 100 + 400 + 100 + 100 + 300 + 100 = \$1500
$$

It seems apparent that, although this method is efficiency-oriented on each individual order, this incremental approach may not be enough to ensure that the overall system is optimized—there are several other heuristic methods that give less expensive results.

Now let's compare the results for our Computerland example to see which heuristic,

TABLE 12-17

PPB Order Pattern for Computerland Example

	Week									
	1	2	3	4	5	6	7	8	9	10
Quantity Received	15	0	17	0	45	0	25	0	45	0

TABLE 12-18

LUC Order Pattern for Computerland Example

Order	Cover Period(s)	Q	C_O	C_H	C_T	C_{Tav}
1	1	5	100	0	100	$20.00
1	1,2	15	100	100	200	13.33*
1	1,2,3	30	100	400	500	16.67
2	3	15	100	0	100	6.67*
2	3,4	17	100	20	120	7.06
2	3,4,5	47	100	620	720	15.32
3	4	2	100	0	100	50.00
3	4,5	32	100	300	400	12.50*
3	4,5,6	47	100	600	700	14.89
4	6	15	100	0	100	6.67*
4	6,7	35	100	200	300	8.57
5	7	20	100	0	100	5.00*
5	7,8	25	100	50	150	6.00
6	8	5	100	0	100	20.00
6	8,9	25	100	200	300	12.00*
6	8,9,10	50	100	700	800	16.00
7	10	25	100	0	100	4.00*

for this one situation, is most attractive. A summary of the various results is provided in Table 12-19.

These results show that the PPB method ($1245) is the most promising. However, it is critical to recognize that the purpose of this comparison is not to establish which method is the panacea; there is no such heuristic. Instead, it is essential to view this as an exercise in expanding your analytical options in assessing lumpy demand inventory problems. Which method is "best" will always be determined by the peculiarities of each individual problem.

TABLE 12-19

Summary of Heuristic Methods; Total System Costs for Computerland Example

Heuristic Method	C_T ($)
Basic EOQ	2890
Lot for lot	1350
Fixed order quantity	2485
Periodic order quantity	1245–4780
Part period balancing	1245
Least unit cost	1500

|12.8| STOCHASTIC SUPPLY-AND-DEMAND INVENTORY-MANAGEMENT SYSTEMS

So far, we have examined inventory models that have assumed known demand rates—either constant (uniform) or lumpy (nonuniform)—and reorder times that either were instantaneous or were made across a defined duration. The original lead time model (EOQ model 2) assumed that the inventory would be decreased at a rate equivalent to the average demand. Further, when the inventory level had dropped to the reorder point, R, an order of Q units of goods was placed. Between the time the order was placed and the time at which the new shipment of goods arrived (lead time), the stock decreased from R to zero. Then, almost magically, as the last unit of goods was consumed, the new order of goods arrived, the stock level was refreshed to Q units, and, and . . . and ducks have lips and Madonna reads Nietzsche.

In reality, either (1) demand *or* lead time are uncertain, or (2) demand *and* lead time are uncertain. These fluctuations are often random.[4]

The two stochastic models presented in this section are

1. Uncertain demand and certain lead time

2. Uncertain demand and uncertain lead time

---

[4]If the demand was variable but scheduled, lumpy inventory methods would be appropriate.

Model 9: Stochastic Inventories Using Safety Stocks; Uncertain Demand and Certain Lead Time

Numerous real-world inventory systems employ *safety stocks* that serve as a hedge against higher-than-expected levels of demand during lead times that could result in highly undesirable stockout episodes. Inventory systems employing safety stocks usually treat demand as a probabilistic variable, whereas they assume lead time to be constant. Since the lead time is assumed to be constant, the basic EOQ model is often used to provide estimates or approximations of the order quantity, Q^*. Although demand is uncertain, the mean demand during lead time is used, in turn, to determine the reorder point, R.

The problem of a stockout is not so easily solved that we can simply toss in some extra inventory units in the form of safety stock. Unfortunately, the extra inventory will add additional holding costs to the overall system cost that could outweigh any benefit it might provide serving as a stockout buffer. Therefore, the quantity of safety stock ultimately selected must reflect the organization's careful tradeoff between excessive holding costs resulting from too much extra inventory and the ill-will and lost sales associated with an inventory level that is too miserly. The additional assumptions of this model include that (1) inventory items are not produced inhouse but are, instead, purchased from outside sources; (2) although stockouts are permitted, there are associated stockout penalties; and (3) unit price, unit ordering cost, unit holding cost, and unit stockout cost are known and constant. An example will illustrate how to determine the optimal amount of safety stock to carry.

EXAMPLE 12.9   WEA SONY TELEVISIONS

Whole Earth Access (WEA), a discount department store headquartered in Berkeley, California, carries a large selection of Sony televisions. Imagine the following scenario: The store has used a fixed order quantity model to determine its inventory procedures for the last 5 years. Unfortunately, sales fluctuations are so significant that WEA has been experiencing stockouts with several of their most important product lines. In particular, the Sony 27-inch color television has been selling out, creating obvious dissatisfaction among WEA buyers. The store manager believes that, to prevent losing these customers to competitors, the store must add safety stock to its present inventory levels. The manager knows that the real issue is the selection of the most appropriate level of safety stock to introduce. To achieve this important task, she begins by gathering the inventory records from the previous sales periods of the Sony television models presently experiencing the current stockout problem. The data collected during the last 40 reordering periods are shown in Table 12-20. The expected value of demand, $EV[D_i]$, during these time periods is

$$EV(D_i) = \sum_{i=1}^{n} P(D_i) \cdot D_i \qquad \text{for } i = 1, 2, \ldots, n \text{ levels of demand}$$

where

$$D_i = i^{\text{th}} \text{ level of demand during lead time}$$
$$P(D_i) = \text{probability of occurrence for } i^{\text{th}} \text{ level of demand}$$

TABLE 12-20

Units of Weekly Demand for Sony Television Example*

Sales during Reorder Period**	Frequency of Sales, f	Probability of Sales	Cumulative Probability of Sales
100	8	.200	.200
200	6	.150	.350
300	12	.300	.650
400	8	.200	.850
500	4	.100	.950
600	2	.050	1.000
	40	1.000	

*In real-world inventory systems, demand will not typically occur in such convenient increments as those illustrated. Nevertheless, similar increments can result if units of goods are withdrawn in fixed lot sizes of 10, 20, or 30 units (Brown and Revelle, 1978, p. 300).

**Average demand during lead time: 300 units/reorder period.

The expected demand is, then,

$$EV[D_i] = (.200)(100) + (.150)(200) + (.300)(300) + (.200)(400)$$
$$+ (.100)(500) + (.050)(600)$$
$$= 300 \text{ units}$$

Currently, WEA has been reordering when inventory levels drop to 300 units for the Sony 27-inch model. From the cumulative frequency column in Table 12-20, the present procedure indicates that no stockout will occur 65 percent of the time. That is, the manager knows from these historical data that, if she reordered only when inventory for the Sony 27-inch model was at 300 units, the demand would be satisfied only 65 percent of the time (i.e., the sum of all probabilities for those occasions when the demand is equal to or less than the reorder point inventory level of 300 units—.200 for 100 units per week plus .150 for 200 units per week plus .300 for 300 units per week). She reasons, then, that the probability of a stockout associated with the ith level of demand, D_i, and the reorder-point inventory level, R, may be defined by the following relationship:[5]

$$P(SO)_{D_i} = \left(\begin{array}{c} \text{cumulative probability} \\ \text{that demand will be} > R \end{array} \right)$$

So, the likelihood of a stockout must include all demand levels *in excess* of the reorder-point inventory level of $R = 300$ units (i.e., .200 for a demand 400 units, .100 for a demand of 500 units, and .050 for a demand of 600 units):

$$P(SO)_{300} = 1 - (.200 + .150 + .300)$$
$$= .35$$

Increasing the present reorder point to 400, 500, and 600 units decreases the likelihood of a stockout to 15, 5, and 0 percent. So, for the present inventory policy, or reordering at 300 units, the probability for a stockout may be characterized fully as in Table 12-21. The manager knows that it is now possible to convert these data into the expected costs

[5]The compliment of the probability of a stockout is referred to as the *service level*, *SL*. That is,

$$SL = 1 - P(SO)_{Di}$$

TABLE 12-21

Relationship Between Quantity of Safety Stock and Stockout Probability

Reorder Point, R	Safety Stock	Cumulative Probability*	Probability of Stockout**
300	0	.650	.350
400	100	.850	.150
500	200	.950	.050
600	300	1.000	.000

*Cumulative probability = probability of no stockout; service level.

**Probability of stockout, $P(SO)$, is $= 1 -$ cumulative probability.

associated with maintaining various safety stock levels. For a specific level of safety stock (or for a given reorder point), this relationship is given by

$$\begin{pmatrix} \text{expected annual} \\ \text{stockout costs} \end{pmatrix} \begin{pmatrix} \text{number of} \\ \text{orders per year} \end{pmatrix} \begin{pmatrix} \text{per-unit} \\ \text{stockout costs} \end{pmatrix} \left[\sum \begin{pmatrix} \text{stockout} \\ \text{probability} \end{pmatrix} \begin{pmatrix} \text{number of units} \\ \text{of shortage} \end{pmatrix} \right]$$

or

$$EC(SO)_R = Nc_{so} \left[\sum_{D_i > R}^{\hat{n}} P(SO)_{D_i} \cdot (D_i - R) \right] \quad \text{for } i = 1, 2, \ldots, \hat{n} \text{ levels of demand greater than reorder point value, } R$$

where

$D_i - R =$ number of units of shortage for a given safety stock (excess of demand over reorder point)

$P(SO)_{D_i} =$ probability of a stockout for i^{th} level of demand, D_i, and reorder point R

$EC[SO]_R =$ expected annual stockout costs associated with inventory policy of reorder point R

$N =$ number of orders placed per year

TABLE 12-22

Inventory Parameters for Sony Television Example

Inventory Parameters	Sony 27-Inch Television
Ordering cost, c_o ($/order)	50
Holding cost, c_h (%/unit/year)	10
Stockout cost, c_{so} ($/unit)	50
Wholesale price of unit, p ($/unit)	600
Number of orders per year, N	10
Demand, D (units/year)	3000

The manager collects the specific cost information concerning the related inventory parameters that will be needed to solve for the expected annual stockout costs associated with a specific reorder point, $EC[SO]_R$. These parameters include ordering cost, holding cost, stockout cost, number of orders placed per year, and wholesale purchase price of the inventory product (if holding costs are expressed as a percentage of the product unit price). These data are shown in Table 12-22. The expected stockout costs associated with maintaining various levels of safety stock can now be found. For example, the stockout costs associated with zero safety stock ($R = 300$ units) are

$$EC(SO)_{300} = Nc_{so} \left[\sum_{i=1}^{n} P(SO)_{D_i} \cdot (D_i - 300) \right]$$

The total expected annual costs associated with reorder points of 300, 400, 500, and 600 units of Sony 27-inch televisions are presented in Table 12-23. The manager now takes into consideration the holding costs. Remember, the holding cost is assumed to be 10 percent of the WEA unit price of $600, or $60.00 per unit per year of safety stock added to the inventory. The cost of carrying this additional inventory is summarized in Table 12-24 and in Figure 12-17. Now the manager is in a position to define the inven-

TABLE 12-23

Stockout Costs for Various Levels of Safety Stock for Sony Television Example

Reorder Point, R	Safety Stock	Demand, D	Units of Stockout	Stockout Probability, $P(SO)$		Expected Total Stockout Cost, $EC[SO]_R$, ($)
300	0	400	100	.200		10,000
		500	200	.100		10,000
		600	300	.050		7,500
					Total	27,500
400	100	500	100	.100		5,000
		600	200	.050		5,000
					Total	10,000
500	200	600	100	.050		2,500
					Total	2,500
600	300	600	0	.000		0
					Total	0

tory operating policy that will minimize overall inventory-system cost for the uncertain-demand WEA experiences with the Sony television product line:

| The inventory costs will be minimized at \$14,500 dollars per year if the company employs a safety stock of 200 units and reorders at 500 units. |

TABLE 12-24

Total Inventory System Costs for Sony Television Example

Reorder Point, R	Safety Stock	Expected Total Stockout Costs	Holding Cost of Safety Stock	Total System Cost
300	0	27,500	0	27,500
400	100	10,000	6,000	16,000
500	200	2,500	12,000	14,500
600	300	0	18,000	18,000

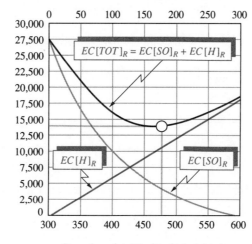

FIGURE 12-17

Total Annual System Costs as Influenced by Reorder Point for Sony Television Example

As you have probably surmised, assessing inventory systems with stochastic demand is not trivial. The next stochastic inventory model adds additional complexity: uncertain demand *and* uncertain lead time.

Model 10: Stochastic Inventories Systems with Uncertain Demand and Uncertain Lead Time

The first stochastic inventory model presented in this section suggested that, in real-world applications, demand is typically probabilistic. It is also very likely that, unless an organization has control over the delivery of goods (such as inhouse production capability), lead time is also uncertain. The stochastic inventory model presented here provides you with a method for evaluating conditions with both probabilistic demand and probabilistic lead time. The additional assumptions included in this model are (1) inventory items are not produced inhouse but are, instead, purchased from outside sources; (2) although stockouts are permitted, there are associated stockout penalties; and (3) unit price, unit ordering cost, unit holding cost, and unit stockout cost are known and constant.

When both demand and lead time are uncertain, the solutions of the optimal order quantity, Q^*, and reorder point, R^*, cannot be found independently. Instead, an iterative solution process must be employed that "homes in" on the values of Q^* and R^* that minimize overall inventory-system costs. As was the case in the first stochastic model, inventory records must be used to construct the necessary random probability distributions: Empirical data describing both the variation of demand during a lead time and the lead time fluctuations must be organized carefully. Although it is beyond the intended scope of this text to include the derivation of the model equations, a summary of the key relationships is presented next.

The total annual inventory cost of the stochastic demand and stochastic lead time model is merely the sum of the annual holding, ordering, and stockout costs. The total annual inventory cost, C_{TOT}, is

$$C_{TOT} = C_H + C_O + (C_{SO})_R$$

where the total annual holding cost, C_H, is

$$\begin{pmatrix} \text{annual total} \\ \text{holding cost} \end{pmatrix} = \begin{pmatrix} \text{per-unit} \\ \text{holding cost} \end{pmatrix} \begin{pmatrix} \text{average} \\ \text{inventory} \\ \text{level} \end{pmatrix}$$

and the average inventory level is given by

$$\begin{pmatrix} \text{average} \\ \text{inventory} \\ \text{level} \end{pmatrix} = \frac{Q}{2} + \begin{pmatrix} \text{safety} \\ \text{stock} \end{pmatrix}$$

The safety stock is

$$\begin{pmatrix} \text{safety} \\ \text{stock} \end{pmatrix} = \begin{pmatrix} \text{reorder} \\ \text{point, } R \end{pmatrix} - \begin{pmatrix} \text{expected demand} \\ \text{during lead time} \end{pmatrix}$$

The expected (average) demand during lead time is

$$\begin{pmatrix} \text{expected demand} \\ \text{during lead time} \end{pmatrix} = \sum_{i=1}^{n} P(D_i) \cdot D_i$$

The total annual holding costs can be expressed as

$$C_H = c_h \left[\frac{Q}{2} + R - \sum_{i=1}^{n} P(D_i) \cdot D_i \right]$$

The total annual ordering cost, C_O, is

$$C_O = c_o \left(\frac{D}{Q} \right)$$

The total annual stockout cost, C_{SO}, associated with a given reorder point, R, is

$$\left(\begin{array}{c} \text{total annual} \\ \text{stockout costs} \end{array} \right) = \left(\begin{array}{c} \text{expected shortage} \\ \text{during lead time} \end{array} \right) \left(\begin{array}{c} \text{per-unit} \\ \text{stockout cost} \end{array} \right) \left(\begin{array}{c} \text{number of} \\ \text{annual reorders} \end{array} \right)$$

and

$$\left(\begin{array}{c} \text{expected shortage} \\ \text{during lead time} \end{array} \right) = \sum_{D_i > R}^{\hat{n}} P(SO)_{D_i} \cdot (D_i - R)$$

Therefore,

$$(C_{SO})_R = N c_{so} \left[\sum_{D_i > R}^{\hat{n}} P(SO)_{D_i} \cdot (D_i - R) \right]$$

Finally, the "working form" of the total annual inventory cost is

$$C_{TOT} = c_h \left[\frac{Q}{2} + R - \sum_{i=1}^{n} P(D_i) \cdot D_i \right] + c_o \left(\frac{D}{Q} \right)$$
$$+ N c_{so} \left[\sum_{D_i > R}^{\hat{n}} P(SO)_{D_i} \cdot (D_i - R) \right]$$

If you examine this rather large equation carefully, you will discover two important points concerning the interrelationship between order quantity, Q, and reorder point, R.

1. As the value of Q grows, the average inventory level and corresponding holding cost will also increase. On the other hand, ordering cost will decrease, since the number of new orders (reorders) will decrease, as will the stockout cost (since the number of lead times will be diminishing). As order quantities decline, the opposite situation will exist: Inventory costs will go down, ordering costs will rise, and stockout cost will also increase as a result of the increasing number of lead times.

2. As the reorder point, R, grows, the holding cost will also increase due to the growth of the average inventory level. Stockout costs will decrease, however, since the number of lead times will drop. Notice that R has no effect on the ordering cost.

So, Q and R influence the total annual inventory costs in different ways. This requires that Q^* and R^* be found independently of each other. Once again, an example will serve to illuminate the solution of this relatively complex model.

EXAMPLE 12.10 ELEGANT 356 CAR DEALER

Elegant 356, of Newport Beach, California, sells classic, restored Porsches from the 1955 to 1965 production years.[6] The average sales price for one of the rare automobiles

6These particular years primarily cover the four-cylinder 356A-, B-, and C-series Porsche "bathtub" models.

TABLE 12-25

Probability Distribution for Demand, Elegant 356 Example

Demand	Frequency, f	P (Demand)
0	5	.2
1	10	.5
2	5	.3

TABLE 12-26

Probability Distribution of Lead Time, Elegant 356 Example

Lead Time	Frequency, f	P (Lead Time)
1	14	.70
2	6	.30

is approximately \$30,000. Finding one of these autos in near-new condition is very difficult, since these models have been historically susceptible to rust and deterioration over the years. Although Elegant 356 has a limited inventory of these cars, sometimes the stock runs out due to unexpectedly high demand. Because of this, experienced buyers constantly investigate potential purchase leads by keeping in touch with 356 Club members as well as by reading the "cars for sale" section of dozens of newspapers from the California, Nevada, Arizona, New Mexico, and Texas areas.[7] Holding costs on each unsold Porsche in stock are estimated at \$500 per year (this includes insurance, upkeep, security, and uninsured damages that sometimes occur unexpectedly). Stockout costs are estimated at \$5000 per unit (customer ill-will and foregone sales), and ordering costs (the expenses associated with searching for, finding, and transporting more units) are assessed to be \$2000 per order. The agency experiences a weekly demand of between zero and two Porsches. Suppose that company ordering policy dictates that buyers actively seek replacement inventory every 2 weeks (regardless of demand or inventory level). Suppose further that it takes anywhere from 1 to 3 weeks for these buyers to find and bring back an acceptable car. Inventory log books reveal the information shown in Tables 12-25 and 12-26 regarding the demand and the lead time distributions. Once you know the demand and lead time distributions, it is possible to use a probability tree to display the various combinations of lead time and demand during lead time (Figure 12-18). The path probabilities for each possible level of demand during the lead time can then be summed to provide the probability distribution of the demand during the lead time (Table 12-27). The expected demand during lead time, $EV(D_i)$ is given by

$$EV(D_i) = \sum_{i=1}^{n} P(D_i) \cdot D_i$$

$$= (0)(.152) + (1)(.410) + (2)(.321) + (3)(.090) + (4)(.027)$$

$$= 1.43 \text{ Porsches}$$

The expected annual demand, assuming a 250 day production year, is

$$EV(D_i) = (1.43)(250) = 357.5 \text{ Porsche automobiles}$$

It is now possible to solve iteratively for the optimal values for order quantity, Q^*, and reorder point, R^*. We find these optimal values using the following procedure.[8] The optimal order quantity is given by

$$Q^* = \sqrt{\frac{2EV(D_i)\,[c_o + c_{so}EC(SO)_R]}{c_h}}$$

The likelihood of a stockout is

$$P(SO)_{D_i} = \frac{c_h Q}{c_{so}EV(D_i)}$$

Since these two equations cannot be solved explicitly, an iterative procedure is employed. First, assume some value for the optimal reorder point, R^*, and solve for Q^*.

---

[7]It is common knowledge among collectors that the "best" cars typically are found in the more arid regions of the country. The Northeast and Southeast, primarily due to weather conditions, have proportionally fewer Porsches in excellent conditions than do the five Southwestern and Western states mentioned.

[8](Moskowitz and Wright, 1979, pp. 628–629)

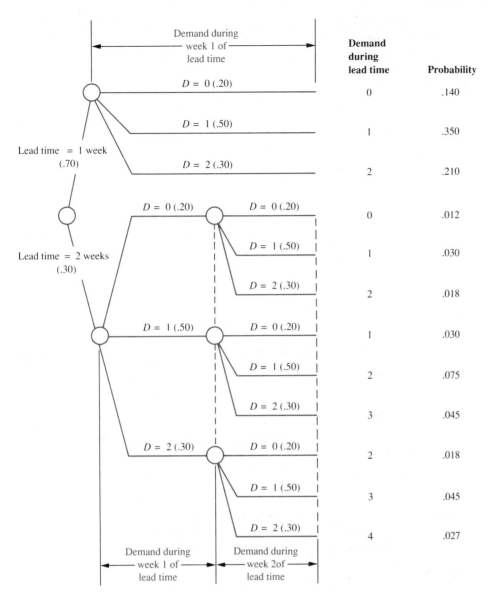

Demand during lead time	Probability
0	.140
1	.350
2	.210
0	.012
1	.030
2	.018
1	.030
2	.075
3	.045
2	.018
3	.045
4	.027

FIGURE 12-18

Probability Tree Illustrating the Expected Demand during Lead Time, Elegant 356 Example

TABLE 12-27

Probability Distribution of Demand during Lead Time, Elegant 356 Example

Demand During Lead Time, *LTD*	Probability of Lead Time Demand, *P(LTD)*	Probability of Stockout, *P(SO)*
0	.14 + .012 = .152	.848
1	.35 + .03 + .03 = .410	.438
2	.21 + .018 + .075 + .018 = .321	.117
3	.045 + .045 = .090	.027
4	.027	.000
	1.000	

Next, use this value of $Q*$ to solve for R. Now, solve again for Q. Repeat this process until the differences between each iteration smooth out. Let's illustrate this procedure now. Assume that the expected stockout costs, c_{so}, are zero. Then,

$$Q* = \sqrt{\frac{(2)(357.5)(2000 + 0)}{500}}$$

$$= 53.48$$

Next, substitute this value into the equation for $P(SO)_{D_i}$:

$$P(SO)_{D_i} = \frac{(500)(53.48)}{(5000)(357.5)}$$

$$= .015$$

Searching Table 12-27, we can see that the R that is associated with the $P(SO)_{D_i}$ value closest to .015 is between 3 and 4. Since $R=3$ is slightly closer, use the value of $P(SO)_{D_i} = .027$ to recalculate $Q*$:

$$Q* = \sqrt{\frac{(2)(357.5)[2000 + (5000)(.027)]}{500}}$$

$$= 55.25 \text{ Porsches}$$

Again, substitute this value into the $P(SO)_{D_i}$ equation:

$$P(SO)_{D_i} = \frac{(500)(55.25)}{(5000)(357.5)}$$

$$= .015$$

Since $P(SO)_{D_i}$ did not change (for three significant figures), R will still be 3. Therefore, the minimum total expected cost occurs when $Q* = 55$ and $R* = 3$.

12.9 ABC ANALYSIS: DEVELOPING A HIERARCHY OF IMPORTANCE AMONG MULTIPLE INVENTORY PRODUCTS

It is quite rare for an organization to have inventory consisting of a single product. When multiple products are to be considered, many organizations use an *ABC Classification System* to assess the relative importance of each product. The motivation for this tier-type grouping is to identify those products that command the greatest investment of inventory dollars, and therefore warrant more sophisticated control and review procedures, like the EOQ type models assessed in this chapter, versus those inventory items that have such little inventory value that the expenses associated with inventory-management techniques cannot be economically sanctioned. These three categories are generally defined as follows:

Group A products consists of the small fraction of the total number of inventory items (10 to 15 percent) that accounts for the majority of the annual total inventory cost (60 to 80 percent) of an organization. It is crucial to control these inventory products closely. Consequently, it is both justifiable and highly advisable to use sophisticated inventory-management systems to keep watch on these products.

Group B products represent about 10 to 25 percent of the product list, and accounts for approximately 20 to 25 percent of the total inventory investment. Although this

group of products does not carry the across-the-board importance as does group A, it may nevertheless be of valuable enough to warrant employment of inventory control procedures.

Group C inventory items are the 50 to 85 percent of products remaining. They constitute the 50 to 80 percent of the inventory costs. These items are sometimes referred to as the "nuts and bolts" or "pencils and paperclips" products that justify little control; the potential savings will likely be outweighed by the expenses associated with any serious inventory-management procedures considered.

An illustration of a typical ABC inventory-classification system is shown in Figure 12-19. To apply the ABC classification procedure, we multiply the per-unit purchase cost associated with each unit of product by that product's total annual dollar demand, and, subsequently, we convert this value into the proportion of the total inventory-dollar investment for all of the products carried in inventory. An example of the classification procedure is illustrated in Table 12-28. Notice that parts 101 and 102 constitute 77.4 percent of the total annual inventory costs and are classified as the group A products. Tight inventory controls are justified for these items. Products 103 and 104 represents 21.1 percent of the total inventory dollars and are defined as group B. The remaining 11 products, account for 73.3 percent of the product list, but constitute only 1.5 percent of the inventory costs; they are placed in group C. A summary of the ABC Classification System for this example is shown in Table 12-29. Of course, this entire pro-

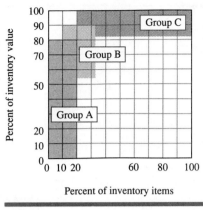

FIGURE 12-19

Illustration of ABC Inventory Classification System

TABLE 12-28

Example of ABC Classification Procedure for a 15-Product Inventory System

Part	Per-Unit Cost ($)	Annual Demand	Total Annual Inventory Value ($)	Percent of Total Inventory Value (%)
101	12,500	40	500,000	43.0
102	1,000	400	400,000	34.4
103	2,000	100	200,000	17.2
104	750	60	45,000	3.9
105	50	200	10,000	0.9
106	20	100	2,000	0.2
107	35	40	1,400	0.1
108	100	10	1,000	0.1
109	75	10	750	0.1
110	50	14	700	0.1
111	150	2	300	0.0
112	10	20	200	0.0
113	10	15	150	0.0
114	3	50	150	0.0
115	1	100	100	0.0
			1,161,750	100.0

TABLE 12-29

Summary of ABC Classification System Example

Group	No. of Products in Group	% of Total No. of Products	Inventory Value	% Inventory Value
A	2	13.33%	$900,000	77.4%
B	2	13.33	$245,000	21.1%
C	11	73.33	$16,750	1.5%

"I'm starting my vacation tomorrow, so I'll leave you 14 newspapers."

cess depends on the judgment of the manager in forming the tier classifications. Further, it is more of a tradition than a necessity to use three levels of classification. Nothing prevents a company from using any number of groups. The primary point of the classification process is to employ inventory-management practices that are discriminating and merit-driven. The decision regarding what amount of resources to spend on inventory management must differentiate between the importance that each of product plays in the overall operation of the business.

12.10 | SINGLE-PERIOD INVENTORIES: THE NEWSBOY PROBLEM

When products either are highly perishable (e.g., meats, poultry, and flowers) or become outdated rapidly (e.g., newspapers, magazines, holiday cards, and calendars), the problem may be viewed as a single-period inventory. The *newsboy problem* is the standard illustration used for this type of inventory setting, because day-old newspapers are viewed as worthless.

The single-period inventory dilemma is that you can order only once. The result of your order quantity is one of three different outcomes. Unfortunately, only one of these outcomes is highly desirable. These outcomes are

1. If you correctly anticipate the demand for your product, you will sell every unit you purchase.

2. If you overestimate demand, you will either lose all the money invested in the overstock or will recapture part of your investment by disposing of the unsold units for some minimal salvage value.

3. If you underestimate demand, you will sell everything. On the other hand, you will lose the opportunity to sell more goods (opportunity cost), and you will create ill-will among those unsatisfied customers. It is also likely that you will lose a portion of these unhappy customers to your competitors.

Now let's employ an example to illustrate how a single-period inventory works.

EXAMPLE 12.11   GODZILLA FOOD IMPORTERS

At 3:00 A.M., 7 days per week, Godzilla Food Importers of Seattle, Washington, picks up, among its many food products, ikura (salmon roe) from JAL Airlines. Just hours earlier, in Japan, the ikura was processed, packed in ice, and sent via JAL; so it arrives in Seattle less than 18 hours after it is removed from the female salmon. Godzilla pays the exporter a wholesale price of $25 per pound—packed in sealed, ice-cooled, 10-pound containers—for the ikura.

The primary customers of Godzilla's business are the many Japanese sushi bars and restaurants in the Seattle area. Godzilla receives approximately $45 per pound for the "same-day" ikura from these customers.[9] For the purposes of these patrons, the ikura must be at its freshest—it is viewed as acceptable for only a single day. Therefore, any ikura that Godzilla has not sold by the late morning—say 10:00 A.M.—must be sold to other outlets. Godzilla freezes all the unsold ikura and resells it to a food broker who

---

[9] Godzilla requires that the ikura be purchased in multiples of 10-pound containers. The ikura cannot be repackaged and sold in any lesser quantity.

services the hotel and specialty-market industry. These secondary commercial outlets, although concerned about quality, do not have the extreme freshness requirements demanded by most of the Japanese restaurants. Godzilla receives approximately $15 per pound for the frozen ikura from the food broker.

Godzilla knows from experience that an average sushi bar uses between 100 and 170 pounds per day. Since Godzilla's customers do not plan any change in their present operations (advertising, expansion, etc.), the company assumes that the demand for the ikura will remain stable. After sitting down with a sampling of 111 daily sales receipts from the past year, Godzilla's accountant extracts and organizes the data regarding ikura sales shown in Table 12-30.

Godzilla's CEO wants to be able to use these data carefully, so that the company will not get stuck with excess ikura. On the other hand, she estimates that Godzilla loses business beyond the foregone sales when it does not purchase enough ikura: Customers will quickly tire of insufficient stock and will take their business elsewhere. In fact, she estimates that, for each pound of demand for ikura that is in excess of the amount actually ordered by Godzilla, $50 is lost due to ill-will and to customers who switch to another food importer. Using these data, how many pounds of ikura should Godzilla order for each day's delivery?

TABLE 12-30

Ikura Sales Data for Godzilla Food Importers

Order Quantity Q, (lbs)	Number of Days $D = Q,t$	Probability of Demand $P(D)$
100	1	.009
110	6	.054
120	15	.135
130	28	.252
140	32	.289
150	18	.162
160	9	.081
170	2	.018
	111	1.000

SOLUTION

For each pound of ikura sold fresh, Godzilla makes $45 minus $25, or $20. If the ikura must be frozen, Godzilla loses $25 minus $15, or $10, per pound. When the demand exceeds the order quantity (supply), Godzilla loses $50 per pound due to customer ill-will and to customers switching to competitors. The general relationship is given by

Profit = ($20/pound demand satisfied) − ($15/pound supply in excess of
demand) − ($50/pound demand in excess of supply)

Since it is rare that the quantity ordered is exactly equal to the demand for a given day, let's examine the two situations that will typically occur.

1. *Order quantity exceeds demand ($Q > D$).* Suppose, for example, that today Godzilla purchases 140 pounds of ikura and that the demand for the day is only 120 pounds. What is the amount for day's profit?

   We are given that the demand satisfied is 120 pounds. Thus, no primary customer goes away unhappy. However, Godzilla must sell the excess 20 pounds of ikura to the broker at a $10-per-pound loss. The profit is, then,

   Profit = (20) (120) − (10) (140 − 120) − (50)(0)
   = 2400 − 200 + 0
   = $2200

2. *Demand exceeds order quantity ($Q < D$).* Now suppose we see what happens when Godzilla is too conservative in estimating daily demand. Pretend that Godzilla purchases 140 pounds of ikura, but the demand for that day was for 160 pounds of the sushi delicacy. What is Godzilla's profit under these conditions?

   We are given that the demand satisfied is only 140 pounds. There is no leftover ikura to freeze, and to resell to the broker. However, a demand for 20 pounds goes unmet, resulting in customer ill will and lost trade. The profit is, then,

   Profit = (20) (140) − (1) (0) − (50)(160 − 140)
   = 2800 − 0 − 1000
   = $1800

Now let's organize all of these risk data concerning order quantities and probabilities of various demand levels so that we can squeeze all possible information from them. Table 12-31 shows the data arranged in a more usable fashion. The numerical columns headers represent the various levels of daily demand for ikura, D; shown opposite these values, in the column footer, are the three-decimal-place numbers representing the probability for that level of demand. The left-row margins represent the quantity of ikura purchased for resale by Godzilla. Finally, the right-column margins represent the anticipated (expected) Godzilla profits that result from the intersection of each order quantity (row) with each level of demand (column).

The results of this expected-profit analysis suggest that it is advisable for Godzilla *always to purchase the maximum 170 pounds of ikura* no matter what the demand. The reason for this outcome is that the penalty for not having leftover ikura, when order quantity is less than demand, is $50 per pound. This setting greatly overshadows the $10-per-pound penalty for having surplus ikura remaining at the end of the daily sales. We can easily illustrate this situation by using *marginal analysis*.

Marginal Analysis Approach   To determine whether more ikura should be purchased for a specific order quantity, we simply calculate the *expected profit* versus the *expected cost* of adding 1 more pound of ikura.[10] These expected values are given by

$$EV[\text{profit}] = p\,(\Delta P)$$
$$EV[\text{cost}] = (1-p)\,(\Delta C)$$

where

$$p = \text{probability of selling at least one more unit of product}$$
$$1-p = \text{probability of not selling one more unit of product}$$
$$\Delta P = \text{marginal profit resulting from adding one more unit of product}$$
$$\Delta C = \text{marginal cost resulting from adding one more unit of product}$$

The idea is to keep adding to the order quantity so long as the expected gain (profit) exceeds the expected loss (cost). We discontinue this incremental addition process when the two expected values are equal. The addition of the next unit will result in an expected loss.

Knowing the point at which the expected profit value and the expected loss value are equal allows the manager to calculate an interesting piece of information: the minimum probability that allows the business—Godzilla, in this case—to add one more unit of product into its inventory. This probability is simply calculated as follows:

$$p(\Delta P) = (1 - p)\,(\Delta C)$$

and, solving for p,

$$p(\Delta P) - \Delta C + p(\Delta C) = 0$$
$$p(\Delta P + \Delta C) = \Delta C$$

Finally,

$$p = \frac{\Delta C}{\Delta P + \Delta C}$$

For the addition of one more unit of product to the inventory to be justified, the chances for selling that additional unit must be *at least* equal to p. Now, let's find the

[10]Turban and Meredith (1988), pp. 614–615, provide an excellent example of marginal analysis.

TABLE 12-31

Godzilla Food Importer Tradeoff Between Order Quantity (Q) and Customer Demand (D) for Ikura

		Level of Demand for Ikura, D (lbs)							Expected Value of Profit, ($)
Order Quantity of Ikura Purchased by Godzilla, Q (lbs)		100	110	120	130	140	150	160	170	
	100	2000	1500	1000	500	0	−500	−1000	−1500	649
	110	2100	2200	1700	1200	700	200	−300	−800	1311
	120	2200	2300	2400	2400	1400	900	400	−100	2036
	130	2300	2400	2500	2600	2100	1600	1100	600	2320
	140	2400	2500	2600	2700	2800	2300	1800	1300	2576
	150	2500	2600	2700	2800	2900	3000	2500	2000	2735
	160	2600	2700	2800	2900	3000	3100	3200	2700	2845
	170	2700	2800	2900	3000	3100	3200	3300	3400	2944
		.009	.054	.135	.252	.289	.162	.081	.018	
					Probability of Demand, $P(D)$					

TABLE 12-32

Marginal-Analysis Solution to the Godzilla Food-Importer Example

Order Quantity, Q (lbs)	Probability of Demand, $P(D)$	Cumulative Probability of $P(D \geq Q)$
100	.009	1.000
110	.054	.991
120	.135	.937
130	.252	.802
140	.289	.550
150	.162	.261
160	.081	.099
170	.018	.018
	1.000	

marginal profit and cost values. If Godzilla sells one additional 10-pound unit, the ΔP is the $20-per-pound profit times the 10 pounds of ikura, or $200. On the other hand, if Godzilla cannot sell that last unit due to an underorder, it suffers a $500 loss associated with foregone sales and customer ill-will.[11] Therefore, $\Delta P = 200, whereas $\Delta C = 500. The magic probability can now be calculated easily:

$$p = \frac{\Delta C}{\Delta P + \Delta C}$$

$$= \frac{500}{200 + 500} = .714$$

Now, let's use some of the probability data from Table 12-31 to form a cumulative probability associated with selling 1 more 10-pound container of ikura for each order quantity. The results are shown in Table 12-32. Here is how to read this table. The chance of selling at least 100 pounds of ikura is 100 percent. You know that Godzilla al-

[11]We find the $500 loss by multiplying the $50 per pound times the 10-pound unit of ikura.

ways sells at least that much. The likelihood of selling 110 pounds is over 99 percent, so ordering that quantity of ikura is fine. In fact, Godzilla can keep adding the 10-pound unit increments until the 130-pound level. At a order quantity of 130 pounds, the optimal level has been found. The next level has a cumulative probability of .550—less than the .714 value needed. So, marginal analysis provides an answer slightly different from that given by the expected value approach.

| 12.11 | ADVANCES IN INVENTORY-MANAGEMENT SYSTEMS FOR MANUFACTURED GOODS: MATERIAL REQUIREMENTS PLANNING (MRP) AND KANBAN

The inventory-management, reorder-point models already discussed in this chapter are most effective when applied to finished goods. In these types of situations, there is an *independent* demand for goods, which is typically estimated by appropriate forecasting methods. In manufacturing, however, inventories consist not only of finished goods, but also of subassemblies, components, and even raw materials. Unfortunately, reorder-point inventory systems do not operate well in a manufacturing environment. Two different types of manufacturing inventory systems that can effectively manage a production-oriented setting will be discussed briefly next. We provide only a simple overview of these complex methods. The reference articles and texts cited at the end of this chapter will provide more detail.

Material Requirements Planning   The demand for manufacturing inventories is *dependent* on the number of units of finished goods already in inventory. Although the demand for the finished product is still forecast, the amount of unfinished inventory constituents can be readily calculated. The technique used to conduct such calculations of the dependent-demand inventory is referred to as *material requirements planning* (MRP). MRP systems are computer-based and are driven by a master schedule: a detailed or "parts-explosion" road map of purchase orders for raw materials and manufacturing orders for production scheduling in the factory. So, if the forecast demand calls for the production of 20,000 Cadillac Sevilles at General Motors, the parts explosion will include a bill of materials (BOM) listing each part needed to assemble the exact number of Cadillacs required by the master schedule. Further, the MRP takes into consideration the parts and raw materials already in inventory or on order; for example, the order of 20,000 Cadillacs may require the purchase and manufacture of only 12,000 sets of component parts, since 6000 units are already on order and an additional 2000 units are in stock (inventory). Assuming independent demand by ignoring the MRP method, the net requirement for each component part would be

$$\begin{pmatrix} \text{net number} \\ \text{of parts} \\ \text{needed} \end{pmatrix} = \begin{pmatrix} \text{number of parts} \\ \text{required to meet} \\ \text{demand for} \\ \text{finished product} \end{pmatrix} - \begin{pmatrix} \text{number of} \\ \text{parts in} \\ \text{inventory} \end{pmatrix}$$

However, the MRP approach, which recognizes the dependent-demand setting in production operations, calculates the net demand as

$$\begin{pmatrix} \text{net number} \\ \text{of parts} \\ \text{needed} \end{pmatrix} = \begin{pmatrix} \text{number of} \\ \text{gross parts} \\ \text{required} \end{pmatrix} - \begin{pmatrix} \text{scheduled} \\ \text{receipts} \end{pmatrix} - \begin{pmatrix} \text{number of} \\ \text{parts in} \\ \text{inventory} \end{pmatrix}$$

MRP systems have several levels of sophistication and have been applied in a number of different ways. Three of them are, briefly,

- *MRP I* is an inventory management system that is focused on the master schedule of finished products of a manufacturing operation. Manufacturing and purchase orders are launched at the appropriate time to support the master schedule. The system takes into account and controls for the number of units in production, as well as the raw material/subassembly/component part inventories, through accurate timing of order placements.
- *MRP II* can balance order quantities and the master schedule to ensure that there is available production capacity. If there is not sufficient capacity, MRP II adjusts for the mismatch either by altering the schedule or by increasing the manufacturing capacity.
- *MRP III* plans and manages the total spectrum of manufacturing elements, including inventory material (both finished and unfinished goods), production capacity, cash flow, equipment, personnel, and facility operations.

The actual implementation of MRP II and MRP III systems has been limited due to expense and complexity.

Zero-Inventory Systems/Kanban   In the early 1980s, interest rates hovered around 20 percent. Accompanying holding costs were so high that many companies with large inventories—especially manufacturing operations—could not carry the expense and went out of business. *Zero inventory* thinking, in which a conscious effort was made to minimize and, if possible, to eliminate inventories became popular during this period. Dramatically reducing the expenses associated with inventories—such as handling costs, costs of perishable goods, internal loss, and theft of inventories— became one of the more important priorities of many businesses.

Although zero-inventory systems are not yet common in the United States, the JIT (just-in-time) system is popular in Japan. In fact, Toyota introduced their own version of JIT called the *kanban* system, in which only the shortage products are produced, and those only when necessary and in the quantity needed—no overstock, no earlier-than-necessary availability. Although kanban is manufacturing-oriented, it has some qualities that are quite different from the similarly focused MRP:

1. Kanban is a manual system, not a computer-based one. It is simpler and less expensive to operate than is an MRP system.

2. Ordering materials is initiated by *actual* usage in the kanban system, not *planned* usage. Forecasting errors regarding demand levels can be accommodated more easily.

3. Kanban is a *pull system*: Parts are pulled out of inventory supplies at locations and times as needed. MRP is a *push system*: The master schedule pushes materials forward, since the usage is based on the planned schedule, not on the actual schedule.

Toyota's version of kanban uses a pair of cards for each inventory part number: the C-kanban card and the P-kanban card. The C-kanban accompanies each delivery container full of a specific part, with a part number, which is rolled out to the production area. A worker who is out of this part takes an empty container and the C-kanban card to the parts storage location. The worker then removes the P-kanban from a full container of that specific part and attaches the C-kanban. The P-kanban is then placed in a special box, signaling the need for more production of that particular part. The full C-kanban container of parts is then rolled back to the assembly area by the worker for immediate usage. As a new part is produced, a bin is filled, and the P-kanban is attached.

Toyota kanban uses two rules zealously:

1. **No production can occur without a P-kanban.** This rule prevents overusage of the production facility. Kanban focuses on immediate usage without a buildup of goods without need—as close to a true zero inventory as possible.

2. **Each container must hold the exact number of parts on the kanban.** This provides rigid enforcement of small stock quantities. There are sometimes as few as two containers for each part number—one empty and waiting for the new production run, and one in use at the assembly area!

Of course, as with any system, kanban has drawbacks. Two of them are these:

1. **The part numbers must be used regularly.** If a particular part is not used regularly, its production is planned using some other method (e.g., reorder point or MRP method).

2. **Setup time for each part number must be rapid.** A streamlined, almost religiously dedicated organization is needed if kanban is to operate properly.

An excellent comparison of reorder point, MRP, kanban, and other types of inventory systems is presented in Richard Schonberger (1985, Chap. 6). An illustration of these systems is presented in Figure 12-20.

12.12 | MICROCOMPUTER SOLUTIONS TO INVENTORY-MANAGEMENT PROBLEMS

The solutions of the IMS models explored in this chapter are highly amenable to microcomputer software solution. The data-entry process is rapid and simple, and the programs offer a far more productive use of a manager's time than arcane pencil-and-paper

FIGURE 12-20

Manufacturing Inventory Systems: A Comparison of Type, Ease of Use, and Inventory Level Requirements

Source: R. J. Schonberger, *Operations Management: Productivity and Quality*, 2nd ed. (Plano, TX: Business Publications, 1985).

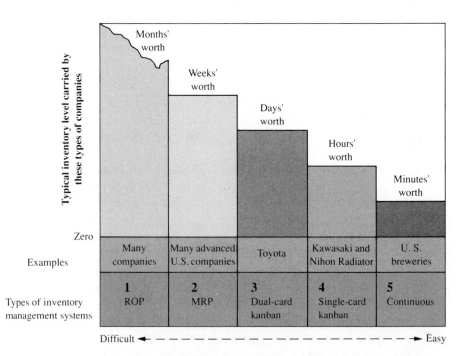

number grinding. We shall solve two of the examples covered in this chapter using two of the microcomputer software packages listed in Section 12.14.

First, we use Chang and Sullivan's *Quantitative Systems for Business* to solve Example 12.3 (EOQ Model 3). Table 12-33 illustrates the solution to problem. Next, the *Micro Manager* quantity-discounts inventory module (EOQ Model 5) is used to solve Example 12.5. These results are shown in Table 12-34. Notice the simplicity of the

```
                EOQ Results for TOYS-R-US
    EOQ Input Data:
        Demand per YEAR (D)  =  50000
        Order or setup cost per order (Co)  =  50
        Holding cost per unit per YEAR (Ch)  =  2
        Shortage cost per unit per YEAR (Cs)  =  4
        Shortage cost per unit, independent of time (c)  =  0
        Replenishment or production rate per YEAR (P) = 1
        Lead time for a new order in YEAR (LT)  =  0
        Unit cost (C)  =  0

    EOQ Ouput:
        EOQ  =  1936.497
        Maximum inventory  =  1290.991
        Maximum backorder  =  645.496
        Order interval  =  0.039 YEARS
        Reorder point  =  -645.496
        Ordering cost  =  1290.991
        Holding cost  =  860.661
        Shortage cost  =  430.330
        Subtotal of inventory cost per YEAR  =  2581.982
        Material cost per YEAR  =  0.000
        Total cost per YEAR  =  2581.982
```

TABLE 12-33

Solution of Toys'R'Us Backorder Inventory, Example 12.3

Reference: Chang and Sullivan, *Quantitative Systems for Business*. Englewood Cliffs, NJ: Prentice-Hall (1986).

```
            PROGRAM:  Inventory Models

        *****  INPUT DATA ENTERED  *****

            Quantity discount model

    Demand (annual)  :  50000 units/year
    Annual working days  :  360 days/year
    Ordering cost  :  $ 50/ order
    Holding cost as percentage  :  20%

    Price levels for minimum order quantity
    -----------------------------------------------
        Levels      Minimum quantity    Price
    -----------------------------------------------
          1            10000.0          2.50
          2             5000.0          2.60
          3             3000.0          2.75
    -----------------------------------------------

            *****  PROGRAM OUTPUT  *****
    -----------------------------------------------
    Quantity per order    10000.00    5000.00    3015.10
    -----------------------------------------------
    Total holding cost     2500.00    1300.00     829.20
    Total ordering cost     250.00     500.00     829.20
    Total purchase cost  125000.00  130000.00  137500.00
    -----------------------------------------------
    Total inventory cost 127750.00  131800.00  139158.30
```

TABLE 12-34

Solution to Chicago Hyatt Regency Table Wine Quantity-Discount Model, Exercise 12.5

Source: Lee and Shim, *Micro Manager*. Dubuque, IA: William C. Brown, (1986).

data-entry process for both software products. You should have little fear of getting lost along the way.

12.13 SUMMARY

The careful management of inventory costs will often make the difference between a healthy and growing business and one in which profit is only a dream. This chapter has examined a number of inventory models within three different families: (1) deterministic EOQ models, (2) heuristic lumpy demand models, and (3) stochastic inventory models.

The use of deterministic inventory models can provide the manager with useful approximations when the real details do not depart significantly from the EOQ model. Unfortunately, the simplicity of such models is often overshadowed by real-world complexities that reach far beyond the models' ranges of applicability; for example, demand is rarely (if ever) known with true certainty, restocking is not instantaneous, and lead times are also unreliable. When demand is uneven or nonuniform, the lumpy heuristic inventory models can be useful. When both demand and lead time considerations are uncertain, stochastic methods can be of great value.

For manufacturing systems, when inventory is not independent, the use of MRP or kanban–zero-inventory methods is rapidly growing in importance and may be the new wave of the near future.

12.14 EXERCISES

The following exercises represent hypothetical, yet realistic, problems settings. Although the exercises are meant to appear "genuine," you should not misinterpret them by thinking that the conditions described are factual.

12-1 Macy's Department Store in Minneapolis sells 1500 Sony televisions per year. The average wholesale cost of each television is $400. Macy estimates ordering costs at $750. Given that the annual holding cost is $6.00 per unit, determine the following:

1. Which EOQ model should be selected? Why?
2. How often should orders be placed?
3. What is the optimal order quantity?
4. What are the annual holding costs?
5. What are the annual ordering costs?
6. What are the total annual costs?

12-2 Software World Corporation (SWC), a discount mail-order house, buys 10,000 copies of *Lotus 1-2-3* each year for resale. The ordering costs are $100 per order; the carrying cost is estimated to be 20 percent of the per-unit price. SWC is trying to determine the optimal order quantity based on the Lotus Corporation's discount price schedule, illustrated in Table 12-2.1.

1. Find the optimal order quantity for each of the four price levels.

TABLE 12-2.1

Lotus 1-2-3 Price-Break Schedule

Quantity Ordered	Unit Price
1 ≤ 999	$250.00
1000 ≤ 4999	$235.00
5000 ≤ 9999	$225.00
≥ 10,000	$218.00

2. What is the largest EOQ that falls in an appropriate price-level and order-quantity range?
3. What is the minimum total inventory cost associated with each price level, using the EOQ found in part 2?

12-3 The University of California at San Francisco (UCSF) Dental School uses 24,000 pairs of latex gloves each school year (this includes use in both laboratory and clinics). The university spends $.50 per pair of gloves. Each order placement costs about $25.00, and holding costs are estimated at 10 percent. The lead time for these gloves is 14 days. Determine the following:

1. What is the optimal order quantity?
2. How many new orders are placed each year?
3. What is the minimum inventory level?
4. What are the minimum total inventory-system costs?

12-4 Assume that the lead time associated with the latex-glove orders for the UCSF Dental School (Exercise 12-3) is 30 days, instead of 14 days. Answer these questions:

1. What is the optimal order quantity?
2. How many new orders are placed each year?
3. What is the minimum inventory level?
4. What are the minimum total inventory-system costs?

12-5 A. J. Canfield Company of Chicago sells 1,100,000 gallons of Diet Chocolate Fudge soda syrup to 11 franchised bottling companies each year. The demand rate is reasonably constant. The annual production capacity at Canfield is 3,000,000 gallons. Canfield estimates that the purging, washing, sterilizing, preparation, and other assembly-line setup costs are $800.00. The cost of producing each gallon of soda syrup is $1.95, and the annual holding costs are about 13 percent. What is the optimal production-lot size for Canfield?

12-6 Off Road Vehicles, Inc., of Cincinnati specializes in AMC Jeep four-wheel-drive vehicles. Its annual demand for such vehicles is 300 units. Each order that it places costs $150; the holding cost is about $125 per year per unit. The company estimates that the stockout cost is about $40 per vehicle. Answer the following questions:

1. What is the optimal order quantity?
2. What is the maximum shortage level?
3. How many orders should be placed each year?
4. What is the amount of time between each order?
5. For what amount of time during each cycle are vehicles available?
6. For what amount of time during each cycle are vehicles out of stock?
7. What are the minimum inventory-system costs?

12-7 Liquor Barn of San Rafael (a discount beer, wine, and liquor outlet) has a 6-week demand schedule for Anchor Steam Beer, as illustrated in Table 12-7.1. The ordering cost from Anchor Steam is $25.00; the holding costs are estimated at $.75 per case per week. The beginning inventory is zero. Answer the following questions:

1. What is the EOQ model order quantity, assuming an average demand across this 6-week period? What is the minimum inventory-system cost?
2. What is the minimal inventory-system cost for the lot-for-lot heuristic method?
3. What is the minimal inventory-system cost for the fixed order quantity heuristic method?
4. What is the minimal inventory-system cost for the periodic order quantity heuristic method?
5. What is the minimal inventory-system cost for the part period balancing heuristic method?
6. What is the minimal inventory-system cost for the least unit cost heuristic method?
7. Of all methods you examined, which one would you select?

TABLE 12-7.1

Six-Week Liquor Barn Demand for Anchor Steam Beer (Cases of Beer)

	Week					
	1	*2*	*3*	*4*	*5*	*6*
Demand	200	125	100	300	150	150

TABLE 12-8.1

Television Discount Price Structure for Macy's Example

Quantity	Unit Price
1–99	$400
100–299	$375
≥ 300	$360

12-8 Macy's (Exercise 12-1) learns that it may be able to take advantage of a new discount price structure for the television sets they purchase. Specifically, the price structure for the televisions is as shown in Table 12-8.1. If the ordering and holding costs remain the same, what is the optimal inventory policy for Macy's?

12-9 The UCSF Dental School (Exercise 12-3) wishes to reconsider the quantity of latex gloves purchased per order, based on the discount price structure, available through their dental-supplies distributor, shown in Table 12-9.1. The ordering and holding costs remain the same. What is the optimal inventory policy for the dental school?

12-10 The Same Old Grind Company sells three green coffee beans from three different countries: Brazil, Africa, and Jamaica. The demand, ordering and holding costs, and per-unit storage costs for each product are shown in Table 12-10.1. The

TABLE 12-9.1

Latex-Rubber-Glove Discount Price Structure for UCSF Dental School

Quantity	Unit Price
< 5000	$.50
5000–9999	$.47
$\geq 10,000$	$.43

TABLE 12-10.1

Inventory Data for Same Old Grind Coffee Products

Parameter	Coffee Type		
	Brazil	*Africa*	*Jamaica*
D_i, lbs/year	60,000	30,000	25,000
c_{o_i}, $/order	40.00	60.00	35.00
c_{h_i}, $/lb/year	.50	.50	.50
v_i, ft^3/lb	.05	.05	.05

TABLE 12-15.1

Six-Month Ford Dealership Demand Schedule for Automobiles

	Month					
	1	*2*	*3*	*4*	*5*	*6*
Demand	60	50	90	40	80	80

maximum space available in the facility for storing these three coffees is 1200 ft^3, and the rental cost for this space is $13.50 per ft^3 per year. What is the minimum inventory-system cost?

12-11 The Yellow Cab Company of Santa Ana, California, uses 600 sets of tires per year for its vehicles. Each set of tires costs the company $185. The ordering costs are approximated at $35 per order, and the holding costs are about 10 percent. If the tire distributor offers the cab company a 4 percent discount for orders of at least 200 sets, should Yellow Cab accept? Assume tires are presently ordered on an EOQ basis.

12-12 Orion Pictures uses 15,000,000 feet of film per year for its various movie productions. It costs $400 to place an order, and holding costs are 20 percent per year (primarily due to spoilage). What is the optimal order quantity? How many orders per year are placed? What is the minimum total inventory costs?

12-13 Whole Earth Access, a discount department store in northern California, sells 4750 VCRs each year. Each order they place for the equipment costs $65.95, the per-unit annual holding cost is $20.00, and the shortage cost is approximated at $35.00 per unit. Determine values for the following:

1. The optimal order quantity.
2. The maximum shortage level.
3. The total number of orders per year.
4. The time between each order.
5. The time during each cycle that the product is available.
6. The time during each cycle that there is a stockout.
7. The minimum system costs.

12-14 Famous Amos Cookie Company's Western regional manufacturing facility in California produces 50,000 pounds of chocolate-chip macadamia-nut cookies each year for sale in its Los Angeles retail-outlet stores. The production costs on this candy product are $1.50 per pound, ordering costs are $50.00, and the holding cost is 15 percent per year. Determine the following:

1. What are the optimal inventory parameters for the present arrangement?
2. What are the optimal inventory parameters if Famous Amos decides to add stock at a rate of 250 pounds per day, rather than to receive batch deliveries? All other operating parameters are the same as in part 1, except the setup cost for each cycle is equal to the ordering cost (i.e., $c_u = \$65.95$).

12-15 A Ford Motor Company dealership in Louisville, Kentucky, has the 6-month demand schedule for automobiles that is illustrated in Table 12-15.1. The ordering cost from Ford is $2000, and the holding cost is estimated at $100 per vehicle per month. The beginning inventory is assumed to be zero. Determine the order quantities and total system costs if the following are true:

1. The inventory system follows the EOQ lumpy demand model.
2. The company is unconcerned about ordering costs but wishes to minimize holding costs.
3. The company can order only fixed quantities of 70 vehicles per order.
4. The company is primarily concerned with the timing of the order.
5. The company wishes to balance holding and ordering costs.
6. The company is primarily concerned with minimizing the *average* per-unit holding and order cost.

References

1. Canen, Alberto G. "An Application of ABC Analysis to Control Imported Material." *Inferfaces* 10 (No. 4: November–December 1980): 22–44.

2. Brown, Kenneth S., and Jack B. Revelle. *Quantitative Methods for Managerial Decisions*. Reading, MA: Addison-Wesley, 1978.

3. Dannenbring, David G., and Martin K. Starr. *Management Science: An Introduction*. New York: McGraw-Hill, 1981.

4. Dumas, Barry M. "Policies for Reducing Blood Wastage in Hospital Blood Banks." *Management Science* 23 (No. 10: October 1977): 1124–1132.

5. Flowers, Dale A. "An Application of Classical Inventory Analysis to a Spare Parts Inventory." *Interfaces* 8 (No. 2: 1978): 76–79.

6. Lieberman, Varda. "On the Hotel Overbooking Problem—An Inventory System with Stochastic Cancellations." *Management Science* 24 (No. 11: November 1978): 1117–1126.

7. Moskowitz, Herbert, and Gordon P. Wright. *Operations Research Techniques for Management*. Englewood Cliffs, NJ: Prentice-Hall, 1979.

8. Narragon, E. A., M. I. Dessouky, and R. E. Devor. "A Prob-

ablistic Model for Analyzing Campus Parking Policies." *Operations Research* 22 (No. 5: September–October 1974): 1025–1039.

9. Schonberger, Richard J. *Operations Management: Productivity and Quality*, 2nd ed. Plano, TX: Business Publications, 1985.

10. Schroeder, Roger G. *Operations Management: Decision Making in the Operations Function*, 2nd ed. New York: McGraw-Hill, 1985.

11. Turban, Efraim, and Jack R. Meredith. *Fundamentals of Management Science*, 4th ed. Plano, TX: Business Publications, 1988.

Inventory-Management Microcomputer Software

There is not a large number of affordable, microcomputer inventory management software packages available. However, as with other types of management science techniques that are not readily available in specialized software packages (e.g., queueing, forecasting), IMS modules are found in numerous multiple-module software products. A few of these products are listed here:

1. *Computer Models for Management Science*, version 2. Erikson and Hall. Reading, MA: Addison-Wesley, 1986.

2. *Decision Support Modeling*. San Juan Capistrano, CA: Decision Support Systems, 1986.

3. *Management Science and the Microcomputer*. Burns and Austin. New York: Macmillan, 1985.

4. *Microcomputer Models for Management Decision-Making*. Dennis and Dennis. St. Paul, MN: West, date?

5. *Microcomputer Software for Management Science and Operations Management*. Render and Stair. Boston: Allyn & Bacon, 1986.

6. *MicroManager*. Sang Lee and Yung Shim. Dubuque, IA: William C. Brown, 1986.

7. *Mr. Quarter Master*. Milford, CT: RJL Systems.

8. *Quantitative Systems for Business*. Chang and Sullivan. Englewood Cliffs, NJ: Prentice-Hall, 1986.

9. *STORM*. Dale Flowers et al. Oakland, CA: Holden-Day, 1986.

CHAPTER 13

PROJECT MANAGEMENT TECHNIQUES

| 13.1 | INTRODUCTION

Project management is a technique that can aid in the planning, scheduling, and monitoring of complex projects characterized by numerous, nonrepetitive jobs called activities. Examples of projects that would use project management include:

- Developing a mass rapid-transit system for a metropolitan area
- Organizing the relocation of a corporate headquarters
- Planning the production of a concert, film, or play
- Developing and marketing a new automobile
- Constructing a high-rise office building

Without thoughtful planning, projects like these are likely to be loaded with unanticipated delays, missed deadlines, poorly allocated resources, and a guaranteed budget overrun. In short, any significantly complex project will almost assuredly cost more

Drawing by Leo Cullum; © 1986
The New Yorker Magazine, Inc.

and take longer to complete than would have been the case had project management been used.

Analysts using project management can discover critical information essential to effective project planning and control. In particular, they can determine, in advance,

1. The individual activities constituting the project

2. The interrelationship among these activities with respect to their chronological sequencing; that is, which activities must be arranged in series (one after the other), and which can be run in parallel (simultaneously)

3. Educated estimates of the time and monies required for the normal completion of each activity

4. The time needed to complete the entire project

5. The activities that are the most likely to extend the project completion date (critical-path activities)

6. The earliest dates that the different activities can be started and finished without changing the project completion date

7. The latest dates that the different activities can be started and finished without changing the project completion date

8. The amount of time that individual activities can be delayed without causing the project to be delayed

The importance of project management to business is wonderfully illustrated by the way the Microsoft Corporation begins their ad for the microcomputer software package, *Microsoft Project*.[1]

| Producing a brochure. Introducing a new product. Moving your entire company across town. Every project has a start date, a completion date, and a date beyond which you absolutely, positively, cannot go. The drop dead date. Blow that date and you've got positively, absolutely no excuses.

Microsoft Project™ tells you which activities are essential to keeping your schedule. And which you can let slide. Give it your best to worst "what-if" scenarios. It tells you what must be accomplished. By whom. By when. At what cost.

Should you decide you can face another drop dead without *Microsoft Project*™, tell us where to send the flowers. |

| 13.2 | TRADITIONAL PROJECT MANAGEMENT METHODS: PERT AND CPM

The most commonly used methods in project management are the program evaluation and review technique (PERT) and the critical-path method (CPM). Although developed independently during the 1950s, these two methods are essentially identical; only two distinctions usually are made. The first difference is the way activity durations are estimated. In CPM, only a single time value is used. For PERT, a three-valued distribution is used to generate a weighted average time. Therefore, CPM can be viewed as a *deterministic* method, whereas PERT is a *stochastic* model. The second distinction is that, whereas PERT focuses exclusively on the planning and management of time, CPM extends its focus to include *time–cost* tradeoffs. Therefore, the ultimate decision regarding which of these two methods to employ will rest largely on two criteria:

[1]*PC World*, Vol. 3, No. 1 (January 1985), 56.

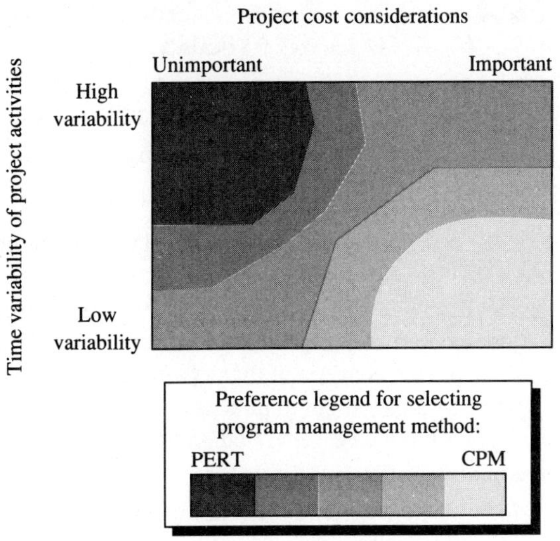

Project cost considerations

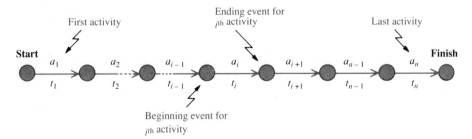

FIGURE 13-1

Project Cost and Variability of Activity Duration Considerations in Selecting Between Program Evaluation and Review Technique (PERT) and Critical-Path Method (CPM)

Preference legend for selecting program management method:

PERT .... CPM

1. The complexity of the project and the variability of project activity durations
2. The budget for the project

The relationship between these two criteria and the two project management techniques is shown in Figure 13-1. Nevertheless, for our purposes, we will not discriminate between the two methods. Both will be explored later in considerable detail. First, the language and symbols of project management will be examined.

13.3 THE JARGON AND NOTATION OF PROJECT MANAGEMENT

There are few symbols for you to worry about in project management. Basically, there are only events and activities. An *activity* is the *ongoing process* of conducting a specific task; the beginning and conclusion of that activity—those *instantaneous slices in time* that mark the start and end of that activity—are called *events*. So, an activity uses resources (amounts of time, money, materials, skills, etc.), whereas an event does not. Pictorially, an event is depicted by a numbered node (circle), whereas an activity is represented by an arc (arrow). Further, the activities are typically numbered and are accompanied by time estimates in parentheses. For example, from the generalized network path of Figure 13-2, a_i represents the ith activity that takes t_i units of time to complete and is bounded by its beginning and ending events. Now, let's see how to construct and analyze a network.

Ending event for
$_i$th activity

First activity
Last activity

Start
Finish

a_1 a_2 a_{i-1} a_i a_{i+1} a_{n-1} a_n

t_1 t_2 t_{i-1} t_i t_{i+1} t_{n-1} t_n

Beginning event for
$_i$th activity

FIGURE 13-2

Standard Project Management Symbols

13.4 PROJECT MANAGEMENT STRUCTURE AND LIMITATIONS

There are two basic rules that we must follow in laying out a project network:

1. Each activity is represented by a single arrow or arc.

2. No two activities can begin and end on the same two event nodes.

Rule 1 is essential in order to provide a unique identity for each activity. The need for rule 2 is a little more subtle and for this reason will be discussed in detail later, when the concept of the *dummy activity variable* is examined. Let it be sufficient to say for now that, without rule 2, spurious constraining relationships would be introduced that would make the analysis of the network impossible.

Before you can begin to plan any project, information regarding the basic elements of a network must be generated and organized. In particular, you will have to, at the bare minimum,

1. Identify each activity (task or job) necessary to complete the project with a unique identification number

2. Estimate how long it will take to complete each activity

3. Identify the predecessor activities for each subsequent activity in the project

There are also several limiting features of PERT-CPM models that the manager must always keep in mind. These include:

1. All activities must be completed before the project can be completed; that is, no task can be partially finished or overlooked.

2. All activities must be completed in chronological order; that is, no later event can occur before all prior events have been completed.

3. No activities can be repeated; that is, no looping can occur.

4. For stochastic activities (PERT), the distribution is limited to the beta-type (Section 13-8).

5. The project must end with one and only one terminal event.

6. The critical path consists of the activities, from beginning to end event, with the longest cumulative time duration. (In the case of PERT, the duration is the mean time lapse.)

Now let's tackle a problem that we will use throughout this chapter to gain experience designing a network.

EXAMPLE 13.1   THE BROADWAY MUSICAL

A theatrical producer has just found a musical that she believes holds great promise as a Broadway musical. She approaches the author-composer and successfully negotiates the stage rights to the play. She also signs the author to adapt the original material for the play. She is well aware now that she is going to have to orchestrate carefully the various artistic (writer, director, musicians, actors, singers, choreographer, and dancers), technical (sound, lighting, costume and set designers), and business staff (advertising, sales, accounting) who represent the wide variety of talent that will be needed to make this play a success. She decides that it would be wise to employ project management to help her organize this complex and delicate project.

TABLE 13-1

Basic Data for Structuring Project Schedule for Broadway Musical

Activity	Expected Completion Time (weeks)	Activity Immediately Preceding
1. Capitalize play, a_1	6	none
2. Writer adaption, a_2	4	1
3. Director search, a_3	4	2
4. Theater search, a_4	6	none
5. Dummy activity 1, a_5	0	3
6. Cast auditions, a_6	2	4,5
7. Hire staff, a_7	3	3
8. Dummy activity 2, a_8	0	7
9. Rehearsals, a_9	4	6,8
10. Costume design and fabrication, a_{10}	6	7
11. Set design and construction, a_{11}	8	7
12. Dummy activity 3, a_{12}	0	10
13. Script revisions, a_{13}	3	9
14. Cast changes, a_{14}	2	9
15. Dummy activity 4, a_{15}	0	14
16. Dress rehearsal, a_{16}	1	11,12,13,15
17. Promotion and advertising, a_{17}	11	3

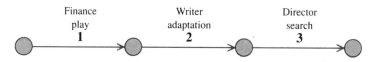

Finance play 1   Writer adaptation 2   Director search 3

FIGURE 13-3

Dependent Activities in Series

First, she knows that it is necessary: (1) to describe all activities comprising the project; (2) to make estimates of the duration of each activity; and (3) to determine, chronologically, how these activities are interrelated (she will be paying special attention to laying out as many in parallel as is possible). Assume Table 13-1 is a result of a considerable investment of her time and energy in undertaking this three-step process. The project begins with the capitalization of the play, a_1. The writer adaption (a_2) and director search (a_3) follow immediately. This sequence requires that the earlier events must be completed before the next activity can begin. So, before the director search can begin, the writer must redraft the original dialogue, music, and dance scenes. Further, neither the writer adaption nor the director search can occur prior to the financing of the play. Figure 13-3 illustrates these dependent activities, which, of course, are drawn in series. The search for the theater to hold the play (a_4) is not dependent on the sequence of activities $a_1 \rightarrow a_2 \rightarrow a_3$, so the producer can conduct a_4 *simultaneously* with $a_1 \rightarrow a_2 \rightarrow a_3$. The organization of these first four activities is represented in Figure 13-4. Using similar logic, and taking care to preserve the two rules discussed earlier, let's complete the entire network of activities depicted in Figure 13-5. It is typically a good idea to view the pictorial layout of a project as primarily a graphical process of trial and error. Often, considerable effort is expended in positioning the various activity arcs together in an esthetically pleasing and technically correct pattern.[2]

---

[2]Some of the more sophisticated project management software packages have network graphic (schematic) options.

FIGURE 13-4

Series and Parallel Activities

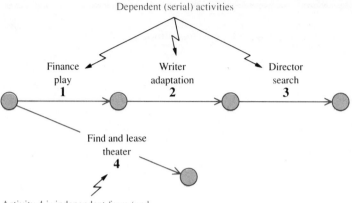

Dependent (serial) activities

Finance play **1**

Writer adaptation **2**

Director search **3**

Find and lease theater **4**

Activity 4 is independent from (and parallel with) activites 1, 2, 3

FIGURE 13-5

Complete Network for Broadway Musical

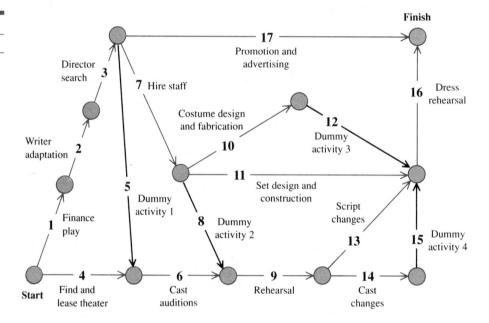

Now that the entire network is illustrated, there are several key points that we must explain. We have used *dummy activity variables*, represented by the broken, or phantom, lines of a_5, a_8, a_{12}, and a_{15}, and we have used *time estimates* to identify those activities that are likely to cause schedule problems and are important to monitor closely.

13.5 DUMMY ACTIVITY VARIABLES

The broken lines in Figure 13-5 are called *dummy activity variables*. Their purpose is most crucial. Dummy activity variables preserve the authenticity of the chronological interrelationships between activities. For example, the requirements in Table 13-1 establish the need for costume design (a_{10}) to be preceded by hiring of the technical and business staffs (a_7) and, also, that rehearsals (a_9) must be preceded by both the cast au-

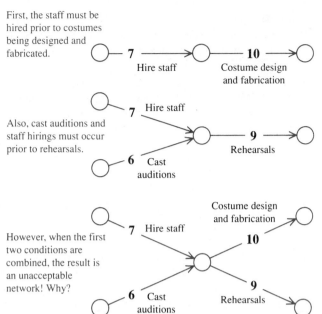

First, the staff must be hired prior to costumes being designed and fabricated.

Hire staff — 7

Costume design and fabrication — 10

Also, cast auditions and staff hirings must occur prior to rehearsals.

Hire staff — 7

Cast auditions — 6

Rehearsals — 9

However, when the first two conditions are combined, the result is an unacceptable network! Why?

Hire staff — 7

Cast auditions — 6

Costume design and fabrication — 10

Rehearsals — 9

FIGURE 13-6

Spurious Requirements Introduced as a Result of Not Using a Dummy Activity

ditions (a_6) and the hiring of the technical and business staffs. So, how can we schematically represent these relationships and retain an accurate and unambiguous accounting of these constraints? Let's examine the various approaches shown in the network sketches of Figure 13-6. As you can see, the final partial network is incorrect, since it suggests that costume design (a_{10}) cannot begin until auditions (a_6) are completed. Of course, no such prerequisite exists. There is no apparent reason why costume design cannot begin while auditions are in progress (final fittings would require the cast to be selected, but it is reasonable to assume that this can take place any time prior to dress rehearsals). So, how can we correctly interrelate staff hiring, costume design, cast auditions, and rehearsals? First, we know that the relationship between staff hiring and costume design is accurately represented by Figure 13-7. Next, staff hiring and rehearsals are correctly shown in Figure 13-8, as is the association between cast auditions and rehearsals (Figure 13-9). However, we run into a serious problem if we try to represent cast auditions and costume design, as we did earlier in Figure 13-6, by Figure 13-10. Instead, we can combine all but this final portion as shown in Figure 13-11. This leaves us with one missing link: Staff hiring is not assured of occurring prior to rehearsals, *as*

Hire staff — 7

Costume design and fabrication — 10

FIGURE 13-7

Sequentially Correct Relationship Between Staff Hiring and Costume Design and Fabrication

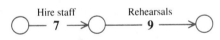

Hire staff — 7

Rehearsals — 9

FIGURE 13-8

Sequentially Correct Relationship Between Staff Hiring and Rehearsals

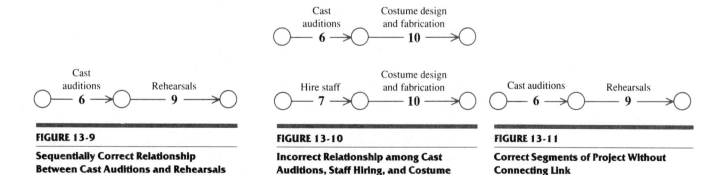

Cast auditions — 6

Rehearsals — 9

FIGURE 13-9

Sequentially Correct Relationship Between Cast Auditions and Rehearsals

Cast auditions — 6

Costume design and fabrication — 10

Hire staff — 7

Costume design and fabrication — 10

FIGURE 13-10

Incorrect Relationship among Cast Auditions, Staff Hiring, and Costume Design and Fabrication

Cast auditions — 6

Rehearsals — 9

FIGURE 13-11

Correct Segments of Project Without Connecting Link

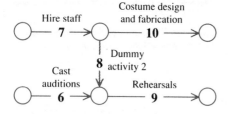

FIGURE 13-12

Corrected Version of Project Segment Using Dummy Activity to Preserve Interrelational Logic

it must be! How can we connect these two activities without forcing the spurious relationship between auditions and costume design that is shown in Figure 13-10? The answer is that we must introduce a phantom bridge (dummy activity), as represented by a broken line connecting staff hiring and rehearsals. This phantom results in a correct network depiction of these four activities—and one dummy activity—as shown in Figure 13-12. It is important to understand that these phantom activities consume neither time nor resources. Their sole purpose is to preempt misleading and incorrect chronological relationships between real activities.

13.6 THE CRITICAL PATH METHOD (CPM)

So far, we have been spending most of our time on understanding the language and schematic representation of a complex project schedule through the use of a network. We know how to identify the individual activities constituting a project, to make estimates of how long each will take, to establish the dependent or independent relationship between each (serial or parallel configuration), and to diagram it chronologically. But this understanding does not provide us with information that any manager obviously must know, such as how much time the total project will take. Since completion can occur only after each individual activity is completed, the total time for the project will be equal to the most time-consuming path through the network. This route is called the *critical path*. To determine this essential piece of information we will have to calculate five key time criteria:

1. Earliest start time for the ith activity, ES_i
2. Earliest finish time for the ith activity, EF_i
3. Latest start time for the ith activity, LS_i
4. Latest finish time for the ith activity, LF_i
5. Slack time for the ith activity, S_i

The earliest start and finish times are, literally, the earliest time that any activity can begin or end, respectively, taking into consideration the time constraints established by precedent activities in the network. The latest start and finish times reflect the latest that an activity can begin or end, respectively, without extending the total time needed to complete the entire project. The slack time reflects the amount of time that any activity can be delayed without extending the project completion time; we find it by measuring the difference between the early and late start ($LS_i - ES_i$) *or* the early finishing and late finishing times ($LF_i - EF_i$) of the activity of interest. If an activity has zero slack, it cannot be delayed without the entire project being delayed. This means that the path through the project of activities that have zero slack time will be the longest path, and these activities are, therefore, the critical-path elements! We shall explain the five time criteria in detail using the Broadway musical example.

The Forward Pass: Earliest Start (ES_i) and Earliest Finish (EF_i) Times

These times are calculated from a process often referred to as a *forward pass*, because the calculations proceed from left to right. The specific method used is adapted from the approach developed by Kenneth Brown and Jack ReVelle (1978). The forward pass presented here incorporates a simple seven-step process, as follows.

Step 1. Set the earliest start time of the first activity equal to zero:

$$ES_1 = 0$$

Step 2. Add the activity completion time of the first activity to the results of step 1. This is the earliest finish time for the first activity. Since ES_1 is equal to zero for the first activity, the earliest finish time will be equal to the estimated activity duration:

$$EF_1 = ES_1 + t_1 = t_1$$

Step 3. Identify each subsequent activity for which all immediate predecessors have calculated earliest start and finishing values.

Step 4. For each activity identified in step 3, define the earliest start time to be equal to the maximum earliest finish time of the immediate predecessor activities.

Step 5. Using the results of step 4, determine the earliest finish time for each current activity by adding the estimated activity completion time to the earliest start time for that activity:

$$EF_i = ES_i + t_i$$

Step 6. Repeat steps 3 through 5 until all earliest start and finish times have been completed.

Step 7. Record the earliest start time, estimated activity time, and earliest finish time for each activity using the time legend pictured in Figure 13-13.

Now, let's employ this process for the Broadway musical.

Step 1. The earliest start time for play capitalization (a_1) is zero; this task can start without delay. The theater search (a_4) is also an initial activity (we have two in this project), so it, too, has an early start time of zero. Therefore, the earliest start times for a_1 and a_4 must be equal:

$$ES_1 = ES_4$$
$$= 0 \text{ weeks}$$

Step 2. The earliest finish times for a_1 and a_4 must equal the sum of the earliest start time plus the estimated activity time:

$$EF_1 = 0 + 6$$
$$= 6 \text{ weeks}$$

and

$$EF_4 = 0 + 6$$
$$= 6 \text{ weeks}$$

Step 3. Writer adaption (a_2) is the only activity for which all immediate predecessors have calculated ES_i and EF_i values.

Step 4. The earliest start time for a_2 is

$$ES_2 = EF_1$$
$$= 6 \text{ weeks}$$

FIGURE 13-13

Legend Used to Indicate Earliest Activity Start, Duration, and Finish Times

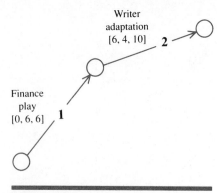

Writer
adaptation
[6, 4, 10]

Finance
play
[0, 6, 6]

FIGURE 13-14

**Earliest Start and Finish Times for
Broadway Musical (Partial Network)**

Step 5. The earliest finish time for a_2 is

$$EF_2 = ES_2 + t_2$$
$$= 6 + 4$$
$$= 10 \text{ weeks}$$

The results of these operations are summarized in the partial network illustrated in Figure 13-14.

Step 6. Now we iterate steps 3 through 5 for the rest of our network. We obtain the following results. Those for director search, a_3, are

$$ES_3 = EF_2$$
$$= 10 \text{ weeks}$$

and

$$EF_3 = ES_3 + t_3$$
$$= 10 + 4$$
$$= 14 \text{ weeks}$$

Those for dummy activity 1, a_5, are

$$ES_5 = EF_3$$
$$= 14 \text{ weeks}$$

and

$$EF_5 = ES_5 + t_5$$
$$= 14 + 0$$
$$= 14 \text{ weeks}$$

The cast audition (a_6) calculations are a bit trickier, because a_6 has two predecessor activities: theater search (a_4) and dummy activity 1 (a_5). Remember that the earliest start time for a_6 must be equal to the maximum latest finish time of these two activities; that is,

$$ES_6 = MAX[EF_4; EF_5]$$
$$= MAX[6;14]$$
$$= 14 \text{ weeks}$$

The earliest finish time for cast auditions is

$$EF_6 = ES_6 + t_6$$
$$= 14 + 2$$
$$= 16 \text{ weeks}$$

Step 7. Figure 13-15 illustrates the earliest start time, activity time, and earliest finish time of each activity in the network.

The Backward Pass: Latest Start (LS_1) and Latest Finish (LF_1) Times

The process for calculating these times is a mirror image of the algorithm used to generate ES_i and EF_i. As you might guess, the procedure is referred to as a *backward pass*,

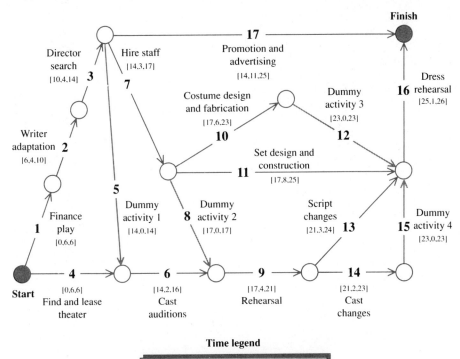

Finish

Director search
[10,4,14] **3**

Hire staff
[14,3,17] **7**

17

Promotion and
advertising
[14,11,25]

Dress
16 rehearsal
[25,1,26]

Costume design
and fabrication
[17,6,23] **10**

Dummy
activity 3
[23,0,23] **12**

Writer
adaptation **2**
[6,4,10]

5

11 Set design and
construction
[17,8,25]

Dummy
activity 1 **8** activity 2
[14,0,14] [17,0,17]

Script
changes
[21,3,24] **13**

Dummy
15 activity 4
[23,0,23]

Finance
1 play
[0,6,6]

Start **4** ——→ **6** ——→ **9** —→ **14** ——→

[0,6,6] [14,2,16] [17,4,21] [21,2,23]
Find and lease   Cast   Rehearsal   Cast
theater   auditions   changes

Time legend

$$\begin{bmatrix} \text{Earliest} & \text{Activity} & \text{Earliest} \\ \text{start } ES_i & \text{duration } t_i & \text{finish } EF_i \end{bmatrix}$$

because the calculations proceed from right to left. This parallel algorithm uses the following six steps:

Step 1. Beginning with the last activity in the network, define the latest finish time, LF_i, to be equal to the total time expended by the project. If there is more than one ending activity, set the LF_i for each ending activity equal to the longest duration early finish time of the total project.

Step 2. Subtract the estimated activity time, t_i, from the latest finish time, LF_i, just calculated in step 1. This difference is equal to latest start time for the activity, LS_i:

$$LS_i = LF_i - t_i$$

Step 3. Identify each predecessor activity for which all immediate successor activities have calculated latest start and latest finish times.

Step 4. For each activity identified in step 3, define the latest finish time to be equal to the minimum latest start time of the immediate successor activities:

$$LF_i = \text{MIN}[LS_{i+1}]$$

Step 5. Using the result of step 4, determine the latest starting time for the current activity by subtracting the estimated time to complete the activity from the activity's latest finish time; that is,

$$LS_i = LF_i - t_i$$

Step 6. Repeat steps 3 through 5 until all latest start, LS_i, and finish, LF_i, have been completed.

FIGURE 13-16

Completed Network of Earliest and Latest
Start and Finish Times for Broadway
Musical Example

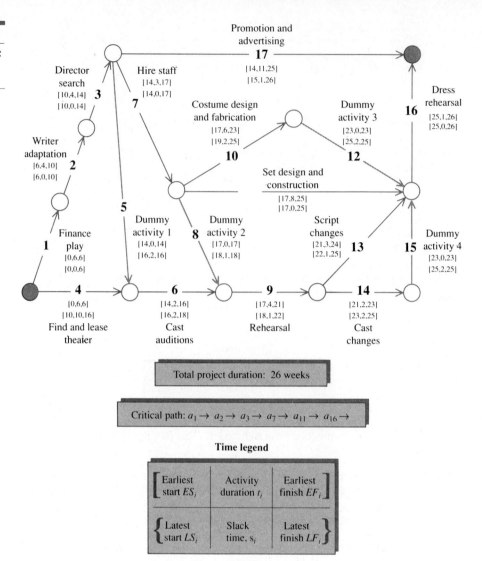

Total project duration: 26 weeks

Critical path: $a_1 \rightarrow a_2 \rightarrow a_3 \rightarrow a_7 \rightarrow a_{11} \rightarrow a_{16} \rightarrow$

Time legend

$\begin{bmatrix} \text{Earliest} \\ \text{start } ES_i \end{bmatrix}$	Activity duration t_i	Earliest finish EF_i
Latest start LS_i	Slack time, s_i	Latest finish LF_i

We can now apply this algorithm to the Broadway musical example example to generate our latest start and finish times.

Step 1. Referring to Figure 13-16, you can see that there are two activities that constitute the end of the project: promotion and advertising (a_{17}) and dress rehearsals (a_{16}). The latest finish times for our last two activities are both equal to the
total time expended by the project; that is, to the maximum earliest finish
time:

$$LF_{17} = LF_{16}$$
$$= 16 \text{ weeks}$$

Step 2. The latest start time for a_{17} is

$$LS_{17} = LF_{17} - t_{17}$$
$$= 26 - 11$$
$$= 15 \text{ weeks}$$

and that for a_{16} is

$$
\begin{aligned}
LS_{16} &= LF_{16} - t_{16} \\
&= 26 - 1 \\
&= 25 \text{ weeks}
\end{aligned}
$$

Step 3. Those activities with all immediate successor activities having defined LS_i and LF_i values are a_{12}, a_{11}, a_{13}, and a_{15} (all succeeded by a_{16}).

Step 4. The latest finish times for the activities identified in step 3 are

$$
\begin{aligned}
LF_{12} &= LF_{11} \\
&= LF_{13} \\
&= LF_{17} \\
&= LS_{16} \\
&= 25 \text{ weeks}
\end{aligned}
$$

Step 5. The latest start times for the four activities in step 4 are

$$
\begin{aligned}
LS_{12} &= LF_{12} - t_{12} \\
&= 25 - 0 \\
&= 25 \text{ weeks}
\end{aligned}
$$

$$
\begin{aligned}
LS_{11} &= LF_{11} - t_{11} \\
&= 25 - 8 \\
&= 17 \text{ weeks}
\end{aligned}
$$

$$
\begin{aligned}
LS_{15} &= LF_{15} - t_{15} \\
&= 25 - 0 \\
&= 25 \text{ weeks}
\end{aligned}
$$

$$
\begin{aligned}
LS_{16} &= LF_{16} - t_{16} \\
&= 26 - 1 \\
&= 25 \text{ weeks}
\end{aligned}
$$

Step 6. Iterating steps 3 through 5 produces all the latest start and finish times, along with the earliest start and finish times generated previously.

The values from step 6 will be displayed after we introduce the last time element in project management: slack time.

Slack (Float) Time   After the earliest and latest start and finish times are completed for the entire project, the *slack* (or *float*) *time* associated with each activity must be determined. The slack time is the amount of time that any given activity can be delayed without affecting the completion time of the overall project. Slack time may be loosely viewed as the amount of extra time that an activity has "to kill" before it becomes a member of the critical path. Therefore, if the slack time of an activity is zero, the activity is a critical-path member. We find slack time for any activity, S_i, by taking the difference *either* between the latest and earliest finish times, $LF_i - EF_i$, or between the latest and earliest start times, $LS_i - ES_i$:

$$
S_i = LF_i - EF_i
$$

or

$$
s_i = LS_i - ES_i
$$

Now that all of the different time elements have been carefully defined, we show the completed Broadway musical illustration in Figure 13-16. The critical path consists of those activities with zero slack that form the longest total activity time between the start and finish of the network. Any delay in these activities will prolong the total project completion time. The Broadway musical critical path consists of the following activities:

$$a_1 \rightarrow a_2 \rightarrow a_3 \rightarrow a_7 \rightarrow a_{11} \rightarrow a_{16}$$

It is important to understand that just because we have defined the critical path does not mean that we need to monitor closely *only* these activities for possible delays. Often, in practice, a noncritical path activity with a short slack time experiences problems but is not closely monitored, and thus pushes the entire project schedule into a time overrun. For this reason, the experienced manager views most activities—especially those with zero or low slack values—as potential problems, and keeps a running account of each.

13.7 | PROJECT COST-TIME TRADEOFFS: COST CRASHING

Sometimes, even painstakingly careful project planning will not ensure completing the project on time or staying within budget limits. When this occurs, managers usually have a choice: (1) do nothing (bite the bullet) and incur any contractual late penalties that may result from an overdue project, or (2) bring in more resources to shorten the critical-path activities (and the corresponding total project duration) so that the due date is met. The selection of a specific strategy depends on the magnitude of the late costs and the noneconomic costs resulting from client ill-will (reputational damage) when there is a project deadline overrun versus the added costs involved in bringing in extra resources needed to keep the project on time. The method used to make this delicate assessment is called *cost crashing*. It is usually possible to decrease the time needed to complete an activity by concentrating greater resources on that activity. This frequently means allocating more skilled people (or the same people, working overtime), additional equipment, or more money, or some combination of these. For example, the Broadway musical can decrease some activities. Financing the play (a_1) may be achieved more readily if the producer is willing to give her investors a better deal—for example, a larger share of the play for each dollar invested, or a higher interest rate on the money borrowed. A theater can be leased (a_4) sooner if a more expensive, readily available building is leased now in lieu of waiting for a more economical space; negotiations with prospective director candidates (a_3) and staff hiring (a_7) can be condensed if higher salaries are offered; time for costume design (a_{10}) and set design (a_{11}) can be decreased if more people in these skill areas are used or if the staff works overtime; promotion and advertising (a_{17}) time can be reduced if a more condensed media blitz is used (more commercials and ads per unit of time). These are just a few examples of how the normal activity completion time can be lessened—for a price.

A step-by-step process illustrating the application of the cost-crashing technique follows.

Step 1. Construct a summary table consisting of the following column headings: (1) activity; (2) expected activity completion times for (a) normal and (b) crash conditions; (3) activity costs for (a) normal and (b) crash conditions; (4) change in activity cost (usually an increase); (5) change in activity

completion time (usually a decrease); and (6) incremental cost per unit time (column 4 divided by column 5).

Step 2. Identify only the critical-path activities that can be "crashed" (noncritical activities can be ignored, because crashing activities with slack will not decrease the earliest completion time for the project).

Step 3. For those activities identified in step 2, construct a summary table identical in format to the one designed in step 1.

Step 4. From the table developed in step 3, select the activity with the smallest incremental cost-per-unit-time quotient (column 6). Use the crash-time value for this activity to replace the normal value used in the original network, and recalculate the new critical path for the project. If, however, this time increment is greater than one unit, it is often circumspect to crash by single-time-unit increments to avoid making larger than necessary time reductions. You will soon see how multiple-time-unit reductions can sometimes shift the critical path midstream, and cause superfluous expenditures on activities no longer critical. If there are two or more activities with the same incremental cost per unit time, make separate critical-path calculations for each, and select the activity that results in the lowest project completion time.

Step 5. From step 4, calculate the sum of time along all network paths. The path with the longest total time is the new critical path (there may be no change from the original network).

Step 6. Repeat steps 2 through 5 until all critical activities are crashed. Display the relationship between project costs and completion time for this network.

Now let's use the Broadway musical to illustrate this six-step algorithm.

Step 1. The summary of cost-crash data is provided in Table 13-2.

TABLE 13-2

Cost-Crash Summary for the Broadway Musical Example

Activity	Normal Cost ($)	Crash Cost ($)	Normal Time (wks)	Crash Time (wks)	$\Delta C/\Delta t$ ($/wk)
1	350,000	500,000	6	4	75,000
2	20,000	20,000	4	4	N/A
3	50,000	95,000	4	2	22,500
4	40,000	60,000	6	2	5,000
5	0	0	0	0	N/A
6	8,000	8,000	2	2	N/A
7	30,000	30,000	3	3	N/A
8	0	0	0	0	N/A
9	100,000	100,000	4	4	N/A
10	25,000	50,000	6	4	12,500
11	100,000	140,000	8	6	20,000
12	0	0	0	0	N/A
13	30,000	30,000	3	3	N/A
14	55,000	55,000	2	2	N/A
15	0	0	0	0	N/A
16	25,000	25,000	1	1	N/A
17	150,000	240,000	11	8	30,000
	983,000	**1,353,000**			

FIGURE 13-17

**Completed Network of Earliest and Latest
Start and Finish Times for Broadway
Musical Example after Crashing Set
Design and Construction (Activity 11)
From 8 to 7 Weeks**

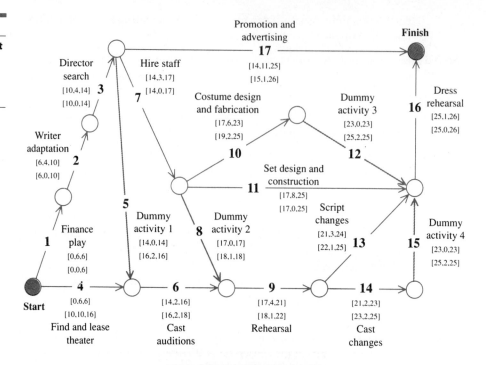

Total project duration: 25 weeks
Total project cost: $1,003,000

Critical paths: $a_1 \rightarrow a_2 \rightarrow a_3 \rightarrow a_7 \rightarrow a_{11} \rightarrow a_{16}$

$a_1 \rightarrow a_2 \rightarrow a_3 \rightarrow a_{17}$

$a_1 \rightarrow a_2 \rightarrow a_3 \rightarrow a_7 \rightarrow a_8 \rightarrow a_9 \rightarrow a_{13} \rightarrow a_{16}$

Time legend

Earliest start ES_i	Activity duration t_i	Earliest finish EF_i
Latest start LS_i	Slack time, s_i	Latest finish LF_i

Step 2. Figure 13-17 shows that the critical activities are

$$a_1 \rightarrow a_2 \rightarrow a_3 \rightarrow a_7 \rightarrow a_{11} \rightarrow a_{16}.$$

Step 3. The network summary table for the critical-path activities is given in Table 13-3. At this point, it would be possible—but not advisable—simply to crash all three critical path activities completely: to decrease a_1 from 6 to 4 weeks, to decrease a_3 from 4 to 2 weeks, and to decrease a_{11} from 8 to 6 weeks. This would lower the $a_1 \rightarrow a_2 \rightarrow a_3 \rightarrow a_7 \rightarrow a_{11} \rightarrow a_{16}$ path from 26 to 20 weeks (and would add $235,000 to the cost of the project). *This would not, however, guarantee that the critical path would remain the same.* In fact, the path will change, as we shall see in step 5.

TABLE 13-3

Summary of Crash Costs for Critical-Path Activities
of the Broadway Musical

Activity	Normal Cost ($)	Crash Cost ($)	Normal Time (wks)	Crash Time (wks)	$\Delta C/\Delta t$ ($/wk)
1	350,000	500,000	6	4	75,000
3	50,000	95,000	4	2	22,500
11	100,000	140,000	8	6	20,000

Step 4. The critical-path activity with the smallest incremental cost per unit time is a_{11}, set design and construction, at \$20,000 per week for 2 weeks. Even though it is possible to crash this activity across the entire 2-week period, *be careful*: Cost crashing over multiple time periods "in one gulp" sometimes causes an unanticipated shift in the critical path. If the path does shift, money may be wasted without the expected accompanying improvement in time savings. Although critical-path shifting is not normally of concern to the manager when using a project management software package, it is important that you understand what really occurs during the solution process if you are to have a sound comprehension of the critical-path technique. It is more prudent to consider a partial crash—sometimes referred to as a *compression*—for this reason.

Step 5. Figure 13-17 shows that the total project duration becomes 25 weeks as a_{11} is compressed from 8 to 7 weeks. Figure 13-18 illustrates what would have happened if a_{11} had been imprudently crashed from 8 to 6 weeks in one step: the project duration would have been reduced by only a single week! What happened? Figure 13-18 shows that, when a_{11} is reduced from 8 weeks to 7 weeks, *two* new critical paths emerge in addition to the original $a_1 \rightarrow a_2 \rightarrow a_3 \rightarrow a_7 \rightarrow a_{11} \rightarrow a_{16}$ critical path: $a_1 \rightarrow a_2 \rightarrow a_3 \rightarrow a_7 \rightarrow a_{17}$ and $a_1 \rightarrow a_2 \rightarrow a_3 \rightarrow a_7 \rightarrow a_8 \rightarrow a_9 \rightarrow a_{13} \rightarrow a_{16}$. The manager is now dealing with three critical paths! Reducing the a_{11} duration from 7 to 6 weeks will have absolutely no effect on the two new routes: neither one contains the crashed activity, a_{11}. Therefore, *all critical paths must have in common the activity being crashed if they are to experience a common reduction in product duration*. Otherwise, significant project funds will be wasted and anticipated time reductions will never be realized.

Step 6. Repeating steps 2 through 5 results in the following two final iterations:

1. Activity a_3 (director search) is common not only to the three critical paths, but also to all possible paths through the network except for those beginning with a_4 (theater search and lease). Further examination of these latter possible paths reveals that any path initiated with a_4 would have such large slack values (9 weeks!) that crashing a_3 by 2 weeks would never shift the critical path. So, reducing a_3 from 4 to 2 weeks in one step is safe and results in a further reduction of the total project to 23 weeks at an additional incremental cost of \$45,000 (Figure 13-19).

2. Since we still have the same three critical paths as in the previous iteration, select the least expensive, uncrashed (or compressed) activity that is common to all. The selection is obvious, because the only common activity

FIGURE 13-18

Earliest and Latest Start and Finish Times
for Broadway Musical Example *If* Set
Design and Construction (Activity 11) Is
Crashed from 8 to 6 Weeks in One Step

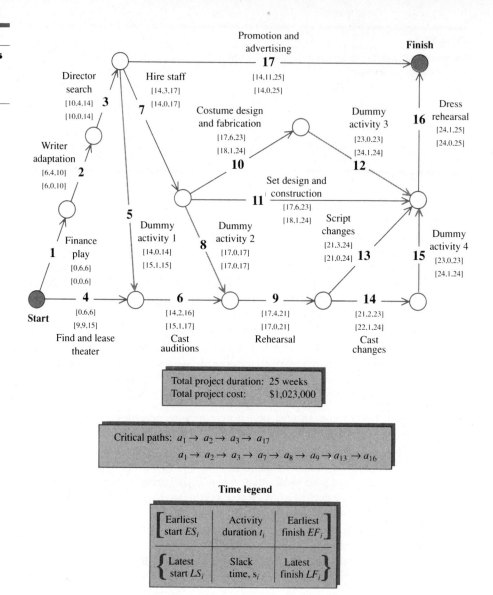

Total project duration: 25 weeks
Total project cost: $1,023,000

Critical paths: $a_1 \rightarrow a_2 \rightarrow a_3 \rightarrow a_{17}$
$a_1 \rightarrow a_2 \rightarrow a_3 \rightarrow a_7 \rightarrow a_8 \rightarrow a_9 \rightarrow a_{13} \rightarrow a_{16}$

Time legend

$$\begin{bmatrix} \text{Earliest} & \text{Activity} & \text{Earliest} \\ \text{start } ES_i & \text{duration } t_i & \text{finish } EF_i \\ \text{Latest} & \text{Slack} & \text{Latest} \\ \text{start } LS_i & \text{time, } s_i & \text{finish } LF_i \end{bmatrix}$$

elements are a_1 and a_3, and the latter is already crashed. Since financing the play, a_1, is common to all critical paths, and the only other noncritical path element, a_4, still has 7 weeks of slack time remaining on it, we can crash it completely without fear of a new path emerging. The cost for this final crash is $150,000 and reduces the total project duration to its ultimate minimum value of 21 weeks (Figure 13-20).

The final crashed project cost is $1,198,000 ($215,000 in crashing costs plus the original $983,000 project cost), and the project can be finished in 21 weeks. Of course, it is possible that the producer may wish to have some intermediate time savings—something between the normal 26 weeks and the minimum 21 weeks. The relationship between project cost and completion time is shown in Figure 13-21.

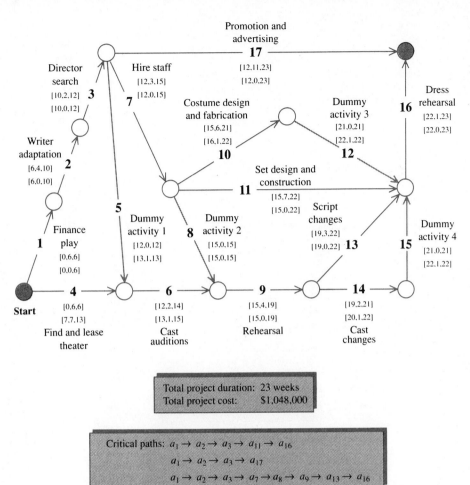

FIGURE 13-19

Earliest and Latest Start and Finish Times
for Broadway Musical Example after
Crashing Director Search (Activity 3)
from 4 to 2 Weeks

Promotion and
advertising

17

[12,11,23]
[12,0,23]

Director
search
[10,2,12] **3**
[10,0,12]

Hire staff
[12,3,15]
[12,0,15] **7**

Dress
rehearsal
16 [22,1,23]
[22,0,23]

Costume design
and fabrication
[15,6,21] **10**
[16,1,22]

Dummy
activity 3
[21,0,21] **12**
[22,1,22]

Writer
adaptation
[6,4,10] **2**
[6,0,10]

Set design and
construction
[15,7,22] **11**
[15,0,22]

Finance
play
1 [0,6,6]
[0,0,6]

Dummy
activity 1
[12,0,12] **5**
[13,1,13]

Dummy
activity 2
[15,0,15] **8**
[15,0,15]

Script
changes
[19,3,22] **13**
[19,0,22]

Dummy
activity 4
[21,0,21] **15**
[22,1,22]

Start

4
[0,6,6]
[7,7,13]

Find and lease
theater

6
[12,2,14]
[13,1,15]

Cast
auditions

9
[15,4,19]
[15,0,19]

Rehearsal

14
[19,2,21]
[20,1,22]

Cast
changes

Total project duration: 23 weeks
Total project cost: $1,048,000

Critical paths: $a_1 \rightarrow a_2 \rightarrow a_3 \rightarrow a_{11} \rightarrow a_{16}$

$a_1 \rightarrow a_2 \rightarrow a_3 \rightarrow a_{17}$

$a_1 \rightarrow a_2 \rightarrow a_3 \rightarrow a_7 \rightarrow a_8 \rightarrow a_9 \rightarrow a_{13} \rightarrow a_{16}$

Time legend

Earliest start ES_i	Activity duration t_i	Earliest finish EF_i
Latest start LS_i	Slack time, s_i	Latest finish LF_i

13.8 STOCHASTIC PROJECT MANAGEMENT: PROJECT EVALUATION AND REVIEW TECHNIQUE (PERT)

When we can make time estimates with a high level of confidence—such as with projects that are repetitive and with which we have considerable experience—a single time value may be sufficient. But what happens if the project does not have these characteristics? What does the manager do when faced with a complex, nonrepetitive project for which there is no previous experience? Our time estimates, in this setting, would be guesses, and the use of a single time value possibly would be naive. It is precisely in these more ambiguous situations that PERT is most useful.

FIGURE 13-20

Earliest and Latest Start and Finish Times
for Broadway Musical Example after
Crashing Financing Play (Activity 1)
from 6 to 4 Weeks

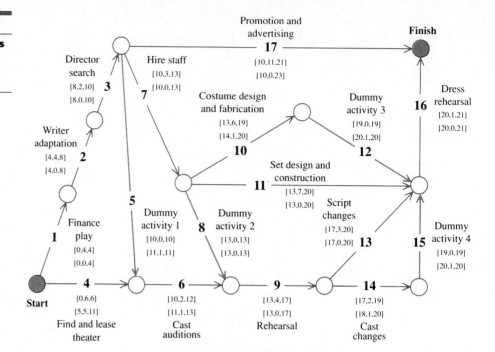

Total project duration: 21 weeks
Total project cost: $1,198,000

Critical paths: $a_1 \rightarrow a_2 \rightarrow a_3 \rightarrow a_7 \rightarrow a_{11} \rightarrow a_{16}$
$a_1 \rightarrow a_2 \rightarrow a_3 \rightarrow a_{17}$
$a_1 \rightarrow a_2 \rightarrow a_3 \rightarrow a_7 \rightarrow a_8 \rightarrow a_9 \rightarrow a_{13} \rightarrow a_{16}$

Time legend

$\begin{bmatrix}$ Earliest start ES_i	Activity duration t_i	Earliest finish $EF_i \end{bmatrix}$
$\{$ Latest start LS_i	Slack time, s_i	Latest finish $LF_i \}$

FIGURE 13-21

Cost-Crashing Tradeoff Considerations
for Broadway Musical Example: Project
Completion Time versus Project Costs

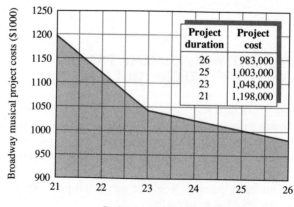

Project duration	Project cost
26	983,000
25	1,003,000
23	1,048,000
21	1,198,000

The PERT approach uses three time estimates to gauge the probability of completion of each of n total activities along a specific path: (1) most optimistic, a; (2) most pessimistic, b; and (3) most likely, m. These three time estimates form a continuous, bounded, and usually skewed probability distribution called the *beta distribution* (Figure 13-22). This distribution, although not mathematically proven to be the most suitable for PERT, has been empirically shown to be quite effective. The mean of this distribution, t_i, is used to represent the expected completion time for the ith activity and is given by the following relationship:

$$t_i = \frac{a_i + 4m_i + b_i}{6}$$

The mean duration along the entire critical path, t^*, is equal to the sum of the individual expected completion times for the activities constituting the critical path:

$$t^* = \sum_{i=1}^{n} \left(\frac{a_i + 4m_i + b_i}{6} \right)$$
$$= t_1 + t_2 + \cdots + t_n$$
$$= \left(\frac{a_1 + 4m_1 + b_1}{6} \right) + \left(\frac{a_2 + 4m_2 + b_2}{6} \right) + \cdots + \left(\frac{a_n + 4m_n + b_n}{6} \right)$$

where

n = number of critical path activities

The beta distribution standard deviation for the ith activity, s_i, is

$$s_i = \sqrt{\left(\frac{b_i - a_i}{6} \right)^2}$$

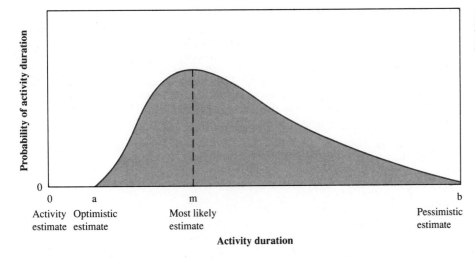

FIGURE 13-22

Beta Probability Distribution

The standard deviation for the expected project completion time, $s*$, is approximated by

$$s* = \sqrt{\sum_{i=1}^{n} \left(\frac{b_i - a_i}{6}\right)^2}$$

$$= \sqrt{\left(\frac{b_1 - a_1}{6}\right)^2 + \left(\frac{b_2 - a_2}{6}\right)^2 + \cdots + \left(\frac{b_n - a_n}{6}\right)^2}$$

Once the critical path is determined, it is possible to determine the probability of completing the expected critical path within a given duration of time by using the standard normal distribution provided in Appendix C.[3] This makes it possible to determine the probability of completing the project, along any path of interest, within a given period by using the mean and standard deviation along that path and the properties of the standard normal distribution. It is important to keep in mind, however, that, in actuality, the set of activities that eventually forms the *realized* critical path may be different from this statistical estimate.

We can easily digest the PERT technique by first using an algorithmic presentation, followed by an application to the Broadway musical.

Step 1. Use the *a-m-b* beta distribution values to calculate activity mean times. Determine the earliest and latest start and finish times for each project activity.

Step 2. From the information generated in step 1, calculate the activity slack times from either $LF_i - EF_i$ or $LS_i - ES_i$.

Step 3. Determine the mean duration of the critical path through the project as indicated by the zero-slack activities.

Step 4. Calculate the cumulative standard deviation for the critical-path activities identified in step 3.

Step 5. Select an acceptable project duration, t_{TOT}. Use this value, along with the *earliest finish time* for the last critical-path activity, EF_n, to calculate the standard normal distribution Z-value given by[4]

$$Z = \frac{t_{TOT} - EF_n}{s}$$

---

[3]Even though the beta distribution is clearly asymmetrical, inferential statistics in general, and the central limit theorem in particular, says that, if we were to select repeatedly random samples of a fixed size from a population—even one that is not normally distributed, such as the beta distribution—and to plot the mean of each of these sample draws, the distribution of these sample means would approach a normal distribution even if the sample size were no larger than 10 to 20! So, in our case, when we randomly sample the beta distributions of each of the activities in our network and then to add them together, the sum of these nonnormal variables results in a distribution that is near normal. Therefore, it is reasonable to assume that the sum of the activity times along the various paths in the network can be approximated by the normal distribution.

[4]The typical statistical form of the Z-value relationship has been "tailored" for project-management terminology. The standard form is

$$Z = \frac{X - \mu}{\sigma}$$

where

μ = mean of the population

σ = standard deviation of the population

X = individual measurement of interest

Step 6. From the findings of step 5 and the normal distribution table in Appendix C, determine the likelihood of being able to achieve this desired project schedule.

Now let's apply this method to the Broadway musical.

Steps 1 and 2. Table 13-4 provides the mean time, earliest and latest start and finish times, and the associated slack for each activity.

Step 3. The critical-path activities are $a_1 \rightarrow a_2 \rightarrow a_3 \rightarrow a_7 \rightarrow a_{11} \rightarrow a_{16}$. The mean project duration along this path is

$$
\begin{aligned}
t^* &= t_1 + t_2 + t_3 + t_7 + t_{11} + t_{12} + t_{16} \\
&= 6 + 4 + 4 + 3 + 8 + 0 + 1 \\
&= 26 \text{ weeks}
\end{aligned}
$$

Step 4. The critical-path standard deviation, s^*, is

$$
s^* = \sqrt{s_1^2 + s_2^2 + s_3^2 + s_7^2 + s_{11}^2 + s_{12}^2 + s_{16}^2}
$$

$$
= \sqrt{\left(\frac{10-2}{6}\right)^2 + \left(\frac{10.5-1.5}{6}\right)^2 + \left(\frac{10-2}{6}\right)^2 + \left(\frac{4-2}{6}\right)^2 + \left(\frac{11-5}{6}\right)^2 + \left(\frac{0-0}{6}\right)^2 + \left(\frac{1.5-.5}{6}\right)^2}
$$

$$
= \sqrt{6.943} = 2.63 \text{ weeks}
$$

Step 5. Suppose, for example, you wish to know the probability of the total project duration, t_{TOT}, lasting no longer than 27 weeks. The corresponding Z-value for this situation is

$$
Z = \frac{27 - 26}{2.63} = .38
$$

TABLE 13-4

Baseline Data for PERT Calculations of Broadway Musical

Activity	a	m	b	t_i	ES_i	EF_i	LS_i	LF_i	S_i
1	2	6	10	6	0	6	0	6	0
2	1.5	3	10.5	4	6	10	6	10	0
3	2	3	10	4	10	14	10	14	0
4	4	6	8	6	0	6	10	16	10
5	0	0	0	0	14	14	16	16	2
6	1.5	2	2.5	2	14	16	16	18	2
7	2	3	4	3	14	17	14	17	0
8	0	0	0	0	17	17	18	18	1
9	3	3.5	7	4	17	21	18	22	1
10	4	6	8	6	17	23	19	25	2
11	5	8	11	8	17	25	17	25	0
12	0	0	0	0	23	23	25	25	0
13	2	3	4	3	21	24	22	25	1
14	.5	1.5	5.5	2	21	23	23	25	2
15	0	0	0	0	23	23	25	25	2
16	.5	1	1.5	1	25	26	25	26	0
17	8.8	10	17.5	11	14	25	15	26	1

Mean project duration = 26.00 weeks

Critical-path standard deviation = 2.63 weeks

FIGURE 13-23

Probability of Completing the Broadway Musical within 27 Weeks

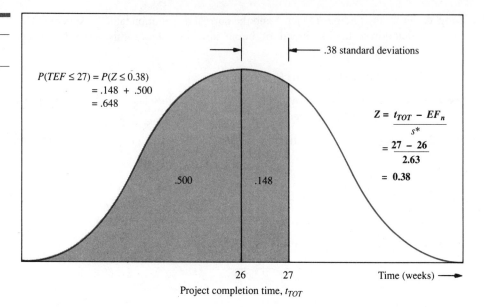

FIGURE 13-24

Probability of Completing the Broadway Musical within the Desired Schedule

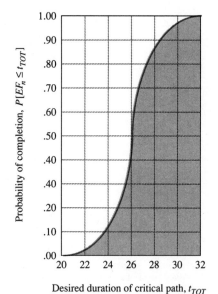

Step 6. Figure 13-23 illustrates how to determine the probability of not exceeding the 27-week limit, $P(EF_n \leq 27)$. This probability is exactly equal to the area under the standard normal distribution to the left of $Z = 0.38$, and represents the proportion of possible project durations equal to or less than 27 weeks:

$$P(EF_n \leq 27) = P(Z \leq 0.38)$$
$$= .148 + .500$$
$$= .648$$

There is, then, a chance of slightly less than two out of three that the project will not exceed 27 weeks.

Using this same procedure, the general relationship between the probabilities of being able to finish the Broadway musical across a range of project durations is pictured in Figure 13-24.

| 13.9 | COST CRASHING USING LINEAR PROGRAMMING

Have you noticed that there is a similarity between the cost-crashing method illustrated in Section 13.7 and another management science technique covered in an earlier chapter? Consider, for a moment, the purpose of cost crashing: to further decrease (*minimize*) a project's normal duration by using additional (*limited*) resources. Heavy-handed hinting aside, there is, indeed, an interesting metaphor between the time and resource tradeoffs of cost crashing and the resource-allocation methods of linear programming (LP). LP provides an alternative method for determining the optimal tradeoff between time and crashing costs. Let's use the Broadway musical example to illustrate this technique next.

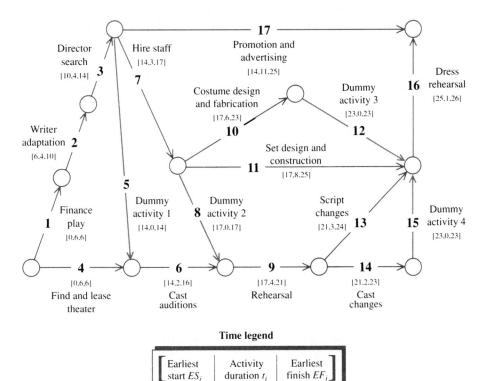

Time legend

$$\begin{bmatrix} \text{Earliest} & \text{Activity} & \text{Earliest} \\ \text{start } ES_i & \text{duration } t_i & \text{finish } EF_i \end{bmatrix}$$

EXAMPLE 13.2   THE BROADWAY MUSICAL, CONTINUED

Suppose the producer is uncomfortable with the 26-week duration needed to prepare for the opening of the Broadway musical. Instead, she would like to see how much it would cost to decrease this time span and to determine how much additional expense these "improvements" will incur. Here is how LP can be used in this situation.

Establish the appropriate notation for the *decision variables*. This step is a little tricky, since the expected times associated with some of the activities are not fixed: Activities can be partially or fully crashed, *as we choose*. So we must define two basic sets of decision variables:

1. The decision variable that will identify the *starting time* or *time of occurrence* of each activity (node) is given by x_j = start time of jth event for $j = A, B, C, \ldots, L$.[5] An illustration of the project's event–activity notation is shown in Figure 13-25.

2. The decision variable that defines the *amount of crash time used* for each activity is y_i = amount of crash time used for i^{th} activity for $i = 1, 2, 3, \ldots, 17$.

The LP procedure will determine the minimum cost associated with crashing the play to a specific duration. The objective function is expressed as[6]

$$\text{Minimize } Z = 75{,}000\, y_1 + 22{,}500\, y_3 + + 5000\, y_4 + 12{,}500\, y_{10} \\ + 20{,}000\, y_{11} + 30{,}000\, y_{17}$$

The constraint equations for the project can now be defined.

---

[5] Although the individual activity numbers had been previously defined in the Broadway musical example, the event nodes had not. Therefore, to avert confusion in the identification of event nodes, letter subscripts are used.

[6] Only those activities that are "crashable" appear in the objective function; all other activities have y_i values equal to zero.

Predecessor Event Constraints   The occurrence (start) time of each event is dependent on the start time for predecessor events, the normal duration of the activity connecting the present event and the predecessor event, and the ultimate amount of crash time *chosen* for this activity.[7] For example, the producer cannot begin to hire staff until the director search is completed. The general form of this relationship is represented by the following expression:

$$\begin{pmatrix} \text{occurrence} \\ \text{time of} \\ \text{ending event} \end{pmatrix} = \begin{pmatrix} \text{occurrence} \\ \text{time of} \\ \text{starting} \\ \text{event} \end{pmatrix} + \begin{pmatrix} \text{normal duration} \\ \text{of activity} \\ \text{connecting ending} \\ \text{and starting events} \end{pmatrix} - \begin{pmatrix} \text{amount of} \\ \text{crash time} \\ \text{for activity} \end{pmatrix}$$

It is probably a good idea to restate this relationship such that the equation form is computer-readable: the variables (occurrence time of ending event, occurrence time of starting event, and actual crash time of activity realized) are collected on the left-hand side of the equation; the constant value (the normal duration of the activity connecting the ending and starting event) is on the right-hand side. This suggested arrangement is

$$\begin{pmatrix} \text{occurrence} \\ \text{time of} \\ \text{ending event} \end{pmatrix} - \begin{pmatrix} \text{occurrence} \\ \text{time of} \\ \text{starting} \\ \text{event} \end{pmatrix} - \begin{pmatrix} \text{amount of} \\ \text{crash time} \\ \text{for activity} \end{pmatrix} = \begin{pmatrix} \text{normal duration} \\ \text{of activity} \\ \text{connecting ending} \\ \text{and starting events} \end{pmatrix}$$

Expressed algebraically, this relationship looks like

$$x_j - x_{j-1} - y_i = t_i$$

where

$$x_j = \text{occurrence time of ending event } j$$
$$x_{j-1} = \text{occurrence time of starting event } j-1 \text{ (predecessor to event } j)$$
$$y_i = \text{amount of crash time for activity } i$$
$$t_i = \text{activity duration}$$

An illustration of the general relationship of the individual terms is provided in Figure 13-26. The predecessor constraints for each of the events are, then,

Event A (start of project/begin *finance play*):

$$x_A = 0$$

Event B:

$$x_B - x_A + y_1 \geqslant 6$$

Since $x_A = 0$, the relationship simplifies to

$$x_B + y_1 \geqslant 6$$

Event C:

$$x_C - x_B + y_2 \geqslant 4$$

---

[7]It is crucial to keep in mind that the manager will select the degree to which a particular activity will be crashed. The maximum amount of crash time possible is, of course, the difference between the normal and fully-crashed times. It is also the case that an event will not be crashed at all if it is not an element of the critical path.

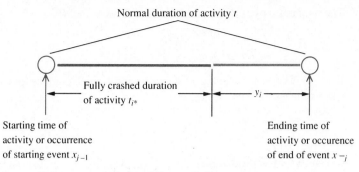

Normal duration of activity t

Fully crashed duration
of activity t_{i*}

y_i

Starting time of
activity or occurrence
of starting event x_{j-1}

Ending time of
activity or occurence
of end of event x_{-j}

Note: y_i = amount of crash time used where $y_i \leq t_{i*}$

t_{i*} = maximum amount time i^{th} activity can be crashed

FIGURE 13-26

**General Decision-Variable Notation
Used for Linear Programming Activity
Time Crashing**

Since activity 2 has a constant duration, $y_2 = 0$, and the equation simplifies to

$$x_C - x_B \geq 4$$

Event D:

$$x_D - x_C + y_3 \geq 4$$

Event E: There are two starting events that feed into the start of event E (events A and D). For predecessor event A,

$$x_E - x_A + y_4 \geq 6$$

This simplifies to

$$x_E + y_4 \geq 6$$

For the dummy predecessor event D,

$$x_E - x_D \geq 0$$

Event F:

$$x_F - x_D \geq 3$$

Event G:

$$x_G - x_E \geq 2$$

Event H:

$$x_H - x_F + y_{10} \geq 6$$

Event I:

$$x_I - x_G \geq 4$$

Event J:

$$x_J - x_I \geq 2$$

Event K: There are four starting events that must be fulfilled that precede K. The constraint equations for the two dummy predecessor events, H and J, are

$$x_K - x_H \geq 0$$
$$x_K - x_J \geq 0$$

The remaining two predecessor events of K are F and I:

$$x_K - x_F + y_{11} \geq 8$$
$$x_H - x_I \geq 3$$

Event L: The two remaining predecessor constraint equations for event L, representing predecessors D and K are, respectively,

$$x_L - x_D + y_{17} \geq 11$$
$$x_L - x_K \geq 1$$

Maximum Crash-Reduction Constraints   The maximum amount of crash reduction possible for any activity is equal to the difference between the normal times and crash times (Table 13-2). For example, the maximum crash reduction possible for activity a_3 (director search) *cannot exceed* $6 - 4 = 2$ weeks (i.e., $y_3 \leq 2$). The Broadway musical maximum crash-reduction constraints are, then,

$y_1 \leq 2$	$y_6 \leq 0$	$y_{11} \leq 2$	$y_{16} \leq 0$
$y_2 \leq 0$	$y_7 \leq 0$	$y_{12} \leq 0$	$y_{17} \leq 3$
$y_3 \leq 2$	$y_8 \leq 0$	$y_{13} \leq 0$	
$y_4 \leq 4$	$y_9 \leq 0$	$y_{14} \leq 0$	
$y_5 \leq 0$	$y_{10} \leq 2$	$y_{15} \leq 0$	

Project Duration Constraint   The producer can now select a specific completion time for the project. Suppose, for the example, the producer wants the new project duration to be no more than 25 weeks. We can state this constraint as

$$x_L \leq 25$$

The result would yield the event times and project cost that would result from a 1-week crash. Of course, this process can be repeated with subsequently lower project duration times of 24, 23, 22, and 21 weeks, until the attempt to find an LP solution yields "no feasible solution."

A summary of the LP cost-crashing formulation of the Broadway musical is as follows:

$$\text{Minimize } Z = 75,000\, y_1 + 22,500\, y_3 + + 5000\, y_4 + 12,500\, y_{10}$$
$$+ 20,000\, y_{11} + 30,000\, y_{17}$$

Predecessor Event Constraints:

(1) $x_A = 0$

(2) $x_B + y_1 \geq 6$

(3) $x_C - x_B \geq 4$

(4) $x_D - x_C + y_3 \geq 4$

(5) $x_E + y_4 \geq 6$

(6) $x_E - x_D \geq 0$

(7) $x_F - x_D \geq 3$

(8) $x_G - x_E \geq 2$

(9) $x_H - x_F + y_{10} \geq 6$

(10) $x_I - x_G \geq 4$

(11) $x_J - x_I \geq 2$

(12) $x_K - x_H \geq 0$

(13) $x_K - x_J \geq 0$

(14) $x_K - x_F + y_{11} \geq 8$

(15) $x_H - x_I \geq 3$

(16) $x_L - x_D + y_{17} \geq 11$

(17) $x_L - x_K \geq 1$

Maximum Crash-Reduction Constraints:

(18) $y_1 \leq 2$ (23) $y_6 \leq 0$ (28) $y_{11} \leq 2$ (33) $y_{16} \leq 0$

(19) $y_2 \leq 0 \ldots$ (24) $y_7 \leq 0 \ldots$ (29) $y_{12} \leq 0 \ldots$ (34) $y_{17} \leq 3$

(20) $y_3 \leq 2 \ldots$ (25) $y_8 \leq 0 \ldots$ (30) $y_{13} \leq 0 \ldots$

(21) $y_4 \leq 4 \ldots$ (26) $y_9 \leq 0 \ldots$ (31) $y_{14} \leq 0$

(22) $y_5 \leq 0 \ldots$ (27) $y_{10} \leq 2 \ldots$ (32) $y_{15} \leq 0$

Project Duration Constraint:

$$x_L \leq 25$$

Regardless of the fact that there are now two methods of conducting project cost crashing, the size of the project will be an overriding issue. That is, as the number of activities that comprise a project schedule grows, the decision to select *either* the incremental, manual method or the LP method to solve cost-crashing situations rapidly becomes less sensible. Project management software—even the lower-cost products used for the educational market—typically include the cost-crash option. Examples of the use of these products are presented in Section 13.11.

13.10 | GRAPHICAL EVALUATION AND REVIEW TECHNIQUE (GERT)

During the 1960s, a radically new project management tool was developed that seemed to overcome almost all of the shortcomings of traditional methods. However, the level of sophistication of the mathematics required for this method, along with the difficulty of developing the information needed to formulate the model, is so great that the method has gained little popularity. Nevertheless, it has such attractive qualities that it deserves some discussion here.

GERT is constructed with event nodes and activities—just as are PERT and CPM. But there the similarity ends. Three characteristics of this unique analytical tool are these:

1. Instead of being structured out of activities that must be done, GERT handles activities that may or may not be completed. It is possible to have activities that you totally fail to achieve, partially achieve, or achieve completely.

2. It is possible to initiate an activity without completing all its predecessor activities.

3. The number of activities required to be completed leading to the node for the first time can be a different value for subsequent passes (Figure 13-27).

4. There are probability distributions associated with each activity branch, resulting in a schematic that resembles part project management, part feedback-control system, and part decision tree.

5. GERT permits an activity to loop from a node back to the same node (Figure 13-28), and can incorporate a variety of probability distributions for each activity time (normal, constant, Erlang, Poisson, etc.), rather than being restricted to just the beta distribution.

There are two kinds of event nodes that dictate the different types of branches in GERT. In addition, it is also necessary to distinguish between the input and output sides

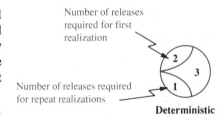

Number of releases required for first realization

Number of releases required for repeat realizations

Deterministic

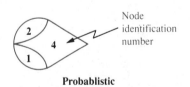

Node identification number

Probablistic

FIGURE 13-27

GERT Input Node Symbolism for Deterministic and Stochastic Activity Branches

FIGURE 13-28

GERT Simple and Complex Branch Looping Schematics

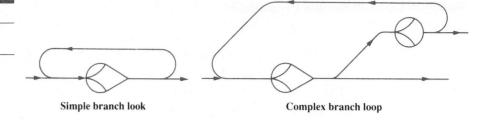

Simple branch look   Complex branch loop

of each node. The two different event node forms and the types of activities branching from them (output branches) are

1. *Deterministic nodes*, in which all activities leaving an event are incorporated if the node is realized. Each activity branch has a probability of 1.0 (just as in PERT and CPM).

2. *Stochastic nodes*, in which only one activity (at most) leaving an event is incorporated *if the node is realized*. All of these activity branches have probabilities of occurrence, the values of which (for all branches) sum to 1.0.

The GERT symbols used for the output activity branches for each of these two types of nodes are shown in Figure 13-29. One of the best examples of the application of GERT is presented by Efraim Turban and N. Paul Loomba (1982). They develop a hypothetical research and development model in which a pharmaceutical company is planning the development of a new drug. The GERT chart illustrating this research project is shown in Figure 13-30.

Probability of occurrence of activities

1.0   1.0   1.0   .10   .30   .60

Deterministic   Probablilistic

FIGURE 13-29

GERT Output Node Symbolism for Deterministic and Stochastic Activity Branches

13.11 | MICROCOMPUTER SOLUTIONS TO PROJECT MANAGEMENT PROBLEMS

Project management software packages are abundant. The packages that can manage thousands of activities, provide graphics and charting capabilities, and balance numerous, multiple resources tend to be expensive. Many more moderate packages are individual models of inexpensive multiple-module management science software products (Chapter 16).

Project management software requires little effort to get the analysis rolling. You should consider (1) whether you want to use a PERT (stochastic) or CPM (deterministic) model, (2) what is the number of activities in your network, (3) what are the number and identification (node numbers) of the predecessor activities for each network activity, (4) what is the duration of each activity (either a single value for CPM or the three-value beta distribution for PERT), and (5) whether you wish to include cost data for each activity so that cost crashing can be conducted as part of the analysis. Examples of microcomputer solutions to the Broadway musical, including cost crashing, are shown in Tables 13-5 (data entry) and 13-6 (solution) using the Lee and Shim software package, *Micro Manager*. Tables 13-7 (data entry) and 13-8 (solution) employ the Chang and Sullivan project management module from *QSB*. Although there are significant similarities between the two software programs, it is interesting to note the slightly different formats used to arrange information.

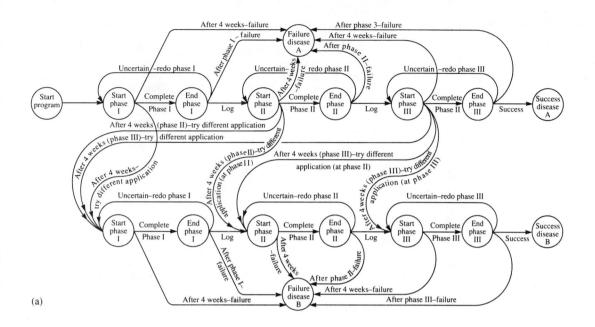

(a)

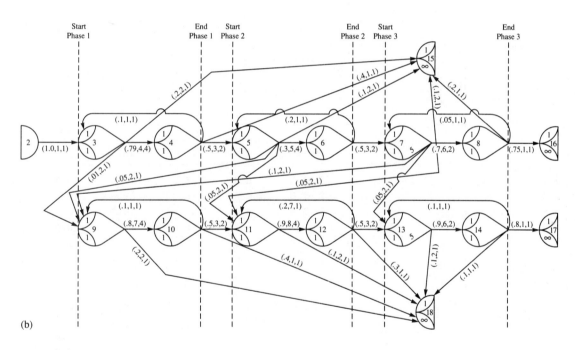

(b)

FIGURE 13-30

Pharmaceutical-Company Research and Development Project (A) and GERT Network (B) for New Drug

Source: E. R. Clayton and L. J. Moore, "PERT versus GERT," *Journal of Systems Engineering* 23 (No. 2: February 1972): 11–19, reprinted in E. Turban and N. P. Loomba (eds), *Cases and Readings in Management Science*, rev. ed. (Plano, TX: Business Publications, 1982.)

TABLE 13-5

CPM with Cost Crashing for Broadway Musical: Input Data

Source: Lee and Shim, *Micro Manager*. Dubuque, IA: William C. Brown, 1986

```
-----------------------------------------------------------------------------
                        Predecessor  Normal   Crashed   Normal    Unit Crash
Activity    Nodes       Activities   Time     Time      Cost      Cost
-----------------------------------------------------------------------------
   1       1 -> 2                      6        4       350000     75000
   2       2 -> 3          1           4        4        20000
   3       3 -> 4          2           4        2        50000     22500
   4       1 -> 5                      6        2        40000      5000
   5       4 -> 5          3           0        0           0
   6       5 -> 7         4 5          2        2        8000
   7       4 -> 6          3           3        3        30000
   8       6 -> 7          7           0        0           0
   9       7 -> 9         6 8          4        4       100000
  10       6 -> 8          7           6        4        25000     12500
  11       6 -> 11         7           8        6       100000     20000
  12       8 -> 11        10           0        0           0
  13       9 -> 11         9           3        3        30000
  14       9 -> 10         9           2        2        55000
  15      10 -> 11        14           0        0           0
  16      11 -> 12   11 12 13 15       1        1        25000
  17       4 -> 12        11           8     150000       30000
-----------------------------------------------------------------------------
```

TABLE 13-6

Analysis of CPM Output for Broadway Musical: Output Data

Source: Lee and Shim, *Micro Manager*. Dubuque, IA: William C. Brown, 1986

```
                    *****  PROGRAM OUTPUT  *****

                        **Analysis of CPM **

-----------------------------------------------------------------------------
                         Activity    Early     Late      Total
        Activity  Nodes  Duration    Start     Finish    Slack
-----------------------------------------------------------------------------
           1      1 -> 2    6.0        0.0       6.0       0.0
           2      2 -> 3    4.0        6.0      10.0       0.0
           3      3 -> 4    4.0       10.0      14.0       0.0
           4      1 -> 5    6.0        0.0      16.0      10.0
           5      4 -> 5    0.0        0.0       0.0       0.0
           6      5 -> 7    2.0       14.0      18.0       2.0
           7      4 -> 6    3.0       14.0      17.0       0.0
           8      6 -> 7    0.0        0.0       0.0       0.0
           9      7 -> 9    4.0       17.0      22.0       1.0
          10      6 -> 8    6.0       17.0      25.0       2.0
          11      6 -> 11   8.0       17.0      25.0       0.0
          12      8 -> 11   0.0        0.0       0.0       0.0
          13      9 -> 11   3.0       21.0      25.0       1.0
          14      9 -> 10   2.0       21.0      25.0       2.0
          15     10 -> 11   0.0        0.0       0.0       0.0
          16     11 -> 12   1.0       25.0      26.0       0.0
          17      4 -> 12  11.0       14.0      26.0       1.0
-----------------------------------------------------------------------------
      The Critical Path (activities):  1-> 2 -> 3 -> 7 -> 11 -> 16
                 The Normal Completion Time = 26
            The Completely Crashed Completion Time = 21
```

```
          **  Summary of the Crashing Procedure  **

    ------------------------------------------------------------
                                Revised                  Revised
               Activities  Time  Completion  Additional  Project
     Step      Crashed     Reduced Time       Cost        Cost
    ------------------------------------------------------------
      0                             26.0                  983000
      1          11        1.0      25.0       20000     1003000
      2          3         2.0      23.0       45000     1048000
      3          1         2.0      21.0      150000     1198000
    ------------------------------------------------------------
     Total                5.0                215000
    ------------------------------------------------------------

         **  Summary of the Critical Path (Activities)  **

    ------------------------------------------------------------
               Project
               Completion
     Step      Time              Critical Path Activities
    ------------------------------------------------------------
      0        26.0       1 -> 2 -> 3 -> 7 -> 11 -> 16
      1        25.0       1 -> 2 -> 3 -> 7 -> 11 -> 16
                          1 -> 2 -> 3 -> 17
                          1 -> 2 -> 3 -> 7 -> 8 -> 9 -> 13 -> 16
      2        23.0       1 -> 2 -> 3 -> 7 -> 11 -> 16
                          1 -> 2 -> 3 -> 17
                          1 -> 2 -> 3 -> 7 -> 8 -> 9 -> 13 -> 16
      3        21.0       1 -> 2 -> 3 -> 7 -> 11 -> 16
                          1 -> 2 -> 3 -> 17
                          1 -> 2 -> 3 -> 7 -> 8 -> 9 -> 13 -> 16
    ------------------------------------------------------------
```

TABLE 13-6

Analysis of CPM Output for Broadway Musical: Output Data, Continued

```
        Input Data of The Problem CPM.MUSICAL     Page 1


Activity Activity  Start  End   Normal    Crash     Normal    Crash
number   name      node   node  duration  duration  cost      cost
  1    <FINANCE >  <1 >   <2 >  <6.0000>  <4.0000>  <350000>  <500000 >
  2    <WRITER  >  <2 >   <3 >  <4.0000>  <4.0000>  <20000 >  <20000  >
  3    <DIRECTOR>  <3 >   <4 >  <4.0000>  <2.0000>  <50000 >  <95000  >
  4    <LEASE   >  <1 >   <5 >  <6.0000>  <2.0000>  <40000 >  <60000  >
  5    <DUMMY#1 >  <4 >   <5 >  <      >  <      >  <      >  <       >
  6    <AUDITION>  <5 >   <7 >  <2.0000>  <2.0000>  <8000  >  <8000   >
  7    <HIRESTAF>  <4 >   <6 >  <3.0000>  <3.0000>  <30000 >  <30000  >
  8    <DUMMY#2 >  <6 >   <7 >  <      >  <      >  <      >  <       >
  9    <REHEARSE>  <7 >   <9 >  <4.0000>  <4.0000>  <100000>  <100000 >
 10    <COSTUME >  <6 >   <8 >  <6.0000>  <4.0000>  <25000 >  <50000  >
 11    <SETDESGN>  <6 >   <11>  <8.0000>  <6.0000>  <100000>  <140000 >
 12    <DUMMY#3 >  <8 >   <11>  <      >  <      >  <      >  <       >
 13    <SCRIPTCH>  <9 >   <11>  <3.0000>  <3.0000>  <30000 >  <30000  >
 14    <CASTCHG >  <9 >   <10>  <2.0000>  <2.0000>  <55000 >  <55000  >
 15    <DUMMY#4 >  <10>   <11>  <      >  <      >  <      >  <       >
 16    <DRESSREH>  <11>   <12>  <1.0000>  <1.0000>  <25000 >  <25000  >
 17    <PROMO   >  <4 >   <12>  <11.000>  <8.0000>  <150000>  <240000 >
```

TABLE 13-7

Cost-Crashing Data Entry for Broadway Musical

Source: Chang and Sullivan, *QSB*. Englewood Cliffs, NJ: Prentice-Hall, 1986

TABLE 13-8

**Cost-Crashing Solution
for Broadway Musical**

Source: Chang and Sullivan, *QSB*. Englewood Cliffs, NJ: Prentice-Hall, 1986

```
For this crash to reduce 1 time unit(s).
Completion time without crashing for CPM.MUSICAL is 26
      Crash activity DIRECTOR 1 time unit(s)  New duration = 3  Incremental cost
      = 22500
      Critical paths for CPM.MUSICAL with completion time = 25  Total cost
      = 1005500
CP # 1  :
      FINANCE     WRITER      DIRECTOR  HIRESTAF  SETDESGN  DRESSREH
      1=======>   2=======>   3=======> 4=======> 6=======> 11=======>  12
For this crash to reduce 2 time unit(s).
Completion time without crashing for CPM.MUSICAL is 26
      Crash activity DIRECTOR 2 time unit(s)  New duration = 2  Incremental cost
      = 45000
      Critical paths for CPM.MUSICAL with completion time = 24  Total cost
      = 1020000
CP # 1  :
      FINANCE     WRITER      DIRECTOR  HIRESTAF  SETDESGN  DRESSREH
      1=======>   2=======>   3=======> 4=======> 6=======> 11=======>  12
For this crash to reduce 3 time unit(s).
Completion time without crashing for CPM.MUSICAL is 26
      Crash activity DIRECTOR 2 time unit(s)  New duration = 2  Incremental cost
      = 45000
      Crash activity SETDESGN 1 time unit(s)  New duration = 7  Incremental cost
      = 20000
      Critical paths for CPM.MUSICAL with completion time = 23  Total cost =
1040000
CP # 1  :
      FINANCE     WRITER      DIRECTOR  HIRESTAF  DUMMY#2    REHEARSE
      1=======>   2=======>   3=======> 4=======> 6=======> 7=======> 9
      SCRIPTCH    DRESSREH
      9=======>   11=======> 12
CP # 2  :
      FINANCE     WRITER      DIRECTOR  PROMO
      1=======>   2=======>   3=======> 4=======> 12
CP # 3  :
      FINANCE     WRITER      DIRECTOR  HIRESTAF  SETDESGN  DRESSREH
      1=======>   2=======>   3=======> 4=======>            6=======>
      11=======> 12
For this crash to reduce 5 time unit(s).
Completion time without crashing for CPM.MUSICAL is 26
      Crash activity DIRECTOR 2 time unit(s)  New duration = 2  Incremental cost
      = 45000
      Crash activity SETDESGN 1 time unit(s)  New duration = 7  Incremental cost
      = 20000
      Crash activity FINANCE 2 time unit(s)  New duration = 4  Incremental cost
      = 150000
      Critical paths for CPM.MUSICAL with completion time = 21  Total cost
      = 1190000
CP # 1  :
      FINANCE     WRITER      DIRECTOR  HIRESTAF  DUMMY#2    REHEARSE
      1=======>   2=======>   3=======> 4=======> 6=======> 7=======> 9
      SCRIPTCH    DRESSREH
      9=======>   11=======> 12
CP # 2  :
      FINANCE     WRITER      DIRECTOR  PROMO
      1=======>   2=======>   3=======> 4=======> 12
CP # 3  :
      FINANCE     WRITER      DIRECTOR  HIRESTAF  SETDESGN  DRESSREH
      1=======>   2=======>   3=======> 4=======> 6=======> 11=======> 12
```

```
-----------------------------------------------------------------------
        CPM Analysis for CPM.MUSICAL           Page 1
-----------------------------------------------------------------------
   Activity  Activity  Earliest  Latest   Earliest  Latest    Slack
   Number    Name      Start     Start    Finish    Finish    LS-E
-----------------------------------------------------------------------
      1      FINANCE    0         0        4.000     4.000    Critical
      2      WRITER     4.000     4.000    8.000     8.000    Critical
      3      DIRECTOR   8.000     8.000    10.000    10.000   Critical
      4      LEASE      0         5.000    6.000     11.000   5.000
      5      DUMMY#1    10.000    11.000   10.000    11.000   1.000
      6      AUDITION   10.000    11.000   12.000    13.000   1.000
      7      HIRESTAF   10.000    10.000   13.000    13.000   Critical
      8      DUMMY#2    13.000    13.000   13.000    13.000   Critical
      9      REHEARSE   13.000    13.000   17.000    17.000   Critical
     10      COSTUME    13.000    14.000   19.000    20.000   1.000
     11      SETDESGN   13.000    13.000   20.000    20.000   Critical
     12      DUMMY#3    19.000    20.000   19.000    20.000   1.000
     13      SCRIPTCH   17.000    17.000   20.000    20.000   Critical
     14      CASTCHG    17.000    18.000   19.000    20.000   1.0000
     15      DUMMY#4    19.000    20.000   19.000    20.000   1.0000
     16      DRESSREH   20.000    20.000   21.000    21.000   Critical
     17      PROMO      10.000    10.000   21.000    21.000   Critical
-----------------------------------------------------------------------
      Completion time = 21        Total Cost = 1198000
-----------------------------------------------------------------------
```

TABLE 13-9

Cost-Crashing Summary for Broadway Musical

Source: Chang and Sullivan, *QSB*. Englewood Cliffs, NJ: Prentice-Hall, 1986

13.12 SUMMARY

Almost any organization can extemporaneously plan, schedule, and monitor a complex project—even though that project may comprise numerous tasks for which little or no experience has been accumulated—so long as budget overruns are of no concern. If the budget is of concern, however, it is important to use project management techniques to streamline this difficult process.

The two most popular tools of project management—the critical path method (CPM) and the program review and evaluation technique (PERT)—are, essentially, identical in concept. The primary thrust of both is first to help the manager to organize the numerous activities that constitute the project into the most streamlined design possible. Then, project management helps the manager to identify the *critical path*: the family of activities that collectively represents the jobs most likely to prolong the project. The identification of the critical-path activities is based on the assumption that the time estimate for each task is reasonably accurate. Unfortunately, in actual application, the variability of completion times for the different activities often results in the critical path shifting to other, sometimes overlooked, project members. This can result in a presumed critical path that is carefully monitored and successfully managed, while the overall project completion date strays off schedule.

When even the best project planning is overcome by unforeseen events, managers can employ additional resources to shorten the critical-path activities (and total project duration). This process is called cost crashing and can, in some instances, bring the project in on time. Two different methods of cost crashing were examined: (1) an incremental, manual approach and (2) a linear programming formulation, which typically relies on computer solution.

A variant of PERT–CPM is offered by the GERT method. This analytical technique, although difficult to model, overcomes many of the limitations inherent in the two more traditional models. Unfortunately, relatively little has been done to popularize GERT since its development in the 1960s.

13.13 | EXERCISES

13-1 For the generic project shown in Figure 13-1.1, determine the following:

1. Estimated project completion time
2. Earliest start and finish times for each activity
3. Latest start and finish times for each activity
4. Slack time associated with each activity
5. Critical path

13-2 Assume that the project depicted in Exercise 13-1 has a $3000-per-day fixed cost under normal conditions. After some thought, the manager of the project estimates that each of the activities can be done more quickly—for a price. The crash times and costs associated with each activity are shown in Table 13-2.1. Establish the cost–time relationship for this project. Illustrate your findings.

13-3 A small project is described by the activity characteristics in Table 13-3.1. Illustrate the network, and find the following information:

1. Estimated project completion time
2. Earliest start and finish times for each activity
3. Latest start and finish times for each activity
4. Slack time associated with each activity
5. Critical path

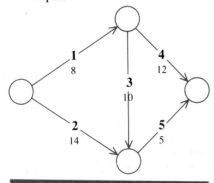

FIGURE 13-1.1

"Generic Project" Network

13-4 Suppose that the city of Santa Fe, New Mexico, is planning to build a new crafts and arts museum, focusing primarily on Native American works. A rough outline of the various tasks (times in weeks) that will need to be accomplished is given in Table 13-4.1. Using these data, determine the following pieces of information for the Santa Fe Museum Arts Commission:

1. What does the project layout look like?
2. Are there any dummy variables in the project? If so, can you explain why they are needed?

TABLE 13-2.1

Cost-Crashing Summary for "Generic Project"

Activity	Crash Cost/Day ($)	Crash Time
1	1500	3
2	2000	6
3	1400	10
4	800	8
5	2500	2

TABLE 13-3.1

Project Sequence Logic and Estimated Activity Durations

Activity	Expected Completion Time (days)	Activity Immediately Preceding
1	12	none
2	24	none
3	9	1
4	36	1
5	18	1
6	27	2,3
7	15	2,3,5
8	39	2,3
9	21	4,6,7

TABLE 13-4.1

Construction-Activity Interrelationships for Santa Fe Museum

Activity	Description	Activity Immediately Preceding	Expected Duration
1	Excavation	—	3
2	Pour foundation	1	1
3	Exterior plumbing	1	4
4	Rough framing	2	7
5	Interior plumbing	4	6
6	Electrical wiring	4	5
7	Roofing	4	3
8	Exterior plastering	2	5
9	Plumbing and electrical inspection	3,5	.5
10	Interior lighting (neon, indirect fluorescent, etc.)	7	2
11	Interior plastering and painting	6,9,10	2
12	Install computerized security system	11	3
13	Exterior painting, detailing	7,8	4
14	Architectural landscaping	13	4

TABLE 13-5.1

Activity Interrelationships for Orion Pictures' *Father Flotsky's Triumph*

Activity	Description	Activity Immediately Preceding	Expected Duration
1	Write script	—	12
2	Develop budget	—	2
3	Design special effects	1	16
4	Auditions and select cast	2	4
5	Select ad agency and develop promotion	2	2
6	Film interior scenes	1,4	4
7	Film exterior scenes	6	2
8	Film special effects	3,6	4
9	Edit film	6,7,8	6
10	Select theaters	5,9	2
11	Preview film	9	2
12	Analyze audience and critic response	11	2
13	Recut film	12	3
14	Distribute film	13	2

3. What are the earliest start and finish times for each activity?

4. What are the latest start and finish times for each activity?

5. What is the total slack time associated with each activity?

6. What are the critical activities and the duration of the critical path?

13-5 Suppose that Orion Pictures is in the process of planning their next film. The movie is loosely based on an old Lenny Bruce comedy sketch of a priest at a prison break, called *Father Flotsky's Triumph*. The various activities (times in weeks) involved in filming this movie are presented in Table 13-5.1. Using this information, determine the following information for the Orion CEO:

1. What does the film schedule look like?

2. Are there any dummy variables in the project? If so, can you explain why they are needed?

3. What are the earliest start and finish times for each activity?

4. What are the latest start and finish times for each activity?

5. What is the total slack time associated with each activity?

6. What are the critical activities and the duration of the critical path?

13-6 A promoter wishes to hold a 3-night jazz concert in Carnegie Hall to commemorate this famed building's one-hundredth anniversary. She is considering such famed musicians and groups as the Wynton Marsalis Quintet, the Stan Getz Quartet, Art Blakey and the Jazz Messengers, the Modern Jazz Quartet, the Jackie McLean Quintet, Carmen McRae, Phil

Woods Quintet, and the Art Farmer Quartet. She is sure that the time estimates are volatile, so she decides to use PERT to analyze the organization of the concert. The activities and associated time estimates are shown in Table 13-6.1. The concert promoter hires you to organize the concert project schedule, and wants to know the following:

1. What does the layout of the concert look like?

2. What is expected duration for the concert project?

3. What are the critical-path elements?

4. What project durations correspond to 90, 95, and 99 percent likelihoods of completion?

5. What is the approximate date that the project should be initiated if the promoter wishes to be 75 percent sure that the concert can be held June 1 through 3?

13-7 The Santa Fe Museum Arts Commission (Exercise 13-4) has developed crash-cost and time data for its new construction project. The commission believes that it may be of paramount importance to accelerate some of the activities in order to meet the desired grand-opening deadline. The financial data are shown in Table 13-7.1. Determine the following information for the Commission:

1. What is the shortest duration for the completion of the film?

2. What total project cost is associated with this shortest duration?

3. Draw the cost-time relationship.

4. Identify the critical path(s) for each incremental step in the crashing procedure.

TABLE 13-6.1

PERT Activities and Time Estimates for Jazz Concert Commemorating One-Hundredth Anniversary of Carnegie Hall

Activity	Description	Immediate Predecessors	Time Estimates a	m	b
1	Select musicians	—	2	5	9
2	Contact artist agents to negotiate contract	1	7	10	21
3	Arrange for travel and hotel accommodations	2	7	10	14
4	Plan concert promotion (radio interviews, newspaper ads, etc.)	2	5	7	10
5	Print concert materials (tickets, posters, programs, etc.)	2	5	7	10
6	Sell tickets	2,5	21	28	35
7	Recheck artist commitments and accommodations	2,3	5	7	14
8	Hire ticket takers and security guards	3	7	14	28
9	Rehearsals	8	2	2	2
10	Present concert	4,6,9	3	3	3

TABLE 13-7.1

Construction-Activity Crashing Times and Expenses for the Santa Fe Museum

Activity	Description	Normal Duration	Crash Time	Crash Cost ($/wk)
1	Excavation	3	2	200,000
2	Pour foundation	1	1	—
3	Exterior plumbing	4	3	75,000
4	Rough framing	7	5	100,000
5	Interior plumbing	6	3	40,000
6	Electrical wiring	5	3	85,000
7	Roofing	3	2	100,000
8	Exterior plastering	5	3	45,000
9	Plumbing and electrical inspection	0.5	0.5	—
10	Interior lighting (neon, indirect fluorescent, etc.)	2	1	30,000
11	Interior plastering and painting	2	1	25,000
12	Install computerized security system	3	2	75,000
13	Exterior painting, detailing	4	2	155,000
14	Architectural landscaping	4	3	25,000

13-8 Let us pretend that the Sharper Image (SI), a San Francisco-based high-tech retailer and mail-order business, is installing a new microcomputer system to manage its entire operation (i.e., payroll, debits, credits, inventory). Terminals at each of SI's many stores will be networked for fast, dependable service. The specific activities that SI will need to accomplish before the system is up and running are listed in Table 13-8.1. Using this information, answer the following questions for SI's CEO:

1. What does the microcomputer project look like?
2. Are there any dummy variables in the project? If so, can you explain why they are needed?
3. What are the earliest start and finish times for each activity?
4. What are the latest start and finish times for each activity?
5. What is the total slack time associated with each activity?
6. What are the critical activities and the duration of the critical path?

13-9 The mean completion time and the standard deviation for the critical path of a particular project are 65.43 days and 18.76 days, respectively. Determine the chances of finishing the project

1. In less than 50 days.
2. In less than 75 days.
3. In more than 80 days.

13-10 For Exercise 13-9, determine the likely number of days for project completion that correspond to the following probabilities:

1. The probability that the project will be completed within this time limit is 67 percent.
2. The probability that the project will be completed within this time limit is 95 percent.

TABLE 13-8.1

Computer-Facility Construction-Activity Interrelationships for Sharper Image

Activity	Description	Activity Immediately Preceding	Expected Duration
1	Build insulated separation enclosure for computer room	—	21
2	Electrical wiring of computer room	1	10
3	Electrical wiring of terminals to computer	2	4
4	Install air conditioning and filter system	2	3
5	Order and wait for computer	—	21
6	Install sprinkler and exhaust vents	4	5
7	Install computer	5, 6	3

3. The probability that the project will exceed this time limit is 67 percent.

4. The probability that the project will be completed within this time limit is 100 percent.

13-11 Using the project completion time found in Exercise 13-1 and the cost-crash information provided in Exercise 13-2, formulate the generic project as though you were going to use linear programming to crash the activities. Define all decision variables.

13-12 Using the linear programming formulation developed in Exercise 13-11, conduct the one-step cost crash with appro-

priate linear programming-software. Are the results in concert with your findings in Exercise 13-2?

13-13 Using the project completion time found in Exercise 13-4 and the cost-crash information provided in Exercise 13-7, formulate the Santa Fe Museum exercise as though you were going to use linear programming to crash the activities. Define all decision variables.

13-14 Using the formulation developed in Exercise 13-13, conduct the cost crashing with appropriate LP software. Are the results in concert with your findings in Exercise 13-13?

References

1. Bellas, C., and A. Salmi. "Improving New Product Planning with GERT Simulation." *California Management Review* 15 (No. 4: Summer 1973): 14–21.

2. Brown, Kenneth S., and Jack B. ReVelle. *Quantitative Methods for Managerial Decisions*. Reading, MA: Addison-Wesley, 1978.

3. Dane, C. W., C. F. Gray, and B. M. Woodworth. "Factors Affecting the Successful Application of PERT/CPM Systems in a Government Organization." *Interfaces* 9 (No. 5: November 1979): 94–98.

4. Digman, L. A., and Gary I. Green. "A Framework for Evaluating Network Planning and Control Techniques." *Research Management* 24 (No. 1: January 1981): 10–17.

5. Halpern, Jonathan, Efstratios Sarisamlis, and Yair Wand. "An Activity Network Approach for the Analysis of Manning Policies in Firefighting Operations." *Management Science* 28 (No. 10: October 1982): 1121–1136.

6. Kurtulus, I., and E. W. Davis. "Multi-Project Scheduling: Categorization of Heuristic Rules Performance." *Management Science* 28 (No. 2: February 1982): 161–172.

7. Pritsker, A. Alan B., and W. William Happ. "GERT: Graphical Evaluation and Review Technique—Part I. *Journal of Industrial Engineering* 17 (No. 5: May 1966): 267–274.

8. Pritsker, A. Alan B., and W. William Happ. "GERT: Graphical Evaluation and Review Technique—Part II. *Journal of Industrial Engineering* 17 (No. 6: June 1966): 293–301.

9. Schonberger, Richard J. "Why Projects Are 'Always' Late: A Rationale Based on Manual Simulation of a PERT/CPM Network." *Interfaces* 11 (No. 5: October 1981): 66–70.

10. Taylor, Bernard W., III, and Laurence J. Moore. "R&D Project Planning with Q-GERT Network Modeling and Simulation." *Management Science* 26 (No. 1: January 1980): 44–59.

11. Turban, Efraim, and N. Paul Loomba. *Cases and Readings in Management Science*, rev. ed. Plano, TX: Business Publications, 1982.

Project Management Microcomputer Software

Project management software is easily the most prolific of all management science software. There are dozens of products from which to choose. A small sampling is given here:

1. *Computer Models for Management Science*, version 2. Erikson and Hall. Reading, MA: Addison-Wesley, 1986.

2. *Confidence Factor*, version 2. Newman et al. Irvine, CA: Simple Software, 1983.

3. *Decision Support Modeling*. San Juan Capistrano, CA: Decision Support Systems, 1986.

4. *Harvard Project Manager*. Mountain View, CA: Software Publishing Company, 1986.

5. *MacProject II*. Cupertino, CA: Claris Computer Corporation.

6. *Management Science and the Microcomputer*. Burns and Austin. New York: Macmillan, 1985.

7. *Microcomputer Models for Management Decision-Making*. Dennis and Dennis. St. Paul, MN: West.

8. *Microcomputer Software for Management Science and Operations Management*. Render and Stair. Boston: Allyn & Bacon, 1986.

9. *MicroManager*. San Francisco: Micro Planning Software, 1989.

10. *Micro Manager*. Sang Lee and Yung Shim. Dubuque, IA: William C. Brown, 1986.

11. *Microsoft Project*. Bellvue, WA: Microsoft Corporation, 1985.

12. *Primavera*. Foster City, CA: Scitor Corporation, 1987.

13. *Quantitative Systems for Business*. Chang and Sullivan. Englewood Cliffs, NJ: Prentice-Hall, 1986.

14. *STORM*. Dale Flowers et al. Oakland, CA: Holden-Day, 1986.

![Chapter icon]

CHAPTER 14

QUEUEING MODELS

THE ANALYTICAL STUDY OF WAITING LINES

14.1 INTRODUCTION

Queueing theory is the mathematical study of waiting lines. The first significant work in this field was done in the early 1900s by a Danish telephone company engineer, A. K. Erlang. He was attempting to model the fluctuation in demand on the telephone facilities and the ability of the telephone company to handle these demands. Waiting lines are a common phenomenon; they occur whenever the current demand for a service exceeds the current capacity to provide that service. Decisions regarding the level of service to offer must be made frequently in business. Providing too much service would involve excessive labor costs. On the other hand, not providing enough service capacity would result in excessively long waiting lines, ill-will, and, possibly, lost business. Therefore, the ultimate and typically elusive goal of the manager is to achieve a financially stable balance between the demand for services and the amount of services provided.

"I've got to go. That guy's still hanging around waiting to use the phone."

14.2 EXAMPLES OF QUEUEING APPLICATIONS

Queueing theory is among the oldest of all management science techniques. Its applications date back to the early part of the twentieth century. More contemporary examples are listed below (full citations can be found in the References at the end of this chapter):

1. Airport passenger security screening (Gilliam, 1979)

2. Bed allocation in a public health-care delivery system (Kao, 1981)

3. Analysis of the 1973 gas shortage (Erikson, 1974)

4. Design of an effective telephone reporting system for the New York State Child Abuse Center (McKeown, 1979)

5. Deployment of emergency service units (Larson, 1975)

6. Travel time analysis of radio-monitored police patrol cars in New York City (Larson and Rich, 1987)

14.3 | STEADY-STATE ASSUMPTIONS OF QUEUEING MODELS

Before we examine the various components that describe a queueing system, it is important to say that everything covered in this chapter is assumed to operate at steady state. This assumption corresponds to the fact that the overwhelming majority of waiting-line problems do, in fact, operate under steady-state or near-steady-state conditions. That is a fortunate simplification to be able to make, since the mathematics involved in the transient phases are most difficult and, in the more complex models are intractable.

14.4 | CHARACTERISTICS OF QUEUEING SYSTEMS

A queueing system may be described by four basic characteristics:

1. *The calling population*: The source from which the customers of your population originate

2. *The service facility*: The place where the customers come to receive some type of product or service

3. *The queue*: The waiting line that forms when the number of customers arriving at the service facility exceeds the immediate capacity of the facility

4. *The served customers*: Those customers who have received the product or service offered at the service facility

The interrelationships among these four elements are shown in Figure 14-1. The first three elements have a variety of characteristics that we must identify to determine the most appropriate queueing model to apply. The fourth element, the served calling units, simply leaves the system. A more detailed discussion of the first three elements follows.

14.5 | THE CALLING POPULATION

The calling population has three properties that must be considered in determining what is the most appropriate queueing model to incorporate.

FIGURE 14-1

Elements of a Queueing System

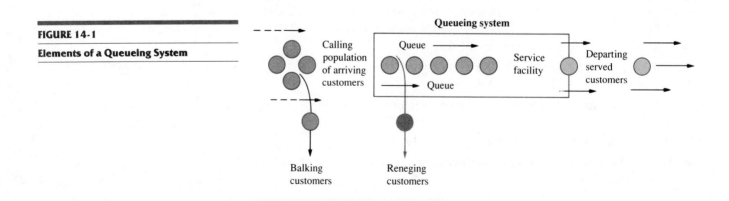

Calling-Population Size

The size of the population is either infinite or finite. In queueing, the term *infinite* is not used in the classical mathematical sense of infinite: It simply means *relatively* large. If the probability of an arrival is not significantly changed when one or more members of the population is receiving service and thus cannot arrive to the system, the population is viewed as infinite (Cook and Russell, 1989). Generally, if the probability of an arrival is not significantly affected by the number of people receiving service, the calling population may be assumed to be infinite (i.e., the proportion of the total population that can receive service at any time is near zero). Most queueing systems are of this type. Examples of infinite calling populations are the people visiting Disneyland or the people visiting Manhattan. A finite population might be the number of kidney-dialysis machines that must be maintained by technicians at Roosevelt Hospital in Manhattan or, possibly, the number of people with good taste who would even consider buying a Madonna album.[1]

Calling-Population Arrival Patterns

The statistical pattern by which the customers of the calling population arrive at the queueing system occurs either according to some predetermined schedule or at random. If the pattern is scheduled, then analytical modeling is unnecessary. If the pattern is random, then it is necessary to determine the specific type of probability distribution of the time between consecutive arrivals. The most common type of arrival pattern is the *Poisson* distribution (pronounced "pwa-suh"). In this case, arrivals to the queueing system occur randomly, but at a certain average rate. An equivalent assumption is that the probability distribution of the time between consecutive arrivals is exponential, and that the number of arrivals during a certain time interval is independent of the number of arrivals that have occurred in previous time intervals (i.e., "memoryless"). The mathematical relationship of the Poisson distribution is

$$P_n(t) = \frac{(\lambda t)^n e^{-\lambda t}}{n!}$$

where

$P_n(t)$ = probability that there will be exactly n customers into the system during a specified time increment, t

λ = mean arrival rate

The pictorial relationship of the Poisson distribution is shown in Figure 14-2.

Although the Poisson distribution represents the arrival pattern for many queueing systems, it does not portray the situation for all settings. It is crucial, therefore, to verify the specific type of arrival pattern for the system under investigation *prior* to the selection of the analytical model. This validation technique is discussed in later in this chapter (Section 14.11).[2]

---

[1] The latter is an example of the extremely rare "zero-population" phenomenon.

[2] It is quite possible that nonanalytical, empirical techniques, such as those discussed in Chapter 15 (*Monte Carlo Simulation*) are more appropriate for waiting-line problems characterized by unorthodox probability distributions.

FIGURE 14-2

Poisson Probability Distribution

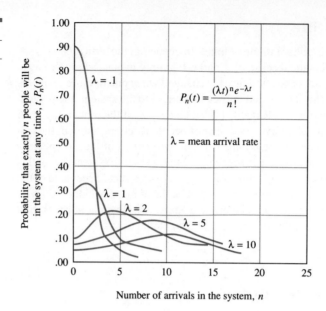

$$P_n(t) = \frac{(\lambda t)^n e^{-\lambda t}}{n!}$$

λ = mean arrival rate

Number of arrivals in the system, n

Calling-Population Behavior

The primary issue, with respect to behavior of the arriving customers, is how the new arrivals will behave with respect to the "condition" of the system. That is, will all new arrivals enter the system and remain regardless of the queue length, or will some *balk* and leave or renege prior to being served? Or, in the case of a multiple-service queue, will the customer switch from one queue to another (a process called *jockeying*) in an effort to decrease her service wait? For a customer who is kept waiting, this type of behavior is quite typical.

▎14.6▎ THE QUEUE

The queue is characterized by the maximum permissible number of customers that it can contain. This number is either potentially *infinite* or *finite*. It is dependent on customer behavior to the physical limitations—available space—of the system. The ease with which we can analytically modeling a queueing system of unlimited length is much greater than that with which we can model a limited queue situation.

▎14.7▎ THE SERVICE FACILITY

There are three basic properties of the service facility to recognize: (1) the queueing system structure, (2) the service-time distribution, and (3) the service discipline.

The Queueing System Structure

The structure can be described as *single phase* or *multiphase*.[3] An example that easily contrasts the two types of structures is the contrast between the shopper in the United

---

[3]It is even possible for a system to be a *zero-phase* or *no-phase* structure if it offers only self-service (Budnick, et al., 1988, p. 768).

"QUIT SHOVING!"

States, who typically purchases produce, fish, fowl, meats, dessert, wine, coffee, and teas at a one-stop supermarket such as Safeway or A & P, and the European shopper, who usually makes individual visits to the numerous stores that specialize in produce, desserts, wine, meats, fish and fowl, and cheese. The American buys everything in one place and stands in line once (single phase), whereas the European may sequentially visit five or six lines prior to finishing shopping for the evening meal (multiphase). In addition, either single phase or multiphase designs can be part of a *single-service* or *multiservice* facility. The system phase is the number of different types of service offered to the customer. When only one type of service is provided, we have a single-phase service facility. When more than one kind of service is provided, we have a multiphase service facility. Further, queueing systems can provide single-service (one facility available) or multiservice facilities. Accordingly, the overall service-facility structure can be any combination of these phases and facilities. An illustration of the different queueing-structure types is represented in Figure 14-3.

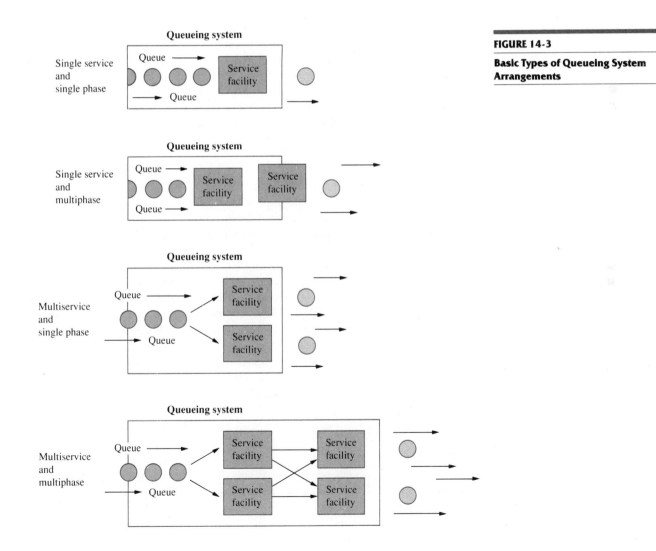

FIGURE 14-4

Exponential Probability Distribution

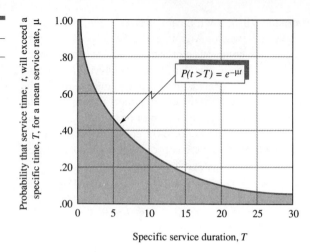

Distribution of Service Time

The service provided the queue member can be either constant or random. If the service time is random, then it is necessary, as in the arrival of members, to determine what specific type of probability distribution the service portrays. In most cases, the service times are distributed exponentially. When this is the case, the probability of completing a service to a member in any subsequent time interval is independent of how much service time has already elapsed for that member. The exponential probability distribution is given by the following formula:

$$P(t > T) = e^{-\mu t}$$

where $P(t > T)$ = the probability that the service time, t, exceeds a specific time, T, for a mean service rate of μ. This relationship is illustrated in Figure 14-4. Another important type of interarrival time distribution is the *Erlang distribution* (also referred to as the *gamma distribution*). This distribution has two parameters and thus can represent an entire family of distributions. The ability to vary these parameters easily gives the Erlang distribution great flexibility in modeling service situations that are characterized by a number of subtasks. The Erlang distribution is of particular value when the type of service to be provided a member consists of k subtasks, each of which has an identical exponential distribution. In reality, however, a task needs only to behave *in total* as though it were the sum of k identically distributed tasks; it does not have to be capable of actual subdivision. The mean service time of each of the k subtasks would then be $1/k\mu$. The mean of the total service time is then $k/k\mu$ or $1/\mu$. This value represents the expected completion time of the entire task. The Erlang probability distribution of the total service time, t, is

$$f(t) = \frac{t^{k-1}e^{-k\mu t}(k\mu)^k}{(k-1)!}$$

Notice that, for the case when $k = 1$, the Erlang distribution becomes the exponential distribution. Also, if $k = \infty$, the service time will become a constant. An illustration of this distribution is shown in Figure 14-5.

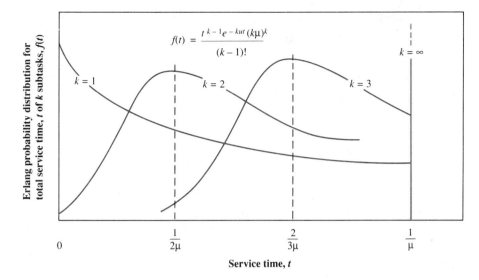

$$f(t) = \frac{t^{k-1}e^{-k\mu t}(k\mu)^k}{(k-1)!}$$

FIGURE 14-5

Erlang Probability Distribution

Service Discipline

The service discipline is the order in which arriving customers of the queueing system are selected for service. The methods employed usually follow one of two styles. The most common method is *first come, first served* (FCFS). The second type of selection procedure follows some sort of *priority* (PRI). Of course, there are also other ways to select members for service, such as selected in *random* order (SIRO) or *first come, last served* (FCLS), but these types occur comparatively rarely.

14.8 QUEUEING SYSTEM NOTATION AND OPERATING PARAMETER DEFINITION

The symbols used for the many different queueing system operating parameters are reasonably standardized, although there may be a minimal amount of variation from one text to another. The notation used for this book is

"No, I didn't take a number. I carry my number around inside me and it's next."

SYMBOL	DEFINITION
λ	Average arrival rate (customers per time period)
μ	Average service rate (customers per time period)
ρ	Utilization factor (proportion of time that the servers are busy) for a single-service facility
n	Number of customers in the system
N	Maximum number of customers allowed in a finite queueing system; maximum queue length is $N = 1$ for a single-service facility
c	Number of service facilities
P_0	Probability that no customers will be in the system[4]

[4]It also follows that the probability that a customer will have to wait, P_w, is equal to $1 - P_0$.

P_n	Probability that exactly *n* customers will be in the system
L	Average number of customers in the system
L_q	Average number of customers in queue
W	Average time in the system for a customer
W_q	Average time in the queue for a customer
M	Poisson probability distribution for arrivals/exponential probability distribution for service
∞	Infinite queue length/infinite calling population.
G	General random probability distribution for service/service priority
E	Erlang random probability distribution for service/service priority
D	Deterministic probability distribution for service

A pictorial representation of how these performance parameters fit into a general queueing model is shown in Figure 14-6. There are numerous combinations of unique queueing models resulting from the various possibilities for each of the four queueing elements discussed earlier. A notation system commonly used for classifying these models is illustrated in Figure 14-7.

As an example, the $(M/M/1)$:$(\infty/\infty/FCFS)$ model is one that has a Poisson arrival distribution and an exponential service distribution with a single server. The queue can accommodate an infinite number of customers who originate in a population of infinite size and are served on a first-come, first-served basis.

The next section will use this system notation to explore the analytical relationships of a number of the most common queueing models. Single-service facility models will be examined first, followed by the multiservice facility models. Examples of each

FIGURE 14-6

General Queueing Model Relationship Between Input Variables and System-Performance Measures

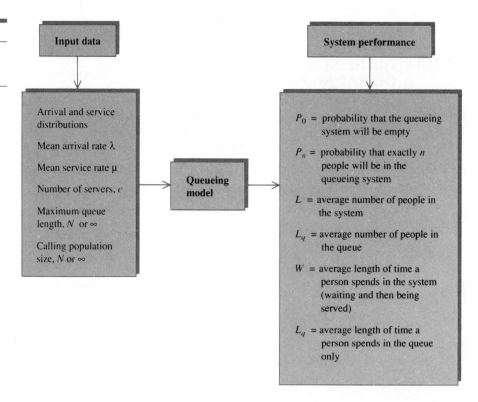

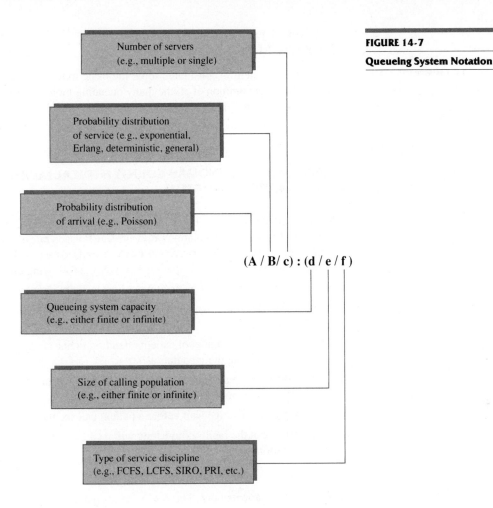

FIGURE 14-7

Queueing System Notation

Number of servers
(e.g., multiple or single)

Probability distribution
of service (e.g., exponential,
Erlang, deterministic, general)

Probability distribution
of arrival (e.g., Poisson)

(A / B/ c) : (d / e / f)

Queueing system capacity
(e.g., either finite or infinite)

Size of calling population
(e.g., either finite or infinite)

Type of service discipline
(e.g., FCFS, LCFS, SIRO, PRI, etc.)

model will be included in the individual presentations. Before we begin, however, it is important to tell you about a very powerful relationship that is known as *Little's queueing formula*. This formula states that the following relationships are true for *all steady-state queueing models*:

$$L = \lambda W \qquad \text{and} \qquad L_q = \lambda W_q$$

Now, the single-service facility queueing models will be explored.

14.9 QUEUEING MODELS FOR THE SINGLE-SERVICE FACILITY

The single-server models presented in this section are

- $(M/M/1) : (\infty/\infty/FCFS)$
- $(M/M/1) : (N/\infty/FCFS)$
- $(M/M/1) : (\infty/N/FCFS)$
- $(M/G/1) : (\infty/\infty/G)$
- $(M/D/1) : (\infty/\infty/G)$
- $(M/E/1) : (\infty/\infty/G)$

TABLE 14-1

Performance Parameters of the Basic Single-Server Model 1—($M/M/1$: (∞/∞/FCFS)

$$P_0 = 1 - \frac{\lambda}{\mu}$$

$$\rho = \frac{\lambda}{\mu}$$

$$P_n = P_0\rho^n$$

$$L = \frac{\lambda}{\mu - \lambda}$$

$$L_q = \frac{\lambda^2}{\mu(\mu - \lambda)}$$

$$W = \frac{1}{\mu - \lambda}$$

$$W_q = \frac{\lambda}{\mu(\mu - \lambda)}$$

The ($M/M/1$) : (∞/∞/FCFS) Model 1 (The Basic Single-Server Model)

This queueing system is considered to be the basic model for the single servers. It is probably the most common of all the many queueing models. Its performance characteristics are given in Table 14-1. An example of the model follows.

EXAMPLE 14.1 MULTNOMAH COUNTY MEDICAL FACILITY FLU VACCINATIONS (MODEL 1)

Assume that patients arrive at the Portland, Oregon, Multnomah County Medical Facility to receive flu vaccine inoculations at an average Poisson rate of 100 per hour. It takes the single nurse at the facility an average of 15 seconds to treat each patient, and the service follows an exponential distribution. Answer the following questions:

1. What are the chances that an arriving patient will not have to wait?

2. What is the likelihood that there will be exactly three patients in the system at any time?

3. What is the average number of patients standing in line at any time? (Do not include the patient receiving the inoculation.)

4. What is the average number of patients in the system at any time, including the person receiving the inoculation?

5. How long is the average wait before a patient can see the nurse?

6. After arriving at the facility, how long will it take for the average patient to receive the inoculation and to leave?

SOLUTION

Given: $\lambda = 100$ patients/hour, $1/\mu = 15$ seconds/patient ($\mu = 4$ patients/minute $= 240$ patients/hour), $\rho = \lambda/\mu = 100/240 = .417$.

1. The probability of the system being empty (no patients waiting in line or being inoculated) at any time is

$$P_0 = 1 - \frac{\lambda}{\mu}$$
$$= 1 - .417$$
$$= .583$$

2. The probability of exactly n patients being in the system at any given time is

$$P_n = P_0\rho^n$$
$$= .583\rho^n$$
$$= .583(.417)^n$$

For the specific case of, say, $n = 3$ patients, the chances of finding exactly n patients in the system is

$$P_3 = .583(.417)^3$$
$$= .101$$

The general relationship for P_n is illustrated in Figure 14-8.

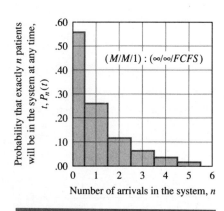

FIGURE 14-8

Probability That There Will Be Exactly n Patients in the System for the Basic Single Server—Model 1

3. The average number of patients in the queue at any time is

$$L_q = \frac{\lambda^2}{\mu(\mu - \lambda)}$$

$$= \frac{(100)^2}{(240)(240 - 100)}$$

$$= .298$$

4. The average number of patients in the system at any time is

$$L = \frac{\lambda}{\mu - \lambda}$$

$$= \frac{.417}{.583} = .715$$

5. The average time a patient spends in the queue prior to receiving the inoculation is

$$W_q = \frac{\lambda}{\mu(\mu - \lambda)}$$

$$= \frac{100}{(240)(140)}$$

$$= .00298 \text{ hour } (10.7 \text{ seconds})$$

6. The average time it takes a patient to pass through the system is

$$W = \frac{1}{\mu - \lambda}$$

$$= \frac{1}{240 - 100}$$

$$= .00714 \text{ hour } (25.7 \text{ seconds})$$

Summary: The Multnomah County Medical Facility has nearly a flythrough level of service. There is almost a 60 percent chance that the system will be empty, and the average patient spends less than 30 seconds in the system.

The $(M/M/1) : (N/\infty/FCFS)$ Model 2 (Single-Server Model with Finite Queue Length)

The only variation between this model and the basic model is that the queue length is now limited. This type of constraint is not unusual—consider the physical limits of many queue systems. The single-server, finite queue model system performance is given in Table 14-2. An example of this type of model follows.

EXAMPLE 14.2 MULTROMAH COUNTY MEDICAL FACILITY FLU VACCINATIONS (MODEL 2)

There exists a situation almost identical to the original flu vaccine problem in Example 14.1. However, because the room used for the inoculations is very small, the facility capacity is limited to a maximum of three people at any one time. What effect does this constraint have on the system-performance parameters calculated earlier?

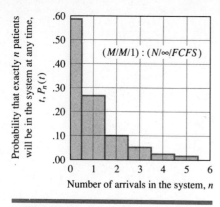

FIGURE 14-9

Probability That There Will Be Exactly *n* Patients in the System for a Single Server with Finite Queue Length—Model 2

TABLE 14-2

Performance Parameters of the Single-Server, Finite Queue Model 2 ($M/M/1$) : (N/∞/FCFS)

$$P_0 = \frac{1 - \rho}{1 - \rho^{N+1}}$$

$$\rho = \frac{\lambda}{\mu}$$

$$P_n = P_0\rho^n \qquad \text{for } n \leq N$$

$$L_q = L - (1 - P_0)$$

$$L = \frac{\rho}{(1 - \rho)} - \left[\frac{(N + 1)\rho^{N+1}}{1 - \rho^{N+1}}\right]$$

$$W_q = \frac{L_q}{\lambda(1 - P_N)}$$

$$W = \frac{L}{\lambda(1 - P_N)}$$

SOLUTION

Given: The utilization factor, ρ, is the same as in model 1: $\rho = .417$. The chance that the system will be empty, P_0, is

$$P_0 = \frac{1 - \rho}{1 - \rho^{N+1}}$$

$$= \frac{1 - .417}{1 - (.417)^4}$$

$$= \frac{.583}{1 - .0302}$$

$$= .601$$

The probability that exactly n people will be in the system at any time is given by

$$P_n = P_0\rho^n \qquad \text{for } n \leq N$$

$$= .601\rho^n$$

Therefore, $P_1 = .251$, $P_2 = .104$, . . . , $P_6 = .003$. This relationship is illustrated in Figure 14-9. The remaining parameters are calculated using the appropriate equations from Table 14-2.

The average number of patients in the system is

$$L = \frac{\rho}{(1 - \rho)} - \left[\frac{(N + 1)\rho^{N+1}}{1 - \rho^{N+1}}\right]$$

$$= \frac{.417}{.583} - \left[\frac{(4)(.417)^4}{1 - (.417)^4}\right]$$

$$= .715 - \frac{(4)(.0302)}{1 - .0302}$$

$$= .715 - .125 = .590$$

The average number of patients waiting to be inoculated (in the queue) is

$$L_q = L - [1 - P_0]$$

$$= .590 - (1 - .601)$$

$$= .590 - .399$$

$$= .191$$

The mean time waiting in line to receive the flu inoculation is

$$W_q = \frac{L_q}{\lambda(1 - P_N)}$$

$$= \frac{.191}{(100)(1 - P_3)}$$

where

$$P_3 = (.601)(.417)^3$$

$$= .0436$$

$$W_q = \frac{.191}{(100)(1 - .0436)}$$

$$= \frac{.191}{95.6} = .0020 \text{ hour } (7.19 \text{ seconds})$$

The average time in the system (time required to wait in line, to receive the flu shot, and to leave the facility) is

$$W = \frac{L}{\lambda(1 - P_N)}$$

$$= \frac{.590}{(100)(.956)} = .00617 \text{ hour } (22.2 \text{ seconds})$$

Notice that, for a system with even a very small queue limitation, the parameters change only slightly from those of the basic model.

The $(M/M/1) : (\infty/N/FCFS)$ Model 3
(Single-Server Model with Finite Calling Population)

The only difference between this model and the basic model 1 is that there is a finite population from which to draw customers. The performance parameters associated with this model are given in Table 14-3 and are illustrated by the following example.

EXAMPLE 14.3   THE DNA RESEARCH LABORATORY MAINFRAME COMPUTER

Suppose that the five Data General mainframe computers used in the DNA research laboratory at the California Institute of Technology need repair after an average of 100 hours of operation. The researchers are presently unhappy with the turnaround time for repair of computers that must be shut down. They think that the repairs should be completed and the computer should be ready for operation again within 2 working days. In addition, the technician complains that she is overworked and needs at least one other person to help in the repair operation. If the technician who repairs the computers requires an average of 25 hours for each computer, what are the values of the system-performance parameters? Do the complaints appear to be reasonable? Assume a repair capability of 40 hours per week.

SOLUTION

Given: $N = 5$, $1/\lambda = 1/100$ hours ($\lambda = .01$ machines/hour) and $1/\mu = 25$ hours ($\mu = .04$ machine/hour), $\lambda/\mu = .25$.

The chance that the technician is free (i.e., is not repairing any of the five computers) is

$$P_0 = \left[\sum_{n=0}^{N} \left(\frac{\lambda}{\mu} \right)^n \frac{N!}{(N-n)!} \right]^{-1}$$

$$= \left[\sum_{n=0}^{5} (.25)^n \frac{5!}{(5-n)!} \right]^{-1}$$

$$= \left[(.25)^0 \frac{5!}{(5-0)!} + (.25)^1 \frac{5!}{(5-1)!} + (.25)^2 \frac{5!}{(5-2)!} + (.25)^3 \frac{5!}{(5-3)!} + (.25)^4 \frac{5!}{(5-4)!} + (.25)^5 \frac{5!}{(5-5)!} \right]^{-1}$$

$$= \left[1 + \left(\tfrac{1}{4}\right)(5) + \left(\tfrac{1}{16}\right)(20) + \left(\tfrac{1}{64}\right)(60) + \left(\tfrac{1}{256}\right)(120) + \left(\tfrac{1}{1024}\right)(120) \right]^{-1}$$

$$= [1 + 1.25 + 1.25 + .94 + .47 + .12]^{-1}$$

$$= .199 \approx .200$$

TABLE 14-3

Performance Parameters of the Single-Server, Finite Calling-Population Model 3—$(M/M/1) : (\infty/N/FCFS)$

$$P_0 = \left[\sum_{n=0}^{N} \left(\frac{\lambda}{\mu} \right)^n \frac{N!}{(N-n)!} \right]^{-1}$$

$$\rho = \frac{\lambda}{\mu}$$

$$P_n = \frac{\left(\frac{\lambda}{\mu} \right)^n N!}{(N-n)!} P_0$$

$$L_q = N - \left[\left(\frac{\mu + \lambda}{\lambda} \right)(1 - P_0) \right]$$

$$L = L_q + (1 - P_0)$$

$$W_q = L_q \left(\frac{W}{L} \right)$$

$$W = \frac{L}{\lambda(N - L)}$$

The probability of exactly n computers being in the system (either being repaired or waiting for repair) at any given time is

$$P_n = \frac{\left(\frac{\lambda}{\mu}\right)^n N!}{(N-n)!} P_0$$

For $n = 1$,

$$P_1 = \frac{\left(\frac{1}{4}\right)^1 5!}{4!} P_0 = 1.25 P_0 = (1.25)(.20) = .25$$

For $n = 2$,

$$P_2 = \frac{\left(\frac{1}{4}\right)^2 5!}{3!} P_0 = \left(\frac{1}{16}\right)(20) P_0 = (1.25)(.20) = .25$$

For $n = 3$,

$$P_3 = \frac{\left(\frac{1}{4}\right)^3 5!}{2!} P_0 = .94 P_0 = .19$$

For $n = 4$,

$$P_4 = \frac{\left(\frac{1}{4}\right)^4 5!}{1!} P_0 = .47 P_0 = .09$$

For $n = 5$,

$$P_5 = \frac{\left(\frac{1}{4}\right)^5 5!}{0!} P_0 = .12 P_0 = .02$$

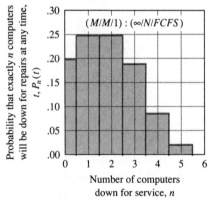

FIGURE 14-10

Probability That There Will Be Exactly *n* Computers Down for Repairs for the Single-Server Model with Finite Calling Population—Model 3

These cases are illustrated in Figure 14-10. The average number of computers waiting to be repaired is

$$L_q = N - \left[\left(\frac{\mu + \lambda}{\lambda}\right)(1 - P_0)\right]$$

$$= 5 - \left[\left(\frac{.04 + .01}{.01}\right)(1 - .20)\right]$$

$$= 5 - (5)(.80) = 1.00 \text{ computer}$$

The mean number of computers waiting for repair or being repaired by the technician at any time is

$$L = L_q + (1 - P_0)$$

$$= 1.00 + (1 - .20)$$

$$= 1.00 + .80 = 1.80 \text{ computers}$$

The mean wait from computer shutdown to finish of repair is

$$W = \frac{L}{\lambda(N-L)}$$

$$= \frac{1.80}{(.01)(5-1.80)} = 56.25 \text{ hours}$$

The mean wait for repair to begin is

$$W_q = L_q\left(\frac{W}{L}\right)$$

$$= \frac{(1.00)(56.25)}{1.80} = 31.25 \text{ hours}$$

Summary: A partial interpretation of these findings show that the chance that a computer that breaks down will have to wait before repair operations can begin (no wait) is .80. There is also an average of 1.00 computers waiting in line at any time for repair. The average time for the laboratory to repair a computer (turnaround time) is 31.25 hours. Since this value is equivalent to almost 4 working days, having only one technician to conduct repairs may be sparse staffing.

The $(M/G/1):(\infty/\infty/G)$ Model 4 (Single-Server Model with Arbitrary Service Times)

All the previous models discussed in this section have assumed exponential service distributions. However, sometimes it is not possible to make such assumptions. Model 4 represents those situations in which the service distribution is arbitrary; for example, it is constant, is normal, or has some other nonexponential form. General or arbitrary service-time models require some estimate of the probability distribution (taken from empirical data or from knowledge of the process, if previous studies have been conducted) so that the mean and variance statistics can be used to solve the various model performance parameters (Table 14-4). In addition to the arbitrary service distribution, this model is applicable to a number of priority disciplines—for example, FCFS, LCFS, and SIRO.

EXAMPLE 14.4 MULTNOMAH COUNTY MEDICAL FACILITY FLU VACCINATIONS (MODEL 4)

Suppose we have a situation identical to that of the flu vaccine model 1 (Example 14.1) except that the service time is normally distributed, with a mean of 15 seconds per patient and a standard deviation of 3 seconds per patient. Calculate all relevant parameters.

SOLUTION

Given: $\lambda = 100/\text{hour}$; $\mu = 240/\text{hour}$; $\sigma = 3$ seconds/patient $= .000833$ hour/patient

TABLE 14-4

Performance Parameters of the Arbitrary Service Time, Single-Server Model 4—$(M/G/1):(\infty/\infty/G)$

$$P_0 = 1 - \left(\frac{\lambda}{\mu}\right)$$

$$\rho = \frac{\lambda}{\mu}$$

$$L_q = \frac{\lambda^2\sigma^2 + \rho^2}{2(1-\rho)}$$

$$L = L_q + \rho$$

$$W_q = \frac{L_q}{\lambda}$$

$$W = \frac{L}{\lambda}$$

The probability of the system being empty is

$$P_0 = 1 - \left(\frac{\lambda}{\mu}\right)$$

$$= 1 - \frac{100}{240} = .583$$

The average number of patients waiting in line for the vaccine at any time is

$$L_q = \frac{\lambda^2\sigma^2 + \rho^2}{2(1 - \rho)}$$

$$= \frac{(100)^2(.000833)^2 + (.417)^2}{(2)(.583)} = .155 \text{ patient}$$

The mean number of patients in the system at any time is

$$L = L_q + \rho$$

$$= .155 + .417 = .572 \text{ patient}$$

The typical time a patient waits in line prior to receiving the vaccine is

$$W_q = \frac{L_q}{\lambda}$$

$$= \frac{.155}{100} = .00155 \text{ hour (5.58 seconds)}$$

The mean total time a patient spends in the health facility is

$$W = \frac{L}{\lambda}$$

$$= \frac{.572}{100} = .00572 \text{ hour (20.59 seconds)}$$

TABLE 14-5

Performance Parameters of the Deterministic (Constant) Service Rate, Single-Server Model 5—$(M/D/1):(\infty/\infty/G)$

$$P_0 = 1 - \left(\frac{\lambda}{\mu}\right)$$

$$\rho = \frac{\lambda}{\mu}$$

$$L_q = \frac{\lambda^2}{2\mu(\mu - \lambda)}$$

$$L = L_q + \rho$$

$$W_q = \frac{L_q}{\lambda}$$

$$W = \frac{L}{\lambda}$$

The $(M/D/1):(\infty/\infty/G)$ Model 5 (Single-Server Model with Constant Service Time)

Production-line-type operations have service distributions that are fairly constant. When this is the case, the standard deviation, σ, is zero. The relationships of such a model are shown in Table 14-5. A typical application of a constant-service-time situation is illustrated next.

EXAMPLE 14.5   THE IMPERIAL CAR WASH

As an illustration of this model, suppose the Imperial Car Wash on La Brea Avenue in Los Angeles experiences a Poisson arrival pattern, with a mean of 18 cars per hour and a reasonably constant service rate of 20 cars per hour. Calculate the performance parameters of this model.

SOLUTION

Given: $\lambda = 18$/hour, $\mu = 20$/hour, $\lambda/\mu = .90$.

The chance of the car wash being empty is

$$P_0 = 1 - \left(\frac{\lambda}{\mu}\right)$$

$$= 1 - \left(\frac{18}{20}\right) = .10$$

The mean number of cars waiting to be washed is

$$L_q = \frac{\lambda^2}{2\mu(\mu - \lambda)}$$

$$= \frac{(18)^2}{(2)(20)(2)} = 4.05 \text{ cars}$$

The average number of cars in the system is

$$L = L_q + \rho$$

$$= 4.05 + .90 = 4.95 \text{ cars}$$

The average amount of time a customer waits prior to having his car washed is

$$W_q = \frac{L_q}{\lambda}$$

$$= \frac{4.05}{18} = .225 \text{ hour } (13.5 \text{ minutes})$$

The total amount of time a customer must wait to get his car washed and to leave the facility is

$$W = \frac{L}{\lambda}$$

$$= \frac{4.95}{18} = .275 \text{ hour } (16.5 \text{ minutes})$$

The $(M/E_k/1) : (\infty/\infty/G)$ Model 6 (Single-Server Model with Erlang Service Times)

If the service task can be broken down into k subtasks, where each subtask has an identical exponentially distributed function, the performance of such a model can be described by the information given in Table 14-6.

EXAMPLE 14.6   THE DELTA AIRLINES TICKET AGENT

Let us pretend that a Delta Airlines ticket agent at Chicago's O'Hare Airport estimates that she performs approximately five different services while waiting on the average customer when she is on call alone: (1) providing general information (ticket prices,

TABLE 14-6

Performance Parameters of the Single-Server, Erlang Service Distribution Model 6—$(M/E_k/1) : (\infty/\infty/G)$

$$P_0 = 1 - \left(\frac{\lambda}{\mu}\right)$$

$$\rho = \frac{\lambda}{k\mu}$$

$$L_q = \frac{(1 + k)\lambda^2}{2k\mu(\mu - \lambda)}$$

$$L = L_q + \rho$$

$$W_q = \frac{L_q}{\lambda}$$

$$W = \frac{L}{\lambda}$$

schedules, gate locations, etc.), (2) ticketing, (3) checking in luggage, (4) assigning seats, and (5) answering the telephone. Each of these services can be divided into five subtasks that take, on the average, 1.00 minute to complete. The mean arrival rate of customers is 10 per hour. Determine all relevant parameters.

SOLUTION

Given: $\lambda = 10$ customers/hour, $\mu = 60/k = 60/5 = 12$ customers/hour.

The chances of an arriving passenger finding the facility empty is

$$P_0 = 1 - \left(\frac{\lambda}{\mu}\right)$$
$$= 1 - \left(\frac{10}{12}\right) = .167$$

The average number of airline passengers waiting for service is

$$L_q = \frac{(1 + k)\lambda^2}{2k\mu(\mu - \lambda)}$$
$$= \frac{(1 + 5)(10)^2}{(2)(5)(12)(12 - 10)}$$
$$= \frac{(6)(100)}{(10)(12)(2)} = 2.50 \text{ passengers}$$

The average number of passengers in the system (those in line and the one being waited on) is

$$L = L_q + \left(\frac{\lambda}{\mu}\right)$$
$$= 2.50 + \left(\frac{10}{12}\right) = 3.33 \text{ passengers}$$

The average wait in line prior to seeing the ticket agent is

$$W_q = \frac{L_q}{\lambda}$$
$$= \frac{2.50}{10} = .250 \text{ hour} (15.00 \text{ minutes})$$

The average duration a passenger spends in the system is

$$W = \frac{L}{\lambda}$$
$$= \frac{3.33}{10} = .333 \text{ hour} (20.00 \text{ minutes})$$

14.10 | MULTISERVICE FACILITY MODELS

The multiservice facilities covered in this section are all assumed to have a Poisson arrival pattern and an exponential service pattern. Even with this simplification, the mathematical complexity of these models is still quite demanding. The additional complications that would be added if we considered the numerous variations of arrival and service patterns would make the models beyond the mathematical scope of this book. These models are

- $(M/M/c) : (\infty/\infty/G)$
- $(M/M/c) : (N/\infty/G)$
- $(M/M/c) : (\infty/N/G)$
- $(M/M/\infty) : (\infty/\infty/G)$

The $(M/M/c) : (\infty/\infty/G)$ Model 7 (Basic Multiple-Server Model)

This queueing model is viewed as the basic one among the multiservice models. It is identical to model 1, except that it has two or more servers. It is used in service disciplines that follow the FCFS, LCFS, or SIRO patterns. The performance parameters are illustrated in Table 14-7.

TABLE 14-7

Performance Parameters of the Basic Multiple-Server Model 7—$(M/M/c) : (\infty/\infty/G)$

$$P_0 = \left[\sum_{n=0}^{c-1} \left(\frac{\lambda}{\mu} \right)^n \left(\frac{1}{n!} \right) + \left(\frac{1}{c!} \right) \left(\frac{\lambda}{\mu} \right)^n \left(\frac{1}{1-\rho} \right) \right]^{-1}$$

$$\rho = \frac{\lambda}{c\mu}$$

$$P_n = \begin{cases} \left(\frac{\lambda}{\mu} \right)^n \left(\frac{1}{n!} \right) P_0 & \text{for } 1 \leq n \leq c \\[2em] \left(\frac{\lambda}{\mu} \right)^n (c!)^{-1} c^{n-c} P_0 & \text{for } c \leq n \leq \infty \end{cases}$$

$$L_q = \frac{\left(\frac{\lambda}{\mu} \right)^c \rho}{c!(1-\rho)^2} P_0$$

$$L = L_q + \left(\frac{\lambda}{\mu} \right)$$

$$W_q = \frac{L_q}{\lambda}$$

$$W = W_q + \left(\frac{1}{\mu} \right)$$

EXAMPLE 14.7 MULTNOMAH COUNTY MEDICAL FACILITY FLU VACCINATIONS (MODEL 7)

A second nurse is added to staff of the flu vaccine Example 14.1, so the situation is now equivalent to a two-server service facility. If the two nurses perform at approximately the same rate, what are the performance characteristics of this system?

SOLUTION

Given: $c = 2$, $\lambda = 100$, $\mu = 240$.

$$P_0 = \left[\sum_{n=0}^{c-1} \left(\frac{\lambda}{\mu} \right)^n \left(\frac{1}{n!} \right) + \left(\frac{1}{c!} \right) \left(\frac{\lambda}{\mu} \right)^n \left(\frac{1}{1-\rho} \right) \right]^{-1}$$

The proportion of time that the facility is busy is

$$\rho = \frac{\lambda}{c\mu}$$

$$= \frac{100}{(2)(240)} = .208$$

The likelihood that the facility will be unused, P_0, is

$$P_0 = \left[(.417)^0 \left(\frac{1}{0!} \right) + (.417)^1 \left(\frac{1}{1!} \right) + \left(\frac{1}{2!} \right)(.417)^2 \left(\frac{1}{1-\rho} \right) \right]^{-1}$$

$$= [1.00 + .417 + (.5)(.174)(1.26)]^{-1}$$

$$= (1.527)^{-1} = .655$$

The probability of having exactly n patients in the system is

$$P_n = \begin{cases} \left(\dfrac{\lambda}{\mu} \right)^n \left(\dfrac{1}{n!} \right) P_0 & \text{for } 1 \leq n \leq c \\[2ex] \left(\dfrac{\lambda}{\mu} \right)^n (c!)^{-1} c^{n-c} P_0 & \text{for } c \leq n \leq \infty \end{cases}$$

So, the probability that there will be exactly one or two patients in the facility is (using the first P_n equation for $1 \leq n \leq c$)

$$P_1 = (.417) \left(\frac{1}{1!} \right)(.655) = .273$$

$$P_2 = (.417)^2 \left(\frac{1}{2!} \right)(.655) = .057$$

The probability that there will be exactly three or four patients in the facility is (using the second P_n equation for $c \leq n \leq \infty$)

$$P_3 = (.417)^3 (2!)^{-1} (2)^1 (.655) = .0050$$

$$P_4 = (.417)^4 (2!)^{-1} (2)^2 (.655) = .0025$$

The probability of exactly *n* members being present in the system for this model is shown in Figure 14-11. The mean number of patients in line at any time is

$$L_q = \frac{\left(\dfrac{\lambda}{\mu}\right)^c \rho}{c!(1-\rho)^2} P_0$$

$$= \frac{\left(\dfrac{100}{240}\right)^2 (.208)(.655)}{2!(1-.208)^2}$$

$$= .0189 \text{ patient}$$

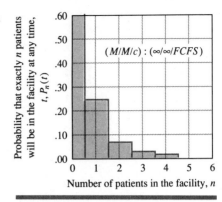

This result is a dramatic decrease over the similar single-server model in Example 14.1. The mean number of patients in the system is

$$L = L_q + \left(\frac{\lambda}{\mu}\right)$$

$$= .0189 + .417 = .436 \text{ patient}$$

The average amount of time a patient waits before seeing a nurse is

$$W_q = \frac{L_q}{\lambda}$$

$$= \frac{.0189}{100} = .000189 \text{ hour } (.68 \text{ second})$$

The mean total time spent in the system is

$$W = W_q + \left(\frac{1}{\mu}\right)$$

$$= .000189 + \left(\frac{1}{240}\right) = .00426 \text{ hour } (15.7 \text{ seconds})$$

The (*M*/*M*/*c*) : (*N*/∞/*G*) Model 8
(Multiple-Server Model with Finite Queue Length)

When the queue length is limited to some finite size, *N*, the performance characteristics of this multiservice model are transformed from those of model 7 to those illustrated in Table 14-8.

EXAMPLE 14.8   MULTNOMAH COUNTY MEDICAL FACILITY FLU VACCINATIONS (MODEL 8)

Assume that the situation described in Example 14.7 has the added constraint that only five patients can be in the facility at any time. Describe the performance of this system.

TABLE 14-8

Performance Parameters of the Multiple-Server, Finite-Queue Model 8—($M/M/c$) : ($N/\infty/G$)

$$P_0 = \left[\sum_{n=0}^{c-1} \left(\frac{\lambda}{\mu}\right)^n \left(\frac{1}{n!}\right) + \left(\frac{1}{c!}\right)\left(\frac{\lambda}{\mu}\right)^n \sum_{n=C+1}^{N} \rho^{n-c} \right]^{-1}$$

$$\rho = \frac{\lambda}{c\mu}$$

$$P_n = \begin{cases} \left(\frac{\lambda}{\mu}\right)^n \left(\frac{1}{n!}\right)P_0 & \text{for } 0 \leq n \leq c \\[2ex] \left(\frac{\lambda}{\mu}\right)^n c^{c-n}\left(\frac{1}{c!}\right)P_0 & \text{for } c \leq n \leq N \end{cases}$$

$$L_q = \frac{\left(\frac{\lambda}{\mu}\right)^c \rho[1 - \rho^{N-c} - (N-c)\rho^{N-c}(1-\rho)]P_0}{c!(1-\rho)^2}$$

$$L = L_q + \left(\frac{\lambda}{\mu}\right)$$

$$W_q = \frac{L_q}{\lambda}$$

$$W = W_q + \left(\frac{1}{\mu}\right)$$

SOLUTION

Given: $\lambda = 100$, $\mu = 240$, $c = 2$, $N = 5$. The utilization factor, ρ, is

$$\rho = \frac{\lambda}{c\mu} = \frac{100}{(2)(240)} = .208$$

The probability that the facility would be empty is

$$P_0 = \left[\sum_{n=0}^{c-1} \left(\frac{\lambda}{\mu}\right)^n \left(\frac{1}{n!}\right) + \left(\frac{1}{c!}\right)\left(\frac{\lambda}{\mu}\right)^n \sum_{n=C+1}^{N} \rho^{n-c} \right]^{-1}$$

$$= \left\{ \left[(.417)^0 \left(\frac{1}{0!}\right) + (.417)^1 \left(\frac{1}{1!}\right) + (.417)^2 \left(\frac{1}{2!}\right) \right] \right.$$
$$\left. + \left(\frac{1}{2!}\right)(.417)^2 \left[(.208)^1 + (.208)^2 + (.208)^3 \right] \right\}$$

$$= \{1.00 + .417 + .087 + (.087)[.208 + .043 + .009]\}^{-1}$$

$$= \{1.504 + .0226\}^{-1}$$

$$= .655$$

The chance of exactly n patients being in the facility at any time is given by the following two relationships:

$$P_n = \begin{cases} \left(\dfrac{\lambda}{\mu}\right)^n \left(\dfrac{1}{n!}\right) P_0 & \text{for } 0 \leq n \leq c \\[2ex] \left(\dfrac{\lambda}{\mu}\right)^n c^{c-n} \left(\dfrac{1}{c!}\right) P_0 & \text{for } c \leq n < N \end{cases}$$

So, the probabilities that there will be one or two patients in the facility are, respectively (using the first P_n equation),

$$P_1 = \frac{(.417)^1}{1!} P_0 = .273$$

$$P_2 = \frac{(.417)^2}{2!} P_0 = .0569$$

For three, four, or five patients, the likelihoods are, respectively (using the second P_n equation),

$$P_3 = \frac{(.417)^3}{2!}(2)^{-1} P_0 = .0119$$

$$P_4 = \frac{(.417)^4}{2!}(2)^{-2} P_0 = .00248$$

$$P_5 = \frac{(.417)^5}{2!}(2)^{-3} P_0 = .0005$$

The chance of having exactly n patients in the system at any time is shown in Figure 14-12. The remaining system performance characteristics include the average number of patients waiting in line:

$$\begin{aligned} L_q &= \frac{\left(\dfrac{\lambda}{\mu}\right)^c \rho \left[1 - \rho^{N-c} - (N-c)\rho^{N-c}(1-\rho)\right] P_0}{c!(1-\rho)^2} \\[2ex] &= \frac{(.417)^2(.655)(.2085)}{(2!)(.7915)}[1 - (.2085)^3 - (3)(.2085)^3(.7915)] \\[2ex] &= (.01895)(.969) = .0189 \text{ patient} \end{aligned}$$

The average number of patients in the facility is

$$\begin{aligned} L &= L_q + \left(\frac{\lambda}{\mu}\right) \\[1ex] &= .0189 + \left(\frac{100}{240}\right) = .439 \text{ patient} \end{aligned}$$

The average wait in line is

$$\begin{aligned} W_q &= \frac{L_q}{\lambda} \\[1ex] &= \frac{.0189}{100} = .000189 \text{ hour } (< 1 \text{ second}) \end{aligned}$$

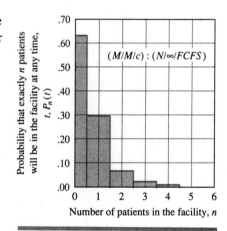

FIGURE 14-12

Probability That There Will Be Exactly n Patients in the Facility for a Multiple-Server with a Finite Queue—Model 8

The total mean time a patient spends in the facility is

$$W = W_q + \left(\frac{1}{\mu}\right)$$

$$= .000189 + \left(\frac{1}{240}\right) = .0044 \text{ hour (15.84 seconds)}$$

The $(M/M/c) : (\infty/N/G)$ Model 9
(Multiple-Server Model with Finite Calling Population)

This model is the multiple-server version of model 3. A simple illustration of this model is discussed next.

EXAMPLE 14.9   THE NAVAL PILOT AIRCRAFT CARRIER LANDING

When a Navy pilot is returning to the aircraft carrier from an exercise, it is not unusual for her aircraft to have only 60 to 90 seconds of fuel remaining—enough for one pass around the aircraft carrier if the two runways are occupied. Analyze the waiting problems that might arise for an eight-plane squadron on an aircraft carrier with two runways, a Poisson aircraft mean arrival rate of one plane every 3 minutes, and an exponential service time of being able to "load" two planes per minute per runway. The performance parameters for this model are shown in Table 14-9.

SOLUTION

Given: $N = 8$ planes, $1/\lambda = 3$ minutes/plane ($\lambda = 1/3$ plane/minute), $\mu = 2$ planes/minute, $c = 2$ runways.

The probability that an arriving aircraft will have no other planes ahead is

$$P_0 = \left[\sum_{n=0}^{c} N! \left[\frac{1}{(N-n)!n!} \right] \rho^n + \sum_{n=c+1}^{N} N! \left[\frac{1}{(N-n)!c!c^{n-c}} \right] \rho^n \right]^{-1}$$

$$= 8! \left[\frac{1}{(8!)(0!)} (.167)^0 \right] + 8! \left[\frac{1}{(7!)(1!)} (.167)^1 \right] + 8! \left[\frac{1}{(6!)(2!)} (.167)^2 \right]$$

$$+ 8! \left[\frac{1}{(4!)(2!)(2)^2} (.167)^4 \right] + 8! \left[\frac{1}{(3!)(2!)(2)^3} (.167)^5 \right]$$

$$+ 8! \left[\frac{1}{(2!)(2!)(2)^4} (.167)^6 \right] + 8! \left[\frac{1}{(1!)(2!)(2)^5} (.167)^7 \right]$$

$$+ 8! \left[\frac{1}{(0!)(2!)(2)^6} (.167)^8 \right]$$

The chance of having n number of aircraft ahead of an arriving aircraft is

$$P^n = \begin{cases} \dfrac{N!\rho^n}{(N-n)!n!} P_0 & \text{for } 0 \leq n \leq c \\[3mm] \dfrac{N!\rho^n}{(N-n)!c!c^{n-c}} P_0 & \text{for } c \leq n \leq N \end{cases}$$

TABLE 14-9

Performance Parameters of the Multiple-Server, Finite Calling-Population Model
9—$(M/M/c) : (\infty/N/G)$

$$P_0 = \left[\sum_{n=0}^{c} N! \left[\frac{1}{(N-n)!n!} \right] \rho^n + \sum_{n=c+1}^{N} N! \left[\frac{1}{(N-n)!c!c^{n-c}} \right] \rho^n \right]^{-1}$$

$$\rho = \frac{\lambda}{c\mu}$$

$$P_n = \begin{cases} \dfrac{N!\rho^n}{(N-n)!n!} P_0 & \text{for } 0 \leq n \leq c \\[3mm] \dfrac{N!\rho^n}{(N-n)!c!c^{n-c}} P_0 & \text{for } c \leq n \leq N \end{cases}$$

$$L_q = \sum_{n=C+1}^{N} (n-c)P_n$$

$$L = \frac{L_q + N\rho}{1 + \rho}$$

$$W_q = \frac{L_q}{\lambda(N-L)}$$

$$W = \frac{L}{\lambda(N-L)}$$

So, for $0 \leq n \leq 2$,

$$P_1 = \frac{(8!)(.267)(.167)^1}{(8-1)!\,1!} = .357$$

$$P_2 = \frac{(8!)(.267)(.167)^2}{(8-2)!\,2!} = .208$$

For $2 \leq n \leq 8$,

$$P_3 = \frac{(8!)(.267)(.167)^3}{(8-3)!\,(2!)(2)^1} = .104$$

$$P_4 = \frac{(8!)(.267)(.167)^4}{(8-4)!\,(2!)(2)^2} = .043$$

$$P_5 = \frac{(8!)(.267)(.167)^5}{(8-5)!\,(2!)(2)^3} = .014$$

$$P_6 = \frac{(8!)(.267)(.167)^6}{(8-6)!\,(2!)(2)^4} = .004$$

$$P_7 = \frac{(8!)(.267)(.167)^7}{(8-7)!\,(2!)(2)^5} = .001$$

$$P_8 = \frac{(8!)(.267)(.167)^8}{(8-8)!\,(2!)(2)^6} = .000$$

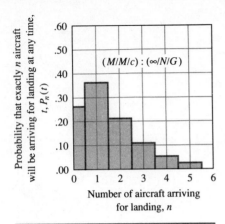

FIGURE 14-13

Probability That There Will Be Exactly n Aircraft Arriving for a Landing for a Multiple-Server with a Finite Calling Population—Model 9

The probability of exactly n planes being in the system at any time is shown in Figure 14-13. The average number of aircraft in a holding pattern (waiting for an approach to land) is

$$L_q = \sum_{n=C+1}^{N} (n-c)P_n$$

$$= (3-2)P_3 + (4-2)P_4 + \cdots + (8-2)P_8$$

$$= .104 + (2)(.044) + (3)(.015) + (4)(.004) + (5)(.001) + (6)(.000)$$

$$= .104 + .088 + .045 + .016 + .005 + 0 = .258 \text{ aircraft}$$

At any time, the average number of aircraft either holding or landing is

$$L = \frac{L_q + N\rho}{1+p}$$

$$= \frac{.258 + (8)(.167)}{1 + .167} = 1.366 \text{ aircraft}$$

The mean wait time prior to landing for any aircraft is

$$W_q = \frac{L_q}{\lambda(N-L)}$$

$$= \frac{.258}{(.333)(8-1.366)} = .117 \text{ minute (7.01 seconds)}$$

The mean time for an aircraft to complete both the holding pattern and the landing process is

$$W = \frac{L}{\lambda(N-L)}$$

$$= \frac{1.366}{(.333)(8-1.366)} = .618 \text{ minute (37.10 seconds)}$$

It is interesting to note that this particular example represents wait times that would be viewed, in most situations, as almost "wait-free." However, this is not the typical situation—it is life or death! In fact, waiting an average of 37 seconds when there is an average of 60 to 90 seconds of fuel remaining may not be good enough!

TABLE 14-10

Performance Parameters of the Multiple-Server, Infinite Number of Servers Model 10—$(M/M/\infty):(\infty/\infty/G)$

$$P_0 = e^{-\lambda/\mu}$$

$$P_n = \frac{e^{-\lambda/\mu}\left(\dfrac{\lambda}{\mu}\right)^n}{n!}$$

$$L_q = 0$$

$$L = \frac{\lambda}{\mu}$$

$$W_q = 0$$

$$W = \frac{1}{\mu}$$

The $(M/M/\infty):(\infty/\infty/G)$ Model 10 (Multiple-Server Model with Infinite Number of Servers)

When the number of service facilities becomes very large (infinite in terms of queueing considerations), the system performance can be described by the equations in Table 14-10.

EXAMPLE 14.10 MULTNOMAH COUNTY MEDICAL FACILITY FLU VACCINATIONS (MODEL 10)

Say Multnomah County has a multiservice facility employing a very large number of nurses. Use the arrival and service-per-nurse rates from Example 14.9. Give the performance parameters of the system.

SOLUTION

Given: $\lambda = 100$/hour, $\mu = 240$/hour, $\rho = \lambda/\mu = .417$, $c = \infty$.

The probability that all nurses are idle is

$$P_0 = e^{-\lambda/\mu}$$
$$= e^{-.417} = .659$$

The chances of exactly n patients being in the facility at any time is

$$P_n = \frac{e^{-\lambda/\mu}\left(\dfrac{\lambda}{\mu}\right)^n}{n!}$$

So, the likelihoods of one, two, or four patients being in the facility at any time are, respectively,

$$P_1 = \frac{(.659)(.417)^1}{1!} = .275$$

$$P_2 = \frac{(.659)(.417)^2}{2!} = .0573$$

$$P_4 = \frac{(.659)(.417)^4}{4!} = .000083$$

With a very large number of servers, the likelihood of any significant number of people being in the system at any time is quite small. This relationship is shown in Figure 14-14. The average number of patients waiting for service is

$$L_q = 0$$

This result is a logical one: If there is an infinite number of nurses to provide the inoculations, then there is enough service for an infinite number of arrivals. There is a nurse available to see every patient at the moment of arrival—no patient has to wait. The average number of patients in the facility is

$$L = \frac{\lambda}{\mu} = .417$$

The mean wait time in the queue—since there are no lines—is

$$W_q = 0$$

The total time a patient spends in the system is

$$W = \frac{1}{\mu}$$
$$= \frac{1}{240} = .00417 \text{ hour (15 seconds)}$$

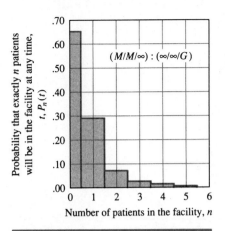

FIGURE 14-14

Probability That There Will Be Exactly *n* Patients in the Facility for a Multiple-Server with An Infinite Number of Servers—Model 10

14.11 VALIDATION OF THE QUEUEING SYSTEM ARRIVAL AND SERVICE PATTERNS: GOODNESS-OF-FIT TESTS

Before any of the many queueing models is selected to analyze a particular problem setting, it is essential to make sure that the assumptions regarding the specific kind of arrival and service rates are appropriate. To determine whether either of these performance parameters follows a known distribution (e.g., exponential, normal, Erlang), a *goodness-of-fit test* should be used to make sure that the actual patterns do not vary significantly from what the theoretical models require. The technique is easier to understand if you have had exposure to a basic course in statistics, but it is fathomable even if you have not. It works like this:

Step 1. Construct the actual probability distributions for the arrival (or service) patterns describing the queueing system under study.

Step 2. Select the theoretical distributions that you think best describe the actual distributions of step 1. Using the appropriate probability distribution equation(s), generate the theoretical distribution(s) to correspond with the ranges of the actual distributions. Use the mean arrival (or service) rates calculated from the actual distributions.

Step 3. Compare the actual and theoretical distributions, one at a time, for the arrival (or service) patterns using the *Kolmogorov–Smirnov (K-S) test* (Appendix C).[5] If the difference between the theoretical and actual distributions for the assumed arrival and service patterns (Poisson, exponential, etc.) exceeds a prescribed critical value, the distribution assumptions are invalidated. If not, the assumed distribution pattern is justified. An example of this method follows.

EXAMPLE 14.11 PHARMACIST'S OFFICE

A pharmacist is interested in better understanding the demand for his services. More particularly, he wants to collect data so that he can best match his on-call staff to meet the typical unpredictable demand that his business attracts. Empirical information collected by the office administrator reveals the probability distribution of arrivals shown in Figure 14-15; the distribution was constructed from 100 randomly selected observations taken over 1-hour periods during a 2-month time span. This arrival pattern is assumed to follow a Poisson distribution. Is this an accurate assumption?

SOLUTION

Step 1. The probability distribution of arrivals constructed by the pharmacist's administrator provides the essential data needed for this step. The only work that remains is to convert the simple probability distribution into a relative cumulative probability distribution to accommodate the requirements of the K-S test (Table 14-11).

TABLE 14-11

Cumulative Probability Distribution of Customer Arrivals for the Pharmacist's Office

n	Actual P_n	Actual cum P_n	Theoretical P_n^*	Theoretical cum P_n^*
0	.000	.000	.000	.000
2	.029	.029	.006	.006
4	.095	.124	.048	.054
6	.229	.353	.149	.203
8	.267	.620	.250	.453
10	.190	.810	.263	.716
12	.114	.924	.187	.903

[5]The chi-square test is the most popular goodness-of-fit test. However, because it uses nominal data, it lacks the "statistically significant" detection ability of the more sensitive ordinal measurements employed by K-S—similar to the difference between a television with a relatively fuzzy picture and one with a high-resolution picture. Because of this advantage over the chi-square test, the K-S test will be used as the goodness-of-fit test of choice.

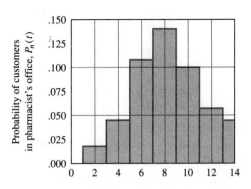

Number of customers in pharmacist's office, n

FIGURE 14-15

Probability Distribution of Customer Arrivals Based on 100 Randomly Selected Observations of the Pharmacist's Office

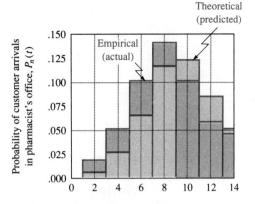

Customer arrival rate for pharmacist's office, λ

FIGURE 14-16

Comparison of Empirical and Theoretical Probability Distributions in Pharmacist's Office for Poisson Arrival Rate of $\lambda = 9.71$ Customers/Hour

Step 2. Let's assume (hypothesize) that the distribution that best describes this arrival pattern is the Poisson function given by

$$P_n(t) = \frac{(\lambda t)^n e^{-\lambda t}}{n!}$$

Step 3. The mean arrival rate, λ, is calculated from the actual distribution developed in step 1; it is 9.71 customers per hour. When this value is substituted into the preceding Poisson equation, we can generate the theoretical distribution that would be anticipated if the arrival pattern were an exact Poisson distribution with a mean value of 9.71 patients per hour. A comparison of the actual (empirical) and theoretical probability distributions is shown in Figure 14-16.

Now we need to see whether the difference in shapes between the actual and theoretical distributions is significant (from a statistical standpoint), or whether the difference can be attributed to sampling error. The K-S test compares the *maximum absolute difference between the relative cumulative frequencies* of these two distributions, and determines whether this difference is significant based on a sample size of 100 observations. If the maximum absolute difference between the relative frequency scores exceeds a specific, critical value, then the difference is viewed as real; if it does not, the difference is not statistically significant (i.e., is random or accidental). The K-S test is

$$D = |\text{cum } P_n^* - \text{cum } P_n|_{\max}$$

where

cum P_n^* = relative cumulative frequency value of theoretical distribution (e.g., normal, Poisson, Erlang, constant).

cum P_n = relative cumulative frequency value of actual distribution

TABLE 14-12

Kolmogorov–Smirnov Goodness-of-Fit Process for Finding the Difference, D, between the Theoretical and Actual Cumulative Probability Distributions for the Pharmacist's Office

n	Actual cum P_n	Theoretical cum P_n*	Absolute Difference, D
0	.000	.000	.000
2	.029	.006	.023
4	.124	.096	.027
6	.353	.239	.114
8	.620	.478	.142*
10	.810	.729	.081
12	.924	.908	.016
14	1.000	1.000	.000

* = maximum absolute difference, D

For the pharmacist, the maximum absolute difference between the two cumulative probability distributions is .142 (Table 14-12). The critical value for D—the *theoretical value* for D that must be equaled or exceeded (assuming an arbitrary 5 percent level of significance)—is given by the relationship

$$D = \frac{1.36}{\sqrt{n}}$$

for sample sizes larger than 35. Since this study uses a sample size of 100, the critical value for D, D^*, is .136. The actual maximum difference measured between the two distributions is larger than the critical value. Therefore, the difference cannot be viewed as accidental: The distributions are significantly different, and the assumption that the arrival pattern of the pharmacist's customers is essentially a Poisson distribution with a mean arrival rate of 9.71 customers/hour is false.[6]

14.12 | OPTIMIZING QUEUEING SYSTEM COSTS

In addition to being able to characterize the system-performance parameters of numerous queueing models, we have an opportunity to use these analytical interrelationships to minimize total system costs. This makes it possible to determine the optimum facility size on the basis of economic considerations, affecting such parameters as service rate, number of service facilities, finite versus infinite queue length, and priority versus nonpriority selection procedures.

Generally, the most common costs associated with queueing problems are (1) those related to providing the service, and (2) those connected with the waiting members of the queueing system. It is a reasonably simple task to estimate the service-associated expenses. They include server costs (salaries) and facility costs (hardware, materials, and maintenance). However, estimating costs dealing with waiting is decidedly more complex. If the waiting members are endogenous (internal) to the organization providing the service, determining the waiting costs accurately is quite simple. For waiting members who are exogenous (external) to the service organization, however, the calculations of waiting costs becomes extremely complex. Examples include costs associated with members who become annoyed with what they view as an excessive wait and who therefore leave (renege), and those who think the queue is too long when they arrive and balk at even entering the queue. Further, there are costs associated with the ill-will of dissatisfied members who pass along their bad feelings to the general population by word of mouth. This latter cost can be even more expensive and can last longer than the immediate cost of losing balking or reneging members. With these reservations in mind, a general description of how to estimate total system costs for the basic single and multiserver models (models 1 and 7) follows.

---

[6]A more significant level of significance—say, 1 percent—would yield different results; for example, $D = 1.63/\sqrt{n} = .163$. Since this value exceeds the largest difference of actual and theoretical cumulative probability values shown in Table 14-12, the difference would be viewed as accidental or random. In addition, it is also possible to take a dramatically different perspective on the use of goodness-of-fit tests; for example, unless the distributions differ by more than 90 or 95 percent, the distributions are assumed similar.

Optimal Service Rates for the Basic
Single-Service Facility Model 1

Usually, the cost relationship is expressed in terms of a linear relationship in dollars per unit of time, as shown by the following relationship:

$$Z = c_s\mu + c_wL$$

where

c_s = marginal cost of service (dollars per member served)

c_w = cost of waiting (dollars per member per unit time)

L = expected number of members in the system

μ = mean service rate (members per unit time)

This relationship is appropriate for any type of simple single-server model at steady-state operation, except for situations where

1. There are members who balk or renege

2. There are finite queues where members are lost after the queue has reached its maximum length, N

The cost relationship can be rewritten as

$$Z = c_s\mu + c_w\left(\frac{\lambda}{\mu - \lambda}\right)$$

The optimum value of μ can be found if the first derivative of Z with respect to μ, $dZ/d\mu$, is set equal to zero. This optimum service-rate value is called μ^*, and is given by

$$\mu^* = \lambda + \sqrt{\frac{\lambda c_w}{c_s}}$$

The corresponding optimal system cost is

$$Z = c_s\mu^* + c_w\left(\frac{\lambda}{\mu^* - \lambda}\right)$$

When we take this derivative we make the assumption that μ is continuous with respect to Z.

As an illustration, let's suppose that the cost per unit time estimates for the service and waiting are $5/hour and $15/hour, respectively. What is the optimum service rate, μ^*, and what is the minimum system cost if λ is 15?

SOLUTION

The optimum service rate is

$$\mu^* = 15 + \sqrt{\frac{(15)(15)}{5}}$$

$$= 15 + 6.71 = 21.71 \text{ people/hour}$$

and the minimum system cost is

$$Z = (5)(21.71) + 15\left(\frac{15}{21.71 - 15}\right) = 108.55 + 33.53 = \$142.08$$

Optimal Number of Service Facilities for the Multiple-Service Facility Model 7

Under steady-state conditions and a linear cost function, the optimum number of service facilities to provide on the basis of cost can be found from the relationship

$$Z = c_s'c + cL$$

where

c_s' = cost per server per unit time

c = number of servers (integer value)

c_w = cost per queue system member per unit time

L = the expected number of customers in the system, L

If Z is assumed to be discontinuous (since c is an integer), marginal analysis can be used to determine the optimal value for c that minimizes system costs. The optimum number of servers, c^*, evolving from this approach is

$$L(c^*) - L(c^* - 1) < \frac{c_s'}{c_w} < L(c^* - 1) - L(c^*)$$

where L^* represents the value of L that is determined for that *specific* value of c^*.

To illustrate the multiple-service-facility cost equations, let's suppose that the ticket office at the Amtrak train station in Atlanta has employees that cost Amtrak an average rate of $10 per hour, and that the average waiting costs for a customer waiting either to receive information regarding the train schedules or to purchase tickets is $5/hour. We find the optimum number of servers, c^*, by solving the last equation for the total hourly system costs (based on the number of people in the system, L, and the number of ticket takers, c) and thus determining minimum value for Z. The results of these calculations are shown in Table 14-13 and are illustrated in Figure 14-17; they reveal that the minimum system costs of $40.20 occur when there are three ($c = 3$) ticket takers.

TABLE 14-13

Queueing System Costs for Model 7

[c_s = $10.00/hour/server, c_w = $5.00/hour/customer]

No. of Servers c	No. of Customers in System L	Wait Time W (min)	Server Costs c_s ($/hour)	Customer Costs c_w ($/hour)	Total Costs Z ($/hour)
2	5.45	3.3	20.00	27.25	47.25
3	2.04	1.2	30.00	10.20	40.20*
4	1.74	1.0	40.00	8.70	48.70
5	1.68	1.0	50.00	8.40	58.40

*Minimum system costs occur when $n = 3$.

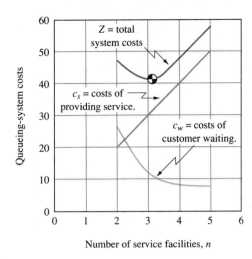

FIGURE 14-17

Illustration of Finding Optimal Number of Service Facilities for the Multiple-Server Model 7

|14.13| MICROCOMPUTER SOLUTIONS TO QUEUEING PROBLEMS

Waiting-line problems are extremely easy to set up and solve with the numerous queueing modules available in most multiple-tool management science packages (see Section 14.15). It is, however, important to anticipate that some of the more exotic models may not be included in every queueing package—for example, non-Poisson/exponential distributions, finite queue length, finite calling-population size.

Microcomputer solutions to several of the queueing model examples presented in this chapter are illustrated next for three different microcomputer software packages. Notice the great similarity of the data entry information used by each program, as well as the information generated by the different solution formats.

Example 1: The data entry and solution to the single-server model with finite queue length, model 2 (Example 14.2) using the queueing module from the QSB software package are shown in Table 14-14.

Example 2: The Micro Manager software package provides a slightly different data entry and solution-output example to the single-server, constant service time model 5 (Example 14.5), shown in Table 14-15.

Example 3: The third and final example of a data entry and computer solution presented is for the multiple-server, finite-population model 9 (Example 14.9). It uses the CMMS software queueing module and is shown in Table 14-16.

|14.14| CONCLUSIONS

This chapter has explored 10 different queueing models. This set constitutes a "drop in the bucket" compared to the numerous potential models that can arise from various combinations of the $(A/B/C)$: $(d/e/f)$ system performance parameters. Although the algebraic solutions to these models are possible, the procedures are typically tedious, and manual solutions are likely to be error-prone. (This is especially true with the more

TABLE 14-14

Microcomputer Solution to the (*M/M/*1) : (*N/∞/FCFS*) Model 2—Single-Server Model with Finite Queue Length

Source: Yi-Long Chang, *Quantitative Systems for Business*. Englewood Cliffs, NJ: Prentice-Hall, 1986.

```
        Input Data Describing the Problem:   QModel#2

M/M/1 with finite queue
Customer arrival rate (lambda) = 100.000
Distribution : Poisson
Number of servers = 1
Service rate per server = 240.000
Distribution : Poisson
Mean service time = .004 hour
Standard deviation = .004 hour
Queue limit = 3
Customer population = Infinity


             Solving the Model for QModel#2
Utilization factor (p) = .4166667
Average number of customers in the system (L) = .5899756
Average number of customers in the queue (Lq) = .1914375
Average time a customer in the system (W) = 6.168122E-03
Average time a customer in the queue (Wq) = 2.001455E-03
The probability that all servers are idle (Po) = .601462
The probability an arriving customer waits (Pw)  = .3985381


P(1) = 0.25061   P(2) = 0.10442    P(3) = 0.04351
P(4) = 0.00000   P(5) = 0.00000
P(6) = 0.00000


6
Σ P(i) = 0.398538
i=1
```

TABLE 14-15

Micro Manager Solution to the (*M/E_k/*1) : (∞/∞/*FCFS*) Model 3—Single-Server Model with Erlang Service Distribution

Source: Lee and Shim, *Micro Manager*. Dubuque, IA: William C. Brown 1986.

```
   PROGRAM:  Queuing Models

          ***** INPUT DATA ENTERED *****
               M/D/1 type

Average service rate:  20
Average customer arrival rate:  18



          ***** PROGRAM OUTPUT *****
Number of customers          Probability
        0                       0.100
        1                       0.090
        2                       0.081
        3                       0.073
        4                       0.066
        5                       0.059

Mean number of customers in the system  :    4.95
Mean number of customers in the queue   :    4.05
Mean time in the system                 :    0.27
Mean waiting time                       :    0.22
Traffic intensity ratio                 :    0.90
```

complex multiple-server models.) Only those businesses without access to electricity should consider any method other than one using computers to solve queueing problems.

When a waiting-line problem is composed of arrival and service patterns that follow *known* probability distributions—primarily Poisson and exponential—the use of

```
COMPUTER   MODELS   FOR   MANAGEMEN T   SCIENCE

                  -=*=-   INFORMATION ENTERED   -=*=-
           ALTERNATIVE CHOSEN  : MULTIPLE SERVER - FINITE POPULATION
           ARRIVAL RATE        : 0.333
           SERVICE RATE        : 2.000
           NUMBER OF SERVERS   : 2
           POPULATION SIZE     : 8

                      -=*=-   RESULTS   -=*=-

           SERVER IDLE (PERCENT)        : 98.611
           EXPECTED NUMBER IN SYSTEM    : 1.358
           EXPECTED NUMBER IN QUEUE     : 0.252
           EXPECTED TIME IN SYSTEM      : 0.614
           EXPECTED TIME IN QUEUE       : 0.114

                  ----------  END OF ANALYSIS  ----------
```

TABLE 14-16

Microcomputer Solution to the ($M/M/c$) : ($\infty N/G$) Model 9—Multiple-Server Model with Finite Calling Population

Source: Erikson and Hall, *Computer Models for Management Science*, Version 2. Reading, MA: Addison-Wesley 1986.

analytical models is an appropriate way to proceed. However, there is considerable disagreement among management scientists regarding the value of queueing theory when the peculiarities of a specific problem have unusual characteristics. In these instances, many analysts argue that the development of a mathematical model can be most difficult, and often impossible, for reasons such as these:

1. Multiple-service facilities, with the possible exception of assembly line operations (where the movements are highly standardized), often exhibit great variability between servers.

2. The arrival rates do not follow a Poisson distribution and/or the service rates are not exponentially distributed.

3. The balking and reneging behavior of people do not occur simply because the queue has reached some predetermined limit; they occur on an individual basis, according to how each arriving member perceives the queue environment. This may result in a person balking or reneging even when the line is far short of its limit.

4. It is not unusual for an organization to change the number of people available to provide service due to a variety of unforeseen events. These intermediate increases or decreases in service rate actually create a non-steady-state condition.

As a result of these types of common occurrences, it is wise to reevaluate the attractiveness of mathematical modeling approaches to waiting lines. This is particularly so when the unpredictability of human behavior is added to the problem setting. In such cases, the alternative approach is the study of waiting lines that does not involve the analyst's ability to develop an accurate algebraic model. This very different, nonmathematical technique is called Monte Carlo simulation; it will be discussed at length in Chapter 15.

This particular issue is argued at length in a series of articles referenced at the end of this chapter (Bhat, 1978; Byrd, Jr., 1978; Kolesar, 1979; Veklerov, 1978).[7]

---

[7]You will find the point-counterpoint tenor of these articles sometimes quite heated, sometimes humorous, certainly nit-picky, and very informative.

14.15 EXERCISES

14-1 A librarian in a small, neighborhood library finds that, on the average, 15 people per hour need service or information from him during a typical day. The arrival of people at the librarian's desk follows a Poisson distribution. The librarian can accommodate one customer every 3 minutes using a near-exponential service pattern. The population of customers is assumed to be infinite, the size of the library is considered infinite, and the librarian operates on a first-come, first-served basis. Under these conditions, determine the following information regarding this library's operation:

1. What queueing model should be used?
2. Calculate all the system-performance parameters for this model.

14-2 The librarian in Exercise 14-1 finds that having a large number of people waiting in line to receive service can often be quite noisy. The library is very small, and he would like the patrons in the nearby reading areas to be undisturbed. He decides to post a notice requesting that the waiting line be limited to a maximum of three people, in addition to the person he is presently serving. Determine the following:

1. What queueing model should be used?
2. How do the system performance parameters of this model compare with those calculated in the original problem (Exercise 14-1)?
3. Do your results make sense? Explain your answer.

14-3 The librarian in Exercise 14-1 does research regarding which patrons from the community use this particular library branch. He discovers that few people outside of the immediate neighborhood use his library. Further, the data he uncovers reveal that many people in the population in the neighborhood are not patrons due to advanced age, poor health, and so on. After some thoughtful computations, he estimates that the total number of regular patrons using this branch is about 50. All other conditions of the original problem remain unchanged. Determine the following:

1. What queueing model should be used?
2. How do the system performance parameters of this model compare with those calculated in the original problem (Exercise 14-1)?
3. Do your results make sense? Explain your answer.

14-4 Suppose that the librarian in Exercise 14-1 discovers to his chagrin that, although his mean-service-rate value is correct, the pattern does not always follow an exponential distribution. In fact, the service pattern varies so significantly that he decides not to make any assumptions about it, and decides instead to treat it as a general distribution. Further, he decides that he is wasting a lot of time always waiting on patrons using a FCFS approach: Often, people in line need only to be pointed in the right direction for a book or periodical, and can be quickly dispatched. Therefore, the librarian decides to use a general service discipline in which he can mix FCFS with SIRO. Determine the following:

1. What queueing model should be used?
2. How do the system performance parameters of this model compare with those calculated in the original problem (Exercise 14-1)?

14-5 The librarian in Exercise 14-1 finds that many patrons, although not intentionally, take far too much time getting help. The librarian estimates that the primary reason for some of the prolonged service times is due to the patron not having organized his or her thoughts—after all, the patron thinks, the librarian's time is free. In an attempt to encourage individuals to phrase their requests concisely, the librarian puts this notice on his desk:

> I will be happy to spend 3 minutes of my time helping you. I will even walk you to the place where the publication you would like is kept, help you with the card catalog, or whatever. But at the end of 3 minutes, I must provide help to the next person waiting in line. For this reason, please make sure you have organized your thoughts regarding exactly the type of help you would like. Thank you.

Determine the following:

1. What queueing model should be used?
2. What effect does this new situation have on the system-performance parameters of the original problem?

14-6 The librarian in Exercise 14-1 estimates that he provides essentially three different services to the library patrons: (1) listening to their questions, (2) helping them to reformulate their request so that it is clear, and (3) telling them the location of the materials they would like. He further estimates that these services are subtasks comprising the overall service operation, and that each has a near identical exponentially distributed relationship and takes about 1 minute to complete. All other considerations of the original problem remained unchanged. Find the following pieces of information:

1. What queueing model should be used?
2. What effect does this new situation have on the system-performance parameters of the original problem?
3. Do your results make sense? Explain your answer.

14-7 Assume the following: The Tassajara Bakery in San Francisco's Haight-Ashbury district has three people waiting on customers to purchase baked goods. The average arrival rate

of customers throughout the day is 75 per hour, and arrivals follow a Poisson distribution. The service provided by the employees follows an exponential distribution, with a mean rate of one customer every 2 minutes per employee. Although the store is relatively small, the lines of customers usually wind out the door and down Cole Avenue. Determine the following information for the bakery:

1. What queueing model should be used?
2. What is the probability that the bakery will be empty during normal business hours?
3. What are the chances that exactly two people will be either standing in line or being waited on?
4. What are the chances that only one person is waiting in line?
5. What is the average number of people in the bakery?
6. What is the average number of people in line?
7. What is the average amount of time a person waits (waits in line, gets help, and leaves)?
8. What is the average amount of time waiting in line only?

14-8 Suppose that the San Francisco City Council decided to pass an ordinance banning any business from having customer waiting lines that spill out onto the sidewalk. Accordingly, businesses must temporarily close their doors to customer traffic when their capacity has been met. Suppose that the Tassajara Bakery discussed in Exercise 14-7 has a limit of 40 customers. All other conditions of the original problem remain the same except for the capacity limitation, and the situation follows a $(M/M/c):(N/\infty/G)$ queueing model. Recalculate the original set of performance characteristics.

1. What percent change is associated with each of the parameters, in contrast to those in Exercise 14-7?
2. Are these changes logical? Explain your answer.

14-9 Suppose that the Tassajara Bakery (Exercise 14-7) decides to make almost everyone in their large bakery available to wait on customers when there is a need. The 25 bakers as well as managerial employees are asked to "pitch in" when demand is high (we overlook the possible congestion that might prevail at the register). Recalculate the original set of performance characteristics of Exercise 14-7. Determine the following:

1. What percent change is associated with each of the parameters, in contrast to those in Exercise 14-7?
2. Are these changes logical? Explain your answer.

14-10 An analysis has assumed that the arrival pattern of customers at the Smooth-Running Auto Tuneup garage chain in Nashville, Tennessee, can be closely approximated by a Poisson distribution. The mean arrival rate has been estimated to be .350 customer per minute. The cumulative frequency distribution for the actual arrival data is shown in Table 14-10.1. Determine if the assumption is statistically defensible at the 5 percent level of significance, using the Kolmogorov–Smirnov goodness-of-fit test.

14-11 Brad Dorsey, a Manhattan commodities exchange broker, rides the elevator daily to his office at work. He thinks that

TABLE 14-10.1

Actual Cumulative Probability Distribution for the Smooth-Running Auto Tuneup Garages

n	Actual cum P_n
0	.268
1	.625
2	.833
3	.937
4	.980
5	.994
6	.998
7	1.000

the amount of time he spends going from his office on one of the intermediate floors to the executive offices and company cafeteria on the forty-seventh floor is quite different from the time he expends getting down to the street level when he leaves for his numerous client appointments. The mean arrival rate and service rate for ascending elevators are 35 people/minute and 50 people/minute, respectively, and those for descending elevators are 60 people/minute and 75 people/minute, respectively. Calculate the following information:

1. For a single server (1 elevator), Poisson arrival pattern, and exponential service pattern (model 1), determine the performance characteristics of the system in both the upward and downward directions.
2. The elevators have a maximum capacity of 10 people. Determine the performance characteristics of the system in both the upward and downward directions.
3. If a second elevator were available for part 1, how would the performance change? Show all performance parameters.
4. If a second elevator were available for part 2, how would the performance change? Show all performance parameters.

Tension mounted as Brad Dorsey rides the elevator to the 47th floor disguised as a mallard duck.

References

1. Bessent, Wailand E. "Student Flow in a University Department," *Interfaces* 10 (No. 2: April 1980): 52–59.

2. Bhat, U. Narayan. "The Value of Queueing Theory—A Rejoinder," *Interfaces* 8 (No. 3: May 1978): 27–28.

3. Bouland, Heber D. "Truck Queues at Country Grain Elevators," *Operations Research* 15 (No. 4: July–August 1967): 649–659.

4. Brigham, Georges. "On a Congestion Problem in an Aircraft Factory," *Operations Research* 3 (No. 4: November 1955): 412–428.

5. Budnick, Frank S., Dennis McLeavy, and Richard Mojena. *Principles of Operations Research for Management.* Homewood, IL: Richard D. Irwin, 1988.

6. Byrd, Jack, Jr. "The Value of Queueing Theory," *Interfaces* 8 (No. 3: May 1978): 22–26.

7. Chelst, Denneth. "A Coal Unloader: A Finite Queueing System with Breakdowns," *Interfaces* 11 (No. 5: October 1981): 12–25.

8. Cook, Thomas M., and Robert A Russell. *Introduction to Management Science,* 3rd ed. Englewood Cliffs, NJ: Prentice-Hall, 1985.

9. Driscoll, M. F., and N. A. Weiss. "Application of Reservation Networks," *Management Science* 22 (No. 5: January 1976): 540–546.

10. Erikson, Warren J. "Analysis of the 1973 Gas Shortage," *Interfaces* 4 (No. 4: August 1976): 47–51.

11. Foote, B. L. "A Queueing Case Study of Drive-In Banking," *Interfaces* 6 (No. 4: August 1976): 31–37.

12. Gilliam, Ronald R. "An Application of Queueing Theory to Airport Passenger Security Screening," *Interfaces* 9 (No. 4: August 1979): 117–123.

13. Jones, Michael T. "Quickening the Queue in Grocery Stores," *Interfaces* 10 (No. 3: June 1980): 90–92.

14. Kao, Edward P. C. "Bed Allocation in a Public Health Care Delivery System," *Management Science* 27 (No. 5: May 1981): 507–520.

15. Kendall, D. G. "Some Problems in the Theory of Queues," *Journal of the Royal Statistical Society* 13 (Series B: 1951): 151–185.

16. Koenigsberg, Ernest, and Richard C. Lam. "Cyclic Models of Fleet Operations," *Operations Research* 24 (No. 3: May–June 1976): 516–529.

17. Kolesar, Peter. "A Quick and Dirty Response to the Quick and Dirty Crowd: Particularly to Jack Byrd's 'The Value of Queueing Theory,'" *Inferfaces* 9 (No. 2, Part 1: February 1979): 77–82.

18. Koopman, Bernard O. "Air-Terminal Queues Under Time-Dependent Conditions," *Operations Research* 20 (No. 6: November–December 1972): 1089–1114.

19. Larson, Richard C. "Approximating the Performance of Urban Emergency Service Systems," *Operations Research* 23 (No. 5: September–October 1975): 845–868.

20. Larson, Richard C., and Thomas F. Rich. "Travel-Time Analysis of New York City Police Patrol Cars," *Interfaces* 17 (No. 2: March–April DATE??): 15–20.

21. McKeown, Patrick G. "An Application of Queueing Analysis to the New York State Child Abuse and Maltreatment Register Telephone," *Interfaces* 9 (No. 3: May 1979): 20–25.

22. Morse, Philip M. "A Queueing Theory, Bayesian Model for the Circulation of Books in a Library," *Operations Research* 27 (No. 4: July–August 1979): 693–716.

23. Taha, Hamdy A. "Queueing Theory in Practice," *Interfaces* 11 (No. 1: February 1981): 43–49.

24. Veklerov, E. "Another Response to 'The Value of Queueing Theory,'" *Interfaces* 9 (No. 1: November 1978): 109–110.

Queueing Microcomputer Software

At the present time, there are few microcomputer software packages that are specialized for queueing analysis. Instead, queueing modules—as part of multiple-module management science software packages—are readily available. A listing of some of these modules follows:

1. *Computer Models for Management Science.* Version 2. Erikson and Hall. Reading, MA: Addison-Wesley, 1986.

2. *DSM.* San Juan Capistrano, CA: Decision Systems Support, 1986.

3. *Management Science and the Microcomputer.* Burns and Austin. New York: Macmillan, 1985.

4. *Microcomputer Models for Management Decision-Making.* Laurie B. Dennis and Terry L. Dennis. Minneapolis, MN: West, 1986.

5. *Microcomputer Software for Management Science and Operations Management.* Render and Stair. Boston: Allyn & Bacon, 1986.

6. *Micro Manager.* Lee and Shim. Dubuque, IA: William C. Brown, 1986.

7. *Microsolve.* Jensen. Student Version, rev. ed. Oakland, CA: Holden-Day, 1985.

8. *Quantitative Systems for Business.* Chang & Sullivan. Englewood Cliffs, NJ: Prentice-Hall, 1986.

9. *STORM.* Flowers et al. Oakland, CA: Holden-Day, 1986.

CHAPTER 15

MONTE CARLO SIMULATION

AN EMPIRICAL MODELING TECHNIQUE
FOR STOCHASTIC MANAGEMENT

| 15.1 | INTRODUCTION

Monte Carlo simulation (MCS) is a nonmathematical method for analyzing real problems that are so complex that any attempt to model them algebraically is too difficult, is economically impractical, or does not depict a satisfactory level of realism.[1] Monte Carlo simulation imitates what happens in a real-world process by collecting empirical data from this process. It literally gathers information concerning what real events occur, how often they occur, and what the duration of each occurrence is (methods used to accomplish this data-collection process most often include either secondary sources, such as performance logs, or actual observations of the events of interest).

Since MCS is a *random* method, the events typifying a particular problem do not follow a schedule, such as a bolt of lightening striking a tree in your yard, winning a lottery, or receiving a "wrong number" telephone call. It is, however, possible to characterize these events by their *probability distributions* (the name for this type of process is *stochastic*).

---

[1]Monte Carlo simulation evolved from one of the most historic projects of modern times: the development of the atomic bomb by the Allied Forces during World War II. *Monte Carlo* was the code name used for the project that studied random neutron diffusion. The research project was, of course, top secret, so it was given a code name that seemed appropriate for a process dealing with random events: Monte Carlo, in reference to the famous gambling casino.

SAMMY DAVIS, JR., DIALS A WRONG NUMBER.

Drawing by Jack Ziegler; © 1985 The New Yorker Magazine, Inc.

The application of MCS is especially suited to waiting line, inventory-management, and project management problems. Although this chapter will concentrate primarily on waiting line simulations, inventory- and project management problems will also be included.

15.2 APPLICATIONS OF MONTE CARLO SIMULATION

The successful applications of MCS are extensive. They include the following:

1. Deployment of emergency medical services (Davis, 1981)
2. Management of a dental practice (Reisman, et al., 1981)
3. Determination of a dispatch policy for a fire company (Ignall, Carter, and Rider, 1982)
4. Planning of crude-oil supply systems (Batra, 1980)
5. Management of operations, planning, and productivity of fast-food restaurants (Stewart and Donno, 1981)
6. Simulation of surgical program policy (Silm, 1981)
7. Emergency deployment of ambulances (Fitzsimmons, 1973)
8. Determination of the optimum size for a substitute-teacher pool in an urban school district (Bruno, 1970)

15.3 THE SIMULATION PROCESS

Simulation models are developed from a general sequence of phases. These phases include three broad procedures:

1. *Problem definition*. The purpose and operationally defined objectives of the problem must be developed. This will include the criteria to be used in assessing the degree of achievement of these objectives. It is not unusual for the elements in this phase to change as greater understanding of the problem is developed by the manager. Suppose, for example, that the purpose of a problem is to examine the difference between two policies of providing private ambulance service to a county hospital. More particularly, the ambulance company would like to know whether it would make more sense for their ambulance fleet to be centrally located or, perhaps, to be divided among several facilities. They decide that they will compare the goodness of each policy on the basis of its profitability to the company and responsiveness to the patient. It now becomes critical to define exactly what is meant by *profitability* and *responsiveness* and how these will be measured.

2. *Model design*. The actual interrelationship of events that constitute the problem must be defined clearly. This can include the development of a flowchart that illustrates the sequencing of activities and decisions or options. (An example flowchart simulating an ambulance response system is shown in Figure 15-1.) In addition, the data collection that will allow the analyst to characterize the random behavior of each activity must be conducted. This is usually the most expensive, time-consuming, and tedious phase of the entire simulation modeling operation, consisting almost entirely of empirical data recording. The result of this phase will be the development of probability distributions for each element of the process being studied.

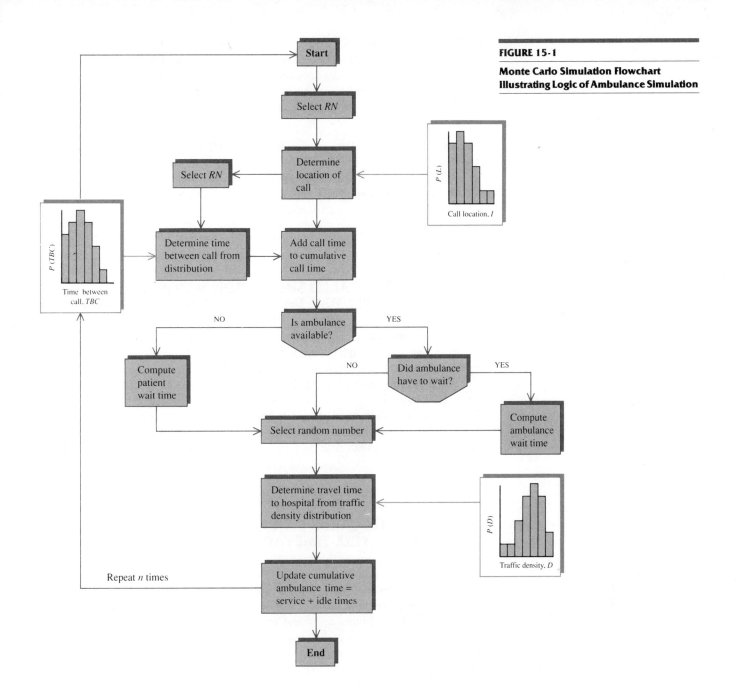

Start

Select *RN*

Determine location of call

Select *RN*

$P(L)$

Call location, *I*

Determine time between call from distribution

Add call time to cumulative call time

$P(TBC)$

Time between call, *TBC*

Is ambulance available?

NO

YES

Compute patient wait time

Did ambulance have to wait?

NO

YES

Select random number

Compute ambulance wait time

Determine travel time to hospital from traffic density distribution

$P(D)$

Traffic density, *D*

Repeat *n* times

Update cumulative ambulance time = service + idle times

End

3. *Model validation.* In addition to making sure that the computer program is operating appropriately, it is also critical to check the validity of the model by several techniques. One technique is to use actual historical data where the system performance is known. The simulation is then run using these data, and the performance of the simulation is compared with the known historical parameter performance to

validate the comparability of the two. Another approach is to change one of the real-world parameters that would cause a definite directional variation from the baseline performance. If the model does not provide you with the same directional change, something is clearly incorrect. For example, an addition of members to the sales force should drive down the mean customer wait time. If it does not, something is wrong.

So that you can become familiar with MCS, we shall illustrate the process with several examples. The first examples will be rudimentary; later ones will depict reasonably complex systems. These examples will cover two basic simulation methods for tracking events in a simulation: (1) the *variable time increment simulation* (VTIS), and (2) the *full cycle-time lapse simulation* (FCTLS).

15.4 MONTE CARLO SIMULATION METHOD 1: VARIABLE TIME INCREMENT SIMULATION (VTIS)

The VTIS begins with a particular probability distribution for arrivals. Each individual arrival is followed through the sequence of remaining events, which characterize the problem on the basis of *clock time*. The simulation is continued for as many new arrivals as occur over some predetermined time increment of interest (24 hours, 1 month, etc.). This makes it possible for the manager to gather extremely detailed information from the simulation that can ultimately be used to compare competing policies (e.g., What is the effect on system performance of offering different levels of service? What is the influence on system costs?).

15.5 MONTE CARLO SIMULATION METHOD 2: FULL CYCLE-TIME LAPSE SIMULATION (FCTLS)

The FCTLS measures the time necessary to complete a *single cycle* run-through of the system event sequence. Although this model also keeps a time calendar on the sequence of events of the problem, *it assumes that a server is available for each run-through*. So, in effect, a FCTLS assumes an infinite level of service. Because of this, it is not possible to compare the effects of different service level policies on customer demand. Although the FCTLS is convenient to use and can provide considerable insight into a problem, the assumption of server availability may often be considered too limiting. It is typically used only for a "first-cut" analysis.

15.6 MONTE CARLO SIMULATIONS FOR CONGESTION PROBLEMS

The application of MCS to waiting line or congestion-type problems is arguably the most common use of the technique in business. We shall present examples that use both the VTIS and FCTLS methods in analyzing waiting line problems.

TABLE 15-1

Empirical Data for Hospital Emergency Room

Time between Arrivals, TBA (minutes)	Number of Observations	Service Time, ST (minutes)	Number of Observations
0–4	60	0–4	20
4–10	100	4–10	60
10–20	30	10–30	100
20–60	10	30–60	20
	200		200

EXAMPLE 15.1 THE BOSTON GENERAL HOSPITAL EMERGENCY ROOM

Consider the following hypothetical scenario: The Boston General Hospital emergency room provides medical attention for patients who seek aid for acute illness or injury. The key events that typify this system are (1) the patient arrivals, and (2) the medical staff service. The arrivals and services are not predictable as a function of time; they do not follow a schedule. They are, instead, random in pattern. Simulate this emergency room for 2 hours of operation beginning at 7:00 A.M. using the empirical data in Table 15-1.

SOLUTION

It is necessary to determine the probability of each event occurring based on the proportion of times that event occurs out of the total number of observations. Also, the event time intervals must be replaced with midpoint values (this assumes that the observations that occur for each event interval are evenly distributed within that interval). These data are shown in Table 15-2. Although Tables 15-1 and 15-2 are essentially the same, there are a few important distinctions. First, for the time-between-arrivals (*TBA*) data, the 0–4 time interval is replaced by its average value of 2 minutes. Next, the number of times that *TBAs* between 0 and 4 minutes occurred, 60, is converted into the probability of having an arrival between 0 and 4 minutes (60/200, or .30). This process is done for each potential outcome of our two events, until we obtain with the probability distributions shown. It is important to remember that these probability distributions are not theoretical: They are taken from observations of actual events! A simulation using these data should clearly parallel the actual performance. A simple process for conducting the simulation requires the use of random numbers (*RNs*), as illustrated in Table 15-3.[2] We select *RNs* for each event for which we have developed probability distributions. We make sure to use enough of these *RNs* so that the desired duration of the time period that we wish to simulate can be "covered." To do this, we must also assign the appropriate *amount* of *RNs* to the various outcomes of each event and, further, assign the *RNs* *in proportion* to the probability of the outcome occurring. Also, the number of digits used per *RN* should be equal to the number of places of accuracy reflected in the probability distributions of each empirical event; for example, the probability that the *TBA* event in the hospital emergency room study will be between 10 and 20 minutes (for an average *TBA* of 15 minutes) is 0.15. Therefore, 15 percent of the *RN* range used to simulate *TBA* must be assigned to the 15-minute outcome. Let's proceed with this *RN* assignment (Table 15-4).

We are almost ready to start the simulation; however, we must first design our simulation table format so that we can interpret our findings easily. The design process does

TABLE 15-2

Probability Distributions for Hospital Emergency Room Events

TBA	p(TBA)	ST	p(ST)
2	.30	2	.10
7	.50	7	.30
15	.15	20	.50
40	.05	45	.10

TABLE 15-3

Table of Random Numbers

97446	30328	05262	77371	13523	62057	44349	85884	94555	23288
15453	75591	60540	77137	09485	27632	05477	99154	78720	10323
69995	77086	55217	53721	85713	27854	41981	88981	90041	20878
69726	58696	27272	38148	52521	73807	29685	49152	20309	58734
23604	31948	16926	26360	76957	99925	86045	11617	32777	38670
13640	17233	58650	47819	24935	28670	33415	77202	92492	40290
90779	09199	51169	94892	34271	22068	13923	53535	56358	50258
71068	19459	32339	10124	13012	79706	07611	52600	83088	26829
55019	79001	34442	16335	06428	52873	65316	01480	72204	39494
20879	50235	17389	25260	34039	99967	48044	05067	69284	53867
00380	11595	49372	95214	98529	46593	77046	27176	39668	20566
68142	40800	20527	79212	14166	84948	11748	69540	84288	37211
42667	89566	20440	57230	35356	01884	79921	94772	29882	24695
07756	78430	45576	86596	56720	65529	44211	18447	53921	92722
45221	31130	44312	63534	47741	02465	50629	94983	05984	88375
20140	77481	61686	82836	41058	41331	04290	61212	60294	95954
54922	25436	33804	51907	73223	66423	68706	36589	45267	35327
48340	30832	72209	07644	52747	40751	06808	85349	18005	52323
23603	84387	20416	88084	33103	41511	59391	71600	35091	52722
12548	01033	22974	59596	92087	02116	63524	00627	41778	24392
15251	87584	12942	03771	91413	75652	19468	83889	98531	91529
65548	59670	57355	18874	63601	55111	07278	32560	40028	36079
48488	76170	46282	76427	41693	04506	80979	26654	62159	83017
02862	15665	62159	15159	69576	20328	68873	28152	66087	39405
67929	06754	45842	66365	80848	15262	55144	37816	08421	30071
73237	07607	31615	04892	50989	87347	14393	21165	68169	70788
13788	20327	07960	95917	75112	01398	26381	41377	33549	19754
43877	66485	40825	45923	74410	69693	76959	70973	26343	63781
14047	08369	56414	78533	76378	44204	71493	68861	31042	81873
88383	46755	51342	13505	55324	52950	22244	28028	73486	98797
29567	16379	41994	65947	58926	50953	09388	00405	29874	44954
20508	60995	41539	26396	99825	25652	28089	57224	35222	58922
64178	76768	75747	32854	32893	61152	58565	33128	33354	16056
26373	51147	90362	93309	13175	66385	57822	31138	12893	68607
10083	47656	59241	73630	99200	94672	59785	95449	99279	25488
11683	14347	04369	98719	75005	43633	24125	30532	54830	95387
56548	76293	50904	88579	24621	94291	56881	35062	48765	22078
35292	47291	82610	27777	43965	31802	98444	88929	54383	93141
51329	87645	51623	08971	50704	82395	33916	95859	99788	97885
51860	19180	39324	68483	78650	74750	64893	58042	82878	20619
23886	01257	07945	71175	31243	87167	42829	44601	08769	26417
80028	82310	43989	09242	15056	48250	04529	96941	48190	69644
83946	46858	09164	18858	12672	55190	02820	45861	29104	75386
00000	41586	25972	25356	54260	95691	99431	89903	22306	43863
90615	12848	23376	29458	48239	37628	59265	50152	30340	40713
42003	10738	55835	48218	23204	19188	13556	06610	77667	88068
86135	26174	07834	17007	97938	96728	15689	77544	89186	41252
54436	10828	41212	19836	89476	53685	28085	22878	71868	35048
14545	72034	32131	38783	58588	47499	50945	97045	42357	53536
43925	49879	13339	78773	95626	67119	93023	96832	09757	98545

Source: Leonard Kazmier, *Statistical Analysis for Business Decisions and Economics*, 2nd ed. (New York: McGraw-Hill, 1973).

TABLE 15-4

Random Number Assignments for the Hospital Emergency Room

TBA	P(TBA)	RN(TBA)	ST	p(ST)	RN(ST)
2	.30	00–29	2	.10	00–09
7	.50	30–79	7	.30	10–39
15	.15	80–94	20	.50	40–89
40	.05	95–99	45	.10	90–99

TABLE 15-5

Simulation Table Format for Hospital Emergency Room

	Arrival Data				Service Data			
Patient No.	RN TBA	TBA	Time of Arrival	RN ST	ST	Service Begins At	Patient Waits	Service Ends At
1	46	7	7:07 A.M.	88	20	7:07 A.M.	0	7:27 A.M.
2	53	7	7:14	23	7	7:27	13	7:34
3	95	40	7:54	—	—	—	—	—
—	—	—	—	—	—	—	—	—

not follow any set formula; it merely uses common sense. The table must include the specific details we need to know about the emergency room. One possible design is to provide a patient arrival number, the clock time at arrival, the service time given to the patient, the amount of time the patient waits prior to being seen, and the clock time at the start and end of the treatment. Let's use the format suggested in Table 15-5 and illustrated in the form of a simplified flowchart (Figure 15-2) to begin our simulation. We will arbitrarily use the last two digits of columns 1 and 10 from Table 15-3.

The simulation begins with, first, determining each patient's *TBA* from his *RN*; for example, an *RN* of 46 falls in the 30–79 *RN* class interval which, in turn, corresponds to an average *TBA* of 7 minutes. The same procedure is followed for the service times. Also, the service begins with each patient depending on the availability of the medical staff. For example, if the staff are still with the earlier patient, the new arrival must wait. Conversely, if medical services are available but there are no patients waiting, there is idle time for the medical personnel. Table 15-5 illustrates that patient 1 arrives at 7:07 A.M. and is seen immediately. The 20 minutes of medical services provided this patient are continuous until 7:27 A.M. This requires patient 2, who arrives at 7:14 A.M., to wait 13 minutes before being treated (this simulation assumes zero turnaround time between patients). Service for patient 2 ends at 7:34 A.M. (7 minutes of treatment time). At this point, no other patients are in the facility, so the medical personnel must wait from 7:34 to 7:54 A.M. for the third patient, resulting in 20 minutes of idle time. We continue the hypothetical simulation for 2 hours, as shown in Table 15-6. This brief simulation period will not give the manager a representative or overall understanding of what the daily 24-hour operation of the facility is really like, but it will provide a beginning level of insight. Our analysis of this limited time period reveals the following findings:

1. A total of 13 patients can be seen between 7:00 A.M. and 9:00 A.M.

2. The medical staff must work until noon before they finish treating the last patient to enter the facility at 8:57 A.M.

[2]Random numbers may be either found in a table (Table 15-3) or generated by software. Spreadsheets such as *Lotus 1-2-3*, *Quatro*, *Wingz*, or *Excel* have random-number-generator programs.

FIGURE 15-2

**Simulation Flowchart for Boston General
Hospital Emergency Room**

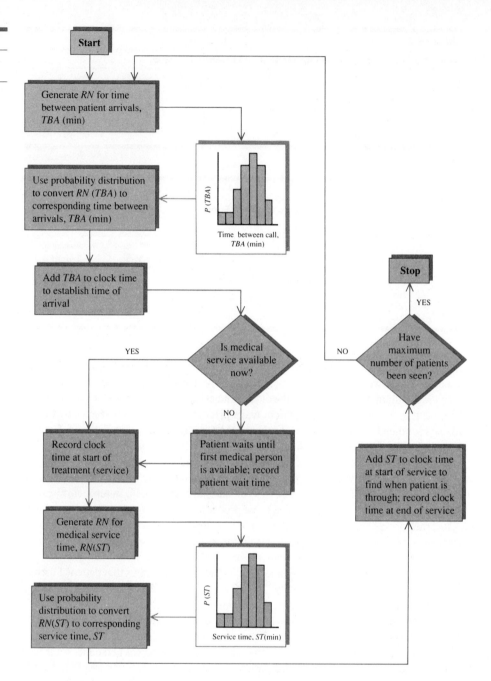

3. The 13 patients wait a total of 904 minutes—an average of almost 70 minutes each before treatment begins.

4. In the time period between 7:00 A.M. and 12:10 noon, the medical staff works 283 out of these 310 minutes (27 idle minutes).

A preliminary conclusion that can be drawn regarding the operation of this emergency room is that it becomes rapidly unstable in terms of its ability to respond to the arriving patients—a clearly unacceptable pattern for a facility such as this. It is obvious that a larger staff would be needed to provide more responsive service. Now let's try a more complex VTIS simulation problem.

TABLE 15-6

Monte Carlo Simulation for Hospital Emergency Room

	Arrival Data			Service Data				
Patient No.	RN (TBA)	TBA	Time of Arrival	RN (ST)	ST	Service Begins At	Patient Waits	Service Ends At
1	46	7	7:07 A.M.	88	20	7:07 A.M.	0	7:27 A.M.
2	53	7	7:14	23	7	7:27	13	7:34
3	95	40	7:54	78	20	7:54	0	8:14
4	26	2	7:56	34	7	8:14	18	8:21
5	04	2	7:58	70	20	8:21	23	8:41
6	40	7	8:05	90	45	8:41	36	9:26
7	79	7	8:12	58	20	9:26	74	9:46
8	68	7	8:19	29	7	9:46	87	9:53
9	19	2	8:21	94	45	9:53	92	10:38
10	79	7	8:28	67	20	10:38	130	10:58
11	80	15	8:43	66	20	10:58	135	11:18
12	42	7	8:50	11	7	11:18	148	12:10
13	67	7	8:57	95	45	11:25	148	12:10
14	56	7	9:04	←14th patient arrives after 2-hour simulation limit				

EXAMPLE 15.2   THE FERRARI AUTOMOBILE AGENCY

Suppose that the owner of a Ferrari agency would like to determine the optimum number of salespeople to employ during normal working hours (nonholiday, and not during clearance sales) based on the objective of maximizing their daily profit. They have collected pertinent data concerning client arrival and salesperson service patterns. In addition, they know the following system properties that are germane to the problem:

1. The service capacities of their salespeople may vary slightly but are essentially, homogeneous.

2. The average salesperson costs the agency $75.00 per day.

3. Each prospective buyer waited on represents an expected profit of $210 to the agency. Five percent of those served will purchase an automobile. The average per-unit contribution to profit of each Ferrari sold is $4200. The resulting expected value is .05 × $4200 = $210.

4. Each salesperson is to start and finish service with her or his client before starting to serve another.

5. Service is on a first-come, first-served basis.

6. The average client will leave if he must wait 10 minutes or longer prior to being served.

7. The agency is open between 10:00 A.M. and 6:00 P.M.

The client-arrival and salesperson-service patterns are shown in Table 15-7. Using these data, simulate the agency's operation for an 8-hour day, and determine the size of the sales force to employ.

SOLUTION

Step 1. The probability distributions and corresponding *RN* range assignments are presented in Table 15-8.

TABLE 15-7

Data on Client Arrival and Salesperson Service for the Ferrari Agency

TBA Interval (minutes)	p(TBA)	ST Interval (minutes)	p(ST)
0–6	.20	0–4	.10
6–20	.60	4–10	.20
20–40	.10	10–20	.50
40–60	.10	20–40	.15
		40–60	.05

TABLE 15-8

Probability Distributions for the Events of the Ferrari Agency

TBA	p(TBA)	RN(TBA)	ST	p(ST)	RN(ST)
3	.20	00–19	2	.10	00–09
13	.60	20–79	7	.20	10–29
30	.10	80–89	15	.50	30–79
50	.10	90–99	30	.15	80–94
			50	.05	95–99

TABLE 15-9

Simulation Table Format for the Ferrari Agency

Client No.	RN (TBA)	TBA	Arrival Time	RN (ST)	ST	Service Begins	Client Waits	Service Ends
. . .	. . .	. . .	. . .	. . .	. . .	. . .	. . .	. . .
	. . .	. . .	. . .	. . .	. . .	. . .	. . .	. . .

Step 2. The design of the simulation table must allow us to determine the time at which each client arrives, the duration of the client's wait prior to being served, the length of the service, and the corresponding clock times of the aforementioned events. One possible format we could use is shown in Table 15-9.

Step 3. Using the table of random numbers, we conduct the simulation for one salesperson (Table 15-10).

We arbitrarily select the first two digits of columns 2 and 3 for the *TBA* and *ST RN*s, respectively. The findings of the simulation for one salesperson show that 10 of the 41 potential clients who arrived at the agency during the day had to wait at least 10 minutes and, consequently, left prior to being waited on. The days profits, P, were, then,

$$P = 210n_c - 75n_s$$
$$= (210)(31) - (75)(1)$$
$$= 6510 - 75$$
$$= \$6425$$

where

n_c = number of clients served

n_s = number of salespeople

Now let's repeat the simulation for two salespeople. If we arbitrarily use the same series of *RN*s for the two random events of arrival and service behavior, a two-salesperson simulation can be easily generated (Table 15-11). For two salespeople, we will not lose any of the 41 arriving clients. The system gross profits are

$$P = (210)(41) - (75)(2)$$
$$= \$8460$$

If we add a third salesperson, we will only increase our daily costs by the additional \$75 salary. Our optimum-size salesforce is clearly two. The values associated with this simulation problem will always make it advantageous to employ enough salespeople to

TABLE 15-10

Monte Carlo Simulation for the Ferrari Automobile Agency Using One Salesperson

Client No.	RN (TBA)	TBA	Arrival Time	RN (ST)	ST	Service Begins	Client Waits	Service Ends
1	30	13	10:13	05	2	10:13	0	10:15
2	75	13	10:26	60	15	10:26	0	10:41
3	77	13	10:39	55	15	10:41	2	10:56
4	58	13	10:52	27	7	10:56	4	11:03
5	31	13	11:07	16	7	11:07	0	11:14
6	17	13	11:10	58	15	11:14	4	11:29
7	09	3	11:13	51	15	11:29	16	*
8	19	3	11:16	32	15	11:29	13	*
9	79	13	11:29	34	15	11:29	0	11:44
10	50	13	11:42	17	7	11:44	2	11:51
11	11	3	11:45	49	7	11:51	6	11:58
12	40	13	11:58	20	15	11:58	0	12:13
13	89	30	12:28	20	15	12:28	0	12:43
14	78	13	12:41	45	7	12:43	2	12:50
15	31	13	12:54	44	7	12:54	0	1:01
16	77	13	1:07	61	15	1:07	0	1:22
17	25	13	1:20	33	15	1:22	2	1:37
18	30	13	1:33	72	15	1:37	4	1:52
19	84	30	2:03	20	7	2:03	0	2:10
20	01	3	2:06	22	7	2:10	4	2:17
21	87	30	2:36	12	7	2:36	0	2:43
22	59	13	2:49	57	15	2:49	0	3:04
23	76	13	3:02	46	15	3:04	2	3:19
24	15	3	3:05	62	15	3:19	14	*
25	06	3	3:08	45	15	3:19	11	*
26	07	3	3:11	31	15	3:19	8	3:34
27	20	13	3:24	07	2	3:34	10	*
28	66	13	3:37	40	15	3:37	0	3:52
29	08	3	3:40	56	15	3:52	12	*
30	46	13	3:53	51	15	3:53	0	4:08
31	16	3	3:56	41	15	4:08	12	*
32	60	13	4:09	41	15	4:09	0	4:24
33	76	13	4:22	75	15	4:24	2	4:39
34	51	13	4:35	90	15	4:39	4	4:54
35	47	13	4:48	59	15	4:54	6	5:09
36	14	3	4:51	04	2	5:09	18	*
37	76	13	5:04	50	15	5:09	5	5:24
38	47	13	5:17	82	30	5:24	7	5:54
39	87	30	5:47	51	15	5:54	7	6:09
40	19	3	5:50	39	15	6:09	19	*
41	01	3	5:53	07	2	6:09	16	*
42	82	30	6:27	← sorry, agency doors closed at 6:00 P.M.				

*Client wait is equal to or exceeds 10-minute limit; client leaves showroom before being served.

eliminate the loss of any clients, so long as the salesperson cost ($75 per day) is less than the expected revenue that is lost from a departed client ($210). An illustration of the relationship between daily gross profits and the number of salespeople is shown in Figure 15-3. Now let's examine the FCTLS simulation model.

EXAMPLE 15.3 THE ST. LOUIS AMBULANCE COMPANY

Suppose that a new hospital is being planned for construction somewhere within the city of St. Louis, Missouri, but the exact site has not yet been selected. Suppose further

TABLE 15-11

Monte Carlo Simulation for the Ferrari Automobile Agency Using Two Salespeople

Client No.	Arrival Time	ST	Server Begins 1	Server Begins 2	Client Waits	Service Ends*
1	10:13	2	10:13		0	10:15
2	10:26	15		10:26	0	10:41
3	10:39	15	10:39		0	10:54
4	10:52	7	10:52		0	10:59
5	11:07	7	11:07		0	11:14
6	11:10	15		11:10	0	11:25
7	11:13	15	11:14		1	11:29
8	11:16	15		11:25	9	11:40
9	11:29	15	11:29		0	11:44
10	11:42	7		11:42	0	11:49
11	11:45	7	11:45		0	11:52
12	11:58	15		11:58	0	12:13
13	12:28	15	12:28		0	12:43
14	12:41	7	12:41		0	12:48
15	12:54	7	12:54		0	1:01
16	1:07	15		1:07	0	1:22
17	1:20	15	1:20		0	1:35
18	1:33	15		1:33	0	1:48
19	2:03	7	2:03		0	2:10
20	2:06	7		2:06	0	2:13
21	2:36	7	2:36		0	2:43
22	2:49	15		2:49	0	3:04
23	3:02	15	3:02		0	3:17
24	3:05	15		3:05	0	3:20
25	3:08	15	3:17		9	3:32
26	3:11	15		3:20	9	3:35
27	3:24	2	3:32		8	3:34
28	3:37	15		3:37	0	3:52
29	3:40	15	3:40		0	3:55
30	3:53	15		3:53	0	4:08
31	3:56	15	3:56		0	4:11
32	4:09	15		4:09	0	4:24
33	4:22	15	4:22		0	4:37
34	4:35	15		4:35	0	4:50
35	4:48	15	4:48		0	5:03
36	4:51	2		4:51	0	4:53
37	5:04	15	5:04		0	5:19
38	5:17	30		5:19	2	5:49
39	5:47	15	5:47		0	6:02
40	5:50	15		5:50	0	6:05
41	5:53	2	6:02		9	6:04
42	6:27	. . .	. . .		. . .	. . .

*All clients were seen prior to the 10-minute time limit.

that a major ambulance company is trying to anticipate the best location among three city districts in which to build its new ambulance station, so that it might be able to get an advantage over its competition. It wishes to base its site-selection decision on its ability to respond to emergency calls. More particularly, it wants to locate the ambulance center so that the average elapsed time between the receipt of the call at the station and the delivery of the patient to the new hospital is minimized. A map of the area is

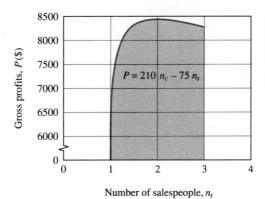

$$P = 210\,n_c - 75\,n_s$$

 District A: Southernmost district in St. Louis. Bordered on the north by Arsenal St.

 District B: Central district. Bordered on the north by Martin Luther King Blvd. and on the south by Arsenal St.

District C: Northernmost district in St. Louis. Bordered on the south by Martin Luther King Blvd.

FIGURE 15-4

District Map for St. Louis Ambulance Location, Monte Carlo Simulation

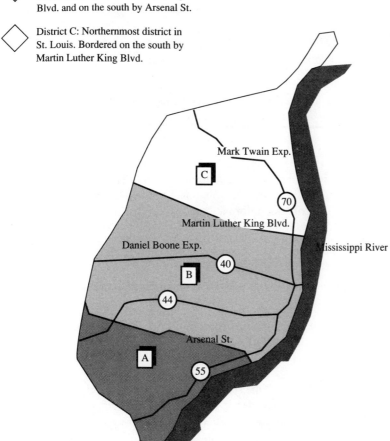

shown in Figure 15-4. The company thinks that the specific factors that are critical to its operation (i.e., those events that are likely to affect its response capability directly) are

1. The location of the neighborhood from which the emergency call originates
2. The accessibility of the patient at the scene, and the company's ability to get the patient into the ambulance
3. The traffic density during the trip
4. The location of the ambulance station
5. The ultimate location of the hospital

Now let's consider the influence of these factors on our goal—minimizing the total time required to get the patient to the hospital.

District of originating call. Depending on the location of the ambulance station, it will take varying amounts of time for the ambulance to make the complete trip from the station to the patient at the emergency origin, and then to the hospital.

Patient accessibility. The patient may be readily accessible to the ambulance crew or may be pinned in the wreckage of an automobile, may be located in the upper floors of a high-rise building, or may have sustained injuries that require special, time-consuming attention (e.g., spinal injuries).

Traffic density. The prevailing traffic conditions at the time of the call could be light, moderate, or heavy.

Ambulance company location. Obviously, the location of the company will have a direct bearing on travel times to the patient and then to the hospital.

Hospital location. This is the same type of consideration as the ambulance location, except that the specific relevant factor is the travel time from the patient location to the hospital.

Suppose now that the ambulance company collects all the data vital to characterizing this problem. This information is shown in Tables 15-12 through 15-15.

SOLUTION

Now we can begin the simulation. There is a variety of different worksheet formats that would do nicely; the one we shall use is shown in Table 15-16. Read the column headings carefully. The entries in columns 2 through 7 are determined randomly by the probability distribution information illustrated earlier in Tables 15-12 through 15-15. The procedure in filling out the worksheet design of Table 15-16 is as follows:

1. Determine the number of calls you desire to simulate, n. Fill in rows 1 through n of column 1 in Table 15-16.
2. From Table 15-3, randomly select n numbers for *each* of columns 2a, 3a, 4a, 5a, and 6a in Table 15-16. These *RN*s will represent

   ■ Column 2a: the district from which the emergency call originates
   ■ Column 3a: the traffic conditions
   ■ Column 4a: the travel time of the ambulance from the station to the patient (minutes)
   ■ Column 5a: the time spent by the ambulance attendants at the patient's location in preparation for the trip to the hospital (minutes)
   ■ Column 6a: the travel time from the patient's location to the hospital (minutes)
3. Calculate the total time lapse between the call for assistance and the delivery of the patient to the hospital by adding columns 4a, 5a, and 6a in Table 15-16.

TABLE 15-12

Probability Distribution of Patient Location

Call from District	Probability of Calls from District	RN
A	.50	00–49
B	.30	50–79
C	.20	80–99

TABLE 15-13

Probability Distribution of Traffic Condition

Traffic Condition	Probability of Condition	RN
Light	.20	00–19
Medium	.50	20–69
Heavy	.30	70–99

TABLE 15-14

Probability Distribution of Preparing Patient for Trip to Hospital

Preparation Time for Patient (min)	Probability of Preparation Time	RN
5	.50	00–49
15	.40	50–89
25	.10	90–99

TABLE 15-15

Probabilities and Corresponding Random Numbers of the Time Required for One-Way Trips Between (1) Ambulance Location in District A and Patient Origin, and (2) Patient Origin to Hospital Location

(1) From Ambulance Located in District A to Patient Located in District

Traffic Conditions	Travel Time	A	B	C
light	10	.80 00–79	.20 00–19	.10 00–09
light	20	.20 80–99	.60 20–79	.80 10–89
light	30	.00 —	.20 80–99	.10 90–99
medium	10	.60 00–59	.20 00–19	.00 —
medium	20	.40 60–99	.50 20–69	.70 00–69
medium	30	.00 —	.30 70–99	.30 70–99
heavy	10	.50 00–49	.10 00–09	.00 —
heavy	20	.50 50–99	.50 10–59	.60 00–59
heavy	30	.00 —	.40 60–99	.40 60–99

Travel Time / **(2) District Patient is Being Moved From to Hospital Located in District A**: A, B, C

(1) From Ambulance Located in District A to Patient Located in District

Traffic Conditions	Travel Time	A	B	C
light	10	.20 00–19	.80 00–79	.20 00–19
light	20	.60 20–79	.20 80–99	.60 20–79
light	30	.20 80–99	.00 —	.20 80–99
medium	10	.20 00–19	.60 00–59	.20 00–19
medium	20	.50 20–69	.40 60–99	.50 20–69
medium	30	.30 70–99	.00 —	.30 70–99
heavy	10	.10 00–09	.50 00–49	.10 00–09
heavy	20	.50 10–59	.50 50–99	.50 10–59
heavy	30	.40 60–99	.00 —	.40 60–99

(2) District Patient is Being Moved From to Hospital Located in District A: A, B, C

(1) From Ambulance Located in District A to Patient Located in District

Traffic Conditions	A	B	C	Travel Time
light	.10 00–09	.20 00–19	.80 00–79	10
light	.80 10–89	.60 20–79	.20 80–99	20
light	.10 90–99	.20 80–99	.00 —	30
medium	.00 —	.20 00–19	.60 00–59	10
medium	.70 00–69	.50 20–69	.40 60–99	20
medium	.30 70–99	.30 70–99	.00 —	30
heavy	.00 —	.10 00–09	.50 00–49	10
heavy	.60 00–59	.50 10–59	.50 50–99	20
heavy	.40 60–99	.40 60–99	.00 —	30

A, B, C / **(2) District Patient is Being Moved From to Hospital Located in District A** — **Travel Time**

TABLE 15-16

Simulation Table Format for the St. Louis Ambulance Location

			Column Number			
1	2a/2b	3a/3b	4a/4b	5a/5b	6a/6b	7
Call No.	Call Origin RN (LOC)	Traffic Density RN (D)	Time to Patient RN (t_1)	Prep Time with Patient RN (t_2)	Time to Hospital RN (t_3)	Total Time Σt
1	...	...	...	...	...	...
2	...	...	...	...	...	...
...	...	...	...	...	...	...

A 10-cycle illustration of this simulation procedure using case 1 (both the ambulance and hospital locations are in district A) follows. To facilitate the ease of following the simulation, we will start at the top of columns 4, 5, 6, 7, 8, and 9 in Table 15-3):

1. Simulate 10 emergency calls using the first two digits from the five-digit numbers in Table 15-3.

2. Now consider the first call. The first two digits of the initial event in the simulation table, column 2a, are 77. We have just simulated the first call, which originated from district B (Table 15-12).

3. The next *RN*, found in column 3a, is 62. This value falls in the 20–69 range representing medium traffic conditions in Table 15-13.

4. The next *RN* is 44 (column 4a); it represents the travel time it will ultimately take for the ambulance to arrive at the patient origin. We find this time by entering Table 15-15 with traffic conditions being medium, the patient being located in district B, and the ambulance coming from district A. The *RN* of 44 falls in the 20–69 *RN* range, which in turn represents a 20-minute trip time to the patient.

5. The *RN* of 85 (column 5a) corresponds to a 15-minute patient-preparation time at the emergency site (Table 15-14) because it falls in the 50–89 *RN* category.

6. The trip from the patient's location to the hospital is simulated from the *RN* of 94 (column 6a). This latter value, using Table 15-15, shows that, under medium traffic conditions, it will take 30 minutes to go from the patient's location in district B to the hospital in district A. The total time from incoming call to the patient delivery at the hospital is 20 + 15 + 30 = 65 minutes.

This process is repeated for 10 calls (Table 15-17).

A summary for cases representing every combination of hospital–ambulance district locations is presented in Table 15-18. More specifically, these findings show the following:

1. The optimum location for both the ambulance company and the hospital is district A (for all combinations of ambulance and hospital locations, the total elapsed trip time is at a minimum for district A).

2. Regardless of where either the ambulance or hospital may be located, the optimum location for the hospital is district A, and, regardless of where the hospital is located, the optimum location for the ambulance is district A.

3. Since only 10 calls were simulated, an accurate overview of the system is not possible, due to relatively large random errors associated with the small sample size.

4. Because of the limitations of the FCTLS method discussed earlier, these findings cannot consider such issues as the effect of the rate at which calls arrive and the ambulance company's ability to provide service (a function of ambulance fleet size as well as location).

5. In addition to the simulation method limitations, other issues, such as variable construction-site cost, maintenance, and security, which might differ according to the district the ambulance company ultimately selects, have not been addressed.[3]

---

[3]It might even make more sense to *decentralize* the company and to have several smaller facilities in different locations, rather than one large facility. All these conditions could be simulated. It simply depends on how much detail you wish to examine and the budget you have available for the simulation study.

TABLE 15-17

Ten-Call Simulation for the St. Louis Ambulance Located in District A
and Hospital Located in District A (Case 1)

Call No.	Call Origin RN/LOC		Traffic Density RN/D		Time to Patient RN/t_1		Prep Time w/Patient RN/t_2		Time to Hospital RN/t_3		Total Time Σt
1	77	B	62	M	44	20	85	15	94	30	65
2	77	B	27	M	05	10	99	25	78	30	65
3	53	B	27	M	41	20	88	15	90	30	65
4	38	A	73	H	29	10	49	5	20	10	25
5	26	A	99	H	86	20	11	5	32	10	35
6	47	A	28	M	33	10	77	15	92	20	45
7	94	C	22	M	13	20	53	15	56	20	55
8	10	A	79	H	07	10	52	15	83	20	45
9	16	A	52	M	65	20	01	5	72	20	45
10	25	A	99	H	48	10	05	5	69	20	35

Average total time = 48 minutes

TABLE 15-18

Summary Total Travel Time (Minutes) for All
Combinations of Ambulance and Hospital Locations

		Hospital Location District		
		A	B	C
Ambulance	A	48	51	53
Location	B	53	52	54
District	C	59	62	64

EXAMPLE 15.4   THE FIRE STATION

Another example of the application of MCS to emergency-service problems has been illustrated in a previous work by Jack Byrd, Jr. (Byrd, 1975). Byrd used the FCTLS method of simulation to help determine the optimum location, among five alternative sites, for a fire station in a community of 25 wards (Figure 15-5). The costs for building the station at each of the five sites are also provided in this figure.

The primary criteria considered to be the most important in determining the "best" location were:

1. Fire damage to the structures (dollars)

2. Number of lives lost

FIGURE 15-5

Potential Fire Station Location Sites and Construction Costs

(Site values have been arbitrarily adjusted to reflect contemporary cost-of-living index.)

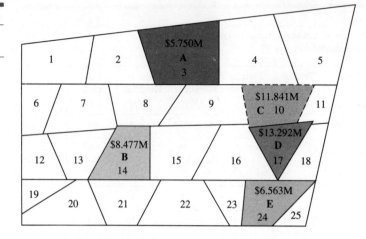

3. The capital costs of building a station at each of the specific potential locations being considered

To evaluate these three criteria, Byrd collected specific supportive historical data:

1. The average travel times between each possible combination of station and ward locations (Table 15-19)

TABLE 15-19

Average Travel Times between Each Possible Combination of Ward and Fire Station Location

Ward No.	Travel Time between Ward and Station (minutes)				
	A	B	C	D	E
1	31	12	22	21	42
2	15	11	17	18	38
3	5	13	13	15	30
4	17	19	9	13	16
5	29	22	10	14	18
6	37	9	23	19	41
7	33	7	17	17	36
8	11	11	12	10	28
9	13	17	9	9	22
10	18	22	5	11	12
11	23	26	8	13	30
12	43	11	29	17	27
13	41	9	26	15	24
14	38	4	18	12	21
15	17	9	15	10	17
16	19	13	12	6	13
17	22	21	8	9	12
18	27	26	9	13	11
19	51	12	31	14	26
20	49	9	28	12	21
21	46	10	23	10	17
22	38	14	18	9	13
23	39	21	14	11	11
24	43	26	13	13	4
25	46	30	13	15	9

2. The community's past history of fires for each ward, which provides the probability of a fire occurring in a particular location to be estimated (Table 15-20, column 2)

3. The average building value of each ward (Table 15-20, column 4)

4. The population density index of each ward, which reflects the relative number of people that would be potentially involved in each fire incident (Table 15-20, column 5); for example, a ward with a population index of two would have twice the number of people involved in a fire as would a ward with an index value of one

5. Probability distributions of the number of buildings involved in a fire as a function of the time it would take the fire-fighting unit to reach the fire (Table 15-21)

6. Probability distributions regarding the percent of the building's value destroyed as a function of time needed by the fire-fighting unit to reach the fire (Table 15-22)

7. Probability distributions of the number of lives lost as a function of the time needed for the fire-fighting unit to reach the fire (Table 15-23)

SOLUTION

The simulation table format designed for this example is shown in Table 15-24. An illustration of how it is used in generating the evaluative criteria used to assess the five alternative locations (some changes, with respect to property value, were made from the data originally shown in Byrd's problem, in an attempt to reflect more contemporary figures) is shown as a simplified flowchart in Figure 15-6.

TABLE 15-20

Probability of Fire, Average Structure Value, and Population Density Index for Each Ward

Ward No.	Percent of Fires in Ward	RN % of Fires	Average Structure Value ($)	Population Density Index
1	3	00–02	350,000	1.0
2	3	03–05	335,000	1.1
3	5	06–10	150,000	1.5
4	5	11–15	170,000	1.5
5	5	16–20	195,000	1.3
6	3	21–23	340,000	1.1
7	3	24–26	160,000	1.4
8	3	27–29	60,000	1.9
9	6	30–35	50,000	2.1
10	4	36–39	75,000	1.6
11	6	40–45	160,000	1.4
12	5	46–50	235,000	1.2
13	5	51–55	225,000	1.2
14	5	56–60	160,000	1.5
15	6	61–66	80,000	1.9
16	4	67–70	60,000	2.0
17	4	71–74	95,000	1.7
18	3	75–77	115,000	1.9
19	4	78–81	240,000	1.0
20	3	82–84	200,000	1.6
21	3	85–87	145,000	1.5
22	3	88–90	105,000	1.7
23	3	91–93	110,000	1.5
24	3	94–96	175,000	1.3
25	3	97–99	225.000	1.2

TABLE 15-21

**Probability Distributions for Number of Buildings Involved
as a Function of Time Required to Reach Fire***

Time to Reach	Number of Buildings Involved in Fire				
Fire (minutes)	*1*	*2*	*3*	*4*	*5*
0–10	95	5	0	0	0
(RN)	*(00–94)*	*(95–99)*			
11–20	80	20	0	0	0
(RN)	*(00–79)*	*(80–99)*			
21–30	70	15	15	0	0
(RN)	*(00–69)*	*(70–84)*	*(85–99)*		
31–40	50	20	20	5	5
(RN)	*(00–49)*	*(50–69)*	*(70–89)*	*(90–94)*	*(95–99)*
>41	40	20	20	10	10
(RN)	*(00–39)*	*(40–59)*	*(60–79)*	*(80–89)*	*(90–99)*

*The value above each italicized random number range indicates the percentage of instances that a specific number of buildings are involved in a fire (e.g., if travel time is 25 minutes and the *RN* for the travel time to the fire location is 54, enter the 21–30 row in column 1 (row 3 because it contains the 25-minute travel time in the range of 21–30) and move to column 1 (because it contains the *RN* of 54 in the range 00–69). The number of buildings involved in the fire can now be read at the heading of column 2—one (1) building.

TABLE 15-22

**Probability Distributions for Percentage of Building
Destroyed as a Function of Time Required to Reach Fire***

Time to Reach	Percentage of Building Value Destroyed			
Fire (minutes)	*25*	*50*	*75*	*100*
0–10	90	10	0	0
(RN)	*(00–89)*	*(90–99)*		
11–20	70	20	10	0
(RN)	*(00–69)*	*(70–89)*	*(90–99)*	
21–30	40	40	10	10
(RN)	*(00–39)*	*(40–79)*	*(80–89)*	*(90–99)*
31–40	30	30	30	10
(RN)	*(00–29)*	*(30–59)*	*(60–89)*	*(90–99)*
>41	10	40	30	20
(RN)	*(00–09)*	*(10–49)*	*(50–79)*	*(80–99)*

*The value above each italicized random number range indicates the proportion of instances that a specific percentage of building destruction occurs (e.g., if travel time is 18 minutes and the *RN* for the travel time to the fire location is 94, enter the 11–20 row in column 1 (row 2 because it contains the 18-minute travel time in the range of 11–20) and move to column 4 (because it contains the *RN* of 94 in the range 90–99). The specific percentage of building destruction that occurs can now be read at the heading of column 4—75 percent.

Let's begin the simulation by analyzing the effectiveness if the station is located at point A. A 10-call FCTLS is illustrated in Table 15-25. Follow closely:

- The first *RN* selected for fire (column 1) is 48 (column 2). From Table 15-20, we can see that an *RN* of 48 corresponds to a fire located in ward 12. The time to get to ward 12 from location A would be 43 minutes (Table 15-19).
- The next *RN* selected, 30, represents the number of buildings involved in the fire (column 6) and corresponds to, using Table 15-21, one building.

TABLE 15-23

Probability Distributions of Number of Lives Lost as a Function of Time Required to Reach Fire*

Time to Reach	Number of Lives Lost			
Fire (minutes)	*0*	*1*	*2*	*3*
0–10	85	15	0	0
(RN)	(00–84)	(85–99)		
11–20	70	20	10	0
(RN)	(00–69)	(70–89)	(90–99)	
21–30	60	20	20	0
(RN)	(00–59)	(60–79)	(80–99)	0
31–40	50	20	20	10
(RN)	(00–49)	(50–69)	(70–89)	(90–99)
>41	40	20	20	20
(RN)	(00–39)	(40–59)	(60–79)	(80–99)

*The value above each italicized random number range indicates the proportion of instances that a specific number of lives lost occurs (e.g., if travel time is 50 minutes and the *RN* for the travel time to the fire location is 55, enter the > 41 row in column 1 (row 5 because it contains the 55-minute travel time in the > 41 range) and move to column 3 (because it contains the *RN* of 55 in the range 40–59). The specific number of lives lost that occurs in this situation can now be read at the heading of column 3—one (1); however, this is for a ward with a population density of 1.0. If the particular ward in question has a higher population density—say, 1.4—multiply the lives lost by this actual population density value—$1.4 \times 1 = 1.4$ lives lost.

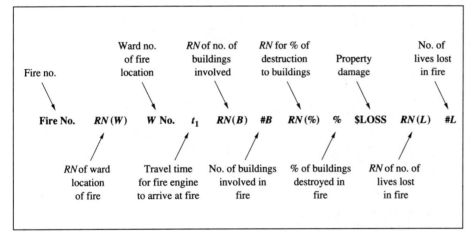

TABLE 15-24

Simulation Table Format for the Fire Station Location

■ The third *RN* (column 7) is 15; it represents the percent of the involved structure(s) destroyed in the fire. When we use this number in concert with Table 15-22, we can see that there is a 50 percent loss of the single structure involved (column 8). The actual property damage resulting from the fire is the product of columns 6, 8, and the average value of a structure from ward 12 (see Table 15-20). The damage is easily calculated and becomes the value of column 9:

Property damage = 1 building × 50 percent loss × \$235,000 = \$117,500

■ The next step is to identify the fourth *RN*, to represent lives lost (column 10). Since 70 is that *RN*, we can now determine the number of lives lost by using this value and the average time it takes to reach the fire (column 4) and the information in Table 15-23. From this information, we find that two lives would be lost. However, this

FIGURE 15-6

Simulation Flowchart of Fire Station Location

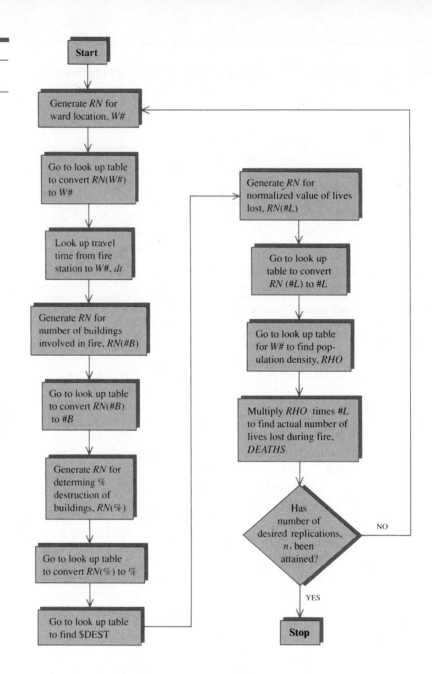

loss of life is for a ward with a population index of 1.00. We must scale up our loss of life by multiplying by the population index of ward 12, which is 1.2 (Table 15-20). Therefore, the number of lives lost is actually 2.4 (column 11).

This exact procedure is continued for each fire examined. The results of the analysis for site A shows that the average property damage is $123,375, with an average of 1.52 lives lost per fire.

TABLE 15-25

Property Damage and Lives Lost for Fire Station at Site A

Fire No.	RN (W)	W No.	RN t(1)	RN (B)	RN No. B	RN (%)	%	$ Loss	RN L	No. L
1	48	12	43	30	1	15	50	117,500	70	2.4
2	18	5	29	65	1	99	100	195,000	40	0.0
3	35	9	13	61	1	60	25	12,500	91	4.2
4	34	9	13	25	1	02	25	12,500	16	0.0
5	24	7	33	71	3	16	25	131,250	82	2.8
6	97	25	46	45	2	47	50	225,000	66	2.4
7	00	1	31	17	1	37	50	175,000	01	0.0
8	24	7	33	98	5	36	50	400,000	59	1.4
9	68	16	19	37	1	07	25	15,000	80	2.0
10	27	8	11	75	1	87	50	30,000	11	0.0
								1,233,750		15.2

TABLE 15-26

Summary of Primary Criteria for the Five-Site Fire Station Simulation

	Fire Station Location Site				
	A	B	C	D	E
1. Average Fire Damage ($1000s)	123.38	64.38	49.00	52.38	109.88
2. Number of Lives Lost	1.52	.86	.67	.47	1.16
3. Station Building Costs ($1000s)	5,750	8,477	11,841	13,292	6,563

These same simulation procedures can be used to determine the effect of having the fire stations at each of the four remaining candidate locations for 10 fires. The simulation summary for the five potential station locations is shown in Table 15-26.

These results, once again, are for illustrative purposes only. Only 10 case runs per site is far too small a sample to give any manager sufficient information on which to base an important decision. In addition, this method of simulation assumes that the station can respond immediately to the fire. To gain greater realism from this simulation, we would have (1) to introduce a probability distribution for the time between incoming calls, so the demand for fire protection is defined; (2) to develop a probability distribution for the time it would take to fight the fire—which would probably likely affected by the amount of time the fire had been burning prior to the arrival of the fire engine, the number of buildings involved in the fire, the materials of the structure, and so on—so that the availability of the responding engine could be established by a specific clock time; and (3) to define the number of fire engines in the company, so that the ability to respond to each call could be determined. It would, of course, also be necessary to make some estimates of the annual costs associated with each fire engine, the cost of a lost life, and so on, before the "best" number of fire engine units to be located at each potential fire station site could be established. All these extra considerations would add significant complexity to the simulation, but would also increase the refinement of the study.

TABLE 15-27

Probability Distribution for Time between Calls for St. Louis Ambulance

Time between Calls, TBC (min)	Average TBC (min)	p(TBC)	RN(TBC)
0 < 4	2	.10	00–09
4 < 10	7	.20	10–29
10 < 20	15	.25	30–54
20 < 40	30	.35	55–89
40 < 60	50	.10	90–99

EXAMPLE 15.5   THE ST. LOUIS AMBULANCE COMPANY REVISITED

Let's assume that exactly the same conditions that existed in Example 15.3 are still acceptable. The only difference is that this study will generate a service demand by adding the additional event of the time between incoming calls (*TBC*) for ambulance requests. It will also be necessary to use a specific value for the number of ambulance units, N, in the company fleet to respond to these calls for each specific simulation run. A representative probability distribution for the time between incoming calls for ambulance assistance is shown in Table 15-27. The simulation format will vary from the original version only by the addition of the *TBC*-related event data. This new event will allow the manager to "clock" the time the call comes in, the time at which the ambulance becomes available to depart to the site, the time at which the ambulance arrives at the site, and so on. The new format would look like this:

1	2	3	4	5	6	7	8	9	10	11	12
Call No.	RN (TBC)	TBC (min)	Clock at Call	Call Origin RN (LOC)	Traffic Density RN (D)	Clock as Ambulance Departs	Prep Time to Patient Site RN (t_1)	Time with Patient RN (t_2)	Time to Hosp. RN (t_3)	Clock as Ambulance Arrival	Total Time Σt

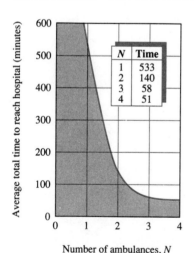

N	Time
1	533
2	140
3	58
4	51

FIGURE 15-7

Average Total Time Patient Must Wait to Reach Hospital as a Function of Ambulance Fleet Size

Some partial results of simulating this system for various ambulance fleet sizes are shown in Figure 15-7 (both the ambulance company and the hospital have been arbitrarily assumed to be located in district A). These refinements, along with running a large enough number of case replications to reduce the sampling error in the simulation, would greatly enhance the usability of the findings. Later in the chapter, we shall explore the importance of running enough replications in our simulation to enhance the credibility of our findings.

We have been concentrating on the simulation of waiting line problems. There are, however, several other significant families of problem settings that are also quite amenable to empirical analysis by Monte Carlo simulation. In the next two sections, we shall explore the use of Monte Carlo simulation in analyzing inventory-management and project-scheduling problems, respectively.

15.7   MONTE CARLO SIMULATIONS FOR INVENTORY MANAGEMENT

As you may remember from Chapter 12, solving the stochastic inventory models analytically is very demanding. It is not uncommon, in fact, to be confronted with re-

lationships that are not explicit and that require tedious, iterative solution procedures. If this is the case, empirical modeling approaches can be as effective in solving stochastic inventory-management systems as they have been in providing insight to waiting line problems. The procedure for formulating the simulation of a stochastic inventory system follows:

Step 1. Determine the probability distribution for demand from inventory records by counting the actual daily demand for the item (use these daily demands to develop a frequency and a relative frequency distribution).

Step 2. Determine the probability distribution for lead time by counting the number of days between the date of ordering the goods to the date of receipt (develop the same information as for demand).

Step 3. Define the inventory policies you wish to compare. Each will be represented by a separate simulation, and the total system costs will be compared. The system with the lowest value will determine the optimum reorder quantity, Q^*, the reorder point, R^*, and the number of units of safety stock to carry, S^*. An example follows to help illustrate the process.

Step 4. Design the simulation table by determining the actual sequence of events that occur in the system being simulated. Allocate probabilities for these events as determined by the use of random number techniques.

EXAMPLE 15.6 THE NEIMAN-MARCUS DEPARTMENT STORE

Consider the following hypothetical example: the Neiman-Marcus department store has noticed that they have been very unsuccessful in trying to predict their customer buying patterns of the exclusive mens ostrich-skin glove line that they carry throughout the year. They have also discovered that there is considerable variability in the amount of lead time of each new order they place with the manufacturer. These circumstances have often resulted in high inventory levels during low demand periods, as well as in stockouts during high demand. Since both demand and lead-time parameters are clearly unpredictable, they decide that simulation is the only sensible approach. Further, they also know that it would be impossible to include some of the operating idiosyncrases of their corporation in an analytical model. Some of these peculiarities include the fact that, although they are conducting sales on a Monday-through-Sunday basis, their order department handles inventory concerns on a Monday-through-Friday schedule. Accordingly, if a new order needs to be placed after the start of business on Friday, it does not go out until the next Monday morning (lead time is always measured from the beginning of the day *after* the reorder point is reached, because that is when the order is placed). Also, Neiman-Marcus receives price breaks (discounts) on the gloves that are sensitive to the number of units ordered. The ordering, holding, and stockout costs are estimated at $100 per order, $.50/unit/day and $25 per unit per stockout period, respectively. Using this information, let's design a simulation for Neiman-Marcus that will help them to determine the combination of R and Q that will result in the minimum total system costs, C_T^*.

SOLUTION

The four-step process for designing the simulation follows:

Steps 1 and 2. Examine the sales (Table 15-28) and shipping (Table 15-29) records from the previous year. Also, examine the price breaks related to the order quantity, provided in Table 15-30.

TABLE 15-28

Customer Demand (Pairs of Gloves)

Demand	D	$p(D)$	$RN(D)$
0–2	1	.20	00–19
3–7	5	.25	20–44
8–12	10	.45	45–89
13–19	16	.06	90–95
20–26	23	.03	96–98
27–35	31	.01	99

TABLE 15-29

Manufacturer Lead Time (Days)

Lead Time	LT	p(LT)	RN(LT)
0–2	1	.10	00–09
3–5	4	.30	10–39
6–8	7	.40	40–79
9–11	10	.15	80–94
12–14	11	.05	95–99

TABLE 15-30

Price Schedule

No. of Pairs Ordered	Unit Price
0–24	$50.00
25–60	$47.50
> 60	$45.00

Step 3. Next, define the IMS policy parameters we want to examine. For our case, we know that we want to compare the effect that different combinations of reorder points and economic order quantities have on the total IMS cost. So, we need to generate simulations for a number of combinations of R and Q, in order to determine R^* and Q^*.

Step 4. The sequence of events that would help to define the operation of the Neiman-Marcus IMS must include the two events for which we have probability distributions, random numbers for each of these events, and any intermediate acts that must be accomplished in the real system that we would perform (e.g., ordering and receiving the goods, tabulating the amount of stockout, a running account of the inventory level, and all associated costs). So, let's try to develop a rough outline of what the *sequence* of these events and actions might be.

First, we need to know what day it is. Next, we must know the beginning inventory level at the start of that day as well as the demand during that day. This will make it possible to determine numerous pieces of information: the final inventory level at the close of the day; whether the reorder point has been reached; the number of stockout units, if any; the possible need to place a new order; the daily average inventory level (remember that holding costs will be based on this value); the order quantity placed and lead time; the day the new shipment arrives; and all IMS costs. One possible version of this simulation format is shown by Table 15-31.

Now, we are ready to run a simulation. The first case will assume an initial inventory level of 100 units, a reorder point of 50 units, and a reorder quantity of 100 units (the initial inventory level is actually unimportant if the simulation covers a sufficient number of periods). Table 15-32 represents a 30-day simulation run for the conditions described. Seven-day progressions of 1s will represent Mondays (1, 8, 15, 22, etc.), those of 2s will represent Tuesdays (2, 9, 16, etc.), and so on. The interpretation of this table is as follows:

1. For day 1, a Monday, a random number of 20 is generated that represents the level of demand for that day. Using Table 15-28, you can see that this *RN* falls in the interval corresponding to a simulated demand of five pairs of gloves. So, at the end of day 1, the stock level will be $100 - 5$ or 95 pairs of gloves. Consequently, the holding costs of $.50/glove/day will be based on the *average inventory* for that day (97.5 units). The holding cost is then computed to be $48.75 for day 1. No other costs occur during this first period.

2. Day 2 has a random number for demand of 35. From Table 15-28, we find that this value also corresponds to a daily demand of five units. The stock level of day 2 will, therefore, end at $95 - 5$ or 90 units. The holding cost, based on an average inventory level of 92.5 units, is $46.25. This process continues until the inventory level reaches the *reorder point* of 50 units. So, let's skip down to day 5.

TABLE 15-31

Monte Carlo Simulation Format for Neiman-Marcus Inventory

Day No.	$RN(D)$	Begin Inventory	Inventory Q_1	Inventory Q_2	Average SO Q_{ave}	$RN(LT)$	LT	C_H	C_{SO}	C_O	C_{TOT}

Day No.	RN(D)	D	Beg. Inv. Q_1	End Inv. Q_2	Ave. Inv. Q_{ave}	S0	RN(T_L)	T_L	C_H	C_{SO}	C_O
1	20	5	100	95	97.5				48.75		
2	35	5	95	90	92.5				64.25		
3	98	23	90	67	78.5				34.25		
4	94	16	67	51	59.0				29.50		
5	4	1	51	50*	50.5				25.25		
6	11	1	50	49	49.5				24.75		
7					CLOSED SUNDAY						
8	51	10	49	39	44.0		43	7**	22.00		100.00
9	49	10	39	29	34.0				17.00		
10	77	10	29	19	24.0				12.00		
11	16	1	19	18	18.5				9.75		
12	51	10	18	8	13.0				6.50		
13	64	10	8	0	4.0	2			2.00	50.00	
14					CLOSED SUNDAY						
‡15	55	10	100	90	95.0				47.50		
16	99	31	90	59	74.5				37.25		
17	53	10	59	49*	54.0				27.00		
18	99	31	49	18	33.5		83	10**	16.75		100.00
19	21	5	18	13	15.5				7.75		
20	1	1	13	12	12.5				6.25		
21					CLOSED SUNDAY						
22	68	10	12	2	7.0				3.50		
23	21	5	2	0	1.0	3			.50	75.00	
24	64	10	0	0	0	10			.00	250.00	
25	48	10	0	0	0	10				250.00	
26	52	10	0	0	0	10					
27	62	10	0	0	0	10				250.00	
28					CLOSED SUNDAY						
‡29	16	1	100	99	99.5				49.75		
30	82	10	99	89	94.0				47.00		
TOTALS									485.75	1150.00	200.00
IMS Monthly Total Costs = $1835.75											

TABLE 15-32

Monte Carlo 1-Month Simulation for Nieman-Marcus Inventory

*Minimum order level violation; launch new order at beginning of next day (Monday through Friday only).

**Lead time until new order is received.

†New order arrives at beginning of day (Monday through Friday only).

Given: Q = 100 units; R = 50 units; C_H = $50/unit/day; C_O = $100/order; C_{SO} = $25/unit.

3. Day 5 begins with an inventory level of 51 pairs of gloves. The simulated demand for that day is one pair of gloves, resulting in an ending inventory level of 50 units. Since this value corresponds exactly to the reorder point in our IMS, a new order for 100 pairs of gloves will be placed at the *beginning of the next day*. However, the next day is Saturday (day 6). Since the Neiman-Marcus order department operates on only a Monday-through-Friday work week, the order cannot be placed until Monday morning (day 8).

4. On Monday (day 8), an order for 100 pairs of gloves is placed. The lead time required for this order, as determined by the $RN(T_L)$ value of 43, is 7 days from the date of order (see Table 15-29). So, the new stock will arrive at the beginning of day 15. The costs for day 8 will consist of the holding costs based on the average inventory level [(.50)(49 + 39)/2] and the $100 order cost.

5. So far, the only costs encountered have been holding and order costs. If we focus on day 13, however, we see that the third cost component occurs when the daily demand, D, exceeds the beginning inventory level for that day, Q_1. The beginning in-

ventory level for day 13 is only eight pairs of gloves, which is not enough to satisfy the demand for 10 units for that day. As a result, there is a *stockout* of two units, resulting in a $50 stockout cost ($25/unit). Do you remember that stockouts can occur only during each lead time? Notice how this happens 2 days *prior* to the arrival of the new order on day 15. The next time a stockout occurs, the effect is far more significant. By the end of day 23, the store experiences a shortage that continues until the delivery of new inventory at the beginning of day 29!

6. By the end of this simulation run, the IMS costs are as follows:

$$C_T = C_H + C_O + C_{SO}$$
$$= \$510.75 + \$175.00 + \$1150.00$$
$$= \$1835.75$$

From this solution, you can see that it is wise to reorder frequently, because the lead time is usually sufficient to cause numerous stockouts unless the inventory level is kept as high as possible. However, since this case uses a specific combination of R and Q, it represents only one possible policy setting. You must now explore new policy settings by running simulations of different combinations of R and Q, in order to find $R*$ and $Q*$. Although this may seem an arduous amount of work, it is not. A microcomputer can do simulation calculations of the size just illustrated in just a few seconds for each case. An illustration of simulating this same problem for the original reorder quantity of 100 pairs of gloves over a reorder-point value range of between 10 and 90 units is shown in Figure 15-8. Do not forget that this is merely a single run. It is essential that it is replicated an appropriate number of times on a computer, so that the large sampling errors associated with small sample sizes can be averted. Later, we shall examine the relationship between the number times a simulation must be replicated to achieve a certain level of credibility (confidence level). Next, however, we will look at a third family of problems that can be analyzed effectively by Monte Carlo simulation: stochastic project management.

15.8 MONTE CARLO SIMULATION OF PROJECT MANAGEMENT

Even though PERT takes the uncertainty of activity times into consideration, it focuses exclusively on the critical-path mean and standard deviation. As discussed before, the completion of the project is also vulnerable to near-critical-path activities—especially if the variability along that path is greater than that along the critical path. For this reason, a more suitable approach to stochastic networks is one that scrutinizes all network paths.

A technique that has attracted considerable interest incorporates a continuous probability distribution for each activity, instead of the PERT beta distribution. The method for generating these probability functions is, typically, subjective. A five-step algorithm is used:

Step 1. Develop the probability distributions for each activity in the network.

Step 2. Determine the random-number assignment profile for the probability distribution of each activity in the project (two-digit random numbers are usually sufficient).

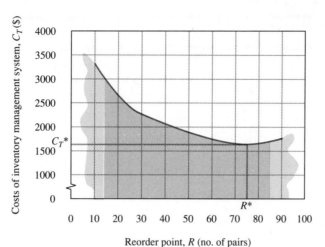

FIGURE 15-8

Determining Reorder Point of the Neiman-Marcus Ostrich-Gloves Inventory Using Monte Carlo Simulation for a Reorder Quantity of $Q = 100$ Pairs

Step 3. From the table of random numbers provided in Table 15-3, page **000**, or through the use of the numerous sources of computer-based random-number generators available in most spreadsheets or databases, establish a simulated time for each activity using the data developed in steps 1 and 2.

Step 4. Using the data from step 3, determine the critical path for the project duration.

Step 5. Repeat steps 2 through 4 for as many replications as desired.

The application of this algorithm to the Broadway Musical presented in Chapter 13 (Example 13.1) provides a useful illustration of the process.

Step 1. The probability distributions of the 13 real (nondummy) activities are illustrated in Table 15-33.

Step 2. The random-number assignment profile (using two-digit random numbers) for the probability distribution of each activity is shown in Table 15-34.

Steps 3-5. Two-digit numbers randomly selected from Table 15-34 are used to establish a simulated time for each activity. The findings of 10 Monte Carlo simulation replications for the Broadway Musical example are shown in Table 15-35.

The first row in Table 15-35 provides the results for replication 1. The critical path for this run is 1-2-3-7-11-16 and takes 23 weeks to complete. Although a sample size of 10 is very limited, the results show that seven different critical paths are potentially possible—an amazing illustration of the broad variety of possible critical-path sets. Replications 7 and 10 reveal, as in the cost-crashing section of this chapter, that it is possible to have several different critical paths present during any single project. This is one of the strengths of the simulation approach in project management: Analytical approaches to network methods do not provide the analyst with such a variety of information, because they rely solely on average or expected times. Even the PERT beta distribution is reduced to a single value. That is why it is so important always to be cautious of the near-critical-path activities that are "lurking in the bushes."

In the next section, we shall examine the critical issue of determining the appropriate number of case replications and sample size to employ.

TABLE 15-33

Probability Distribution of Activities for Broadway Musical

Time (weeks)	1	2	3	4	5*	6	7	8*	9	10	11	12*	13	14	15*	16	17
0																.01	
1		.05				.10								.30		.95	
2	.01	.17	.20			.80	.25						.30	.45		.04	
3	.04	.25	.25			.10	.50		.30				.45	.15			
4	.10	.20	.20	.10			.25		.40				.25	.05			
5	.10	.10	.15	.25					.25	.25	.05			.05			
6	.30	.10	.10	.35					.04	.30	.15						
7	.25	.05	.05	.25					.01	.25	.20						
8	.16	.04	.04	.05						.10	.20						.05
9	.03	.02	.01								.20						.15
10	.01	.01	.01								.15						.25
11		.01									.05						.20
12																	.15
13																	.05
14																	.05
15																	.04
16																	.03
17																	.02
18																	.01
19																	
20																	

*Dummy activities 5, 8, 12, and 15.

TABLE 15-34

Two-Digit Random Number Assignments for Activity Durations, ti, of Broadway Musical*

Time (weeks)	1	2	3	4	6	7	9	10	11	13	14	16	17
0												00	
1		00–04			00–09						00–19	01–95	
2	00	05–21	00–19		10–89	00–24				00–29	30–74	96–99	
3	01–04	22–46	20–44		90–99	25–74	00–29			30–74	75–89		
4	05–14	47–66	45–64	00–09		75–99	30–69	00–09		75–99	90–94		
5	15–34	67–76	65–79	10–34			70–94	10–34	00–04		95–99		
6	35–64	77–86	80–89	35–69			95–98	35–64	05–19				
7	65–89	87–91	90–94	70–94			99	65–89	20–39				
8	90–95	92–95	95–97	95–99				90–99	40–59				00–04
9	96–98	96–97	98						60–79				05–19
10	99	98	99						80–94				20–44
11		99							95–99				45–64
12													65–79
13													80–84
14													85–89
15													90–93
16													94–96
17													97–98
18													99
19													
20													

*Dummy activities 5, 8, 12, and 15 omitted.

TABLE 15-35

Ten Simulation Runs of Broadway Musical

Trial No.	a_1 RN	t	a_2 RN	t	a_3 RN	t	a_4 RN	t	a_6 RN	t
1	15	4	21	2	49	4	32	5	13	2
2	83	7	68	5	83	6	71	7	52	2
3	17	5	52	4	18	2	36	6	86	2
4	63	6	46	3	12	2	50	6	60	2
5	91	8	76	5	63	4	07	4	83	2
6	52	6	60	4	02	2	33	5	79	2
7	14	4	83	6	33	3	98	8	94	3
8	68	7	61	4	66	5	20	5	18	2
9	70	7	32	3	79	5	54	6	62	2
10	26	5	29	3	05	4	98	3	87	4
Totals		59		39		36		56		22
Mean		5.9		3.9		3.6		5.6		2.2

Trial No.	a_7 RN	t	a_9 RN	t	a_{10} RN	t	a_{11} RN	t	a_{13} RN	t
1	54	6	75	9	82	4	71	2	54	1
2	76	4	32	4	08	4	96	11	59	3
3	67	3	97	6	55	6	61	9	04	2
4	80	4	24	3	72	7	67	9	51	3
5	79	4	52	4	66	7	15	6	58	3
6	79	4	30	4	36	6	58	8	43	3
7	16	2	59	4	98	8	57	8	36	3
8	37	3	68	4	61	6	88	10	76	4
9	62	3	62	4	10	5	70	9	23	2
10	87	4	56	4	58	6	25	7	95	4
Totals		34		41		61		86		31
Mean		3.4		4.1		6.1		8.6		3.1

Trial No.	a_{14} RN	t	a_{16} RN	t	a_{17} RN	t
1	71	2	54	1	06	9
2	47	2	37	1	30	10
3	93	4	42	1	05	9
4	12	1	13	1	13	9
5	15	1	33	1	90	15
6	65	2	63	1	64	11
7	67	2	41	1	66	11
8	44	2	40	1	11	9
9	61	2	04	1	44	10
10	92	4	62	1	59	11
Totals		22		10		104
Mean		2.2		1.0		10.4

Trial No.	Critical Path(s) Activities**	Duration (wks)
1	B	23
2	B	34
3	D	25
4	B	25
5	A	32
6	B	25
7	A, B, E, F	24
8	B	30
9	B	28
10	C, D, E, G	25

Mean = 27.1 weeks

**A = 1-2-3-17
B = 1-2-3-7-11-16
C = 1-2-3-7-8-9-13-16
D = 1-2-3-7-8-9-14-15-16
E = 1-2-3-5-6-9-13-16
F = 1-2-3-7-10-12-16
G = 1-2-3-5-6-9-14-15-16

15.9 DETERMINING THE MOST APPROPRIATE SAMPLE SIZE AND THE NUMBER OF REPLICATIONS

One of the most important concepts learned from inferential statistics is that the reliability of your finding is directly influenced by the size of your sample. Very small sample sizes are more likely to have intolerably high errors associated with them than are, say, moderate-sized samples.[4] Of course, the higher the error, the less reliable the findings.

An effective way to drive down the sampling error is to increase the sample size. So, as the number of case replications used in a specific simulation is increased, the difference between the means of the population performance associated with the real process and that of your simulation will increase.

[4] The term *error* typically refers to the difference between a population and sample mean.

FIGURE 15-9

**Relationship between the Number of
Replications and the Mean Value of the
Simulated Parameter**

If the number of replications is small, the
simulated value of a given parameter will vary
significantly from one replication to another.
However, as the number of replications
increases, there is a dramatic decrease in this
variability. The optimal number of replications is
related by

$$n = \left(\frac{Z\sigma}{E}\right)^2$$

where

Z = level of confidence desired in simulation
results

σ = standard deviation of simulated
parameter

E = tolerable error

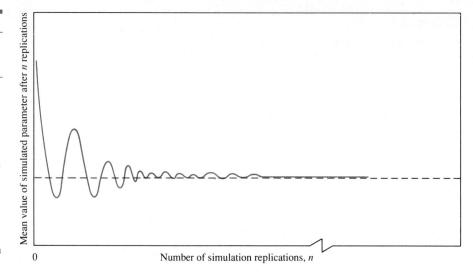

When we conduct Monte Carlo simulation, two crucial issues, both sensitive to sample size, arise:

1. How many measures of each empirical event must be collected to provide a
database of the correct size for a credible simulation?

2. How many replications must be conducted for a given simulation problem to
achieve an acceptable level of confidence?

The determinations of what size database sample to collect and of how many simulation
replications to run are different issues. Nevertheless, the underlying concept is the
same.

Although there is no definitive technique for determining the optimal number of replications to employ, it is important for a manager to examine the change of the average
outcome from one replication to another.[5] As the number of replications grows, the
mean simulation performance values will begin to smooth out, and the change will approach zero. A qualitative illustration of this relationship is provided in Figure 15-9.
The statistical relationship for determining the "optimal" sample size is given by:

$$n = \left(\frac{Z\sigma}{E}\right)^2$$

where

n = optimal sample size of the database or optimal number of simulation runs

Z = a function of the desired level of confidence you wish for your findings (typically 95 percent)

σ = population standard deviation of the variable (empirical event) you are
measuring

E = the amount of error you believe can be tolerated in your findings (the difference between the actual population mean value of the variable and the mean of
the sample)

[5]It is not unusual to run 100 to 1000 case replications for a typical simulation.

To determine the appropriate sample size to use for the overall problem, *we must make individual estimates for each event in the simulation sequence*. We must develop measures of standard deviation, and must define acceptable error measures for each event random variable. The error tolerance values, E, can be subjectively decided; however, the generation of reasonably accurate measures of variability is not so simple. There are, in fact, several ways to estimate the standard deviation of an event random variable. We shall examine several options using the travel time between station and ward location for the fire station of Example 15.4.

1. When the standard deviation of the random variable can be calculated from existing data, and the total population is small enough to make this task feasible, do so (i.e., calculate the variability directly from all possible combinations of travel time from the station to each of the 25 wards). This situation is almost too good to be true. Usually, if you are fortunate enough to have access to the total body of population data, economic considerations will force you to use random sampling methods to estimate the true population standard deviation, σ, rather than to calculate it directly.

2. If you know the range that the random variable covers, you can estimate the population standaard deviation (i.e., divide the range of the travel time values by 4).[6] However, be sure that you have confidence in the range values representing the population data before you proceed. If you do not, read on.

3. If neither opportunity described in settings 1 and 2 is available, select a random pilot sample of the random variable population. Assume, for this example, that we decide to select five wards from the total of 25 wards. Calculate the standard deviation, s, for the sample of five wards. Let this value represent a crude estimate of σ. If random sampling procedures are not available, sample by the most reasonable means possible. As before, calculate s and let it represent an approximation of σ.[7]

Now let's illustrate these three approaches using the variable of travel time between the fire station located at, say, site A and the 25 wards.

Calculate σ Directly from Population Data (Method 1)

We can easily calculate the standard deviation for the travel times from station location A to each ward using the following equation:

$$\sigma = \sqrt{\frac{\sum X^2}{n} - \left(\frac{\sum X}{n}\right)^2}$$

$$= \sqrt{\frac{26{,}827}{25} + \left(\frac{751}{25}\right)^2}$$

$$= 13.33 \text{ minutes}$$

---

[6]This step is based on the fact that about 95 percent of all possible outcomes are within approximately $\pm 2\sigma$ of the mean value. This provides a more conservative estimate than, say, dividing through by a factor of 6, which would represent the data within $\pm 3\sigma$ of the population mean (essentially 99.74 percent is approximately equal to 100 percent of the data in the distribution).

[7]If you have a population that is small enough to allow you measure "everybody," do so! Do not sample. The selection of a sample size of five taken from a population of 25 was done for illustrative reasons only.

Calculate σ Using the Range of Measures as an Estimate (Method 2)

The relationship is an approximation of the range of the data found:

$$\sigma = \frac{\text{high measure} - \text{low measure}}{4}$$

$$= \frac{51 - 5}{4} = 11.50 \text{ minutes}$$

Calculate σ Using a Small Pilot Sample (Method 3)

Assume we selected five wards at random and that they were 06, 21, 07, 11, and 02. The sample standard deviation, s, can be used as an approximation of the population standard deviation, σ, and is calculated from

WARD	TRAVEL TIME
06	37
21	46
07	33
11	23
02	15

Consequently,[8]

$$\sigma \approx s = \sqrt{\frac{1}{n-1}\left[\sum X^2 - \frac{(\sum X)^2}{n}\right]} \sqrt{\frac{N-n}{N-1}}$$

$$= \sqrt{\frac{1}{5-1}\left[5328 - \frac{(154)^2}{5}\right]} \sqrt{\frac{25-5}{25-1}}$$

Thus, the standard deviation for the travel time, based on the pilot sample, is

$$s = 11.04 \text{ minutes}$$

The estimated sample size (number of simulation replications) needed to justify, say, a 95 percent level of confidence in your findings and an acceptable error tolerance of, say, 2 minutes for the travel time variable between station A and the 25 wards is, then,

$$n = \left(\frac{Z\sigma}{E}\right)^2$$

$$= \left[\frac{(1.96)(11.04)}{2}\right]^2$$

$$= 117$$

---

[8]The second factor in the expression, $\sqrt{\frac{N-n}{N-1}}$, represents the finite population correction factor, *FPCF*.

The *FPCF* is required when the sample size n is equal to or greater than 5 percent of the population size N. Since we have chosen a sample size of 5, $n/N = 25$ percent—much larger than the 5 percent limit.

where

$Z = 1.96$ for a 95 percent level of confidence

$E = 2.00$ minutes

The sample size, n, using the three different methods yields

METHOD NO.	SAMPLE SIZE, n
1	164
2	128
3	117

So, it appears that between 100 and 200 replications of the simulation would provide the manager with the desired level of reliability and accuracy.

To further illustrate the importance of the relationship between the number of simulation run replications and model accuracy, we can replicate Example 15.4 for 200 calls using Microsoft Corporation's Excel 1.5 spreadsheet software (Table 15-36).[9] The mean values for (1) the fire-engine travel time to each ward, dt (column C), and (2) the dollar destruction to the buildings, $DEST (column H) are calculated for 2, 5, 10, 25, 50, 100 and 200 replications, and are presented in Table 15-37. Notice how quickly these values smooth out as the number of replications increases.

It is important to recall that we assumed the primary variable of interest to be the travel time between a station at location A and any of the 25 wards. Additional calculations for the other random event variables must also be analyzed similarly. *The sample size ultimately selected must be based on the random event variable that requires the largest sample size.* Accordingly, the other random variables that must be considered in the experiment are the number of buildings involved, the percent destruction of buildings, the property damage in dollars, and the number of lives lost.

15.10 MICROCOMPUTER SOLUTIONS TO MONTE CARLO SIMULATION

There are numerous Monte Carlo simulation software packages. Most require that the user learn a simulation language. The commands are similar in nature to the structures that are needed for the more powerful database packages.

Typically, the complexity of the simulation language is directly proportional to the sophistication of the simulation package. Regardless of this, the energy expended in learning to use any of these packages is well worth the investment. Once the particular simulation is structured, the manager can easily run hundreds or even thousands of replications of the particular problem in just a few seconds.

15.11 CONCLUSIONS

If it is possible to do mathematical modeling of a business problem *effectively*, simulation methods are usually bypassed. However, there are many conditions in which there are events that cannot be adequately characterized mathematically. This occurs when

"Thank you, Burrows, for that descriptive insight into the nuclear arms race."

[9]Included with the data for 200 replications are the built-in command formulas used to operationalize the spreadsheet.

TABLE 15-36

Monte Carlo Simulation of
Fire Station Location

	A	B	C	D	E	F	G	H	I	J	K	L
1	\multicolumn{12}{c}{TABLE 15-36. MONTE CARLO SIMULATION OF}
2	\multicolumn{12}{c}{FIRE STATION LOCATION EXAMPLE}
3												
4	RN			RN		RN			RN			
5	(¥#)	¥#	dt	(#B)	#B	(%)	%	$DEST	(#L)	#L	RHO	DEATHS
6	0.52	13	41	0.09	1	0.19	25	56250	0.67	0	1.2	0
7	0.72	17	22	0.87	3	0.12	75	71250	0.82	2	1.7	3.4
8	0.01	1	31	0.68	2	0.71	75	262500	0.80	1	1	1
9	0.99	25	46	0.98	5	0.99	100	225000	0.70	3	1.2	3.6
10	0.83	20	49	0.02	1	0.67	25	50000	0.71	0	1.6	0
11	0.52	13	41	0.16	1	0.11	50	112500	0.96	0	1.2	0
12	0.86	21	46	0.27	1	0.88	50	72500	0.12	0	1.5	0
13	0.74	17	22	0.10	1	0.88	25	23750	0.44	0	1.7	0
14	0.09	3	5	0.24	1	0.60	25	37500	0.40	0	1.5	0
15	0.66	15	17	0.04	1	0.23	25	20000	0.94	0	1.9	0
16	0.44	11	23	0.94	3	0.16	100	160000	0.40	2	1.4	2.8
17	0.66	15	17	0.73	1	0.82	50	40000	0.79	1	1.9	1.9
18	0.64	15	17	0.10	1	0.49	25	20000	0.37	0	1.9	0
19	0.88	22	38	0.11	1	0.59	25	26250	0.18	0	1.7	0
20	0.61	15	17	0.54	1	0.85	25	20000	0.04	0	1.9	0
21	0.54	13	41	0.11	1	0.49	50	112500	0.18	0	1.2	0
22	0.86	21	46	0.62	3	0.60	75	108750	0.76	2	1.5	3
23	0.63	15	17	0.71	1	0.55	50	40000	0.51	1	1.9	1.9
24	0.26	7	33	0.75	3	0.44	75	120000	0.99	2	1.4	2.8
25	0.10	3	5	0.31	1	0.27	25	37500	0.94	0	1.5	0
26	0.03	1	31	0.59	2	0.47	50	175000	0.73	1	1	1
27	0.10	3	5	0.41	1	0.64	25	37500	0.10	0	1.5	0
28	0.78	19	51	0.01	1	0.33	25	60000	0.14	0	1	0
29	0.05	2	15	0.13	1	0.41	25	83750	0.70	0	1.1	0
30	0.23	6	37	0.68	2	0.35	75	255000	0.44	1	1.1	1.1
31	0.45	11	23	0.99	3	0.12	100	160000	0.64	2	1.4	2.8
32	0.53	13	41	0.85	4	0.96	100	225000	0.30	3	1.2	3.6
33	0.19	5	29	0.27	1	0.85	25	48750	0.37	0	1.3	0
34	0.56	13	41	0.24	1	0.50	50	112500	0.75	0	1.2	0
35	0.35	9	13	0.39	1	0.51	25	12500	0.80	0	2.1	0
36	0.86	21	46	0.44	2	0.04	50	72500	0.78	1	1.5	1.5
37	0.35	9	13	0.17	1	0.59	25	12500	0.16	0	2.1	0
38	0.09	3	5	0.39	1	0.04	25	37500	0.46	0	1.5	0
39	0.50	12	43	0.78	3	0.31	75	176250	0.05	2	1.2	2.4
40	0.48	12	43	0.77	3	0.03	75	176250	0.29	2	1.2	2.4
41	0.92	23	39	0.27	1	0.27	25	27500	0.56	0	1.5	0
42	0.18	5	29	0.24	1	0.20	25	48750	1.00	0	1.3	0
43	0.69	16	19	0.79	1	0.04	50	30000	0.88	1	2	2
44	0.06	3	5	0.82	1	0.37	25	37500	0.74	0	1.5	0
45	0.21	6	37	0.36	1	0.38	50	170000	0.45	0	1.1	0
46	0.91	22	38	0.94	4	0.13	100	105000	0.39	3	1.7	5.1
47	0.80	19	51	0.18	1	0.09	50	120000	0.20	0	1	0
48	0.51	13	41	0.51	2	0.51	75	168750	0.99	1	1.2	1.2
49	0.10	3	5	0.29	1	0.49	25	37500	0.76	0	1.5	0
50	0.83	20	49	0.93	5	0.26	100	200000	0.16	3	1.6	4.8
51	0.80	19	51	0.39	1	0.45	50	120000	0.73	0	1	0
52	0.43	11	23	0.22	1	0.88	25	40000	0.60	0	1.4	0
53	0.88	21	46	0.82	4	0.59	100	145000	0.89	3	1.5	4.5
54	0.33	9	13	0.84	2	0.86	50	25000	0.93	1	2.1	2.1
55	0.36	9	13	0.97	2	0.80	75	37500	0.55	2	2.1	4.2
56	0.97	25	46	0.84	4	0.30	100	225000	0.77	3	1.2	3.6
57	0.04	2	15	0.73	1	0.96	50	167500	0.13	1	1.1	1.1
58	0.19	5	29	0.67	1	0.42	50	97500	0.58	1	1.3	1.3
59	0.25	7	33	0.39	1	0.19	50	80000	0.29	0	1.4	0
60	0.79	19	51	0.66	3	0.50	75	180000	0.86	2	1	2
61	0.14	4	17	0.48	1	0.08	25	42500	0.35	0	1.5	0
62	0.04	2	15	0.13	1	0.97	25	83750	0.18	0	1.1	0
63	0.54	13	41	0.88	4	0.44	100	225000	0.38	3	1.2	3.6
64	0.90	22	38	0.27	1	0.31	25	26250	0.72	0	1.7	0
65	0.41	11	23	0.94	3	0.51	100	160000	0.19	2	1.4	2.8
66	0.06	2	15	0.95	2	0.59	75	251250	0.87	2	1.1	2.2
67	0.52	13	41	0.75	3	0.43	75	168750	0.73	2	1.2	2.4
68	0.22	6	37	0.00	1	0.27	25	85000	0.16	0	1.1	0
69	0.53	13	41	0.92	5	0.32	100	225000	0.94	3	1.2	3.6
70	0.66	15	17	0.36	1	0.70	25	20000	0.05	0	1.9	0
71	0.42	11	23	0.78	2	0.88	50	80000	0.73	1	1.4	1.4
72	0.77	18	27	0.81	2	0.18	75	86250	0.13	2	1.9	3.8
73	0.93	23	39	0.01	1	0.34	25	27500	0.63	0	1.5	0
74	0.03	2	15	0.48	1	0.06	25	83750	0.32	0	1.1	0
75	0.43	11	23	0.25	1	0.33	25	40000	0.67	0	1.4	0
76	0.61	14	38	0.62	2	0.42	75	120000	0.33	1	1.5	1.5
77	0.26	7	33	0.96	5	0.91	100	160000	0.29	3	1.4	4.2

	A	B	C	D	E	F	G	H	I	J	K	L
78	0.02	1	31	0.11	1	0.98	25	87500	0.45	0	1	0
79	0.18	5	29	0.58	1	0.86	50	97500	0.86	0	1.3	0
80	0.81	19	51	0.49	2	0.33	50	120000	0.80	1	1	1
81	0.58	14	38	0.70	3	0.31	75	120000	0.33	2	1.5	3
82	0.33	9	13	0.57	1	0.40	25	12500	0.13	0	2.1	0
83	0.55	13	41	0.57	2	0.76	75	168750	0.78	1	1.2	1.2
84	0.41	11	23	0.87	3	0.26	75	120000	0.99	2	1.4	2.8
85	0.75	18	27	0.83	2	0.12	75	86250	0.24	2	1.9	3.8
86	0.02	1	31	1.00	5	0.76	100	350000	0.23	3	1	3
87	0.05	2	15	0.63	1	0.14	25	83750	0.30	0	1.1	0
88	0.84	20	49	0.09	1	0.12	25	50000	0.36	0	1.6	0
89	0.21	6	37	0.41	1	0.32	50	170000	0.17	0	1.1	0
90	0.53	13	41	0.66	3	0.24	75	168750	1.00	2	1.2	2.4
91	0.82	20	49	0.88	4	0.81	100	200000	0.66	3	1.6	4.8
92	0.45	11	23	0.43	1	0.71	50	80000	0.23	0	1.4	0
93	0.98	25	46	0.57	2	0.60	75	168750	0.60	1	1.2	1.2
94	0.00	1	31	0.30	1	0.80	50	175000	0.06	0	1	0
95	0.43	11	23	0.80	2	0.12	50	80000	0.47	1	1.4	1.4
96	0.56	14	38	0.05	1	0.87	25	40000	0.52	0	1.5	0
97	0.92	23	39	0.07	1	0.02	25	27500	0.42	0	1.5	0
98	0.69	16	19	0.64	1	0.31	25	15000	0.67	0	2	0
99	0.87	21	46	0.52	2	0.48	75	108750	0.72	1	1.5	1.5
100	0.57	14	38	0.79	3	0.69	75	120000	0.88	2	1.5	3
101	0.76	18	27	0.30	1	0.71	25	28750	0.05	0	1.9	0
102	0.36	10	18	0.36	1	0.63	25	18750	0.26	0	1.6	0
103	0.89	22	38	0.33	1	0.40	50	52500	0.58	0	1.7	0
104	0.42	11	23	0.79	2	0.47	50	80000	0.72	1	1.4	1.4
105	0.79	19	51	0.76	3	0.75	75	180000	0.96	2	1	2
106	0.40	10	18	0.71	1	0.96	50	37500	0.58	1	1.6	1.6
107	0.86	21	46	0.55	2	0.74	75	108750	0.60	1	1.5	1.5
108	0.65	15	17	0.67	1	0.92	25	20000	0.78	0	1.9	0
109	0.65	15	17	0.61	1	0.14	25	20000	0.78	0	1.9	0
110	0.66	15	17	0.76	1	0.57	50	40000	0.31	1	1.9	1.9
111	0.00	1	31	0.28	1	0.83	25	87500	0.41	0	1	0
112	0.43	11	23	0.96	3	0.54	100	160000	0.47	2	1.4	2.8
113	0.67	16	19	0.93	2	0.06	75	45000	0.35	2	2	4
114	0.82	20	49	0.76	3	0.08	75	150000	0.48	2	1.6	3.2
115	0.01	1	31	0.05	1	0.41	25	87500	0.49	0	1	0
116	0.20	5	29	0.91	3	0.48	100	195000	0.60	2	1.3	2.6
117	0.27	7	33	0.75	3	0.39	75	120000	0.30	2	1.4	2.8
118	0.95	24	43	0.92	5	0.54	100	175000	0.75	3	1.3	3.9
119	0.59	14	38	0.64	2	0.56	75	120000	0.78	1	1.5	1.5
120	0.11	3	5	0.32	1	0.01	25	37500	0.14	0	1.5	0
121	0.86	21	46	1.00	5	0.77	100	145000	0.18	3	1.5	4.5
122	0.76	18	27	0.17	1	0.96	25	28750	0.19	0	1.9	0
123	0.56	14	38	0.73	3	0.05	75	120000	0.97	2	1.5	3
124	0.07	3	5	0.27	1	0.10	25	37500	0.00	0	1.5	0
125	0.17	5	29	0.64	1	0.56	50	97500	0.39	1	1.3	1.3
126	0.76	18	27	0.75	2	0.95	50	57500	0.46	1	1.9	1.9
127	0.47	12	43	0.92	5	0.30	100	235000	0.99	3	1.2	3.6
128	0.16	5	29	0.72	2	0.02	50	97500	0.80	1	1.3	1.3
129	0.78	18	27	0.06	1	0.09	25	28750	0.75	0	1.9	0
130	0.05	2	15	0.04	1	0.20	25	83750	0.09	0	1.1	0
131	0.98	25	46	0.68	3	0.78	75	168750	0.68	2	1.2	2.4
132	0.50	12	43	0.52	2	0.62	75	176250	0.48	1	1.2	1.2
133	0.06	2	15	0.95	2	0.64	75	251250	0.31	2	1.1	2.2
134	0.81	19	51	0.67	3	0.49	75	180000	0.97	2	1	2
135	0.55	13	41	0.66	3	0.88	75	168750	0.80	2	1.2	2.4
136	0.02	1	31	0.25	1	0.19	25	87500	0.73	0	1	0
137	0.79	19	51	0.38	1	0.33	50	120000	0.48	0	1	0
138	0.54	13	41	0.68	3	0.08	75	168750	0.15	2	1.2	2.4
139	0.78	19	51	0.77	3	0.37	75	180000	0.67	2	1	2
140	0.30	8	11	0.57	1	0.48	25	15000	0.48	0	1.9	0
141	0.72	17	22	0.99	3	0.67	100	95000	0.92	2	1.7	3.4
142	0.49	12	43	0.35	1	0.07	50	117500	0.39	0	1.2	0
143	0.65	15	17	0.65	1	0.48	25	20000	0.01	0	1.9	0
144	0.19	5	29	0.64	1	0.58	50	97500	0.52	1	1.3	1.3
145	0.29	8	11	0.54	1	0.14	25	15000	0.04	0	1.9	0
146	0.85	21	46	0.17	1	0.10	50	72500	0.98	0	1.5	0
147	0.79	19	51	0.76	3	0.55	75	180000	0.16	2	1	2
148	0.36	10	18	0.68	1	0.41	25	18750	0.96	0	1.6	0
149	0.13	4	17	0.01	1	0.29	25	42500	0.20	0	1.5	0
150	0.71	16	19	0.99	2	0.39	75	45000	0.41	2	2	4
151	0.39	10	18	0.94	2	0.97	75	56250	0.83	2	1.6	3.2
152	0.63	15	17	0.50	1	0.53	25	20000	0.10	0	1.9	0
153	0.47	12	43	0.62	3	0.62	75	176250	0.33	2	1.2	2.4
154	0.28	8	11	0.11	1	0.05	25	15000	0.73	0	1.9	0

TABLE 15-36

Monte Carlo Simulation of Fire-Station Location

	A	B	C	D	E	F	G	H	I	J	K	L	M
155	0.93	23	39	0.64	2	0.39	75	82500	0.27	1	1.5	1.5	
156	0.66	15	17	0.28	1	0.39	25	20000	0.76	0	1.9	0	
157	0.62	15	17	0.87	2	0.61	50	40000	0.93	1	1.9	1.9	
158	0.95	24	43	0.93	5	0.14	100	175000	0.67	3	1.3	3.9	
159	0.95	24	43	0.71	3	0.84	75	131250	0.63	2	1.3	2.6	
160	0.40	10	18	0.60	1	0.69	25	18750	0.33	0	1.6	0	
161	0.89	22	38	0.31	1	0.79	50	52500	0.84	0	1.7	0	
162	0.76	18	27	0.46	1	0.92	50	57500	0.77	0	1.9	0	
163	0.05	2	15	0.89	2	0.20	50	167500	0.92	1	1.1	1.1	
164	0.69	16	19	0.21	1	0.08	25	15000	0.95	0	2	0	
165	0.42	11	23	0.57	1	0.54	50	80000	0.11	0	1.4	0	
166	0.92	23	39	0.00	1	0.42	25	27500	0.51	0	1.5	0	
167	0.19	5	29	0.20	1	0.13	25	48750	0.46	0	1.3	0	
168	0.98	25	46	0.97	5	0.01	100	225000	0.70	3	1.2	3.6	
169	0.97	25	46	0.41	2	0.27	50	112500	0.11	1	1.2	1.2	
170	0.14	4	17	0.41	1	0.36	25	42500	0.47	0	1.5	0	
171	0.51	12	43	0.73	3	0.94	75	176250	0.61	2	1.2	2.4	
172	0.58	14	38	0.87	3	0.78	75	120000	0.26	2	1.5	3	
173	0.05	2	15	0.69	1	0.56	25	83750	0.86	0	1.1	0	
174	0.58	14	38	0.67	2	0.43	75	120000	0.83	1	1.5	1.5	
175	0.75	18	27	0.70	1	0.42	50	57500	0.62	1	1.9	1.9	
176	0.82	19	51	0.58	2	0.33	75	180000	0.09	1	1	1	
177	0.02	1	31	0.70	2	0.56	75	262500	0.74	1	1	1	
178	0.50	12	43	0.52	2	0.37	75	176250	0.07	1	1.2	1.2	
179	0.35	9	13	0.02	1	0.91	25	12500	0.86	0	2.1	0	
180	0.47	12	43	0.69	3	0.78	75	176250	0.32	2	1.2	2.4	
181	0.73	17	22	0.25	1	0.40	25	23750	0.10	0	1.7	0	
182	0.62	15	17	0.75	1	0.41	50	40000	0.16	1	1.9	1.9	
183	0.88	22	38	0.82	3	0.42	75	78750	0.12	2	1.7	3.4	
184	0.31	9	13	0.80	1	0.30	50	25000	0.40	1	2.1	2.1	
185	0.39	10	18	0.27	1	0.05	25	18750	0.69	0	1.6	0	
186	0.37	10	18	0.60	1	0.89	25	18750	0.41	0	1.6	0	
187	0.16	4	17	0.88	2	0.89	50	85000	0.20	1	1.5	1.5	
188	0.62	15	17	1.00	2	0.46	75	60000	0.46	2	1.9	3.8	
189	0.83	20	49	0.42	2	0.51	50	100000	0.39	1	1.6	1.6	
190	0.05	2	15	0.26	1	0.24	25	83750	0.38	0	1.1	0	
191	0.87	21	46	0.26	1	0.51	50	72500	0.33	0	1.5	0	
192	0.68	16	19	0.93	2	0.07	75	45000	0.90	2	2	4	
193	0.83	20	49	0.31	1	0.83	50	100000	0.12	0	1.6	0	
194	0.76	18	27	0.62	1	0.38	50	57500	0.13	1	1.9	1.9	
195	0.64	15	17	0.46	1	0.99	25	20000	0.76	0	1.9	0	
196	0.85	20	49	0.73	3	0.86	75	150000	0.37	2	1.6	3.2	
197	0.90	22	38	0.62	2	0.80	75	78750	0.07	1	1.7	1.7	
198	0.82	19	51	0.10	1	0.19	50	120000	0.05	0	1	0	
199	0.00	1	31	0.85	3	0.40	75	262500	0.73	2	1	2	
200	0.21	6	37	0.99	5	0.29	100	340000	0.05	3	1.1	3.3	
201	0.80	19	51	0.08	1	0.99	25	60000	0.38	0	1	0	
202	0.07	3	5	0.44	1	0.76	25	37500	0.07	0	1.5	0	
203	0.47	12	43	0.03	1	0.13	25	58750	0.25	0	1.2	0	
204	0.63	15	17	0.47	1	0.57	25	20000	0.67	0	1.9	0	
205	0.51	12	43	0.82	4	0.94	100	235000	0.82	3	1.2	3.6	
206							Mean=	$99,469				1.308	
207							Totals=	$19,893,750				261.6	
208													
209													
210													
211		A6:	=	RAND()									
212		B6:	=	VLOOKUP(A6,$A$271:$B$370,2)									
213		C6:	=	VLOOKUP(B6,$T$101:$U$125,2)									
214		D6:	=	RAND()									
215		E6:	=	IF(C6>=41,VLOOKUP(D6,$A$271:$Q$370,7),IF(C6>=31,VLOOKUP(D6,$A$271:$Q$370,6),									
216				IF(C6>=21,VLOOKUP(D6,$A$271:$Q$370,5),IF(C6>=11,VLOOKUP(D6,$A$271:$Q$370,4),									
217				VLOOKUP(D6,$A$271:$Q$370,3)))))									
218		F6:	=	RAND()									
219		G6:	=	IF(C6>=41,VLOOKUP(D6,$A$271:$Q$370,12),IF(C6>=31,VLOOKUP(D6,$A$271:$Q$370,11),									
220				IF(C6>=21,VLOOKUP(D6,$A$271:$Q$370,10),IF(C6>=11,VLOOKUP(D6,$A$271:$Q$370,9),									
221				VLOOKUP(D6,$A$271:$Q$370,8)))))									
222		H6:	=	VLOOKUP(B6,$T$101:$U$125,3)*G6/100*1000									
223		I6:	=	RAND()									
224		J6:	=	IF(C6>=41,VLOOKUP(D6,$A$271:$Q$370,17),IF(C6>=31,VLOOKUP(D6,$A$271:$Q$370,16),									
225				IF(C6>=21,VLOOKUP(D6,$A$271:$Q$370,15),IF(C6>=11,VLOOKUP(D6,$A$271:$Q$370,14),									
226				VLOOKUP(D6,$A$271:$Q$370,13)))))									
227		K6:	=	VLOOKUP(B6,$T$101:$U$125,4)									
228		L6:	=	J6*K6									

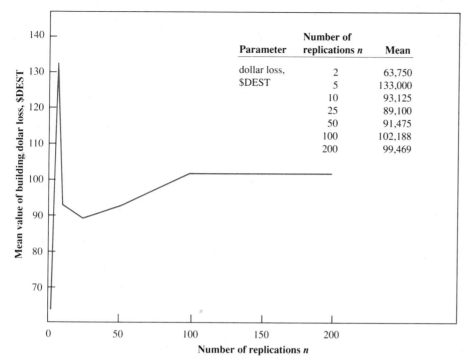

Parameter	Number of replications n	Mean
dollar loss,	2	63,750
$DEST	5	133,000
	10	93,125
	25	89,100
	50	91,475
	100	102,188
	200	99,469

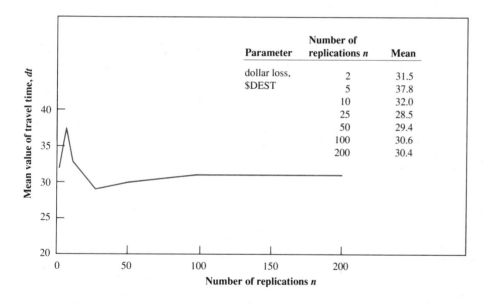

Parameter	Number of replications n	Mean
dollar loss,	2	31.5
$DEST	5	37.8
	10	32.0
	25	28.5
	50	29.4
	100	30.6
	200	30.4

problems include intangible considerations, such as the caprice of human behavior. Attempting to "quantify" such abstract considerations is foolish. Monte Carlo simulation methods may be just what is needed in such instances. As with any analytical technique, Monte Carlo simulation must be used with great caution. It is imperative that you be able to portray accurately the sequence of events that characterize the problem under study. This is typically a *very* expensive and time-consuming process, which can lead to either an indispensable, informative finding or a wasteful, misleading representation of the real process. The outcome will depend almost entirely on how skillful you are in recording the empirical observations and on the finances available to conduct the data collection process.

15.12 | EXERCISES

15-1 A 30-day random sample of daily receipts generated by a fast-food restaurant is illustrated in Table 15-1.1. Using these data, complete the following:

   1. Determine the midpoint values associated with each daily receipt range interval.
   2. Develop the probability distribution for daily receipts using two decimal places of accuracy.
   3. Select the random number range associated with the probability distribution values of part 2.
   4. Determine the midpoint values of daily receipts are associated with each of the following *RNs*: 33, 07, 75, 87, 21, 67, 13, 01, 41, 98.
   5. Using the *RNs* of part 4 (in sequence), simulate 10 days of receipts and determine the mean daily sales based on this limited sampling.
   6. Repeat part 5 by randomly selecting another 10 *RNs*, and generate the sample mean sales value.

TABLE 15-1.1

Thirty-Day Sample of Sales Receipts for Fast-Food Restaurant

Receipts ($/day)	Frequency of Occurrences
0 < 1000	8
1000 < 2000	15
2000 < 5000	5
5000 < 10,000	2

TABLE 15-2.1

Daily Gross Profits Associated with Rented, Unrented, and Stockout Automobile Units at Thrifty Car Rental

Automobile Status	Mean Gross Profits ($/day)
Rented	28.00
Unrented	−8.00
Stockout*	−3.00

*The unrented cost is associated with holding cost-type expenses (e.g., insurance, security, deterioration); the stockout cost is composed of customer ill-will and permanent market-share loss to competitors as a result of the unit shortage.

TABLE 15-2.2

Thrifty Car Rental Agency Customer Arrival Probability Distribution

Time between Rentals, TBR (min)	p(TBR)
0 < 4	.30
4 < 10	.40
10 < 30	.25
30 < 60	.05

7. Combine the findings of parts 5 and 6 and determine the mean sales for this 20-day sample.
8. Randomly select another 20 *RNs* and combine the corresponding sales values with the findings in part 7 to provide a 40-day sales sampling. Calculate the mean for this sample. Plot the sample means for parts 5, 7, and 8 as a function of the sample size associated with each mean.
9. Calculate the standard deviation associated with the sampling distributions of parts 5, 7, and 8. Plot the relationship between the sample standard deviation and the sample size for these three distributions.
10. Calculate the expected value of sales using the data of parts 1 and 2. Compare the sample means of parts 5, 7, and 8 with this expected value. Briefly, what possible relationship do you think exists between this expected value and the three distribution sample means?

15-2 Suppose the Thrifty Car Rental Agency at Tucson Airport would like to determine the optimal fleet size to employ for the specific level of daily demand they have experienced. They have the financial information regarding rented, unrented, and stockout (shortages) units shown in Table 15-2.1. The demand for auto rentals is represented by the time between customer arrivals (*TBA*) is shown in Table 15-2.2. What is the effect of fleet sizes of 20, 30, 50, and 100 units on the overall gross daily profits for Thrifty based on a 6 A.M. to 12 midnight simulation? (Assume that a rented car does not return during the same day of rental.)

15-3 Following is a hypothetical scenario built around the Xerox Corporation in Atlanta. Suppose the corporation is concerned about employing a staff of field representatives that is large enough to be responsive to their client repair needs. In particular, they would like to have a decent overview of what the relationship is between the number of field representatives they employ and the average time their clients wait until repair service is initiated. Xerox thinks that the key events they will need to simulate are the probability distributions of the time between calls by their clients (*TBC*), the travel time by the field reps to the client (t_1), and the repair time (t_2). These data, readily available from the Xerox repair logs of the past several years, are shown in Table 15-3.1. The typical Xerox client business is open between 8:30 A.M. and 5:30 P.M., Monday through Friday.

ASSIGNMENT

   1. Simulate an 8-hour work day for Xerox assuming various numbers of field representatives (start with $N = 1$ to get a "baseline" feel for the problem).
   2. Assume that the mean costs associated with each field representative are $90 per day, and that the cost associated with the time it takes between when the incoming call is received and the time the rep arrives at the client's business is

COPYRIGHT © 1971 by Gahan Wilson. Reprinted by permission of SIMON & SCHUSTER, INC.

"Something's gone horribly wrong with the copying machine!"

$50 per hour. What is the optimum number of field representatives to employ?

15-4 Airport Shuttle is an airport ground-transportation service that takes air travelers to and from the major airports in the Washington, D.C., area. The business uses commercial buses that seat approximately 60 people. Air travelers board the buses at a centralized terminal for the trip to the airport and are unloaded at the airport; new passengers board for the ride back to the depot, the bus returns to the depot, and, finally, unloads the returning passengers.

Conduct a simulation exercise on an average Airport Shuttle operating day: 6:00 A.M. to 12:00 midnight. Here are the particulars to keep in mind:

■ The simulation is to concentrate on optimizing system travel to the airport only (as opposed to optimizing roundtrip travel).
■ The revenue generated from a one-way fare is $15 per person.
■ The cost to the service—such as ill will and market share lost to competition—associated with not having the capacity to provide a ride to a prospective traveler is $3 per customer.

Use the following data to conduct the simulation. The rate of arrivals of travelers at the bus depot, broken into four time intervals during the operating day, is shown in Table 15-4.1. The probability distribution representing the bus drop-off and passenger "reload" time variability, t_1, is illustrated in Table 15-4.2. The probability distribution associated with the travel time to the airport, t_2, is represented by Table 15-4.3. The probability distributions for the bus travel times on the return trip from the airport, t_3, is presented in Table 15-4.4.

Design a simulation table and determine the bus fleet size that provides the company with maximum profits.

15-5 Convert the Example 15.4 into a variable time increment study (VTIS) that examines the effect on the system performance of using different numbers of fire engines. Variables are property damage per day and number of lives lost per day.

TABLE 15-3.1

Xerox Key-Event Probability Distributions

TBC	p(TBC)	t_1	p(t_1)	t_2)	p(t_2
0 < 10	.20	0 < 10	.25	0 < 10	.30
10 < 30	.50	10 < 20	.50	10 < 30	.50
30 < 60	.30	20 < 30	.25	30 < 60	.15
				60 < 120	.05

TABLE 15-4.1

Airporter Bus Customer Arrival Rate (*TBC*) at Depot Broken into Four Time Segments during Operating Day

6:00–10:00 A.M.		10:00 A.M.–4:00 P.M.		4:00–8:00 P.M.		8:00–12:00 P.M.	
TBC	p(TBC)	TBC	p(TBC)	TBC	p(TBC)	TBC	p(TBC)
0 < 1	.50	0 < 1	.10	0 < 1	.50	0 < 1	.10
1 < 3	.25	1 < 3	.25	1 < 3	.25	1 < 3	.25
3 < 9	.25	3 < 9	.50	3 < 9	.25	3 < 9	.25
9 < 19	.00	9 < 19	.15	9 < 19	.00	9 < 19	.25
19 < 29	.00	19 < 29	.00	19 < 29	.00	19 < 29	.15

TABLE 15-4.2

Airporter Bus Travel Time to Airport Broken into Four Time Segments during Operating Day (t_1)

6:00–10:00 A.M.		10:00 A.M.–4:00 P.M.		4:00–8:00 P.M.		8:00–12:00 P.M.	
t_1	p(t_1)	t_1	p(t_1)	t_1	p(t_1)	t_1	p(t_1)
18 < 24	.15	18 < 24	.35	18 < 24	.10	18 < 24	.85
24 < 30	.40	24 < 30	.45	24 < 30	.30	24 < 30	.15
30 < 40	.35	30 < 40	.20	30 < 40	.45	30 < 40	.00
40 < 60	.10	40 < 60	.00	40 < 60	.15	40 < 60	.00

TABLE 15-4.3

Time Required to Drop Off Passengers at Airport and to Pick Up New Customers for Return Trip to Depot (t_2)

t_2	p(t_2)
0 < 6	.50
6 < 12	.30
12 < 30	.20

TABLE 15-4.4

Airporter Bus Return Travel Time from Airport to Depot Broken into Four Time Segments during Operating Day (t_3)

6:00–10:00 A.M.		10:00 A.M.–4:00 P.M.		4:00–8:00 P.M.		8:00–12:00 P.M.	
t_3	p(t_3)	t_3	p(t_3)	t_3	p(t_3)	t_3	p(t_3)
18 < 24	.00	18 < 24	.35	18 < 24	.00	18 < 24	.85
24 < 30	.40	24 < 30	.45	24 < 30	.30	24 < 30	.15
30 < 40	.30	30 < 40	.20	30 < 40	.40	30 < 40	.00
40 < 60	.30	40 < 60	.00	40 < 60	.30	40 < 60	.00

TABLE 15-5.1

Probability Distribution Data for Incoming Fire-Alarm Calls

Time between Calls, *TBC* (min)	Frequency of Occurrences, *f*
0 < 10	20
10 < 30	60
30 < 60	60
Total observations = 200	

TABLE 15-5.2

Probability Distributions for Time Needed to Fight Fire as a Function of Time Required to Reach Fire*

Time to Reach	Time Needed to Fight Fire			
Fire (minutes)	5	20	45	90
0–10	90	10	0	0
(RN)	(00–89)	(90–99)		
11–20	70	20	10	0
(RN)	(00–69)	(70–89)	(90–99)	
21–30	50	30	15	5
(RN)	(00–49)	(50–79)	(80–94)	(95–99)
31–40	30	40	20	10
(RN)	(00–29)	(30–69)	(70–89)	(90–99)
> 41	10	20	40	30
(RN)	(00–09)	(10–29)	(30–69)	(70–99)

*The value above each italicized random number range indicates the percentage of instances that a specific amount of time is needed to fight a fire (e.g., if travel time is 38 minutes and the *RN* for the travel time to the fire location is 71, enter the 31–40 row in column 1 (row 4 because it contains the 38-minute travel time in the range of 31–40), and move to column 4, since it contains the *RN* range that captures 71 (70–89). The time needed to fight the fire can now be read at the heading of column 4—45 minutes.

Assume that the fire station is to be located in district B. The number of fire engine units to include in the study is up to you. The probability distribution for the incoming calls is provided in Table 15-5.1. The probability distribution for the time required to fight each fire is shown in Table 15-5.2. On resolution of each fire, the engine unit is to return to the station, unless it is the next unit available to respond to an outstanding incoming call. In that case, the fire unit is to leave for the next call, as soon as available, from its present location. You are to provide the *RNs* of each event (either manually select the random numbers from an *RN* table or use the random number generator in your spreadsheet). Assume that the cost of a life lost is $200,000 and that the daily amortized cost of a fire engine (which will include maintenance, equipment, and personnel) is $10,000. The simulation is to cover a 24-hour time period (12 midnight to 12 midnight).

ASSIGNMENT

1. Illustrate (plot) the relationship between (1) the number of fire engines, (2) the property damage, and (3) the lives lost during the 24-hour simulation period.

2. Convert lives lost during the 24-hour simulations to dollar values, and find the optimal fire-engine fleet size to employ so that the total system costs (cost of property damage plus cost of fire-engine-units operation plus cost of lost human lives) are minimized.

15-6 Simulate one work day (8 hours) for the Ferrari Automobile Agency presented in Example 15.2 with the following changes from the original problem:

1. Each salesperson costs the agency $300 per day (this figure includes health insurance, disability, etc.).

2. The chance that a potential buyer will renege and leave the agency is related to the amount of time the buyer spends without a salesperson in the following manner: none will leave if waited on within 4 minutes of arrival at the agency; 30 percent will leave if made to wait between 4 up to 8 minutes unattended; another 50 percent will leave if left alone between 8 to 12 minutes; the remaining 20 percent will leave after 12 minutes.

3. The proportion of people buying a Ferrari out of the total number that visit the agency is 2.5 percent of those who are attended by a salesperson.

4. The mean profit margin on each Ferrari is $10,000.

The arrival and service probability distributions remain the same. Determine the least-cost number of salespeople to employ based on the simulation findings.

15-7 Calculate the optimal number of simulation replications to use for the fast-food restaurant discussed in Exercise 15-1, using the sample data for cash receipts. Assume that the allowable error is $10 and that you desire a 95 percent level of confidence in your findings.

15-8 Calculate the optimal number of simulation replications to use for the Thrifty Car Rental Agency problem discussed in Exercise 15-2, using the data on customer demand for auto rentals. Assume that the allowable error is 2 minutes for the *TBC* value, and that you desire a 95 percent level of confidence in your findings.

15-9 For the Xerox Corporation problem discussed in Exercise 15-3, use the three probability distributions of (1) the time between calls by their clients, *TBC*, (2) the travel time by the field representatives to the client, t_1, and (3) the repair time, t_2. Determine the optimal number of replications to use for the overall simulation. Assume that the allowable error is 2 minutes for each event, and that you desire a 95 percent level of confidence in your findings.

15-10 For the Ferrari Automobile Agency of Example 15.2, use the two probability distributions of customer time between arrival, *TBA*, and salesperson service time, *ST*, to determine the number of replications to use for the overall simulation if the desired accuracy is 3 minutes, with a corresponding 99 percent level of confidence.

TABLE 15-5.3

Travel Times between Wards for Fire Station Location Simulation

	1	2	3	4	5	6	7	8	9	10	11	12	13	14	15	16	17	18	19	20	21	22	23	24	25
1	5																								
2	8	6																							
3	17	8	7																						
4	24	8	9	5																					
5	28	17	15	10	7																				
6	6	18	19	26	28	5																			
7	8	9	14	19	25	5	7																		
8	10	8	10	14	17	13	7	7																	
9	16	11	10	10	10	18	12	9	7																
10	22	13	15	10	8	23	17	13	10	7															
11	30	15	20	13	7	28	25	19	17	7	5														
12	11	21	20	27	30	7	10	21	25	33	35	7													
13	11	11	17	23	26	8	7	16	21	27	30	7	5												
14	12	11	13	19	22	9	7	11	17	22	26	11	9	4											
15	18	13	13	20	21	14	12	9	10	17	20	18	13	9	4										
16	30	16	19	22	20	20	15	15	10	13	15	24	16	13	4	4									
17	35	32	23	25	20	28	25	19	17	10	10	29	20	21	12	4	5								
18	38	35	27	25	20	34	30	24	22	13	10	33	25	26	22	9	5	4							
19	13	17	23	31	34	10	13	20	29	33	35	5	6	12	20	25	30	34	3						
20	15	18	21	30	31	12	16	17	27	28	30	11	7	9	16	18	25	32	6	3					
21	21	18	18	30	29	18	19	15	22	25	27	13	12	10	10	15	21	27	12	6	3				
22	32	21	18	30	27	19	20	17	19	21	23	19	17	14	7	12	17	22	18	12	6	4			
23	32	32	25	28	24	31	25	21	17	17	20	28	25	21	12	9	13	17	24	18	12	8	4		
24	40	35	31	28	24	36	31	25	20	18	18	32	30	26	20	12	10	12	30	24	18	13	8	4	
25	45	40	36	30	25	40	35	30	25	20	20	37	34	30	24	18	14	12	36	30	24	19	14	8	4

References

1. Batra, Pradeep. "Planning a Crude Oil Supply System through Simulation," *Omega* 8 (No. 4: 1980): 493–497.

2. Bruno, James E. "The Use of Monte Carlo Simulation Techniques for Determining Optimal Size of Substitute Teacher Pools in Large Urban School Districts," *Socio-Economic Planning Sciences* 4 (No. 4: December 1970): 415–428.

3. Byrd, Jack, Jr. *Operations Research Models for Public Administration.* Lexington, MA: Lexington Books, 1975.

4. Davis, Samuel G. "Analysis of the Deployment of Emergency Medical Services," *Omega* 9 (No. 6: 1981): 000–000.

5. Fitzsimmons, James A. "A Methodology for Emergency Ambulance Deployment," *Management Science* 19 (No. 6: February 1973): 000–000.

6. Ignall, E., G. Carter, and K. Rider. "An Algorithm for the Initial Dispatch of Fire Companies," *Management Science* 28 (No. 4: April 1982): 366–378.

7. Kao, Edward P. C., and Grace G. Tung. "Bed Allocation in a Public Health Care Delivery System," *Management Science* 27 (No. 5: May 1981): 507–520.

8. Levin, Richard I. *Statistics for Management*, 4th ed. Englewood Cliffs, NJ: Prentice-Hall, 1975.

9. Reisman, A., et al. "On the Design of Alternative Obstetric Anesthesia Team Configurations," *Management Science* 23 (No. 6: February 1977): 545–556.

10. Reisman, A., et al. "Application of Simulation Gaming to Dental Practice Management," in *Applications of Management Science*, Vol. 1. PLACE: JAI Press, 1981, pp. 293–326.

11. Riccio, NAME, and NAME Litke. "Making a Clean Sweep: Simulating the Effects of Illegally Parked Cars on New York City's Mechanical Street-Cleaning Efforts," *Operations Research* 34 (No. 5: September–October 1986): 661–666.

12. Swart, William, and Luca Donno. "Simulation Modeling Improves Operations, Planning, and Productivity of Fast Food Restaurants," *Interfaces* 11 (No. 6: December 1981): 35–47.

13. Zilm, Frank. "Simulation and Surgery: Planning a Complex Service," *Health Care Planning and Marketing* VOL. NO. (No. ?: October 1981): 000–000.

Microcompputer Software for Monte Carlo Simulation

A sampling of microcomputer software available for Monte Carlo simulation analyses is presented here. The majority of packages require a PC-DOS-type host microcomputer, although several of the products operate on a Macintosh system (indicated with an asterisk (*). In addition, some products that have educational versions with dramatically reduced costs.

1. *Actsim*. Reston, VA: Lake Ann Software.
2. *Crystal Ball*. Denver: Market Engineering Corporation.
3. *Extend*. San Jose, CA: Imagine That!
4. *Micro-PASSIM*. College Place, WA: Walla Walla College.
5. *Minuteman Software. Stow, MA: GPSS/PC*.
6. *PC Model*. San Jose, CA: Simulation Software Systems.
7. *Siman*. State College, PA: Systems Modeling Corporation.
8. *SIMPLE 1*. Campbell, CA: Sierra Simulations & Software.
9. *Simscript II.5*. La Jolla, CA: CACI.
10. *Simulations*. Winston-Salem, NC: Actuarial Micro Software.
11. *Slam II*. West Lafayette, IN: Pritsker & Associates.
12. *Solon*. Minneapolis: Y. J. Stephanedes.
13. *Tutsim*. Palo Alto, CA: Applied.

MICROCOMPUTER SOFTWARE FOR MANAGEMENT SCIENCE

16.1 | INTRODUCTION

You have been strongly urged throughout this text to use microcomputer software whenever possible to analyze management science problems. In this chapter, we shall further illustrate the value of this philosophy by presenting, in detail, a number of management science software packages—mostly inexpensive ones—that are capable of solving every type of problem presented in this textbook. View this chapter as a demonstration of the software products that can make life easy (or, certainly, easier) for any manager confronted with real-life situations. Two different types of software are illustrated in this chapter:

1. Individual or *specialty* software packages that use single techniques, (e.g., linear programming or project scheduling).

2. *Multiple-module* software packages that provide a variety of tools. A typical collection, for example, might include linear programming, PERT/CPM, queueing, and inventory models.

The specialty packages *generally* have a larger capacity and can solve more complex problems than the multiple-module software. However, the multiple-module products can offer those users interested in exposure to a variety of management science software a significant economic savings over the purchase of a number of specialty packages.

This chapter is organized into sections corresponding to most of the management science tools discussed in the earlier chapters. The only exception to this arrangement is the section at the close of the chapter, which examines multiple-module products. Specifically, the following types of software will be presented: (1) decision trees, (2) multiattribute utility methods, (3) linear programming, (4) Markov analysis, (5) project management (PERT/CPM), (6) inventory management, (7) queueing, and (8) forecasting.

Although the packages included in this chapter are current, new products will have entered the marketplace by the time you read this material. That does not reduce the significance of this chapter, since the general use of these types of software products will remain essentially unchanged.

We shall make a special effort to illustrate software from a broad spectrum of styles, so that you will be able to get a good feel for the kinds of features that might best suit your tastes. Some of these products are selected for demonstration simply because they provide an interesting contrast in style with other product(s). It is essential that you *not* infer that the products presented are the best available. That is not the purpose of this chapter; in fact, it would be inappropriate to impose that kind of value judgment on you.

Since people who are not yet management science practitioners will be the primary users of the software packages discussed in this textbook, special attention will be on the features that are particularly important to the beginner and intermediate user. These general features include the following:

1. *User friendliness.* Is the documentation well written, and does it contain good examples? Are the menu instructions simple? Is there comprehensive error handling? Is there graphics capability?

2. *Data entry and editing ease.* Does the software use line-by-line input? Does it offer spreadsheet entry? Can both prompted data entry or batch input be used? Does the editing menu allow for extensive changes?

3. *Ability to store problems as data or text files.* Can the problem be saved as a data file or as a text file? Can only the formulation be saved, or can the entire problem, including the solution, be saved as well? Can the data be easily exported as a text file to a spreadsheet or word-processor program?

Later, in the sections concentrating on a particular management science tools, specific features unique to the individual techniques will be mentioned.

16.2 DECISION TREE

The three decision-tree software packages presented in this section are (1) Arborist, (2) Micro Manager, and (3) Quantitative Systems for Business (QSB). Arborist is aimed at the intermediate to high-end business and engineering user whose demand is for large problem capacities and graphical capability (e.g., risk analysis of nuclear-power facilities). Micro Manager and QSB have significant capabilities but lack the node capacity and graphics component of Arborist. Some of the specific features of these three packages are summarized in Table 16-1. These three decision-tree packages can address surprisingly large problems: The node capacities range from between 80 to

TABLE 16-1

Decision-Tree Model Options for Abortist, Micro Manager, and Quantitative Systems for Business Software Packages

Decision Tree Features	Software Package*		
	Arborist	Micro Manager	QSB
1. Spreadsheet format	no[1]	no	yes
2. Size (number of nodes)	> 1000	100	80
3. Expected value calculations	yes	yes	yes
4. EV corrected for NPV	yes	no	no
5. Expected utility calculations	yes	yes	yes
6. Develops utility relationships[2]	no	no	no
7. Bayes' calculations	no	yes	yes
8. Tree graphics	yes	no	no
9. Color capability	yes[3]	no	no
10. Solution identifies optimal strategy	yes[3]	yes	yes
11. No. significant figures in answer	> 10	3	8
12. Printouts use file names	yes	no	yes
13. User-defined branch names	yes	no	yes
14. No. char. avail. for branch names	> 20	0	8
15. Change/editing capabilities:			
15.1 Change probabilities	yes	yes	yes
15.2 Change payoffs	yes	yes	yes
15.3 Add branches	yes	no	yes
15.4 Delete branches	yes	no	yes
16. Save/retrieve data file	yes	yes	yes
17. Save data as text file[4]	yes	no	no
18. Save graphics file	yes	no	no
19. System operating environment	IBM[5]	IBM[5]	IBM[5]
20. Approximate sales price	$595	$30	$30

1 = Arborist decision tree is developed graphically; 2 = Reference lottery method; 3 = Arborist uses three-color scheme for identifying overall tree display (light blue), current position of interest in tree (white), and the optimal strategy (magenta); 4 = ASCII, SYLK, etc.; 5 = IBM-PC/XT/AT and compatibles (MS-DOS).

100 for the two smaller programs—QSB and Micro Manager, respectively—to over 1000 for Arborist! (Few management science textbooks present sequential decision-tree problems that exceed a need for more than 40 nodes.) It is interesting to note that QSB and Micro Manager have Bayes' revision options for posterior probability analysis, whereas Arborist does not. The distinguishing design features selected for comparing these decision-tree software products include (1) *data-entry format*, (2) *editing ease*, and (3) *user branch identification*.

Decision-Tree Data-Entry Format

Generally, most management science models will have data-entry formats that are either (1) spreadsheet, or (2) individually prompted or batch-entry modes. However, decision trees also lend themselves to graphical data-entry formats as well.

SOFTWARE PACKAGE	DATA ENTRY FORMAT
1. Arborist	Multicolor, graphic format data entry; allows the manager to structure the tree from branches and root, decision, chance, undefined, and end nodes
2. Micro Manager	Individually prompted or batch entry
3. QSB	Spreadsheet entry

The graphical data-entry process for Arborist is accomplished through the four windows illustrated in Figure 16-1. Micro Manager uses either (1) the individually prompted branches or (2) batch input method. An example of the latter approach is illustrated in Table 16-2. The data-entry procedure for QSB provides a spreadsheet that exactly fits the number of decision branches of your tree (Table 16-3).

Decision-Tree Editing Capabilities

Both the Arborist and QSB packages provide full editing capability: QSB can quickly modify the payoffs and probabilities, as well as add and delete branches from the existing tree from a full-screen, spreadsheet-style editor, whereas Arborist provides a complete editing menu for the graphic decision-tree display. Micro Manager can change probabilities and payoff values only—there are no options for adding or deleting existing branches because branch numbers must follow *sequentially*. These modifications can be ultimately managed by redesigning and renumbering the tree's branch and node numbers.

Decision-Tree User Branch Identification

It is important for the user to be able quickly to understand the node and branch numbering arrangement of a decision tree. This is particularly important when the program does not have the graphical capability to illustrate the tree. The opportunity to name the tree branches will provide an immediate comprehension that use of mere numbers will not: It is very helpful to know that a specific branch is the "market" decision branch, M, following the unfavorable forecast, $P(F')$, rather than that it is branch 10, connected by nodes 4 and 9. Arborist—in addition to its decision-tree graphs—and QSB offer this valuable option; Micro Manager provides a numerical branch labeling system only.

FIGURE 16-1

Arborist Decision-Tree Graphic Data-Entry Windows

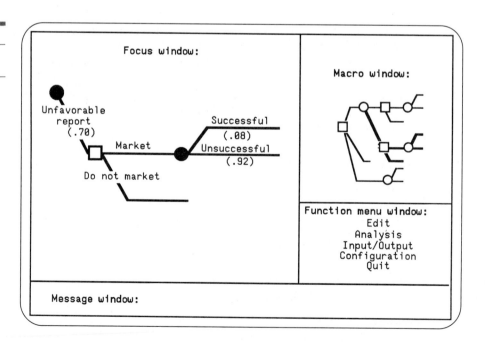

TABLE 16-2

Batch Input Format of Micro Manager Decision-Tree Program

```
<< PURPOSE >>

DECISION TREE determines the optimum alternative that should be selected
among various paths of a decision tree.  It also computes the expected value
of the optimum alternative.  The program can handle up to 100 nodes in a
decision tree.

<< BATCH INPUT >>

Type in the values of the following input data requirements, after creating a
new file.  You may enter as many values as you want in a line, separating
them by commas for alphabetic characters and by commas or blank spaces for
numeric values.  However, the input data must be exactly in the following
order:
1.  Number of branches
2.  For each branch
       starting node number
       ending node number
       probability (0 at decision node)
       conditional payoff (0 if not available)

 ** Sample Batch Input Data Set (United Airlines Example, Ch. 1, Fig. 1-11) **
 15                       ; fifteen branches
 1,2,.00,0               ; start and end node, probability, and payoff at branch 1
 1,13,.00,0              ; start and end node, probability, and payoff at branch 2
 1,14,.00,0              ; start and end node, probability, and payoff at branch 3
 2,3,.30,0               ; start and end node, probability, and payoff at branch 4
 2,4,.70,0               ; start and end node, probability, and payoff at branch 5
 3,5,.00,0               ; start and end node, probability, and payoff at branch 6
 3,6,.00,-.50            ; start and end node, probability, and payoff at branch 7
 4,9,.00,0               ; start and end node, probability, and payoff at branch 8
 4,12,.00,-.50           ; start and end node, probability, and payoff at branch 9
 5,7,.85,24.50           ; start and end node, probability, and payoff at branch 10
 5,8,.15,-9.00           ; start and end node, probability, and payoff at branch 11
 9,10,.08,24.50          ; start and end node, probability, and payoff at branch 12
 9,11,.92,-9.00          ; start and end node, probability, and payoff at branch 13
 14,15,.31,25.00         ; start and end node, probability, and payoff at branch 14
 14,16,.69,-8.50         ; start and end node, probability, and payoff at branch 15
```

Decision-Tree File-Saving Capability

All three decision-tree software packages save information in a data file for future retrieval. Arborist saves both decision tree text (payoffs, probabilities, branch identification information) and graphics (tree layout, as well as the color identification of the optimal strategy) in a data file. However, none of the programs can save the data as a text file that can be exported to other documents (e.g., word-processing, spreadsheets, or page-layout programs).

16.3 | MULTIATTRIBUTE UTILITY METHODS (MAUM)

MAUM software is readily available, inexpensive, and simple to use. Two products will be presented in this section: Decision Analyst and DecisionMap. A list of features likely to be important to the MAUM user is shown in Table 16-4 for these two programs.

```
Enter Data for Decision Tree Analysis

Before entering data, you have to prepare a decision tree with
numbered nodes and numbered branches.  The program can solve decision
trees with up to 80 branches.  The nodes and brances should be
numbered sequentially from 1.  The number of the start node should be
lower than the number of the end node for every branch.  Each node can
be either a decision node or a chance node represented by 1 or 2,
respectively.  For each branch, you may have probability, payoff/cost
value, and name with it.  The following data entry is performed branch
by branch (United Airlines Study, Chapter 1, Figure 1-11):


        How many branches are there in your decision tree?  15


    Do you want to maximize (1) or minimize (2) criterion?  (Enter 1 or
                            2)?  1


            Enter Data for Decision Tree Analysis Page 1
```

Branch number	Branch name	Start node	End node	Start node type	Probability	Payoff/cost
1	<H >	<1 >	<2 >	<1 >	< >	< >
2	<N >	<1 >	<13 >	<1 >	< >	<0 >
3	<M >	<1 >	<14 >	<1 >	< >	< >
4	<P(F) >	<2 >	<3 >	<2 >	<.30 >	< >
5	<P(F') >	<2 >	<4 >	<2 >	<.70 >	< >
6	<M >	<3 >	<5 >	<1 >	< >	< >
7	<M' >	<3 >	<6 >	<1 >	< >	<-.50 >
8	<P(S/F) >	<5 >	<7 >	<2 >	<.85 >	<24.50 >
9	<P(S'/F) >	<5 >	<8 >	<2 >	<.15 >	<-9.00 >
10	<M >	<4 >	<9 >	<1 >	< >	< >
11	<M' >	<4 >	<12 >	<1 >	< >	<-.50 >
12	<P(S/F') >	<9 >	<10 >	<2 >	<.08 >	<24.50 >
13	<P(S'/F')>	<9 >	<11 >	<2 >	<.92 >	<-9.00 >
14	<P(S) >	<14 >	<15 >	<2 >	<.31 >	<25.00 >
15	<P(S') >	<14 >	<16 >	<2 >	<.69 >	<-8.50 >

MAUM Data-Entry Format

The main menu illustrating the data-entry commands for Decision Analyst is shown in Table 16-5. The user is chronologically walked (prompted) through the eight-step menu until a detailed MAUM model has been developed. An illustration of the multi-level criteria (attribute) selection and weighting scheme for the "Buy a Car" problem (Chapter 3, Exercise 3.3) is given in Table 16-6. Later, a composite score is calculated for each alternative (not shown). The alternatives are ranked by these scores. Finally, a detailed report generator provides an explanation of the results by analyzing the strong and weak attribute performance points of each alternative.

Although DecisionMap uses the same substantive model-developing procedure as Decision Analyst, the former program uses a visual–graphical orientation for its data-entry process and solutions presentation. Illustrations of the multilevel attribute set in

TABLE 16-4

Microcomputer Software Features of MAUM Models for the Decision Analyst and Decision-Map Programs

	Software Programs	
MAUM Features	Decision Analyst	Decision-Map
1. Maximum no. of alternatives	> 50	5
2. Maximum no. of attributes	> 50	3–65
3. Attribute weighting provision	yes	yes
4. Graphical illustrations	no	yes
5. Compare alternatives by aggregate score	yes	yes
6. Compare alternatives by individual attribute scores	yes	yes
7. Report generator	yes	yes
8. Host microcomputer	IBM	Macintosh
9. Provision for alternative names	yes	yes
10. Provision for attribute names	yes	yes
11. Printouts use file names	yes	yes
12. Change/editing capabilities:	yes	yes
13. Store/retrieve data file	yes	no
14. Store data as text file	yes	no
15. Minimum required RAM	128K	128K
16. Approximate retail price	$100	$35

TABLE 16-5

Main Data-Entry Menu of Decision Analyst

```
+---------------------------------------------------------------+
                ********   MAIN MENU   ********
===============================================================
---------------------------------------------------------------
    <1>   DEFINE THE PROBLEM      (Why is a decision necessary?)
    <2>   STATE DECISION PURPOSE  (What are you trying to achieve?)
    <3>   DEFINE YOUR CRITERIA    (What are your objectives?)
    <4>   SORT & LIST YOUR CRITERIA (List criteria sorted by value)
    <5>   DEFINE YOUR ALTERNATIVES (List all practical solutions)
    <6>   WEIGHT/SCORE ALTERNATIVES (Evaluate to find best 'score')
    <7>   TEST FOR MURPHY'S LAW   (Assess consequences of each option)
    <8>   DRAW CONCLUSIONS & CHOOSE (Print final decision summary)


    <R>  Revise COMPANY NAME, AUTHOR, DATE, DISK DRIVES or DISKSIZE
    <S>  Switch to a DIFFERENT DECISION . . or change DECISION TITLE


    NOTE:  Current decision name is dname on drive d:
               . . Help file is on d:


            Please enter your choice or <Q> to Quit __

---------------------------------------------------------------
```

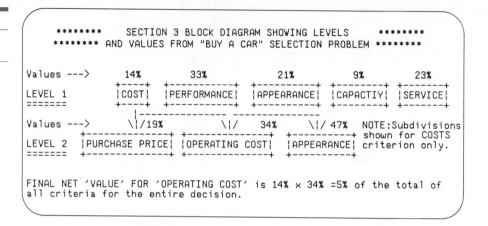

```
********      SECTION 3 BLOCK DIAGRAM SHOWING LEVELS      ********
******** AND VALUES FROM "BUY A CAR" SELECTION PROBLEM ********

Values --->      14%        33%          21%        9%        23%
            +----+    +-----------+   +----------+  +--------+  +-------+
LEVEL 1     |COST|    |PERFORMANCE|   |APPEARANCE|  |CAPACTIY|  |SERVICE|
=======     +----+    +-----------+   +----------+  +--------+  +-------+
            |---------------  ----------------
Values --->      \|/19%            \|/  34%      \|/ 47%   NOTE:Subdivisions
            +--------------+   +--------------+   +----------+  shown for COSTS
LEVEL 2     |PURCHASE PRICE|   |OPERATING COST|   |APPEARANCE|  criterion only.
=======     +--------------+   +--------------+   +----------+

FINAL NET 'VALUE' FOR 'OPERATING COST' is 14% x 34% =5% of the total of
all criteria for the entire decision.
```

FIGURE 16-2

DecisionMap Multilevel Factors (Attributes) for "Buy a Car" Problem

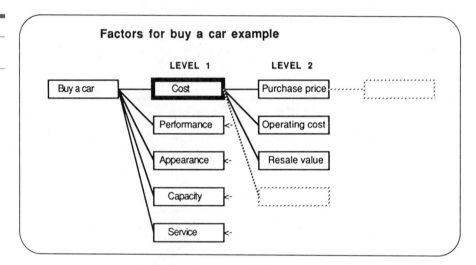

Factors for buy a car example

the solution of a MAUM problem by DecisionMap are presented in Figure 16-2 for the "Buy a Car" problem.[1] Figure 16-3 shows the final evaluation of the three alternative car models considered.

16.4 | LINEAR PROGRAMMING

The three linear programming software programs explored in this section are Microsolve, STORM, and LINDO-PC. A summary of the specific features offered in these three programs is presented in Table 16-7. The *model size* of these two programs varies between capacities of 40 to 100 decision variables and 25 to 50 constraints. All the programs have almost identical *sensitivity-analysis* options. The primary design features that clearly distinguished the packages are (1) *data-entry format*, (2) *editing options and ease*, (3) *decision-variable naming and indexing capabilities*, and (4) *file-storage flexibility* (data and text file formats).

[1]DecisionMap refers to *factors*, rather than to attributes.

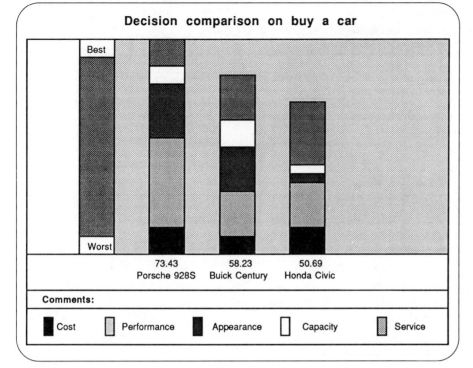

FIGURE 16-3

Final Comparison of Three Alternatives in the "Buy a Car" Problem Using DecisionMap

LP Data-Entry Format

The two most common forms of data entry use either an "$R \times C$" spreadsheet whose size conforms to the number of decision variables (number of columns, C) and the number of constraints (number of rows, R) or individually prompted data entry (or batch input) of the objective function and constraint decision-variable coefficients, right-hand-side values (resource levels), and constraint relationships ($\leq$, $=$, $\geq$). Neither data-entry format is inherently superior to the other; which is better depends on the type of problem formulation. A few qualitative examples of when it may be advantageous to use one LP data-entry format in lieu of the other follow:

1. *Spreadsheet formats* typically facilitate data entry best when

   - The formulation comprises a moderate to large number of decision variables, with a low proportion of zero coefficients and a moderate to large number of constraints.
   - The user is inexperienced with LP microcomputer software—a person is often more confident when there is visual connection between the formulated LP problem and the spreadsheet layout.

2. *Individually prompted or batch-data entry* is usually more effective with

   - Small $R \times C$ formulations.
   - Moderate to large $R \times C$ formulations when either a significant numbers of zero-coefficient constraint variables are present or the proportion of decision variables to constraints is small (the batch-input strings are short).
   - The user is experienced with LP formulation and microcomputer usage.

TABLE 16-7

**Summary of Microsolve, STORM, and LINDO-PC Linear
Programming Microcomputer Software Features**

LP Features	Software Packages		
	Microsolve	*STORM*	*LINDO-PC*
1. Model size (#var × #con)	100×50	40×25	100×50
2. Printouts use file names	yes	yes	yes
3. User-defined names	no	yes	yes
4. User-defined row (con) names	no	yes	no
5. Max no. char. avail. for decision-variable indices ($x_{ij \ldots m}$)	15	1	4
6. Change/editing capabilities:			
6.1 Change *OF* type (max/min)	yes	yes	yes
6.2 Delete constraints	yes	yes	yes
6.3 Add constraints	no	yes	yes
6.4 Change const. coefficients	yes	yes	yes
6.5 Delete variables	yes	yes	yes
6.6 Add variables	yes	yes	yes
6.7 Change *OF* coefficients	yes	yes	yes
6.8 Change *RHS* values	yes	yes	yes
6.9 Change const. relationship, i.e., $\leq, =, \geq$	yes	yes	yes
7. Spreadsheet input format	no	yes	no
8. Need zero coef. input (Y/N)	no	no	no
9. Sensitivity analysis:			
9.1 Dual solution	yes	yes	yes
9.2 *RHS* ranging	yes	yes	yes
9.3 *OF* coefficient ranging	yes	yes	yes
10. Store/retrieve data file	yes	yes	yes
11. Store data as text file	no	yes	yes
12. Iterations available for viewing	yes	yes	yes
13. Approximate sales price	$50	$40	$30
14. Special features	†	‡	*
15. Host microcomputer	IBM	IBM	IBM

* = Has built-in integer decision-variable options (branch and bound)

† = Allows constraints to be entered with upper and lower bounds; e.g., $b \leq \Sigma; a_i x_i \leq B$

‡ = Automatic scaling

The Microsolve data entry is shown in Table 16-8 for the German car dealer study introduced in Chapter 4, Exercise 4.3. Each problem is entered in rows of equations. The rows are identified by the type of objective function (OBJMAX/ or OBJMIN) the solution is to follow, and the corresponding constraints (CON#) are entered *exactly* as formulated. Any terms (decision variables) with zero constraints are completely omitted.

The STORM spreadsheet data-entry format for the German car dealer study is shown in Table 16-9. The LINDO-PC data entry for the German car dealer study is very similar to the Microsolve procedure: The problem is entered exactly as formulated (Table

```
┌──────────────────────────────────────────────────────────┐
│                                                          │
│            MICROSOLVE/OPERATIONS RESEARCH                │
│               REVISED EDITION IBM-PC                     │
│                  STUDENT VERSION                         │
│  ------------------------------------------------------  │
│              NUMBER OF VARIABLES (<100): 3              │
│              NUMBER OF CONSTRAINTS (<50): 9            │
│  DATA ENTRY:                                            │
│                                                          │
│            OBJMAX/    9000X1+6000X2+12500X3             │
│            CON1/      120X1+115X2+148X3<=5000           │
│            CON2/      27000X1+20000X2+32500X3<=800000   │
│            CON3/      X1<=25                            │
│            CON4/      X2<=35                            │
│            CON5/      X3<=8                             │
│            CON6/      X3<=6                             │
│            CON7//     X1>=12                            │
│            CON8/      X2>=12                            │
│            CON9/      X3>=4                             │
│                                                          │
└──────────────────────────────────────────────────────────┘
```

TABLE 16-8

Data Entry for German Car Dealer Using Microsolve Linear-Programming Model

```
┌─────────────────────────────────────────────────────────────────┐
│ ┌──────────────┤ STORM EDITOR : Linear Programming Module├─────┐ │
│ │  Title:   GERMAN CAR DEALER STUDY                           │ │
│ │  Number of variables    :     3                            │ │
│ │  Number of constraints  :     9                            │ │
│ │  Starting solution given:    NO                            │ │
│ │  Objective function     :    MAX                           │ │
│ ├─────────────────────────────────────────────────────────────┤ │
│ │           PORSCHE   BMW   MERCEDES  TYPE    RHS    RANGE    │ │
│ │ OBJ COEFF  9000.  6000.   12500.   xxxx   xxxx    xxxx     │ │
│ │ SPACE       120.   115.     148.   <=     5000.   INF.     │ │
│ │ BUDGET    27000. 20000.   32500.   <=   800000.   INF.     │ │
│ │ MAX POR       1.     0.       0.   <=       25.   INF.     │ │
│ │ MAX BMW       0.     1.       0.   <=       35.   INF.     │ │
│ │ MAX MER       0.     0.       1.   <=        8.   INF.     │ │
│ │ SALES MER     0.     0.       1.   <=        6.   INF.     │ │
│ │ MIN POR       1.     0.       0.   >=       12.   INF.     │ │
│ │ MIN BMW       0.     1.       0.   >=       12.   INF.     │ │
│ │ MIN MER       0.     0.       1.   >=        4.   INF.     │ │
│ │ VARBL TYPE    +      +        +    xxxx   xxxx    xxxx     │ │
│ │ LOWER BOUND -INF.  -INF.   -INF.   xxxx   xxxx    xxxx     │ │
│ │ UPPER BOUND  INF.   INF.    INF.   xxxx   xxxx    xxxx     │ │
│ │ INIT SOLN     0.     0.       0.   xxxx   xxxx    xxxx     │ │
│ │                                                            │ │
│ │                                                            │ │
│ │                                                            │ │
│ ├─────┤No entry                    │ ->          │─────┤    │ │
│ └─────────────────────────────────────────────────────────────┘ │
└─────────────────────────────────────────────────────────────────┘
```

TABLE 16-9

STORM Editor Screen of the German Car Dealer Using Linear-Programming Module

```
MAX  9000 X1 + 6000 X2 + 12500 X3
SUBJECT TO
 2)     120X1+115X2+148X3 <  5000
 3)     27000X1+20000X2+32500X3 <  800000
 4)     X1 < 25
 5)     X2 < 35
 6)     X3 < 8
 7)     X3 < 6
 8)     X1 > 12
 9)     X2 > 12
10)     X3 > 4
```

16-10). One minor difference between the LINDO-PC and Microsolve programs is that the former uses row numbers, rather than constraint numbers. Also, LINDO-PC does not require the user to define the size of the problem prior to beginning the data-entry process.

LP Editing Capabilities

Most LP software packages offer similar editing capabilities. However, the ease with which these modifications can be accomplished is significantly affected by the type of data-entry form used by the program, as discussed in the last section. Generally, the spreadsheet format is easier to edit: The user simply moves around the appropriate cells through the use of the cursor keys or a mouse, and changes the necessary values freely. Prompted or batch data entry usually has individual, one-at-a-time element editing capability. Therefore, when the editing changes are numerous, nonspreadsheet formats can be quite tedious. The Microsolve general editing menu, including the specific changes available for the "change a constraint" (option 2), is shown in Table 16-11. The STORM spreadsheet editor display (Table 16-9) accommodates rapid data editing. The user uses the arrow keys to move the cursor over any cell value she wishes to change, and types in the new values, followed by striking the Enter key. That's it! The LINDO-PC data-editing process is similar in style, but is more extensive in scope, than that of Microsolve: The former program allows addition of new constraints, whereas the latter program does not. The problem-editing options for LINDO-PC are provided in Table 16-12.

LP Decision-Variable Naming and Indexing: Problem Notation Clarity

Linear programming problems can be analyzed more easily if multiple indexing can be employed to define each decision variable (such as x_{ijk}) more explicitly, and if names can be used to identify more accurately the constraint equations and, in simplified formulations, the decision variables.[2]

[2]It is not feasible to provide names for complex decision variables due to space limitations imposed by almost all LP software: even the 15 spaces provided in Microsolve are not enough to identify explicitly the x_{3215} decision variable illustrated above. Try it. Decision-variable naming is likely to be limited to the one- or two-index variety (i.e., x_i or x_{ij}).

TABLE 16-11

Microsolve Editing Menu for
Linear-Programming Problems: Constraint
Change Option

```
                    CHANGE DATA ROUTINE

    ENTER THE TYPE OF CHANGE YOU WANT.

        1. CHANGE THE OBJECTIVE FUNCTION
        2. CHANGE A CONSTRAINT
        3. CHANGE A BOUND
        4. CHANGE A VARIABLE NAME
        5. CHANGE OR ADD A VARIABLE
        6. DELETE A VARIABLE
        7. DELETE A CONSTRAINT
        8. ORDER VARIABLES ALPHABETICALLY
           PRESS 'ENTER' FOR MAIN MENU


    ENTER AN OPTION NUMBER: 2

                    CHANGING CONSTRAINT

    LIST OF CONSTRAINT NAMES
            CON1  CON2  CON3  CON4  CON5
            CON6  CON7  CON8  CON9


    ENTER NAME OF CONSTRAINT YOU WANT CHANGED OR ENTER 'STOP'
    TO STOP. **

    TO CHANGE A CONSTRAINT NAME ENTER 'NAME'
    TO CHANGE A RIGHT HAND SIDE ENTER 'RHS'
    TO CHANGE A RELATION ENTER 'REL'
    TO CHANGE A COEFFICIENT ENTER THE NAME OF THE VARIABLE WHOSE
    COEFFICIENT IS TO BE CHANGED.
    TYPE 'STOP' TO STOP.
```

- *Constraint names* bring the computer input and results to life: It is easier to appreciate the shadow price of a specific product or service than it is to understand that of "variable 3." It is possible that a technocratic, insensitive geek can find meaning in this type of ill-defined, antiseptic nomenclature. A manager, however, probably would like the data to be as self-explanatory as possible.
- *Decision variable indexing* facilitates the comprehension of production scheduling, transportation, and assignment problems. Without indexing, interpreting the solution and postoptimality analysis of a moderate-sized problem requires a "directory" of decision variables. A manager, for example, must be able to quickly determine that the twenty-seventh decision variable (x_{27}) is really the number of units of product 3, manufactured by the second shift in the first month, for sale in the fifth month. In this problem, it would be far better to use an x_{ijkl} decision-variable formulation so that the combination of identifying features that truly describes the decision variable is explicit: x_{3215}.

A summary of problem clarity features of the three LP programs explored in this section is provided in Table 16-13.

TABLE 16-12

LINDO-PC Editing Menu for Linear-Programming Problems

```
@lindo
LINDO  (USF 24 JUNE 87)
:cat
```

6.PROBLEM EDITING COMMANDS

ALTER   USE "ALTER" TO EDIT THE CURRENT MODEL. THE FORMAT
          FOR THE COMMAND IS "ALTER row-id var-id". "row-id"
          IS THE ID OF THE ROW YOU WANT TO EDIT AND "var-id"
          IS THE NAME OF THE VARIABLE WHOSE COEFFICIENT YOU
          WANT TO CHANGE. LINDO WILL THEN PROMPT YOU FOR THE
          NEW VALUE. IF YOU WISH TO CHANGE THE RHS,
          DIRECTION, OR NAME OF A ROW USE A "var-id" OF
          EITHER "RHS", "DIR", OR "NAME".
            NOTES:
            - VALID DIRECTIONS FOR THE OBJECTIVE ARE "MAX" OR
             "MIN"; FOR ALL OTHER ROWS USE "<", "=", OR ">".
            - DO NOT TRY TO DELETE A ROW WITH "ALTER". USE
             "DELETE" INSTEAD.

EXT   PERMITS YOU TO ADD CONSTRAINT ROWS TO A PREVIOUSLY
          DEFINED MODEL. ENTER NEW ROWS AS YOU WOULD FOR
          "MAX" OR "MIN". DO NOT TYPE THE KEYWORDS "MAX",
          "MIN", OR "SUBJECT TO". NEW ROWS WILL BE APPENDED
          TO THE END OF THE MODEL. INDICATE END OF
          EXTENSIONS BY TYPING END.

DEL   TYPE "DELETE row-id" TO DELETE ROW "row-id" FROM
          THE CURRENT MODEL. YOU CANNOT DELETE THE
          OBJECTIVE.

SUB   TYPE "SUB var-id bound" TO ENTER OR CHANGE A SIMPLE
          UPPER BOUND FOR A VARIABLE, WHERE "var-id" IS A
          VARIABLE NAME AND "bound" IS A NUMERIC BOUND. FOR
          LARGE PROBLEMS, SUBS ARE MORE EFFICIENT FOR STATING
          CONSTRAINTS LIKE: X<10.

APPC   TYPE "APPC var-id" TO APPEND A NEW COLUMN TO THE
MODEL   WITH NAME "var-id". FOLLOW THIS WITH THE ROW AND
VALUE   SEPARATED BY A SPACE. END BY ENTERING A 0 FOR THE
ROW.   A COLUMN NAME OF "RHS" WILL CAUSE THE INPUT TO BE
          INTERPRETED AS A NEW RHS.

TABLE 16-13

Summary of Problem Clarity Features for Microsolve, STORM, and LINDO-PC Linear-Programming Models

LP Program	Problem Clarity
Microsolve	The user has no ability to provide names to either the constraints or the decision variables when using Microsolve. However, the 15 spaces provided for indexing decision variables are extremely helpful in explicitly formulating multiperiod-shift product-line problems.
STORM	STORM offers nearly the opposite features of Microsolve with respect to problem clarity features. The user can name both constraint and decision variables, but must use a default, single-subscript decision variable.
LINDO-PC	Decision variables can be given names of up to four characters; however, row (constraint) names are not possible in the PC version of LINDO.

LP File-Storage Flexibility

The ability to store a problem formulation and solution as data files for reuse is very important. The time required and accompanying aggravation commonly experienced in reformulating a particular problem every time it must be solved are conveniently averted. It is also useful to be able to store each problem as a text file, so that the formulation and solution can be downloaded into a page-layout or word-processing program for report generation. All three programs presented in this section provide these options with one exception: Microsolve will not save the problem as a text file.

16.5 | MARKOV ANALYSIS

The two programs examined in this section to illustrate the styles of use and kinds of capabilities of Markov analysis (MA) software are Quantitative Systems for Business (QSB) and Computer Models for Management Science (CMMS). The program features that the user-manager might look for in an MA package include those shown in Table 16-14. Some of the key features to be used to assess the desirability of any MA program are (1) *market-share analysis*, (2) *absorbing-state analysis*, (3) *editing capabilities*, and (4) *file-storage flexibility* (data and text formats).

TABLE 16-14

Markov Analysis Model Options of the QSB and CMMS Programs

	Software Package	
	CMMS	QSB
1. Spreadsheet format	no	yes
2. Number of states	25	50
3. Market-share options:		
3.1 Max no. forecast periods	25	32,000
3.2 nth period market shares	yes	yes
4. Steady-state probabilities	yes	yes
5. Mean first passage times	yes	yes
6. Expected recurrence times	yes	yes
7. Absorbing-state options:		
7.1 Fundamental matrix	yes	no
7.2 Mean time to absorption	yes	no
7.3 Conditional probabilities	yes	no
8. Printouts use file names	no	yes
9. User-defined state names	no	yes
10. No. char. avail for state names	2	6
11. Change/editing capabilities:		
11.1 Add states	no	yes
11.2 Delete states	yes	yes
11.3 Change initial market share	yes	yes
12. Store/retrieve data file	yes	yes
13. Store data as text file	yes	no
14. Host microcomputer	IBM	IBM
15. Approximate retail price	$30	$30

Markov Market-Share Analysis

The ability to forecast market shares for a specified number of time periods into the future is one of the most common uses of MA. The only information needed for any MA program to provide future market-share values is simply the present-period market-share distribution and the transition probability matrix. A market-share analysis of the Bloomingdale's accounts receivable study from Chapter 10 (Example 10.2) using QSB is shown in Table 16-15. The market-share process using CMMS is illustrated in Table 16-16. You may have noticed that CMMS does not print out all market shares across the two projected time periods; only the last—in this case, the second—future time period is calculated. The program must be rerun for each *specific* time period of interest for market-share values.

Markov Absorbing-State Analysis

It is increasingly important to use MA applications in helping to determine optimal maintenance policy procedures. Often, this type of analysis will require solving prob-

---

TABLE 16-15

Two-Period Market-Share Analysis for Bloomingdale's Accounts Receivable Using QSB Markov Analysis Software Program

```
                  MKV  Data  Entry  for  BDSARS

Please observe the following conventions when entering a problem:
(1) Respond to the questions that seek general information about a problem.
(2) Then enter the names of the states unless using defaults.
(3) Then enter the initial state probability vector, if known.
(4) Then enter the transition probability matrix.
(5) After you enter your data, press the ENTER key.
(6) On the same screen page, you may correct errors by pressing the BACKSPACE
key to move the cursor to the required position.
(7) When you are satisfied with the data on a page, press the SPACE BAR.
(8) When entering a problem, press the Esc key to go to a prvious page; press
the / key to go to the next page.

How many states are there in your problem: (Enter number ⁻ 50)  <3>
Do you know the initial state probability vector (Y/N) ?  <Y>
Do you want to use the default names of states (S1,...,Sn)  (Y/N) ?  <N>
Enter the Names of States using at most 6 characters (To use default names,
i.e., S1,...,Sn, press the ENTER key)
          States:
          1: <Π1   > 2: <Π2    > 3: <Π3    >
Enter the Initial State Probability Vector for BDSARS
              Π1:  .200  Π2:   .500  Π3:   .300
Enter the Transition Probability Matrix for BDSARS Pg 1
     From      To
     Π1        Π1: .900__  Π2: .100__  Π3:  .000__
     Π2        Π1: .130__  Π2: .720__  Π3:  .150__
     Π3        Π1: .020__  Π2: .110__  Π3:  .870__
_____
              Option  Menu  for  Solving  BDSARS
   When solving a problem, you can display every iteration of the Markov
process.  You may specify the number of iterations (< 32000); otherwise, the
program continues iterations until approximate steady state is found.  Steady
state is attained as the differences of probabilities of the same state
between consecutive periods are < 1.0E-6.
_____
Option
1 ---- Solve and display each iteration
2 ---- Solve and display the final iteration
3 ---- Solve without displaying any iteration
4 ---- Specify the maximum number of iterations
5 ---- Return to the function menu
_____
              Initial State Probabilities -- Iteration 0
              Π1:  .200  Π2:  .500  Π3:  .300
                State Probabilities -- Iteration 1
              Π1:  .251  Π2:  .413  Π3:  .336
                State Probabilities -- Iteration 2
              Π1:  .287  Π2:  .359  Π3:  .354
```

TABLE 16-16

Two-Period Market-Share Analysis for
Bloomingdale Department Store Accounts
Receivable Using CMMS Markov Analysis
Software Program

```
            **  INFORMATION ENTERED  **

        TOTAL NUMBER OF STATES  (1 TO 12)  ?3
        NUMBER OF ABSORBING STATES (0 TO 12)  ?0

                    PROBABILITIES.
                        ROW 1
        PROBABILITY FOR COL. 1 (0 TO 1)  ? .900
        PROBABILITY FOR COL. 2 (0 TO 1)  ? .100
        PROBABILITY FOR COL. 3 (0 TO 1)  ? .000

                        ROW 2
        PROBABILITY FOR COL. 1 (0 TO 1)  ? .130
        PROBABILITY FOR COL. 2 (0 TO 1)  ? .720
        PROBABILITY FOR COL. 3 (0 TO 1)  ? .150

                        ROW 3
        PROBABILITY FOR COL. 1 (0 TO 1)  ? .020
        PROBABILITY FOR COL. 2 (0 TO 1)  ? .110
        PROBABILITY FOR COL. 3 (0 TO 1)  ? .870

                        OPTIONS.
        MEAN FIRST PASSAGE TIMES  (1=YES, 2=NO)  ? 2
        EQUIL FIRST PASSAGE TIMES  (1=YES, 2=NO)  ? 2
        RECURRENCE TIMES           (1=YES, 2=NO)  ? 2
        MARKET SHARE ANALYSIS      (1=YES, 2=NO)  ? 1

                    MARKET SHARE
        FUTURE PERIOD (ANY NUMBER)   ? 2

        MARKET SHARE FOR STATE 1 (0 TO 1)  ? .200
        MARKET SHARE FOR STATE 2 (0 TO 1)  ? .500
        MARKET SHARE FOR STATE 3 (0 TO 1)  ? .300

              MARKET SHARE ANALYSIS

        START PERIOD:  1
        END PERIOD:  3

        MARKET SHARE IN PERIOD 3
            .287    .359     .354

              **  END OF ANALYSIS  **
```

lems with absorbing states. Of the two MA software packages examined in this section, only CMMS can provide this kind of information. The process used for generating absorbing-state analysis requires that the transition probability matrix be arranged in a particular format: The absorbing states must be moved to occupy the top rows of the transition probability matrix so that they form an identity matrix in the upper-left corner. The life expectancy of professional baseball players study (Chapter 10, Example 10.4) is solved using the CMMS program as shown in Table 16-17.

Markov Editing Capabilities

The ability to add or delete states, as well as to alter transition matrix probabilities, after the problem is formulated and saved is an important feature. One package—QSB—can conduct all three of these editing functions. The menu for modifying an MA problem is shown in Table 16-18.

Markov File-Storage Flexibility

Both CMMS and QSB can save problems as data files; only CMMS can also store the problem as a text file for downloading into a page-layout or word-processing program.

TABLE 16-17

Absorbing-State Calculations of the Life Expectancy of Professional Baseball Players Using the CMMS Markov Analysis Model

```
              TOTAL NUMBER OF STATES   (1 TO 12)  ?4
              NUMBER OF ABSORBING STATES  (0 TO 12)   ?2
                          PROBABILITIES.
                             ROW 1
              PROBABILITIES FOR COL. 1 (0 TO 1)  ? 1
              PROBABILITIES FOR COL. 2 (0 TO 1)  ? 0
              PROBABILITIES FOR COL. 3 (0 TO 1)  ? 0
              PROBABILITIES FOR COL. 4 (0 TO 1)  ? 0
                             ROW 2
              PROBABILITIES FOR COL. 1 (0 TO 1)  ? 0
              PROBABILITIES FOR COL. 2 (0 TO 1)  ? 1
              PROBABILITIES FOR COL. 3 (0 TO 1)  ? 0
              PROBABILITIES FOR COL. 4 (0 TO 1)  ? 0
                             ROW 3
              PROBABILITIES FOR COL. 1 (0 TO 1)  ? .6
              PROBABILITIES FOR COL. 2 (0 TO 1)  ? .2
              PROBABILITIES FOR COL. 3 (0 TO 1)  ? .1
              PROBABILITIES FOR COL. 4 (0 TO 1)  ? .1
                             ROW 4
              PROBABILITIES FOR COL. 1 (0 TO 1)  ? .1
              PROBABILITIES FOR COL. 2 (0 TO 1)  ? .8
              PROBABILITIES FOR COL. 3 (0 TO 1)  ? .05
              PROBABILITIES FOR COL. 4 (0 TO 1)  ? .05


                      ** INFORMATION ENTERED **

              TOTAL NUMBER OF STATES  : 4
              NUMBER OF ABSORBING STATES  : 2

                          TRANSITION TABLE
                             STATES
              1.000   .000   .000   .000
               .000  1.000   .000   .000
               .600   .200   .100   .100
               .100   .800   .050   .050

                          FUNDAMENTAL MATRIX
              STATES
              3    3.333   3.333
              4    1.667   6.667

                          TIME TO ABSORPTION
              STATES    TIME
              3         6.666
              4         8.334

                          CONDITIONAL PROBABILITES
              STATES
              3    .500   .500
              4    .500   .500
                      **  END OF ANALYSIS **
```

TABLE 16-18

QSB Option Menu for Modifying a Markov Analysis Problem

```
--------------------------------------------------------------------
                  Option Menu for Modifying BDSARS
--------------------------------------------------------------------


      Option
          1 ---- Modity the initial probability vector
          2 ---- Modify the transition probability matrix
          3 ---- Add one state
          4 ---- Delete one state
          5 ---- Display and/or print input data
          6 ---- Return to the function menu

--------------------------------------------------------------------
```

16.6 | PROJECT MANAGEMENT (PERT/CPM)

Project management (PM) models are the most widely purchased of all the management science software programs in business. The two project management programs examined in this section are MacProject and Quantitative Systems for Business (QSB). The activity capacity ranges from between 200 and 2000 activities. A detailed breakdown of the contents of each of these packages is shown in Table 16-19. The distinguishing features selected for examining this model are (1) *data-entry ease*, (2) *editing ease*, (3) *graphics*, (4) *user-defined activity identification capability*, and (5) *cost crashing*.

TABLE 16-19

Project Management Model Features of QSB, MacProject, and CMMS Programs

Features	Software Package		
	QSB	*MacProject*	*CMMS*
1. Data-entry format	spreadsheet	graphical	prompted
2. PERT *and* CPM offered	yes	CPM	yes
3. No. activities per project	200	2000	100
4. No. resources per project	1	50	1
5. No. resources per activity	1	6	1
6. User-defined branch names	yes	yes	no
7. Cost crashing	yes	no*	no
8. Step-by-step cost crashing	yes	no*	no
9. Graphics	no	yes	no
10. Simulation	no	no	no
11. $P(t \leq x) = ?$	yes	no	no
12. Printouts use file names	yes	yes	no
13. User-defined activity names	yes	yes	no
14. No. characters available for activity name	8	> 30	0
15. Change/editing capabilities:			
15.1 Change beginning node no.	yes	yes	yes
15.2 Change ending node no.	yes	yes	yes
15.3 Add activities	yes	yes	no
15.4 Delete activities	yes	yes	no
15.5 Change time estimates	yes	yes	yes
15.6 Change cost estimates	yes	yes	no
16. Store/retrieve data file	yes	yes	yes
17. Store data as text file	no	yes	yes
18. Host microcomputer	IBM	Macintosh	IBM/Apple II
19. Approximate sales price	$30	$125	$30

*Crashing can be accomplished by editing critical path times and cash flows; however, no automatic crashing option is available.

Project Management Data-Entry Format

Neither the spreadsheet data-entry format nor the prompted or batch-entry format is very helpful in providing the user with a good feel for the PERT/CPM problem structure. Fortunately, project management problems also lend themselves to graphical data entry (as was the case in the decision-tree section of this chapter). The three PM microcomputer programs illustrated in this section include one spreadsheet-oriented data entry model, QSB, one prompted/batch-entry model, CMMS, and a graphics-oriented data-entry package, MacProject. The data-entry process using the Broadway musical study (Chapter 13, Example 13.1) in these three software programs is shown in Table 16-20 for QSB, in Table 16-21 for CMMS, and in Figure 16-4 for MacProject.

The graphical data entry of the MacProject software program provides an immediate visual understanding of the interrelationship among activities that is impossible to obtain with the other two data-entry methods. Also notice that MacProject eliminates the need to establish dummy activities—this aspect of the analysis is performed automatically.

Project Management Editing Capabilities

There are a number of editing functions that are crucial to project management problems. These include the ability (1) to change beginning and ending node numbers, (2) to change activity time and cost estimates, and (3) to add and delete activities. The QSB PM model provides all these editing options, as does MacProject, although the latter program does not require that activities be numbered. Instead they are graphically introduced into the schedule, with earlier activities placed farther to the left than later activities. The CMMS program is limited to changing beginning and ending node num-

TABLE 16-20

Spreadsheet Data-Entry Screen for QSB PERT Model

PERT Entry for PLAY Page 1

Activity number	Activity name	Start node	End node	Optimistic Time	Most likely Time	Pessimistic Time
1	<FINANCE >	<1 >	<2 >	<2 >	<6 >	<10 >
2	<WRITER >	<2 >	<3 >	<1.5 >	<3 >	<10.5>
3	<DIRECTOR>	<3 >	<4 >	<2 >	<3 >	<10 >
4	<LEASE >	<1 >	<5 >	<4 >	<6 >	<8 >
5	<DUMMY #1>	<4 >	<5 >	<0 >	<0 >	<0 >
6	<AUDITION>	<5 >	<7 >	<1.5 >	<2 >	<2.5 >
7	<STAFF >	<4 >	<6 >	<2 >	<3 >	<4 >
8	<DUMMY #2>	<6 >	<7 >	<0 >	<0 >	<0 >
9	<REHEARSE>	<7 >	<9 >	<3 >	<3.5 >	<7 >
10	<COSTUME >	<6 >	<8 >	<4 >	<6 >	<8 >
11	<SET DSGN>	<6 >	<11 >	<5 >	<8 >	<11 >
12	<DUMMY #3>	<8 >	<11 >	<0 >	<0 >	<0 >
13	<SCRIPT >	<9 >	<11 >	<2 >	<3 >	<4 >
14	<CAST CHG>	<9 >	<10 >	<.5 >	<1.5 >	<5.5 >
15	<DUMMY #4>	<10 >	<11 >	<0 >	<0 >	<0 >
16	<DRESS >	<11 >	<12 >	<.5 >	<1 >	<1.5 >
17	<PROMO&AD>	<4 >	<12 >	<8.8 >	<10 >	<17.5>

```
        **   INFORMATION ENTERED   **

        17,3
        2,6,10,0
        1.5,3,10.5,1,1
        2,3,10,1,2
        4,6,8,1,1
        0,0,0,1,4
        1.5,2,2.5,1,5
        2,3,4,1,4
        0,0,0,1,7
        3,3.5,7,2,6,8
        4,6,8,1,7
        5,8,11,1,7
        0,0,0,1,10
        2,3,4,1,9
        .5,1.5,5.5,1,9
        0,0,0,1,14
        .5,1,1.5,4,11,12,13,15
        8.5,10,17.5,1,3
```

NOTE: EACH LINE OF THE *CMMS—* BATCH MOCE DATA
ENTRY PROCESS REPRESENTS THE OPTIMISTIC, MODAL, AND
PESSIMISTIC TIME ESTIMATES OF EACH PERT ACTIVITY
(SEPARATED BY COMMAS), FOLLOWED BY THE NUMBER OF
PREDECESSOR ACTIVITIES, AND THE ACTIVITY NUMBER OF
EACH PREDECESSOR ACTIVITY.

TABLE 16-21

PERT Batch Mode Data Entry of Broadway Musical Using CMMS Program

Note: Each line of the CMMS batch-mode data-entry process represents the optimistic, modal, and pessimistic time estimates of each PERT activity (separated by commas), followed by the number of predecessor activities, and the activity number of each predecessor activity.

FIGURE 16-4

PERT-CPM Data Entry for Broadway Musical Using MacProject

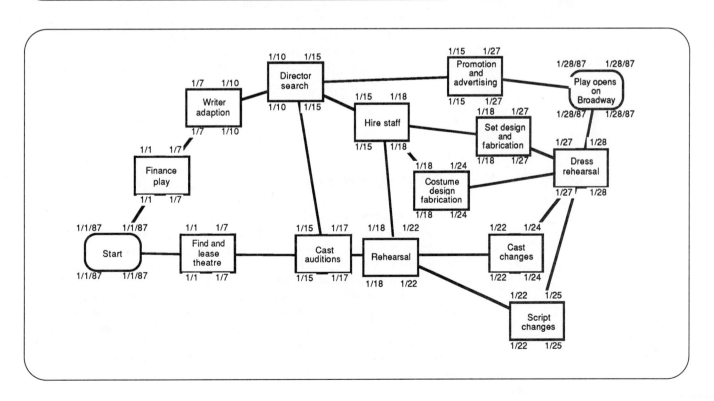

bers and activity time estimates. Although there is no stated limit to adding activities in CMMS, the program's need for chronologically ordered activities is disrupted when node numbers are changed. Since this will make it necessary to renumber the activities in the chart, in order to reestablish a chronological relationship among the branches, adding or deleting activities becomes impractical.

Project Management Graphics

It is helpful to be able to see the arrangement of the various activities of the project under study. Of the three models examined in this section, only MacProject has this important capability (Figure 16-4).

Project Management User-Defined Activity Identification

It is useful to be able to know the interrelationship of activities in a project. When a PM model does not have graphical capabilities, the ability to provide names for each activity is very useful: The knowledge that "activity A precedes activities B and C" does not provide the cognitive recognition that "questionnaire mailing" is preceded by "questionnaire design" and "questionnaire pilot testing." Of the two nongraphical models in this section, only QSB allows activity branch names.

Project Management Ability to Conduct Cost Crashing and to Determine the Probability of Completing a Project within a Given Duration

The interrelationships between project completion time and both project expense and the probability of finishing the project within a specific duration are vital measures of performance. These two options add significantly more power to project management software than when the user is given merely the early and late start and finish times, slack, and critical-path activity identifications. The only module of the three illustrated in this section that offers both cost-crashing and probability estimate options is QSB. Neither of the other two software programs offer either of these computational features.

16.7 INVENTORY MANAGEMENT SYSTEM (IMS)

Inventory management system (IMS) software are simpler and easy to use. Virtually none of the complexity that typifies such software as linear programming or decision-tree analysis is present. The user simply selects the type of IMS model he wishes to use and the appropriate input parameters (demand, lead time, holding cost, ordering costs, etc.), and he is off and running. That's it!

The two IMS software programs used in this section are Micro Manager and QSB. Some features of IMS software that are likely to be important to the user-manager are shown in Table 16-22. This section will concentrate on examining a subset of these features to illustrate how the user might contrast different IMS software package offerings. These selected features are (1) *data entry*, (2) *data editing*, and (3) *number of different EOQ and non-EOQ models offered* (production run, backorders, etc.).

TABLE 16-22

Inventory-Management-System Program Model Features for the QSB and CMMS Programs

| IMS Features | Software Package | |
	Micro Manager	QSB
1. Spreadsheet format	no	yes
2. Graphic display of results	no	yes
3. IMS models offered:		
3.1 Basic EOQ	yes	yes
3.2 EOQ with lead time	yes	yes
3.3 EOQ with backorders	yes	yes
3.4 EOQ with single production	yes	yes
3.5 EOQ with multiple production	no	no
3.6 EOQ with quantity discounts	yes	yes
3.7 EOQ with resource constraints	no	no
3.8 Lumpy demand	no	no
3.9 Simulation models	yes	no
4. Printouts use file names	no	yes
5. User-defined state names	no	yes
6. Char. avail for file names	no	6
7. Change/editing capabilities	yes	yes
8. Store/retrieve data file	yes	yes
9. Store data as text file	yes	no
10. Host microcomputer	IBM	IBM
11. Approximate retail price	$30	$30

IMS Data-Entry Process

The two programs selected for this section use the prompted data-entry format. (The spreadsheet data-entry format for IMS is unnecessary unless the problem deals with multiple-product-line information.) The Micro Manager data entry for the MUNI Transportation District of San Francisco study is given in Table 16-23. The QSB data entry for the Chicago Hyatt Regency table wine quantity-discount model (Chapter 12, Example 12.5) is illustrated next in Table 16-24.

IMS Data-Editing Options

The data-editing features of the Micro Manager and QSB programs are shown in Tables 16-25 and 16-26, respectively. The primary difference between the two editing options is that QSB uses a general menu, whereas the Micro Manager menu changes to reflect the input data used for a specific IMS model.

IMS Model Options

The two programs featured in this section offer a somewhat different menu of IMS models (although the majority of models are common to both software packages). The Micro Manager and QSB menus of IMS model options have already been shown in Tables 16-23 and 16-24, respectively (as well as earlier, in Table 16-22).

TABLE 16-23

**Micro Manager Basic EOQ Model
Data Entry for the MUNI Transportation
District of San Francisco**

```
<< PURPOSE >>

INVENTORY MODELS determines the economic order quantity (EOQ) (either
with or without shortage) and the optimum lot size.  The output will
present the order quantity (either with or without discount
situation), order frequency, reorder point, inventory cycle, total
inventory cost, and/or the maximum required inventory level.  For the
inventory problem with uncertain demand rates and leaad times, a
simulation program is presented in SIMULATION.


     Inventory Models
             1  Basic economic order quantity (EOQ) model
             2  Receipt model
             3  Economic lot-size (ELS) model
             4  Quantity discount model
             5  Inventory model with planned shortages
             6  Inventory model with safety stocks


     Enter a model number (1 to 6): 1


             Basic economic order quantity (EOQ) model
             Enter annual demand (units/year): 5000
             Enter annual working days (360 by default): 360
             Enter ordering cost ($/order): 250
             Enter holding cost ($/unit/year): 40
```

TABLE 16-24

**QSB Data-Engry Procedure for the
Chicago Hyatt Regency Table Wine
Quantity-Discount Model**

```
                   INVT Data Entry for CHRTW

Please observe the following conventions when entering a problem:
(1) The Esc key allows you to reenter data from the beginning.
(2) The / key allows you to reenter data for the previous question.
(3) To enter the default value, just press the ENTER key.

Select one of the options for entering your model:

1 -- Deterministic Economic Order Quantity (EOQ)
2 -- Deterministic discount analysis
3 -- Single-period probablistic demand problem
0 -- Return to the function menu

                 Discount analysis Data Entry for CHRTW

EOQ Input Data:
Demand per year (D) = 50000
Order or setup cost per order (Co) = 50
Holding cost per unit per year (Ch) = .55
Shortage cost per unit per year (Cs) = 4
Shortage cost per unit, independent of time (π) = 0
Replenishment or production rate per year (P) = 1
Lead time for a new order in year (LT) = 0
Unit cost (C) = 2.75

How many discount breaks do you want to analyze ? 2
Enter the discount breaks beginning with the first(lowest) price
level:
Discount break #1
Break quantity ? 5000
Discount (%) ? 5.45

Discount break #2
Break quantity ? 10000
Discount (%) ? 9.09
```

```
            ***** CHANGEABLE INPUT DATA *****


    Basic EOQ
        (1) Demand (annual) : units/year
        (2) Annual working days :360 (default)
        (3) Ordering cost : $/order
        (4) Holding cost : $/unit/year


        Enter number (1 to 4) you want to change: 1
        Current annual demand: 5000
        Enter new annual demand (units/year):   5300


        Do you wish to make another correction (YES/NO)?
```

TABLE 16-25

Micro Manager Inventory Management System Edit Menu (Demand Change)

```
                    Modify Inventory Data

    You may change one of the following inventory data:
        1  -- Demand
        2  -- Order or set-up cost
        3  -- Holding cost
        4  -- Shortage cost per unit time
        5  -- Shortage cost independent of time
        6  -- Replenishment or production rate
        7  -- Lead time
        8  -- Unit cost
        9  -- Selling price
        10 -- Salvage value
        11 -- Shortage cost (newsboy problem)
        12 -- Display and/or print data
        0  -- Return to the function menu


    Enter the option number ?
```

TABLE 16-26

QSB Inventory Management-System Edit Menu

16.8 QUEUEING ANALYSIS

Queueing analysis software is as simple to run as is the inventory-management system software discussed in the previous section. A general list of queueing model features is presented in Table 16-27 for the three software programs used in this section: Computer Models for Management Science (CMMS), Quantitative Systems for Business (QSB), and Microcomputer Models for Management Decision-Making (MMMDM). The particular features examined in this section are (1) *data-entry process*, (2) *data-editing process*, and (3) *selection of different queueing models*.

TABLE 16-27

Queueing Analysis Microcomputer Software
Features for the MMMDM, QSB, and CMMS Programs

Queueing Features	Software Packages MMMDM	CMMS	QSB
1. Cost analysis	no	yes	no
2. Graphic display of results	no	yes	no
3. Queueing models offered:			
3.1 $[M/M/1]:[\infty/\infty/FCFS]$	yes	yes	yes
3.2 $[M/M/1]:[N/\infty/FCFS]$	yes	yes	yes
3.3 $[M/M/1]:[\infty/N/FCFS]$	yes	yes	yes
3.4 $[M/M/1]:[\infty/\infty/G]$	yes	yes	no
3.5 $[M/G/1]:[\infty/\infty/G]$	no	no	yes
3.6 $[M/D/1]:[\infty/\infty/G]$	yes	yes	yes
3.7 $[M/E/1]:[\infty/\infty/G]$	no	no	no
3.8 $[M/M/c]:[\infty/\infty/G]$	no	no	yes
3.9 $[M/M/c]:[N/\infty/G]$	yes	yes	no
3.10 $[M/M/c]:[\infty/N/G]$	no	yes	yes
3.11 $[M/M/\infty]:[\infty/\infty/G]$	no	no	no
4. Printouts use file names	no	yes	yes
5. Char. avail. for file names	no		6
6. Change/editing capabilities	yes		yes
7. Store/retrieve data file	yes		yes
8. Store data as text file	yes		no
9. Host microcomputer	IBM	IBM	IBM
10. Special features	*		†
11. Approximate sales price	$30	$30	$30

* = MMMDM can analyze single servers with varying service rates.

† = QSB can analyze multiple servers with varying service rates.

Queueing Analysis Data-Entry Process

About the only type of nongraphic data-entry process used for queueing problems is the prompted or batch-input mode. Spreadsheet data entry is not necessary, since the input parameters do not necessarily lend themselves to a table format. The data-entry processes for CMMS, QSB, and MMMDM are shown in Tables 16-28, 16-29, and 16-30, respectively.

Queueing Analysis Data-Editing Options

The data-editing menus for CMMS, QSB, and MMMDM are shown in Tables 16-31, 16-32, and 16-33, respectively.

16.9 FORECASTING

The microcomputer forecasting software available, although not rare, is not as plentiful as many of the other software types. Further, most of the inexpensive software does not contain the more sophisticated forecast methods (e.g., Box–Jenkins). It is likely that,

```
        ** COMPUTER MODELS FOR MANAGEMENT SCIENCE **
    DATA ENTRY
            1.   SINGLE SERVER
            2.   SINGLE SERVER WITH FINITE QUEUE LENGTH
            3.   SINGLE SERVER WITH FINITE CALLING POPULATION
            4.   SINGLE SERVER WITH ARBITRARY SERVICE TIME DISTRIBUTION
            5.   MULTIPLE SERVER
            6.   MULTIPLE SERVER WITH FINITE QUEUE LENGTH
            7.   MULTIPLE SERVER WITH FINITE CALLING POPULATION


    ENTER A NUMBER FOR YOUR SELECTION FROM THIS MENU (1 TO 7) ? 7


    ARRIVAL RATE :
    SERVICE RATE:
    NUMBER OF SERVERS:
    PERFORM ECONOMIC ANALYSIS (1=YES, 2=NO) ? 1
    SERVICE COST RATE (ANY NUMBER) ?
    WAITING COST RATE (ANY NUMBER) ?
```

TABLE 16-28

CMMS Data-Entry Menu for Multiple Server, Finite-Population Queueing Model

```
                    QSM Model Entry Menu


    Please observe the following conventions when entering a problem:
    (1)  The Esc key allows you to reenter data from the beginning.
    (2)  The / key allows you to reenter data for the previous question.
    (3)  After entering data, the function menu allows you to modify data.

How many servers (up to 200) ? ____
Are all servers identical (Y/N) ? ____
Available distributions for service/interarrival time are:
  1 -- Exponential
  2 -- Erlang
  3 -- Uniform
  4 -- Normal
  5 -- Constant

What is the service time distribution (1-5) ? ____
What is the mean service time ? ____
How many queues (up to 20, default = 1) ? ____
What is the queue length limit (< 100, default =100) ? ____
Queue dispatching rules are:
  1 -- FIFO (First in First Out)
  2 -- LIFO (Last in First Out)
  3 -- Random

What is the dispatching rule (1-3) ? ____
What is the mean interarrival time in minutes ? ____
Available distributions for service/interarrival time are:
  1 -- Exponential
  2 -- Erlang
  3 -- Uniform
  4 -- Normal
  5 -- Constant
What is the interarrival time distribution (1-5) ? ____
```

TABLE 16-29

QSM Main Data-Entry Menu for Queueing Model

TABLE 16-30

MMMDM Data-Entry Menu for Multiple Server, Finite-Population Queueing Model

```
                    DATA ENTRY: GENERAL


QUEUING MODELS:
        (1) SINGLE SERVER
        (2) MULTIPLE SERVERS
        (3) SINGLE SERVER, VARIABLE SERVICE TIME
        (4) SINGLE SERVER, FINITE QUEUE LENGTH
        (5) SINGLE SERVER, FINITE POPULATION
        (6) MULTIPLE SERVER, FINITE POPULATION


WHICH MODEL (1-6) DO YOU WISH TO RUN ? 6


        *** MULTIPLE SERVER, FINITE POPULATION ***
   WHAT IS THE MEAN ARRIVAL RATE ?
   WHAT IS THE MEAN SERVICE RATE ?
   HOW MANY SERVERS ARE THERE ?
   WHAT IS THE SIZE OF THE POPULATION ?
   DO YOU WANT TO DO ECONOMIC ANALYSIS (Y/N) ?
   CALCULATE PROBABILITY OF n CUSTOMERS IN SYSTEM (Y/N) ?
   WHAT n DO YOU WANT TO USE ?
   DID YOU MAKE ANY MISTAKES (Y/N) ?
   WHICH LINE DO YOU WISH TO CHANGE ?
```

TABLE 16-31

CMMS Queueing Model Data-Editing Menu

```
           COMPUTER MODELS FOR MANAGEMENT SCIENCE

              -=*=-  DATA EDIT MENU  -=*=-


     1 = ARRIVAL RATE
     2 = SERVICE RATE
     3 = ADD ECONOMIC ANALYSIS
     4 = RETURN TO PROGRAM MENU


     ENTER A NUMBER FOR YOU SELECTION FROM THIS MENU  2


     ENTER SERVICE RATE
```

TABLE 16-32

QSB Queueing Model Data-Editing Menu

```
              Option Menu for Modifying a QSB Problem
     Option
          1 ---- Modify service time and distribution
          2 ---- Add one server
          3 ---- Delete one server
          4 ---- Modify queue limit and dispatching rule
          5 ---- Add one queue
          6 ---- Delete one queue
          7 ---- Modify interarrival time and distribution
          8 ---- Display and/or print input data
          9 ---- Return to the function menu
```

TABLE 16-33

MMMDM Queueing Model
Data-Editing Menu

```
                ******************
                *                *
                *  QUEUING THEORY *
                *                *
                ******************


        HERE IS WHAT YOU ENTERED:
                (1) SINGLE SERVER, FINITE POPULATION
                (2) MEAN ARRIVAL RATE = 1
                (3) MEAN SERVICE RATE = 4
                (4) POPULATION SIZE = 5


        DID YOU MAKE ANY MISTAKES (Y/N) ? Y
        WHICH LINE DO YOU WISH TO CHANGE (1 TO 4) ? 3
        WHAT IS THE MEAN SERVICE RATE ?
```

if you need to do a serious forecast, you will have to purchase a more specialized, higher-priced software product than those illustrated in this chapter.

The two forecast programs selected for this section are STORM and MMMDM. The general features that the potential user might consider when examining forecast software are illustrated in Table 16-34. The STORM data-entry screen using the Sun-

TABLE 16-34

STORM and MMMDM Forecasting Microcomputer Software Features

	Software Program	
Forecast Features	STORM	MMMDM
1. Graphic display of results	no	yes
2. Host computer	IBM	IBM
3. Forecast models offered:		
3.1 Simple moving average	no	yes
3.2 Weighted moving average	no	yes
3.3 Simple exponential	yes	yes
3.4 Trend exponential	yes	yes
3.5 Seasonal exponential	yes	no
3.6 Trend-seasonal exponential	yes	yes
3.7 Simple regression	no	yes
3.8 Multiple regression	no	no
3.9 Holt–Winters	no	no
3.10 Box–Jenkins	no	no
3.11 Optimal smoothing-constant search	yes	yes
4. Accuracy measurements offered:		
4.1 MAD	yes	yes
4.2 MAPE	yes	no
4.3 MSE	yes	yes
4.4 Tracking signal	no	yes
5. Printouts use file names	yes	no
6. Change/editing capabilities	yes	yes
7. Store/retrieve data file	yes	no
8. Store data as text file	yes	no
9. Approximate sales price	$30	$30

```
|------------------|STORM EDITOR : Forecasting Module|------------------|
|     Title:    FORECASTING SUNBELT AIRLINES TICKET SALES          |
|     Number of time series              :      1                 |
|     Maximal length of any series       :      12                |
|                                                                 |
|                                                                 |
|-----------------------------------------------------------------|
|                        SERIES    1        |                     |
|     DATA TYPE                    INT                            |
|     DATA RANGE                   POS                            |
|     SEASON LNG                   4                              |
|     MODEL VAL                    0                              |
|     PLAN HORIZ                   1                              |
|     LEVL ALPHA                   0.2                            |
|     TRND ALPHA                   0.2                            |
|     SEAS ALPHA                   0.2                            |
|     SEARCH  ?                    YES                            |
|     STEP SIZE                    0.1                            |
|     MODEL                        BEST                           |
|     PERIOD 1                     70000                          |
|     PERIOD 2                     60000                          |
|     PERIOD 3                     105000                         |
|     PERIOD 4                     100000                         |
|     PERIOD 5                     75000                          |
|     PERIOD 6                     75000                          |
|     PERIOD 7                     110000                         |
|     PERIOD 8                     105000                         |
|     PERIOD 9                     85000                          |
|     PERIOD 10                    75000                          |
|     PERIOD 11                    120000                         |
|     PERIOD 12                    125000                         |
|-----|  Enter the type of data (Integer/Real)      | -> |--------|
```

belt Airlines ticket sales study (Chapter 11, Example 11.1) is shown in Table 16-35. STORM also has the capability to enter up to four separate sets of historical data at a time, so more than one forecast can be conducted at once. Table 16-36 illustrates the MMMDM data entry for the same study using the program's exponential-smoothing model option.

16.10 MULTIPLE-MODULE MANAGEMENT SCIENCE

Management science microcomputer software specialty packages, such as those that address linear programming or project scheduling, have been readily available for the past 5 to 7 years. The prices for these packages typically range from several hundred to well over a thousand dollars. Recently, however, a number of inexpensive (less than $75), multiple-module management science microcomputer software packages have become available. The standard collection typically includes linear programming,

```
FORECASTING MODELS:

(1) MOVING AVERAGES
(2) EXPONENTIAL SMOOTHING
(3) REGRESSION ANALYSIS

WHICH MODEL (1-3) DO YOU WISH TO RUN? 2

                ****************************
                *                          *
                *   EXPONENTIAL SMOOTHING  *
                *                          *
                ****************************

HOW MANY PERIODS DO YOU HAVE (1-100) ? 12
ENTER ACTUAL VALUE FOR EACH PERIOD
            PERIOD       ACTUAL
            ------       ------
              1            70
              2            60
              3           105
              4           100
              5            75
              6            75
              7           110
              8           105
              9            85
             10            75
             11           120
             12           125

FORECAST FOR THE INITIAL PERIOD = 65
ALPHA (0<ALPHA<1) = .1
BETA (0<BETA<1) = .0

DID YOU MAKE ANY MISTAKES (Y/N) ? N

DO YOU WANT TO USE THE SEARCH OPTION TO FIND THE BEST
VALUE FOR ALPHA/OR BETA (Y/N) ?

ARE YOU DONE WITH THIS PROBLEM (Y/N) ?
```

PERT/CPM, queueing, inventory, and network models. It is now possible for users to have access to a wide array of management science products at a very low cost. Further, based on the exposure to these multiple-module products, the user can determine *from experience* which higher-power specialty packages, if any, would be useful to purchase.

Comparison of 10 Software Packages

The multiple-module software products reviewed, with few exceptions, are designed almost exclusively for the IBM PC and compatibles operating system (MS-DOS).[3] The software products illustrated in this section are *Micro Manager*, *Microsolve*, *Decision Support Modeling*, *STORM*, *Management Science and the Microcomputer*, *Microcomputer Software for Management Science and Operations Management*, *Computer Models for Management Science*, *Confidence Factor*, *Quantitative Systems for Business*, and *Microcomputer Models for Management Decision-Making*. The number and type of models that the different packages offer vary from four to well over 20 modules, as illustrated in Table 16-37. The information in this table focuses on the array of *features* offered by the individual packages; it does *not* address the design and operational

[3] A few of these packages also have versions designed for the Apple II microcomputer.

TABLE 16-37

Multiple Module Management Science Software Package Model Options

Models Included in Software	*1	2	3	4	5	6	7	8	9	10
Linear programming	•	•	•	•	•	•	•	•	•	•
Integer programming	•	•	•		•		•		•	
Transportation method	•	•		•	•	•	•		•	•
Assignment method	•	•	•	•	•	•	•		•	•
Network models										
Shortest route	•	•			•		•		•	•
Maximum flow	•	•			•		•		•	•
Minimum spanning tree	•	•			•		•		•	•
Nonlinear programming			•	•						
Goal programming	•		•							
Dynamic programming	•								•	
Markov analysis	•				•		•		•	
Decision trees	•		•				•	•		
MAUM								•		
Queueing analysis	•	•	•	•		•	•			•
Inventory control	•		•	•	•	•	•			
PERT/CPM	•		•	•	•	•	•	•		
Monte Carlo simulation	•				•	•			•	
Forecasting				•	•	•			•	•
Other models†	1,2	3	1,4,10	3,5–7	2	6,8,9	2		2	
Approximate unit cost	$35	$50	$39	$69	$35‡	$25	$35	$67‡	$30‡	$20
Required RAM	128K	128K	192K	256K	64K	64K	128K	128K	64K	64K
No. diskettes	2	1	3	2	1	1	1	2	2	1

*1–Lee & Shim, Micro Manager; **2**–Jensen, Microsolve; **3**–DSS, Decision Support Modeling (DSM); **4**–Flowers et al., STORM; **5**–Burns & Austin, Management Science Models and the Microcomputer (MSMM); **6**–Render & Stair, Microcomputer Software for Management Science and Operations Management (MSMSOM); **7**–Erikson & Hall, Computer Models for Management Science (CMMS); **8**–Simple Software, Confidence Factor; **9**–Chang & Sullivan, Quantitative Systems for Business (QSB); **10**–Dennis & Dennis, Microcomputer Models for Management Decision-Making (MMMDM).

†**1**–Break-even analysis; **2**–Decision-matrix analysis; **3**–Statistical techniques; **4**–Net-present-value (NPV) and internal-rate-of-return analysis (IRR); **5**–Facility layout; **6**–Assembly-line balancing; **7**–Production scheduling; **8**–Game theory; **9**–Aggregate planning; **10**–Materials resource planning (MRP).

‡The educational pricing policy for Confidence Factor is to charge an initial copy cost of $389 plus $50 per copy thereafter. For an average of 20 students per class, this would average $67/student copy (telecon with Fred Newman, 3-18-86). MSMSOM and QSB software are included *free* with purchase of Allyn-Bacon or Prentice-Hall MS texts, respectively.

"Emperor has no clothes—but selling them anyway to VaporSoft, MicroOz, Windware, and MegaMind."

quality of each. Some of these 10 packages include statistical as well as operations and production management models. Although details regarding these models are not included, a footnote in Table 16-37 provides additional information regarding these exclusions.

16.11 SUMMARY

There are hundreds of inexpensive management science microcomputer software products currently available. These products vary dramatically in the user-interface design and in the size and complexity of the problems they can solve, as well as in the speed of solution. The richness of the spectrum of software from which you can choose is more than adequate for sophisticated industrial-strength problems. There is no need to face the drudgery and mind-numbing experience of attempting to solve business analysis problems manually; appropriate management science programs are bountiful and inexpensive.

TABLE 16-38

Microcomputer Software Product Bibliography

Name of Software	Source	A	B	C	D	E	F	G	H	I	J	K	L
Actsim	Lake Ann Software												L
ALPAL	Kinko's Academic Courseware Exchange												L
AMPS	Micro Vision			C									
Arborist	Texas Instruments, Scientific Press	A											
Computer Models for Management Science	Prentice-Hall Publishing Company	A					F	G		I	J	K	
The Confidence Factor	Simple Software	A	B	C						I			
Crystal Ball	Marketing Engineering Corporation											K	
DATA	Tree Age Software	A											
Decision Analysis Techniques	Lionheart Press	A											
Decision-Analyst	Executive Software		B										
DecisionMap	Softstyle, Inc.		B										
DSM	Decision Systems Support									I	J	K	
Expert Choice	Decision Support Software, Inc.		B										
Extend	Imagine That, Inc.!												L
FLP	Bid and Awards, Inc.			C									
Lightyear	Lightyear		B										
LINDO/PC	The Scientific Press			C									
Logical Decision	Logical Decisions	A											
LP/80	Decision Science Software			C									
LP83	Sunset Software			C									
LP88	Easter Software Products			C									
MacProject	Apple Computer Corporation									I			
Management Science and the Microcomputer	Macmillan Publishing Company						F	G	H	I	J	K	
Micro Manager	Wm. C. Brown	A		C	D	E	F		H	I	J		
Micro-PASSIM	Walla Walla College												L
MicroBO	Stratix								H				
Microcomputer Models for Management Decision-Making	West Publishing Company							G					
Microcomputer Software for Management Science and Operations management	Allyn and Bacon Publishing Company							G	H	I	J	K	
MicroGANTT	Earth Data Corporation									I			
MicroManager	Micro Planning Software									I			
Microsolve	Holden-Day Publishing Company			C	D							K	
Microsolve/Goal Programming via Multiplex-1	Holden-Day Publishing Company					E							
MicroTSP	McGraw-Hill Publishing Company								H				
Milestone	Digital Marketing Corporation									I			
GPII/PC	Minuteman Software												L
MIP83	Sunset Software				D								
MP7-MIPROG	SCI Computing				D		F						
Mr. Quarter Master	RJL Systems										J		
PC Model	Simulation Software Systems												L
Primavera Project Planner	Primavera Systems, Inc.									I			
Quantitative Systems for Business	Prentice-Hall Publishing Company				D			G	H	I	J	K	
Siman	Systems Modeling Corporation												L
Simple 1,	Sierra Simulations and Software												L
Simscript II.5	CACI												L
Simulations	Actuarial Micro Software												L
Slam II	Pritsker and Associates												L
SmartForecasts	SmartSoftware, Inc.								H				
SOLON	Y. J. Stephanedes												L
STORM	Holden-Day Publishing Company								H	I	J	K	
Supertree	SDG Decision Systems	A											
Tutism	Applied												L
Xtrapolator	Stratix								H				

Key: **A** Decision Analysi **B** MAUM **C** Linear Programming **D** Integer Programming **E** Goal Programming **F** Network Programming
G Markov Analysis **H** Forecasting **I** Project management **J** Inventory management **K** Queueing **L** Monte Carlo

References

1. Assad, Arjang A., and Edward A. Wasil. "Microcomputers and the Teaching of Operations Research," *Computers and Operations Research* (January 1986).

2. Jensen, Paul A. "Microcomputers in the Instruction of Operations Research," *Inferfaces* 13 (No. 5: October 1983): 18–24.

3. Oberstone, Joelee. "A Comparison of Several Multiple Module Management Science Microcomputer Software Packages for Use in MBA Programs," *OR/MS Today*, ???.

4. Sharda, Ramesh. "Linear Programming on Microcomputers: A Survey," *Interfaces* 14 (No. 2: November–December 1984): 27–38.

5. Sharda, Ramesh. "A Summary of OR/MS Software on Microcomputers." Publication No. 85-8, College of Business Administration, Oklahoma State University, Stillwater, April 1985.

FUTURE VIEWS OF MANAGEMENT SCIENCE

INTRODUCTION

This book has presented a collection of some of the most important tools that management science can use in tackling complex business problems. All these tools have a shortcoming in common: They are aimed at *specific, well-defined* (or at least reasonably well-defined) problem settings. In reality, problems are rarely that neat. The scope of real problems is often so large that "optimal" or "best" decisions directed by one management science technique spill over into areas addressed by other management science techniques. In addition, the technical aspects of a complex problem are inextricably intertwined with other, disparate fields such as organizational behavior, finance, marketing, and strategy. Certainly, problems in these other fields cannot be approached optimally by solely technical methods, so what we typically end up with is a decision that manages a *portion* of a problem.[1] This shortcoming is certainly understandable: We simply do not have the means to respond rapidly to these multidisciplinary problems in a truly comprehensive way. At present, we must often settle for the expedience of patchwork, incremental approaches. How, then, does this inability to address complex, fuzzy problems comprehensively affect the stance managers will take in addressing complex problems in the future, and, additionally, what bearing will these factors have on the evolution of the *discipline* of management science?

It is my educated guess that the *methods* of management science are not likely to change dramatically during the next decade or, perhaps, much longer. However, epic changes are likely to occur in several areas at least superficially unrealted to methodology. These areas include: (1) the new user population—the broader variety of people able to use management science techniques and (2) the way in which management science will be incorporated within larger, more diverse problem solving apparatus.

1. **The population of users of management scientist methods is going to become continually more diverse.** The initial "practitioners" of management science were an elite core of physical scientists (primarily mathematicians and physicists) who developed and used operations research techniques in technical applications (e.g., military science and engineering). The application of management science methods to the social sciences, such as business, education, health care, and city planning

---

[1] It is even conceivable that this partial management may create a larger problem in terms of the overall system.

was relatively unexplored in the early years. Now, however, the methods of management science are even being used in the arts and humanities (e.g., theatre, film, and television). How did this expansion come about? The startling growth of the personal computer (microcomputer) industry and the incorporation of computers in education—even at the early grade school levels—has created a new generation of users who are comfortable with the use of computers and view them as essential (even fun) in performing their everyday work routines.

Tomorrow's manager will emerge from the new population of users. He or she will become more a director of data than a data generator and quantitative analyst. I also foresee a considerable need for new managers to be skilled in the manipulation of diverse data forms using micro or minicomputer systems that have sophisticated problem solving components.

2. **Management science methods will be incorporated within larger, more diverse problem solving apparatus.** If an organization is to be successful it must be able to make consistently good decisions in a tangled environment of ever-growing complexity. A company's ability to access, analyze, and interpret the specific market data that is crucial to its operations at any one time will make the difference between that company's going under, merely surviving, or prospering. To accomplish the increasingly difficult task of digesting huge amounts of varied forms of data, businesses will have to employ new methods of information management. Management science will be one of the many techniques that will be "built in to" an organization's *problem solving apparatus*. The complexity and heightened competition in each market will drive any company desiring long-term survival and growth toward highly accessible databases that can manage and manipulate multiple forms of data in an easy-to-use manner and that can provide the manager with near-immediate "what if?" and "what's best?" answers in numerous scenarios. *Expert systems* and *decision support systems* are two new approaches to managerial problem solving that hold promise for greater comprehensiveness.

Expert Systems

Imagine that you have a resident expert problem solver in your organization who is always there to trouble-shoot and solve difficult problems that are otherwise intractable. Now suppose that you have just been told some bad news: The expert has decided to leave the company—permanently—to live in New Zealand. Regardless of where she is going to live, her expertise will no longer be available to the company. What are you going to do? Possibly you would like to pick her brain or to have her run some intensive workshops so that she might impart a portion of her vast warehouse of diagnostic and problem solving knowledge. However, if her presentation is inappropriately organized and given without consideration of how to best "bottle" her knowledge for long-term use and reuse, the "transferred expertise" will quickly disappear. Sooner or later, the company's ability to manage similar problems requiring her type of expertise will diminish, and it will be lost without her. The ideal solution for the company would be to develop a *process* that rigorously captures the diagnostic, problem solving skills of its soon-to-be-departed resident expert. If the company could accomplish this significant task, it would have captured its expert's specific knowledge in the form of *artificial intelligence*. Further, if the company could then structure the knowledge into a medium more permanent than human memory—such as incorporating the diagnostic process

into a user-friendly computer program that would prompt, explain, and teach users—it would have transformed the knowledge into an *expert system*.[2]

An expert system (ES) can be viewed as consisting of two major parts: (1) the **user environment** and (2) the **developmental environment**.[3] The user environment is made up of the following components:

1. *The manager (user)*: Anyone wishing to solve a complex problem using the ES.

2. *User interface*: An ES relies on the user to provide it with the facts about the specific problem under investigation. A flexible ES must assume that many users are not capable of providing this information using highly technical data entry processes. If the manager is such a user, he or she must be able to talk with the ES using simple forms of communication such as *graphic displays* and *natural computer languages* that are closer to English than the oftentimes rigorous code required by most of the more traditional computer languages such as Pascal and C.

3. *Workplace*: The ES stores information concerning each new problem. The developmental environment components are:

   ■ *The knowledge engineer*: The person who collects, transforms, and simulates the skills of other experts, databases, books—any appropriate source—to a computerized software program.
   ■ *Knowledge base*: The collection of factual (database, algorithms, etc.) and informal knowledge (heuristics, rules, models, etc.) necessary to analyze and solve the problem in question.
   ■ *Inference engine*: The computer program that simulates the "expert's brain." This component provides the methodology for using, interpreting, reasoning, and explaining the hows and whys of the information in the knowledge base. The engine selects the specific information needed and organizes it into the appropriate sequence of steps needed for a solution.

   A generalized ES structure is shown in Figure EP-1.

As an example, suppose that you want to plan an ES that will help a manager to determine what kind of management science model to use in any given problem setting. A *spartan* depiction of how this ES might be constructed is represented by the following logic chart, which primarily focuses on the component dealing with resource allocation (Figure EP-2).

Of course, much greater detail must be developed for each component. Suppose, for example, that we wish to continue the resource allocation portion of this ES. More specifically, let's assume that the manager reaches the point where he or she knows that the situation requires the formulation of a linear programming problem. The following sequence represents one way to elicit the appropriate information:

Step 1. What is the goal, relative to your problem? What are you trying to achieve for your business or organization? Restate this goal as a single objective, for example, "maximize profits" or "minimize overall system operating costs."

Step 2. Use the single objective defined in step 1 to identify the *mix of goods or services* that the business uses to generate profits or that contribute to the system

---

[2]The complexity of this task is magnified since part of any problem solving process has qualitative or (worse yet) intuitive components. Unfortunately, these fuzzy elements must also be quantified so that anyone using the computer program is prompted in terms of operationally defined rules and variables.

[3]Efraim Turban, *Decision Support and Expert Systems: Managerial Perspectives*. New York: Macmillan Publishing Company, 1988.

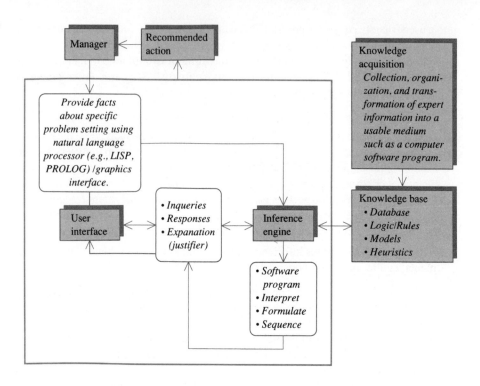

costs. For example, if your company sells automobiles, the product mix will be the combination of automobile models that are sold. This will include the identification of all characteristics that differentiate one product/model from another (e.g., [1] make—Buick, Cadillac, Oldsmobile, Toyota; [2] body style—four door sedan, two door, convertible; [3] exterior color—red, white, gray, silver, blue; [4] interior color—black, red, blue, brown, tan; [5] option packages—deluxe, sporty, basic). In addition, identify other relevant considerations: *when* the goods or services are to be provided, *by whom, where*, etc.[4]

Step 3. Use the information developed in step 2 to define the decision variable that represents the specific mix of goods or services that characterizes your operation. The decision variable is algebraically represented by $x_i, x_{ij} \ldots$, etc. If we continue with a simplified version of the car dealer example, x_{ij} can be the number of units of the ith make automobile of the jth exterior color purchased wholesale by the dealer for retail resale.

Step 4. What are the per unit contribution or consumption rates associated with each decision variable with respect to the organization's objective? Use this infor-

---

[4]Use a different letter of the alphabet to represent each of these differentiating characteristics. For example, if the company sells only white and black Buicks and Cadillacs, then the differentiating characteristics will be make and color, and the two letters will be, say i and j. These letters will represent the x_{ij} decision variable that defines the mix of goods or services that depicts the primary focus of the business; thus, x_{ij} is equal to the number of ith make cars (either Buick or Cadillac) of the jth color (either black or white) that are sold by the car agency.

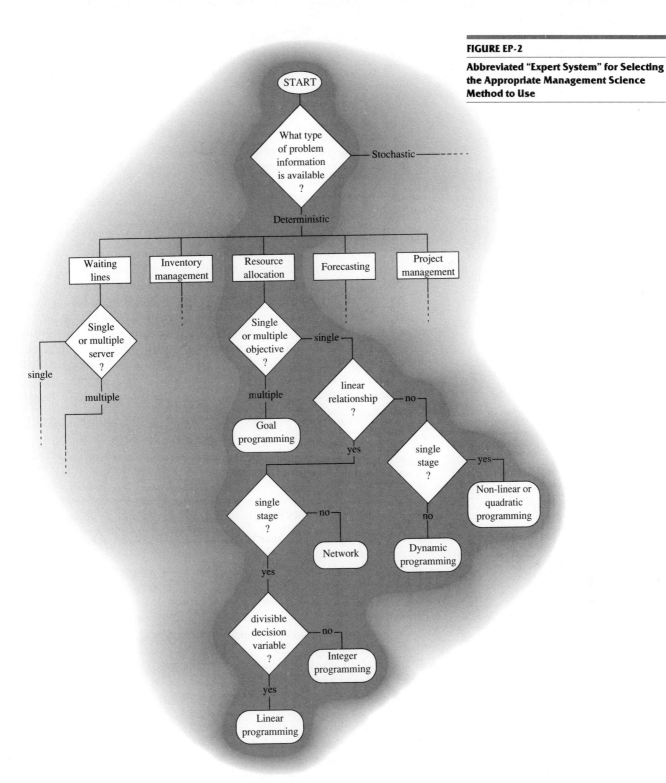

mation to construct the *objective function*. For example, suppose the dealer sells only Buicks ($i = 1$) and Cadillacs ($i = 2$) and that the only colors available for either make are black ($j = 1$) and white ($j = 2$). If the per unit profit margin is $3000 and $5000 for Buick and Cadillac, respectively, and if color has no influence on these figures, the objective function will be:

$$\text{Maximize profit, } Z = 3000x_{11} + 3000x_{12} + 5000x_{21} + 5000x_{22}$$

Step 5. What are the types and specific levels of limited (or scarce) resources that the business can use in reaching the optimal level of objective satisfaction? Identify the budget, salesperson hours, repair shop hours, floor space, minimum inventory requirements, manufacturer minimum and maximum purchase requirements, demand, and all policy constraints that the organization must observe. This information provides the *right-hand side* values of the constraint equations.

Step 6. For each limited resource listed in step 5, estimate the per unit contribution or consumption associated with each unit combination of decision variable. This information will define the *constraint coefficients* for each limited resource. For example, suppose the maximum budget for car purchases is $100,000. You must attempt to estimate accurately the per unit consumption of that budget for each combination of automobile purchased by the agency for resale. Suppose that the average agency cost for each Buick is $12,000 and for each Cadillac, $16,000. The *constraint equation* for the budget can now be developed:

$$12,000x_{11} + 12,000x_{12} + 16,000x_{21} + x_{22} \leq 100,000$$

The remainder of the process is illustrated in the flow chart of Figure EP-3. ESs will likely be developed as components of larger problem solving structures such as decision support systems.

Decision Support Systems

A decision support system (DSS) can be broadly viewed as a special kind of organizational survival kit that can help a manager to deal effectively with unscheduled, complex, unstructured problems crucial to the company's existence. A well-designed DSS has the ability to tackle problems much more complex than those more traditional, less comprehensive problem solving techniques—such as statistical or financial analysis—can encompass. Unfortunately, there has been little success in *generalizing* the process of DSS development, which has been limited thus far to large, lucrative industries such as airlines and pharmaceuticals.

A DSS typically consists of several key components: the database; the computer models; the computer hardware; and the user interface. It is important to make a few points particularly about databases and computer models.

Database   Every business collects various kinds of information that is used in its overall operation. These clusters of organized data—commonly referred to as *databases*—provide the company with strategic information regarding its product inventory, employees, competitors, and customers.[5] Each database is made up of numer-

---

[5]There may also be data that the company does not personally collect but, rather, purchases or subscribes to in the form of syndicated databases (e.g., unemployment rates, import and export information, industrial and stock market indicators, and foreign investments).

Start

Step 1. What is the goal of your problem? Restate this goal as a single objective such as maximize profits or minimize costs.

Step 2. What is the specific mix of goods or services that best describes your *do* business (e.g., what does your business that helps it to achieve profits?)
Describe how the goods or services (#2) are used to satisfy your objective (#1).
• optimal product mix
• blending
• production schedule
• etc, etc.

Step 3. Define the *decision variable* that represents the specific mix of good or services that characterize your business $x_{ij} \ldots m$ (e.g., x_{ijkl} is the number of units of the ith product stocked in the jth month for sale in the kth month at the 1th store).

Step 4. Describe the per unit rate of contribution (or consumption) for each decision variable in helping your business achieve its maximum profit or minimum cost. This is the *objective function.*

Step 5. Make a list of the kinds and amounts of each scarce resources that your business needs to operate (e.g., budget; labor hours for production, sales, assembly, and service; space; demand; minimum inventory; maximum availability; policy requirements, etc.). This will define the *RHS* values of each constraint.

Step 6. For a specific limited resource, determine the per unit rate of contribution (or consumption for each decision variable. This defines the *resource constraint coefficients.*

Step 7. Enter the objective function and all constraint equations into an appropriate LP software package. Solve for the optimal solution and conduct sensitivity analysis.

Step 8. Using the computer solution, determine the optimal objective function value along with (1) all binding constraints and (2) all slack (non-binding) constraints.

Step 9. Consider if it makes sense to reallocate resources from non-binding to binding constraints (i.e., would it be sensible to "cash in" excess resources to reallocate to more scarce resources?)

Step 10. Relax all but budget constraint. Rerun for "family" of budget values only (ignore all other constraints). These new runs will likely result in single product optimal solutions (de novo-type programming). Add in other resource constraints as deemed important to problem to see how additional resources influence product mix.

End

FIGURE EP-3

Formulating a Linear Programming Model

ous, unique pieces of information called *fields*. In the case of the customer database, the fields may provide the company with detailed information regarding which product(s) a specific customer purchases, how frequently these purchases are made, the purchase quantity, the location of the store or warehouse that provides the customer with the product(s), customer payment arrangement (e.g., credit or cash), and customer credit history (e.g., percentages of "pay on time," credit carried for 30–60 days, 60–90 days, the greater than 90 days). A product inventory database will likely consist of fields such as those describing each product and each product component by a part number, weekly-monthly-quarterly demand by region or by the store or warehouse that distributes the product, product pricing, and product discount quantity policy.

There are several important considerations regarding the design characteristics of a database. These include:

1. A database must be capable of sharing information with other databases.[6] The kinds of databases that can be integrated to share information are called *relational databases*. The following example illustrates the importance of relational databases:

> A company wishes to estimate the optimal inventory level of its numerous products in each of its 7 regional distribution centers. The demand for each product found in the inventory database is linked with the customer demand for the different products by region. This linkage of the product inventory and customer databases helps the company to match the regional demand with the amount of inventory to carry in each regional distribution center.

> In actual use, the relational design will make the boundaries between the multiple databases appear *seamless* so that during the operation of the DSS, the manager will feel that there is only one database. For this reason, DSSs typically refer to a *database*, not databases.

2. There should be as little *redundancy* in the database as possible. This will allow for simplified data entry, minimal data storage space, rapid data retrieval times, and a simplified data editing process.[7] As an example, if the pricing of a specific product is regionally sensitive, this information can be carried in specific fields of the product inventory portion of the database *exclusively*, not carried also as a field in the customer database component.

3. The database must be *independent* of both the computer software programs (and languages) that use it and the computer hardware being used to run the DSS. To put it another way, the database must not "care" if it is being accessed by a VAX mainframe using machine code language or a Macintosh microcomputer using LISP. Further, the database is unaware if the data are being gathered for use in a forecasting, financial analysis, or multiple regression software program. The information in the database is unrestrictedly "there" for use in any way by any program and host computer environment that the manager is using.

Computer Models The computer models of the DSS are used to create, modify, and manipulate the database. The models are *transparent* to the manager to the degree that he or she does not have to be aware of the language or the operational intricacies of each model. It is essential, however, that the manager/user interface with the models be extremely "friendly," and that these models have the ability to prompt and provide "why," "what if," and "what's best" information, along with assistance and coaching when needed. An illustration of a "typical" DSS is shown in Figure Epilogue-4.

---

[6]For example, there may be an important interrelationship between the current success of, say, a high-quality ice cream manufacturer, recent shifts in public opinion regarding foods containing high cholesterol and hydrogenated fats, and a competitor's introduction of a new, nondairy, low-fat, no cholesterol chocolate fudge ice cream product. If the ice cream manufacturer sends mailers to its customers that elicit the likelihood of their giving up ice cream in favor of another product such as the competitor's, and the response is positive, it may be a good idea for the manufacturer to introduce a new healthy ice cream substitute product also.

[7]Even though databases are relational and changes in a particular field will result in near-simultaneous changes in any other identical field, carrying these redundant pieces of information requires additional (and unnecessary) storage space.

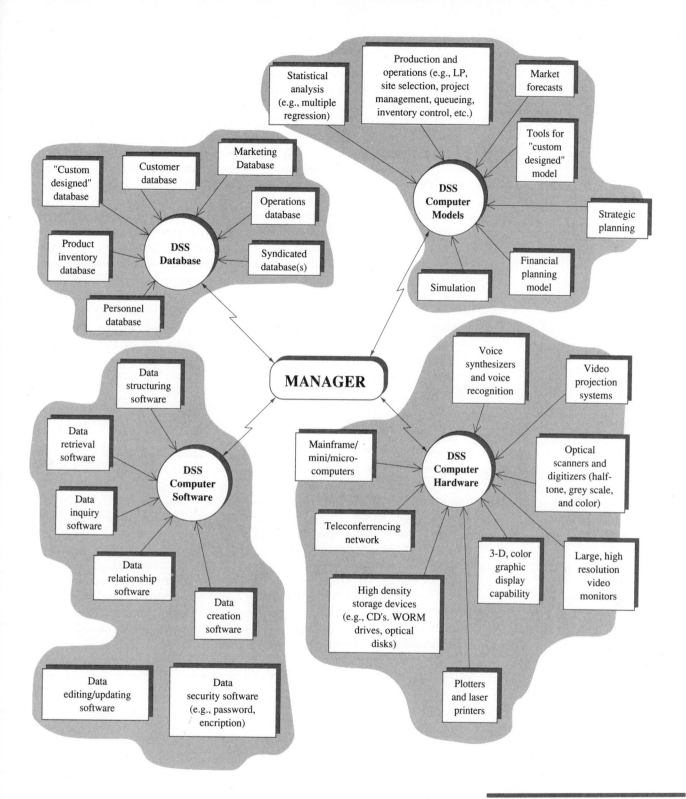

FIGURE EP-4

Typical Decision Support System for Business and Management

SUMMARY

Management science will develop in at least two important directions: (1) the profile of the people who use management science methods will become more variegated and (2) the field itself will likely be taken in under the umbrella of larger, more sophisticated problem solving systems. Although decision support and expert systems hold considerable promise, to date the development and generalizability of such complex systems have been limited to highly specialized, immense industries such as pharmaceuticals and airlines. These "success stories" are rare exceptions. Reports of the present ability to apply these systems in a consistently successful way are more a reflection of wishful thinking than of reality. It is unlikely that any but organizations that are well financed and highly committed toward managing ongoing change will ever be able to afford, develop, and implement a decision support or expert system.

That there has been limited success in operationalizing DSSs and ESs is likely closely related to the "weak link" of almost all management science problem solving efforts: the inability to *implement*.[8] When even the most specialized of management science methods fail, it is usually because of the inability of an organization to implement, to get the department or other structural element of the organization affected by the problem to accept and incorporate the changes necessary to the solution of the problem. Certainly it is even more difficult if the system to be implemented is so highly sophisticated that it affects disparate, often competitive areas within an organization. However, therein lies the potential "trump card" for these more complex systems. DSSs and ESs have the potential to manage problems that cannot be viewed as neatly contained within the confines of a single department, problems that spill over and threaten the very existence of an entire organization, problems in other words, that put all departments at risk.

Moreover, in the future the term *risk* will take on a new meaning: Few markets will support more than two or three serious competitors. Missed opportunities or delays in responses to problems today could mean that an organization will not be a viable competitor tomorrow. DSSs and ESs have the potential to *unite* an entire organization's problem solving efforts. They alone can provide tools comprehensive enough to cope with the intimidating dilemmas threatening an organization's vitality.

In the past, implementation of quantitative problem solving methods has largely been left to the technical personnel developing these approaches. Management scientists as a group are not highly skilled at working with the nontechnical people who are typically the end-users of their efforts. This is a crucial problem often overlooked by the post mortem critics of failed implementation projects. In the future, organizations will typically go outside the quantitative analysis arena to embrace only skilled human/ organization behavior professionals who can expertly facilitate the kind of sweeping organizational changes demanded by DSSs and ESs. Only then will there be a dramatic increase in the probability of getting one of these systems up and running within an organization.

---

[8]Failure at implementation occurs, in my opinion, because of two highly related components: (1) The technique suggested is not appreciated as a workable replacement for the method currently being used (which may include the well-known "method by omission"), and (2) the people responsible for implementing the new approach are not sufficiently skilled at personal communication and interaction.

References

1. Assad, Arjang A., and Bruce L. Golden, "Expert Systems, Microcomputers, and Operations Research." *Computers & Operations Research* 13 (Nos. 2–3 1986): 303.

2. Brown, D. C. "The Anatomy of a Decision Support System." *Business Marketing* (June 1985).

3. Class, R. L. "A DSS for Airline Management." *Data Base* (Winter 1977).

4. Harmon, Paul, Rex Maus, and Wm. Morrissey. *Expert Systems: Tools & Applications*. New York, John Wiley, 1988.

5. Holsapple, Clyde W., and Andrew B. Whinston. *Business Expert Systems*. Homewood, Ill.: Richard D. Irwin, 1987.

6. Rauch-Hindin, Wendy B. *A Guide to Artificial Intelligence: Fundamentals and Real-World Applications*. Englewood Cliffs, NJ: Prentice-Hall, 1986.

7. Rauch-Hindin, Wendy B. *Artificial Intelligence in Business, Science, and Industry*, Vols. I and II. Englewood Cliffs, NJ: Prentice-Hall, 1986.

8. Sprague, R. H., Jr. "A Framework for the Development of Decision Support Systems." *M.I.S. Quarterly*, December 1980.

9. Sprague, R. H., Jr., and E. D. Carlson. *Building Effective Decision Support Systems*. Englewood Cliffs, NJ: Prentice-Hall, 1982.

10. Sprague, R. H., Jr., and H. J. Watson, eds. *Decision Support Systems: Putting Theory into Practice*. Englewood Cliffs, NJ: Prentice-Hall, 1986.

11. Turban, E. *Decision Support Systems and Expert Systems*. New York: Macmillan, 1988.

12. Waterman, Donald A. *A Guide to Expert Systems*. Reading, Mass.: Addison-Wesley, 1986.

BASIC PROBABILITY CONCEPTS

|A.1| INTRODUCTION

An appreciation for probability relationships is inescapably tied to an understanding of decision analysis. Yet, different people interpret English assertions including reference to the notion of probability in vastly different ways (Table A-1). We need to grasp what

TABLE A-1

Interpreting Probability Phrases (Arranged in Order of Median Percentage)

Probability Phrases	Specific Interpretation (in Percent)				
	Lowest	Lower Quartile	Median	Upper Quartile	Highest
1. There is no probability, no serious probability that	0	1	3	5	40
2. It is very improbable that	1	5	9	10	80*
3. It is very unlikely that	1	5	10	12	30
4. It is quite unlikely that	1	7	10	15	35
5. There is little chance that	2	10	12	20	49
6. There is a slight chance that	2	10	15	20	54
7. The possibility is low that	3	15	20	24	45
8. It is unlikely that	4	18	20	29	45
9. It is improbable that	4	12	22	30	82
10. The probability of . . . is relatively constrained.	5	20	27	35	65
11. There is a possibility that	5	25	35	45	70
12. There is a chance that	1	26	35	50	70
13. The chances are better than even that	51	57	60	60	87
14. It is likely that	40	65	70	79	95
15. There is a good chance that	30	65	71	75	90
16. It is probable that	20	61	73	80	98
17. There is a much better than even chance that	55	70	74	78	92
18. They will probably	50	65	75	78	95
19. There is a high probability that	40	80	85	90	98
20. There is a high likelihood that	60	80	85	90	97
21. The probability of . . . is very high.	71	85	90	95	100

*Eighty percent may seem like an absurd interpretation of "It is very improbable that . . ." This phrase, however, seems to be particularly ambiguous. Responses included 80, 70, 55, and 35 percent.

Source: Robert D. Behn and James W. Vaupel, *Quick Analysis for Busy Decision Makers* (New York: Basic Books, 1982), 76.

is meant by *probability* if we are to make intelligent selections among different strategies. A manager who cannot volunteer compelling reasons for her choices will have neither a credible reputation nor, correspondingly, a productive track record. In a given instance of decision making, any manager can be lucky. Even when we overlook important considerations, it is not impossible that we will make a *good decision* in that the outcome is desirable—such as a successful product launching or a terrific investment. No manager, however, is consistently lucky. It takes considerable skill and understanding of the decision setting to accumulate an impressive batting average over the long haul.

The probability that a particular strategy will be successful or not is one of the primary considerations that a manager must include in considering whether to choose that option. Expensive forecasts are commonly conducted to help the manager dispel the uncertainty clouding this final outcome. The ability to understand the probabilities surrounding the events intrinsically tied to each decision setting is one of the most important keys to making consistently good decisions. It is therefore essential for managers to have a working knowledge of the basic concepts of probability.

A.2 CONCEPTS OF PROBABILITY

It is traditional to introduce the concepts of probability with examples such as:

- What are your chances of drawing a jack of diamonds from a standard deck of 52 cards?
- What is the likelihood of drawing a face card and a red card in two simultaneous card selections?
- What would you say your chances are of rolling a 10 on a fair set of dice?
- What is the probability of drawing a red marble when you randomly select from one of two opaque urns: one urn contains 70 percent red marbles and 30 percent white marbles; the other urn holds 25 percent red marbles and 75 percent white marbles?

In this appendix, we will instead use business-related situations to introduce the basic relationships of probability in the hope that learning these concepts will be more interesting and simpler. We begin with an examination of the Manufacturers and Developers of Microcomputer Products (MADOMP), a collection of chief executive officers (CEOs) of companies that specialize in the production of hardware and software products for microcomputers.

TABLE A-2

Membership of Manufacturers and Developers of Microcomputer Products (MADOMP)

	Managers	Engineers	
Hardware developers	30	20	*50*
Software developers	70	30	*100*
	100	*50*	*150 Totals*

EXAMPLE A.1 MANUFACTURERS AND DEVELOPERS OF MICROCOMPUTER PRODUCTS

A professional society membership is made up entirely of women from a variety of microcomputer hardware and software developers. Both the hardware and software developer groups are divided into two subgroups: managers and engineers. The society meets several times per year to establish operating and design standards for their industry. In May of each year, the hardware and software developers meet separately in their two groups, followed in October by a joint meeting of both groups. The exact composition of this group is illustrated in Table A-2. The following definition of probability

terms describe the different combinations of MADOMP member attributes (i.e., manager, engineer, hardware, software):

$P(B_1)$: Probability that the member is a hardware developer

$P(B_2)$: Probability that the member is a software developer

$P(M)$: Probability that the member is a manager

$P(M_1)$: Probability that the member is a manager hardware developer

$P(M_2)$: Probability that the member is a manager software developer

$P(F)$: Probability that the member is an engineer

$P(F_1)$: Probability that the member is an engineer hardware developer

$P(F_2)$: Probability that the member is an engineer software developer

We shall continue this example in a moment.

A.3 PROBABILITY BASICS: SAMPLE SPACES, UNIONS, AND INTERSECTIONS

There are basic terminology and properties used to describe probability relationships that are essential for the manager to grasp. A collection of these points are discussed next.

EXAMPLE A.2   MADOMP CONTINUED

SAMPLE SPACE

A sample space (S) is a visual presentation of all of the possible events (E_i) that could occur in a particular situation. It is assumed that the different events comprising the sample space are mutually exclusive and collectively exhaustive. The probability of any specific event occurring is given by

$$P(E_i) = \frac{\text{number of ways in which } E_i \text{ can occur}}{\text{number of events in } S}$$

The probability of randomly selecting a member of MADOMP from the hardware group is

$$P(B_i) = \frac{\text{total number of hardware developer members}}{\text{total membership in MADOMP}}$$

$$P(B_i) = \frac{50}{150} = .33$$

Venn diagrams are commonly used to illustrate a sample space. Figure A-1 illustrates the Venn diagram for the MADOMP example.

The probability of occurrence of any event in the sample space must have a value between 0 and 1.0. This requirement is expressed as

$$0 \le P(E_i) \le 1 \quad \text{for all } j$$

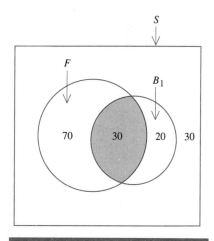

FIGURE A-1

Sample Space (Venn Diagram) for MADOMP Membership

Thus, if the occurrence of an event is impossible, the probability of that event will be 0. If the event is certain to occur, the associated probability is 1.0. Events typically have neither of these extreme probability values.

The sum of all the likelihoods of occurrence associated with each event in the sample space is 1.0. So,

$$\sum_{j=1}^{n} P(E_j) = 1$$

Therefore, the sum of the individual probabilities of selection of each member of MADOMP must be equal to 1.0.

The *compliment* of any event, E_i, is E_i'. As an example, the probability of a engineer being randomly selected from MADOMP is $P(F)$, whereas the probability of a engineer *not* being selected (i.e., a manager being selected) is $P(F')$, the compliment of $P(F)$. The general relationship is given by

$$P(E_i) + P(E_i') = 1$$

or by

$$P(E_i') = 1 - P(E_i)$$

The most common types of events that occur in business settings are *compound events*. Such events typically take place in one of two ways in the sample space: unions and intersections.

UNION

The chance that either or both events E_i and E_j will occur is called the *union* of E_i and E_j. This union is represented by the probability notation $P(E_i \ E_j)$. The probability of *mutually exclusive (independent) events* occurring in this way, called the *rule of addition* or the *additive law of probability*, is represented by the following relationship:

$$P(E_1 \cup E_2 \cup \cdots \cup E_n) = P(E_1 \text{ or } E_2 \text{ or } \ldots \text{ or } E_n)$$
$$= P(E_1) + P(E_2) + \cdots + P(E_n)$$
$$= \sum_{i=1}^{n} P(E_i)$$

For two *mutually exclusive independent events*, E_1 and E_2, the additive law is

$$P(E_1 \cup E_2) = P(E_1) + P(E_2)$$

For two *dependent events*, E_1 and E_2, the additive law is

$$P(E_1 \cup E_2) = P(E_1) + P(E_2) - P(E_1) \cdot P(E_2)$$

The second right-hand-side term, $P(E_1) \cdot P(E_2)$, can also be expressed as $P(E_i \cup E_j)$; that is,

$$P(E_1 \cup E_2) = P(E_1) + P(E_2) - P(E_i \cup E_j)$$

We'll discuss independent probability calculations in greater detail later in this appendix.

INTERSECTION

The intersection of events E_i and E_j is the event that both E_i and E_j will occur and is given by $E_i \cup E_j$. The general expression for the probability that any number of *independent events* can occur is the *multiplication rule*, given by

$$P(E_1 \cup E_2) \quad \cdots \quad E_n) = P(E_1) \text{ and } E_2 \text{ and } \ldots \text{ and } E_n)$$
$$= P(E_1) \cdot P(E_2) \cdot \cdots \cdot P(E_n)$$

The relationships we have discussed are basic tenants of probability. In the following sections, we'll examine more specific applications that incorporate these rules.

A.4 COUNTING WITHOUT COUNTING: PERMUTATIONS AND COMBINATIONS

Sometimes, it is helpful to be able to determine the number of possibilities associated with the selection of some members of a sample in a particular order or arrangement. In particular, let's look at two useful counting formulas: permutations and combinations.

Permutations define how many different sequences of r objects can be formed when the objects are sampled from a set of n objects, and if each r object is not used more than once. The relationship for calculating this number is

$$P_r^n = \frac{n!}{(n-r)!}$$

Suppose that MADOMP is having new elections for the office of president and vice president at their joint meeting in October this year. According to the election rules, the three members from each of the hardware and software groups that received the most votes at the preliminary elections held in May will be eligible to be in the final runoff. How many different combinations of president and vice president are possible? Assume that the two candidates with the most votes will be appointed president and vice president.

For $r = 2$ and $n = 6$,

$$P_2^6 = \frac{6!}{(6-2)!} = \frac{6!}{4!} = 6 \cdot 5 = 30$$

So, there are 30 different possible combinations of president and vice president from the six finalist candidates.

Combinations examine the number of different ways in which the same set of r objects can be selected from a set of n objects *without regard to sequence*. The factorial relationship for calculating this combination is

$$C_r^n = \frac{P_r^n}{r!} = \frac{n!}{r!(n-r)!}$$

How many different "people" combinations of president and vice president are possible? Assume we have no interest in identifying which of the two people selected is president and which is vice president—we want to know the number of different combinations of the two top vote getters. The number of combinations is

$$C_2^6 = \frac{6!}{2!(6-2)!} = \frac{6!}{2!4!} = \frac{6 \cdot 5}{2} = 15$$

A.5 | MARGINAL PROBABILITIES

The marginal probability of an event is simply the chance that a specific single event will occur. For the MADOMP example, the probability of randomly selecting a person out of the total membership who is a software developer, $P(B_2)$, is 100/150 or .67. Another example of a marginal probability can be represented by the likelihood of randomly selecting someone out of the hardware developer group who is an engineer, $P(F_1)$. This probability is represented by the number of engineers out of the total membership in the hardware developer group: 20/50, or .40.

A.6 | CONDITIONAL PROBABILITIES

A *conditional probability* is the chance that an event will occur, *given* some earlier event that has already taken place. So, the expression for the probability of selecting an engineer software developer from the general membership, given that an engineer hardware developer was previously selected, is $P(F_2/F_1)$. As we shall see, however, it is crucial for the manager to know whether the earlier selection influences the chances of the later selection (*statistically dependent events*) or does not (*statistically independent events*). We'll discuss the relationships for conditional probabilities under statistical dependence and independence next.

Statistically Independent Conditional Probabilities

The conditional probability of an event (E_i) occurring when that event has been preceded by an earlier independent event (E_j) is given by

$$P(E_i/E_j) = P(E_i)$$

Examples of a statistically independent conditional probability include

1. The probability that an engineer will be selected from the software group $P(F_2)$ after an engineer hardware developer $P(F_1)$ was initially selected, which is given by the expression

$$P(F_2/F_1) = P(F_2)$$
$$= 30/100$$
$$= .30$$

The earlier selection of an engineer hardware developer in no way influences the chances of an engineer from the software group being selected on the second selection.

2. The probability that a manager $P(M_1)$ will be selected from the hardware group after the initial selection of an engineer software member $P(F_2)$, given by

$$P(M_1/F_2) = P(M_1)$$
$$= 30/50$$
$$= .60$$

Statistically Dependent Conditional Probabilities

The conditional probability of an event (E_i) occurring when it has been preceded by an earlier independent event (E_j) is given by

$$P(E_i/E_j) = P(E_i \text{ and } E_j)/P(E_j)$$

Given that an engineer is selected, the chance that she is a software developer is

$$
\begin{aligned}
P(F_2/F) &= P(F \text{ and } F_2)/P(F) \\
&= P(F) \cdot P(F_2)/[P(F) \cdot P(F_1/F) + P(F) \cdot P(F_2/F)] \\
&= (60/150) \cdot (30/50)/[(60/150) \cdot (20/50) + (60/150) \cdot (30/50)] \\
&= (.40)(.60)/[(.40)(.40) + (.40)(.60)] \\
&= .24/[.16 + .24] \\
&= .24/.40 \\
&= .60
\end{aligned}
$$

It is important to understand the meaning of an expression of conditional probability. The concept is tricky and *very* important:

- The numerator represents the probability of selecting an engineer software developer.

- The denominator represents *all* the ways in which an engineer could have been selected—the probability of selecting an engineer hardware developer as well as the probability of selecting an engineer software developer.

- The ratio of numerator to denominator is, then, the fraction of times the selected engineer is a software developer compared to all the ways in which an engineer can be selected (i.e., the probability of selecting an engineer software developer *given* the person selected was an engineer).

A.7 JOINT PROBABILITIES

A joint probability of two or more events is the likelihood that these events will occur either simultaneously or in rapid succession. It is important, however, to know whether the occurrence of one event influences that of the other (*statistically dependent events*) or not (*statistically independent events*). We'll examine the relationships for joint probabilities under statistical dependence and independence next.

Statistically Independent Joint Probabilities

The joint probability of the occurrence of two *independent* events is represented by

$$P(E_i \text{ and } E_j) = P(E_i) \cdot P(E_j)$$

An equivalent Boolean algebra form of $P(E_i \text{ and } E_j)$ is $P(E_i \quad E_j)$—discussed earlier as the *intersection* of two events—can also be used. So, the chances that an engineer will

be drawn out of the hardware developer group and a manager drawn out of the software developer group is

$$P(F_1 \text{ and } M_2) = P(F_1) \cdot P(M_2)$$
$$= (20/50) \cdot (70/100)$$
$$= .28$$

These two events are statistically independent, because the selection of either event in no way influences the opportunity for selection of the other event.

Statistically Dependent Joint Probabilities

The joint probability of two *dependent* events occurring is given by

$$P(E_1 \text{ and } E_2) = P(E_1) \cdot P(E_2/E_1)$$

So, the chance that an engineer hardware developer and a manager software developer will be drawn out of the total MADOMP membership on two successive random selections is

$$P(F_1 \text{ and } M_2) = P(F_1) \cdot P(M_2/F_1)$$
$$= (20/150) \cdot (70/149)$$
$$= .0626$$
$$\approx .06$$

The joint probability of selecting two engineer software developers from the software group in two successive draws is

$$P(F_2 \text{ and } F_2) = P(F_2) \cdot P(F_2/F_2)$$
$$= (30/100) \cdot (29/99)$$
$$= .0879$$
$$\approx .09$$

Finally, the chance that no software developers will be drawn out of the total membership on two successive draws is

$$P(B_1 \text{ and } B_1) = P(B_1) \cdot P(B_1/B_1)$$
$$= (50/150)(49/149)$$
$$= .1096$$
$$\approx .11$$

This joint event could be restated as, "The chance that two hardware developers will be selected on two successive draws."

|A.8| REVISING PRIOR ESTIMATES: BAYES' THEOREM

It is most common to reassess earlier estimates based on newly available information. One of the most useful techniques used to update old estimates is Bayes' theorem, which is given by the following relationship for a decision setting involving two events:

$$P(S_i/F) = \frac{P(S_i) \cdot P(F/S_i)}{\sum\limits_{j=1}^{n} P(S_j)P(F/S_j)} = \frac{P(S) \cdot P(F/S)}{P(S) \cdot P(F/S) + P(S') \cdot P(F/S')}$$

where

$P(S_i/F)$ = probability that the ith outcome event (e.g., either success or failure) will actually occur given that prediction F has already been made

$P(S_i)$ = probability that the ith outcome event (e.g., either success or failure) will actually occur without the help of any forecast (e.g., favorable or unfavorable prediction)

$P(F/S_i)$ = probability that forecast F will occur given that the ith outcome event (e.g., either success or failure) is already known; this type of information is typically empirical data, taken from previous experiences

$\sum\limits_{j=1}^{n} P(S_j)P(F/S_j)$ = the sum of the probabilities of all the ways in which the prediction F can occur (i.e., j represents the different outcome events that can occur when there are n different outcome events; for most examples in this text, $n = 2$: success or failure; this term also represents the marginal probability of the prediction F)

An example of Bayes' theorem was illustrated earlier in the section *Statistically Dependent Conditional Probabilities*. Nevertheless, given the importance of the concept, let's look at another example. What is the probability of randomly selecting a hardware developer from the MADOMP membership if you already know that the person selected is a manager?

$$P(B_1/M) = \frac{P(B_1) \cdot P(M/B_1)}{\sum\limits_{j=1}^{2} P(B_j)P(M/B_j)}$$

$$= \frac{P(B_1) \cdot P(M/B_1)}{P(B_1) \cdot P(M/B_1) + P(B_2) \cdot P(M/B_2)}$$

$$= \frac{(50/150) \cdot (30/50)}{(50/150) \cdot (30/50) + (100/150) \cdot (70/100)}$$

$$= \frac{(.33)(.60)}{(.33)(.60) + (.67)(.70)} = .297 \approx .30$$

A.9 THE BINOMIAL AND NORMAL PROBABILITY DISTRIBUTIONS: DISCRETE AND CONTINUOUS RANDOM VARIABLES

Managers typically wrestle with risky situations. Their primary concern is, inevitably, "What are the chances of random event X occurring?" Or, "How close does our sample information come to the true population measurement?" However, to answer questions

such as these intelligently—to make defensible estimates of such matters—the manager must be able to define the event in terms of the probability distribution that characterizes its behavior. Although there are many different probability distributions, they all fall into one of two general categories: discrete and continuous random variables.

Discrete probability distributions are limited to a finite, sometimes very small, number of possible outcome values (e.g., whether someone is female or male). *Continuous probability distributions* represent variables that can assume an infinite number of values within a given range, including fractional or noninteger (e.g., the temperature in a room). Two probability distributions—one discrete and one continuous—will be discussed in this appendix. They are (1) the binomial distribution (discrete), and (2) the normal distribution (continuous).

The Binomial Probability Distribution

One of the most widely used probability distributions of a discrete random variable is the *binomial probability distribution* (BPD). We can use the BPD whenever the event can take on only one of two possible outcomes: yes or no, success or failure, male or female, above 30 years old or less than or equal to 30 years old, and so on. Responses on a questionnaire are commonly dichotomous, such as, "Are you for or against capital punishment?" Questions such as these proliferate on marketing surveys and the well-known Harris, Nielsen, and Gallup polls. Crucial decisions evolve from the binomial responses to these questions, which are used to predict events such as the outcomes of congressional or presidential elections. Staff of television shows, hoping to continue a series past the 13-week trial period, watch the ratings carefully.[1]

Binomial distributions are characterized by several properties:

1. There are *n* identical "trials." The trials can be a number of identically conducted interviews, a sample of identically distributed questionnaires, and so on.

2. The trials are measured dichotomously; only one of two possible outcomes occurs. Typically, the desired outcome is referred to as "success"; any others are aggregated under "failure."

3. There is a probability, *p*, associated with the likelihood of success on each trial that remains constant. The probability of being unsuccessful is *q* or $(1 - p)$. If it is known that 58 percent of the voters in a particular district are registered Democrats, the probability of "success" of randomly selecting a Democrat from this district is .58. If, in the random selection of, say, 50 registered voters, 51 percent are Democrats, the proportion of registered Democrats is still assumed to be 58 percent. The 51-percent reading would more likely reflect the degree of randomness in the selection of the sample.

4. Each trial is independent of the outcomes of all other trials. For example, the response to one questionnaire is assumed to not influence the response to any other questionnaire.

5. The measurement centers on the number of successful outcomes, *X*, observed during a total of *n* trials.

Number five . . . peanut butter side down.

---

[1]It is important to note that a binomial probability distribution is not limited to issues of only two categories. Say, for example, that a pollster wished to determine the proportion of support for a particular candidate in, say, a field of five candidates. Randomly distributed questionnaires (or interviews) would ask respondents which one of the five the latter would support. Since the focus is on the *level* of support for a specific candidate, all the responses could be reduced to "those who support candidate *X*" and "those who do not support candidate *X*," a dichotomous description.

The probability of experiencing *exactly X* successes in *n* trials of a binomial probability distribution is:[2]

$$P(X) = \frac{n!}{X!(n-X)!} p^X q^{n-X}$$

where

n = number of trials (or sample size)

X = number of successful outcomes

p = probability of a successful outcome

q = probability of an unsuccessful outcome, $1 - p$

Influence of the $p - q$ Values and Sample Size on the Geometry of the Binomial Distribution   The shape of the BPD is influenced by the $p - q$ proportions *when the sample size is small*. An illustration of the effect of the $p - q$ proportions on the BPD geometry for sample sizes of 5, 10, 15, and 30 is provided in Figures A-2 through A-4. In Figure A-2, when $p = .1$ $(q = .9)$, the distribution is positively (right) skewed. The degree of skew is clearly more dramatic the smaller the sample size, n. As the proportions of p and q become equal $(p = q = .5)$, such as in Figure A-3, the distributions becomes exactly symmetrical (bell-shaped), regardless of sample size without skew. In Figure A-4, the value of p increases to .9 $(q = .1)$. In this latter case, however, the direction of the skew, although identical in degree, is opposite in direction to that of the skew in Figure A-2. Also of significance is that the influence of extreme $p - q$ values on the shape of the distribution is dramatically reduced as n grows. In fact, there is a relatively small effect for the $n = 30$ sample size in Figures A-2 $(p = .1)$ and A-4 $(p = .1)$.

Sample Calculations for the Binomial Probability Distribution   The binomial equation solves for the probability that exactly X successful outcomes will occur in a sample size of n trials if the probability for success is p. However, in addition to finding the probability that a particular sampling will contain exactly X outcomes, a manager may sometimes find it essential to determine the probability of finding "*at least X*" outcomes or "*no more than X*" outcomes. Therefore, we'll discuss examples of how we can enhance the usability of the BPD.

EXAMPLE A.3   Binomial Probability Distribution 1: The Heart Surgeon

A heart surgeon reportedly has a 70 percent success rate on a specific type of intricate cardiac surgery. If a sample of 10 cases of this type of surgery are randomly selected, what is the probability that

1. Exactly six will be successful?

2. Less than six will be successful?

3. At least six will be successful?

---

[2]Factorial (!) notation is very simple—do not be intimidated; $n!$ is simply $(n-1)(n-2)(n-3) \ldots (2)(1)$. There are, however, two points to remember. First, zero factorial is equal to 1.0 (i.e., $0! = 1$). Second, any number raised to the zero power is equal to 1.0 (i.e., $X^0 = 1.0$).

FIGURE A-2

Influence of Sample Size on Symmetry of Binomial Distribution with $p = .1$ and $q = .9$

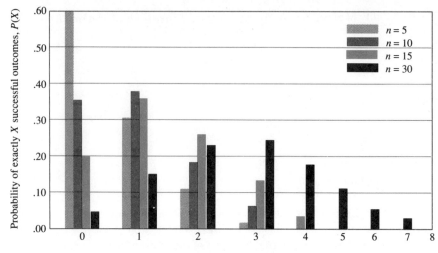

ANSWERS

Question 1

This question addresses the binomial equation "as is." So, the probability that the surgeon's sample of 10 cases will have exactly six successes is $P(6)$. Since $n = 10$, $p = .70$ ($q = 1 - p = .30$), and $X = 6$,

$$P(6) = \frac{10!}{6!(10-6)!}(.70)^6(.30)^{10-6}$$

$$= \frac{10!}{6!4!}(.70)^6(.30)^4$$

FIGURE A-3

Influence of Sample Size on Symmetry of Binomial Distribution with $p = .5$ and $q = .5$

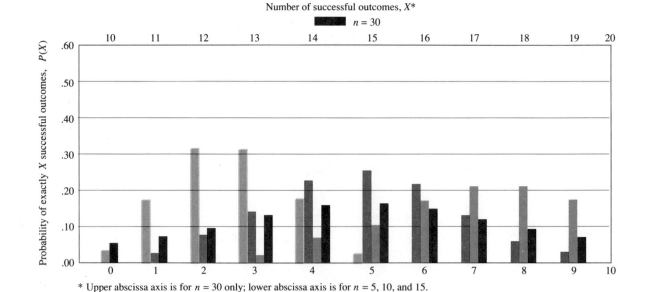

* Upper abscissa axis is for $n = 30$ only; lower abscissa axis is for $n = 5$, 10, and 15.

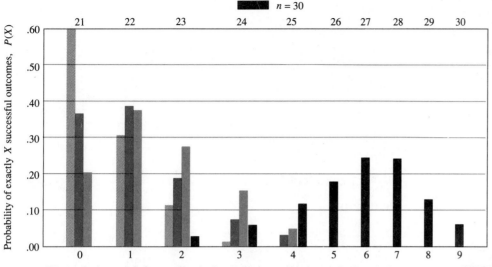

*Upper abscissa axis is for $n = 30$ only; lower abscissa axis is for $n = 5$, 10, and 15.

$n = 5$ $n = 10$ $n = 15$

Number of successful outcomes, X

FIGURE A-4

Influence of Sample Size on Symmetry of Binomial Distribution with $p = .9$ and $q = .1$

For example, 6! is simply

$(6)(5)(4)(3)(2)(1)$

So, if you have a ratio of two factorials such as 10!/6!, you can write

$$\frac{10!}{6!} = \frac{(10)(9)(8)(7)(6)(5)(4)(3)(2)(1)}{(6)(5)(4)(3)(2)(1)}$$

or, recognizing that the common portion of the factorial in the numerator and denominator will cancel each other, you can simplify the expression as

$$\frac{10!}{6!} = (10)(9)(8)(7)$$

Now let's solve $P(6)$. The chances that the surgeon's sample will have exactly six successes is

$$P(6) = \frac{(10)(9)(8)(7)}{(4)(3)(2)(1)}(.70)^6(.30)^4$$

and

$$P(6) = \frac{(5040)}{24}(.117649)(.0081)$$
$$= .20012$$

So, there is only about one chance in five that the sample will contain exactly six successful surgeries.

Question 2

The probability that there will be less than six successful surgeries in the sample of 10 is the probability of having zero, one, two, three, four, or five successful cases in the

sample; that is, $P(X < 6) = P(0) + P(1) + P(2) + P(3) + P(4) + P(5)$. So,

$$P(0) = \frac{10!}{0!(10-0)!}(.70)^0(.30)^{10-0}$$
$$= \frac{(10!)}{(1)(10!)}(1)(.30)^{10}$$
$$= .0000059049$$

$$P(1) = \frac{10!}{1!(10-1)!}(.70)^1(.30)^{10-1}$$
$$= \frac{(10!)}{(1)(9!)}(.70)^2(.30)^9$$
$$= .00013776$$

$$P(2) = \frac{10!}{2!(10-2)!}(.70)^2(.30)^{10-2}$$
$$= \frac{(10!)}{(2!)(8!)}(.70)^2(.30)^8$$
$$= \frac{(10)(9)}{(2)(1)}(.49)(.0000656)$$
$$= .00144648$$

$$P(3) = \frac{10!}{3!(10-3)!}(.70)^3(.30)^{10-3}$$
$$= \frac{(10!)}{(3!)(7!)}(.70)^3(.30)^7$$
$$= \frac{(10)(9)(8)}{(3)(2)(1)}(.343)(.0002187)$$
$$= .00900$$

$$P(4) = \frac{10!}{4!(10-4)!}(.70)^4(.30)^{10-4}$$
$$= \frac{(10!)}{(4!)(6!)}(.70)^4(.30)^6$$
$$= \frac{(10)(9)(8)(7)}{(4)(3)(2)(1)}(.2401)(.000729)$$
$$= .03676$$

$$P(5) = \frac{10!}{5!(10-5)!}(.70)^5(.30)^{10-5}$$
$$= \frac{(10!)}{(5!)(5!)}(.70)^5(.30)^5$$
$$= \frac{(10)(9)(8)(7)(6)}{(5)(4)(3)(2)(1)}(.1681)(.00243)$$
$$= .10294$$

Finally,

$$P(X < 6) = .0000 + .0001 + .0014 + .0090 + .0368 + .1029$$
$$= .1502$$

Question 3

The probability that at least six of the sample surgeries selected will be successful is the complement of the answer to question 2. That is,

$$P(X \geq 6) = 1 - P(X < 6)$$
$$= 1 - .1502$$
$$= .8498.$$

The Binomial Probability Distribution Mean and Standard Deviation   It is also possible to characterize the BPD in terms of measures of its mean, denoted by the Greek letter mu—μ; and of its standard deviation, denoted by the Greek letter sigma—σ. That is, the mean of a BPD is given by

$$\mu = np$$

So, for Example A.3, the average number of successful operations anticipated in a sample size of 10 cases is

$$\mu = (10)(.70) = 7$$

The standard deviation for the BPD is

$$\sigma = \sqrt{npq}$$
$$= \sqrt{(10)(.70)(.30)}$$
$$= \sqrt{2.1} = 1.45$$

It is easy to see that calculating a binomial probability is not simple when the sample (trial size), n, is large. In fact, it is generally accepted that the binomial formula should be used only when *either or both* of the np and nq products are ≤ 5. The binomial example just concluded fell into that category (e.g., $np = (10)(.70) = 7$, *but* $nq = (10)(.30) = 3$, so the binomial formula must be used). If, on the other hand, *both* np and nq are greater than 5, we can use another relationship that is far easier: We can use the *normal distribution* to approximate the binomial distribution when n is "large." This option will be discussed in the next section. Let's try one more example of the BPD before moving on.

EXAMPLE A.4   BINOMIAL PROBABILITY DISTRIBUTION 2: THE MARKETING STUDY

Small bottles of a new men's designer cologne are being distributed, at no cost, in the men's designer clothes section of Macy's department store in San Francisco. The manufacturer of the cologne wants feedback concerning consumers' opinions of this new product. Each person handed a gift bottle is asked to try the product and to answer a brief questionnaire before they leave the premises. The key question assesses the probability that the patron will purchase the product if it is brought to market. The possible responses each patron may choose are A = definitely, B = possibly, C = unlikely, D = no. After 2 days spent distributing the cologne and collecting responses, the staff put the questionnaires into a large box, mixed them up, and randomly selected six of them. The six responses are distributed as follows: A = 1 response, B = 2 responses, C = 1 response, D = 2 responses.

The manufacturer thinks that marketing the cologne would not be worthwhile unless two of the six responses are favorable—which they define as either A or B. Answer the following questions for the manufacturer based on the sample findings and the assumption that the sample is truly random:

1. What is the probability that at least two out of every six patrons in the men's cologne market will buy the cologne?

2. What is the probability that no more than one out of six patrons will buy the cologne?

ANSWERS

For our purposes, it is best to set aside the reliability surrounding such a small sample selection and the notion that it is possible to collect something that approaches a random sampling of the manufacturer's true consumer population group. With these weighty concerns shelved, we can answer the two questions.

Question 1

The probability that at least two out of six people in the men's cologne market will buy the cologne is $P(X \geq 2)$, where $X = 3$, $n = 6$, $p = 1/3$, and $q = 2/3$. Therefore,

$$P(X \geq 2) = P(2) + P(3) + P(4) + P(5) + P(6)$$

It is also possible to gain the same information more rapidly from the fact that the sum of all the possible outcomes must be equal to 1.0. Then,

$$P(X \geq 2) = 1 - P(X < 2)$$
$$1 - [P(0) + P(1)]$$

Selecting the latter approach will save a significant amount of time. We can now easily find the probability that at least two out of six people will buy the cologne. First, $P(0)$ is

$$P(0) = \frac{6!}{0!(6-0)!}\left(\frac{1}{3}\right)^0\left(\frac{2}{3}\right)^6$$

$$= \frac{6!}{(1)(6!)}(1)(.08779)$$

$$= (1)(1)(.08779)$$

$$= .08779$$

and $P(1)$ is

$$P(1) = \frac{6!}{1!(6-1)!}\left(\frac{1}{3}\right)^1\left(\frac{2}{3}\right)^5$$

$$= \frac{(6)}{(1)}\left(\frac{1}{3}\right)(.1317)$$

$$= .2634$$

Finally, $P(X \geq 2)$ is

$$P(X \geq 2) = 1 - P(X < 2)$$

$$= 1 - [P(0) + P(1)]$$

$$= 1 - [.0878 + .2634]$$

$$= .6498$$

There is about a 65 percent chance that the cologne manufacturer's market exceeds the company's hope of capturing two out of every six purchasers.

Question 2

The probability that no more than one out of six people will buy the cologne is $P(X \leq 1)$. However, $P(X \leq 1)$ is just another representation of $P(X < 2)$. So, $P(X \leq 1)$ is

$$P(X \leq 1) = P(0) + P(1)$$

$$= .0878 + .2634$$

$$= .3502$$

Voila!

Now let's turn our attention to a probability distribution that measures continuous random variables and is the most widely used distribution: the normal distribution.

The Normal Probability Distribution

No one has escaped the curve—the dreaded bell-shaped curve. We've all had experiences with it, such as "grading on the curve." The normal probability distribution (NPD), or bell-shaped curve, is the backbone of inferential statistics. The properties of the NPD allow the accurate estimation of population characteristics based on amazingly small (randomly drawn) sample sizes.[3]

---

[3]The television Nielsen ratings are based on the responses of a sample of 1300 "Nielsen family" members that, in turn, represent approximately 50,000,000 households—a sample-to-population proportion of .000026.

A high percentage of human beliefs and personality traits can be approximated accurately by the properties of the NPD. Further, many physical science phenomena follow, exactly or nearly exactly, the properties of the NPD. Many business phenomena can also be accurately approximated by the NPD. For these reasons, the normal distribution is, ostensibly, the most important of all probability distributions.

As with the BPD, the NPD has defining characteristics:

1. The geometry of the curve follows a symmetrical bell shape; there is no skew.

2. The mean (as well as the median and the mode) of the distribution is measured underneath the center (peak) of the curve.

3. The standard deviation, along with the mean, of the NPD satisfies the following relationships regarding the percentage of the total area underneath the curve: 68.26 percent of this area is found between $\mu \pm 1\sigma$; 95.54 percent lies between $\mu \pm 2\sigma$; 99.74 percent between $\mu \pm 3\sigma$. This relationship is true for any normal distribution, regardless of the values of μ and σ (Figure A-5). The formula for the NPD is

$$f(X) = \frac{1}{\sigma \sqrt{2\pi}} e^{-\frac{1}{2}\left[\frac{(X - \mu)}{\sigma}\right]^2}$$

where

$f(X)$ = probability function of a normal random variable value, X, for a given mean, μ, and standard deviation, σ (i.e., the frequency of occurrence of normal random variable, X)

X = normal random variable value

σ = standard deviation of X

μ = mean of X

e = 2.7182 . . .

π = 3.1416 . . .

Computing the area between various intervals under the normal probability distribution would be a tedious task for even a single combination of μ and σ. Computing these same areas for the infinite combinations of μ and σ is impossible. Fortunately, a single table is available that allows us to determine quickly any area (and corresponding probability) of interest for all possible sets of μ and σ: that table is the *standard normal distribution*. This table defines the area under any normal curve as a function of a Z-*score*. The Z-score is merely a transformed score of a specific measurement value of X; it is no different from representing a particular Fahrenheit degree value by its equivalent centigrade value. The Z-score merely nor-

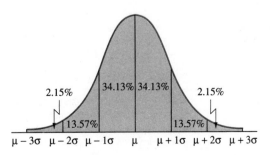

FIGURE A-5

Percentage of Area Under the Normal Distribution as a Function of the Distance from the Mean, in Multiples of the Standard Deviation

malizes a given *X*-score by measuring its distance from the mean of the distribution in units of the standard deviation:[4]

$$Z = \frac{X - \mu}{\sigma}$$

The *Z*-table—or standard normal distribution table as it is often called—is presented in Table A-3.

Now let's see how we can use this table in an example.

EXAMPLE A.5   NORMAL PROBABILITY DISTRIBUTION 1: MEASURING RELATIVE SALARY PERFORMANCE

Greg Walcraft is most unhappy with his present job. He has tried everything to please his boss: He's always on time, he dresses impeccably, and he is well mannered. At lunch last week, in a conversation with three colleagues who work in essentially the same position as himself, Walcraft learned that he had the lowest salary of anyone present. After delicately confronting his manager, Ms. Strong, Walcraft is assured that he is doing very well, regardless of what he might have heard. Strong guarantees Walcraft that he is, in fact, making more money than three-fourths of the other people with similar educational and professional experience performing similar jobs. She also suggests that a sample size of three colleagues is not necessarily representative of the entire population of employees in an equivalent position. Unconvinced by these assurances, Walcraft goes to his labor union and collects information regarding the salaries of all of

[4]The numerator of the *Z*-score is the distance from the score, *X*, to the mean, μ, of the distribution. The denominator, σ, is the standard deviation (spread) of the distribution. The ratio of numerator to denominator forms a *Z*-ratio or *Z*-score that describes how far a particular score of interest, *X*, is from the mean.

Ironically, it was young Greg Walcraft's blind acceptance of his business school's advice to "dress like your boss" that cost him further opportunities within the corporation.

TABLE A-3

Areas Under the Standard Normal Curve

Normal Deviate Z	.00	.01	.02	.03	.04	.05	.06	.07	.08	.09
.0	.0000	.0040	.0080	.0120	.0160	.0199	.0239	.0279	.0319	.0359
.1	.0398	.0438	.0478	.0517	.0557	.0596	.0636	.0675	.0714	.0753
.2	.0793	.0832	.0871	.0910	.0948	.0987	.1026	.1064	.1103	.1141
.3	.1179	.1217	.1255	.1293	.1331	.1368	.1406	.1443	.1480	.1517
.4	.1554	.1591	.1628	.1664	.1700	.1736	.1772	.1808	.1844	.1879
.5	.1915	.1950	.1985	.2019	.2054	.2088	.2123	.2157	.2190	.2224
.6	.2257	.2291	.2324	.2357	.2389	.2422	.2454	.2486	.2518	.2549
.7	.2580	.2612	.2642	.2673	.2704	.2734	.2764	.2794	.2823	.2852
.8	.2881	.2910	.2939	.2967	.2995	.3023	.3051	.3078	.3106	.3133
.9	.3159	.3186	.3212	.3238	.3264	.3289	.3315	.3340	.3365	.3389
1.0	.3413	.3438	.3461	.3485	.3508	.3531	.3554	.3577	.3599	.3621
1.1	.3643	.3665	.3686	.3708	.3729	.3749	.3770	.3790	.3810	.3830
1.2	.3849	.3869	.3888	.3907	.3925	.3944	.3962	.3980	.3997	.4015
1.3	.4032	.4049	.4066	.4082	.4099	.4115	.4131	.4147	.4162	.4177
1.4	.4192	.4207	.4222	.4236	.4251	.4265	.4279	.4292	.4306	.4319
1.5	.4332	.4345	.4357	.4370	.4382	.4394	.4406	.4418	.4429	.4441
1.6	.4452	.4463	.4474	.4484	.4495	.4505	.4515	.4525	.4535	.4545
1.7	.4554	.4564	.4573	.4582	.4591	.4599	.4608	.4616	.4625	.4633
1.8	.4641	.4649	.4656	.4664	.4671	.4678	.4686	.4693	.4699	.4706
1.9	.4713	.4719	.4726	.4732	.4738	.4744	.4750	.4756	.4761	.4767
2.0	.4772	.4778	.4783	.4788	.4793	.4798	.4803	.4808	.4812	.4817
2.1	.4821	.4826	.4830	.4834	.4838	.4842	.4846	.4850	.4854	.4857
2.2	.4861	.4864	.4868	.4871	.4875	.4878	.4881	.4884	.4887	.4890
2.3	.4893	.4896	.4898	.4901	.4904	.4906	.4909	.4911	.4913	.4916
2.4	.4918	.4920	.4922	.4925	.4927	.4929	.4931	.4932	.4934	.4936
2.5	.4938	.4940	.4941	.4943	.4945	.4946	.4948	.4949	.4951	.4952
2.6	.4953	.4955	.4956	.4957	.4959	.4960	.4961	.4962	.4963	.4964
2.7	.4965	.4966	.4967	.4968	.4969	.4970	.4971	.4972	.4973	.4974
2.8	.4974	.4975	.4976	.4977	.4977	.4978	.4979	.4979	.4980	.4981
2.9	.4981	.4982	.4982	.4983	.4984	.4984	.4985	.4985	.4986	.4986
3.0	.49865	.4987	.4987	.4988	.4988	.4989	.4989	.4989	.4990	.4990
4.0	.49997									

© 1977 by Harcourt Brace Jovanovich, Inc., and reproduced with their permission from *Statistical Analysis for Decision Making*, 2nd ed., by Morris Hamburg.

the people in his job category. He ultimately calculates the annual salary mean, μ, of the population of similar positions as $31,500 and the standard deviation, σ, as $3472. Answer the following questions:

1. If Walcraft's annual salary is $28,600, what proportion of people in his job category earn more money?

2. If Walcraft's annual salary is $35,970, what proportion of people in his job category earn more money?

3. What proportion of employees in Walcraft's job category earn between $28,600 and $35,970 per annum?

4. What salary would Walcraft have to make to support the manager's claim that he makes more money than three-fourths of the other employees in his job category?

Question 1

The Z-score corresponding to Walcraft's annual salary of $28,600 is

$$Z = \frac{X - \mu}{\sigma}$$

$$= \frac{28,600 - 31,500}{3472}$$

$$= \frac{-2900}{3472} = -.84$$

Table A-3 provides the proportion (area) between the mean and the Z-value of .84. Although the Z-value calculated is −.84, due to perfect symmetry, only the right-hand side of the standard normal distribution is provided. This is sufficient, since the proportion of area between a Z-value of .84 and the mean is identical to the proportion of area located between the mean and a Z-value of −.84. This proportion is

$$P(-.84 < Z < 0) = P(0 < Z < .84)$$
$$= .2995$$

However, the proportion of salaries that are greater than $28,600 (a.k.a. $Z = -.84$) includes not only the porportion of .2995 but also the proportion of salaries that are *above* the mean: an additional area of .5000:

$$P(Z > -.84) = P(0 < Z < .84) + P(Z > 0)$$
$$= .2995 + .5000$$
$$= .7995$$

Therefore, the total proportion of salaries that exceeds Walcraft's is .7995 (i.e., a little less than 80 percent of people in similar positions earn more than Walcraft does). An illustration of this relationship is shown in Figure A-6.

Question 2

The Z-score equivalent to Walcraft's $35,970 annual salary is

$$Z = \frac{X - \mu}{\sigma}$$

$$= \frac{35,970 - 31,500}{3472}$$

$$= \frac{4470}{3472} = 1.29$$

FIGURE A-6

Proportion of Salaries Greater than Greg Walcraft's $28,600 Annual Income ($\mu$ = $31,500; σ = $3472)

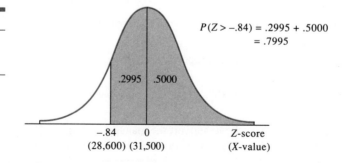

$P(Z > -.84) = .2995 + .5000$
$= .7995$

.2995 .5000

−.84   0   Z-score
(28,600) (31,500)   (X-value)

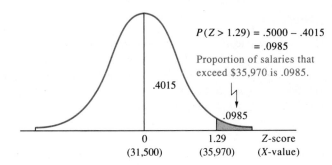

$P(Z > 1.29) = .5000 - .4015$
$= .0985$
Proportion of salaries that exceed $35,970 is .0985.

.4015

.0985

0   1.29   Z-score
(31,500) (35,970) (X-value)

We find the proportion of scores greater than this value from the proportion of the area under the curve beyond—to the right of—this Z-score. Since the Z-table gives us only the value between the mean and the Z-score in question, we subtract this latter area from the entire area in the right-hand half, .5000, to obtain the correct value. That is,

$$P(Z > 1.29) = .5000 - P(0 < Z < 1.29)$$
$$= .5000 - .4015$$
$$= .0985$$

Less than 10 percent of employees in similar jobs earn more money than Walcraft does (Figure A-7).

Question 3

We find the proportion of salaries between $35,970 and $28,600 by summing the area under the standard normal curve located between the mean and the corresponding Z-values of these two salaries (Figure A-8):

$$P(\$28,600 < X < \$35,970) = P(-.84 < Z < 1.29)$$
$$= P(-.84 < Z < 0) + P(0 < Z < 1.29)$$

However, since $P(-.84 < Z < 0) = P(0 < Z < .84)$,

$$P(\$28,600 < X < \$35,970) = P(0 < Z < .84) + P(0 < Z < 1.29)$$
$$= .2995 + .4015$$
$$= .7010$$
$$= .70$$

Approximately 70 percent of the people in a similar job category earn a salary between these two values.

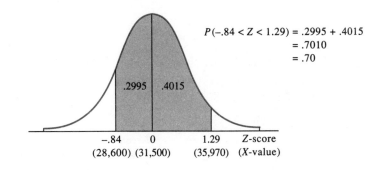

$P(-.84 < Z < 1.29) = .2995 + .4015$
$= .7010$
$= .70$

.2995   .4015

-.84   0   1.29   Z-score
(28,600) (31,500) (35,970) (X-value)

Question 4

This time, instead of calculating an area, we are trying to find the specific salary, X, that is equal to or higher than three-fourths of all salaries in this job category. That is the same as saying that this salary has 75 percent of the area under the standard normal distribution below it—to the left of it (i.e., all the area in the left-hand side *plus* half the area in the right-hand side). The salary, X, is given by

$$X = \mu + Z\sigma$$

Before this equation can be solved, the Z-value located at the seventy-fifth percentile mark must be found. Although the Z-value has .7500 of the area under the normal curve to the left of its location, the table value provides only the .2500 area between it and the mean of zero. The nearest Z-value corresponding to the .2500 area is .67 (.2486). This information is shown in Figure A-9. We can now calculate the corresponding seventy-fifth percentile rank salary value, X:

$$
\begin{aligned}
X &= Z\sigma + \mu \\
&= (.67)(3472) + 31,500 \\
&= 2326.24 + 31,500 \\
&= \$33,826.24
\end{aligned}
$$

Using the Normal Probability Distribution to Approximate the Binomial Probability Distribution   The NPD, even though it is continuous, may be used to approximate discrete BPD data accurately. Recall from the earlier illustration in our discussion of BPD (Figures A-3 through A-5), that the skew in the BPDs diminished significantly as the sample size increased. From a statistical standpoint, it is usually quite accurate to approximate binomial data with the normal distribution, as long as the np and nq products both exceed some minimal value. Although there is disagreement over what this minimum threshold value should be, the majority of references suggest np and nq products between 3 and 10. For expediency, let's select the minimum value of 5. Now let's see how well the NPD can approximate the BPD data.

FIGURE A-9

Finding the Salary, X, Corresponding to the Seventy-Fifth Percentile Rank ($\mu = \$31,500$; $\sigma = \$3472$)

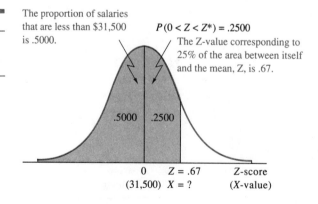

The proportion of salaries that are less than $31,500 is .5000.

$P(0 < Z < Z^*) = .2500$

The Z-value corresponding to 25% of the area between itself and the mean, Z, is .67.

.5000   .2500

0   Z = .67   Z-score
(31,500) X = ?   (X-value)

EXAMPLE A.6 APPROXIMATING THE BINOMIAL PROBABILITY DISTRIBUTION WITH THE NORMAL PROBABILITY DISTRIBUTION 2: MANAGEMENT TURNOVER RATE

Fred Barnwall is sales manager of a high-tech company in Cambridge, Massachusetts. Barnwall believes that the turnover rate of his salespeople is too high. The costs associated with advertising for, interviewing, recruiting, and training new employees is cutting deeply into the company's profits. Based on research he conducted regarding the turnover rates in similar organizations, Barnwall finds that there is a 25 percent chance that a salesperson will resign before 3 years of employment with the company. Barnwall decides to conduct a small study. He randomly selects a sample of 20 salespeople that have left the company during the past 18 months; he finds that eight of these people had been on the job for less than 3 years. Can you tell Barnwall whether the company's turnover rate is a cause for alarm, in light of the industry standard of 25 percent? Use both (1) the BPD and (2) the NPD to approximate the binomial distribution to support your answer.

Manager Fred Barnwall senses a mood shift among his salespeople

ANSWER

Question 1

Estimate using the BPD. The given information is

$n = 20$

$X = 8$

$p = .25$

$q = .75$

The fact that eight out of 12 employees left the company before their third anniversary concerns Barnwall. After all, eight-twelfths, or 75 percent, is more than the 25 percent industrywide attrition rate. These company figures, however, are based on a sample of only 20. The question Barnwall wants answered is, "How likely is it that eight or more salespeople leaving is a random occurrence (i.e., has no statistical significance)?" That is,

$P(X \geq 8) = ?$

If binomial tables are not available, solving the binomial equation from $X = 8$ through $X = 20$ will be very tedious. Fortunately, it is possible to calculate the complimentary event—the probability that *less than* eight salespeople resigned—and then to subtract the sum of these values from 1.0.

$P(X \geq 8) = 1 - P(X < 8)$

The binomial equation reveals the following information:

$$P(X < 8) = P(7) + P(6) + P(5) + P(4) + P(3) + P(2) + P(1) + P(0)$$
$$= .1124 + .1686 + .2023 + .1897 + .1339 + .0669 + .0211 + .0032$$
$$= .8981$$

Therefore, the *random* chance that at least eight or more salespeople would have quit their jobs in less than 3 years is

$$P(X \geq 8) = 1 - P(X < 8) = 1 - .8981 = .1019$$

It is up to Barnwall to interpret this probability as either evidence supportive of his suspicions or as calming information. In general, however, the smaller this probability, the less likely it is that the outcome is random or accidental, and the more basis there is for concern.

Question 2

Estimate using the NPD. Next, let's use the normal distribution as an approximation of the binomial distribution. In this instance, although we use precisely the same information, the normal approximation requires that we use the mean and standard deviation. The mean of the binomial data is

$$\begin{aligned}
\mu &= np \\
&= (20)(.25) \\
&= 5
\end{aligned}$$

The standard deviation is

$$\begin{aligned}
\sigma &= \sqrt{npq} \\
&= \sqrt{(20)(.25)(.75)} \\
&= \sqrt{3.75} = 1.936
\end{aligned}$$

Now it is possible to use the normal distribution to find the probability that eight or more salespeople resigning their jobs before 3 years of service is a random occurrence. First, we find the Z-value corresponding to the X-value of 8

$$\begin{aligned}
Z &= \frac{|X - .5| - \mu}{\sigma} \\
&= \frac{|8 - .5| - 5}{1.936} = 1.29
\end{aligned}$$

The Z-formula for approximating the binomial distribution with the normal distribution contains a *continuity correction factor* of .5 to improve the accuracy of the estimate.[5] Finally, from the standard normal distribution (Figure A-10),

$$P(X \geq 8) = P(Z \geq 1.29)$$

and

$$\begin{aligned}
P(Z \geq 1.29) &= .5000 - .4015 \\
&= .0985
\end{aligned}$$

[5] A continuity correction factor of .5 is subtracted from the low end and added to the high end of any range being assessed. If, for example, the manager wished to know the probability of between eight and twelve salespeople resigning, the range would include 7.5 to 12.5.

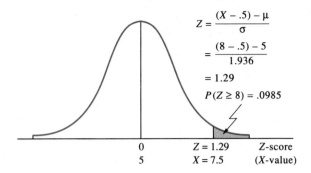

$$Z = \frac{(X - .5) - \mu}{\sigma}$$

$$= \frac{(8 - .5) - 5}{1.936}$$

$$= 1.29$$

$$P(Z \geq 8) = .0985$$

0	Z = 1.29	Z-score
5	X = 7.5	(X-value)

FIGURE A-10

Approximating the Binomial Probability Distribution with the Normal Probability Distribution for $p = .25$, $n = 20$, $P(X \geq 8)$

This answer is only slightly different from the binomial estimate of .1019. Even for this small sample size, the normal approximation of the binomial data results in only a small error in the estimate:

$$\% \text{ Error} = 100 \left(\frac{\text{binomial approximation} - \text{normal approximation}}{\text{binomial approximation}} \right)$$

$$= 100 \left(\frac{.1019 - .0985}{.1019} \right)$$

$$= 3.33\%$$

Now you have had an abbreviated exposure to probability concepts. The basics presented here will help you to appreciate more readily situations that place uncertainty and risk between you and an informed decision. Chapters 1 and 2 provide further reinforcement on most of these concepts through numerous application examples.

APPENDIX B

MATRIX ALGEBRA BASICS

B.1 | INTRODUCTION

A matrix is a rectangular format for presenting data (usually numbers). Each matrix is described by its size. For example, an $m \times n$ matrix represents has dimensions of m rows and n columns. If the number of rows and columns are equal ($m = n$), the matrix is called *square matrix* of the order n. A generalized matrix format, with element a_{ij} found at the intersection of the ith row and j^{th} column, is

$$
\mathbf{A} = \begin{bmatrix}
a_{11} & a_{12} & \cdots & a_{1j} & \cdots & a_{1n} \\
a_{21} & a_{22} & \cdots & a_{2j} & \cdots & a_{2n} \\
\cdots & \cdots & \cdots & \cdots & \cdots & \cdots \\
a_{i1} & \cdots & \cdots & a_{ij} & \cdots & a_{in} \\
\cdots & \cdots & \cdots & \cdots & \cdots & \cdots \\
a_{m1} & a_{m2} & \cdots & a_{mj} & \cdots & a_{mn}
\end{bmatrix}
$$

Sometimes a matrix will consist of only a single row or a single column. These types of matrices are referred to as *row vectors* and *column vectors*, respectively, and can be represented by single subscript notation, such as

$$
\mathbf{A} = \begin{bmatrix} a_1 & a_2 & \cdots & a_n \end{bmatrix}
$$

or

$$
\mathbf{A} = \begin{bmatrix}
a_1 \\
a_2 \\
\cdot \\
\cdot \\
\cdot \\
a_n
\end{bmatrix}
$$

Once organized in a matrix, data can be effectively illustrated or manipulated using appropriate algebraic operations. These procedures are discussed next.

B.2 | MATRIX OPERATIONS

A number of important algebraic operations can be helpful in manipulating matrices. These specific operations include (1) multiplying a constant times a matrix (referred to as *scalar multiplication*) and (2) finding the transpose of a specific matrix.

Scalar Multiplication

If you wish to multiply a matrix, $\mathbf{A}$, by a constant, k, multiply each matrix element, a_{ij}, by the constant value, k. So, if

$$\mathbf{A} = \begin{bmatrix} a_{11} & a_{12} & a_{13} \\ a_{21} & a_{22} & a_{23} \end{bmatrix}$$

then

$$k\mathbf{A} = \begin{bmatrix} ka_{11} & ka_{12} & ka_{13} \\ ka_{21} & ka_{22} & ka_{23} \end{bmatrix}$$

Transposing a Matrix

Sometimes, it is necessary to interchange the row and column elements of a matrix. In instances such as this, the ith row elements become the jth column elements (and vice versa). A matrix $\mathbf{A}$ and its corresponding transpose, $\mathbf{A}^T$, is

$$\mathbf{A} = \begin{bmatrix} 5 & 0 & 8 \\ 4 & 7 & 3 \end{bmatrix}$$

and

$$\mathbf{A}^T = \begin{bmatrix} 5 & 4 \\ 0 & 7 \\ 8 & 3 \end{bmatrix}$$

As you can see, it is not necessary for the original matrix to have square dimensions in order to have a transpose.

B.3 | MATRIX ALGEBRA

There are several essential algebraic manipulations commonly used in matrix operations. These include (1) matrix addition and subtraction, and (2) matrix multiplication.

Matrix Addition or Subtraction

To perform either an addition or a subtraction operation, the matrices must have the same number of rows and columns (i.e., be of the same order). Suppose that a second matrix, $\mathbf{B}$, is introduced:

$$\mathbf{B} = \begin{bmatrix} 4 & 4 & 1 \\ 3 & 2 & 8 \end{bmatrix}$$

The sum of **A** and **B** is then

$$\mathbf{A} + \mathbf{B} = \begin{bmatrix} 5 & 0 & 8 \\ 4 & 7 & 3 \end{bmatrix} + \begin{bmatrix} 4 & 4 & 1 \\ 3 & 2 & 8 \end{bmatrix}$$

$$= \begin{bmatrix} (5+4) & (0+4) & (8+1) \\ (4+3) & (7+2) & (3+8) \end{bmatrix}$$

$$= \begin{bmatrix} 9 & 4 & 9 \\ 7 & 9 & 11 \end{bmatrix}$$

The difference between **A** and **B** is

$$\mathbf{A} - \mathbf{B} = \begin{bmatrix} 5 & 0 & 8 \\ 4 & 7 & 3 \end{bmatrix} - \begin{bmatrix} 4 & 4 & 1 \\ 3 & 2 & 8 \end{bmatrix}$$

$$= \begin{bmatrix} (5-4) & (0-4) & (8-1) \\ (4-3) & (7-2) & (3-8) \end{bmatrix}$$

$$= \begin{bmatrix} 1 & -4 & 7 \\ 1 & 5 & -5 \end{bmatrix}$$

Matrix Multiplication

Matrix multiplication does not require that the matrices have identical dimensions. However, it is necessary that the number of columns of the first matrix be equal to the number of rows of the second matrix. For two matrices, **A** and **B**,

$$\mathbf{A} = \begin{bmatrix} 7 & 1 \\ 3 & 0 \\ 5 & 4 \end{bmatrix} \qquad \mathbf{B} = \begin{bmatrix} 1 & 8 & 9 & 0 & -4 \\ -3 & 2 & 6 & 5 & 0 \end{bmatrix}$$

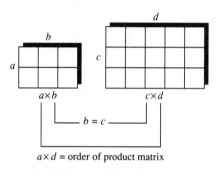

$a \times d$ = order of product matrix

FIGURE B-1

Order of Product Matrix in Matrix Multiplication

This requirement results in a product matrix, **C**, which has an order equal to the number of rows in the first matrix multiplied by the number of columns in the second matrix. This relationship is illustrated in Figure B-1. So, if the first matrix has an order of 3×2 and the second matrix has an order of 2×5, the order of the product matrix will be 3×5. We calculate the product matrix elements, c_{ij}, by summing the products formed by multiplying the ith row value in **A** by the corresponding j^{th} column value in **B**. The multiplication solution of the two matrices will illuminate this process:

$$\mathbf{C} = \mathbf{AB} = \begin{bmatrix} 7 & 1 \\ 3 & 0 \\ 5 & 4 \end{bmatrix} \begin{bmatrix} 1 & 8 & 9 & 0 & -4 \\ -3 & 2 & 6 & 5 & 0 \end{bmatrix}$$

$$\mathbf{C} = \begin{bmatrix} ((7)(1)+(1)(-3)) & ((7)(8)+(1)(2)) & ((7)(9)+(1)(6)) & ((7)(0)+(1)(5)) & ((7)(-4)+(1)(0)) \\ ((3)(1)+(0)(-3)) & ((3)(8)+(0)(2)) & ((3)(9)+(0)(6)) & ((3)(0)+(0)(5)) & ((3)(-4)+(0)(0)) \\ ((5)(1)+(4)(-3)) & ((5)(8)+(4)(2)) & ((5)(9)+(4)(6)) & ((5)(0)+(4)(5)) & ((5)(-4)+(4)(0)) \end{bmatrix}$$

$$\mathbf{C} = \begin{bmatrix} 4 & 58 & 69 & 5 & -28 \\ 3 & 24 & 27 & 0 & -12 \\ -7 & 48 & 69 & 20 & -20 \end{bmatrix}$$

This multiplication process suggests that **AB** is not typically equivalent to **BA**. That is, there is a mismatch between the column elements in **A** and the row elements in **B**.

The Inverse Matrix Form

In Chapters 4 through 6, we spent considerable time wrestling with the simplex method of solving simultaneous linear equations of the $m \times m$ order. Inverse matrices are used to solve simultaneous linear equation sets such as those comprising the linear programming resource constraint set. An identity matrix, $\mathbf{I}$, occurs if there are two square matrices, $\mathbf{A}$ and $\mathbf{D}$, that have the following relationship:[1]

$$\mathbf{I} = \mathbf{DA} = \mathbf{AD}$$

If so, matrix $\mathbf{D}$ is the inverse of matrix $\mathbf{A}$, and

$$\mathbf{D} = \mathbf{A}^{-1}$$

and

$$\begin{aligned}\mathbf{I} &= \mathbf{AD} \\ &= \mathbf{AA}^{-1} \\ &= 1\end{aligned}$$

We find the inverse of a matrix, if one exists, using the method suggested by Turban and Meredith (1988). Assume that we have a matrix given by

$$\mathbf{A} = \begin{bmatrix} a_{11} & a_{12} \\ a_{21} & a_{22} \end{bmatrix}$$

To find the inverse, we take the following steps:

Step 1. Add an identity matrix of the same order to the right side of the original matrix, $\mathbf{A}$:

$$\begin{bmatrix} a_{11} & a_{12} & 1 & 0 \\ a_{21} & a_{22} & 0 & 1 \end{bmatrix}$$

Step 2. Manipulate the rows using the Gauss–Jordan elimination method, so that the identity matrix is on the left side:

$$\begin{bmatrix} 1 & 0 & d_{11} & d_{12} \\ 0 & 1 & d_{21} & d_{22} \end{bmatrix}$$

The resulting right-hand matrix, $\mathbf{D}$, will then be the inverse of $\mathbf{A}$:

$$\mathbf{D} = \begin{bmatrix} d_{11} & d_{12} \\ d_{21} & d_{22} \end{bmatrix} = \mathbf{A}^{-1}$$

As an illustration of this procedure, assume that we want to find the inverse of

$$\mathbf{A} = \begin{bmatrix} 2 & 6 \\ 3 & 5 \end{bmatrix}$$

---

[1] The identity matrix, $\mathbf{I}$, is simply a square matrix consisting of 1s through the main diagonal and 0s elsewhere. For a simple 2×2 matrix, $\mathbf{I}$ is

$$\mathbf{I} = \begin{bmatrix} 1 & 0 \\ 0 & 1 \end{bmatrix} = 1$$

Step 1. An equal-order identity matrix is added to the right side of the original matrix:

$$\begin{bmatrix} 2 & 6 & 1 & 0 \\ 3 & 5 & 0 & 1 \end{bmatrix}$$

Step 2. The Gauss–Jordan elimination method uses basic matrix operations to form the identity matrix on the left side of the original matrix. First, divide the elements of the top row by 2 (this forces a 1 into the a_{ij} cell).

$$\begin{bmatrix} 1 & 3 & \frac{1}{2} & 0 \\ 3 & 5 & 0 & 1 \end{bmatrix}$$

Next, multiply the first row by -3 and add it to the second row.

$$\begin{bmatrix} 1 & 3 & \frac{1}{2} & 0 \\ (3-3=0) & (5-9=-4) & \left(0-\frac{3}{2}=-\frac{3}{2}\right) & (1-0=1) \end{bmatrix}$$

Now, divide row 2 by -4.

$$\begin{bmatrix} 1 & 3 & \frac{1}{2} & 0 \\ \left(\frac{0}{-4}=0\right) & \left(\frac{-4}{-4}=1\right) & \left(\left(-\frac{3}{2}\right)\left(-\frac{1}{4}\right)=\frac{3}{8}\right) & \left(\frac{1}{-4}=-\frac{1}{4}\right) \end{bmatrix}$$

Finally, multiply row 2 by 3 and subtract it from row 1.

$$\begin{bmatrix} (1-0=1) & (3-3=0) & \left(\frac{1}{2}-\frac{9}{8}=-\frac{5}{8}\right) & \left(0-\left(-\frac{3}{4}\right)=\frac{3}{4}\right) \\ 0 & 1 & \frac{3}{8} & -\frac{1}{4} \end{bmatrix}$$

and

$$\begin{bmatrix} 1 & 0 & -\frac{5}{8} & \frac{3}{4} \\ 0 & 1 & \frac{3}{8} & -\frac{1}{4} \end{bmatrix}$$

The inverse matrix is

$$\begin{bmatrix} -\frac{5}{8} & \frac{3}{4} \\ \frac{3}{8} & -\frac{1}{4} \end{bmatrix}$$

Let's check to make sure that we do, indeed, have the inverse matrix:

$$\begin{bmatrix} 2 & 6 \\ 3 & 5 \end{bmatrix}\begin{bmatrix} -\frac{5}{8} & \frac{3}{4} \\ \frac{3}{4} & -\frac{1}{4} \end{bmatrix} = \begin{bmatrix} \left(2\left(-\frac{5}{8}\right)+6\left(\frac{3}{8}\right)=1\right) & \left(2\left(\frac{3}{4}\right)+6\left(-\frac{1}{4}\right)=0\right) \\ \left(3\left(-\frac{5}{8}\right)+5\left(\frac{3}{8}\right)=0\right) & \left(3\left(\frac{3}{4}\right)+5\left(-\frac{1}{4}\right)=1\right) \end{bmatrix}$$

Now let's examine the ability of an inverse matrix to solve an $m \times m$ set of linear equations. Suppose that we have a set of linear equations defined by the relationship

$$\mathbf{Ax} = \mathbf{b}$$

where **x** and **b** are *column vectors* of the (decision) variable and right-hand-side (resource level) elements of a linear (LP constraint) equation. That is,

$$\mathbf{A} = \begin{bmatrix} a_{11} & a_{12} & \cdots & a_{1j} & \cdots & a_{1n} \\ a_{21} & a_{22} & \cdots & a_{2j} & \cdots & a_{2n} \\ \cdots & \cdots & \cdots & \cdots & \cdots & \cdots \\ a_{i1} & \cdots & \cdots & a_{ij} & \cdots & a_{in} \\ \cdots & \cdots & \cdots & \cdots & \cdots & \cdots \\ a_{m1} & a_{m2} & \cdots & a_{mj} & \cdots & a_{mn} \end{bmatrix}, \quad \mathbf{x} = \begin{bmatrix} x_1 \\ x_2 \\ \cdot \\ \cdot \\ \cdot \\ x_n \end{bmatrix}, \quad \mathbf{b} = \begin{bmatrix} b_1 \\ b_2 \\ \cdot \\ \cdot \\ \cdot \\ b_n \end{bmatrix}$$

If the inverse matrix of $\mathbf{A}^{-1}$ exists, multiply both sides of the linear equation, $\mathbf{Ax} = \mathbf{b}$ by it. Then,

$$\mathbf{A}^{-1}(\mathbf{Ax}) = \mathbf{A}^{-1}(\mathbf{b})$$

and

$$\mathbf{x} = \mathbf{A}^{-1}\mathbf{b}$$

It is a simple procedure to solve for **x** if we can first find the inverse matrix, $\mathbf{A}^{-1}$. Let's illustrate this procedure next with the aid of an example.

General Manager Harold Stang makes a mental note to check all materials coming from this product manager's area.

TABLE B-1

New Products Resource Allocation for Stang Precision Instruments

Product	Cost	Product and Labor Hours
Laryngoscope	$200	3
Proctoscope	$600	5
Total	*$1,400,000*	*13,000 hours*

EXAMPLE B.1   STANG PRECISION INSTRUMENTS

Stang Precision Instruments (SPI) specializes in providing the dental market with the highest quality precision endodontic reams—the files used to perform root canals—that money can buy. Regardless of the company's success, General Manager Harold Stang, grandson of the company's founder, Arnold Stang, is uncomfortable about SPI's being so specialized and is considering expanding the company's product line. In particular, Harold would like to examine the strategy of adding two new products: (1) a laryngoscope—an instrument used by ear, nose, and throat specialists to view a person's larynx—and (2) a proctoscope—an instrument used to . . . uh, used to . . . , well, an instrument used by another kind of medical specialist. Harold's marketing department has indicated that these products have not been modernized since their introduction to the medical profession over 60 years ago. Further, the engineering department at Stang Precision has a new method of inexpensively including a pencil laser beam in both instruments that will, as one of the product managers put it, shed new light on the subject. Marketing is convinced that it can capture both the laryngoscope and proctoscope markets with this modernized, high-tech approach. Harold calls a meeting of his product managers to discuss the situation.

For the first year of manufacturing and marketing these two new products SPI feels it would have to set aside about $1,400,000 of its overall budget and 13,000 hours. The unit costs and production time associated with these products are shown in Table B-1. The equations representing these resource limits are:

$$200x_1 + 600x_2 = 1,400,000$$
$$3x_1 + 5x_2 = 13,000$$

Rewriting these equations in matrix form yields:

$$\begin{bmatrix} 200 & 600 \\ 3 & 5 \end{bmatrix} \begin{bmatrix} x_1 \\ x_2 \end{bmatrix} = \begin{bmatrix} 1,400,000 \\ 13,000 \end{bmatrix}$$

where

$$\mathbf{A} = \begin{bmatrix} 200 & 600 \\ 3 & 5 \end{bmatrix}$$

We already have solved for a nearly identical inverse matrix. Earlier, the first row elements were 2 and 6 rather than 200 and 600. If exactly the same procedure is followed, the new identity matrix will be:

$$\mathbf{A}^{-1} = \begin{bmatrix} -\frac{5}{800} & \frac{3}{4} \\ \frac{3}{800} & -\frac{1}{4} \end{bmatrix}$$

Multiply both sides of the original matrix form by $\mathbf{A}^{-1}$:

$$\begin{bmatrix} -\frac{5}{800} & \frac{3}{4} \\ \frac{3}{800} & -\frac{1}{4} \end{bmatrix} \begin{bmatrix} 200 & 600 \\ 3 & 5 \end{bmatrix} \begin{bmatrix} x_1 \\ x_2 \end{bmatrix} = \begin{bmatrix} -\frac{5}{800} & \frac{3}{4} \\ \frac{3}{800} & -\frac{1}{4} \end{bmatrix} \begin{bmatrix} 1,400,000 \\ 13,000 \end{bmatrix}$$

If we multiply the 2 matrices on the right-hand side of the equation, we will be able to solve for the optimal number of laryngoscopes (x_1) and proctoscopes (x_2). This multiplication follows:

$$\begin{bmatrix} -\frac{5}{800} & \frac{3}{4} \\ \frac{3}{800} & \frac{1}{4} \end{bmatrix} \begin{bmatrix} 1,400,000 \\ 13,000 \end{bmatrix} = \begin{bmatrix} \left(-\frac{5}{800}\right)(1,400,000) + \left(\frac{3}{4}\right)(13,000) \\ \left(\frac{3}{800}\right)(1,400,000) + \left(-\frac{1}{4}\right)(13,000) \end{bmatrix}$$

$$= \begin{bmatrix} -8750 + 9750 \\ 5250 - 3250 \end{bmatrix}$$

$$= \begin{bmatrix} 1000 \\ 2000 \end{bmatrix}$$

and

$$\begin{bmatrix} x_1 \\ x_2 \end{bmatrix} = \begin{bmatrix} 1000 \\ 2000 \end{bmatrix}$$

The unique solution of the two simultaneous linear equations is: $x_1 = 1000$ units of laryngoscopes and $x_2 = 2000$ units of proctoscopes.

References

1. Budnick, Frank S., Dennis McLeavey, and Richard Mojena. *Principles of Operations Research for Management*, 2nd ed. Homewood, IL: Irwin, 1988.
2. Cook, Thomas M., and Robert A. Russell. *Introduction to Management Science*, 4th ed. Englewood Cliffs, NJ: Prentice-Hall, 1989.
3. Roscoe, K., and Patrick G. McKeown. *Quantitative Models for Management Science*, 2nd ed. PLACE?: Kent, 1984.

4. Spivey, W. Allen, and Robert M. Thrall. *Linear Optimization*. New York: Holt, Rinehart & Winston, 1970.
5. Turban, Efraim, and Jack R. Meredith. *Fundamentals of Management Science*, 4th ed. Plano, TX: Business Publications, 1988.
6. Wagner, Harvey M. *Principles of Operations Research: With Application to Managerial Decisions*. Englewood Cliffs, NJ: Prentice-Hall, 1969.

TABLE OF CRITICAL VALUES OF *D* IN THE KOLMOGROV-SMIRNOV TWO-SAMPLE TEST

Large Samples: Two-Tailed Test*

Level of Significance	Value of D so Large as to call for rejection of H_0 at the indicated level of significance, where D = maximum $\lvert S_{n1}(X) - S_{n2}(X) \rvert$
.10	$1.22 \sqrt{\dfrac{n_1 + n_2}{n_1 n_2}}$
.05	$1.36 \sqrt{\dfrac{n_1 + n_2}{n_1 n_2}}$
.025	$1.48 \sqrt{\dfrac{n_1 + n_2}{n_1 n_2}}$
.01	$1.63 \sqrt{\dfrac{n_1 + n_2}{n_1 n_2}}$
.005	$1.73 \sqrt{\dfrac{n_1 + n_2}{n_1 n_2}}$
.001	$1.95 \sqrt{\dfrac{n_1 + n_2}{n_1 n_2}}$

Adapted from Smirnov, N. 1948. Tables for estimating the goodness of fit of empirical distributions. *Ann. Math. Statist.*, **19**, 280–281, with the kind permission of the publicher.

INDEX